SHIPWRECK!

A Comprehensive Directory of Over 3,700 Shipwrecks on the Great Lakes

■

INCLUDES:

The most dangerous spot on the Lakes
Largest freighters lost
The most dangerous decade
Treasure ships

■

DAVID D. SWAYZE

Harbor House Publishers, Inc., 221 Water Street, Boyne City, Michigan 49712
Manufactured in the United States of America

Swayze, David D., 1946-
SHIPWRECK: A comprehensive directory of over
3,700 shipwrecks on the Great Lakes / David D. Swayze.

ISBN 0-937360-12-0
Library of Congress Catalog Number 92-189076

Contents

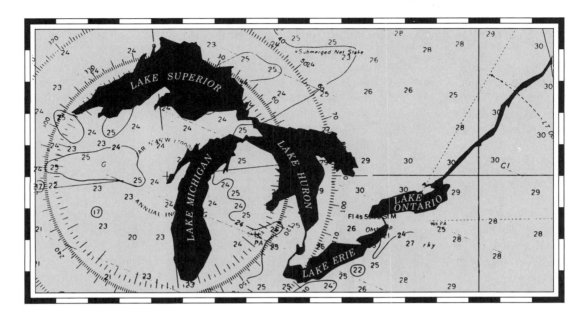

DEDICATION

With love to my wife Margie and my daughters Becky and Lesley,
all of whom thought me a lunatic, but supported me wholeheartedly anyway.

*"They that go down to the sea in ships, that do business in
great waters; these see the works of the Lord and His wonders
in the deep. For He commands and raises the stormy wind,
which brings up the waves. These men mount up to heaven,
they go down again to the depths and their soul is melted
because of this trouble. They reel to and fro, and stagger like
a drunken man, then come to their wit's end."*

Psalms 107: 23-7

Preface

Why prepare a volume of information such as this? Practically every library in the Great Lakes region has a book or two on the subject of Great Lakes shipwrecks. The works of Dana Bowen and Dwight Boyer are well-known, highly readable pieces of Lakes lore. Writer/historians such as Dr. Julius Wolff, Frederick Stonehouse and John O. Greenwood turn morsels of research data into fascinating documents on the wrecks of specific areas or times. Listings of shipwrecks exist as well. Bowen enumerated 500 in his *Shipwrecks of the Lakes* (1952) and researcher Erich Karl Heden compiled a list of about 1,500 known shipwrecks in his *Directory of Shipwrecks of the Great Lakes* (1966).

Great Lakes historians are not in close accord as to how many ships have been lost in the region. Estimates have emerged stating that anywhere from 5,000 to 10,000 serious accidents have occurred, with perhaps 40 percent being total losses. In fact, there is not much agreement as to what constitutes a loss. Newspaper articles are a major source of information concerning wrecks, particularly those of the 19th Century, but these accounts are variable as to the seriousness of a particular wreck. Some tend to call any accident that resulted in financial cost to the owners as a loss, while others called almost any occurrence that delayed a ship's schedule or damaged the vessel a disaster. In addition, literally hundreds of vessels were reported as lost, only to turn up again days or even weeks later.

At first glance, reports such as these seem to be exaggerated, but thought given to the conditions under which newspapers worked in earlier times helps to put the inaccuracies in a fairer light. The 20th Century was well underway before wireless radio became common on Lakes vessels. A ship that was going to make port days late often had no way of making her situation known. Many a vessel was given up as lost in a treacherous Lakes gale, only to show up days later, battered but still afloat, having sheltered from the storm in the lee of some uninhabited island or distant bay. In remote areas a report of a grounded ship "up the beach" might come from a mail carrier, fisherman or trapper and be days old when received.

After a few days of stormy weather, there would even be doubt as to whether the ship would be visible. Many stranded ships were broken up by giant storm-driven combers or pushed off the bar by an offshore current to sink in deeper water. But in a high percentage of cases, a ship put on the rocks by a gale was on her way the next day due to a lightening of her cargo, a clever salvager, or a fortuitous change of wind. Even if a report of a salvaged vessel were to eventually reach a news desk, ships not lost in a storm were much less newsworthy than those that were, and late arrivals of boats previously considered wrecked were often not reported at all.

Old newspaper reports, then, often need to be confirmed through other sources. One commonly-used type of reference is the loss report of insurance companies. Unfortunately, these only cover ships that were insured and the wreck reports were subject to the same types of handicaps as newspaper accounts. To further complicate research, many wrecks were declared to be total losses by their underwriters, only to be resurrected, rebuilt and returned to service, sometimes under the same name, but often under a different one. Fortunately, as one moves through time toward the present, the reports become more and more accurate. Not to say that all modern accounts are error-free, but mistakes are easier to weed out and facts easier to confirm.

One can see how "non-wrecks" complicate information gathering, but perhaps even more significant are the vessels lost and never reported. Up until the late 1800s, there was little overall organization to the Great Lakes shipping industry, and there was virtually no reliable way to report arrivals and departures. With the ships themselves often being the fastest form of communication, even a large vessel claimed by an angry lake might not be missed for days. By then her position when lost could only be guessed at; her wreckage already having been cast ashore.

A singular example is the famous sailing ship GRIFFIN (LE GRIFON), built by the explorer LaSalle, and sent from Green Bay home to New France in the fall of 1679 with a crew of six and heavily laden with a cargo of valuable furs. The tiny brig never reached her destination, a fact that remained unreported until LaSalle himself returned to Montreal much later. She is still overdue today, and a 300-year debate continues as to where she might lie.

Official lists of vessels such as the series *Merchant Vessels of the United States* provide information on the ships themselves, and, after 1900, some data on wrecks. But even as late as the 1870s, many unregistered schooners and steamboats just sailed from port to port on no particular schedule, picking up and delivering cargoes and passengers when and where they could. These "coasters" were often skippered by their owners, crewed by a few itinerant sailors, and not obliged to call any town home port. Even to this day, there are stories of little ships like this that just sailed off over the horizon and were never seen again. Just how many of these tramps were lost during the early days of Great Lakes shipping will probably never be known, but rumors suggest that the number may be in the hundreds.

And what of the loss of life? Thousands of men, women and children have drowned, frozen or burned in Lakes accidents, but reports of this mortality are often contradictory or non-existent. It is a great tragedy when a sailor disappears in a swirl of foam, and an even greater one when succeeding generations forget that he existed. Yet this occurs over and over again in shipwreck reports. Again, reporters of earlier times were hampered by poor communications and inaccurate record-keeping. Passenger manifests and crew lists were often carried aboard the ship itself and, in case of a disaster, were lost along with the vessel. As late as 1915, in the tragic capsizing of the excursion steamer *EASTLAND* at Chicago, it was months before the large number of dead could be determined with any degree of confidence, since no passenger list was kept, and many passengers who came aboard with passes were not even counted. Even today there is still some debate over the actual number of casualties in this infamous accident.

Moreover, the membership of the crews of merchant vessels was as fluid as the medium the ships travelled upon. Up until the 1950s, it was uncommon, if not unheard of, for a ship to finish the season with the same crew that began it. Officers often stayed with the same boat for many years, but the hands moved around quite a bit. In addition, and for a variety of reasons, many sailors of times past used fictitious names and manufactured personal data. The head office or any other agency ashore would likely not have an accurate idea of who, or even how many, were aboard their ship at a given time, no matter how conscientious the record-keepers might be. Many vessels were equipped with a watertight canister containing a crew list, to be jettisoned in the event of a sinking, but in a desperate emergency, such precautions are not the first thing on a seaman's mind. If the ship were to sail to her doom, the final tally of lost crew might in the end be left to the memory of a wet and frozen survivor.

Ultimately, time destroys information on vessel disasters just as surely as wind, water and ice destroy the ships themselves. And just as a sunken lake steamer may still exist but be out of our reach, so the details of her demise may be almost irretrievably buried in a mountain of other information. The further one progresses from an event, the more difficult it becomes to obtain accurate information about it. Lake buffs are very familiar with the details of the loss of the bulk carrier EDMUND FITZGERALD and her crew in 1975, but what of the sloop ONTARIO, reported lost on Lake Ontario in 1783 with as many as 200 casualties? Perhaps even more to the point, who has ready knowledge of the loss of the hundreds of small ships such as the schooner W C GRISWOLD that sunk with her crew of six in 1872? Where some ship disasters have entire books written about them, thousands of others are recorded in just a few sentences or words.

This volume, then, attempts to report on these many ships and the people who sailed with them. With a few exceptions, only significant losses of commercial vessels are included (i.e. those which involved loss of life or total loss of the vessel). To further narrow the topic, fatal accidents are only included if they involved significant damage to the ship. Some exceptions include wrecks where the vessel was declared lost, but later recovered, recoveries involving excessive loss or expense to the owners, and wrecks of unusual historical interest. The exceptions are noted in the text.

The reader may note that many vessels whose remains are still visible do not appear in this volume. For example, the Saginaw River has up to a dozen or more visible wrecks, but only one or two are on this list. Most often, vessels whose remains can still be seen are not wrecks in the sense used in this work. They are generally not accidental losses at all, but are vessels which were no longer usable and were just scuttled or tied to a tree to rot. There were literally thousands of these on the Lakes—mostly wooden ships—and many of them can still be seen, especially around once-busy Lakes ports. Conversely, wooden vessels that were abandoned on some lonely beach due to storm damage or fires, usually ended up contributing most or all of their timbers for local construction or firewood. Even today, planking and broken spars from magnificent vessels wrecked decades ago wash up after storms and wind up in beach fires or as garden decorations.

An effort has also been made to provide information on the ships themselves as they were at the time of the loss. Since wreck reports do not always correlate shipwreck information with data on the vessel, sometimes the ship data has, of necessity, been conjectural. Where such is the case, the reader will be told that the information has involved educated guesswork by use of the words "probably" or "possibly".

One of the most important duties of historians, both amateur and professional, is to compile and keep accurate memory of events past. Historians of the Great Lakes have preserved, to a tremendous degree, the accounts of ships and crews that were and are such a part of our past. The information contained in this volume is merely a compilation of data gathered by previous reporters. Though Great Lakes shipwrecks still happen, the era when men and women took their lives in their hands daily by setting out on the "sweetwater seas" is, thankfully, past. We are therefore in the luxurious position of being able to rummage around in an almost encapsulated piece of the past, and continue to rummage until we discover all of the information therein. Collecting information is one of the most benign and satifying forms of collecting. It does not vandalize, hoard, nor even disturb the object of collection. In many cases, it can clarify or increase our understanding of the subject matter. This book represents years of collecting and sorting reports from dozens of different sources, but it is not a complete listing. It tries only to bring a large volume of information together into a small volume of paper. Sources have been compared and weighed as to credibility in an effort to obtain the most accurate possible data. In situations where reliable resources are contradictory, both sets of data are given, with the most probable presented first. No data has been modified, embellished or abandoned without documentation, thus the reader will find some sets of data which are almost identical, but which cannot be combined. . .yet.

Future research will perhaps shed some light upon inaccuracies and provide missing information. The author has no doubt that many readers will have valuable information on specific areas or incidents. For this edition, he has done his best to provide at least some detail on the major shipwrecks of the Great Lakes, from LaSalle's *GRIFFIN* of 1679 to the 384-foot gasoline tanker *JUPITER* of 1990.

Introduction

Handling a large volume of information has one aspect in common with handling a ship and its crew. A set of rules and definitions of terms have to be established if everything is to run smoothly. Sailors worldwide have always developed ways of looking at their surroundings that is uniquely theirs; lakers are no exception. Every point of land and gull-covered rock has its own nickname, each ship acquires its own personality and temperament and every piece of equipment aboard its individual, sometimes unprintable, name. Even the generic term "ship," used in reference to large commercial vessels, becomes "boat" in Lakes jargon. Those who go to work "on the boats" learn the language quickly as part of their everyday lives while landsmen need to expend considerable effort to interpret. This volume does not attempt to define or even use the thousands of words in the Lakes sailors' lexicon, but in the context of the shipwreck, a degree of clarification is in order.

VESSEL TYPES—Design of ships used on the Great Lakes followed much the same patterns as marine vessels, with hundreds of kinds of vessels being developed for more and more specific purposes. A detailed description of the numerous different types of Lakes vessels is beyond the scope of this work, but a glossary of common parlance is almost essential to understanding the information provided herein. Please note that the terminology used applies to privately owned vessels. Military ships use many of the same terms, but in quite different ways.

Barge—A vessel that is designed or converted to be towed by another ship is known as a "barge". A barge's hull is usually the shape of a regular ship, as opposed to the flat-ended and flat-bottomed "scow." Barges may be cargo-carriers or used for many other types of utility work. See also "schooner-barge", "steam barge", etc.

Bark or barque—In strictest terms, a bark is a sailing ship with three or more masts, with the mizzen (furthest aft) mast fore-and-aft rigged (sails aligned with the long axis of the hull), and the others being square-rigged. In actual usage, it appears that any three-masted ship with mixed fore-and-aft and square rig was referred to as a bark. Square-rigged ships were good in open water, but required larger crews than comparably-sized schooners and were more difficult to maneuver in confined channels and harbors, thus the "schooner" became the preferred type of sailing vessel and most barks were eventually converted to schooners. The term "barkentine" is sometimes used interchangably with "bark".

Break-bulk carrier—In the days when many railroads used ships to move cargoes and passengers across bodies of water, the break-bulk carrier was developed. Freight from rail cars was loaded onto these ships on one side of the lake, then reloaded onto a new set of cars on the other side. The break-bulk carrier was supplanted by the "carferry" for hauling rail cargoes.

Brig—The Lakes brig was generally a two-masted ship with the foremast square-rigged and the mizzen fore-and-aft rigged. The type is technically known as a "brigantine" or "hermaphrodite brig", saltwater brigs had all masts square-rigged. As ship design progressed, this type of rig was supplanted by the schooner, just as the bark had been, and many brigs were converted to the more maneuverable schooner type, which required a smaller crew.

Bulk freighter or bulk carrier—As the name implies, a bulk freighter is a ship intended to carry bulk—as opposed to package—cargoes. They were generally loaded through hatches in the top of the main deck. The largest ships on the Lakes today are of this type. Common bulk freight includes grain, iron ore and coal.

Canaller—A canaller is a ship designed to fit the dimensions of the Welland Canal, and thus able to move cargoes among all the Great Lakes and into the Atlantic as well. The term is generally used to describe ships of this size in the days before the opening of the St. Lawrence Seaway.

Carferry—A carferry is a ship designed to transport loaded or empty railroad cars, and sometimes passengers, and move them across bodies of water, usually on a fixed route.

Carferries may be either powered or barges and may accommodate one to many rail cars. Some modern carferries will also carry automobiles. See also "ferry".

Coaster—This term is an abbreviated form of "coastal ship" and refers to a type of vessel used to shuffle such cargoes and passengers as were available among small ports. Coasters were usually relatively small vessels that ran on rather loose schedules and were often much-beloved by the people of the ports they served. On saltwater this type of ship is often called a "tramp".

Collier—The collier is a ship primarily designed to carry coal. Few of these operated on the Lakes, this duty being performed by the many bulk carriers available. On saltwater colliers were often used by navies to carry bunker coal for refueling warships.

Composite steamer—Before iron and steel came into general use as materials for constructing ships, some vessels were built using iron structure in the hulls for strength and wooden planking for flexibility, economy and availability. The composite-hulled steamer was an intermediate type, and only a few were built before metal hulls came into general use.

Dredge—A dredge is a piece of equipment mounted on a vessel and used to scoop or suction up lake bottom, usually to reform a channel or harbor to improve navigation. Some dredge vessels were self propelled, but most were barges or scows.

Excursion steamer—An excursion steamer is a vessel designed to carry passengers on relatively short trips, such as the day trips to amusement parks or fairs that were in vogue in the first few decades of this century. This type of ship can carry many people, but has few or no accommodations for overnight guests. See also "passenger steamer".

Ferry—A "ferry" is a vessel designed to transport some commodity over a single, relatively short, fixed route many times a season. "Automobile ferries," "passenger ferries," and "carferries" are all common types.

Freighter—Any vessel designed primarily to transport cargo rather than passengers can be termed a freighter. In the context of this volume, the term is used in reference to steamers only, though most schooners could be described as freighters as well.

Launch—A boat of a few tons, usually steam or internal combustion engine powered and often meant to be used as a pleasure craft, is known as a "launch". The term is becoming obsolete in favor of "cruiser", "runabout", etc.

Lighter—A lighter is a vessel used to take on the cargo of another vessel, and either hold that cargo or transfer it to shore. A lighter is often an auxiliary salvage ship, used to help "lighten" a stranded vessel to aid removal, hence its name. Lighters are also used to move cargos from deep-draft ships to shore in shallow or dockless ports.

Lumber hooker—A lumber hooker is a specialized type of bulk freighter. These relatively small ships would move among the dozens of lumber ports on the Upper Lakes, picking up wood cargoes and perhaps a barge or two for transshipment to the south. Often a cargo of coal or package freight would then be loaded aboard for the return trip. The lumber hooker passed

away with the lumbering era.

Mackinaw boat—The Mackinaw was a type of small sailing vessel of one mast and very shallow draft, used in the early days of the history of the Lakes to move small cargoes to camps of trappers or lumbermen along the shore. The Mackinaw type still exists as a modern pleasure craft.

Montreal canoe—This was a type of large canoe used by early Lakes traders and trappers to move several tons of trade goods or furs about the area. The vessel could be either paddled or sailed by its crew of four or more, and was also called a "voyageur's canoe".

Motor vessel or motor ship—This term is applied to any relatively large vessel with a propulsion system other than steam. Motor vessels most often use an internal combustion engine to power a large electric motor which turns the prop.

Package freighter—A vessel designed primarily to carry packaged freight (such as barrelled or bagged foodstuffs, boxed household goods and even large items such as machinery) is termed a package freighter. These vessels generally had doors in the side for ease of loading and were often equipped with comfortable accommodations for passengers. The term may be applied to either steamers or sailing ships, but is here applied only to steamers.

Packet—The packet is a type of small package freighter used for largely local movement of goods.

Passenger steamer—Many Lakes buffs sigh at the passing of the days when fast passenger steamers carried travellers from port to port on the Great Lakes. These sidewheel or propeller ships often had luxurious accommodations rivalling the ocean liners of the day. Passenger steamers often carried freight as well.

Propeller—In the early 19th Century the screw propeller was developed as a method of ship propulsion. The propeller-powered ship or "propeller" immediately began to take over the cargo and passenger trade from paddlewheel steamers and schooners. Propellers had many advantages over sidewheelers. They transmitted more of their power to propulsion, were more maneuverable, were less effected by foul weather and their machinery took up far less room than in their paddle-powered contemporaries. The term "propeller" has fallen into general disuse now that virtually all ships are propelled this way. In this book, the term has been used in places where the vessel is described as such in reference material.

Rabbit—This is a slang term applied to the many small package and bulk freighters that had all of their deckhouses, engineering spaces, and cabins aft. These little ships, very popular in the late 19th and early 20th Centuries, could move quickly from port to port, due in part to their small size and limited cargo capacities.

Sandsucker—The sandsucker was a specially-designed ship used to harvest the abundant white sand from lake bottoms for use in the construction and iron-casting trades. These ships had equipment to suck sand up from the bottom, filter it out of the water and deliver it to some port. A sandsucker could be either a powered ship or a barge.

Schooner—"Schooner" is a term often used to describe

any sail ship used on the Lakes, but actually a refers to a rather specific type of sail vessel. The schooner is a boat of two or more masts (up to five were used), with all masts being fore-and-aft rigged. The typical commercial vessel was a "topsail schooner" with two tiers of fore-and-aft sails per mast. Some lakers also carried a square or triangular (raffee) topsail on the foremast. Nearly all commercial Lakes schooners were of wooden construction. If a sail vessel is known to have been constructed of some other material, it will be described as such in the text, otherwise readers may assume wood (usually oak) was used. Schooners were generally designed to carry any type of cargo, and could often accommodate a few passengers as well, especially in the early days. The descriptive term "merchant schooner" has often been used in this text to describe the generalized freight-and-passenger schooner. Thousands of these craft once plied the Great Lakes, but the last commercial sailing ships were gone by the mid-1930s.

Schooner-barge—This type of vessel became very important in Lakes commerce in the latter quarter of the 19th Century. It was a relatively large vessel equipped with sails and masts, but designed mainly to be towed. If necessary, and conditions were good, the schooner-barge was usually able to set sail and move under her own power. Most of these ships were regular schooners that were toward the end of their useful life and had been cut down to a barge by the removal of topmasts and some spars. Others were specifically built to be schooner-barges.

Schooner-scow or scow-schooner—This was essentially a narrow-beamed scow with the fore-and-aft rig of a schooner. These relatively small vessels' flat bottoms made them able to pull into very shallow water to pick up cargoes of lumber or other freight, often allowing them to be loaded directly from shore. At their peak, several hundred schooner-scows were in the trade.

Scow—A scow is a vessel with a flat bottom and square ends, designed to be towed for short distances and used for a variety of tasks. Scows usually do their work while riding at anchor, since their flat bottoms make them relatively stable, and are thus used for dredging, salvage work, pile driving, etc.

Screw—The term "screw" is often used to describe relatively small propeller-driven vessels. It is often modified by a term denoting the vessel's type of power (e.g. "oil screw" or "steam screw").

Ship—This term has several meanings and is included here for clarity. In this volume the noun "ship" is used in its most general way, to denote any significantly-sized vessel. A ship can also be a very specific type of large sailing vessel.

Sidewheel steamer or sidewheeler—Before the advent of the propeller-driven ship, most self-powered vessels on the Lakes were sidewheelers. Their huge paddles on each side of the hull gave the ships broad beams and made them difficult to load, but the ships were still powerful and impressive looking. The power of the engines was often transferred to the driveshaft by a distinctive, diamond-shaped walking beam which protruded above the top deck of the ship. Perhaps partially because of the nostalgia they evoked, sidewheelers continued to be used in the passenger trade well after they had been supplant-

ed by propellers (qv) for freight hauling.

Sloop—The sloop was probably the smallest variety of sailing vessel used regularly in Lakes commerce. Sloops were single-masted, fore-and-aft rigged vessels. The usual commercial rig was main and topsail, plus one or two jibs. Though the sloop has gone out of existence as a merchant ship, it is still by far the most common type of vessel for sail yachts.

Steam barge—With the growth of the bulk freight trades on the Great Lakes, special vessels were developed to carry grain, metallic ores and lumber. The important line of development that led to the modern bulk carrier included the "steam barge". This was just a large empty hull with cabins placed forward and aft, and with engineering areas at the extreme after end. The cargo was normally poured in through hatches in the main deck, and the loss of the hatch covers in heavy weather was the cause of the demise of many ships. Steam barges were generally of high cargo-carrying capacity and low horsepower for their size.

Steamer—The general term "steamer" denotes any vessel that is driven by a steam powerplant.

Sternwheel steamer or sternwheeler—This is another type of paddle steamer which had the paddles at the rear of the vessel. This configuration, combined with the vessels' flat bottoms and shallow drafts, allowed them to nose into a cargo-loading area, then back out. These same features, which made them ideal for riverine trade, rendered them difficult and dangerous to use in stormy water. For this reason, only a few were ever used on the Lakes, and those were generally for intra-harbor use.

Tanker—A tanker is a ship designed primarily for the transporting of bulk liquids such as gasoline and oil. Many Lakes tankers were barges.

Tender—The "tender" is a vessel with the primary purpose of servicing other ships. On the Lakes, tenders were used to supply lightships and lighthouses and to service navigational buoys. The term "tender" is also used to describe vessels that were unresponsive to the helm, or slow to recover from wave-induced listing or sharp turns.

Tug—The "tug" was (and is) the "all purpose vehicle" of the world of navigation. Tugs served a large variety of functions, including cargo hauling, fishing, and salvage work. The most common function of the tug was to push or pull other vessels to docks, around harbors and up and down waterways. In the schooner era, tugs were kept busy towing long lines of the sailing ships along crowded connecting waterways, where tacking was impossible.

Turret steamer—The "turret steamer" was a steel ship with the midships cabins supported above the main deck by a "turret" of steel, and a significant "tumblehome" (sides curving inward toward the top). Similar in concept to the "whaleback" (qv), most turret steamers were of European build.

Whaleback—A uniquely Great Lakes design, the "whaleback" was a ship with rounded sides, a blunt, spoon-shaped prow, and with the cabins being supported above the cigar-shaped hull by fore and aft "turrets." Captain A. MacDougall, their designer, said it made more sense to "invite the waves aboard" rather than resist them. The ships, dubbed "pigboats" by lakemen of the time, rode with decks nearly awash when loaded, thus isolating their forward and after crews in heavy weather.

Yacht—A yacht is a vessel of any size and with any type of propulsion that is used primarily as a pleasure craft; that is, for cruising or racing.

Yawl or yawl-boat—Most commercial vessels of any size carried a small "yawl" for use by the officers and crew to get ashore when the ship lay at anchor and as a lifeboat in an emergency. Most ship's yawls could be either sailed or rowed.

NAMES OF SHIPS—Each vessel is assigned an official name. It may be as prosaic as DREDGE #8 or as romantic as WINGS OF THE WIND, but it is always the official way of referring to that vessel, at least in print. Unfortunately, individuals reporting on ships and shipwrecks were not always aware of these given designations. In addition, many past reporters did not share our current preoccupation with proper spelling. Lighthouse keepers, harbormasters, and even newspaper reporters tended to show great creativity in the spelling of ship names, particularly if the name was one unfamiliar to the observer.

The author has found at least five different spellings of the name of the French minesweeper CERISOLES, which disappeared in Lake Superior in 1918. Misspellings and use of ships' nicknames turns simple compilation of data into complicated detective work. Government listings, shipyard records, and even photographs can help in this clarification. For example, a photo of a boat referred to in a number of works as "Gales Staples", shows the name GALE STAPLES in elegant Roman letters on her bow.

A significant number of vessels began their careers under one name and met their demise under another, perhaps with other name changes in between. The usual reason for renaming was new ownership, but often an extensively rebuilt ship would slide down the ways with a new moniker as well as new planking.

In some cases, a vessel was renamed to hide her original identity. In 1860, the little schooner AUGUSTA rammed the passenger steamer LADY ELGIN in a fog off Winnetka, Illinois. In a sinking condition, the AUGUSTA made a run for shore, her crew not realizing that the massive sidewheeler was fatally holed and would soon founder with a loss of almost 300 lives. Even though her crew was absolved of guilt in not standing by to pick up survivors, the schooner became such a pariah that her name was changed to COLONEL COOK in an attempt to mask her original identity. It was under that name that she sank in a Lake Erie storm in 1895. In this volume, only initial names (where known) and final names are provided.

ARRANGEMENT OF ENTRIES—There are several different and distinct schemes for the arrangement of material such as this. Some authors, such as Dana Bowen and Frederick Stonehouse, have used the chronological listing. Compilers of dive charts and writers, such as Steve Harold, concentrating on localized areas, have used geographical listings that move along a coastline, identifying vessels along the way. Others arrange by builder or owner, then alphabetize within these categories. A common method among official agencies has been to alphabetize within larger categories by using the first letter of the vessel's official name (e.g. HELEN TAYLOR precedes HELENA).

Thus *Merchant Vessels of the United States, Lloyd's Register of Ships, Canadian Steams Vessels,* and others are ideal references for those who already know the vessel's official name, and wish to find information.

However, in many cases a reader will not have the entire offical name of the vessel to use as a reference point. When a ship is named after an individual or city, the researcher may have only the part of the namesake's name to steer by. In the press and in popular literature, vessels with compound names are often referred to by their last names, sometimes by their full names, and almost never by their first names. For example, a number of articles have been written about a schooner with the last name REEVES that foundered in Tawas Bay, Michigan, in the last century, with a load of copper. However, authors vary enough on the first name that a reader wishing to find more information may be looking for KITTY REEVES or ERMA B REEVES or even E REEVES. In a long list of names, it may be very time-consuming if one starts out looking with the wrong name.

A similar problem arises with the names of city boats. A vessel often cited in the readings as "City of Muskegon" was really named, simply, MUSKEGON, and a tug often shown as "Col. Davis" actually bore the name CAL DAVIS. Indices, where provided, can help reduce some of these types of problems, but it is the author's opinion that the easiest to use form of organization should be in the text itself, and that the index should only be supplemental.

How, then, to make the use of this book as a reference as simple as possible for the reader? A standard alphabetical listing seems to be the most streamlined solution for a large number of entries. Vessels named for individuals are arranged by the person's last name, and ships named for cities or states are alphabetized by the proper noun (e.g. ROUSE SIMMONS falls after SIMCOE, rather than ROTARIAN, and CITY OF TORONTO follows TORONTO). So that the reader will not lose the sound of the ship's appellation, names have been left in their natural order. Thus the schooner ROUSE SIMMONS is listed as such and not as "Simmons, Rouse," which obviously loses some of the effect of the original name. Apologies are offered to purists who prefer listing by first letter of first name (after all, "Fitzgerald, Edmund," is a person, while EDMUND FITZGERALD is the name of a ship).

VESSEL INFORMATION—The shipwreck information in this volume will be much more meaningful if data is provided on the vessels themselves. With this in mind, the following information has been provided where available: Length in feet at the waterline (overall length has been used if that is the only measurement available); gross tonnage (note that the Canadian and American systems of figuring tonnage differ greatly); plus year and location of launch.

In cases where it has been possible to do so, a sketch of the silhouette of the vessel has been added. These are scale drawings meant to show the general features of the vessel, and are not meant to be accurate in every detail. Sketches have been taken from photographs, artist's renderings, and written descriptions.

LOCATIONAL DATA—For purposes of this work, the Great Lakes have been described in this manner:

• Lake Erie extends from the mouth of the Detroit River

to Niagara Falls and the outflow of the Welland Canal at Port Dalhousie.

• Lake Huron includes Georgian Bay and the North Channel, St. Marys River, and the Lake proper from the present Mackinac Bridge to the head of the St. Clair River.

• Lake Michigan includes the Chicago Canal System, Green Bay, and the lake itself to the site of the present Mackinac Bridge.

• Lake Ontario includes the lake proper from Niagara Falls to the head of the St. Lawrence River.

• Lake Superior includes the lake itself to the Soo Locks.

• The Detroit-St. Clair River complex components have been treated as separate entities, with their respective watershed rivers.

• In general, accidents occurring on inland lakes and waterways have not been included unless they had significant loss of life or are of particular historical interest.

An attempt has been made to locate every accident described in this book as to its general location on a map or chart. This has been a major research project in itself. Many location names have changed (some several times), since accidents happened. Some reports use local names which do not appear on any map or chart, while others reflect confusion over the use of the same name for locations on different lakes (e.g. each of the lakes has a "Long Point" and a "Presque Isle").

Multiple reports on the same vessel have served to clarify most of these problems, but there are a small number of locations shown which have defied identification. The author has tried to pass information concerning specific obscure places on to the reader by giving the location in relation to some known town or landmark. Divers or others who desire to pinpoint wreck positions should consult local records. Readers should be able to identify the general locations of most wrecks on a good roadmap.

ANTHROPOMORPHISM/GENDER—Since this work is of an historical nature, the author has chosen to use the traditional practice of mariners in describing their vessels in the female gender, regardless of the name of the ship. Avid readers of sea lore are aware that sailors have always ascribed to vessels the qualities of humans, both good and bad, and referred to their vessel in the respectful manner one would use in reference to their mother.

This personification is probably rooted in the utter dependence that a sailor has upon the vessel for life and livelihood. Some writings go so far as to refer to the crew as the ship's "children". A boat that had survived a storm may therefore have been said to have "protected her crew" and "fought through the gale to bring them home", actions of the crew notwithstanding. Likewise, a ship that had suddenly capsized with loss of life might be said to have "drowned her sailors" on purpose and with evil intent. Incidentally, some other cultures have the tradition of referring to vessels in the masculine.

Another traditional gender-related practice used in this volume is that of referring to the members of a ship's crew as "crewmen" or "seamen." The author has attempted to use these words only when it was known or was reasonable to assume that those involved were men. In practice, very few commercial ships carried women on board, except as passengers, until the turn of the century. Beginning around that time, ships' officers would sometimes hire a woman—usually a wife or relative of some other crew member—as a cook or steward on board a commercial boat. Although many more women work the boats today than in the past, crews of lakers and ocean-going vessels are still predominantly men.

TYPES OF ACCIDENTS—All ship losses described herein may be assumed to be accidental unless otherwise indicated. Vessels that had outlived their usefulness were, in times past, often taken out on a lake and scuttled or burned in lieu of dismantling. Sometimes an entrepreneur would destroy a ship as a spectacle for paying crowds. The two-masted schooner LYMAN M DAVIS, one of the last commercial sailing ships on the Lakes and veteran of 60 years of service, was burned for the pleasure of an amusement park crowd at Toronto in 1934.

But in the present volume we are concerned only with accidents that resulted in the loss of vessel or crew, and though each loss has a uniqueness about it, almost all accidents fall within the confines of a few limited categories.

Gales and storms—More than half of all accidental vessel losses were caused by temperamental Great Lakes weather. People who live by the freshwater seas tell visitors "if you don't like the weather, stick around for a while and it will change". Saltwater sailors that have plied the inland seas can tell you that Lake storms are markedly different from the sea-going variety, but they can be just as dangerous and deadly as those fabled gales of the Seven Seas.

Lake storms can arise with terrifying speed and without warning. Mirror smooth water can be whipped into a killing frenzy in an hour's time. Temperatures can drop from balmy to arctic before the stove can be stoked up, and wind can shift 180° faster than a big ship can be turned to meet it.

In the Big Storm of 1913, skippers reported huge waves coming from one point on the compass while 60 mile-per-hour winds assaulted their ships from an entirely different direction. Ten big steel freighters were lost in that infamous gale—capsized or twisted in half or driven under by the combination of terrors described. Storm-stirred lake waves have a much smaller frequency than their ocean cousins, and large vessels may be attacked by four or five at once, while smaller ships may find themselves with air under their keels as they span the gap between greybeards.

Sail vessels are often blown down or capsized. Heavily laden bulk carriers have been known to climb the side of a big sea, then simply dive to the bottom in the trough that follows. Green water can wash right over the deck and remove hatch covers and even deckhouses, clearing the way for other waves to invade the holds and engineering spaces. Ships losing steerageway or attempting to turn can be pushed around sideways—"into the troughs"—where crews, cargoes and gear are buffeted and tossed about, until the ship just surrenders. Unfortunately, the words "foundered" or "sunk," which are often used in reports to describe such losses, do not even begin to describe what a ship and her crew may go through before she is simply overwhelmed by the elements and slides beneath the maelstrom to the dark, cool, calm resting place below.

Strandings—No matter how much a sailor loves the life

aboard ship, his home is still on land. But the shore is no friend to his ship. Vessels that can withstand the biggest of waves with ease are quickly destroyed when thrown upon the rocks by a storm. The Lakes seem so vast when one looks out to the horizon on a calm day, but in heavy weather a skipper can feel positively claustrophobic with the shore only ten miles away and the seas running towards it. The fact is that many of the shipping lanes on the Lakes pass within hailing distance of deadly reefs and shoal water. Storm-beset vessels may have to struggle mightily just to stay off the rocks. In days past, sailing vessels and barges were particularly vulnerable to the conspiracy of wind and wave. This one-two punch would rip a ship's sails to tatters, or part her towing hawsers, then push her up on some reef or beach. Once she was aground, the waves could really begin their evil work, lifting a ship and dropping it like a galley cook cracking an egg. It was a stout ship indeed that could last more than a few hours under those torturous conditions.

Ships broken up by the action of waves were not always cast ashore by storms. Navigational error, inaccurate charts, or inadequate watch often sent ships aground. If the vessel was not rescued quickly, big waves would rush in to administer the *coup de grace* in the next storm. Wooden and steel ships alike were doomed if left on their bellies for too long.

Even as late as December of 1989, the U.S. Coast Guard Bouy Tender MESQUITE was destroyed in this way. Jammed on a rocky bar near Keweenaw Point, the veteran steel ship was slowly but inexorably dashed to pieces, despite confident predictions of an early rescue. Within a month of her grounding, she was declared to be a constructive total loss, and by the time she was lowered to her grave the next summer, the spit-and-polish "cutter" had been reduced to a ragged shadow of a military ship.

Fires and explosions—Where strandings were a major cause of the loss of sailing ships and schooner-barges, fire was often the culprit in the loss of wooden steamers, a breed which dominated Lakes trade for 75 years. Steam boilers required high heat to operate, and the more power that was needed, the bigger the fire. A steamer hard-pressed by a storm might need all the fire she could get, but the contents of a full firebox could easily be dumped out on the deck of a heaving ship. Thus many vessels caught fire while underway, and some lost the race to the shore that was necessary for survival under such conditions.

Other ships were destroyed by fire when they were just sitting at their docks. Idle steamers often kept a banked fire going all the time. This was done to provide steam power when needed and to prevent moving parts from seizing. In a great many instances, a fire left untended was responsible for the the loss of an otherwise perfectly seaworthy vessel, and sometimes spread to docks, warehouses, and other ships as well. Occasionally it was the other way around, and some unfortunate schooner or steamer was consumed by a dock fire or even a forest fire.

At least three significant ships were lost in the Great Chicago Fire of 1871. Unfortunately for historians, fire was also used as a method of disposing of vessels sent to the shipbreakers for scrapping, and many reports do not distinguish between accidental fires and the demolition of a stripped vessel that had outlived its usefulness.

Steam boilers had another drawback. If they were not perfectly built or were imperfectly maintained, they could explode when placed under high pressure. Boiler explosions could destroy a ship in many ways. Small vessels such as tugs were often demolished outright by the blast, while others were set afire by the burning coal and red-hot boilerplate that was sprinkled about. Still others had some portion of their own machinery cast through their hulls and sank as a result. Ships sometimes survived these explosions, but crewmen were often killed or scalded, and many vessels were gone forever.

Ice damage—Anyone who has lived along the shores of one of the Great Lakes can attest to the power of moving ice. Locals smirk when a novice cottage owner decides to leave his supposedly sturdy dock in the water for the winter, then returns in the spring to find that both pilings and decking have gone to join the bones of many ships that also made the mistake of challenging the ice.

In late fall and early spring, ships are crushed, holed and sometimes dismembered by the frozen version of their element. In Lake Superior, roving ice floes have sunk unwary vessels as late as the end of May. When the lake purges itself in the spring, huge fields of ice still rudely elbow their way past helpless freighters waiting above the Soo, and rivers such as the St. Marys, the St. Clair, and the Detroit become moving masses of battering rams. Vessels caught in the path of such a juggernaut risk loss or heavy damage.

Collisions—The "rules of the road" for Great Lakes commerce have developed gradually over the past 200 years. For a long time ships simply went where they pleased, and there were few enough that the possibility of two vessels finding themselves occupying the same bit of lake at the same time was remote. As more and more vessels tried to service the same growing ports and travelled the same routes, collisions became more and more common.

Maritime laws regarding passing and rights-of-way went on the books and fixed shipping lanes were established (though for quite some time the lanes for U.S. and Canadian vessels did not coincide). But with a growing number of ships on the Lakes at once, with heavily used ports such as Cleveland and Milwaukee drawing dozens of vessels to the same spot, and with lanes becoming compressed in dangerous zones such as Pointe Aux Barques and Pelee Passage, a certain number of collisions were almost inevitable.

The Laws of Physics usually declared the larger ship in such a meeting the automatic winner, but in cases like that of the LADY ELGIN and the AUGUSTA, this was not the inevitable result. In the 1881 collision between the brand-new iron-hulled steamer BRUNSWICK and the loaded wooden schooner CARLINGFORD, both ships were lost, even though the schooner was less than half the BRUNSWICK's size and had been rammed broadsides.

Boats collided with other objects quite often, and more than a few did not survive. For example, the popular steel-hulled excursion steamer TASHMOO struck a floating obstruction or "deadhead" and sank in 1936. The wooden steamer ROBERT R RHODES came out second best in a duel with a bridge in 1921. And the freighter CHARLES B PACKARD struck a submerged wreck and sank in

Pelee Passage in 1906.

Then there were the dozens of vessels that were destroyed in collisions with breakwaters, piers, jetties and other man-made obstructions. In all, collisions of one sort or another accounted for about 15 percent of all vessels destroyed.

Other losses—Some of the most interesting cases of destroyed vessels are the result of some rare or freak occurrence. Tugs crushed by ships in harbor, vessels struck by lightning or waterspouts, boats dragged down when their companions sank, and freight carriers lost due to misloading or poor stowage of equipment are just a few of the freakish accidents that spelled the end for lakers. In May of 1964, the two small passenger and automobile ferries JAMES W CURRAN and JOHN A McPHAIL were being towed to Georgian Bay for refitting when the CURRAN was struck by a freak waterspout and sank. The hapless McPHAIL, though undamaged otherwise, was still chained to her companion, and simply followed her to the bottom.

Another freakish weather occurrence was (and is) the "white squall". Little mentioned in meteorology books, the white squall was a well-known and feared phenomenon to the men of the sail era. The windstorm was small and localized, but very violent. It would come "out of the clear blue" and could rip a schooner's sails to shreds, tear off masts and spars, or "knock her down" in a few moments, without the forewarning of dark clouds.

A significant number of sail vessels were reportedly destroyed on otherwise calm days by white squalls, including a few that were just found floating by passing ships. The change to steam-powered vessels spelled an end to disasters caused by the squalls, but pleasure sailors still occasionally report the strong winds that come out of nowhere.

"Sailed through a crack in the lake"—Perhaps most fascinating and mysterious of all are the ships that left port and, as the official records understate, "have not since reported". Legends and ghost stories have grown around these vessels that just sailed out of port and out of all knowledge of men, leaving little or no trace behind. Of these the steel steamer BANNOCKBURN is perhaps the most famous, but the rolls show scores of vessels like the bark GRIFFIN, the schooner EMERALD, and the twin warships INKERMANN and CERISOLES, that just disappeared, without a shred of identifiable evidence to prove that they were not the victims of Gitchee Manitou, the Chippewa god that controlled the Lakes.

Any mass of information of this scope, gleaned as it has often been from the sometimes murky history of an often undeveloped region can hardly claim to be absolutely accurate. However, it is believed that this volume represents the most complete and accurate body of data yet assembled on the subject of Great Lakes shipwrecks. Perhaps individuals with more intimate knowledge of specific localities or events can help to fill in gaps in information and correct errors. Future editions of this work may be a combination of the efforts to provide the complete picture of Great Lakes shipwrecks.

The ultimate goal of this work is an ambitious one. It is hoped that it will stimulate historians (both amateur and professional), boating enthusiasts, sport divers, and anyone else who enjoys freshwater and blue skies, to an even bigger desire to study and appreciate the Great Lakes. Our freshwater seas are one of the earth's premier resources, and it remains for we who love them to protect both the Lakes and their fascinating history. □

Dave Swayze
Mt. Pleasant, MI
September, 1990

Directory of Great Lakes shipwrecks

Number of sources used for each entry follows in brackets [ ].

C L ABBELL ■ Merchant schooner
Lake Michigan: The ABBELL struck bottom and wrecked in the shoal water surrounding Waugoschance Point, Michigan in 1861. The location is pronounced "wawg-uh-shantz," but was called "Wobbleshanks" by sailors. [2]

ABBIE ■ Merchant schooner of 87 t. and 88 ft., launched in 1886 at Ludington, MI
Lake Michigan: This little schooner with her cargo of bark foundered off Manistee, Michigan on November 8, 1905. No lives were lost in the incident. [3]

GEORGE M ABELL or **ABLE** ■ Merchant schooner of 146 t.
Lake Erie: On August 20, 1871, the ABELL went on a reef near Port Burwell, Ontario, and broke up. [2]

ABEONA ■ Merchant schooner of 100 tons
Lake Ontario: On October 11, 1877, the ABEONA sank one mile west of Point Austin, near Big Sandy Creek. She was downbound with lumber at the time. One source says she was of British registry. [2]

ABERCORN ■ Wooden bulk freight steamer of 261 t. and 126 ft., launched at Marine City, MI in 1873
Lake Huron: This "rabbit" was destroyed by fire in the harbor at Goderich, Ontario, on September 5, 1904. Her remains were abandoned in place. [4]

ABERDEEN ■ Merchant schooner, probably the 1,045 t., 211 ft. schooner launched at W Bay City, MI in 1892
Lake Michigan: This big sailing vessel beached and broke up in a storm near Grand Haven, Michigan, in November of 1898. [2]

ABERDEEN ■ Wooden bulk freight steamer of 142 t. and 100 ft., launched at Picton, Ontario in 1894
Lake Ontario: On March 11, 1918, the small "rabbit" ABERDEEN caught fire and was destroyed at Picton, in the Bay of Quinte area. [3]

ABERNETHY ■ 260 t. vessel of unreported type
Lake Erie: This ship was destroyed by fire at Pelee Island on October 24, 1914. [1]

ABIGAIL ■ Merchant schooner
Lake Huron: Conflicting reports show this vessel lost in either the main part of Georgian Bay or in the North Channel in 1892. [2]

ABYSSINIA ■ Bulk freight schooner-barge of 2,037 t. and 305 ft., launched at W Bay City, MI in 1896
Lake Erie: One of the largest vessels of this type ever to ply the Lakes, the ABYSSINIA met her end on Oct. 18, 1917. In a heavy gale she was lost from the tow of the steamer MARUBA, went ashore near Buffalo and broke up. [3]

ACACIA ■ 188 t. vessel of unreported type, but she may be the 102 ft. schooner-barge of that name built at Smith's Falls, Ont. in 1875
Lake Ontario: This small carrier went hard aground on Main Duck Island, in the center of the approach to the St. Lawrence River, on May 2, 1903. She may have been recovered. [2]

ACADIA ■ Steam freighter of 806 t. and 177 ft., launched in 1866 at Hamilton, Ont.
Lake Superior: On November 5, 1896, this 30-year-old steamer was driven ashore by a gale near the Michipicoten River, Ontario. Her crew was rescued, but the vessel itself was broken up under the pounding of storm waves. [4]

ACME ■ Propeller freighter, probably the 320 t., 124 ft. ship launched as the steamer MUSIC at New Jerusalem, OH in 1874
Lake Huron: The ACME was reported to have foundered in midlake in 1893. [2]

ACME ■ Steam tug
Lake Erie: While breaking ice near Buffalo in the spring of 1902, the tug ACME was rammed from behind by the steamer WILKESBARRE. Her crew was taken off by the steamer before the tug sank. [2]

ACONTIOUS ■ Merchant schooner
Lake Huron: This sailing ship went missing with all hands in a fall, 1887 gale. [2]

ACORN ■ Merchant schooner
Lake Huron: In 1876 the schooner ACORN foundered near Sand Beach (now Harbor Beach), Michigan. [1]

ACORN ■ Schooner (probably yacht)
Lake Erie: This sail vessel is reported to have sunk fol-

lowing a collision with the propeller TROY near West Sister Island in July of 1849. [1]

ADA ■ Merchant schooner
Lake Huron: This schooner sank within sight of Collingwood, Ontario, in Georgian Bay, in 1859. [1]

ADAIN ■ Merchant schooner of 62 t.
Lake Huron: This tiny schooner was wrecked by storm waves and sank near Grindstone City, at the tip of Michigan's "thumb," on October 18, 1890. [2]

ADAIR ■ Merchant schooner
Lake Huron: This schooner is listed by two sources as having been lost in two adjacent places. One report says she went ashore and broke up on Charity Island in 1886, the other says on Oak Point, nine miles to the east, in 1891. Both locations are in upper Saginaw Bay. [2]

GEORGE W ADAMS ■ Bulk freight schooner-barge of 1,444 t. and 231 ft., launched at Toledo in 1875
Lake Erie: On December 11, 1895, while in tow of the steamer CALEDONIA, the ADAMS sank near Colchester Shoal. The barge was trapped in early winter ice and her hull was crushed. [3]

ADDIE ■ Merchant schooner of 30 t. and 64 ft., launched at Benton Harbor, MI, in 1872
Lake Michigan: This diminutive schooner, carrying a cargo of household goods, sank in a storm near Frankfort, Michigan, on October 5, 1897. It was her second major Lake Michigan accident—she sank in 1887 as well, but was recovered. [2]

ADDIE B ■ Merchant schooner
Lake Huron: This sailing ship was stranded near Caseville, Michigan in 1888 and declared a total loss. [1]

ADELAIDE ■ Sidewheel passenger and package freight steamer of 230 t., built in 1830 at Chippawa, Ont.
Lake Erie: This early freighter suffered two major accidents in her 10 year career. She was almost destroyed by a boiler explosion and fire in 1830 or 31, in which three lives were lost, and was wrecked on the lake in 1840. [3]

ADELE ■ Tug, perhaps the 9 t., 48 ft. vessel built in 1889 at Mt Clemens, MI
Lake Huron: Few details are reported on the loss of this tug, reportedly destroyed by fire at Drummond Island, Michigan, in 1936. [1]

ADIRAMLED ■ Wooden bulk freight steamer of 706 t. and 191 ft., launched as the CITY OF FREMONT at Cleveland in 1866

Lake Ontario: On June 18, 1912, in Dutch John Bay, this veteran steamer met her fate. When her 46-year-old hull could not take the strain of a heavy load of railroad rails and coal, her seams opened and she sank. [3]

ADMIRAL ■ Wooden passenger and package freight steamer of 49 tons
Lake Michigan: The tiny ADMIRAL was in Chicago harbor when her boilers exploded and she sank with the loss of four lives December 31, 1884. [1]

ADMIRAL ■ Steel tug of 130 t. and 90 ft., built as the W H MEYER at Manitowoc, WI in 1922
Lake Erie: This tug was towing the loaded steel tanker-barge CLEVECO (qv) on December 2, 1944, when she encountered a terrific storm off Cleveland. The ADMIRAL radioed her plight, but went down with all 14 hands before a rescue could be accomplished. The CLEVECO was also lost. Both wrecks were later located. [5+]

ADRIATIC ■ Merchant bark
Lake Huron: Details are lacking in the report of the loss of this ship near Thunder Bay, Michigan, following a collision in 1872. [1]

ADVANCE ■ Scow or schooner-scow of 49 t.
Lake Erie: This vessel was reported to have sunk after a collision with the steamer U S GRANT at Put-in-Bay in July of 1871. [1]

ADVANCE ■ 84 t. vessel of unrecorded type
Lake Ontario: This small ship was reported stranded and lost on the shore of Nicholson Island, near Wellington, Ontario on October 14, 1871. [1]

ADVANCE ■ Bulk freight schooner of 180 t.
Lake Michigan: All six crewmen lost their lives when this ship sank ten miles north of Port Washington, Wisconsin, on September 8, 1885. She was carrying a cargo of wood at the time. [3]

ADVANCE ■ Propeller freighter of 358 t. and 175 ft., launched in 1884 at St Catherine's, Ont., as the steamer SIR S L TILLEY (qv)
Lake Huron: This propeller had been seriously damaged in a fire in 1899, but had not been rebuilt until the 1920's. In December of 1927, the ADVANCE went on the rocks off Manitoulin Island, and was so badly damaged (and probably of so little value) that she was declared a total loss. [3]

ADVENTURE ■ Small merchant schooner
Lake Ontario: While transporting a cargo of stone, the ADVENTURE foundered with all three hands off Grand River, Ontario, in October of 1848. [1]

ADVENTURE ▪ Wooden bulk freight steamer of 149 t. and 104 ft., built as a schooner at Detroit in 1875, converted to steamer in 1897
Lake Erie: This ADVENTURE, laden with a cargo of lime, caught fire and was destroyed close to shore at Kelley's Island on October 7, 1903. [3]

AETNA ▪ Schooner
Lake Michigan: The AETNA ostensibly went down about 1890 in the Manitou Passage. She was reportedly under full sail with a cargo of coal when she sank in calm weather. [1]

AFRICA ▪ Passenger and package freight propeller of 482 t. and 136 ft., launched in 1873 at Kingston, Ont.
Lake Huron: On October 14, 1895 this ship encountered a heavy gale on the lake. She had almost made Georgian Bay when she struck a reef near Cove Island, broke up and foundered with all 13 of her crew. In a previous accident, she was almost destroyed by fire in 1888 and was rebuilt at Kingston, Ontario. [5+]

AGATE ▪ Merchant schooner
Lake Huron: This vessel is reported to have gone ashore and broken up at Presque Isle, near Alpena, Michigan, in 1856. [1]

AGAWA ▪ Steel bulk freight steamer of 3,759 t. and 379 ft., launched in 1902 at Collingwood, Ont., as a barge
Lake Huron: On December 7, 1927, this carrier stranded on Manitoulin Island and was declared a total loss by her underwriters. However, clever salvage work released her and she was rebuilt and returned to service as the steamer ROBERT P DURHAM and later HERON BAY. She was scrapped in 1966. [5]

AGNES W ▪ Wooden bulk freight steamer of 1,593 t. and 264 ft., launched as the ROSWELL P FLOWER at Milwaukee in 1887
Lake Huron: While attempting to enter the St Mary's River in a storm, this steamer stranded on Drummond Island and was pounded to pieces. The accident occurred on July 12, 1918. [3]

AHNAPEE ▪ Merchant schooner of 118 t.
Lake Michigan: This carrier, along with her cargo of railroad ties, was lost when she sank 2.5 miles north of Sheboygan, Wisconsin, on June 9, 1884. [2]

AIMIE ▪ Steamer of 10 t.
Lake Erie: The AIMIE was a tiny steamer that stranded and was destroyed by waves north of Presque Isle, near Erie, Pennsylvania on November 20, 1880. [1]

AJAX ▪ Steam freighter
Lake Huron: Saginaw Bay was the site of the destruction of this ship by fire in 1872. Other details are unavailable. [1]

H C AKELEY or **ACKLEY** or **ACKELEY** ▪ Bulk freight steambarge of 1,187 t., new at the time of the accident
Lake Michigan: Six of this steamer's crew were lost when the AKELEY foundered. In a heavy gale, she encountered the disabled tug PROTECTION (qv). She took the tug in tow, but the storm soon broke her rudder off, and the helpless steamer was forced into the wave troughs. Her cargo of corn shifted, causing her to list, take water and slowly sink. She released the tug, drifted away and sank the next day. The two-mast schooner DRIVER, disabled by the storm herself, was by chance passing by and saved all but six of the AKELEY's crew. The accident happened off Holland, Michigan, on November 13, 1883. [4]

ALAMEDA ▪ Barge
Lake Erie: Anchored off Pelee Island in a storm, the ALMEDA's stern was wrenched off and she sank on May 22, 1880. [1]

ALASKA ▪ Merchant schooner
Lake Huron: According to one report, the ALASKA went aground and broke up on Bois Blanc Island in the Straits of Mackinac in 1884. [1]

ALASKA ▪ Wooden bulk freight steamer of 510 t. and 140 ft., launched at Spring Wells (Detroit), MI in 1878 as a passenger steamer
Lake Huron: While waiting out a late season storm on Christmas Eve of 1910, this steamer caught fire and was destroyed. The accident happened a few miles from Tobermory, Ontario, at the tip of the Saugeen (Bruce) Peninsula. [5]

ALBACORE ▪ Package and bulk freight schooner of 337 t. and 144 ft., launched at Port Dalhousie, Ont. in 1872
Lake Ontario: After a storm blew out her sails, the helpless two-master was washed into a seawall near Oswego, New York and battered to pieces by waves. The date was September 12, 1900. [2]

ALBANY ▪ Merchant schooner
Lake Huron: In 1843 this sail vessel was reported to have gone aground and wrecked in the Straits of Mackinac. [1]

ALBANY ▪ Sidewheel passenger and package freight steamer of 669 t. and 210 ft., launched at Detroit in 1846
Lake Huron: A tremendous gale on November 26, 1853 drove the ALBANY over a bar and into shoal water near Presque Isle, Michigan. Plans were made to haul her back to open water, but before they could be accomplished, she was wrecked by big combers. None of her passengers or crew were lost. [3]

ALBANY ▪ Steel bulk freight steamer of 1,918 t. and 267 ft., launched at Wyandotte, MI in 1885
Lake Huron: While traversing the converging shipping lanes above Pointe Aux Barques in a fog, the ALBANY collided with the steamer PHILADELPHIA (qv) and sank. Eight of her crew were reported lost (one source says 24), and her cargo of grain as well, in this November 7, 1893, accident. [5 +]

ALBATROS IV ▪ 16 t. vessel of unreported type
Lake Ontario: On August 22, 1953, this boat was reported destroyed by fire in Toronto Harbor. [1]

ALBATROSS ▪ Bulk freight schooner of 140 ft. overall length, launched at Port Dalhousie (pronounced Duh-Lucy), Ont. in 1871
Lake Huron: On October 21, 1911, this veteran schooner took water and sank in Georgian Bay. [1]

ALBEMARLE ▪ Merchant schooner, probably built at Buffalo in 1867
Lake Huron: This ship is reported to have foundered in a storm near Point Nipigon in the Straits of Mackinac in 1867. [1]

ALBERTA ▪ Steel passenger and package freight steamer
Lake Superior: Fog played a part in the collision between this freighter and the steam barge JOHN M OSBORNE (qv) near Whitefish Point. Both ships sank in the accident, which occurred on July 27, 1884, but although she was carrying a full complement of crew and passengers, only one of the ALBERTA's people was lost, and that was in an attempt to rescue crewmen from the OSBORNE. The ship was later recovered. [3]

ALBERTA ▪ Wooden bulk freight steamer of 122 t. and 103 ft. overall, built as a schooner at Cape Vincent, New York in 1886
Lake Ontario: On October 8, 1902, this carrier was at a wharf at Trenton, Ontario when she caught fire and was totally destroyed. [3]

ALBERTA ▪ Vessel of unreported type
Lake Superior: A single report shows this ALBERTA as having foundered at Thunder Bay, Ontario, on December 22, 1917. [1]

ALBION ▪ Wooden bulk freight steamer of 380 t. and 138 ft., launched at Brockville, Ont., as the steamer BRISTOL. Sometimes reported as a schooner
Lake Huron: This lumber-carrying vessel was destroyed when she went on the rocks near treacherous Pointe Aux Barques, northeast of Grindstone City, Michigan on October 3, 1887. [4]

ALDRICH ▪ Salvage tug
St. Clair River: The ALDRICH was a Reid salvage tug reported to have sunk in December of 1899. [1]

WILLIAM ALDRICH ▪ Lumber schooner of 192 t. and 124 ft., launched in 1856 at Two Rivers, WI
Lake Michigan: The ALDRICH was knocked down in a white squall in 1891, resulting in the drowning of one of her crew. She was righted and went on to a 60-year career of service on the Lakes. [2]
Lake Michigan: No lives were lost when the ALDRICH went ashore and broke up off Davenport, Michigan, near Point Epoufette. The ship was lost on June 9, 1916. Ironically, the word Epoufette means "place of rest" in French. [3]

ALERT ▪ Merchant brig
Lake Michigan: The ALERT was a small sailing vessel that went hard ashore on Waugoschance Point, near the western end of the Straits of Mackinac, and was wrecked. The year was 1844. [1]

ALERT ▪ Bulk freight schooner-barge of 600 t. and 146 ft., launched at Trenton, MI, in 1871
Lake Michigan: This vessel was in tow of the steamer DUNCAN CITY with a cargo of stone when she broke loose, swamped and sank in heavy weather. The accident occurred near S. Manitou Island on Sept. 16, 1904. [2]

ALETHA B ■ Fishing tug
Lake Erie: A violent storm overtook this fishing boat while she was going about her business, sinking her in 1974 with the loss of two of her crew. She was later recovered, rebuilt and renamed GLEN L. [1]

ALEXANDER ■ Sidewheel steamer of 111 t. and 104 ft., launched in 1865 at Sandusky, OH, as the steamer GENERAL SHERMAN
Lake St Clair: This small vessel caught fire and was destroyed four miles from Belle River, Ontario, on October 4, 1879. [3]

ALEXANDRIA ■ Steam freighter of 201 t. and 97 ft., launched in 1902 at Chatham, Ont.
Lake Huron: Little Current, Ontario, at the north end of Georgian Bay was the site of the loss of this vessel by fire in 1927. [2]

ALEXANDRIA ■ Wooden passenger/package freight steamer of 508 t. and 188 ft., launched as the towing steamer ALEXANDRA at Montreal in 1866
Lake Ontario: Carrying a cargo of foodstuffs, this aged ship was blown ashore under the Scarborough Bluffs, east of Toronto, on August 3, 1915. She was later broken up by waves. [3]

ALGERIA ■ Bulk freight schooner-barge of 2,038 t. and 285 ft., launched at W Bay City, MI, in 1896
Lake Erie: On May 9, 1906, after loading a cargo of iron ore at Cleveland, the hull of this large wooden carrier gave way and she sank near a harbor breakwall with the loss of two of her crew of twelve. [5]

ALGERIAN ■ Schooner or steamer
Lake Superior: This vessel sank somewhere along the Minnesota shore (most likely near Split Rock) in 1875, taking seven of her crew down with her. [2]

ALGOMA ■ Steel passenger steamer of 1,733 t. and 262 ft., launched at Clyde, Scotland, in 1883
Lake Superior: In one of the worst disasters in Lake Superior history, this new steel vessel, thought to be one of the sturdiest afloat, was driven aground on Isle Royale on November 7, 1883. The tremendous storm that had sent her aground tore the ship apart with the loss of 48 lives. The wreck was eventually pushed off the rocks by waves and sank. She was relocated by divers in 1978. [5+]

ALGOMA ■ Dredge
Lake Michigan: During a gale that battered the lake on November 18, 1919, this work vessel foundered off Manitowoc, Wisconsin. [1]

ALGOMA ■ Sidewheel passenger and package freight steamer of 758 t. and 163 ft., built as the CITY OF TORONTO at Niagara, Ont., in 1839, rebuilt in 1863 and lengthened
Lake Huron: In the winter of 1877, this venerable steamer sank from unreported causes at Collingwood, Ontario, in Georgian Bay. The year of this accident is also reported as 1870. [3]

ALGONQUIN ■ Merchant schooner of 50 t. and 54 ft., launched in 1838 at Cleveland
Lake Superior: This tiny sailing ship sank at the head of the Lake, near Duluth, in 1856. [2]

ALGOSOO ■ Steel bulk freight steamer of 3,429 t. and 346 ft., launched in Lorain, OH, in 1901 as the steamer SATURN
Lake Superior: The veteran freighter ALGOSOO struck bottom in big waves as she was rounding treacherous Whitefish Point in November of 1965. The steamer sank in relatively shallow water and though she was recovered, she was too old and badly damaged to be repaired, and was scrapped. [2]

ALICE G ■ Steam tug
Lake Huron: This tug went ashore and was a total loss near Tobermory, Ontario, in 1927. [1]

ALICE L ■ Gas fishing tug
Lake Superior: Caught in a late season gale, this vessel and one of her crew were lost on December 2, 1929, east of Grand Marais, Michigan. [2]

CITY OF ALLEGAN ■ Gas sternwheeler of 18 t., launched in 1908
Lake Michigan: This brand-new excursion ship was completely destroyed in a fire that occurred on the Kalamazoo River at Allegan on June 26, 1908. [1]

ALLEGHANY ■ Steam freighter, probably the 402 t., 167-footer launched in 1856 at Milwaukee
Lake Huron: This steamer is reported to have gone aground and wrecked on Summer Island near Thunder Bay, Michigan in 1896, but the position is probably misreported. The site of the wreck may be in Lake Michigan, south of the Garden Peninsula. [2]

ALLEGHENY ■ Lumber schooner-barge of 664 t. and 187 ft., launched in 1873 at Erie, PA
Lake Superior: Laden with a cargo of lumber, the ALLEGHENY broke away from her towing steamer in a gale on June 6, 1913. She stranded on a bar near Vermilion Point, Michigan, and broke up with a loss of one of her crew. [3]

ALLEGHENY ■ Steel motor vessel of 900 t. and 143 ft., launched in 1940
Lake Michigan: The ALLEGHENY was a training vessel for the Great Lakes Maritime Academy at Traverse City, Michigan. On January 27, 1978, she rolled over at her winter dock from the weight of accumulated ice on her upperworks. She may have been scrapped following the accident. [1]

ADA E ALLEN ■ Wooden propeller of 170 t. and 90 ft., launched in 1872 at Walpole Island, Ont., rebuilt in 1878 and 81
Detroit River: The ADA E ALLEN caught fire and was destroyed opposite Amherstburg, Ontario, on November (or September) 21, 1887. [2]

E B ALLEN ■ Propeller (possibly schooner) passenger and package freighter of 275 t. and 111 ft., launched at Ogdensburg, NY, in 1864
Lake Huron: The grain-laden ALLEN was reported lost following a collision with the bark NEWSBOY. The November 18, 1871, sinking occurred off Thunder Bay Island, near Alpena, Michigan. None of her crew was lost. [3]

HARRY L ALLEN ■ Steel bulk freight steamer, launched as the JOHN B COWLE
Lake Superior: This freighter caught fire at Duluth on January 20, 1978. She was damaged so severely that she was declared a total loss. [1]

WALTER B ALLEN ■ Merchant schooner of 296 t. and 137 ft., launched in 1866 at Ogdensburg, NY
Lake Michigan: This two-master was being towed in for repairs at Manitowoc, Wisconsin, when she foundered in a gale on April 16, 1880. Her temporary crew was rescued. [1]

ALLIE ■ 60 ton vessel of unreported type
Lake Ontario: One brief report says that the ALLIE was lost on September 30, 1875, near Belleville, Ontario, in the Bay of Quinte area. [1]

J M ALLMENDINGER ■ Bulk freight steamer of 183 t. and 104 ft., launched in 1883 at Benton Harbor, MI

Lake Michigan: This small lumber-carrying steamer was lost on November 26, 1895. She ran into a blinding snowstorm on that date, and went ashore to be destroyed by waves at Fox Point, north of Milwaukee. [3]

ALMA ■ Merchant schooner, probably the 94 t. schooner of this name launched at Sarnia, Ont. in 1855
Lake Ontario: This vessel reportedly foundered in mid-lake with all hands on October 22, 1866. [1]

ALOHA ■ Bulk freight schooner-barge of 552 t. and 182 ft., launched as a schooner at Mt Clemens, MI in 1888
Lake Ontario: While under tow of the steamer C W CHAMBERLAIN, this converted schooner sank in a storm on October 28, 1917. Though her location near Kingston, Ontario, was known, no salvage of the ship was attempted. [2]

ALPENA ■ Passenger and package freight sidewheeler of 643 t. and 170 ft., launched at Marine City, MI, in 1867
Lake Michigan: In one of the best known of Lakes disasters, the passenger steamer ALPENA was overtaken by a storm and went missing on October 15, 1880, with between 60 and 101 passengers and crew. She was last seen off Racine, Wisconsin and is thought to lie somewhere near Holland, Michigan. [5+]

ALPENA ■ Tug
Lake Erie: The loss of the tug ALPENA occurred on June 20, 1943 in the harbor at Huron, Ohio. On that date, she collided with the big steamer EDMUND W MUDGE and sank with the loss of one of her crewmen. [1]

ALTA ■ Bulk freight schooner-barge of 935 t. and 198 ft., launched in 1884 at W Bay City, MI
Lake Superior: Laden with lumber and under the tow of the tug W H MEYER, this carrier met her demise during a storm when she stranded in shoal water and was broken up by big waves. The accident occurred at Grand Island, off Munising, Michigan on October 5, 1905. No lives were lost. [5+]

ALTADOC ■ Steel bulk freight steamer of 3,815 t. and 356 ft., launched at W Bay City, MI, in 1901 as the steamer LAKE SHORE, later INDUS
Lake Superior: The loss of this big ship occurred on December 8, 1927, on Michigan's rugged Keweenaw Peninsula. On that date she was beset by a heavy storm and became so encrusted with ice that she was rendered help-

less. She was driven ashore and broke up in heavy seas that followed, but no lives were lost. Her deckhouse was used as a hotel on nearby Keweenaw Point for years. [5+]

ALTAIR ■ Merchant schooner
Lake Huron: The schooner ALTAIR was reported to have gone aground and wrecked on Chantry Island, Ontario, in 1864. [1]

ALTON ■ Gas screw passenger launch of 7 t. and 42 ft., launched in 1905 at Sandusky, OH
Lake Erie: This tiny shuttle boat was destroyed by fire at Lakeside, Ohio, in 1921. [1]

ALVA B ■ Steam tug of 83 t. and 73 ft, launched in 1890 at Buffalo
Lake Erie: The steam tug ALVA B sank after striking bottom in heavy weather off Avon Lake, Ohio. Lights from a local amusement park were apparently mistaken for harbor lights. She was lost on November 1, 1917. Her propeller is on display at Avon Lake. [3]

ALVA D or **D ALVA** ■ Tug of 15 t.
Lake Huron: This tiny vessel was destroyed by a fire that occurred on Collins Inlet in Georgian Bay on August 25, 1914. [2]

ALVINA ■ Schooner-scow of 95 t. and 89 ft., launched at Fair Haven, MI, in 1865
Lake Huron: This tiny cargo vessel foundered some distance off Sturgeon Point, near Harrisville, Michigan, in 1900. [2]

ALZORA ■ 33 t. vessel of unreported type
Lake Erie: In October of 1895 this small carrier was lost by sinking off the south side of Long Point. [1]

AMARANTH ■ Bulk freight schooner-barge of 272 t. and 134 ft., launched in 1864 at Milan, OH
Lake Huron: In a sudden storm on September 7, 1901, this ship was blown ashore near Ft. Gratiot, at the southern end of the lake. Her tow steamer JOHN H PAULY took the crew off in a daring action. The vessel was subsequently pounded to pieces by storm waves, despite salvage efforts. [5+]

AMAZON ■ Propeller freighter of 1,496 t. and 245 ft.
Lake Michigan: While carrying a full load of provisions, this large (for the time) steamer struck the Grand Haven

Bar in a storm and broke up. Fortunately, no lives were lost. The accident occurred on October 29, 1879 (one source says 1880). [4]

AMBOY ■ Bulk freight schooner-barge of 894 t. and 209 ft., built as the schooner HELENA at Cleveland in 1874
Lake Superior: On November 29, 1905, this barge and her tow steamer GEORGE SPENCER (qv) encountered one of the largest storms in Lakes history. Despite a day-long struggle, the coal-laden ships were driven ashore near Thomasville, Ontario, and wrecked. None of the six crew of the AMBOY were lost. [4]

AMELIA ■ Merchant schooner
Lake Erie: This sailing ship foundered with all hands in a gale on August 12, 1861. She was carrying a cargo of iron ore and was off Fairport, Ohio, when lost. Her sails and part of her rigging were found floating, but details of her demise came from a "message in a bottle" thought by historians to be authentic. [4]

AMELIA ■ Merchant schooner
Lake Huron: According to one account, this ship foundered off Goderich, Ontario, in 1864. She was recovered and rebuilt as a barge, but soon sank again (no details on second accident). [1]

AMERICA ■ Sidewheel steamer of 221 t. and 141 ft., launched at Niagara, Ont., in 1840
Lake Ontario: The old paddlewheeler AMERICA was lost off Kingston, Ontario when she foundered there in 1874. [1]

AMERICA ■ Wooden propeller of 600 t.
Lake Erie: This ship was stranded on the northeast corner of Pelee Island and went to pieces in an 1854 storm. [1]

AMERICA ■ Bulk freight schooner, possibly the 271 t., 139 ft. AMERICA built in 1849 at Clayton, NY
Lake Michigan: While traversing Green Bay in 1907 with a load of iron ore, this ship went aground on Chambers Island and broke up. [2]

AMERICA ■ Steel passenger and package freight steamer of 937 t. and 182 ft., launched in 1898 at Wyandotte, MI
Lake Superior: On June 7, 1928, reportedly in good weather, this popular passenger ship struck a reef at Washington Harbor, Isle Royale, and sank. Though the ship and her cargo of general merchandise were lost, all of her passengers and crew were saved. A wreck diver was lost on her in 1970. [5+]

The most dangerous spot on the lakes

Often when Great Lakes buffs gather, you will hear debates on the question, "What is the most dangerous spot in the Great Lakes/Seaway System?"

Everyone seems to have a favored location, and a list of disasters to back it up. Whitefish Bay, Duluth Harbor, Straits of Mackinac, Porte des Mortes, Thunder Bay, Pelee Passage, Buffalo Harbor and Kingston, Ontario, are all areas with a record of bringing ships to an untimely end.

But there is no other place in the entire basin that can compare, in sheer numbers of vessels lost, with the area surrounding Pointe Aux Barques, at the tip of Michigan's Thumb. The appellation was assigned by the French, who ostensibly named it after a rock formation in the area that has the uncanny resemblance to the prow of a sailing ship. The name, which means "point of boats", turned out to be ironic in the extreme, since at least 80 vessels have left their hulls within 20 miles of the formation.

The lake bottom within this radius is a maze of reefs, bars and shallow areas. Currents that sweep in from the open lake and up the coast of Saginaw Bay deposit sand in random ways, causing bars to come and go, and even the casual boater can point to places where ankle-deep shallows have appeared where charts say none should exist! Some charted reefs extend miles out into the lake, and come dangerously close to the shipping lanes. Parts of the bottom are extremely rocky and studded with pinnacles and boulders.

Ships travelling to and from the busy ports of Saginaw and Bay City, Michigan, must make a turn around the end of the point when bound for Lower Lakes ports at a point where the shipping lane is quite narrow, and is a convergence zone for vessels from the north as well.

A look at any map shows the exposed position of the Point. It juts out into the widest part of the lake and is thus battered by storms sweeping in from nearly every point of the compass save due south. The most common westerly storms sweep across the mouth of Saginaw Bay to catch northbound ships unawares as they emerge from the lee of the Thumb. In addition, the proximity of land and shallower (hence warmer) water to the cooler deep parts of the lake make the area particularly susceptible to fog, especially in the spring and fall.

The combination of these factors has given the area its justly-deserved reputation as "the most dangerous spot

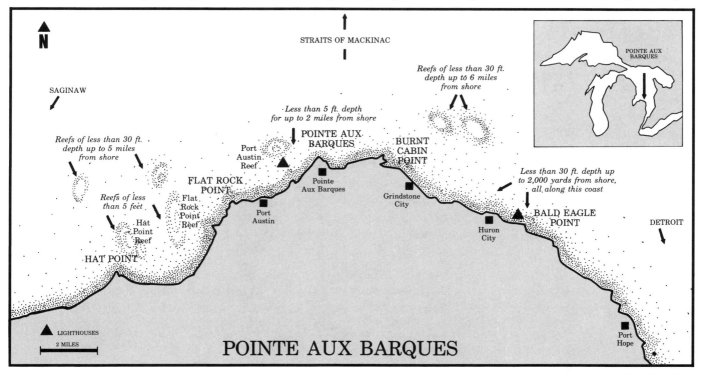

on the Lakes," and have made it the final resting place for the following vessels:

SOUTHWESTERN (1850); MONSON (1851); CRISPIN (1853); JOHN J. AUDUBON (1854); ST. CLAIR, WIMAN (1855); MAIME (1858); TROY (1859); ROCKET (1860); HURON, KEYSTONE STATE (1861); ANDOVER (1862); QUEEN CITY (1863); L.D. COWAN, WILLARD JOHNSON (1865); EUREKA (1869); MICHIGAN, MOHAWK, MOHEGAN (1870); DISPATCH, MIRANDA, MONTEZUMA (1871); R.T. LAMBERT, RURAL, STRANGER, SULTAN, VALENTINE (1873); MERCHANT, WAURECAN (1875); S.S. COE, MASSILON (1876); BERLIN, A. BOODY, J.T. MINER (1877); JACOB BETSCHY (1879); GEORGE W. HOLT (1880); AUSTIN, ENTERPRISE, H. HYDE (1883); JOSEPH (1885); C.P. WILLIAMS (1886); ALBION, ARK, MONA, MORRIS, OSCEOLA (1887); ADDIE B, EMEU, A.M. FOSTER (1888); ADAIN, E COHEN,

EUGENE, CHARLES C RYAN (1890); B.F. FERRIS, H.C. PATTER (1891); RACINE, NAIAD, L. SEATON (1892); ALBANY, PHILADELPHIA, VOLUNTEER (1893); S.P. AMES, ARCTIC, A.E. EVERETT, S.H. KIMBALL, SUPERIOR (1895); PILOT (1896); MAGGIE ASHTON, GRACE A RUELLE, HUNTER SAVIDGE (1899); LENA BEHM (1900); ANDREW JACKSON (1901); JOHN MINER, JULIA MINOR (1902); METROPOLE (1903); IRON CHIEF, WYOMING (1904); MARGRETTA (1907); GOV. SMITH (1904); FRANK H GOODYEAR (1910); AZOV (1911); SACRAMENTO (1917); CHARLES A KING, SANTIAGO (1918); FREDERICK A LEE (1936); JAMES W CURRAN, JOHN A McPHAIL (1964); DANIEL J. MORRELL (1966); BARBARA LYNN (1990).

In addition, at least some of the dozens of vessels which were lost at an unknown or unreported postion may also lie around Pointe Aux Barques. □

The Great Lakes schooner

When one thinks of Great Lakes commerce, it is natural to bring to mind the big steel ore boats, with their cabins forward and aft and their long, open decks. They are almost a symbol of the Lakes themselves. But it was the schooner that built the area. These sail ships were carrying goods to establish and sustain laketowns decades before the first steam whistles were heard. Before the railroads and highways were built, the schooner was the only connection between the developed East and frontier towns like Detroit, Chicago, Milwaukee and Duluth.

Schooners came in all shapes and sizes, from the tiny two-masted coasters that were little larger than a small sail yacht, to five-masted giants like the huge, 1200-ton DAVID DOWS. The typical schooner was a vessel of about 130 feet in length, 25 feet in beam and nine feet in depth. This size was handy in tight places, economical to operate in terms of crew, and relatively inexpensive to construct. Schooners of this size could use the Welland Canal of the late 1800s to move cargoes around Niagara.

The typical schooner was built of white oak, an abundant tree in the Midwest at that time, though some were constructed of other hardwoods, and a few even of pine and fir. She carried two or three masts, fore and aft rigged, with a mainsail and a gaff topsail on each. Many schooners also carried a square or triangular topsail on the foremast. She usually had a cabin aft, and several large holds. The three-masted schooner carried a crew of two officers and five to seven hands, and would often take on a few passengers as well.

Under normal conditions a well-built oak schooner could be expected to last about 15 to 20 years, but many were used for 30 or 40 years, and some into their 70s. A schooner that could no longer withstand the rigors of sailing was often cut down for use as a schooner-barge. This would involve the removal of her topmasts (and often some of the mains as well). The vessel would then be towed behind a steamer to increase cargo volume. In theory, a schooner-barge could set sail if pressed and make it to port under her own power. In practice, though, the barges usually only needed to strike out on their own when their steamers were in trouble due to weather. By then the barges' meager sails (which were often in poor condition, due to lack of use) were of little help.

The last operating schooner on the Lakes was the J T WING, built on the east coast, which ran into the late '30s and was put on display at Belle Isle, Detroit. She was put to the torch in the '50s to make way for the Dossin Great Lakes Museum. □

AMERICA ■ Salvage tug
Detroit River: Six of this tug's crew of 13 drowned when she capsized off Belle Isle, at Detroit. The October 21, 1941 accident occurred while she was attempting to pull the big steel freighter B F JONES off a bar. [2]

AMERICA ■ Oil screw of 13 tons
Lake Michigan: This little vessel encountered a sudden storm on May 5, 1950, and sank five miles off Sturgeon Bay, Wisconsin. [1]

AMERICAN ■ Wooden passenger/package freight steamer
Lake Erie: This early steamer's boiler exploded while she was underway and well offshore in July of 1850. She sank with the loss of 11 lives. [2]

AMERICAN EAGLE ■ Wooden passenger steamer of 161 t. and 145 ft., launched in 1880 at Sandusky, OH
Lake Erie: Pride in a ship's power and speed was the cause of many Lakes disasters. Six lives were lost when the AMERICAN EAGLE's boiler exploded while she was racing another steamer off Kelley's Island on May 18, 1882. [2]
Lake Erie: After 28 seasons in the passenger trade, this small boat was destroyed by fire at her winter layup dock at Maumee, Ohio on December 21, 1908. This vessel also gave her name to "American Eagle Reef" in the Erie Islands, which she discovered by hitting it. [4]

AMERICAN EAGLE ■ Tug of 34 t. and 57 ft.
Lake Erie: A victim of collision near the busy port of Cleveland, this tug sank 3 miles offshore on June 10, 1891. [1]

AMERICAN SAILOR ■ Bulk freight barge of 429 t.
Lake Erie: This is one of three barges reportedly sunk in a storm off Barcelona, New York, on November 2, 1937. She was in tow of the tug BALLENAS and went down with a cargo of sulphur. See also AMERICAN SCOUT, BETTY HEDGER. [2]

AMERICAN SCOUT ■ Bulk freight barge of 422 t.
Lake Erie: This carrier is one of three barges that sank off Barcelona, New York, in a November 2, 1937, storm. She was laden with a cargo of sulphur and was in tow of the tug BALLENAS at the time. See also AMERICAN SAILOR, BETTY HEDGER. [2]

AMERICAN UNION ■ Merchant schooner or bark of 543 t.
Lake Huron: On May 6, 1894, this ship was caught in a spring storm and foundered several miles off Presque Isle, Michigan. [3]

S P AMES ■ Merchant schooner of 43 t. and 61 ft.,
launched at Bay City or Montrose, MI, in 1879
Lake Huron: It is reported that this sail vessel went ashore at Pointe Aux Barques, Michigan, in 1895, and was wrecked. [2]

LILLY AMIOT ■ Gas launch of 14 t. and 45 ft., launched at Cheboygan, MI, in 1873
Lake Michigan: The AMIOT was at Ellison Bay on Plum Island, Wisconsin, when she struck a rocky ledge, exploded and burned on June 6, 1909. [3]

AMITY ■ Sidewheel steamer of 217 t. and 102 ft., launched in 1856 at Chatham, Ont.
Lake Erie: The AMITY became another of the many victims of Long Point when she was wrecked there in October of 1864. [1]

ANABEL II ■ Oil screw of 62 t.
Lake Michigan: This small vessel met her end when she caught fire at her dock and was destroyed. The blaze occurred January 12, 1956, at Sturgeon Bay, Wisconsin. [1]

ANCHOR BAY ■ Steel tug
St. Clair River: The U S Army Corps of Engineers tug ANCHOR BAY was reported to have grounded, then exploded and sunk near Harsen's Island, at the mouth of the river on December 12, 1968. One crewman was killed and three injured in the accident. [2]

ANDASTE ■ Steel self-unloading steam sandsucker of 573 t. and 266 ft., launched at Cleveland in 1892
Lake Michigan: The exact location of this "semi-whaleback" steamer's demise is not known, but she disappeared on September 9, 1929, while hauling a load of gravel from Grand Haven, Michigan to Chicago. Some historians estimate her position as 14 miles directly off Holland, Michigan. Probably overloaded, she went down from unknown causes with all 25 of her crew. When built, she was the sister ship of the steamer CHOCTAW (qv), but had been shortened 20 ft. [5]

BOB ANDERSON ■ Tug of 118 t. and 100 ft., built in 1859 at Cleveland
Lake Superior: The ANDERSON caught fire and burned to the waterline in shallow water on July 29, 1899. The accident occurred near Grand Marais, Minnesota, while the tug was towing a large raft of sawlogs. [2]

JESSIE ANDERSON ■ Schooner of 252 t. and 114 ft., launched in 1861 at Sandusky, OH
Lake Erie: On October 30, 1871, the schooner JESSIE ANDERSON sank with all hands near Long Point's "Old Cut." [2]

MAJOR ANDERSON ▪ Merchant schooner of 143 t. and 95 ft., launched in 1861 at Oswego, NY
Lake Huron/Michigan: In 1863 the MAJOR ANDERSON went ashore on Middle Island, near Alpena, Michigan, and was heavily damaged. She was recovered and later lost on Lake Michigan, but there are no details on the final accident. [3]

ANDOVER ▪ Merchant schooner
Lake Huron: This sail vessel was reported to have gone ashore and wrecked at Pte Aux Barques on Michigan's "thumb," in 1861. [1]

DAVID ANDREWS ▪ Bulk freight schooner of 150 t.
Lake Ontario: This schooner was carrying a cargo of rye when she was driven ashore at 4 Mile Point, near Oswego, New York. None of the crew was lost in the April 12, 1880, accident. [2]

ANGLO-SAXON ▪ Barge or schooner-barge, probably the former bark built at Port Dalhousie, Ont., in 1864
Lake Huron: A storm claimed this vessel, which foundered in the Straits of Mackinac in 1887. [2]

ANN ▪ Merchant schooner
Lake Erie: An early victim of Lake Erie's dreaded Long Point, this ship was lost there in 1827. It is reported that several lives were lost along with her. [2]

ANN ARBOR #1 ▪ Wooden steam carferry of 1,128 t. and 260 ft., launched at Toledo, OH in 1892
Lake Michigan: A March 7, 1910 fire consumed this vessel and her 20 rail cars of lumber, 4 miles off Manitowoc, Wisconsin. She was recovered and rebuilt, even though she had been declared a total loss. [4]

ANN MARIA ▪ Lumber schooner of 256 t. and 135 ft., launched at Conneaut, OH in 1864
Lake Huron: On October 7, 1902, this veteran schooner, laden with coal, was wrecked on a pier at Kincardine, Ontario. Four of her six crew were lost. [4]

ANNA MARIA ▪ Merchant schooner
Lake Michigan: On October 15, 1880, this schooner capsized off Two Rivers, Wisconsin. [1]

ANNA MILDRED ▪ 19 t. vessel of unreported type
Lake Ontario: This little vessel exploded and sank three miles off Port Dalhousie, Ontario, on July 9, 1950. [1]

ANNA RUTH or **ANNE RUTH** ▪ Tug and freight packet of 27 t., launched in 1920
Lake Superior: Pringle's Bay, on Edward Island near Thunder Bay, Ontario, was the site of the disastrous fire that ruined this combination tug and packet boat. She was lost on December 9, 1928. [3]

ANNANDALE ▪ Bulk freight schooner-scow of 180 t. and 123 ft., launched at Kingston, Ont. in 1868
Lake Ontario: This veteran shallow-draft vessel stranded and broke up on Charity Shoal, west of Sacket's Harbor, New York, on October 3, 1905. [2]

ANNIE LAURA ▪ Wooden sandsucker of 244 t. and 133 ft., launched in 1871 at Marine City, MI
St. Clair River: This aged wooden vessel caught fire and was destroyed after being beached near Algonac, Michigan, on August 10, 1922. The wreck was later removed as a hazard. [3]

ANNIE LAURIE ▪ Steam tug of 31 t. and 84 ft., launched at Buffalo in 1874
Lake Erie: This tug sank from unknown causes one mile off the entrance to the Erie, Pennsylvania, harbor on August 19, 1893. [1]

ANNIE MARIA ▪ Merchant schooner
Lake Huron: This ship was reported to have met her end when she foundered on Stony Island, in 1869. [1]

ANTELOPE ▪ Schooner-barge of 523 t. and 187 ft., launched in 1861 at Newport, MI
Lake Superior: In a relatively mild fall storm, this vessel opened her seams and sank off Michigan Island in the Apostles group. The date of her loss was Oct. 7, 1897. [3]

ANTELOPE ▪ Schooner-barge
Lake Huron: This barge was destroyed by fire on the Saginaw River in 1885. [1]

ANTELOPE ▪ Merchant schooner of 32 t. and 56 ft., launched as the ELLEN G COCHRAN in 1878
Lake Michigan: Four lives were lost (probably her entire crew), when this tiny sailing vessel sank in a storm near Grand Haven, Michigan, on November 15, 1894. [2]

E L ANTHONY ▪ Tug of 14 t.
Lake Michigan: The ANTHONY was reportedly destroyed by fire and sank in Chicago Harbor in July of 1885. [1]

MARIA ANTOINETTE ▪ Merchant schooner of 87 t. and 73 ft., launched in 1826 at Sandusky, OH
Lake Erie: This early lake schooner was lost in 1829, when she went ashore and was dashed to pieces in a storm. She was wrecked near Sandusky. [1]

ANZAC ▪ Tug of 9 t.
Lake Erie: This tiny vessel was reported lost to fire 18 miles southeast of Port Burwell, Ontario, on May 6, 1947. [1]

APPELONA ▪ Vessel information unreported, but may be the 37 t., 45 ft. schooner launched in 1814 at Henderson, NY
Lake Ontario: Little information is available about this vessel, reported to have disappeared on the lake with all hands. [1]

APPOMATTOX ▪ Wooden bulk freight steamer of 2,643 t. and 310 ft., launched at W Bay City, MI in 1896
Lake Michigan: This steamer was near Milwaukee when she became the victim of fog. On November 2, 1905, while carrying a cargo of coal, she ran hard aground and was so badly damaged that she was abandoned. [3]

ARAB ▪ Lumber schooner of 158 t.
Lake Michigan: On November 7th, 1883, the lumber-carrying ARAB grounded near Arcadia, Michigan, in a storm. Quick work by salvagers rescued her before she could be broken by waves, but on November 13, while being towed across to Racine by the tug PROTECTION (qv) for repairs, she capsized and sank for good with the loss of one life. [4]

ARABIA ▪ Package and bulk freight bark or schooner of 309 t. and 131 ft., launched in 1853 at Kingston, Ont.
Lake Huron: While carrying her cargo of corn across Georgian Bay, this 3-mast sail vessel encountered a gale and was beached near Echo Island. She slipped into deep water soon after. Her crew survived the October 1, 1884 accident without loss. The wreckage was located in 1973. [4]

ARABIAN ▪ Merchant brig
Lake Huron: In 1856, this small vessel struck shoal water and sank near Goose Island, 10 miles west-northwest of Mackinac Island. [2]

ARBUTUS ▪ Steam tug of 34 t., launched in 1887
Lake Superior: At the height of the Prohibition Era, in November of 1921, this tug was stopped and her crew arrested for rumrunning. While being escorted in by a Revenue Cutter, she encountered a heavy gale off Grand Marais, Michigan, on the 24th and sank with her cargo of liquor, but with no loss of life. Reports that she disappeared with all hands (and her cargo) are erroneous. [5]

ARCADIA ▪ Wooden bulk freight steamer of 230 t. and 118 ft., launched at Milwaukee in 1888
Lake Michigan: Several contradictory reports exist concerning the loss of this steamer in a storm at Big Sable Point, Michigan, in 1907. The number of lives lost is reported as 4, 9, or 10, the date as April 11, April 23 or sometime in January, and the ship is said to have either foundered or gone aground and broken up in place. [5]

ARCOLA ▪ Sternwheel freight steamer of 170 t., launched in 1856
Lake Superior: On April 2, 1859, this paddlewheeler was damaged by the action of an ice floe and sank at Reece's Landing, Minnesota. Though reported for Lake Superior, this accident may have occurred on the Mississippi River. [1]

ARCTIC ▪ Sidewheel steamer
Lake Superior: A single report states that this vessel went down off the Huron Islands, near Point Abbaye, Michigan, in 1860, but that it has been mostly salvaged or carried away by divers. [2]

ARCTIC ▪ Propeller packet of 53 t. and 64 ft., launched at Manitowoc, WI in 1881. One source says 400 t. and 194 ft.
Lake Huron: This small vessel was reported to have struck rocks and foundered south of Sand Beach (now Harbor Beach), Michigan, in September, 1893. [3]

ARCTIC ▪ Merchant schooner of 185 t. and 112 ft., launched at Ashtabula, OH, in 1853
Lake Huron: In September of 1895, this veteran schooner was lost in a collision nine miles north-northwest of Pte Aux Barques, Mich., after a collision with the vessel CLYDE. She was travelling in ballast at the time. [3]

ARCTURUS ▪ Bulk freight barge
Lake Huron: This barge or schooner-barge foundered in Saginaw Bay in 1888. [1]

ARGO ▪ Merchant schooner of 14 t. and 36 ft., launched in 1873 at Boothbay, ME, as the sail yacht LIZZIE T DAVIS
Lake Michigan: This small carrier was reported lost near Ludington, MI, on July 3, 1905, but with no loss of life. [1]

ARGO ▪ Package freight steamer of 1,089 t. and 174 ft., launched at Wyandotte, MI, in 1896 (one source says Toledo)
Lake Michigan: Caught by a heavy gale on October 20, 1905, this freighter and her cargo of general merchandise were driven ashore near Holland, Michigan. The ship later broke up under the pounding of storm waves. [3]

ARGO ▪ Lumber schooner of 68 ft.
Lake Michigan: The ARGO was a sailing vessel reported to have stranded and broken up on the beach between Big Sable Point and Manistee, Michigan, in April of 1907. Fourteen lives were lost. [1]

ARGO ▪ Tanker barge of 421 t.
Lake Erie: On October 20, 1937, this barge sank 3 miles off Pelee Island. It is reported that oil still slowly leaks from her, marking her grave with a thin slick. [2]

ARGONAUT ▪ Wooden bulk freight steamer of 1,119 t. and 213 ft., built as a schooner at Detroit in 1873
St. Clair River: On October 13, 1906, this carrier was destroyed by fire at her dock at Marysville, Michigan. [2]

ARGUS ▪ Steel bulk freighter of 7,000 t. and 436 ft., launched as the LEWIS WOODRUFF at Lorain, OH, in 1903
Lake Huron: One of the largest vessels ever lost on the Lakes, the ARGUS was assaulted by tremendous seas in the big storm of November 10-14, 1913. On the 12th, she broke in half and sank with all 25 of her crew, west of Kincardine, Ontario. The wreck was located in 1972. [5 +]

ARIADNE ▪ Bulk freight schooner of 138 t.
Lake Ontario: A storm drove this schooner ashore near New York's Big Sandy Creek on December 2, 1886, with the loss of three of her crew. The ship and her cargo of barley were both a total loss. [2]

ARIEL ▪ Armed schooner of 75 t., launched on Lake Erie in 1813
Lake Erie: Not much is known of this four gun schooner which served with the U S Navy in the War of 1812, except that she was wrecked on Lake Erie in 1814. [1]

ARIEL ▪ Merchant schooner of 166 t. and 126 ft. launched as a sidewheel steamer at Sandusky, OH, in 1854
Lake Huron: The schooner ARIEL was newly back in service after having been rebuilt at Detroit following an 1868 fire, when she went hard aground in Georgian Bay near Collingwood, Ontario. The vessel became a total wreck in the 1870 accident. [2]

ARIZONA ▪ Wooden package freight steamer of 201 ft. overall, launched in 1868 at Cleveland
Lake Superior: On November 17, 1887, this package freighter's highly combustible cargo of oils and acid burst into flame and ignited the ship. Flames drove the engine crew on deck before they could shut her down. With the

ARIZONA's prow against the breakwater at Marquette, Michigan, and her engine running full, the crew abandoned ship, whereupon she turned and pursued them up the breakwater, preceded by a plume of poisonous smoke. She finally went up on the beach and burned out. The hull was later recovered and rebuilt as a bulk freighter. [5]

ARK ▪ Cargo barge
Lake Huron: This vessel foundered with four of her crew in midlake in 1866. [1]

ARK ▪ Merchant schooner
Lake Huron: The ARK was another of at least 70 vessels lost near Pte Aux Barques, Michigan. She stranded and was lost at Grindstone City, in 1887. [1]

ARLINGTON ▪ Steel bulk freight canaller of 244 ft. and about 3,000 t., launched at Wyandotte, MI in 1913 as the steamer F P JONES
Lake Superior: Downbound with a load of wheat, this steel ship was overtaken by a violent gale/blizzard. Literally torn open by the storm, she sank near Superior Shoals on May 1, 1940, with the loss of one of her crew of 17. [5 +]

ARMENIA ▪ Bulk freight schooner-barge of 2,040 t. and 285 ft., launched at W Bay City, MI, in 1896
Lake Erie: The ARMENIA was one of the largest schooner-barges ever built for the Lakes trade. On May 9, 1906, she encountered a terrific spring gale in Pelee Passage and sank when she simply took in more water than her pumps could handle. She lies 3.8 miles off Pelee Island's abandoned lighthouse. None of her crew of seven were lost. Later in the same year, her wreckage was struck by the steamer CHARLES B PACKARD (qv), which sank. [5]

PHILIP D ARMOR or **ARMOUR** ▪ Wooden steam freighter of 1,991 t. and 264 ft., launched in 1889 at Detroit
Lake Erie: The ARMOR was lost when she struck a reef near Erie, Pennsylvania, on November 13, 1915. After her crew had abandoned ship, the vessel slipped into deeper water and sank. [3]

C W ARMSTRONG ▪ Tug
Lake Huron: A dockside fire spelled the end for this tug in 1870. She was destroyed at Bay City, Michigan, on the Saginaw River. [1]

B W ARNOLD ■ Wooden lumber hooker of 944 t. and 202 ft., launched in 1885 at Bay City, MI
Lake Superior: Laden with lumber and towing a barge, this ship met her firey end on November 21, 1896. On that date, while just west of the Portage Ship Canal across the Keweenaw Peninsula, she caught fire and was destroyed. Her crew abandoned ship without injury. [2]

W W ARNOLD ■ Package and bulk freight schooner of 426 t., launched in 1863 at Buffalo
Lake Superior: The ARNOLD was downbound with a load of ore and several passengers on November 4, 1869, when she was struck by a violent gale. The storm literally tore the schooner apart and she went down with the loss of all 11 aboard at the mouth of the Two Hearted River in Michigan's Upper Peninsula. [4]

ARROW ■ Merchant schooner of 281 t.
Lake Michigan: The schooner ARROW was stranded and lost six miles from Milwaukee in November of 1869. [1]

ARROW ■ Merchant schooner of 69 t.
Lake Michigan: On April 30, 1883, this sailing ship sank three and a half miles from Two Rivers, Wisconsin. [2]

ARUNDELL ■ Wooden or iron bulk freighter of 339 t. and 166 ft., launched in 1886 at Buffalo
Lake Michigan: While moored at a dock at Douglas, Michigan, the ARUNDELL caught fire and was destroyed. The accident happened on October 18, 1911. [2]

CITY OF ASHLAND ■ Passenger and package freight steamer of 85 t.
Lake Superior: On August 8, 1887, this small steamer was lost when she foundered in a gale near Washburn, Wisconsin. One life was lost in the accident. [1]

ASHTABULA ■ Steel steam carferry of 2,670 t. and 338 ft., launched at St. Clair, MI in 1906
Lake Erie: Just offshore from her namesake city of Ashtabula, Ohio, this veteran carferry was lost in a collision with the steamer BEN MOREELL on September 18, 1958. She settled with her upperworks above water and was later recovered for scrap. [2]

MAGGIE ASHTON ■ Merchant schooner
Lake Huron: The ASHTON was reported to have gone on the rocks and wrecked at Pointe Aux Barques, Michigan, in 1899. [1]

ASIA ■ Wooden passenger/package freight steamer of 350 t. and 136 ft., launched at St Catharine's, Ont., in 1873
Lake Huron: In one of the most disastrous accidents on the Lakes, this ship was lost on September 14, 1882, carrying 123 passengers and crew with her to the bottom of Georgian Bay. Laboring in a storm with a heavy cargo of general merchandise, she was reportedly stranded, then crushed by a huge wave and sunk near Lonely Island. Only two people survived. [5+]

ASP ■ Merchant schooner (coaster) of 57 t., built as the armed sloop ELIZABETH at Mississauga, Ont. in 1808
Lake Ontario: This War of 1812 naval veteran was captured by the Americans during the war and later rebuilt as a coaster. She was transporting lumber on October 9, 1820, when she foundered in a storm off the Salmon River, NY, in Mexico Bay. Nine of her eleven crew were lost. [4]

JOHN JACOB ASTOR ■ Merchant and fishing schooner of 112 t., launched in 1835 at Pointe Aux Pins, Ont. Her parts were cut and formed at Lorain, OH, and shipped to Superior for assembly.
Lake Superior: The little ASTOR, first reported commercial vessel on Lake Superior, was nearing Copper Harbor, Michigan, with a load of furs and trade goods when she struck a reef and foundered. None of her crew was lost in the September 21, 1844 accident. Her anchor was recovered in 1970. [5+]

ATALANTA ■ Merchant schooner
Lake Michigan: This schooner was one of the hundreds that went ashore in storms and were torn to pieces by the pounding of waves. Her particular demise came in 1878 on Sleeping Bear Point, Michigan. [1]

ATHABASKA ■ Steel steamer of 2,348 t. and 263 ft., launched in 1903 at Glasgow, Scotland, as the steamer ATHABASCA
Lake Huron: A collision with the vessel GENERAL caused this steamer to founder on November 30, 1910, near Lonely Island, in upper Georgian Bay. She sustained heavy damage and it was questionable whether she could be repaired. She was extensively rebuilt, lengthened and put back into service in 1911. [3]

ATHENA ■ Merchant schooner of 12 t., this may be the 12 t., 32 ft. ATHENE built at W Bay City, MI, in 1892
Lake Ontario: This tiny vessel was destroyed by fire at Hamilton, Ontario, on August 20, 1897. [2]

ATHENIAN ■ Merchant schooner of 372 t., launched in 1856 at Buffalo
Lake Huron: This schooner was wrecked off Oscoda, MI, in 1880, but details concerning her demise are lacking. [2]

ATHENS ■ Bulk freight schooner-barge of 2,073 t. and 289 ft., launched at W Bay City, MI, in 1897
Lake Huron: Another of the dozen or so very large wooden schooner-barges constructed at the Davidson Yard in the 1890's, this ship was lost on October 7, 1917. In tow of the steamer LUCKNOW (qv), she encountered heavy seas off Southampton, Ontario, and broke her back. She sank with five of her eight crew. [5]

ATLANTA ■ Bulk freight schooner of 600 t. and 172 ft., launched at W Bay City, MI in 1890
Lake Superior: In use as a towbarge and laden with coal, the ATLANTA was struck by a gale, whereupon she broke her towline and went to pieces off Deer Park, MI. Five of her seven crew were lost in the May 4, 1891 accident. [5]

ATLANTA ■ Wooden freighter of 1,501 t. and 201 ft., launched at Cleveland in 1891
Lake Michigan: On March 18, 1906, the steamer ATLANTA was running offshore near Port Washington when fire was discovered among her cargo of porcelain and general merchandise. Before it could be brought under control, the fire caused the loss of the ship and one of her crew of 40. [5+]

ATLANTIC ■ Merchant schooner
Lake Erie: This early schooner was lost in 1840 when she collided with the steamer BUFFALO and sank six miles east of Cleveland. [1]

ATLANTIC ■ Sidewheel passenger steamer of 1,155 t. and 267 ft., launched at Detroit in 1849
Lake Erie: In perhaps the most famous of the early Lakes disasters, the ATLANTIC was lost on August 20, 1852. Bound for Detroit on a night run, she collided with the propeller freighter OGDENSBURG and sank off Long Point. Estimates of loss of life vary from 150 to over 250. [5+]

ATLANTIC ■ Wooden bulk freight steamer of 158 t. and 112 ft., launched at Buffalo in 1880
Lake Huron: This freighter was reported lost off the lumber docks at Harrisville, MI in 1895. [2]

ATLANTIC ■ Wooden passenger and package freight steamer of 422 t. and 162 ft., launched in 1880 at Owen Sound, Ont. as the steamer MANITOULIN (qv)
Lake Huron: The popular steamboat ATLANTIC was on the lee side of the Pancake Islands, in eastern Georgian Bay, when disaster struck. Loaded with a highly flammable cargo of hay and coal oil, she caught fire and was destroyed on Nov. 10, 1903 (some sources give the year as 1902). She had been almost completely destroyed by fire previously, in 1882. [5+]

ATLANTIS ■ Oil screw of 15 t.
Lake Erie: This small vessel was destroyed by a storm that she encountered off Erieau, Ontario, on November 21, 1958. [1]

ATLAS ■ Merchant schooner
Lake Ontario: The ATLAS became an early victim of lake gales when she foundered 6 miles northwest of Oswego, NY. She went down in 1839. [1]

ATLASCO ■ Bulk freight barge of 1,224 t. and 218 ft., launched in 1881 at Buffalo as the steam package freighter RUSSELL SAGE
Lake Ontario: Laden with a cargo of coal, this barge was struck by a summer gale and sank off South Bay Point, 30 miles W of Kingston, Ontario. Her crew were all rescued in the August 17, 1921 accident. [2]

SAMUEL T ATWATER ■ Lumber schooner-barge of 322 t., launched in 1866 at Charlotte, NY
Lake Huron: Laden with a cargo of lumber, the ATWATER was lost when she went ashore and was wrecked on Manitoulin Island in 1895. [2]

JOHN J AUDUBON ■ Merchant brig
Lake Huron: This small sailing vessel was lost as the result of a collision near Pointe Aux Barques, MI in 1854. [2]

AUGUSTA ■ Steam tug 31 t. and 66 ft. overall, launched in 1883 at Port Robinson, Ont.
Lake Ontario: On December 7, 1909, this vessel was consumed by fire at Port Dalhousie, Ontario, near the north entrance to the Welland Canal. [2]

AURANIA ■ Steel bulk freight steamer of 3,218 t. and 352 ft., launched as a schooner-barge at Chicago in 1895
Lake Superior: The steamer AURANIA was one of many victims of spring ice in eastern Lake Superior. Trapped in pack ice near Parisienne Island above the Soo Locks in April of 1909, her steel hull was was slowly crushed. Her crew eventually abandoned her and she sank on the 29th, within sight of a number of other trapped vessels. The wreck was located in 1972. One source says she was iron-hulled. [5+]

AURORA ■ Wooden bulk freight steamer of 2,282 t. and 290 ft., launched at Cleveland in 1887
Detroit River: Early formation of pack ice in the river contributed to the demise of this steamer on December 12, 1898. While trapped in the ice off Bois Blanc (Bob-Lo) Island, she caught fire and was gutted before the flames could be brought under control. The hull was later recovered and converted to a barge. The year of the accident is also reported as 1888. [3]

AUSTIN ■ Merchant schooner
Lake Huron: This sail vessel was lost off her namesake town of Port Austin, MI, when she sank in 1883. Seven crew were also victims of the accident. [1]

D S AUSTIN ■ Merchant schooner of 282 t. and 135 ft., launched at Cleveland in 1872
Lake Michigan: The AUSTIN was lost near the mouth of the harbor at Ludington, Michigan, when she sank on November 7, 1898. [2]

AUSTRALASIA ■ Steam freighter of 1,829 t. and 282 ft., launched in 1884 at W Bay City, MI
Lake Michigan: Whitefish Bay, near Jacksonport, Wisconsin, was the site of the demise of this ship in October of 1896. Laden with a cargo of coal, she was consumed by fire and sank in the bay. [3]

AUSTRALIA ■ Merchant schooner of 159 t. and 109 ft.
Lake Michigan: This small schooner was outbound with a cargo of cedar posts when she was slapped down and sunk by a white squall just outside the entrance to the harbor at Holland, Michigan, on September 30, 1888. One source reports this accident as having happened on Lake Erie in 1880. [3]

WALDO A AVERY ■ Wooden bulk freight propeller of 1,294 t. and 240 ft., launched in 1884 at W Bay City, MI
Lake Michigan: This wooden steamer was lost to fire west of Mackinaw City, Michigan, in 1893. Though she was thought to be a total loss, her hull was later recovered and rebuilt as the steamer PHENIX. [3]

AVIS ■ Gas screw packet of 12 t.
Lake Michigan: This small supply vessel sank in the harbor at S. Manitou Island, Michigan on January 1, 1939. [1]

AVON ■ Wooden propeller freighter of about 300 t. and 132 ft., launched in 1857 at Kingston, Ont.
Lake Huron: This propeller vessel is reported to have foundered in a gale near Presque Isle, Michigan, in October of 1869. [2]

AVON ■ Wooden package freight steamer of 1,702 t. and 251 ft., launched in 1871 at Buffalo
Lake Superior: While bucking heavy seas near Pte Aux Pins (Ont.), above the Soo, this freighter caught fire on June 30, 1901. Her crew escaped, but the vessel and her cargo of flour and general freight were declared a total loss. However, she was eventually recovered and rebuilt at great expense. [3]

AYCLIFFE HALL ■ Steel bulk freight canaller of 1,904 t. and 253 ft., built in England in 1928
Lake Erie: Another victim of the shipping bottleneck around the end of Long Point, the freighter AYCLIFFE HALL collided with the steamer EDWARD J BERWIND and sank 18 miles off the point. The accident occurred on June 11, 1936. Luckily, none of her crew were lost. [5+]

MARY D AYRE ■ Merchant schooner of 337 t. and 144 ft., launched at Saginaw, Michigan as the 516 t. bark JESSE HOYT, in 1854
Lake Michigan: On May 17, 1896, the AYRE was lost in a collision at an unreported position. Five, perhaps all, of her crew, were lost. She was without cargo at the time. [3]

AZOV ■ Lumber schooner of 195 t. and 116 ft., launched at Wellington, Ont. in 1866
Lake Huron: This schooner was carrying a cargo of piling logs when she was overwhelmed by a storm on October 25, 1911. She capsized near Pte Aux Barques, Michigan and drifted ashore on the Canadian side days later. [4]

AZTEC ■ Wooden lumber hooker of 835 t. and 180 ft., launched at Marine City, MI in 1889
St. Clair River: This old vessel met her end on the Belle River at her home port of Marine City, Michigan. She caught fire and was destroyed there on November 9, 1923. [3]

B C & Co ■ Freight barge
Lake Huron: It was reported that this barge sank in the Saginaw River at Saginaw in 1870, but details are lacking. [1]

MELVIN S BACON ■ Merchant schooner of 614 t. and 182 ft., launched in 1874 at Vermilion, OH
Detroit River: The schooner BACON was the victim of a collision on November 16, 1915. On that date, she was rammed and sunk by the steamer JOSEPH SELLWOOD. [2]

BADGER ■ Crane-equipped barge of 140 ft. overall, launched at Duluth in 1914
Lake Erie: While working over the wreck of the steamer BRITON (qv), this barge struck bottom and became a total loss. Her final accident occurred in 1929 off Point Abino, Ontario. [2]

BADGER STATE ■ Merchant bark of 302 t. and 150 ft., launched in 1853 at Buffalo
Lake Michigan: This sail vessel was reported stranded and wrecked, a total loss, off Sleeping Bear Point on November 16, 1870. [3]

BADGER STATE ■ Wooden bulk freight steamer of 864 t. and 213 ft., launched in 1862 at Buffalo as a passenger steamer
St. Clair River: The BADGER STATE suffered a tragic fire in which 15 of her crew were lost. She was discovered to be ablaze at her dock at Marine City, Michigan, on December 6, 1909. When it became apparent that the fire could not be contained, she was cut loose, whereupon she drifted to Fawn Island and burned herself out. [4]

BADGER STATE ■ Oil screw tug of 45 t.
Lake Michigan: This tug was lost off Northport, Michigan, near the mouth of Grand Traverse Bay, when she foundered on November 9, 1939. One of her crew was lost with her. [2]

HORACE H BADGER ■ Lumber schooner of 263 t. and 129 ft., launched as the schooner KATE GILLETT, at Conneaut, OH in 1867
Lake Erie: Struck by a violent storm on June 11, 1903, this coal-carrying vessel was driven on the breakwater at Cleveland, OH. She subsequently broke up in place. [3]

BAHAMA ■ Merchant schooner of 333 t. and 136 ft., launched in 1863 at Oswego, New York
Lake Huron: This sailing ship was reported to have foundered off Alpena, Michigan, in an 1895 gale. [2]

NINA BAILEY ■ Schooner of 30 t.
Lake Michigan: This schooner reportedly sank at the north pier at St. Joseph, MI on November 1, 1880. [1]

TIMOTHY BAKER ■ 215 t. vessel of unreported type
Lake Erie: The BAKER is reported to have stranded off Pelee Island on October 1, 1887. She probably broke up in place. [1]

H P BALDWIN ■ Merchant schooner of 495 t. and 177 ft., launched in 1866 at Detroit
Lake Michigan: One life was lost when this schooner capsized and sank one mile north of Indiana Shoals. The loss occurred in August of 1908, when the ship was laden with

a cargo of grain. She was also heavily damaged in an accident near Cleveland in 1881. [4]

S C BALDWIN ■ Wooden bulk freight propeller of 412 t. and 160 ft., launched in 1871 at Wyandotte, MI
Lake Michigan: The steamer S C BALDWIN was lost on August 27, 1908, when she grounded in a storm, then capsized and sank at Twin River Point. One of the crew was lost along with the vessel and her cargo of stone. She was nearly destroyed in a previous accident on Lake Huron in 1876. [5+]

BALTIC ■ Freight barge
Lake Huron: The BALTIC was reported driven ashore in a gale and wrecked on Long Point (probably actually North Point) at Thunder Bay, Michigan in 1872. [1]

BALTIC ■ Bulk freight schooner of 164 t., launched at Wellington Square, Ontario, in 1867
Lake Ontario: None of the crew were lost, but the BALTIC and her cargo of barley were destroyed when the ship went ashore in a squall and broke up near Oswego, NY, on Nov. 24, 1894. See also DANIEL G FORT. [3]

BALTIC ■ Propeller freighter, of 1,324 t and 182 ft., built as the steamer FRANCIS SMITH at Owen Sound, Ont. in 1867
Lake Huron: On September 5, 1895, this steamer was destroyed at her wharf at Collingwood, Ontario, by an accidental fire. One source gives 1896 as the year. [5+]

BALTIMORE ■ Sidewheel passenger/package freight steamer of 513 t. and 170 ft., launched at Monroe, MI in 1847
Lake Michigan: This wooden vessel was bringing a load of supplies to Sheboygan, Wis., when she struck bottom near the port and stranded. She went aground on September 17, 1855 and was later broken up by wave action. [3]

BALTIMORE ■ Wooden bulk freight steamer of 1,160 t. and 212 ft., launched at Gibraltar, MI, in 1881 as the steamer ESCANABA
Lake Huron: All 14 crew were victims of a deadly storm that sank this coal-laden freighter on May 24, 1901. Her remains still lie on the bottom southeast of Au Sable, Michigan. [5]

BALTIN ■ Merchant brig
Lake Erie: This little sailing vessel was lost in 1855. In that year she went on a reef near Port Stanley, Ontario, and was destroyed. [1]

CITY OF BANGOR ▪ Steel auto carrier of 4,202 t. and 445 ft., launched in 1896 at W Bay City, MI
Lake Superior: The CITY OF BANGOR was carrying 248 new Chrysler automobiles to Duluth when she was blasted by a gale and lost her way on November 30, 1926. She went hard aground on Keweenaw Point. Most of the cars were recovered by driving them across the ice to shore, but the big ship would not budge and was left to break up. [4]

BANNER ▪ Bulk freight schooner-barge of 470 t. and 140 ft., launched in 1847 at Conneaut, OH
Lake Huron: The BANNER was struck by a northeast gale on November 11, 1888, and driven helplessly on a reef off Fish Point, near Oscoda, Michigan. The vessel soon sank, but her crew still had time to abandon ship. [3]

BANNOCKBURN ▪ Steel bulk freight steamer of 1,620 t. and 245 ft., launched in 1893 in Scotland
Lake Superior: The mysterious loss of the BANNOCKBURN is one of the most well-known ghost stories of the Great Lakes. On November 22, 1902 she was downbound with a load of grain when a terrific storm swept across the lake. The steel ship and her 21-man crew have not since reported, nor has any wreckage ever been identified. Many a lakeman has claimed to have seen her misty form sweep silently past on moonless nights, still making for a lower lakes port. [5+]

BANSHEE ▪ Propeller freighter of 119 ft. (probably 166 t.), launched in 1852, Portsmouth, Ont.
Lake Ontario: Little information has been reported on the accident in which this steamer foundered on the lake in August of 1861. [1]

BARBARA LYNN ▪ Diesel tug of 60 ft., launched in 1953
Lake Huron: Bound Monroe to Alpena, Michigan, on October 1, 1990, the tug BARBARA LYNN, with two construction barges in tow, was struck by a near-gale. Twelve-foot seas capsized the vessel and sank her about 12 miles north of Huron City, Michigan. Three members of her four-man crew were able to swim to the barges and were eventually rescued by helicopter, but the fourth crewmen lost his life. [4]

MAJOR BARBARA ▪ Bark
Lake Michigan: Blinded by smoke from the great Peshtigo Forest Fire on the other side of the Lake, the MAJOR BARBARA went ashore and was wrecked at Big Sable Point, Michigan. The date was October 8, 1871. This fire was one of the largest ever recorded in the Geat Lakes

Basin. It began on the same day, but 225 miles to the north of, the Great Chicago Fire of 1871. [1]

BARBARIAN ▪ Merchant schooner of 357 t. and 136 ft., launched in 1855 at Oswego, NY
Lake Michigan: An October, 1898 gale claimed this schooner and her cargo of railroad ties. She was near Milwaukee when she was blown ashore and wrecked beyond recovery. [2]

J BARBER ▪ Wooden propeller of 306 t. and 124 ft.
Lake Michigan: Five of the BARBER's crew were lost when she burned while 14 miles off Michigan City, Indiana, and sank. The accident took place in 1871. [1]

JAMES BARDON or **BARTON #7** ▪ Tug of 69 ft.
Lake Superior: This small tug was lost to fire in the harbor at Duluth on November 10, 1890. One source says she was lost in June. [3]

BARGE A ▪ Barge or schooner-barge of 410 t.
Lake Michigan: This vessel broke in half and sank in the harbor at Racine, Wisconsin, on May 15, 1900. [1]

BARGE No 1 ▪ Wooden railroad ferry-barge of 1,544 t. and 309 ft., launched at W Bay City, MI, in 1895
Lake Huron: Normally used as a railroad carferry, this big barge was carrying a cargo of lumber and crated chickens when she encountered heavy seas on November 8, 1918. She grounded on North Point of Thunder Bay, Michigan, broke in half, and slipped into deep water. Her crew escaped before she sank. [4]

BARGE No 2 ▪ Wooden railroad ferry-barge of 1,598 t. and 310 ft., launched in 1895 at W Bay City, MI
Lake Michigan: Due to an error in loading, this big ferry-barge capsized and sank in the harbor at Chicago, causing the loss of the lives of three of her crew. [3]

BARGE No 3 and **BARGE No 4** ▪ Identical wooden railroad ferry-barges of 1,581 t. and 306 ft. each, launched in 1896 at Toledo, OH
Lake Erie: These two big railroad barges were under tow of the big tug S M FISCHER and loaded with pulpwood when a violent storm overtook them on Nov. 12, 1900. They quickly became unmanageable in the heavy seas and the tug was forced to take their crews off and cut the barges loose. Both foundered near Long Point. [4]

BARGE No 7 ■ Barge of 78 t.
Detroit River: This unpowered vessel was reported to have sunk off the docks at Windsor, Ontario, on October 16, 1958. [1]

BARGE 104 ■ Steel whaleback barge of 1,295 t. and 276 ft., launched at W Superior, WI, in 1892
Lake Erie: This big "'pigboat'" was being towed into the harbor at Cleveland in a heavy gale when she went out of control and struck the breakwater. She sank quickly in the November 10, 1899 accident, but with no loss of life. One source gives 1898 as the year. [3]

BARGE 115 ■ Steel whaleback barge of 256 ft., launched at W Superior, WI, in 1892
Lake Superior: No 115 was lost on Pie Island, in the mouth of Thunder Bay, Ont. In December, 1899, she broke away from her tow steamer and went shore on the island. [1]

BARGE 129 ■ Steel whaleback barge of 1,310 t. and 292 ft., launched at W Superior, WI, in 1893
Lake Superior: On October 13, 1902, this big barge was heavy with iron ore when she broke her towline off Vermilion Point, Michigan. In trying to reconnect with her tow vessel, the steamer MAUNALOA, she was rammed and sank quickly. No lives were lost. [5+]

M P BARKALOW ■ Package and bulk freight schooner of 121 t. and 104 ft., launched in 1871 at Perry, OH
Lake Erie: The BARKALOW was riding out a storm at anchor off South Bass Island when she sank, taking three of her crew and her cargo of salt to the bottom with her. She went down on April 26, 1902. [2]

JOHN J BARLUM ■ Bulk freight schooner-barge of 1,185 t. and 222 ft., launched at Toledo in 1890
Lake Erie: This big wooden ship was outbound with a cargo of coal when she filled and sank five miles off the entrance to Sandusky (Ohio) Bay, near Marblehead Lighthouse. The loss occurred on September 8, 1922. [2]

BURT BARNES ■ Merchant schooner of 134 t. and 95 ft., launched at Manitowoc, WI, in 1882
Lake Ontario: One of the last working schooners on the Lakes, the BARNES was bound for Picton, Ontario, with a cargo of coal on September 3, 1926. She foundered 12 miles short. One source gives 10 miles off Long Point, Lake Erie as her position. [3]

FRANK C BARNES ■ Tug of 46 t. and 67 ft., launched in 1892 at Manistee, MI
Lake Ontario: The small BARNES is one of those vessels

that simply "sailed through a crack in the lake." She disappeared with all hands on November 1, 1915. [3]

F T BARNEY ■ Merchant schooner
Lake Huron: Two different sources report the loss of this vessel following a collision below Nine Mile Point, near Rogers City, Michigan in 1868. The wreck was rediscovered recently, and is now under investigation by divers. [3]

WILLIAM H BARNUM ■ Wooden steam freighter of 1,212 t. and 218 ft., launched at Detroit in 1873
Lake Huron: In the spring the Straits of Mackinac are often still dotted with floating sheets of ice. On April 3, 1894, the BARNUM was underway east of Mackinaw City when her hull was cut by ice and she sank. Her crew was able to abandon the steamer before she went down. The vessel was partially salvaged in 1969. [5]

H A BARR ■ Bulk freight schooner-barge of 1,119 t. and 217 ft., launched in 1893 at W Bay City, MI
Lake Erie: The BARR was in tow of the steamer THEANO (qv) on August 24, 1902, when she and her consort were struck by a violent storm. The barge broke her towline and sank 30 miles off Port Stanley, Ontario. [3]

COMMODORE BARRIE ■ Sidewheel steamer launched in 1833 at Kingston, Ont.
Lake Ontario: The COMMODORE BARRIE was reported as lost in May of 1842, the victim of a collision. [1]

M J BARTELME ■ Steel bulk freight steamer of 3,400 t. and 352 t., launched at W Bay City, MI, in 1894 as the steamer JOHN J McWILLIAMS
Lake Michigan: This freighter was in ballast when she stranded on the southeast tip of Cana Island on October 4, 1928. Release efforts failed and the ship was destroyed by waves. [3]

BARTLETT ■ Tug
Lake Huron: Fire destroyed this tug, probably the 40 ft., 10 t. screw tug A F BARTLETT built at Bay City, MI, in 1871, on the Saginaw River at Bay City, Michigan, in 1884. [1]

BENJAMIN BARTON ■ Merchant schooner
Lake Erie: This schooner was blown ashore and wrecked by a gale at an unrecorded location on Nov. 20, 1838. [1]

BESSE or **BESSIE BARWICK** ■ Merchant schooner of 273 t.
Lake Superior: A westerly gale pushed this schooner off the safe shipping lanes and into the shallows surrounding Michipicoten Island. She foundered there in October of 1887, but her crew escaped the wreck. [3]

BATCHAWANA ■ Wooden bulk freight steamer of 674 t. and 209 ft., launched as the ROBERT A PACKER in 1881 at W Bay City, MI
Lake Superior: This carrier became a victim of fire when she was destroyed at Coppermine Point, Ontario. No lives were lost in the June 27, 1907, incident. [5+]

ELI BATES ■ Schooner of 265 t.
Lake Erie: Nine crewmen were lost when this sailing ship foundered seven miles north of the harbor at Ashtabula, Ohio, in November of 1871. [2]

STEVEN S BATES ■ Merchant brig or schooner of 199 t.
Lake Michigan: The BATES was loaded with a cargo of posts and hardware when she stranded five miles north of Grosse Point, Illinois. The vessel was not recovered after the April 23, 1883, accident, and broke up where she lay. [2]

GERALDINE BATTLE ■ Bulk freight barge of 146 ft., launched at Buffalo in 1893 as the passenger steamer PURITAN
Welland Canal: This barge was unloading her cargo of gravel at Thorold, Ontario, in the Welland Canal, when she caught fire and was completely destroyed. She was lost on October 21, 1916. [1]

THOMAS FREE BATTLE ■ 19 t. vessel of unreported type
Lake Erie: This vessel was reported destroyed by fire at Port Maitland, Ontario, on September 7, 1907. [1]

BAVARIA ■ Bulk freight schooner-barge
Lake Ontario: All eight crew lost their lives when this barge was lost from the tow of her steamer D D CALVIN (qv), in a November, 1889 gale. Her crew thought she was doomed and abandoned her, but were drowned before reaching land. The ship, with her cargo of sawlogs, drifted ashore on Long Point, at the east end of the lake, and was recovered and returned to service. [3]

BAVARIAN ■ Iron sidewheel passenger and package freight steamer of 427 t. and 176 ft., launched in 1873 at Montreal on the burned-out hull of the steamer KINGSTON (qv)
Lake Ontario: This short-lived steamboat was in transit about 15 miles off Bowmanville, Ontario, when she caught fire and was burned to a shell. The November 5, 1873 accident claimed the lives of 14 of those aboard. Her iron hull was recovered and used as the basis for the steamer ALGERIAN. [4]

BAVARIAN ■ Merchant schooner
Lake Huron: No lives were lost when this sail vessel went aground and broke up on Cape Smith, Manitoulin Island. [1]

BAY CITY ■ Steamer
Lake Erie: This steamer went on a reef near Port Burwell, Ontario, in 1862, and was destroyed. [1]

BAY CITY ■ Bulk freight steam barge of 450 t.
Lake Erie: Laden with a cargo of coal, this bulk freighter sank five miles east of the harbor at Erie, Pennsylvania, on November 20, 1880. [1]

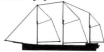

BAY CITY ■ Bulk freight schooner-barge of 306 t. and 140 ft., launched at E Saginaw, MI, in 1857
Lake Huron: While docking in a storm on Thunder Bay, Michigan, this old carrier was blown into a pier and wrecked beyond repair. The vessel was abandoned after the November 29, 1902, accident. She had also been heavily damaged in an incident on Lake Erie in 1880. [3]

BAY STATE ■ Propeller freighter, possibly the 59 t., 53 ft. vessel built near Saginaw, MI, in 1874
Lake Ontario: The BAY STATE is reported to have "gone missing" with all hands. Details on the accident are unavailable. [1]

BAYANNA ■ Steel passenger/package freight steamer of 1,643 t. and 249 ft., launched as the steamer ARAGON at Wyandotte, MI, in 1896
Lake Ontario: This ancient steamer was still a popular passenger vessel when she struck an obstruction and sank near Deseronto in Ontario's Bay of Quinte area on Dec. 1, 1962. No lives were lost in the accident and the ship was subsequently raised, but found to be beyond economical repair. In 1964 she was purposely gutted by fire in lieu of dismantling, and her hull was cut up for scrap. [3]

BAYPORT ■ Tug
Lake Huron: Three of the six-man crew of this tug were lost when she was hooked by her own tow cable and capsized at Collingwood, Ontario, on June 22, 1959. [1]

JOHN BEAN, Jr ■ Schooner of 157 t.
Lake Michigan: On September 30, 1886, the JOHN BEAN sank in the harbor at Muskegon, Michigan. [1]

BEAVER ■ Passenger and package freight schooner, built in 1771
Lake Erie: This sailing ship, part of Commodore Grant's fleet of trading and exploring vessels, was brand new when she sank two or three miles west of the present harbor entrance at Lorain, Ohio. It was reported that she was carrying a valuable cargo when she went down with all seven hands in 1771. [4]

BEAVER ■ Merchant schooner
Lake Huron: The BEAVER was reported to have been lost when she went ashore and was wrecked at Nine Mile Point, near Cheboygan, Michigan, in 1861. [1]

BEAVERSTONE ■ Wooden steamer of 18 t., built in 1882
Lake Superior: Another of the many vessels battered to pieces on shore by wave action was the little BEAVER-STONE, which grounded in a storm at Black Bay, Ontario, on May 14, 1926. [2]

B H BECKER ■ Motor tug of 19 t.
Lake Huron: The little tug BECKER was lost when she encountered heavy seas and sank off Greenbush (9 miles north of Oscoda), Michigan, on August 10, 1937. [3]

PHILIP BECKER ■ 21 t. vessel of unreported type
Lake Ontario: The BECKER and her crew of three were lost when the little ship foundered ten miles off Oswego, New York, on November 17, 1879. She was in ballast at the time. [1]

R H BECKER ■ Bulk freight schooner-scow of 140 t. and 114 ft., launched at Dover Bay, OH in 1867
Lake Michigan: This aged sailing scow was loaded with a cargo of lumber when she was lost in a storm on May 1, 1908. The BECKER was off Sheboygan, Wisconsin when she capsized and sank. [2]

J L BECKWITH ■ Steam screw packet of 104 t. and 59 ft., launched at Buffalo in 1873
Lake Superior: The BECKWITH was broken up on Sandy Point by a storm which struck her on July 26, 1912. [4]

ALICE M BEERS ■ Lumber schooner of 211 t. and 110 ft., launched in 1864 at Algonac, MI
Lake Michigan: On September 4, 1902, this lumber carrier was lying to outside the harbor at Glen Arbor, Michigan, in a storm. The force of the onrushing waves broke her anchor chains and she struck a harbor entry marker and sank. [5]

LENA BEHM ■ Merchant schooner of 33 t. and 59 ft., launched at Grand Haven, MI, in 1886
Lake Huron: The tiny schooner LENA BEHM was underway off Port Hope, Michigan, when she caught fire and was destroyed in 1900. [2]

DANIEL BELL ■ Wooden steam freighter
Lake Huron: This steamer was reported as destroyed by fire at the head of Saginaw Bay, near Bay City, in 1859. [1]

JANE BELL ■ Bark of 447 t.
Lake Michigan: The bark JANE BELL was loaded with cordwood and traversing Green Bay, when she was struck by a sudden storm, capsized, and sank five miles west of Chambers Island Light. The accident occurred in October of 1881. [1]

BELLE ■ Steam freighter
Lake Huron: This steamer was reported to have been struck by a storm and foundered at an unreported location on Georgian Bay in 1852. [1]

BELLE ■ 65 t. vessel of unreported type
Lake Ontario: This vessel was lost by foundering near Port Dalhousie, Ontario, in November of 1887. [1]

BELLE ■ Bulk freight schooner-barge of 104 t. and 94 ft., launched at Manitowoc, WI, in 1856
Lake Michigan: This 52-year-old ship was in tow of the steamer FLETCHER when she encountered a heavy gale on December 12, 1908. Both were downbound with lumber cargoes. The strain of the plunging barge was too much for the towline—she broke it and foundered near Big Sable Point, Michigan. [2]

BELLE LAURIE ■ Merchant schooner of 36 t. and 59 ft., launched at Sturgeon Bay, WI, in 1876
Lake Michigan: The tiny BELLE LAURIE was reported to have foundered in Garrett Bay, Wisconsin, on August 10, 1894. [2]

BELOIT ■ Merchant schooner of 105 t.
Lake Michigan: The BELOIT was the victim of a November storm that drove her ashore and tore her apart near Michigan City, Indiana, in 1882. [1]

A J BEMIS ■ Tug of 49 t., launched in 1859 at Buffalo
Lake Huron: This tug caught fire and was destroyed just off shore at the busy lumber port of Alpena, MI, in 1872. [2]

PHILO T BEMIS ■ Tug
Lake Huron: The tug BEMIS succumbed to fire at Alpena, MI, in 1879. Repairs were begun to restore her to service, but she was abandoned before they were completed. [2]

BEN HUR ■ Wrecking schooner of 314 t., launched at Dunville, Ont. in 1874
Lake Huron: This vessel was working to salvage the schooner M E TREMBLE (qv) when she was rammed and sunk by the tethered schooner-barge SUPERIOR on November 8, 1890. All of her crew were rescued. The accident occurred near Port Huron, Michigan. [2]

E G BENEDICT ■ Merchant schooner of 154 t. and 104 ft.
Lake Erie: The BENEDICT was another victim of an equinoctial storm when she was blown ashore to break up on November 19, 1891. Her remains lie near Port Burwell, Ontario. None of her crew were lost. [1]

BENNINGTON ■ Wrecking barge of 250 t., launched in 1891
Lake Superior: Both crewmen were lost when this vessel foundered, reportedly in fair weather, off Whitefish Point, on September 5, 1908. [3]

C B BENSON ▪ Merchant schooner of 299 t. and 137 ft., launched at Port Clinton, OH, in 1873
Lake Erie: All seven hands lost their lives on October 14, 1893, when this coal-laden sailing ship was wrecked in a storm. Her hull lies off Gravelly Bay, near Port Colborne, Ontario. See also KATE WINSLOW. [3]

JAMES H BENTLEY ▪ Merchant schooner, 575 t. and 170 ft.
Lake Huron: This grain-laden three-master foundered in a November, 1878, storm that struck her off 40 Mile Point, at the east end of the Straits of Mackinac. [2]

JOHN BENTLEY ▪ Merchant schooner
Lake Huron: The sailing ship JOHN BENTLEY was struck by a white squall on Georgian Bay in 1886, and sank near Cabbage Head. [1]

BENTON ▪ Wooden bulk freight steamer of 305 t. and 152 ft., launched at Buffalo in 1867
Detroit River: While docked at the Ford Rouge Plant on the Rouge River, the freighter BENTON caught fire and was destroyed. She was unloading a cargo of partially-finished wooden automobile parts at the time of her demise on August 1, 1909. [2]

BERLIN ▪ Merchant schooner of 260 t. and 111 ft.
Lake Huron: This schooner went ashore on Burnt Cabin Reef near Point Aux Barques, Michigan, and broke up on November 8, 1877. She was downbound with a load of limestone at the time of the accident, in which four of her crew lost their lives. [4]

BERMUDA ▪ Merchant schooner of 394 t., launched at Oswego, NY, in 1896
Lake Superior: Grand Island, in front of Munising, Michigan, was the site of the loss of this iron ore laden schooner. She foundered there with no loss of life in October of 1870. [3]

BERMUDA ▪ 115 ft. vessel of unreported type
Lake Ontario: This vessel is reported to have foundered off Port Granby, Ontario, on November 6, 1880. [1]

LOTTA BERNARD ▪ Sidewheel package and bulk freight steamer of 190 t. and 125 ft., built at Port Clinton and fitted at Sandusky, OH, in 1869
Lake Superior: The LOTTA BERNARD was one of the earliest examples of the "rabbit" type of steamer (all cabins aft). She was carrying a cargo of general merchandise when she foundered in a storm off Encampment Island. Three of her crew were lost in the October 30, 1874, accident. [4]

FRANCIS BERRIMAN ▪ Merchant bark
Lake Huron: This sailing ship was wrecked in a collision which took place in Thunder Bay, Michigan, in 1877. [1]

COMMODORE JACK BERRY ▪ Tug of 57 t. and 71 ft., launched at Saugatuck, MI, in 1885
Lake Superior: Fire destroyed this tug at Superior, Wisconsin, on October 30, 1899. Her crewmen all survived the accident. [1]

BERWYN ▪ Bulk freight schooner of 269 t. and 134 ft., launched in 1866 at Algonac, MI as the R C CRAWFORD
Lake Michigan: The BERWYN stranded and broke up two miles from Pilot Island Light while trying to traverse the treacherous Porte des Mortes (Death's Door) entrance to Green Bay. The accident occurred on November 22, 1908, but, fortunately, none of the schooner's crew were lost. [2]

BESSEMER ▪ Bulk freight steamer of 590 t.
Lake Superior: This steamer was just off the north end of the Portage Ship Canal across the Keweenaw Peninsula when she was struck by a storm and sank on October 6, 1889. She was loaded with iron ore when she went down. [2]

BETHLEHEM ▪ Wooden passenger/package freight steamer of 2,633 t. and 298 ft., built in 1888 at Cleveland
Lake Michigan: In an early fall gale, on September 23, 1910, this big steamer went ashore on the southwest side of S. Manitou Island. It took several days for the vessel to be relieved of her cargo of general merchandise by her crew and the island's lifesavers. She was declared a total loss, and is reported to have broken up, but she may have been recovered. [2]

JACOB BETSCHY ▪ Wooden bulk freight steamer of 434 t.
Lake Huron: The BETSCHY was loaded with a cargo of shingles and wheat when she went on a reef near Port Austin, Michigan, on September 3, 1879. [3]

J BIGLER ▪ Schooner-scow of 351 t. and 150 ft.
Lake Superior: The flat-bottomed J BIGLER was lost in 1884, when she foundered off the lower entry to the Keweenaw Waterway. [1]

P H BIRCKHEAD ▪ Wooden bulk freight steamer of 568 t. and 157 ft., launched at Marine City, MI, in 1870
Lake Huron: Alpena, Michigan, was the site of the loss of this freighter on September 30, 1905. On that date, she was pulling away from the docks when she caught fire and burned ⅔ of a mile off shore. All of her crew of 13 escaped the blaze. The BIRCKHEAD had an unusual twin tandem arch hull construction. [5]

BIRDIE ▪ Merchant schooner of 13 t.
Lake Huron: This tiny schooner sank in upper Lake Huron off Hammond Bay, Michigan, on October 7, 1892. [2]

H B BISHOP ■ Merchant schooner
Lake Huron: This vessel was reported to have foundered in a severe storm on Georgian Bay in the year 1852. [1]

BISMARK ■ 75 t. vessel of unreported type, perhaps the schooner BISMARCK, built at Port Dalhousie, Ont., in 1871
Lake Ontario: Another of the hundreds vessels lost by stranding was the BISMARK, which went aground near Port Credit, Ontario, on September 13, 1878. [1]

HARVEY BISSEL ■ Bulk freight schooner-barge of 496 t. and 162 ft., launched at Toledo in 1866
Lake Huron: There are several versions of this vessel's ultimate demise, but in the most reliable, the BISSEL was in tow with a cargo of lumber when she was blasted by a sudden and violent gale off False Presque Isle, Michigan, on November 28, 1905. The old ship literally went to pieces in the big greybeards, but her crew was rescued by the tow vessel. [5]

BLACK HAWK ■ Merchant brig of 384 t.
Lake Michigan: This BLACK HAWK was a large brig that was lost when she sank in a storm with all hands and a cargo of stained glass. The accident occurred at Pointe Aux Becs Scies (now Point Betsie), Michigan, in November of 1862. [2]

BLACK HAWK ■ Merchant schooner
Lake Michigan: The schooner BLACK HAWK disappeared with all hands on the lake in November of 1887. [2]

BLACK MARLIN ■ Tug
Lake Erie: This towing vessel was reported lost near Avon Point, west of Cleveland. [1]

BLACKBIRD ■ Vessel of unreported type
Lake Ontario: It is reported that this vessel went missing with all hands, but details are unavailable. [1]

JAMES G BLAINE ■ Bulk freight schooner-barge of 555 t. and 177 ft., launched at Little Sturgeon Bay, WI, in 1867 as the schooner PENSAUKEE
Lake Ontario: This vessel was in tow of the tug WILLIAM G PROCTER on July 8, 1908, when she broke her towline and went ashore before she could be recaptured. The 41-year old ship was left to be broken up by waves near Oswego, New York. [4]

E R BLAKE ■ Merchant schooner of 201 t. and 121 ft., launched in 1867 at Milwaukee

Lake Huron: The BLAKE was reported to be well out of sight of land when she caught fire and was destroyed in 1898. [1]

EMMA BLAKE ■ Merchant schooner
Lake Erie: This sail vessel was blown out of control by a storm which struck her in the harbor at Cleveland on October 17, 1870. She was dashed against a railroad pier and quickly sank with all hands. [2]

J W BLAKE ■ Merchant schooner
Lake Huron: In 1855, this schooner piled up on the rocks at Sturgeon Bay, Michigan, and was a total loss. [1]

B W BLANCHARD ■ Wooden bulk freight steamer of 1,142 t. and 212 ft., launched at Cleveland in 1872
Lake Huron: Treacherous North Point Reef, on Thunder Bay, Michigan, claimed the BLANCHARD as a victim on November 28, 1904. She was inbound with a two-barge tow when she struck the reef in a storm, broke in half, and sank. [4]

BLAZING STAR ■ Lumber schooner of 265 t. and 137 ft.
Lake Michigan: In November of 1887, this lumber-laden ship went ashore and broke up on Fisherman Shoal, near Washington Island, Wisconsin. [1]

E D BLISH ■ Merchant schooner
Lake Huron: This schooner left port and was never heard from again, sinking with all hands in mid-lake in 1864. [1]

A T BLISS ■ Lumber schooner-barge of 437 t. and 168 ft., launched at E Saginaw, MI, in 1881
Lake Michigan: Loaded with a cargo of stone, the BLISS ran into a gale on November 4, 1903, and was overwhelmed ten miles off Ludington, Michigan. [3]

BLUE BELLE or **BLUE BELL** ■ Merchant schooner of 122 t.
Lake Michigan: This schooner sank in a white squall just off the harbor entrance at Sheboygan, Wisconsin. The date of the accident is unreported. [2]

BLUE COMET ■ Steel steam tanker launched at Chester, PA, in 1923
Lake Michigan: One crewman lost his life when this vessel's cargo of 500,000 gallons of gasoline exploded and burned at Calumet, IL, sometime in the 1930s. The ship was recovered and rebuilt. She was scrapped in 1964. [2]

BESSIE BOALT ■ Merchant schooner of 164 t.
Lake Michigan: This little schooner was laden with lumber when she became stranded and was lost four miles northeast of Two Rivers, Wisconsin, in Sept. of 1872. [2]

BOAZ ■ Lumber schooner of 127 t. and 114 ft., launched at Sheboygan, WI, in 1869
Lake Michigan: This sailing vessel encountered a gale in northern Lake Michigan and was driven hard aground on November 10, 1900. The ship's resting place was in North Bay, near Bailey's Harbor, Wisconsin. [2]

JOHN J BOLAND, Jr ■ Steel bulk freighter of 1,149 t. and 253 ft., built as the freighter TYNEVILLE at Newcastle-upon-Tyne, England, in 1928
Lake Erie: A fierce westerly storm struck this coal-laden steamer as she was passing Barcelona, New York, on October 5, 1932. She quickly capsized and sank in the blow, with the loss of four lives. [5]

BOLIVIAN ■ Merchant schooner
Lake Huron: This vessel was reported stranded and lost in 1877, near Sand Beach (Harbor Beach), Michigan. [1]

SAMUEL BOLTON ■ Schooner-barge of 330 t. and 150 ft., launched at Bay City, MI, in 1867
Lake Huron: The schooner-barge SAMUEL BOLTON was reported to have run aground in fog near Richmondville, Michigan, and broken in two. None of her crew was lost in the 1893 accident. [2]

BON VOYAGE ■ Wooden steam coaster of 500 t. and 153 ft., launched at Saugatuck, Michigan, in 1891
Lake Superior: The steamer BON VOYAGE was lost when she caught fire and was run aground near the south entrance to the Portage Ship Canal on May 10, 1901. Four of her 40 passengers and crew lost their lives in the accident. [5]

HIRAM R BOND ■ Scow of 230 t. and 113 ft., launched in 1888 at Milwaukee as a steamer
Lake Michigan: This vessel was lost off Milwaukee on May 29, 1905, when she was rammed in a fog and sunk by the big carferry PERE MARQUETTE 20. Her crew were all rescued. [1]

O M BOND ■ Merchant schooner of 315 t. and 137 ft., launched in 1873 at Oswego, NY
Lake Erie: The two-master O M BOND was lost when she foundered near Point Aux Pins, Ontario, with the loss of two of her crew. She was carrying a load of wheat at the time of the October 14, 1886 sinking. The location of this accident is also given as Lake Ontario, off Port Dalhousie. The BOND had also sunk near Sand Beach, Michigan, on Lake Huron, in 1879, and was recovered. [4]

BONNIE DOON ■ Merchant schooner
Lake Huron: This schooner was reported ashore and wrecked on Bois Blanc Island, in the Straits of Mackinac, in 1867. [1]

BONNIE DOON ■ Merchant sloop
Lake Huron: This vessel's demise came in 1880, when she succumbed to fire at Meldrum Bay in the North Channel. This could be the same sail vessel as above. [1]

BONNIE MAGGIE ■ Steam freighter of 203 t. and 111 ft., launched in 1859 at Sandusky, OH, as the steamer BONNIE BOAT
Lake Huron: Northerly storms concentrate as they are forced into the narrowing throat of Lake Huron, east of Michigan's thumb. This freighter was one of many caught in this trap and thrown ashore near Kincardine, Ontario. She was broken up in place by wave action. This 1868 accident is also reported under her previous name. [2]

A BOODY ■ Merchant schooner of 287 t. and 137 ft., launched in 1863 at Toledo
Lake Huron: Stranded on a reef and declared a total loss at Pte Aux Barques, Michigan, in 1887, she was subsequently salvaged and rebuilt as the schooner E A FULTON. [3]

BOSCOBEL ■ Schooner-barge of 504 t. and 167 ft., built on the hull of a burned-out passenger steamer and launched at Algonac, Michigan, in 1876
Lake Huron: This vessel was caught in midlake by a moderate blow, while in tow of the steamer D F ROSE, on August 1, 1909. The old hull could not take the strain and she opened her seams and sank. [2]

BOSTON ■ Sidewheel steamer of 775 t., launched at Detroit in 1846
Lake Michigan: This brand-new paddle steamer was reported to have sunk in the bay at Milwaukee in November of 1846. [1]

BOSTON ■ Wooden steam freighter
Lake Ontario: On September 28, 1854, this steamer collided with the bark PLYMOUTH and sank near Oak Orchard, New York. [2]

CITY OF BOSTON ■ Wooden freighter
Lake Huron: This steamer is reported to have sunk following a collison with an unreported vessel in the Straits of Mackinac in 1868. [1]

BOTHNIA ■ Wooden bulk freight steamer of 833 t. and 178 ft., launched at Garden Island, Ontario, in 1895, as the steamer JACK
Lake St. Clair: This wooden vessel was lost when she sank in the St. Clair Flats after being rammed by the steel steamer S S CURRY. One of her crew was drowned in the June 26, 1912 accident. [2]

MARY N BOURKE ■ Bulk freight schooner of 920 t. and 219 ft., launched at Baraga, MI, in 1889
Detroit River: The big schooner MARY N BOURKE caught fire at Detroit, burned to the waterline and sank on September 29, 1914. This incident also reported as having happened in the Pine River, at St. Ignace, Michigan, but is probably in error. [2]

ERASTUS BOWEN ■ Package freight schooner of 52 t.
Lake Michigan: This schooner was laden with a cargo of household goods when she became stranded and was lost off Grosse Point, Illinois, in April of 1851. [1]

C M BOWMAN ■ Propeller freighter of 88 t. and 92 ft., launched at Port Elgin, Ont., in 1897
Lake Huron: On December 13, 1915, the small steamer C M BOWMAN was blown ashore and wrecked on Vail's Point, in Georgian Bay. [3]

BOXER ■ Merchant schooner
Lake Erie: This early Lakes' schooner was reported to have sunk at the mouth of Ohio's Grand River in 1818. No loss of life was recorded. [1]

ISABELLA J BOYCE ■ Wooden sandsucker of 368 t. and 138 ft., launched at Manitowoc, WI, in 1889 as a freighter
Lake Erie: In the early decades of the 20th Century the sandsucker was a common vessel, especially on relatively shallow Lake Erie. The vessel was designed to drop anchor over a sandy area then, by means of a suction pipe, pick up a load of sand and water. On board, the sand was filtered out, then delivered to some waiting consumer. The fine Lake Erie sand was much in demand in the construction industry and in the iron-casting plants, where it was used in the process of molding such items as engine blocks. Sandsuckers were often old vessels that had been converted from another type, and were thus susceptible to accidents. One of a number of this type of ship lost on Lake Erie, the ISABELLA J BOYCE grounded on Middle Bass Island on June 6, 1917, then was destroyed by fire. [3]

MARY H BOYCE ■ Wooden bulk freight steamer of 864 t. and 181 ft., launched in 1888 at Grand Haven, MI
Lake Superior: The bulk freighter MARY H BOYCE was in service for 40 years, until she was destroyed by an accidental fire at Fort William (Thunder Bay) Ontario, in 1928. The final disposition of the hull is in some question. Some sources saying she was scuttled, while others say she was dismantled in 1936. [4]

J OSWALD BOYD ■ Fuel tanker of 1,806 t. and 244 ft., built in Scotland in 1913
Lake Michigan: On November 11, 1936, this tanker, laden with 900,000 gallons of gasoline, ran hard aground on Simmons Reef on the north side of Beaver Island. No lives were lost in the initial accident, but the tanker exploded and burned in January of 1937. See MAROLD II for more details. [5]

COLONEL BRACKETT ■ Steamer or schooner of 187 t. and 115 ft.
Lake Huron: The COLONEL BRACKETT was in ballast when she ran on the Harbor Beach, Michigan, breakwater in a gale and was destroyed. The accident occurred on April 24, 1890. [2]

ALVA BRADLEY ■ Merchant schooner of 934 t. and 190 ft., launched at Cleveland in 1870
Lake Superior: According to one report, this sailing vessel was driven ashore and wrecked at Shot Point, near Marquette, Michigan, on October 20, 1887. She may have been recovered. [1]

ALVA BRADLEY ■ Merchant schooner. May be the same ship as above.
Lake Michigan: Carrying steel billets, this vessel sank seven miles off North Manitou Island on Oct. 13, 1894. [2]

CARL D BRADLEY ■ Self-unloading steel bulk carrier of 10,028 t. and 640 ft., launched at Lorain, OH, in 1927
Lake Michigan: The second largest vessel ever lost on the Lakes, the BRADLEY foundered on November 18, 1958. Running in ballast, the big steamer was blasted by a teriffic storm while abreast of the Beaver Island group. Riding up on a huge greybeard, the long ship broke in two and sank near Gull Island. An extensive air-sea search yielded only two freezing survivors. The other 33 crewmen were lost. [5+]

CHARLES H BRADLEY ■ Wooden bulk freight steamer of 804 t. and 210 ft. launched in 1890 at W Bay City, MI
Lake Superior: On October 9, 1931, this ship was traversing Portage Lake in the Portage Ship Canal, when she met with a fatal accident. The steamer struck a bar and was rammed from behind by her tow, the barge GRAMPIAN. She caught fire following the crash, and the BRADLEY and her cargo of pulpwood were completely destroyed. [5+]

KATE BRAINARD ■ Schooner
Lake Huron: In 1871, the KATE BRAINARD foundered near Kincardine, Ontario. [1]

D R BRAMAN ■ Merchant schooner
Lake Huron: This schooner foundered off the mouth of the Black River, south of Alpena, in 1870. [1]

BRANDON ■ Schooner-barge of 517 t.
Lake Superior: The BRANDON was in one of the most remote stretches of water on the Great Lakes when she foundered in a storm 40 miles southwest of Isle Royale. Fortunately, all of her crew survived the September 29, 1888 sinking. [3]

BRANDYWINE ■ Sloop
Lake Erie: This one-mast sailing vessel capsized and sank off Barcelona, New York, in 1846. Three of her crew were drowned. [1]

BRANT ■ Schooner-scow of 53 t. and 74 ft., launched in 1857 at Sandusky, OH
Lake Huron: The position of this vessel when she went down on the lake in 1859 in a storm is either unknown or unrecorded. [1]

JESSE H BRECK ■ Merchant schooner of 430 t. and 142 ft., launched in 1873 at Port Dalhousie, Ont.
Lake Ontario: All seven crewmen were lost when this schooner capsized and sank in a storm, close in to 9-mile Point, New York. One report places the loss at 9-mile Point, Lake Huron. The accident happened on May 17, 1890 and by the next year the BRECK had been recovered and rebuilt as the schooner H M STANLEY. [3]

MARION L BRECK ■ Bulk freight schooner of 396 t. and 127 ft., launched as the schooner WILLIAM PENN at Garden Island, Ont., in 1858
Lake Huron: This schooner met her demise on Bear's Rump Shoal, near Tobermory, Ontario, after grounding

there on October 7, 1907. She was laden with the unusual cargo of brick pieces at the time. [3]

JOHN BREDIN ■ Merchant bark of 430 t. and 142 ft., launched in 1862 at Port Dalhousie, Ont.
Lake Huron: Three lives were lost when this windjammer foundered off Lexington, MI, on July 21, 1899. [4]

C G BREED ■ Bulk freight schooner of 385 t.
Lake Erie: On November 14, 1879, the BREED was delivering a load of wheat when she was struck by a sudden squall and capsized. Five lives were lost in the incident, which occurred near Ashtabula, Ohio. [1]

BRENTON ■ Merchant schooner of 54 t. and 70 ft., launched in 1882 at Gibraltar, MI
Lake Huron: This small sailing ship simply "went missing" in 1899. It is presumed that her crew perished with her. She had also sunk but had been recovered near Cleveland in 1896. [3]

BRENTON ■ Oil screw of 29 t.
Lake Michigan: The BRENTON is reported to have sunk 8 miles off Frankfort, Michigan, on Sept. 19, 1937. [1]

WILLIAM BREWSTER ■ Steel bulk freighter, built at Superior, WI
Lake St Clair: The BREWSTER was lost near Walpole Island after being rammed and sunk on June 15, 1943. She was reportedly of British registry, and may have been recovered. [4]

JOHN B BREYMAN ■ Tug
Lake Erie: This tug was destroyed by fire at Toledo, Ohio, on June 28, 1926. [1]

BRICK ■ Vessel of unreported type
Lake Huron: On October 15, 1900, this vessel struck famous Flowerpot Island, at the mouth of Georgian Bay, and sank. [1]

H P BRIDGE ■ Merchant bark
Lake Huron: The BRIDGE was the victim of a collision that occurred southeast of Thunder Bay Island, Michigan, in 1869. [1]

BRIDGEBUILDER X ■ Oil screw of 53 t.
Lake Michigan: The BRIDGEBUILDER was a relatively small vessel that sank at an unreported location on December 15, 1950. [1]

BRIDGEWATER ■ Merchant schooner
Lake Michigan: The reef and shoals around Waugoschance Point, in the western Straits of Mackinaw, claimed another victim when this vessel ran aground and was lost there in 1875. [1]

JOHN BRIGHT ■ 30 t. vessel of unreported type
Lake Ontario: Fire claimed another victim when the JOHN BRIGHT was accidentally burned at Belleville, Ontario, on October 9, 1879. [1]

BRIGHTIE ■ Lumber schooner-barge of 600 t. and 182 ft., built in 1868 at Cleveland
Lake Michigan: This 60-year-old tow vessel finally gave up and sank when her seams opened one mile off Whitehall, Michigan, on August 23, 1928. One source says one of her crew was lost with her. [3]

BEN BRINK ■ Schooner-barge of 317 t. and 156 ft. overall, launched in 1888 at Detroit
Lake Superior: On September 12, 1890, this barge was lost from her towing steamer in a storm near Eagle Harbor, Michigan. She was driven ashore and wrecked in the shallows, with the loss of the lives of six of her crew. [3]

JENNIE BRISCOE ■ Steam barge of 82 t., launched in 1870 at Detroit
Detroit River: This small bulk freighter was lost in a collision with the propeller FREE STATE near Grosse Ile, Michigan, in September of 1870. [2]

BRITISH LION ■ Merchant schooner
Lake Erie: This vessel was reported destroyed in a gale off Erie, Pennsylvania, on October 27, 1891. [1]

BRITON ■ Steel package/bulk freight steamer of 2,348 t. and 296 ft., launched in 1891 at Cleveland
Lake Erie: A faulty navigation light on shore caused this big steel steamer to run aground and wreck near Point Abino in a storm. The accident occurred on November 13, 1929. See also barge BADGER. [4]

R C BRITTAIN ■ Wooden bulk freight steamer of 213 t. and 142 ft., launched in 1877 at Saugatuck
St. Clair River: The R C BRITTAIN was heavily damaged by a fire at Sarnia, Ontario, in 1912. It was deemed possible to rebuild her, so she was laid up. Though she was never repaired, it was not until 1926 that she was finally scrapped without having returned to service. [3]

BRITTANIC ■ Bulk freight steam barge of 1,122 t. and 219 ft., launched in 1888 at W Bay City
Detroit River: One crew member was lost when this big steamer sank with her cargo of iron ore on August 9, 1895. She was subsequently recovered and rebuilt (see SARNOR). [2]

BROCKVILLE ■ Propeller freighter of 136 ft., launched in 1863 at Brockville, Ont.
Lake Huron: The steamer BROCKVILLE was reported ashore and wrecked at Au Sable Point, Michigan, in

November of 1865. This may have occurred at Big Sable Point, Lake Michigan. [1]

ELIZABETH BRODER ■ Merchant schooner built about 1849 at Owen Sound, Ont.
Lake Huron: The year of this schooner's demise is not recorded, but it is known that she was lost when she went on the rocks and broke up on Manitoulin Island. [2]

ALVIN BRONSON ■ Merchant schooner of 192 t.
Lake Michigan: On April 29, 1888, this small ship sank off the Port Sherman area of Muskegon, MI, harbor. [1]

BROOKLYN ■ Propeller freighter built prior to 1871
Detroit River: On October 22, 1874, this steamer suffered a devastating boiler explosion that blew her bottom out and killed 13 of her crew. She went down off Fighting Island, near Wyandotte, Michigan. [2]

BROOKLYN ■ Merchant schooner of 319 t. and 140 ft., launched in 1864 at Clayton, NY
Lake Huron: This schooner went ashore and was wrecked near Alpena, Michigan, on May 15, 1892. [2]

J S BROOKS ■ 252 t. schooner
Lake Ontario: The schooner J S BROOKS sank in the Black River Bay, near Sacket's Harbor, New York, on November 4, 1856. She was reportedly carrying a cargo of steel billets at the time. One report says her safe contained $1 million. [2]

BROTHERS ■ Merchant schooner
Lake Huron: This wooden vessel's hull was crushed and she sank after being caught in an ice field near Goderich, Ontario, early in 1869. [1]

BROWN BROTHERS ■ Propeller freighter of 64 t. and 75 ft., launched in 1915 at Port Stanley, Ont.
Lake Erie: The small steamboat BROWN BROTHERS sank five miles off Long Point on October 28, 1959. [2]

FAYETTE BROWN ■ Merchant schooner
Lake Erie: The BROWN foundered in Pelee Passage on June 4, 1891. She was later removed as a hazard to navigation. [2]

IDA MAY or **I. MAY BROWN** ■ Merchant schooner of 20 t. and 52 ft., launched in 1884 at Charlevoix, MI
Lake Michigan: A tiny two mast schooner, the BROWN was lost near Michigan City, Indiana, when her cargo of gravel shifted and capsized her. Her crew made it ashore safely, and the ship later drifted to the beach, but was a total loss. Lost July 7, 1895. [3]

WILLIAM J BROWN ■ Bulk freight steam barge of 365 t. and 140 ft. launched in 1856 as the steamer NEPTUNE
Lake Michigan: The iron ore-laden steamer WILLIAM J BROWN was lost near Green Island, in Green Bay, when she exploded and sank in a gale on October 21, 1886. [2]

WILLIAM O BROWN ▪ Package and bulk freight schooner of 400 t.
Lake Superior: This schooner was loaded with wheat when she was driven ashore by a gale and broke up near Point Maimanse, Ontario. Six of the nine aboard were lost in the November 28, 1872 accident. [4]

WILLIE BROWN ▪ Tug of 19 t. and 47 ft., launched in 1871 at Buffalo
Lake Huron: The tug WILLIE BROWN was reported lost to fire on the Saginaw River at East Saginaw in 1889, but she was still listed in registration in 1906. [2]

BROWNVILLE ▪ Sidewheel passenger and package freight steamer of 94 t. and 85 ft., launched at Brownville, NY, in 1830
Lake Erie: This early steamer was reportedly destroyed by fire during her first year of service, 1830. The location of the wreck has not been reported. [1]

BRUCE MINES ▪ Sidewheel steam freighter of 126 ft., built at Montreal in 1842.
Lake Huron: The BRUCE MINES foundered in a storm off Cape Hurd, near Tobermory, Ontario, on November 28, 1854. Though some reports say she went down with all hands, only one of her 25 passengers and crew was lost. The fact that her people landed in a desolate spot and were missing for two weeks probably contributes to the misreporting. [5]

KATE L BRUCE ▪ Merchant schooner of 307 t.
Lake Huron: A case of a ship that "sailed throught a crack in the Lake," the KATE BRUCE disappeared in upper Lake Huron on November 8, 1877. The schooner, her crew of eight, and her cargo of wheat were last seen off 40 Mile Point, Michigan. [4]

ROBERT BRUCE ▪ Merchant schooner
Lake Erie: This schooner was blown upon a reef near Port Burwell, Ontario, and was wrecked in 1856. [2]

BRUNO ▪ Steam freighter of 359 t. and 136 ft., launched in 1863 at Montreal
Lake Huron: With a load of wheat and the barge LOUISA in tow, this carrier struck Magnetic Reef, south of Cockburn Island in Georgian Bay, and sank. The loss occurred on November 13, 1890. [5]

BRUNSWICK ▪ Iron bulk freight steamer of 1,120 t. and 228 ft., built at Detroit in 1881
Lake Erie: This brand new bulk freighter was lost in a disastrous accident off Dunkirk, New York, on November 12, 1881. On a night of fitful snow squalls, she rammed the loaded schooner CARLINGFORD (qv) and stove in her bows. After ascertaining that the schooner's crew was abandoning ship, the steamer turned and made a run for shore. She sank a few miles short, with the loss of three of her crew and her cargo of hard coal. [4]

BUCEPHELUS ▪ Propeller freighter
Lake Huron: Ten crewmen drowned when this steamer foundered in Saginaw Bay on November 13, 1854. [3]

BUCEPHELUS ▪ Merchant schooner
Lake Huron: The schooner BUCEPHELUS was lost when she sank on Saginaw Bay in 1879. [1]

BUCKEYE ▪ Freight barge
Lake Huron: This vessel was destroyed by fire and sank in Georgian Bay in 1885. [1]

BUCKEYE STATE ▪ Merchant bark
Lake Michigan: Stranded off S Milwaukee Point in November of 1852, the BUCKEYE STATE was later broken up by the pounding of waves. [1]

BUCKINGHAM ▪ Merchant schooner
Lake Huron: Another of the many ships lost on Saginaw Bay, this one sank in 1870. [1]

EDWARD BUCKLEY ▪ Wooden lumber hooker of 415 t. and 154 ft., launched in 1891 at Manitowoc, WI
Lake Huron: On Sept. 1, 1929, this small steamer caught fire in Georgian Bay. She was beached on the east side of Manitoulin Island and burned to a total loss. [4]

JAMES BUCKLEY ▪ 7 t. vessel of unreported type
Lake Erie: The tiny JAMES BUCKLEY was destroyed by fire in the harbor at Port Stanley, Ontario, on November 20, 1890. [1]

JAMES BUCKLY ▪ Bulk freight schooner-barge of 442 t. and 166 ft., launched at Quebec City in 1884
Lake Ontario: This schooner-barge was lost when she was sent out of control by a storm and grounded on the coast of Jefferson County, New York. The carrier went on the rocks on October 16, 1912, and later slipped off and sank in deeper water. [2]

W G BUCKNER ▪ Merchant schooner of 107 t., built before 1847
Lake Michigan: The small sailing vessel W G BUCKNER was reported lost on the lake in 1848. [1]

RALPH BUDD ▪ Steam freighter
Lake Superior: May 16, 1929 was the date of the loss of the steamer RALPH BUDD. She reportedly stranded and broke up. [1]

BUDDY ▪ Tug
Lake Michigan: Proof that, even in the current age, work on a tug can be dangerous came when this tow vessel was struck by the barge she was towing and sank. The tug sank in midlake, off Manistee, on May 11, 1966, but all of her crew escaped with their lives. [2]

BUENA VISTA ■ Merchant schooner of 172 t. built prior to 1847
Lake Michigan: This vessel was reported as wrecked on the lake in 1875. [1]

BUFFALO ■ Wooden tug of 60 t. and 68 ft., launched at Buffalo in 1887
Lake Superior: On April 29, 1907, this tug sank off Harrington Island, near Duluth, for unknown reasons. She was recovered and completely rebuilt in 1914. [2]

CITY OF BUFFALO ■ Merchant bark
Lake Huron: This sail ship was struck by a storm in the year 1875 and sank off the end of the piers at Sand Beach (now Harbor Beach), Michigan. [1]

CITY OF BUFFALO ■ Steel passenger and package freight steamer of 2,940 t. and 340 ft., launched in 1896 at Wyandotte, MI
Lake Erie: Many a fine vessel has been lost to fire while docked for the winter or preparing for her spring runs. Such was the case with the steel CITY OF BUFFALO when she caught fire at her winter moorings at Cleveland on March 22, 1938, and was destroyed. Fortunately, no lives were lost in the blaze. [5+]

BULGARIA ■ Propeller freighter of 1,188 t. and 280 ft., launched in 1887 at W Bay City, MI
Lake Michigan: On June 4, 1906, this big steamer struck Fisherman Shoal, in Porte Des Mortes (Death's Door), Wisconsin. Her crew was not harmed, but the vessel was declared a total loss. She was later recovered, however, and served the iron and coal trade until being scrapped in 1915. [2]

KATE BULLY ■ Lumber schooner of 380 t., launched at Corunna, Ont., in 1866
Lake Michigan: Built by a local Corunna man who wanted to go to sea, the KATE BULLY was struck by a sudden squall and capsized on October 4, 1869. The ship was off Little Sable Point, Michigan, with a cargo of railroad ties, when the accident happened, though her remains ended up on the beach near Sleeping Bear. Six of her ten were lost, and the survivors had floated for 40 hours before being rescued. She may have been the only vessel ever built at Corunna. [5]

SARDIS BURCHARDS ■ Merchant schooner
Lake Huron: This schooner was reported wrecked offshore in the Straits of Mackinac in 1879. [1]

H B BURGER ■ Bulk freight schooner of 191 t.
Lake Michigan: Lumber-laden and inbound, the BURGER is reported to have foundered two miles south of the Chicago waterfront on May 21, 1883. [1]

BURLINGTON ■ Wooden propeller launched in 1837 at Oakville, Ont.
Lake Ontario: The steamer BURLINGTON was reported as having been destroyed by fire at Toronto in March of 1841. [1]

BURLINGTON ■ Brig of 117 t., launched at Cleveland in 1842
Lake Erie: The small two-masted BURLINGTON was destroyed when she went hard aground on a reef near Port Bruce, Ontario, in 1852. [2]

BURLINGTON ■ Propeller freighter of 277 t. and 137 ft., built at Buffalo in 1857, though one report says she was launched at Bay City, MI
Lake Huron: This steamer was destroyed by fire at Meldrum Bay, in the North Channel, in 1895. [2]

BURLINGTON ■ Steel bulk freight steamer of 2,024 t. and 255 ft., launched in 1897 at Cleveland as the steamer MINNEAPOLIS
Lake Michigan: On December 6, 1936, this steamer went hard aground at the entrance to the harbor at Holland, Michigan, with no loss of life. Over the succeeding winter, she was broken up by ice and waves. [2]

RICHARD BURNS ■ Bulk freight barge of 565 t. and 178 ft., launched as the schooner-barge J B LOZEN in 1890 at Mt. Clemens, MI
St. Clair River: The BURNS was traversing the St Clair Flats area at the mouth of the river when she sprang a leak and sank on Nov. 4, 1921. The ship was later removed for scrap and her cargo of coal was recovered. [2]

ROBERT BURNS ■ Vessel information unreported
Lake Erie: This early ship was reported to have foundered near E Sister Island Reef in 1850. [1]

ROBERT BURNS ■ Merchant brig
Lake Huron: This little ship, reportedly the last full-rigged brig on the Lakes, sank east of Bois Blanc Island, in the Straits of Mackinac, in 1869. Ten lives were lost. [1]

GENERAL BURNSIDE ■ Merchant schooner of 307 t. and 137 ft.
Lake Erie: The GENERAL BURNSIDE was reported to have sunk in the vicinity of Southeast Shoal Light, in July of 1892. [1]

GEORGE T BURROUGHS ■ Wooden steam sandsucker of 130 t. and 109 ft., launched at Chicago in 1881 as a freighter
St. Clair River: On May 31, 1905, the BURROUGHS collided with the steamer C F BIELMAN and sank. [2]

JOHN BURT ■ Merchant schooner of 348 t. and 131 ft., launched at Detroit in 1871
Lake Ontario: This schooner was coming in to Oswego, New York, harbor in a gale and with a cargo of grain, when she went hard aground on a reef and broke up. Two lives were lost in the accident, which occurred on September 26, 1892. [3]

WELLS BURT ■ Merchant schooner of 756 t.
Lake Michigan: The big schooner WELLS BURT was laden with a cargo of coal when she foundered on May 20, 1883. All ten hands were lost when she went down five miles off Evanston Point, Illinois. [4]

CHARLES H BURTON ■ Package and bulk freight schooner of 514 t. and 158 ft., launched at Bangor, MI (Bay City) in 1873 as the schooner GLENBULAH
Lake Erie: This coal-laden schooner was driven ashore 4.5 miles east of Barcelona, New York, and broke up. The accident happened on October 10, 1905. [3]

LOMIE A BURTON ■ Lumber schooner of 215 t. and 131 ft., launched at Chicago in 1873
Lake Michigan: Bound to Chicago with a load of lumber, the BURTON ran aground on North Manitou Island in Nov. of 1911. After being pulled off the rocks, she proceeded on her way, but made it only as far as South Manitou, about 8 miles, before she sank on the 17th. [5]

BUTCHER'S BOY ■ Wooden propeller of 214 t. and 96 ft., launched at Bay City, MI in 1879, probably as the steamer A H MORRISON
Lake Huron: The small steamer BUTCHER'S BOY was lost in 1902 when she foundered at Christian Island in southeastern Georgian Bay. [3]

BUTCHER'S MAID ■ Wooden propeller of 129 t. and 80 ft., launched in 1871 at Oshkosh, WI as the steamer KAMINISTIQUIA
Lake Superior: This little steamer was caught in a storm and driven ashore at Porphyry Point, on the North Shore. She broke up in place following the October, 1886 grounding. [1]

HANNAH BUTLER ■ 126 t. vessel of unreported type
Lake Ontario: This vessel was lost when she struck a reef and broke up in a storm near Salmon Point, Ontario, on November 26, 1887. [1]

MARSHALL F BUTTERS ■ Wooden lumber hooker of 376 t. and 164 ft., launched in 1882 at Milwaukee
Lake Erie: The old steamer BUTTERS was heavily laden with shingles and lumber when she was struck by a following gale in western Lake Erie on October 21, 1916. The vessel began to simply come apart in the big waves,

but her crew was saved in a courageous rescue before the BUTTERS sank near Southeast Shoals. [5+]

L C BUTTS No 1 ■ Merchant schooner of 504 t. and 173 ft., launched at Banks (Saginaw), MI, in 1873
Lake Michigan: The schooner L C BUTTS was trying to negotiate the island-studded entrance to Green Bay in a storm when she struck the shallows near Fish Island. Storm waves soon began their deadly work of reducing the coal-laden vessel to matchwood. The accident happened in 1891. One report says this loss occurred in the Nipigon Strait in northern Lake Huron. [3]

JOHN BY ■ Sternwheel steamer launched in 1832 at Kingston, Ont.
Lake Ontario: One of the few sternwheelers to venture out into the open lake, the JOHN BY had reason to regret it. The steamer was wrecked near Port Credit, a few miles from Toronto, Ontario, in 1833. [1]

BYTOWN ■ Sidewheel steamer launched in 1836 at Kingston, Ont.
Lake Ontario: The the new steamer BYTOWN was reported wrecked near Kingston, Ontario, in October of 1837. [1]

C D #2 ■ Cargo barge of 94 t.
Lake Erie: This unpowered vessel foundered 3.5 miles west of Erieau, Ontario, on August 30, 1940. [2]

C O D ■ Merchant schooner of 266 t. and 140 ft.
Lake Erie: Laden with a cargo of wheat, this carrier was lost when she beached 3 miles west of Port Burwell, Ontario. One life was lost in the October 22, 1887 accident. [2]

CABOTIA ■ Wooden bulk freighter of 1,530 t. and 244 ft., launched in 1880 at Gibraltar, MI as the steamer HIAWATHA
Lake Ontario: The big steamer CABOTIA was wrecked on Main Duck Island on August 25, 1919. The old vessel split her hull going on the beach, and was deemed unrepairable by her owners. [2]

THOMAS H CAHOON ■ Lumber schooner-barge of 431 t. and 166 ft., launched at Saginaw, MI, in 1881
Lake Huron: The THOMAS H CAHOON was lost in the North Channel on October 11, 1913. On that date, while in tow of the steamer CHAMBERLAIN and loaded with lumber, she was struck by a heavy gale. Her towline parted and the barge was flung ashore on Innes Island, where she broke up. [5]

CALATCO #2 ■ Oil screw tug of 101 t.
Lake Ontario: This tug was lost to fire in the harbor at Oswego, New York, on November 13, 1946. She was valued at over $100,000. [1]

CALEDONIA ■ Schooner
Lake Michigan: Carrying a cargo of flour and salt pork, the schooner CALEDONIA was blown ashore and wrecked near Sleeping Bear Point in 1862. [1]

CALIFORNIA ■ Wooden propeller freighter of 450 t. and 137 ft., launched in 1873 at Toronto
Lake Michigan: The CALIFORNIA was lost on October 3, 1887, when she was overwhelmed and sunk by huge gale-driven waves. The accident occurred one mile off St Helena Island, about seven miles west of the present Mackinac Bridge north anchorage. The number of lives lost is variously reported as 5, 9 or 14. She was carrying a cargo of general merchandise at the time. The vessel was later recovered and rebuilt as the steamer EDWARD S PEASE (qv). [5]

CALIFORNIA ■ Schooner, perhaps a yacht
Lake Erie: A single, brief report states that this sail vessel was lost by stranding on Niagara Reef, at the west end of the lake, in 1959. [1]

BERTIE CALKINS ■ Merchant schooner of 248 t. and 134 ft., launched at Two Rivers, WI, in 1874
Lake Ontario: October 3, 1919, was the date of the loss of this schooner by foundering near Belleville, Ontario, in the Bay of Quinte area. She may have been recovered. [3]

CALUMET ■ Bulk freight steamer of 1,529 t. and 256 ft.
Lake Michigan: This freighter was bucking a heavy gale and blizzard on Nov. 28, 1889, when she was discovered to be leaking. She was run up on the beach near Ft. Sheridan, Illinois and her crew was saved, but the wave-battered steamer and her cargo of coal were lost. [2]

D D CALVIN ■ Wooden bulk freight steamer of 485 t. and 175 ft., launched at Garden Island, Ont., in 1883
Lake Ontario: On April 11, 1910, while fitting out for the coming season, the CALVIN caught fire, burned and sank at Garden Island. [1]

HIRAM A CALVIN ■ Sidewheel steamer of 309 t. and 144 ft., launched at Garden Island, Ont., in 1868
Lake Ontario: The HIRAM A CALVIN was the victim of an accidental fire at the shipyards at Garden Island, Ontario, in December of 1895. [1]

CAMANCHE ■ Merchant schooner of 322 t.
Lake Ontario: The life of one of the CAMANCHE's crew was reported lost along with the ship when she foundered near Point Peninsula, New York, on Nov. 27, 1886. [1]

CAMBRIA ■ Sidewheel passenger/package freight steamer of 180 ft., built in 1877 at Quebec City as the large steam tug CHAMPION
Lake Erie: On July 16, 1902, the CAMBRIA was traversing the old Welland Canal with passengers, when she struck the rocks surrounding Reid's Island hard and stayed put. She was soon recovered, but was too badly damaged to be repaired. The ship had also been partially wrecked in 1897 when she struck a log raft and went ashore to avoid sinking. [3]

CAMBRIDGE ■ Merchant schooner of 445 t. and 162 ft.
Lake Superior: The schooner CAMBRIDGE was downbound with a load of iron ore in August of 1873, when she encountered a storm. The vessel was thrown on a rocky shore, where she broke up. [1]

COLONEL CAMP ■ Merchant bark
Lake Huron: The CAMP reportedly sank following a collision in the Straits of Mackinac in 1856. [1]

MYRTLE CAMP ■ Merchant schooner of 48 t. and 68 ft., launched at Manitowoc in 1892
Lake Michigan: The schooner MYRTLE CAMP sank on May 18, 1894. She went down off Deadman's Point, north of Menominee, Michigan, in Green Bay. [2]

T H CAMP ■ Fishing tug of 59 t. and 64 ft. launched in 1876 at Cape Vincent, NY
Lake Superior: The fishing tug T H CAMP had been chartered to carry lumber camp supplies and was engaged in that trade when she struck a reef near Madeline Island, in the Apostles Group, and sank on November 16, 1900. No lives were lost in the incident. [3]

FANNY CAMPBELL ■ Vessel of unreported type
Lake Huron: A single report states that this ship was lost on the lake in September, 1899. [1]

P N CAMPBELL ■ 33 t. vessel of unreported type
Lake Huron: This vessel was reportedly destroyed by fire at Manitoulin Island in November of 1898. [1]

PEARL B CAMPBELL ■ Steam tug of 22 t. and 55 ft., launched in 1883 at Saugatuck, MI
Lake Superior: After rescuing the schooner-barge HENRY A KENT (q.v., see also CHARLES J KERSHAW) from a beach near Marquette, the CAMPBELL was returning to Duluth in a storm when she sank with all 7 hands. The accident occurred near the Huron Islands on December 27, 1895. [4]

RALPH CAMPBELL ▪ Merchant schooner of 227 t. and 127 ft., launched in 1855 at Cleveland
Lake Erie: Long Point claimed the schooner RALPH CAMPBELL as a victim on October 14, 1909. On that date the ship swamped in a storm and was pushed ashore, where she was pounded to pieces by wave action. [2]

CANADA ▪ Merchant bark of 758 t. and 199 ft., built as a sidewheel steamer at Chippawa, Ont., in 1846
Lake Michigan: This sail vessel, originally a steamer, had been seized by the U.S. in 1849 and rebuilt as a bark. She was recorded as lost on the lake in 1855, but her position was unreported. [1]

CANADA ▪ Propeller freighter of 143 t., launched at Detroit in 1858
Lake Huron: In 1883 this small steamer was reported sunk and lost off Rockport, Michigan, near Rogers City. [2]

CANADA ▪ Propeller freighter of 644 t. and 142 ft., launched in 1872 at Hamilton, Ontario
Lake Huron: The steamer CANADA caught fire and was destroyed at Port Huron, Michigan, in October of 1892. The hull was abandoned, but was later recovered and rebuilt as the barge EUREKA (qv). [4]

CANADA ▪ Steamer of 2,445 t.
Lake St. Clair: This big steamer was lost on the lake when she collided with the tug MITCHELL'S BAY and sank on November 2, 1916. [1]

CANADA #2 ▪ 85 t. vessel of unreported type
Lake Erie: This little vessel was wrecked in a storm in April of 1902, and sank three miles east of Toledo harbor entrance. [1]

CANADIAN ▪ Merchant schooner of 153 t. (one source says 260 t.)
Lake Huron: On November 5, 1880, this schooner foundered and was lost near Clara Island, in the Whaleback area of the North Channel. [3]

FRANK CANFIELD ▪ Steam tug of 48 t. and 67 ft., launched in 1875 at Manistee, MI
Lake Michigan: The tug CANFIELD was pushed ashore near Big Sable Point, Michigan, in an April 11, 1904 gale. The vessel broke up and sank before all of her crew could be rescued, and three were lost. [2]

CANISTEO ▪ Wooden passenger and package freighter of 600 t., launched at Buffalo in 1862
Lake Michigan: While traversing the narrow channel around the end of Waugoschance Point, at the east end of the Straits of Mackinac, this steamer was wrecked in a collision with the schooner GEORGE MURRAY. The ship and her cargo of flaxseed were lost in the October 14, 1880 incident, but her crew and passengers escaped. [3]

CANISTEO ▪ Wooden bulk freight steamer of 595 t. and 182 ft., launched in 1886 at Mt. Clemens, MI
Lake Huron: The steamer CANISTEO was lost to a 1920 fire which occurred near Port Huron, Michigan. The hulk was recovered and scrapped. [2]

CANOBIE ▪ Wooden bulk freight steamer of 1,031 t. and 268 ft., launched at Detroit in 1887 as the steamer IRON KING
Lake Erie: The steamer CANOBIE was 30 miles off Port Colborne on November 1, 1921, when she was assaulted by a big storm which inflicted heavy damage to her. The battered ship was able to limp into port at Erie, Pennsylvania, but was too badly damaged to be repaired. She was subsequently stripped of usable items and put to the torch. [3]

CAPELLA ▪ Merchant schooner of 25 t.
Lake Michigan: This little schooner succumbed to the Lake and sank three miles north of the harbor at Racine, Wisconsin, on May 9, 1883. [1]

CAPRON ▪ Lumber schooner of 170 t.
Lake Michigan: The CAPRON was lost on Halloween, October 31, 1898, when she foundered in a storm off Bailey's Harbor, Wisconsin. She was carrying a cargo of lumber at the time. [1]

J F CARD ▪ Lumber schooner of 276 t. and 137 ft., launched at Vermilion, OH, in 1864
Lake Huron: A westerly storm pushed the schooner J F CARD off her course and onto the rocks near Inverhuron, Ontario, on November 15, 1900. The vessel broke up in place, but the CARD's crew escaped. [3]

CARDINAL ▪ Steel freighter of 1,930 t. and 250 ft., launched in 1927 at Haverton Hill, England, as the steamer WINDSOLITE
Lake Erie: A modern victim of reef-strewn Pelee Passage, the steamer CARDINAL was lost there in May of 1974. She struck a rocky shoal and went down in shallow water. The vessel was later recovered for scrap. [1]

M D CARDINGTON ▪ Merchant schooner
Lake Huron: In 1873 this schooner was reported to have gone aground and wrecked near Au Sable Point, south of Oscoda, Michigan. [1]

W S CARKIN ■ Steam tug of 15 t., launched at Bay City, MI, in 1874
Lake Huron: The tug W S CARKIN sank at an unreported position on the open lake in 1887. [2]

CARLINGFORD ■ Bulk freight schooner of 470 t., launched at Port Huron in 1869
Lake Erie: The CARLINGFORD was lost in a collision with the new iron bulk freighter BRUNSWICK (qv) on November 12, 1881. One of her crew died in the scramble to abandon the rapidly foundering schooner, but the rest of them escaped. The vessel sank off Dunkirk, New York, although one report says she drifted below the surface and came to rest 30 miles away, near Port Colborne, Ontario. [3]

CARLOTTA ■ Gas screw
Lake Superior: The CARLOTTA was lost as a result of fire while she was underway. The 1913 incident occurred off Grand Island, near Munising, Michigan. [1]

CAROLINE ■ Merchant schooner or may be the propeller built at Kingston, Ont., in 1825
Lake Huron: An 1832 victim of the lake's ire, this vessel capsized and sank in a storm near the Duck Islands, off Manitoulin. [2]

CAROLINE ■ Wooden steam gunboat, launched in 1822 at Charleston, SC
Lake Ontario: This American warship was commandeered on the Niagara River by Canadian rebels on December 29, 1837. During the fracas that ensued, the vessel was accidentally set afire and was abandoned. She drifted down the river and finally went over the Niagara Falls and was destroyed, with one life lost. [3]

CAROLINE ■ Merchant schooner of 60 t. launched at Presque Isle, PA, in 1812 as the armed sloop PORCUPINE
Lake Michigan: The CAROLINE, as the sloop PORCUPINE, was a veteran of Commodore Perry's victory at Put-in-Bay during the War of 1812. After the war she served as a Revenue Cutter and was later converted to a merchantman. She finally sank on Spring Lake, near Grand Haven, Michigan, in 1855, due to the aged condition of her hull. Parts of her hull were later salvaged and cut into souvenirs. A historical society has recovered most of the rest. [4]

HONORA CARR ■ Merchant schooner of 107 t. and 95 ft., built as the schooner MAPLELEAF
Lake Erie: One life was lost when this coal-laden schooner foundered offshore, two miles southwest of Point Abino, on September 4, 1886. [2]

CARRIER ■ Retired schooner of 187 t. and 123 ft., launched at Marine City, MI, in 1865
Lake Michigan: After many years of cargo service and a stint as the clubhouse for a yacht club, the CARRIER was being towed away for scrapping when she sank off Waukegan, Illinois, in October of 1923. [2]

F CARRIN ■ Merchant steamer
Lake Huron: The CARRIN was reported to have foundered in a storm at an unknown position in 1912. [1]

CARRINGTON ■ Merchant schooner of 215 t.
Lake Michigan: While outbound with a cargo of pig iron, this schooner struck Hat Island Reef in October of 1870. She stuck fast and was later broken up by wave action. [1]

CARRINGTON ■ Wooden tug
Lake Superior: While towing a log raft on May 17 of 1885, this tug caught fire and was destroyed off Baraga, Michigan. [1]

E M CARRINGTON ■ Bulk freight schooner of 121 t.
Lake Michigan: Five lives were lost when this lumber-laden schooner became waterlogged in a storm and sank in midlake off Milwaukee. The ship and crewmen were lost on November 5, 1880. [1]

E T CARRINGTON ■ Steam tug of 58 t. and 76 ft., launched in 1876 at Bangor, MI
Lake Superior: The little tug E T CARRINGTON was lost in a gale when she foundered near her homeport of Duluth on August 23, 1907. [2]

M D CARRINGTON ■ Steam tug of 64 t. and 67 ft., launched in 1875 at Buffalo
Lake Superior: The extreme tension on the hawsers strung between towed vessels and those towing them was the cause of a significant number of Lakes accidents. The CARRINGTON was towing a vessel in Duluth Harbor when she got out of line with her charge, capsized and quickly sank on September 1, 1901. One of her crew was lost in the accident. [2]

J J CARROLL ■ Oil screw fish tug of 77 t. and 59 ft., launched in 1925 at Sandusky, OH
Lake Erie: The fish tug J J CARROLL was reported destroyed by fire at Pelee Island in 1929. [1]

J J CARROLL II ■ Oil screw fish tug of 30 t. and 63 ft., launched in 1908 at Sandusky, OH as the oil screw JOS. T SLOAT
Lake Erie: The small motor vessel CARROLL was lost on October 12, 1939, when she struck a bar and foundered just offshore, six miles east of Fairport, Ohio. [1]

MAGGIE CARROLL ■ Steam tug of 16 t. and 49 ft., launched in 1883 at Duluth
Lake Superior: This little tug was destroyed by fire on the Superior, Wisconsin side of Duluth-Superior Harbor. She was lost on September 28, 1893. [3]

JAMES C CARRUTHERS ■ Steel bulk freight steamer of 9,500 t. and 550 ft., launched at Collingwood, Ont., in 1913
Lake Huron: The CARRUTHERS was the newest and

largest of the ten Long Ships that were lost with all hands on Huron in the "Big Storm" of 1913. In her first season of operation, she was laden with over 10,000 tons of wheat when the grandfather of storms struck her on November 11. The giant steamer was simply overwhelmed and sank near Kincardine, Ontario, with all 25 of her crew. [5+]

COLONEL CARRY ■ Merchant bark
Lake Huron: The schooner COLONEL CARRY was lost in 1854, when she foundered off Goderich, Ontario. [1]

J S CARTER ■ Merchant schooner
Lake Huron: This vessel was moving through the Mississagi Strait, at the northwest end of Manitoulin Island, when she plowed into a shallow, rocky area and was destroyed. The reef where the 1890 accident happened is now known as "Carter Rock." [1]

W J CARTER ■ Wooden bulk freight steamer of 235 t. and 122 ft., launched in 1886 at Milwaukee
Lake Ontario: The small bulk carrier W J CARTER was lost when she sprang a leak in a gale and was lost near Point Petre, on July 28, 1923. She was full-laden with coal at the time. [2]

CARTHAGINIAN ■ Merchant schooner of 405 t. and 139 ft., launched at Oswego, NY
Lake Ontario: This two-mast schooner was reported lost on the lake in 1867. [1]

JACQUES CARTIER ■ Wooden steam passenger and package freighter of 74 t. and 85 ft., launched at Detroit in 1870
Lake Huron: This diminutive steamer was reported as wrecked near Goderich, Ontario, in an October, 1878 storm. [3]

CARTIERCLIFFE HALL ■ Steel bulk freight steamer of 730 ft., launched in Germany in 1960 as the steamer RUHR ORE. Lengthened and renamed in 1976
Lake Superior: A tragic fire struck this big carrier off Copper Harbor, Michigan, on June 5, 1979. Six men died in the blaze, which caused $4.5 million in damages to the ship and her cargo of corn. She was extensively rebuilt and returned to service. [1]

CASCADEN ■ Merchant schooner of 138 t.
Lake Huron: This small carrier was lost when she foundered off Long Point, near Tobermory, Ontario, in October of 1871. [2]

CASE ■ Wooden bulk freight steamer of 2,278 t. and 301 ft., launched as the JAMES C LOCKWOOD at Cleveland in 1889
Lake Erie: East Sister Island, at the western end of the lake, was the final resting place for this big steamer. On May 1, 1917, she was discovered to be leaking and was beached. The ship broke up in place and was a total loss, but her cargo of coal was recovered. [4]

GEORGE M CASE ■ Bulk freight schooner of 344 t. and 137 ft.
Lake Erie: On October 14, 1888 or 86, the schooner GEORGE M CASE, laden with a cargo of corn, sank eight miles off Port Colborne, Ontario. [2]

REED CASE ■ Schooner of 330 t.
Lake Superior: The REED CASE is reported to have foundered near the Portage Ship Canal on October 19, 1888. One life was lost when she went down. [1]

WILLIAM CASE ■ Package and bulk freight schooner of 266 t. and 137 ft., launched in 1855 at Cleveland
Lake Erie: This schooner was heavy laden with coal when she encountered heavy weather on July 26, 1906. The 51-year-old vessel's aged seams could not take the strain and she filled and sank five miles north-northeast of Colchester Light. [3]

CASPIAN ■ Steam freighter
Lake Erie: No lives were lost when this steamer foundered just off Cleveland, in 1852. [2]

CASTALIA ■ Merchant brig of 242 t. and 119 ft., launched in 1847 at Sandusky, OH
Lake Huron: This little ship was overcome by a violent gale and sank near Cove Island, on Georgian Bay, in 1871. [2]

LAUREN CASTLE ■ Tug of 98 ft
Lake Michigan: On November 5, 1980, the big tug LAUREN CASTLE was towing the disabled tanker AMOCO WISCONSIN up Grand Traverse Bay, when a navigational error caused her to touch bottom. As she slowed she was rammed from behind by the tanker. The tug quickly sank seven miles north of Traverse City, Michigan, with the loss of one of her four crew. [3]

W B CASTLE ■ Steam tug of 172 t. and 114 ft., launched in 1862 at Cleveland
Lake Superior: This big tug succumbed to fire in Duluth Harbor on November 30, 1898. [2]

CATARACT ■ Merchant schooner of 426 t. and 138 ft., launched at Sandusky, OH, in 1856
Lake Erie: This hapless schooner was almost new when she was wrecked on Long Point in 1857. [1]

CATARAQUI ■ Sidewheel steamer launched in 1836 at Kingston, Ont.
Lake Ontario: The new steamer CATARAQUI was destroyed by fire at Kingston, Ontario in April of 1840. [1]

CATARAQUI ■ Propeller freighter of 101 t. and 91 ft., launched in 1847 at Portsmouth, Ont.
Lake Ontario: This small steamer was reported as lost on the Lake in 1864. [1]

E S CATLIN ■ Schooner-barge of 372 t., launched at Banks (Saginaw), MI, in 1869
Lake Erie: The CATLIN was lost when she stranded and went to pieces five miles east of Ashtabula, Ohio, in 1876. [2]

CATTARAUGUS ■ Merchant schooner of 309 t., launched at Oswego, NY, in 1857
Lake Ontario: This two-master was reported to have been lost on the lake in 1864. [1]

CAVALIER ■ Merchant schooner of 268 t. and 140 ft., launched in 1867 at Quebec City
Lake Huron: On August 31, 1906, this schooner filled in heavy weather and sank off Chantry Island. [3]

CAYUGA ■ Merchant schooner of 60 t., built before 1847
Lake Ontario: This little schooner was reported as wrecked on the lake in 1854. [1]

CAYUGA ■ Steel bulk freighter of 1,939 t. and 290 ft., launched in 1889 at Cleveland
Lake Michigan: The dangerous Skillagalee Shoal area, where the shipping channel narrows to only a few hundred yards, was the site of the loss of this big steamer. On May 1, 1895, the grain-laden ship collided with the lumber hooker JOSEPH L HURD (qv) and sank. Her crew made it to shore safely. [3]

CECILIA or **CECELIA** ■ Merchant schooner of 167 t., may be the bark built at Port Dalhousie, Ont., in 1865

Lake Michigan: This small schooner was stranded and lost near Jacksonport, Wisconsin, in September of 1885. [1]

CEDARVILLE ■ Self-unloading steel bulk freighter of 8,222 t. and 588 ft., launched at River Rouge, Michigan, in 1927 as the A F HARVEY
Lake Huron: This very big steamer, laden with a full load of limestone and groping her way through a fog, collided with the Norwegian steel freighter TOPJALSFJORD and sank in the Straits of Mackinac, two miles east of the Mackinac Bridge. Ten of her crew went down with the ship in the May 7, 1965 accident. The wreckage of the big ship is a popular dive target. [5+]

CELTIC ■ Bulk freight schooner-barge of 716 t. and 190 ft., launched at W Bay City, MI, in 1890
Lake Huron: Upbound and laden with a cargo of coal, this vessel broke her towline and disappeared with all 8 hands in a gale on Nov. 29, 1902. Her wreckage later washed up on the southeast point of Cockburn Island. [5+]

CELTIC ■ Propeller freighter of 698 t. and 131 ft. launched in 1874 at Hamilton, Ont.
Lake Erie: The steamer CELTIC was lost in a collision in May of 1892. The accident occurred off Rondeau, Ontario. [1]

CERISOLES ■ Armed steel or wooden minesweeper of 630 t. and 143 ft., launched in 1918 at Ft. William, Ont.
Lake Superior: Built for the French navy, this minesweeper was on her maiden voyage, bound for delivery in France, when disaster struck. Travelling with her sisters INKERMANN (qv) and SEBASTOPOL, and a crew of 38, she simply disappeared in a strong gale on November 24, 1918, somewhere between Ft. William and the Soo. No identifiable wreckage, nor the remains of any of her crew, was ever found. Many spellings of her name have been encountered. [5+]

CHALLENGE ■ Propeller freighter
Lake Huron: In the days of wooden steamships, boiler explosions and fires were a fairly common occurence. This propeller succumbed to such a fate on June 22, 1853, when she blew up and burned at Cheboygan, Michigan. Five of her crew lost their lives in the accident. [2]

CHALLENGE ■ Merchant schooner of 150 t., launched at Rochester, NY, in 1853
Lake Michigan: It was reported that this schooner sank off Sheboygan, Wisconsin, in 1871. [1]

CHALLENGE ■ Tug, perhaps the 11 t., 58 ft. tug CHALLENGE built at Bay City, MI, in 1870
Lake Huron: This tug was destroyed by fire in 1880 at East Saginaw, Michigan, about 15 miles up the Saginaw River. [2]

CHALLENGE ■ Merchant schooner of 87 t. and 82 ft., launched at Manitowoc, WI, in 1852
Lake Michigan: The schooner CHALLENGE was lost in December of 1901 when she stranded on a reef near Bailey's Harbor, Wisconsin, and was reported wrecked. [2]

CHALLENGE ■ Lumber schooner of 97 t.
Lake Michigan: This little vessel and her cargo of wood were reported lost on September 5, 1910, when she sank in a storm off Sheboygan, Wisconsin. May be the same ship as the 1901 wreck, above. [1]

PORTER CHAMBERLAIN ■ Wooden bulk freight steamer of 280 t. and 134 ft., launched at Marine City, MI, in 1874
Lake Huron: The CHAMBERLAIN was lost on Georgian Bay on November 11, 1901. The little steamer had a cargo of lumber when she grounded, then caught fire and was destroyed. [3]

SELAH CHAMBERLAIN ■ Steam barge (one source says schooner) of 1,207 t. and 212 ft.
Lake Michigan: Five lives were lost when this big vessel was lost off Sheboygan, Wisconsin. The wood-carrying ship was groping her way through a thick fog on October 13, 1886 when she collided with another vessel and sank quickly. [2]

CHAMPION ■ Merchant schooner of 205 t., launched at Milwaukee in 1844
Lake Huron: The schooner CHAMPION was passing through the Straits of Mackinac in 1847, when she fetched up on the west end of Bois Blanc Island, and was lost. [2]

CHAMPION ■ Wooden tug of 264 t. and 134 ft, launched in 1868 at Detroit
Lake Erie: This big tug was famous for her long tows of schooners up and down the Detroit River. She met her end at Put-in-Bay, on South Bass Island, in 1903, when she was destroyed by an accidental fire. [2]

CHAMPLAIN ■ Steam packet
Lake Michigan: An early Lake Michigan steamer, the CHAMPLAIN was reported to have been driven ashore four miles south of St. Joseph, Michigan, by a gale. Passengers and crew were rescued, but the ship broke up in place. The loss occurred on May 3, 1840. [1]

CHAMPLAIN ■ Wooden passenger and package freighter of 438 t.
Lake Michigan: With a full complement of crew and passengers, and a cargo of general merchandise, this steamer caught fire off Charlevoix, Michigan. She made a run for shore in an effort to save the lives of her people, but 22 were still lost on June 16, 1887. Her wreckage may lie near Fisherman's Island, though one source says she was recovered and rebuilt as the steamer KANSAS. [3]

ZACH CHANDLER ■ Lumber schooner-barge of 727 t. and 194 ft., launched at Detroit in 1867
Lake Superior: On October 29, 1892, this big schooner-barge was carrying her usual load of lumber when she and her tow steamer JOHN MITCHELL ran into a heavy gale. The tow cable parted, and the almost helpless barge was broken up by the big waves. Seven of her eight crew members made it to shore, but one sailor was lost. [5]

J P CHAPIN ■ Merchant schooner of 121 t.
Lake Michigan: A May, 1877, accident claimed this schooner when she sank off Michigan City, Indiana. [1]

W T CHAPPELL ■ Package and bulk freight schooner of 40 t. and 72 ft., launched in 1877 at Sebewaing, MI
Lake Superior: The little CHAPPELL was battered by a storm that she encountered on October 24, 1902. She sprang a leak in the big combers, blew don and sank off Vermilion Point, Michigan. [5]

CHARGER ■ Merchant schooner
Lake Erie: The CHARGER is reported to have sunk at the mouth of the Detroit River on August 7, 1890. [1]

CHARLEY ■ Merchant schooner of 50 t. and 113 ft., launched in 1863 at Detroit
Lake Superior: This little two-master was wrecked at the mouth of Minnesota's Beaver River on May 10, 1881. [1]

CHARLIE ■ Merchant schooner
Lake Superior: The CHARLIE was lost with all hands somewhere near Whitefish Point, in 1877. She simply "went missing." [2]

CHARLOTTE ■ Gas screw of 13 t.
Lake Michigan: This tiny vessel was reported to have foundered at Michigan City, Indiana, in July of 1945. [1]

CHASKA ■ Schooner-scow of 72 ft. and 50 t., launched in 1869 at Duluth
Lake Superior: This little vessel was wrecked near Duluth in 1870, with no loss of life. She was reportedly the first vessel built at Duluth. [1]

CHATTANOOGA ■ Bulk freight schooner-barge of 2,329 t. and 308 ft., built at W Bay City, MI, in 1898
Lake Erie: This enormous schooner-barge was wrecked on Lake Erie in the fall of 1925. She was later raised but was in too poor a condition to be returned to service and was scrapped. [2]

CITY OF CHEBOYGAN ■ Merchant schooner
Lake Huron: A single report claims that this schooner was driven ashore and wrecked near Detour, MI, in 1880. [1]

CHECOTAH ■ Bulk freight schooner-barge of 658 t. and 199 ft., launched as the GEORGE D RUSSELL in 1870 at Toledo, OH
Lake Huron: The CHECOTAH was off Port Sanilac, Michigan, when she was overcome by a storm and sank on October 30, 1906. No lives were lost. [3]

CHENANGO ■ Schooner-barge of 384 t.
Lake Superior: The towline connecting this schooner-barge to her tow steamer, the JAY C MORSE, parted in a sudden squall and the CHENANGO was driven aground on Wood Island Reef, near Munising, Michigan. The loss occurred on November 20, 1875, when the ship was downbound with a load of pig iron. Fortunately, her crew escaped before the ship broke up. [2]

CHENANGO ■ Wooden package freighter of 690 t. and 175 ft., launched at Detroit in 1887
Lake Erie: This vessel was in transit off Erie, Pennsylvania, when she was partially consumed by fire and sank on April 11, 1890. She was refloated and rebuilt as the steamer LIZZIE MADDEN (qv). [3]

CHENANGO ■ Propeller freighter
Lake Huron: It was reported that this ship was lost on the lake in 1891. [1]

O W CHENEY ■ Tug of 56 t. and 66 ft.
Lake Erie: The tug CHENEY was lost in a June 23, 1902 accident. On that date, she collided with the steamer CHEMUNG and sank seven miles west of Buffalo and four miles offshore. The year of this accident is also given as 1903. [3]

CHEROKEE ■ Steam freighter, possibly the 1,304 t. 208 ft. ship built in 1889 at Marine City, MI (only ship of this name on the lakes capable of maneuvering two barges)
Lake Huron: A somewhat cryptic report says that this ship was lost on Saginaw Point with two barges in 1913. If this is the ship described above, it was recovered. [1]

CHESAPEAKE ■ Sidewheel passenger and freight steamer of 412 t. and 172 ft., launched at Maumee, OH, in 1838 (one source says 1828)
Lake Erie: The CHESAPEAKE was off Conneaut, Ohio, on June 9, 1847, when she struck the loaded schooner JOHN F PORTER (qv) and sank. Sources vary as to the number of lives lost (1,6,7 or 13). One report says that the ship was popular as an offshore gambling casino. [5]

CHICAGO ■ Wooden passenger and package freight steamer, probably the 166 t. vessel built at St. Joseph, MI, in 1835
Lake Erie: The steamer CHICAGO was an early victim of Sturgeon Point, west of Buffalo. In November of 1842 the vessel was driven ashore there by a violent gale and wrecked. [1]

CHICAGO ■ Steam freighter, perhaps the same vessel as above
Lake Erie: This ship was lost in Buffalo Harbor on August 1, 1849, when she caught fire and was destroyed. No lives were lost in the incident. [2]

CHICAGO ■ Steel package freight steamer of 3,195 t. and 324 ft., launched at Buffalo in 1901
Lake Superior: The big freighter CHICAGO was no match for one of the powerful gales that sweep the Big Lake in the fall. On October 23, 1929, the ship was swept onto the shore of Michipicoten Island and broken up by wave action. Fortunately, her crew escaped with their lives. [3]

CHICAGO BOARD OF TRADE ■ Package and bulk freight schooner of 423 t. and 153 ft., launched in 1863 at Manitowoc, WI
Lake Erie: One of the many victims of Erie's fitful storms was this schooner that was lost on November 21, 1900. While riding deep with a cargo of iron ore and battling a gale on the western end of the Lake, she struck Niagara Reef, stranded and went to pieces. [3]

CHICAGO HARBOR ■ Tug
Lake Michigan: This utility vessel was reported lost off downtown Chicago in July of 1892.

CHICKAMAUGA ■ Bulk freight schooner-barge of 2,472 t. and 322 ft., launched at W Bay City, MI, in 1898
Lake Huron: The giant schooner-barge CHICKAMAUGA was downbound with a load of iron ore and in the tow of the steamer CENTURION when she was beset by huge, storm-driven seas on September 12, 1919. The long hull could not take the stress and began to leak badly. The vessels tried to make it to Harbor Beach, Michigan, but the barge sank just outside the harbor, after her crew had been taken off. The wreckage was removed in 1920. [5+]

CHICORA ■ Passenger and package freight steamer of 1,122 t. and 217 ft., launched at Detroit in 1882
Lake Michigan: The CHICORA is one of those vessels which "sailed through a crack in the lake," disappearing with all 25 hands and leaving little evidence behind. The steamer left Milwaukee on a late season run with a load of flour on January 21, 1895, but never made port at St. Joseph. Sudden squalls and roving ice floes probably did the ship in somewhere off St. Joseph. According to one report, the ship's dog was found wandering on the beach near St. Joseph a few days after the accident. [5+]

CHICOUTIMI ■ Sidewheel steamer of 110 t. and 93 ft., launched at Levis, Quebec in 1881
Lake Ontario: The small sidewheeler CHICOUTIMI was lost in 1898. She was destroyed by fire in the harbor at Toronto. [1]

CHINA ■ Propeller freighter of 130 ft. (about 333 t.), launched in 1872 at Kingston, Ont.
Lake Ontario: This propeller was destroyed by fire at Kingston, Ontario, in October of 1872. [1]

CHINA ■ Merchant schooner of 314 t.
Lake Huron: The CHINA was bucking big seas in Georgian Bay on November 20, 1883, when she met her end. Diving into the trough of a wave, she struck bottom and quickly sank near Cape Hurd, Ontario. [3]

CHIPPEWA ■ Merchant schooner
Lake Superior: One of the few vessels trading on Lake Superior in the 1840s, the CHIPPEWA was lost when she ran on Sawtooth Reef, near the top of the Keweenaw Peninsula, and was lost in November of 1847. [1]

CHIPPEWA ■ Propeller steamer of 94 t.
Lake Huron: This small steamer was reported wrecked or abandoned at the mouth of Georgian Bay's Musquash River, in 1906. [1]

ALVAH S CHISHOLM, Jr ■ Wooden steam sandsucker of 170 ft., launched at Marine City, MI, in 1900
Lake Erie: One of a number of vessels used for mining sand and gravel from the lake bottom, the CHISHOLM burned at her dock at Sandusky, Ohio, on May 11, 1935. For awhile it was thought she might be repairable, but her hulk was towed several miles out and blown up in 1937. [2]

HENRY CHISHOLM ■ Wooden bulk freight steamer of 1,775 t. and 256 ft., launched at Cleveland in 1880
Lake Superior: Reef-studded Isle Royale has been the final resting place for many an unwary ship since the early days of Lakes commerce. The CHISHOLM was tossed onto the Rock of Ages Reef, at the southwest end, by an October 20, 1898, storm. The ship was subsequntly broken up by weather and her cargo of barley lost, but her crew made it to shore in lifeboats. [2]

CHOCTAW ■ Steel bulk freight steamer of 1,574 t. and 278 ft., launched at Cleveland in 1892
Lake Huron: The CHOCTAW was an unusual-looking vessel, similar to the whalebacks in design and sister to the steamer ANDASTE (qv), before the latter was converted to a sandsucker. Her low freeboard may have contributed to her loss on July 12, 1915. While travelling in a fog off Presque Isle, Michigan, the freighter collided with the steamer WAHCONDAH. With a large hole below her waterline, she quickly went to the bottom. Some reports say as many as ten of her crew were lost, but most say all survived. [5+]

CHOCTAW ■ Propeller packet of 53 t. and 75 ft., launched in 1911 at Collingwood, Ont.
Lake Erie: In January of 1923, the small steamer CHOCTAW was destroyed by fire at her dock at Port Stanley, Ontario. [1]

SAMUEL J CHRISTIAN ■ Steam tug of 55 t. and 71 ft., built in New Jersey and launched in 1868
Detroit River: This veteran tug and three of her crew were lost when the vessel sank in the river on October 19, 1901

T S CHRISTIE ■ Wooden bulk freight steamer of 769 t. and 160 ft., launched in 1885 at W Bay City, MI
Lake Michigan: Nearly 50 years old at the time of her loss on November 7, 1933, the CHRISTIE was caught by a bliz-

zard/gale and driven ashore at Barr Creek, four miles northeast of Manistee, Michigan. Her crew made it to shore, but the old wooden hull could not take the battering and the vessel soon went to pieces. [3]

CHURCHILL ■ Schooner or schooner-barge of 1,010 t. and 202 ft.
Lake Michigan: After being lost from the tow of a steamer, this big sailing ship foundered off Waukegan, Illinois. Two lives were lost in the October 13, 1898, incident. [3]

CIBOLA ■ Sidewheel steamer of 962 t. and 252 ft., launched in 1888 at Deseronto, Ont.
Lake Ontario: The sidewheeler CIBOLA was at her dock at Lewiston, New York, on the Niagara River, when she caught fire and was destroyed in July of 1895. [1]

CINCINNATI ■ Wooden freighter, perhaps the 116 t. vessel launched at Sandusky in 1836
Lake Huron: This steamer was reported ashore and wrecked near Forestville, Michigan, (south of Harbor Beach) in 1854. [1]

CIRCASSIAN ■ Merchant schooner
Lake Michigan: In 1860 the schooner CIRCASSIAN was reported sunk at White Shoals, near the Beaver Islands. [1]

CISCOE ■ Steam passenger and freight packet of 25 t. and 44 ft., launched in 1891 at Cleveland
Lake Michigan: On May 19, 1910, this tiny vessel caught fire near Sleeping Bear Point and was destroyed. The hulk sank six miles from shore, but none of those aboard were lost. [3]

CITIZEN ■ Merchant schooner of 54 t.
Lake Michigan: The little schooner CITIZEN was lost when she went aground and was abandoned six miles north of Chicago in May of 1853. [1]

CITY QUEEN ■ Tug of 42 t.
Lake Huron: This tug was reported to have sunk near "Manitou Dock" on August 27, 1924. [2]

CLARA ■ Merchant schooner of 21 t.
Lake Michigan: The Lakes were alive with small vessels like the CLARA, tiny sailing vessels of relatively low value that shuttled between ports with whatever cargoes they could muster. Many were unregistered and uninsured, making it nearly impossible to even estimate their number. This little sailing ship and her one-man crew were reported lost on the lake on August 23, 1887. She was hauling a cargo of lumber at the time. [2]

CLARENCE E ■ Gas packet of 13 t.
Lake Superior: A fire of unknown origin caused the loss of this small carrier when she was destroyed at Superior, Wisconsin, on June 30, 1938. [2]

CLARION ■ Merchant brig
Lake Michigan: The CLARION was a small sailing ves-

sel that was lost when she ran into the shallows and wrecked in the area of Skillagallee, in upper Lake Michigan, 1860. [1]

CLARION ■ Composite package freighter of 1,712 t. and 254 ft., launched at Wyandotte, MI, in 1881
Lake Erie: The steamer CLARION is well-known because of her unusual cargo. She was upbound with a pair of locomotives aboard when she encountered a heavy gale and was driven north of her chosen course and into the shallows at Southeast Shoal, near Point Pelee. The ship jammed fast and then caught fire and was destroyed. Reports of the number of crew lost vary from 12 to 32, with 15 lost of the 21 aboard being the most reliable estimate. It is not known whether her cargo was recovered. [5+]

ALVIN CLARK ■ Merchant schooner of 220 t. and 113 ft., launched at Trenton, MI, in 1846
Lake Michigan: This three-masted schooner was lost on Green Bay on June 29, 1864, while travelling in ballast. She went down in a terrific gale with three of her five crew. In 1968-69, a schooner thought to be the CLARK was recovered almost intact, and is now on display at Menominee, Michigan. [3]

LUCY J CLARK ■ Bulk freight schooner
Lake Huron: The schooner CLARK was laden with a cargo of wood when she was struck by a stiff wind and capsized off Cross Village, Michigan, near the Skillagallee shoal area. Three of her crew were lost in the November 11, 1883 accident. [2]

S C CLARK ■ Steam freighter
Lake Huron: Little information is available on this steamer, reported destroyed by fire off Port Sanilac, Michigan, in 1893. [1]

J C CLARKE ■ Wooden steam freighter of 175 t. and 96 ft., launched at Marine City, MI, in 1865 as the steamer T D DOLE
Lake Huron: Engaged in the Sarnia-Port Huron trade, this old steamer was reported to have burned to a total loss at a dock at Port Huron, Michigan, in 1905. [3]

JAMES CLARKE or **CLARK** ■ Steam tug of 48 t. and 79 ft., launched in 1883 at Goderich, Ont.
Lake Huron: The tug JAMES CLARKE was reported destroyed by fire in August of 1896. Two Ontario locations are given for her demise. One places her in Owen Sound, Georgian Bay, while the other says she was lost in St Michael's Bay, Manitoulin Island. [2]

CLAY TILE ■ Freight scow of 206 t.
Lake Huron: This unpowered vessel sank in the Saginaw River on July 11, 1943.

Treasure Ships

The Lakes abound with rumors and reports of the loss of vessels laden with gold and silver, gems and other glittering cargoes. Indeed, there are a number of recorded recoveries of riches from the bottoms of the Lakes.

In 1841, the passenger sidewheeler ERIE left Buffalo with a manifest of German and Dutch immigrants who were hoping to make a new start in the west. These hardy folks were not the ragged, destitute travellers one might envision. In fact, many were quite wealthy, and planned to purchase significant tracts of farmland when they reached Milwaukee or Chicago.

Alas, the ship fell victim to a boiler explosion and fire in which as many as 175 souls and their dreams were lost. No one knows how much paper money, securities and other flammables were destroyed in the blaze, but when the burned-out hull of the ERIE was raised from the bottom of her namesake lake a decade later, almost $200,000 in melted gold and silver coinage was in her bilges.

Many other vessels sank with safes loaded with passengers' valuables and other riches. The G P GRIFFITH near Cleveland in 1850, the luxury yacht GUNILDA on Lake Superior in 1911, the sidewheel liner ALPENA off Holland, Michigan in 1880, and dozens of others.

In addition to the flashy precious metals and jewelry that make salvagers' eyes sparkle, numerous ships carried valuable, if heavier, cargos of ores and manufactured goods. The PEWABIC and the KITTY REEVES, both Lake Huron victims, were laden with copper ore of high purity and with a value that increases almost daily. Several ships are known to have been lost with non-perishables such as stained glass and stainless steel wire.

Of course this is all academic, salvage laws being what they are, but it is still exciting to know that one's runabout may be passing over some glittering hoard a few fathoms below.

But what of the real big treasure—treasure like that which has been discovered off the coast of Florida in the last few years? Are there galleons from the Spanish Main packed with gold lying about on the Lakes beds? Rumors persist, especially on Lake Erie, of ships having gone down with chests of dubloons. Let's examine a well-known example.

One vessel often mentioned by gold hunters is the French-flagged frigate La JEAN FLORIN, reportedly lost off the present site of Barcelona, New York in 1721, with a payroll of gold pieces. Research can cast some light on a report such as this. Soldiers at France's two garrisons above Lake Erie, Detroit and Michilimackinac, were generally not paid in gold specie, but in goods and in "chits" that could be cashed in when the soldier reached an area where cash could be spent.

After the loss of the GRIFFIN in 1679, there is record of only one decked ship on the Lakes above Niagara Falls, a small sloop, until the Comte de Frontenac acquired the permission to build two trading vessels at Niagara in 1726. Until that time, and indeed well after, goods were transported mostly by the "Montreal canoe," a large canoe of three or four tons capacity, which could be easily portaged and pulled up on shore in bad weather.

The term "frigate," as used at the time, applied to a relatively large (24 or more guns) warship. Such a ship would, of necessity, either have been built above Niagara Falls (no record), or portaged around the Falls (also, no record). It is also questionable whether the need for a ship designed to bombard shore emplacements and engage other warships would have justified the expense of bringing it to Lake Erie, since at that time there were no other big warships, and all of the forts belonged to the French. There is, of course, the possibility that the word "frigate" is used to describe what the English and Americans called a "frigate-built" merchantman, that is, a merchant vessel with a frigate-shaped hull.

1721 was a time of relative peace for the French. Much of their war fleet would have been engaged in exploration or have been based in home waters in the Atlantic or Mediterranean. Their big Mediterranean port of Marseilles is located less than 200 nautical miles from the coastal city of Barcelona, Spain. French ships bound for Gibraltar and the Atlantic would routinely pass within a few leagues of the Spanish port. Perhaps this is where the La JEAN FLORIN lies.

Speculative, it is agreed, but this exercise shows one must be cautious when accepting reports of treasure unquestioningly. Perhaps we would be better advised to consider only a vessel's historic, rather than monetary, value. If the La JEAN FLORIN does lie somewhere off the New York lakeshore, its discovery will certainly fill a blank spot in our knowledge of the French in North America.□

Tanker explosions

In the early 1990s there is a great deal of interest in the possibility of tanker accidents on the Great Lakes and their possible effects. It is ironic, therefore, that the biggest tanker explosion and fire ever to occur on the Lakes happened in September of 1990. It destroyed the motor vessel JUPITER and her cargo of almost a million gallons of gasoline.

The vessel was unloading at her dock in the Saginaw River at Bay City, Michigan, when a fire began on the pier and spread to the ship, causing a terrific explosion and a fire that burned for several days. Smoke from the fire could be seen at least 50 miles away, and the JUPITER was so badly burned that parts of her inner hull melted. Considering the magnitude of the blast and fire, it is fortunate that only one sailor lost his life in the accident, and that environmental damage was minimal.

The JUPITER disaster involved the largest tanker to be lost, and the largest cargo destroyed, but it was definitely not the first large tanker explosion. On October 29, 1951, the tanker-barge MORANIA #130 was being guided into the harbor at Buffalo by her consort tug DAUNTLESS #12. She carried in her tanks 800,000 gallons of gasoline. In attempting to pass the pair, the steel freighter PENOBSCOT made an error and rammed the MORANIA. The barge exploded instantly, engulfing all three vessels in a mass of flame and smoke.

The fire continued for several days before finally burning itself out, destroying the barge and tug and doing severe damage to the PENOBSCOT's forward end. The final death toll was 11; two on the barge, seven of eight aboard the DAUNTLESS, and two of the freighter's crew.

On January 1, 1937, a big explosion rocked the normally peaceful, thinly populated Beaver Islands. The 244-foot tanker J OSWALD BOYD, which had gone aground on Simmons Reef, north of the main island on November 11 of the previous year, had exploded with nearly 200,000 gallons of gasoline aboard. A former yacht and now Beaver Island supply and mail steamer, the MAROLD II, had been contracted to lighter the fuel from the big vessel. About 800,000 gallons had been removed when, on the quiet, pristine New Year's Day of 1937, something went wrong with the operation.

Beaver Islanders heard the big blast from their town of St. James, but it was quite some time before the details of the accident could be worked out, for the BOYD was now a flaming mass of tangled wreckage, and the MAROLD had practically disappeared. The most reliable reports on the accident say that the MAROLD was carrying a crew of five when she was blown to pieces.

Another tanker accident, but one about which there seems to be little information, was the steel tanker BLUE COMET. She was reported to have exploded and burned in the harbor at Calumet. Illinois, sometime in the 1930s. One crewman died in the mighty conflagration. The vessel was said to have been carrying about a half million gallons of gasoline.

Of course, there have also been tankers lost in other types of accidents involving tankers. The final resting place of the tank-barge CLEVECO can reportedly still be located on calm days by an oil slick. The Great Lakes are fortunate to have never suffered a tanker disaster that turned into an environmental disaster.

Lost vessels named after States and Provinces

Number of vessels of that name in parentheses:

ALASKA (2), ALBERTA (3), ARIZONA (1), CALIFORNIA (2), COLORADO (1), DELAWARE (3), FLORIDA (6), IDAHO (2), ILLINOIS (2), INDIANA (3), IOWA (1), KANSAS (1), LOUISIANA (1), MAINE (3), MANITOBA (1), MICHIGAN (5), MINNESOTA (2), MISSOURI (1), MONTANA (2), NEVADA (1), NEW BRUNSWICK (1), NEW HAMPSHIRE (1), NEW YORK (2), NORTH CAROLINA (1), OHIO (4), ONTARIO (8), OREGON (4), VERMONT (1), WISCONSIN (4), WYOMING (2), YUKON (1)

There was also a STATE OF MICHIGAN, a STATE OF OHIO, a GEORGIAN, a KENTUCKIAN, and two SCOTIA's, though the latter may have been named after Scotland.

HENRY CLAY ■ Merchant brig of 59 t., built prior to 1847
Lake Huron: The little two-stick HENRY CLAY sank in the Straits of Mackinac, near Point Nipigon, in 1850. [2]

HENRY CLAY ■ Passenger and package freight steamer
Lake Erie: On October 25, 1851, this famous old steamer capsized in a heavy gale and sank near Long Point. 16 to 19 lives were lost in the accident. Her cargo of baled wool reportedly washed up on the Canadian shore for months. [4]

CLAYTON ■ Merchant bark
Lake Huron: This bark sank at an unreported position after a collision in 1868. [1]

CLAYTON BELLE ■ Merchant schooner of 300 t.
Lake Huron: Four lives were lost when this schooner sank following an April 10, 1882, accident. The CLAYTON BELLE was off Lexington, MI, when she collided with the schooner THOMAS PARSONS (qv) and was lost. [4]

NORMAN P CLEMENT ■ Steel steam acid tanker of 261 ft. overall, launched in England in 1924.
Lake Huron: This tanker was the only ship on the Lakes to be built specifically for transporting acid. On October 23, 1968, she was destroyed by an explosion and fire which occurred on Georgian Bay. The hulk was later scuttled in deep water. [3]

D M CLEMSON ■ Steel bulk freight steamer of 5,531 t. and 448 ft., launched in 1903 at Superior, WI
Lake Superior: In one of the mysteries of the Lakes, the big freighter D M CLEMSON simply "went missing" on December 1, 1908. Laden with a cargo of coal, the steamer encountered a heavy gale and blizzard and went down at an unknown position with all 24 of her crew. Little evidence of what may have happened was ever found. The CLEMSON was the largest U.S. ship lost, worldwide, in 1908. [5+]

CLETUS ■ Wooden lumber hooker
Lake Huron: One obscure report states that this ship sank in a storm around the turn of the century, and that her crew was rescued by the schooner ROUSE SIMMONS (qv). [1]

CLEVECO ■ Steel tanker-barge of 2,441 t. and 250 ft., launched in 1913 at Superior, WI as the S.O. & Co. #85.
Lake Erie: On December 2, 1942, this loaded oil barge and her consort, the steel tug ADMIRAL (qv), were struck by an extremely violent storm off Cleveland. After surviving a severe buffeting for hours, the barge found herself tethered to a tug which had already sunk! The crew radioed for help and cut the towline in an effort to save her. But despite concerted efforts of the Coast Guard and other nearby vessels, the CLEVECO sank with the loss of all 18 of her crew. [5+]

CLEVELAND ■ Wooden steamer, perhaps the 574 t. passenger/freighter built on Lake Erie in 1852
Lake Superior: This steamer was reported to have gone ashore near the Two Hearted River on the Upper Peninsula shoreline, in 1868. None of her crew were lost. [2]

CLEVELAND ■ Wooden freighter
Lake Huron: This steamer was reported to have burned while underway near the Charity Island, at the mouth of Saginaw Bay, in 1880. [1]

CITY OF CLEVELAND ■ Steam freighter, probably the 1,924 t., 272 ft. vessel launched at Wyandotte in 1886, but perhaps built at Cleveland in 1882
Lake Huron: The CITY OF CLEVELAND was downbound on October 17, 1901, with a cargo of coal when she caught fire and was destroyed near Perseverance Island, at the mouth of Georgian Bay. Her crew escaped. [4]

CITY OF CLEVELAND III ■ Steel sidewheel passenger steamer of 4,400 t. and 390 ft., launched in 1907 at Wyandotte, MI
Lake Huron: Three lives were lost when this popular passenger boat was rammed by the Norwegian freighter RAVNEFJELL off Harbor Beach, Michigan, on June 25, of 1950. She was struck directly on her port paddlewheel and was deemed too expensive to repair, so she was sent to the scrapyard. During her dismantling in 1954, the vessel caught fire and was gutted. [4]

H G CLEVELAND ■ Merchant schooner of 264 t. and 137 ft., launched in 1862 at Black River, OH
Lake Erie: The schooner H G CLEVELAND and her cargo of limestone were lost on August 13, 1899, when the vessel sank seven miles from the harbor at Cleveland. [2]

CLIFTON ■ Steel whaleback bulk freighter of 3,500 t. and 308 ft., launched in 1892, at W Superior, WI as the SAMUEL MATHER
Lake Huron: This self-unloading whaleback was downbound with a load of crushed stone when she was struck by a powerful gale on September 22, 1924. The big steamer went down about 30 miles west by northwest of Oscoda, Michigan, with the loss of all 27 of her crew. [5+]

DEWITT CLINTON ■ Wooden passenger and package freighter
Lake Michigan: One of the earliest steamers operating on Lake Michigan, the CLINTON foundered off Milwaukee on October 11, 1839. Five lives were lost in the accident. [1]

GEORGE R CLINTON ■ 320 t. vessel of unreported type
Lake Huron: On October 17, 1890, the GEORGE R CLINTON was stranded and wrecked near the north harbor marker at Kincardine, Ontario. [1]

CLIPPER ■ Small merchant schooner
Lake Ontario: This schooner was laden with a cargo of lumber when she went ashore and wrecked near Oak Orchard, New York, in 1860. [1]

COASTER ■ 29 t. vessel of unreported type
Lake Erie: A victim of stranding, this little boat became a total loss off Point Pelee, on October 17, 1880. [1]

R G COBURN ■ Wooden passenger and freight propeller of 867 t. and 193 ft., launched in 1870
Lake Huron: The loss of this steamer on October 15, 1871, is subject to a number of contradictory reports. The one-year-old ship foundered with a cargo of either grain or copper ore and the loss of 32 of 75 aboard. The location of the accident is given variously as Presque Isle, Saginaw Bay, or Harbor Beach, Michigan, or on Lake Superior. The Presque Isle report has the most support. [5+]

TOM COCHRANE ■ Merchant steamer
Lake Huron: The steamer TOM COCHRANE was wrecked on the rocks near Sturgeon Point, south of Alcona, Michigan, in 1862. [1]

S S COE ■ Tug
Lake Huron: The tug S S COE was lost to fire in 1876. The little vessel burned out and sank near Port Austin, Michigan. [1]

ALICE COFFEE ■ Merchant schooner
Lake Huron: A single report shows this schooner as lost near Detour, Michigan, with no date given. [1]

E COHEN ■ Lumber schooner-barge of 205 t., built as a 265 t. brig
Lake Huron: Laden with a cargo of lumber and lath, the towed vessel E COHEN was lost on shallow Port Hope Reef on October 18, 1890. As a brig, she was stranded and heavily damaged on Lake Erie in 1877. [3]

ANNIE COLEMAN ■ Merchant schooner
Lake Superior: This schooner was accidentally run on a reef in dense fog on July 19, 1879. She went ashore in a desolate area near the mouth of the Hurricane River, nine miles west of Grand Marais, Michigan. None of the crew were lost, and one source says they walked 70 miles to Marquette to obtain assistance. [3]

COLFAX ■ Merchant schooner
Lake Huron: The island-studded waters near Detour, Michigan, have claimed many ships, this schooner among them. She sank there in 1870. [1]

JAMES B COLGATE ■ Steel whaleback bulk steamer of 1,713 t. and 302 ft., launched at W Superior, WI, in 1892
Lake Erie: One of the most violent gales ever recorded on Lake Erie struck this coal laden steamer on October 21, 1916. The big steel vessel reportedly rode up on a big wave and then just dove to the bottom off Long Point. Of the 26 aboard, only her captain survived. The big steamer MERIDA (qv) had been lost further up the lake in the same storm. [5+]

COLLINGWOOD ■ Merchant schooner of 44 t.
Lake Huron: On July 19, 1878, this schooner was destroyed by fire ½ mile from Byng Inlet, Ontario. [2]

COLLINGWOOD ■ Merchant schooner of 258 t.
Lake Michigan: Five lives were lost when this schooner capsized, drifted ashore and was wrecked near Milwaukee, in November of 1882. She was carrying a load of cedar posts and poles at the time. [2]

CITY OF COLLINGWOOD ■ Passenger and package freight steamer of 893 t. and 226 ft., launched at Owen Sound, Ont., in 1893
Lake Huron: This steamer was lost in the harbor of her namesake city of Collingwood, Ontario. She caught fire at her berth there on June 19, 1905, and was destroyed. [5]

E K COLLINS ■ Wooden passenger steamer launched at Newport (now Marine City) MI, in 1853
Detroit River: 23 lives were lost when this steamer caught fire, burned and sank near Amherstburg, Ontario, on October 8, 1854. [2]

M L COLLINS ■ Merchant schooner of 231 t. and 130 ft., launched in 1854 at Toledo
Lake Michigan: The old schooner M L COLLINS was carrying a load of lumber when she went aground near Waugoschance Point in April, 1893, though one source says 1903. The vessel broke up before she could be released. [2]

COLONIAL ■ Wooden bulk freight steamer of 1,501 t. and 244 ft., launched at Cleveland in 1882 or 1885
Lake Erie: While fighting a heavy storm off Rondeau, Ontario, the COLONIAL was discovered to be leaking badly and in danger of sinking. She was run onto the beach and her crew was saved, but the vessel broke up following the November 13, 1914 accident. [2]

COLONIAL ■ Iron or composite-hulled passenger and auto carrier of 538 t. and 215 ft., built in 1885 at Cleveland as the sidewheel passenger steamer DARIUS COLE, converted to propeller in 1907
Lake Erie: Four lives were lost when this veteran steamer caught fire and was destroyed off Barcelona, New York, on September 2, 1925 or '26. She sank in shallow water and was later recovered for scrapping. [5+]

COLONIAL ■ Oil screw tug of 27 t.
Lake Huron: This little tug was reported stranded and wrecked in the Straits of Mackinac on November 1, 1939. [1]

COLONIST ■ Propeller freighter of 341 t. and 134 ft., launched in 1855 at Sarnia, Ont.
Lake Huron: The COLONIST was reported to have wrecked in a storm in the Straits of Mackinac in November of 1869. [2]

COLORADO ■ Wooden package freight propeller of 1,472 t. and 252 ft., launched in 1867 at Buffalo, NY
Lake Superior: The many forest fires that accompanied the lumbering industry were hazardous to ships as well as a danger to those ashore. On September 19, 1898, the COLORADO was approaching Eagle River, Michigan, with a cargo of flour when her navigators were blinded by forest fire smoke. The vessel went hard aground on Sawtooth Reef and broke up. [3]

COLUMBIA ■ Merchant brig of 177 t. and 91 ft., launched in 1842 at Sandusky, OH
Lake Michigan: It is reported that this vessel is the famous brig that delivered the first load of copper ore from the Keweenaw and brought the first locomotive to Marquette. She was lost in Green Bay in 1859, when she stranded near Sherwood Point and broke up. [3]

COLUMBIA ■ Wooden steamer, possibly Canadian
Lake Huron: Little is known about this ship, reported lost in a storm on the Lake in 1866. [1]

COLUMBIA ■ Barge
Lake Huron: This unpowered vessel was reported to have been destroyed by a gale in the fall of 1880. The accident occurred near Harrisville, Michigan. [1]

COLUMBIA ■ Wooden passenger and package freight steamer of 400 t. and 137 ft., launched at Hamilton, Ont., in 1873

Lake Michigan: This steamer, 16 of her people and her cargo of corn were lost when she foundered in a gale off Frankfort, Michigan. The accident took place on September 10, 1881. [5]

COLUMBIAN ■ Lumber schooner of 356 t. and 131 ft., launched at Fort Howard, WI, in 1864
Lake Erie: This lumber carrier encountered a storm on September 4, 1913, was wrecked and sank off Dunkirk, New York. [2]

COLUMBUS ■ Steam freighter of 439 t. and 150 ft., launched in 1874 at Detroit as the steamer JOHN OWEN
Lake Superior: The COLUMBUS met her end when she was destroyed by fire at her dock at Gargantua, Ontario, on September 10, 1909. [4]

COLUMBUS ■ Gas screw passenger boat of 26 t. and 60 ft., launched at Sandusky, OH, in 1905
Lake Erie: This little motor vessel was unlucky enough to be destroyed in the harbor at Sandusky, Ohio, by a freak tornado which sank her in the spring of 1924. [1]

COMET ■ Merchant schooner
Lake Erie: This small schooner was lost off Dunkirk, New York, on November 11, 1835. She was carrying a load of iron when she foundered with the loss of all hands. [1]

COMET ■ Sidewheel passenger and package freight steamer of 337 t. and 176 ft., launched at Portsmouth, Ont., in 1848
Lake Ontario: Known along the lake ports as a hard-luck ship, the COMET had suffered a number of serious accidents in her career. Her only fatal one occurred in May of 1861 (also given as 1851), when she was almost destroyed by an explosion and fire following a collision at Oswego, New York, with the loss of eight lives. She may have been rebuilt following the accident. [2]

COMET ■ Merchant schooner of 339 t.
Lake Michigan: This sail vessel was lost when she was driven ashore in a November, 1870 gale and broke up one mile south of Frankfort, MI. [1]

COMET ■ Wooden package and bulk freight propeller of 744 t. and 181 ft., launched at Cleveland in 1856
Lake Superior: The freighter COMET was lost, and 11 of her 21 crew were drowned in a bizarre collision which occurred on busy Whitefish Bay. On the night of August 26, 1875, the COMET, carrying a cargo of ores and pig iron, was preparing to pass the big sidewheel steamer MANITOBA, when misunderstood signals caused her to veer in front of the other ship. The COMET was rammed amidships and quickly sank. The wreckage of the vessel was discovered in 1980. [4]

COMET ■ Steam tug of 32 t. and 67 ft., launched in 1881 at Muskegon, MI
Lake Michigan: A victim of fire, the tug COMET was off Two Rivers, Wisconsin, when she was destroyed on October 12, 1897. Fortunately, none of her crew was lost in the incident. [2]

COMMERCE ■ Wooden passenger and package freight steamer of 134 ft., launched at Portsmouth, Ont., in 1848
Lake Erie: The COMMERCE had boarded a detachment of soldiers at Port Maitland, Ontario, and was outbound on May 6, 1850, when she suffered a disastrous accident. In reportedly good weather, she collided with the steamer DESPATCH and quickly sank, with the loss of 41 lives. She was recovered and rebuilt as the steamer REINDEER (qv). [4]

COMMERCE ■ Merchant schooner
Lake Michigan: The schooner COMMERCE was reported to have stranded, then sunk on the west side of Seul Choix Point, on the south coast of Michigan's Upper Peninsula, in 1899. [1]

COMMERCE ■ Merchant schooner or brig
Lake Huron: This sail vessel was reported lost at an unknown position on the Lake in the Big Storm of 1905, on October 20. [2]

COMMERCE ■ Bulk freight barge of 327 t. and 142 ft., launched in 1857 at Sandusky, OH, as a brig. This may be the same vessel as one or more of the above ships of the same name.
Lake Michigan: While carrying a cargo of lumber across the Lake on November 19, 1909, the barge COMMERCE was torn away from her towing steamer in a blizzard and gale. The helpless vessel was tossed ashore near Sheboygan, Wisconsin, and quickly broken up by breakers. Her crew was able to make it to shore. [4]

COMMODORE ■ Bulk freight schooner-barge of 586 t. and 176 ft., launched in 1880 at Carrollton, MI
Lake Erie: The schooner-barge COMMODORE and her towing steamer JAY GOULD (qv), were upbound with coal on June 17, 1918, when they encountered gale winds and rapidly building waves near Southeast Shoal. The barge was soon in trouble and capsized and sank within two hours of the breaking of the storm. The big steamer MATAAFA (qv) was standing by to lend assistance, and took the COMMODORE's crew off just before she went down. [4]

COMRADE ■ Bulk freight schooner-barge of 910 t. and 199 ft., launched in 1883 at Buffalo
Lake Superior: An unusual southeasterly gale struck this big schooner-barge and her towing steamer COLUMBIA as they were approaching the west side of the Portage Ship Canal on September 13, 1890. The strain of the storm against the iron-ore laden barge was too much for her

towline, and she was cast out to fend for herself. The steamer fought her way to shelter, but the COMRADE and her crew of eight lost their battle with the elements somewhere between the Keweenaw and Isle Royale. [3]

A W COMSTOCK ■ Merchant schooner
Lake Superior: The small schooner COMSTOCK was lost off Stannard Rock, east of the Keweenaw Peninsula, in 1895. [1]

J B COMSTOCK ■ Bulk freight schooner-barge of 326 t. and 139 ft., launched at Algonac, MI, in 1891
Lake Huron: Attempting to find shelter from storm-driven waves, the J B COMSTOCK and her tow steamer LANGELL BOYS (qv) set anchor in the lee of the Duck Islands, off Manitoulin, on October 8, 1906. The big greybeards would not be denied, however, and dragged the lumber-laden barge into the shallows to break up. Fortunately, her crew was able to abandon her safely. [2]

CITY OF CONCORD ■ Wooden bulk freight steamer of 385 t. and 144 ft., launched at Cleveland in 1868 as a passenger steamer
Lake Erie: This veteran steamer made her last voyage on September 27, 1906. On that date, she was carrying a cargo of coal up the Lake and was nearing Point Pelee when an angry gale struck, sinking the CITY OF CONCORD, and drowning two of her crew. [3]

CONDOR ■ Merchant schooner
Lake Michigan: The schooner CONDOR was reported to have been lost near Skillagallee Reef, east of the Beaver Islands, in 1862. [1]

CONDOR ■ Schooner of 30 t., launched at Sheboygan, WI, in 1871
Lake Michigan: The small two-masted schooner CONDOR was lying at anchor in the Kalamazoo River, at Singapore, Michigan, when the breakup of river ice came on April 1, 1904. Before she could be moved, the little vessel was crushed and sank. [1]

CONDOR ■ Bulk freight barge of 193 ft. overall, launched at Montreal in 1888
Lake Ontario: Bound for Montreal with a cargo of coal, the CONDOR went aground on the south side of Point Traverse, 30 miles west southwest of the head of the St Lawrence River. The accident happened on August 7, 1921. [1]

CONDUCTOR ■ Merchant schooner
Lake Erie: This schooner was the subject of one of the most thrilling and heroic rescues in Lakes history. On November 24, 1854, the schooner was driven hard onto Long Point by an icy gale, and immediately began to break up and sink. Her crew clung to her masts as she settled on the bottom, but were too frozen to make it to shore through the maelstrom. "Mother" Becker, a young

woman living with her children on the desolate point nearby, built a beach fire to encourage the crew to try to make it. When they were still unable, she swam the icy, storm-driven surf ½ mile to the ship and back nine times, and brought them all ashore herelf. The CONDUCTOR went to pieces soon after, but the crewmen all survived to add their thanks to the many honors bestowed upon the courageous Mrs. Becker. [4]

CONEMAUGH ■ Wooden package freighter of 1,609 t. and 251 ft., launched in 1880 at W Bay City, MI
Lake Erie: The narrow passage between Pelee Island and Point Pelee is a bottleneck to shipping moving to and from the Upper Lakes. In heavy weather such as the gale that struck on November 21, 1906, it can be especially difficult for a loaded ship. The steamer CONEMAUGH was trying to breast big seas and make it to more open water when she struck the Point and stuck fast. The big freighter later broke up, but her crew managed to escape. [3]

CHESTER A CONGDON ■ Steel bulk freight steamer of 6,530 t. and 532 ft., launched at S. Chicago in 1907 as the steamer SALT LAKE CITY
Lake Superior: Usually the weather on the Lakes simply ignores the puny works of shipbuilders and sailors, but occasionally there seems to be a genuine malevolence in the actions of wind and wave. The staunch steel freighter CONGDON was groping through a heavy fog near Isle Royale's convoluted reefs when she struck bottom, jamming fast near Canoe Rocks on November 7, 1918. The giant freighter and her cargo of wheat seemed to be easily salvageable, so tugs were summoned to pull her off the reef. Before this could be accomplished, one of the big gales that sweep the Lake once in a decade tore the ship to pieces and pushed her wreckage into deeper waters, where it still lies today. The CONGDON was one of the largest vessels ever sunk on the Lakes up to that time. [5+]

OMAR D CONGER ■ Steam passenger ferry of 200 t. and 93 ft., launched at Milwaukee in 1887
Lake Huron: The CONGER was at her accustomed dock on the Black River at Port Huron on March 26, 1922, when disaster struck. Without warning, the cross-river ferry exploded with such violence that parts of her were strewn all over the town of Port Huron. Four people died in the the explosion. Some reports say that she had a load of unregistered explosives aboard at the time. [5+]

CONGERCOAL ■ Wooden bulk freight steamer of 333 t. and 175 ft., launched at Mt. Clemens in 1882
Lake Ontario: On May 10, 1917, this freighter became a victim of fire at Little Sodus Bay, New York. She report-

edly caught fire in the harbor, burned to the waterline and sank. [4]

CONGRESS ■ Wooden propeller freighter of 452 t. and 140 ft., launched at Cleveland in 1861
Lake Huron: There is some disagreement over whether this steamer was recovered after her 1868 accident or not. On October 26, she was stranded on Thunder Bay Island in heavy weather. She may have broken up in place, but one report says that she was recovered and wrecked at another location in 1893. [2]

CONGRESS ■ Wooden bulk freight steamer of 1,320 t. and 265 ft., launched at Cleveland in 1867 as the steamer NEBRASKA
Lake Michigan: While docked in the harbor at South Manitou Island, Michigan, this steamer caught fire and began to blaze furiously while loading a cargo of lumber. To prevent the flames from spreading to the dock and surrounding forests, a courageous tug skipper got a line on her and towed her out into the lake, where she was burned to the water and sank. [4]

A B CONMEE ■ Propeller freighter of 133 t. and 81 ft., launched at Owen Sound in 1881 as the steamer SUPERIOR
Lake Superior: The diminutive steamer A B CONMEE was lost in May of 1937, when she foundered near Thunder Bay, Ontario. [1]

CONSTELLATION ■ Merchant brig
Lake Michigan: This little vessel was reported stranded in a November, 1857 storm. Her hulk was abandoned to break up near Waukegan, Illinois. [1]

CONSTITUTION ■ Merchant schooner, possibly the 84 t., 71 ft., vessel built in 1825 at Sandusky, OH
Lake Erie: The tall bluffs near Port Bruce, Ontario, have beckoned a number of ships to disaster. One such victim was the schooner CONSTITUTION, blown ashore there by a southwest gale in 1859 and broken up by waves built up across 150 miles of open lake. [2]

CONSTITUTION ■ Sidewheel steamer
Lake Erie: The sidewheeler CONSTITUTION was lost on July 27, 1847, when she struck a pier in the harbor at Sandusky, Ohio, and sank. Her machinery was later recovered. [1]

CONSUELO ■ Vessel of unreported type
Lake Erie: Five lives were lost when this ship capsized off Marblehead, near Sandusky, on May 1, 1875. Since ships that capsize and don't sink are usually righted and returned to service, this may be the same vessel as the schooner that was reported wrecked in the North Channel of Lake Huron in 1885 and later recovered. [3]

CONSUELO ■ Steam freighter of 142 t.
Lake Huron: On November 9, 1887, this boat was reported to have foundered nine miles north by northeast of Harbor Beach, Michigan. [2]

CONTEST ■ Merchant schooner of 206 t.
Lake Michigan: Driven ashore near Whitehall, Michigan, by an October, 1882 gale, the schooner CONTEST broke up in place, a total loss. [2]

CONTINENTAL ■ Wooden bulk freight steamer of 1,506 t. and 244 ft., launched at Cleveland in 1882
Lake Michigan: Wooden vessels that encountered heavy weather when they were without cargo to ballast them were often buffeted about unmercifully by big seas. Such was the case with the steamer CONTINENTAL, thrown ashore at Rowley Point, near Two Rivers, Wisconsin, to break up on December 12, 1904. [2]

L J CONWAY ■ Bulk freight schooner of 90 t.
Lake Michigan: The CONWAY was loaded with corn and oats when she was hit by a storm on November 17, 1896. The schooner was wrecked near shore at Fowler Creek, north of White Lake, Michigan, with the loss of five lives. One source says she went down on Lake Huron in 1886. [3]

COLONEL COOK ■ Package and bulk freight schooner of 322 t. and 128 ft., launched as the schooner AUGUSTA at Oswego, NY, in 1855
Lake Erie: The COLONEL COOK was lost when she foundered well offshore on April 27, 1895. The wreckage of the little ship washed ashore between Lorain and Cleveland. Hers would be just another of the many losses of this type if it had not been for her background, for this is the little schooner that gained infamy as the AUGUSTA by ramming the passenger steamer LADY ELGIN (qv) in 1860, then leaving the scene. Even though she was in danger of foundering herself and her crew did not suspect that the steamer was sinking, the little vessel garnered such hatred that she changed her name and went to sea and did not return to the Lakes for many years. See also MOJAVE. [5+]

EMILY COOPER ■ Merchant schooner
Lake Michigan: On May 18, 1894, this sailing ship was lost when she went ashore and broke up near Manitowoc, Wisconsin. [1]

LOTTIE COOPER ■ Lumber schooner of 252 t. and 131 ft., launched at Manitowoc, WI, in 1876
Lake Michigan: This little schooner and her cargo of lumber were lost when she capsized off Sheboygan, Wisconsin, on April 9, 1894. One life was lost in the accident. [3]

COQUETTE ■ Merchant schooner
Lake Erie: Stranded near Put-in-Bay, this schooner was lost in October of 1858. [1]

CORA B ■ Tug of 31 t. and 62 ft., launched in 1874 at Bay City, MI

Lake Superior: This tug was reported destroyed by fire in the harbor at Duluth on July 5, 1890. [1]

CORAL ■ Steam freighter of 119 t. and 86 ft., launched at Wallaceburg, Ont. in 1871
Lake Huron: The tiny steamer CORAL was reported to have foundered in mid-lake, in 1887. [2]

CORALIA ■ Steamer, possibly the 4,330 t., 413 ft. steel steamer launched at Cleveland in 1896
Lake Superior: The CORALIA was reported to have gone aground at Point Isabelle, near the tip of the Keeweenaw Peninsula, on November 25, 1905. She was probably recovered. [2]

CORDELIA ■ Schooner-scow of 31 t. and 58 ft., launched in 1865 at Sandusky, OH
Little information is available on the loss of this flat-bottomed schooner, except that she sank in 1884. [1]

CORISANDE ■ Bulk freight schooner-barge of 145 ft., launched in 1873 at Marine City, MI
Lake Huron: This 40-year-old vessel was sunk by a storm which struck her at Sarnia, Ontario, in 1913. Though within reach of salvagers, she was abandoned in place. [2]

MINNIE CORLETT ■ Merchant schooner of 107 t.
Lake Michigan: On March 24, 1876, the schooner MINNIE CORLETT foundered off Livesaving Station number 7. One life was lost in the accident. [1]

CORMORANT ■ Wooden lumber hooker of 977 t. and 218 ft., launched in 1873 at Cleveland
Lake Superior: This small lumber ship was destroyed by fire in the Apostle Islands, on October 30, 1907. She was taking on a load of sawlogs when she caught fire and burned to the waterline. No lives were lost, and the burned out hulk was removed to a position just off Red Cliff, Wisconsin, and scuttled. [4]

CORMORANT ■ Oil screw of 18 t.
Lake Ontario: The small CORMORANT was lost on October 17, 1958, when she foundered five miles north of Oswego, New York. [1]

CORNELL ■ Steam tug of 65 t. and 72 ft., launched at Buffalo in 1888 as the tug GRACE DANFORTH
Lake Erie: The tug CORNELL simply went missing with all eight hands, somewhere on the lake on December 22, 1922. Her position at the time was unknown, nor has her wreckage ever been discovered. [4]

MAY CORNELL ■ Bulk freight schooner of 8 t. and 32 ft., launched at Manistee in 1882
Lake Michigan: One of the smallest commercial vessels recorded, the MAY CORNELL went down on September 30, 1894. She was carrying a load of shingles when she

foundered one mile from the lighthouse at Big Sable Point, Michigan. [2]

ERASTUS CORNING ■ Merchant bark of 291 t.
Lake Michigan: The ERASTUS CORNING was one of the last barks operating on the Lakes when she was wrecked in May of 1889. Caught in a spring blow, she was driven ashore on Poverty Island, south of Fairport, Michigan, and abandoned to break up. [2]

CORNWALL ■ Vessel of unreported type
Lake Erie: It has been reported that this vessel sank on East Sister Island Reef in 1865. [1]

CORSAIR ■ Merchant schooner
Lake Huron: The schooner CORSAIR foundered off Sturgeon Point, north of Harrisville, Michigan, in 1872. [1]

CORSICAN ■ Merchant schooner of 210 t. and 112 ft., launched in 1862 at Olcott, NY
Lake Huron: The CORSICAN was inbound with a cargo of coal when she collided with another vessel off Thunder Bay Island, and sank with the loss of either six or eight lives, probably her whole crew. The disaster occurred on June 2, 1893. [4]

HENRY CORT ■ Steel bulk freight whaleback of 2,235 t. and 320 ft., launched in 1892 at Superior, WI as the whaleback steamer PILLSBURY
Lake Michigan: One of the largest of Alexander McDougall's whalebacks, the CORT was finishing her 42nd year on the Lakes when she was lost on November 30, 1934. On that date she was harried by a wicked gale and, while trying to make it into Muskegon harbor, was thrown on a breakwall. She sank in shallow water, but was in danger of going to pieces with her crew still aboard when the U.S. Lifesaving Service arrived. All were taken off safely, but one brave lifesaver lost his life in the rescue. The CORT had been sunk previously, at Bar Point in 1917. [4]

CORTEZ ■ Bulk freight schooner
Lake Ontario: The wheat-laden schooner CORTEZ was near Stoney Creek, New York, on November 12, 1880, when she was hit by a storm and foundered. [1]

COSSACK ■ Bulk freight schooner of 318 t.
Lake Erie: December 17, 1881, was the date that this schooner sank in a storm near the entrance to the harbor at Cleveland. [1]

COTTONWOOD ■ Bulk freight steamer of 261 ft., launched in 1918 at Ecorse, MI
Lake Superior: The steamer COTTONWOOD was carrying a load of stone when she was driven hard ashore at

Coppermine Point, Ontario, by a strong westerly gale. After the December 2, 1926, accident, the vessel was thought to be a total loss. Salvagers, though, thought they could free her and succeeded the following spring. The salvage operation and repairs to the vessel cost over $100,000. [3]

COURIER ■ 65 ft. tug
Lake Superior: The small tug COURIER was lost to fire on November 27, 1891, at Superior, Wisconsin. [2]

COURTLAND or **COURTLANDT** ■ Bulk freight bark, built about 1867
Lake Erie: About 7 people lost their lives when this sailing ship met with disaster on June 21, 1868. The bark was involved in a collision with the sidewheeler MORNING STAR (qv) in which she was literally "run over" and destroyed by the big paddle wheels, off Lorain, Ohio. She was reportedly carrying iron ore at the time, though one source says coal. [3]

L D COWAN ■ Merchant schooner
Lake Huron: Pte Aux Barques, Michigan, claimed another victim in this schooner, which wrecked there in 1865. [1]

WILLIAM COWIE ■ Propeller freighter, possibly the 208 t., 133 ft. vessel launched at Marine City, MI, in 1868, but this ship was still in registry in 1892
Lake Huron: The COWIE was reported destroyed by fire at Cheboygan, Michigan, in 1890. She may have been returned to service. [2]

JOHN B COWLE ■ Steel bulk freight steamer of 4,731 t. and 420 ft., launched at Port Huron in 1902
Lake Superior: In addition to being one of the most congested traffic areas on the Great Lakes, Whitefish Bay is also subject to some of the most dangerous weather. On July 12, 1909, a thick fog smothered the area, and a number of big steamers were groping their way through it. The JOHN B COWLE, with a cargo of ore, was moving through the soup when she was rammed by one of the largest vessels on the lake at the time, the big steel bulk carrier ISAAC M SCOTT (qv). The COWLE reportedly sank in three minutes, with the loss of 14 of her 24 crew. Divers located the wreck in 1972. [5+]

GEORGE M COX ■ Steel passenger steamer of 1,792 t. and 259 ft., launched at Toledo in 1901 as the PURITAN
Lake Superior: Running at 17 knots in patchy fog on May 27, 1933, the big steamer GEORGE M COX came into the vicinity of Isle Royale in a little too cocky a style. She struck a rock pinnacle at speed and rode up until she was virtually impaled upon the rock. Famous photos of her in distress show the long ship with her forward 110 feet of keel out of the water, and her fantail awash. She was

enroute to pick up passengers for her first cruise since refitting and renaming and thus had only 18 passengers plus her crew aboard. All of these escaped in the boats, but the steamer could not escape her fate. She broke up and slipped into deeper water the following October. [4]

EMMA L COYNE ▪ Barge or schooner-barge
Lake Michigan: Laden with iron ore, this barge was lost when she stranded on a reef to the southwest of St. Martin's Island, in the mouth of Green Bay, in 1869. She subsequently broke up. [1]

CRAFTSMAN ▪ Barge of 165 t.
Lake Ontario: The barge CRAFTSMAN was reported to have foundered on June 3, 1958, two miles north of Oswego, New York. [1]

JOHN W CRAMER ▪ Steamer of 23 t.
Lake Erie: Horseshoe Reef lies just outside a shipping lane, a few miles from Buffalo. The CRAMER became one of a number of vessels whose bones lie on the reef when she grounded there on October 17, 1884, and broke up. [1]

THOMAS CRANAGE ▪ Wooden bulk freighter of 2,219 t. and 305 ft., launched at W Bay City, MI, in 1893
Lake Huron: The CRANAGE was the largest wooden steamer afloat when she was built, and by September 25, 1911, she was a mainstay of the grain trade. On that date, she was navigating Georgian Bay in a storm, when she went hard aground on Watcher's Reef, near Hope Island. Immediate salvage efforts saved her cargo of wheat, but the ship itself could not be rescued before big seas broke her up. [5+]

J L CRANE ▪ Lumber schooner-barge of 548 t. and 187 ft., launched in 1891 at Marine City as the schooner-barge THEO S FASSETT
Lake Superior: This lumber-hauler was no stranger to disaster. She had had several previous mishaps, including a near-fatal one on Lake Huron in 1898 (as the FASSETT). The end came on Nov. 5, 1925, when in the tow of the steamer HERMAN H HETTLER (qv), she was struck by a terrific gale with winds recorded up to 80 mph. Witnesses say that, when opposite Crisp Point, MI, she rode up on a big wave, broke her towline and dove to the bottom, taking all seven of her crew with her. For several years her broken masts were visible above the surface. [5]

CREAM CITY ▪ Wooden bulk freighter of 875 t. and 166 ft., launched in 1884 at Trenton as the steamer RHODA EMILY

Lake Huron: The northern edge of Lake Huron is dotted with islands and reefs and is difficult to navigate safely, even in good weather. To this day, the entrys to the St. Marys River are sometimes closed by foggy conditions. The CREAM CITY was groping for the False Detour Passage on July 1, 1918, with two schooner-barges in tow, when she struck Wheeler's Reef. Though she did not seem to be in any danger, the steamer would not budge from her perch. Several salvage attempts failed, and the wooden vessel, still on the bar, caught fire and was destroyed in 1925. [5]

CREOLE ▪ Tug of 14 t.
Lake Huron: The tug CREOLE became the victim of an accidental blaze when she caught fire and was destroyed at the mouth of the Wye River, near Midland, Ontario, on November 17, 1905. [2]

CREVOLA ▪ Merchant schooner
Lake Erie: One brief report states that the schooner CREVOLA went ashore and was wrecked in an 1865 storm. The ship was lost near Port Bruce, Ontario. [1]

CRISPIN ▪ Merchant brig
Lake Huron: The small, two-masted CRISPIN was lost in 1853 on Pte Aux Barques, when she stranded on a reef. [1]

HANS CROCKER ▪ Merchant bark of 473 t. and 139 ft., launched in 1856 at Milwaukee
Lake Michigan: The "curse of of the eleventh month" removed this sailing ship from the rolls. On November 29, 1879, she began to leak while battling a gale, and went down off Kenosha, Wisconsin. The ship was lost, but her crew was rescued. [2]

CROMWELL ▪ Schooner
Lake Huron: Listed as having gone down off Harbor Beach, Michigan, in 1888, this is probably the same vessel as the OLIVER CROMWELL, below. [1]

OLIVER CROMWELL ▪ Steam propeller of 291 t. and 138 ft., launched at Buffalo in 1853 as the steamer DAYTON
Lake Huron: A somewhat tangled web of reports surround this ship. She is probably the vessel that sank in a collision near Mackinac Island in 1857 and was raised and rebuilt, reportedly in 1871. Her final demise came at Harbor Beach, Michigan, in 1888, when she sank in the harbor October 2. This and the report for the CROMWELL above may be one, two or even three separate vessels. [4]

E G CROSBY ▪ Steel passenger and freight steamer of 260 ft. overall, launched at Toledo in 1903
Lake Michigan: This 32-year-old vessel and two other old ships, the schooner LUCIA A SIMPSON (qv) and the wooden steamer PETOSKEY (qv) were tied to a layup

dock, possibly awaiting scrapping, when they were destroyed by an accidental fire on December 5, 1935. The conflagration destroyed all three at Sturgeon Bay, Wisconsin. [3]

BELLE P CROSS ■ Wooden lumber hooker of 298 t. and 135 ft., launched in 1870 at Trenton, MI
Lake Superior: On April 23, 1903, the CROSS was struck by a blinding blizzard and gale near the Minnesota shoreline. She struck a reef near Danger Castle (Gooseberry R.) and went to pieces, spewing her cargo of cedar posts into the lake next to her own flotsam. [3]

WILLIAM CROSTHWAITE ■ Lumber schooner of 371 t. and 150 ft., launched at Banks (now part of Bay City) MI, in 1866
Lake Erie: The venerable schooner WILLIAM CROSTHWAITE went down on September 6, 1906. Running down the Lake with a cargo of lumber, she collided with the schooner HOMER WARREN and sank near Kelley's Island. [1]

WILLIAM S or **W S CROSTHWAITE** ■ Bulk freight schooner-barge of 673 t. and 197 ft., launched at Saginaw, MI, in 1873
Lake Superior: The CROSTHWAITE was lost to an unusual accident on November 13, 1904. She was riding comfortably at anchor in Whitefish Bay, and her crew had brought a stove on deck to heat water for laundry. The stove became overheated and set the deck of the barge afire. The crew abandoned ship as the CROSTHWAITE burned to the waterline and sank. [4]

J S CROUSE ■ Steam freighter of 82 t. and 90 ft., launched in 1898 at Saugatuck, MI
Lake Michigan: The rabbit J S CROUSE was lost when she was sent ashore by a gale on the southwest side of Sleeping Bear Bay, near Glen Haven, Michigan. The accident occurred on November 15, 1919, when the CROUSE was carrying a full cargo of lumber and potatoes. [2]

J R CROWE ■ Steam propeller of 91 t. and 96 ft., launched in 1870 at Chatham, Ont.
Lake Erie: The little steamer J R CROWE was wrecked when she was shoved ashore by an October, 1872 gale. Despite salvage efforts, the new ship broke up on the beach near Leamington, Ontario. [1]

BERTIE CROWELL ■ Merchant schooner of 16 t.
Lake Erie: This tiny sailing vessel was lost when she sank near the Quarry Docks, southeast of Marblehead Point, on October 8, 1884. [1]

WILLIAM R CROWELL ■ Tug of 56 t.
Lake Michigan: The early tug CROWELL was lost in December of 1853 off Michigan City, Indiana, when she sprang a leak and went down six miles offshore. [1]

CUBA ■ Bulk freight schooner, launched at 3 Mile Bay, NY, in 1844
Lake Ontario: On May 6, 1847, this schooner sank following a collision with the steamer GENESEE CHIEF. The sail vessel was near Point Breeze, New York, with a cargo of wheat at the time. [1]

JOHN W CULLEN ■ Schooner
Lake Huron: The schooner CULLEN was reported as abandoned north of Frying Pan Island, though the purpose for the abandonment—whether accidental or instead of scrapping—is not reported. [1]

CULLIGAN ■ Wooden bulk freight steamer of 1,748 t. and 263 ft., launched in 1883 at W Bay City, MI, as the steamer GEORGE T HOPE
Lake Superior: This big wooden steamer, heavily laden with iron ore, was battling a storm on September 27, 1912, and was holding her own against the big seas that washed over her and forced their way through the seams in her hull. Then, off Grand Island, Michigan, her pumps failed, rising water doused her boiler fires, and there was nothing for the crew to do but abandon her to sink. [3]

OLIVER CULVER ■ Merchant schooner of 450 t. and 145 ft., launched at Charlotte, NY (Rochester), in 1855
Lake Michigan: Laden with lumber, the schooner OLIVER CULVER was just outside the harbor entrance at Two Rivers, Wisconsin, when she foundered. The date was December 4, 1882. [2]

CUMBERLAND ■ Brig
Lake Huron or *Michigan:* Two reports show a brig named CUMBERLAND as wrecked. These may be the same ship or two different vessels, or even two different versions of the same wreck. One shows her as wrecked off Milwaukee (no date given), while the other states she was destroyed at an unreported position in Lake Huron, in 1856. [2]

CUMBERLAND ■ Sidewheel passenger and package freight steamer of 418 t. and 205 ft., launched at Port Robinson, Ont., in 1871
Lake Superior: None of her passengers or crew were lost,

but the CUMBERLAND and her cargo of general merchandise were a total loss in a July 26, 1877, accident. Skirting around the southwest end of Isle Royale in good weather, the steamer struck Rock of Ages Reef and settled to the bottom. Subsequent heavy weather tore her to pieces and deposited the remains on a point opposite the wreck, a location now known as "Cumberland Point." [5+]

M J CUMMINGS ■ Bulk freight schooner of 330 t. and 137 ft., launched at Oswego, NY, in 1874
Lake Michigan: The CUMMINGS was approaching Milwaukee with a cargo of coal, when she suffered a fatal accident on May 18, 1894. Six of the schooner's crew drowned when the vessel sank in 15 feet of water, ¾ mile off the harbor entrance. [4]

CUPID ■ Gas screw of 47 ft, launched in 1917 at Ashtabula, OH
Lake Erie: The CUPID was a small utility vessel that foundered off Cedar Point, near Sandusky, Ohio, on June 27, 1919. [1]

CURLEW ■ Merchant schooner of 80 t. and 80 ft., launched in 1866 at Port Huron, MI
Lake Michigan or *Lake Huron:* Reported to have been forced ashore four miles north of Sturgeon Point, Michigan, on November 24, 1879, the actual site may be north of Sturgeon Bay Point, Lake Michigan, or Sturgeon Point, Lake Huron. As with so many other sailing vessels driven ashore, she was in ballast when stranded. The vessel may have been recovered and be the same as below. [3]

CURLEW ■ Merchant schooner
Lake Huron: The schooner CURLEW was reportedly lost when she foundered in the Saginaw River in 1890. [1]

JAMES W CURRAN ■ Steel motor ferry
Lake Huron: The passenger and automobile ferry JAMES W CURRAN and her consort JOHN A McPHAIL (qv) were victims of a bizarre accident which occurred off Pointe Aux Barques, Michigan, in May of 1964. On that date, the CURRAN was being towed to an Ontario port for refitting when she was struck by a tornado and sank. Fortunately, no lives were lost in the incident. She had served for years in the cross-river trade at the Soo. [1]

C F CURTIS ■ Wooden lumber hooker of 691 t. and 196 ft., launched at Green Bay, WI, in 1874
Lake Superior: With a full load of lumber and two big barges in tow, this steamer was struck by one of the most violent storms ever recorded on the big lake. The CURTIS was literally torn apart by tremendous seas, and went down with all hands off Grand Marais, Michigan. Both barges were also lost in the November 19, 1914 blow. See

SELDEN E MARVIN and ANNIE M PETERSON. [5+]

GOVERNOR CUSHMAN ■ Steam freighter
Lake Erie: On May 1, 1868, the GOVERNOR CUSHMAN was destroyed by a boiler explosion which killed 12 persons aboard, and caused the total loss of the ship. Buffalo harbor was the site of the accident. [1]

CUYAHOGA ■ Wooden propeller freighter
Lake Huron: This steamer was reported lost when she sank near Sarnia, Ontario, in 1866. [1]

CUYAHOGA ■ Merchant brig, perhaps the 243 t., 121 ft. vessel built at Cleveland in 1855
Lake Erie: One brief report says that the brig CUYAHOGA was sunk by a "white squall" on the Lake. No date or other detail is given. [1]

GLEN CUYLER ■ Package and bulk freight schooner of 49 t. and 72 ft., launched at Pultneyville, NY, in 1859
Lake Huron: Several monster storms swept the Lakes in the fall of 1905. The worst of these occurred October 18-21, destroying several big steel steamers and a number of lesser ships. This kind of violent weather does not overlook such tiny and aged vessels as the two-masted schooner GLEN CUYLER, which was overwhelmed and went down in midlake on the 20th. [3]

CYCLONE ■ Bulk freight barge, launched as the steamer PITTSBURGH
Lake Huron: The barge CYCLONE was reported to have sunk off the gypsum quarry at Alabaster, Michigan, at the upper end of Saginaw Bay, in 1885. [1]

CYGNET ■ Freight barge
Lake Huron: This barge exploded and burned on Saginaw Bay in 1875, according to one report. [1]

CYGNET ■ Steam tug, probably the 26 t. vessel launched at Bay City, MI, in 1865
Lake Huron: The CYGNET was lost to fire in 1882. She was reported destroyed at Cheboygan, Michigan. [1]

CYGNET ■ Steam screw tug of 12 t. and 42 ft., launched at Buffalo in 1878
Lake Huron: A victim of a terribly destructive gale that ripped across the Lakes (see GLEN CUYLER), the small tug CYGNET was lost when she was tossed ashore and broken up on the 19th of October, 1905. She met her end in the Straits of Mackinac. [1]

CYPRUS ■ Steel bulk freight steamer of 4,900 t. and 420 ft., launched at Lorain, OH, in 1907
Lake Superior: Sometimes even the best and most modern vessel that the shipbuilder can put out on the lake is no

match for the fury of an equinoctial storm. The CYPRUS was of a proven design and was only 21 days old when she was blasted by a big gale on October 11, 1907. The proud ship was downbound with a full load of iron ore and was 19 miles off Deer Park, Michigan, when she turned turtle and sank, taking 21 of her 22 crew to a waterly death with her. She apparently was pushed around abeam of the storm-driven seas, and the violent rocking caused her cargo to shift. [5+]

CZAR ■ Merchant schooner
Lake Huron: Some of the limestone outcrops that supported the commercial quarry at Presque Isle, lurk just under the surface, offshore from the northern Michigan town. These have claimed a good number of the ships that have come for a limestone cargo. The CZAR was one of these, wrecked and sunk on a reef just off the beach in 1875. [1]

D & C ■ Tug of 9 t.
Lake Superior: This small vessel struck a reef and sank near Grenfell Rock on November 19, 1957. [1]

D.R.L.C. #2 ■ Contruction scow of 46 t.
Lake Erie: The unpowered vessel D.R.C.L. #2 was trapped by an advancing storm and sank off Port Crewe, Ontario, on November 20, 1955. [1]

DACOTAH ■ Bulk freight schooner of 144 ft. overall, launched in 1867 at Fairport, OH
Lake Huron: The schooner DACOTAH was lost on Sept. 24, 1901, when she was forced ashore and wrecked by a gale at an unreported position on Georgian Bay. [1]

DACOTAH or **DAKOTAH** ■ Wooden freighter
Lake Erie: This vessel was reported to have been carrying a valuable cargo of copper ingots and cash when she went missing with all 24 hands off Clear Creek, Ontario, in midlake. The date of her loss was November 24, 1860. A conflicting report says that she went aground near Angola, New York, on the 11th, and broke up. [5]

DAGMAR ■ Fishing tug of 14 t.
Lake Superior: This fisherman is reported to have sunk off Isle Royale on June 1, 1935. [1]

DAHLIA ■ Schooner of 210 t.
Lake Erie: The schooner DAHLIA was reported beached and lost near Port Burwell, Ontario, in 1857. High bluffs along this part of the Lake contributed to unpredictable winds and the loss of quite a number of sailing vessels. [1]

H DAHLKE ■ Steel bulk freight steamer of 166 ft. overall, launched in 1907 at Manitowoc, WI
Detroit River: Cargo problems caused the demise of this

steamer on December 22, 1938. On that date, she was at a dock at Sandwich, Ontario (now part of Windsor), when her cargo shifted and she capsized and sank. She was deemed beyond economical repair and was cut up for scrap. [1]

DAISY ■ Steam tug of 17 t., built at Detroit in 1881
Lake Huron: Fire claimed the tug DAISY as a victim at Port Hope, on Michigan's "thumb," in 1895. [1]

DAISY ■ Steam tug of 18 t. and 57 ft., launched at Vermilion, OH, in 1896
Lake Erie: This tug was lost to a fire which destroyed her at Lorain, Ohio, on April 15, 1909. [2]

DALHOUSIE ■ Wooden propeller freighter of 144 ft. (about 350 t.), launched in 1869 at St Catharine's, Ont.
Lake Ontario: The steamer DALHOUSIE was destroyed by fire in the harbor at Charlotte, NY, in Sept. of 1872. [1]

DALHOUSIE ROVER ■ 47 t. vessel of unreported type
Lake Erie: This vessel is reported to have sunk in Lock #1 of the Welland Canal on June 29, 1946. She was subsequently raised to clear the canal, but was declared too heavily damaged for repair and was scrapped. [1]

LINCOLN DALL ■ Lumber schooner of 207 t. and 115 ft., launched in 1869 at Chicago
Lake Michigan: The lumber-carrying schooner LINCOLN DALL was lost on May 18, 1894 off Glencoe, IL. A spring storm drove the vessel on a reef and she went to pieces with the loss of one of her crew before help arrived. [3]

MARGARET DALL ■ Lumber schooner of 149 t. and 112 ft., launched at Michigan City, IN, in 1867
Lake Michigan: This little sail vessel, which normally was engaged in the lumber trade, was bound northward with a hold full of potatoes when she was caught by a wicked storm on Nov. 16, 1906. She attempted to put into the harbor at South Manitou Island, MI, but was driven on the rocks north of the lighthouse. She was close enough to the beach for her crew to walk ashore, but too badly damaged to be saved. She broke up the following winter. [5+]

PETER DALTON ■ Steam tug of 63 t. and 99 ft., launched at Grand Haven, MI, in 1883
Lake Huron: In 1896 it was reported that this tug had sunk in mid-lake. [2]

GEORGE DANA ■ Barge or schooner-barge
Lake Huron: This vessel was reported lost at an unrecorded position on the Lake in 1876. [1]

LILLIE DANAY ■ Merchant schooner
Lake Huron: Kincardine, Ontario, was the reported location of the wreck of this sailing ship in 1865. [1]

LILY DANCEY ■ Merchant schooner
Lake Huron: This vessel was reported to have foundered near Port Elgin, Ont., in 1856. This report and that of the schooner LILLIE DANAY may refer to the same incident. [1]

F L DANFORTH ■ Steam tug of 29 t. and 58 ft., launched in 1857 at Buffalo
Lake Huron: The many hard-working wooden tugs that helped bigger vessels around harbors and along waterways in the 19th Century were highly susceptible to fires. Their engines were large and powerful for their size, and their high-pressure boilers required high heat to function most efficiently. The F L DANFORTH caught fire due to an overheated boiler in the Duluth-Superior Harbor and burned to the waterline on June 21, 1892. [2]

F L DANFORTH ■ Bulk freight schooner of 715 t. and 193 ft., launched in 1872 at Tonawanda, NY
Lake Michigan: The big schooner F L DANFORTH was loaded with corn on April 20, 1893, when she was driven ashore and wrecked near Chicago. [2]

DARIEN ■ Merchant schooner
Lake Huron: Little information is reported about this schooner, said to have been stranded and lost at Presque Isle, Michigan, in 1870. [1]

DART ■ Merchant schooner of 26 t.
Lake Michigan: This tiny two-stick schooner went ashore and broke up in a storm near Two Rivers, Wisconsin. The date is given variously as October 26 or 28, 1883, or December of 1882. [3]

MARY A DARYAW ■ Merchant schooner of 206 t. and 124 ft., launched in 1866 at Port Huron, MI as the schooner KEWAUNEE
Lake Ontario: This little two-master was one of the last working schooners on the Lakes, and one of the oldest. Laden with a cargo of coal, she was driven onto the shore of Simcoe Island, Ontario, by a storm. Though still largely intact, she was not recovered, and her hulk was destroyed by fire in 1927. [3]

J C DAUN ■ Merchant schooner
Lake Erie: Eight lives were reportedly lost when this sailing ship capsized and sank off Conneaut, Ohio, in 1847. [2]

DAUNTLESS ■ Merchant schooner
Lake Huron: Martin's Reef, in the Straits of Mackinac, was the location of the destruction of this sailing vessel in 1870. She reportedly went aground and was wrecked. [1]

DAUNTLESS ■ Merchant schooner
Lake Huron: Reports show that a vessel or vessels of this name were wrecked ashore in the Port Huron/Sarnia area in either 1889 or 1895. These may be two separate incidents or two reports of the same one. [2]

DAUNTLESS ■ Propeller steamer launched at Levis, Que, in 1871
Lake Ontario: The steamer DAUNTLESS was reported as wrecked and lost at Oswego, New York, in 1905. [1]

DAUNTLESS #12 ■ Diesel tug
Lake Erie: This tug was destroyed and seven of her eight crew lost in a tragic accident in Buffalo harbor on October 29, 1951. She was pushing a loaded gasoline barge when the barge was rammed by the steamer PENOBSCOT (qv) and exploded. A total of 11 sailors died in the incident. See also MORANIA #130. [2]

FRED DAVIDSON ■ Tug of 30 t.
Lake Huron: The small tug DAVIDSON was lost on September 4, 1916, when she sank off Pointe Au Baril, on the Ontario coast opposite the mouth of Georgian Bay. One source gives the year as 1886. [3]

JAMES DAVIDSON ■ Wooden package and bulk freight steamer of 1,456 t. and 230 ft., launched at Bay City, MI, in 1874
Lake Huron: This large bulk freighter was carrying a load of coal to Alpena on the day that she was lost. On October 4, 1883, she encountered a big storm while approaching the lumber town and was thrust onto a reef off Thunder Bay Island. There she quickly went to pieces from the pounding of waves, and sank in nearby deep water. Her crew was rescued. [5]

JOSIE DAVIDSON ■ Steam tug of 28 t. and 59 ft., launched in 1884 at Chicago
Lake Superior: One of a number of tugs lost to fire in the Duluth-Superior Harbor was this little vessel, which burned there on May 5, 1900, with no loss of life. [3]

GEORGE T DAVIE ■ 680 t. vessel of unreported type
Lake Ontario: Little detail is given on the loss of the DAVIE, reported sunk in deep water three miles north of Pigeon Island, on April 18, 1945. [1]

CHARLES H DAVIS ■ Wooden bulk freight steamer of 390 t. and 150 ft., launched in 1890 at W Bay City, MI
Lake Erie: The CHARLES H DAVIS was heavily loaded with limestone and offshore from Cleveland when she was discovered to be leaking on June 13, 1903. The leakage overcame her pumping capacity before she could make port, and she went down. She was one of the few Lakes-built ships constructed of pine. [3]

CAL DAVIS ■ (usually listed as COL. DAVIS) Steam tug
Lake Huron: Another of the dozens of Lakes tugs lost to fire was the CAL DAVIS, burned at Port Huron in 1889. [2]

DAN DAVIS ■ Merchant schooner
Lake Michigan: The schooner DAN DAVIS was driven up on the beach by a storm and broken up. The accident occurred at Port Sheldon, Michigan, eight miles north of Holland, in 1886. [1]

GEORGE DAVIS ■ Merchant schooner
Lake Erie: The schooner GEORGE DAVIS was one of a number of sail vessels wrecked under the bluffs near Port Burwell, Ontario. She piled ashore and broke up there in an 1863 storm. [1]

GEORGE DAVIS ■ Merchant schooner of 298 t. and 135 ft.
Lake Erie: On October 26, 1895, this schooner was hit by a violent storm, stranded and lost on the beach near Port Maitland, Ontario. [1]

GEORGE DAVIS ■ Merchant schooner of 15 t. and 47 ft., launched at Sebewaing, MI, in 1882
Lake Huron: A tiny vessel such as the schooner GEORGE DAVIS could truly be at the mercy of a storm of almost any size. In 1901 she was driven ashore in Saginaw Bay by heavy weather and broke up. [2]

J A DAVIS ■ Merchant schooner
Lake Michigan: A single brief report states that the DAVIS was lost in a white squall. See also J C DAVIS. [1]

J C DAVIS ■ Merchant schooner of 97 t., built before 1847
Lake Michigan: This small vessel was reported to have been blown down and capsized off Grand Haven, Michigan, in 1868. May be the same vessel as J A DAVIS, above. [2]

J H DAVIS ■ Merchant schooner of 47 t. and 83 ft., launched at Gibraltar, MI, in 1887
Lake Huron: The small schooner J H DAVIS was lost at an unknown position on the Lake when she was swamped by a squall in 1893. [2]

MINNIE DAVIS ■ Merchant schooner of 173 t. and 95 ft., launched in 1862 at Port Burwell, Ont., as the schooner ALVINA
Locational data is not available on the accident which ended the career of the schooner MINNIE DAVIS in 1892. Carrying a cargo of coal, she was rammed by the schooner HUNTER SAVIDGE (qv) and quickly sank. [2]

WILLIAM B DAVOCK ■ Steel bulk freight steamer of 7,200 t. and 420 ft., launched in 1909 at St. Clair, MI
Lake Michigan: The great "Armistice Day Storm" of November 11-13, 1940 was the last day afloat for several large vessels (see ANNA C MINCH, NOVADOC), and caused severe damage to a half-dozen others. The worst loss was the big steamer WILLIAM B DAVOCK. Bound for Chicago with a load of coal, she was hit by the most violent part of a terrible storm, and went down on the 11th with the loss of all 33 of her crew. It is theorized that she was simply overwhelmed by tremendous waves, though some say she may have collided with the ANNA C MINCH (qv). Even her position was not known with certainty until the wreck was located off Pentwater, Michigan in 1982. [5+]

DAWN ■ Merchant schooner
Lake Huron: This schooner was lost in the Straits of Mackinac in 1859. The cause of the accident, which cost the lives of five of her crew, has been reported as either a collision or a sinking by a white squall. [2]

DAWN ■ Merchant schooner of 26 t. and 60 ft., launched at Milwaukee in 1888
Lake Michigan: The tiny schooner DAWN sank on September 18, 1903, off the entrance to the harbor at Kewaunee, Wisconsin. [2]

DAY SPRING ■ Package and bulk freight schooner of 600 t. and 182 ft. (one source says she was considerably smaller than this)
Lake Michigan: Most weather-related founderings occur in the gale-torn fall and spring months, when large, rapidly-building equinoctial storms sweep the Lakes clear of ships. But a few vessels are lost in the more pleasant summer months, and the big schooner DAY SPRING was one of these. On August 1, 1904, while downbound with her holds full of sawdust, she was struck by a localized gale and sank 15 miles off White Lake, north of Muskegon, Michigan. [3]

DAYTON ■ Merchant schooner
Lake Erie: On October 25, 1844, the schooner DAYTON was caught in a big gale, capsized and sank with all hands. [1]

JULIA DEAN ■ Merchant brig
Lake Michigan: This two-master was wrecked on a reef near Skillagallee (Isle Aux Galets), Michigan, in 1855. [1]

J P DECONDRES or **DESCONDRES** ■ Lumber schooner of 146 t.
Lake Michigan: The DECONDRES was laden with a cargo of wood products when she became stranded one mile north of Milwaukee, on June 3 in 1882 or 83. [2]

DEER ■ Steam tug, probably the 47 t., 76 ft., tug of this name launched at Grand Haven in 1892
Lake Huron: This small tug became another victim of fire when she was destroyed off Au Gres, Michigan, in upper Saginaw Bay, in 1908. [2]

DEER ■ Vessel information unreported
Lake Ontario: This vessel is reported to have simply "gone missing" with all hands. [1]

DEFIANCE ■ Merchant schooner of 111 t., launched in 1905
Lake Michigan: On November 19, 1909, the schooner DEFIANCE was stranded, a total loss, at the mouth of the Bark River. The wreck location is ten miles south of Escanaba, Michigan, in upper Green Bay. [1]

DELAWARE ■ Wooden passenger and package freight steamer of 170 t., launched in 1833 at Huron, OH
Lake Michigan: The steamer DELAWARE was thrown ashore and broken in half by a storm in June of 1836. The ship was a total loss, but all passengers and crew escaped safely. Location was probably near New Buffalo, Michigan, though some sources say she was lost off Niles, 24 miles inland. [3]

DELAWARE ■ Merchant schooner
Lake Ontario: This schooner was loaded with a cargo of iron pigs when she was driven ashore near Port Weller, Ontario, and was wrecked. The date of the stranding was November 25, 1887. [1]

DELAWARE or **DELEWARE** ■ Propeller freighter of 1,450 t. and 231 ft.
Lake Huron: The wooden propeller DELAWARE went on a reef one mile offshore in Hammond Bay, Michigan. Sources give two different dates for the accident, one says November 25, 1883 and another 1887. She may have been recovered and rebuilt as CHARLES B HILL (qv). [3]

DELIGHT ■ 14 t. vessel of unreported type
Lake Erie: This small vessel was reported to have been destroyed by fire at Richards Landing in August of 1899. [1]

NANCY DELL ■ Lumber schooner of 106 t. and 105 ft., launched in 1879 at Port Sheldon, MI
Lake Michigan: The NANCY DELL was lost when she stranded and broke up ashore near Middle Village, Michigan, opposite Beaver Island. The schooner was wrecked on June 21, 1902. [3]

DELTA ■ Bulk freight schooner-barge of 269 t. and 134 ft., launched in 1890, at Algonac, MI
Lake Michigan: The schooner-barge DELTA was being towed into the harbor at Holland, Michigan, on August 21, 1919, when she was wrecked. Heavily laden with lumber, she broke her towline near the harbor entrance and, before she could set her limited sails, went on the breakwater and was torn to pieces by waves. [3]

DELVER #1 ■ 305 t. vessel of unreported type, but possibly a dredge
Lake Ontario: On June 15, 1914, the DELVER sank in the harbor at Port Dalhousie, Ontario. Details are unavailable. [1]

EDWARD U DEMMER ■ Steel bulk freight steamer of 4,651 t. and 423 ft., launched in 1899 at Wyandotte, MI, as the steamer ADMIRAL
Lake Huron: The big steel freighter EDWARD U DEMMER was loaded with coal and approaching Thunder Bay, Michigan, in a heavy fog when she met her fate on May 20, 1923. Out of the fog came the steel steamer SATURN and struck the DEMMER almost bows-on. Even though the accident took place about 30 miles offshore from Harrisville, Michigan, there were other vessels in the area to rescue the steamer's crew, but the DEMMER herself sank and was lost in deep water. [5]

JAMES DEMPSEY ■ Wooden bulk freight steamer of 841 t. and 183 ft., launched in 1883 at Milwaukee as the steamer JIM SHERIFFS (qv)
Lake Michigan: The bulk freighter JAMES DEMPSEY was destroyed by fire at Manistee, Michigan, on December 10, 1922. [2]

SENATOR DERBYSHIRE ■ Wooden bulk freight steamer of 1,312 t. and 220 ft., launched at W Bay City, MI, in 1897, as the steamer BERMUDA
Lake Ontario: On October 11, 1924, this wooden freighter caught fire and was destroyed off the lighthouse at Point Petre, Ontario. Her crew was rescued by a passing steamer. [3]

DESMOND ■ Steam-powered sandsucker of 456 t. and 149 ft., launched at Port Huron, MI, as a freighter
Lake Michigan: All seven crewmen aboard the sandsucker DESMOND drowned when the vessel rolled over in a gale that struck her on December 8, 1917. The accident took place off South Chicago. The wreck was located in 1978. [5+]

DETROIT ■ Armed sloop of about 50 t., probably built at Erie, PA
Lake Erie: This vessel was reportedly the first American-flagged vessel on Lake Erie. In 1797, she was upbound with a cargo of military supplies when she was lost three miles off Erie, Pennsylvania. [1]

DETROIT ■ Armed brig, built as the brig ADAMS, probably at Detroit
Lake Erie: This 14-gun brig had a short but eventful career as a warship during the War of 1812. Purchased by the Americans at Detroit in 1812 and named ADAMS, she was captured by the Royal Navy in August and renamed DETROIT. On October 12 she was lying to in the Niagara River when she was recaptured by American raiders. During the gun battle that ensued, the ship was set afire, either purposely or by accident, and burned to the waterline near Squaw Island. [3]

DETROIT ■ Schooner or steamer of 1,039 t. and 239 ft., launched in Buffalo in 1859. One source says she went from a sidewheeler to a propeller to a schooner.
Lake Huron: The DETROIT was reported to have gone ashore near Harrisville, Michigan, in a March, 1872, storm. She subsequently broke up under the pounding of waves and was lost. [3]

DETROIT ■ Bulk freight schooner, launched as the MARY BATTLE
Lake Michigan: This schooner was reported ashore and lost on November 4, 1886. Conflicting reports place her loss in either of two locations. One says she went on a reef near Skillagalee light, while the other gives her position as Summer Island, 75 miles due east of the first. [3]

DETROIT ■ Wooden steamer
Lake Huron: This early steamer went down after a collision with the brig NUCLEUS in Saginaw Bay. The loss occurred in 1854. [1]

CITY OF DETROIT ■ Bulk freight steamer
Lake Erie: This freighter was reported lost four miles offshore from Barcelona, New York. She sank on September 3, 1873, with a cargo of copper ore. One report says she had gold in her safe. [2]

CITY OF DETROIT ■ Package and bulk freight propeller of 653 t.
Lake Huron: The loss of the freighter CITY OF DETROIT was one of the worst disasters in the history of Saginaw Bay. The boat was laden with a cargo of wheat and barrelled flour when she sailed into a storm on December 4, 1875, and never sailed out. All 20 of her crew were lost with the ship. One source gives 1863 as the year. [3]

GEORGE B DICKENSON ■ Steam tug
Lake Huron: The tug GEORGE B DICKENSON was the victim of an 1886 collision. The vessel was lost in Saginaw Bay, just off Bay City, Michigan. [1]

DICKINSON ■ Merchant brig
Lake Michigan: It is reported that, on November 17, 1886, this sail vessel was driven ashore to break up near Frankfort, Michigan. [1]

WILLIAM DICKINSON ■ Steam tug of 78 t. and 78 ft., launched in 1893 at Benton Harbor, MI
St. Clair River: The busy St. Clair River, due to its position as a narrow water route connecting Lakes Huron and St. Clair, was the site of many tug losses. One of these was the WILLIAM DICKINSON, which caught fire and was destroyed below Marine City, Michigan, on September 6, 1923. [1]

EMMA DIETRICH ■ Vessel details unavailable
Lake Erie: Sugar Loaf Reef, which protects the approach to Port Colborne, Ontario, was the site of the loss of this vessel in May of 1903. [1]

DINAH ■ 16 t. vessel of unreported type
Lake Erie: This little boat was lost off Long Point when she foundered near there on July 4, 1910. [1]

DISCOVERY ■ Schooner of 20-100 t.
Lake Superior: In the days before the Soo locks were built, merchant vessels to be used on Lake Superior were either hauled around the St. Marys Rapids on skids or were built above them. On the rare occasion when a vessel was to be brought back down to Lake Huron, it was sometimes possible to "shoot the rapids," thus saving the time and expense of portaging back around the rapids. The DISCOVERY was one of those that tried to run the whitewater and didn't make it. She was lost in the fall of 1829. [2]

DISPATCH or **DESPATCH** ■ Steam tug
Lake Huron: Forest fires were an all-too-common occurrence in the lumbering days in the Great Lakes basin. The loggers stripped the branches off trees right where they fell and left huge amounts of this highly flammable "slash" wherever they worked. The result was often a great fire that destroyed everything in its path and gave off tremendous clouds of smoke. Ships caught in this could be blinded and become easy prey for the reef-studded coasts of the Lakes. Such a victim was the DISPATCH. Reportedly towing five barges around the tip of Pointe Aux Barques, she wrecked on the point on October 10, 1871, when she lost her way in smoke from a big fire to the west (at the time, both the Chicago Fire and the Peshtigo Fire were burning). No information is given on her tow barges. [4]

DISPATCH ■ Gas screw of 15 t. and 49 ft. launched in 1905 at Sandusky, OH as the gas screw COL. WOODWARD
Lake Huron: This small tug or packet was lost to fire on the St. Mary's River, in 1931. She had sunk in the harbor at Sandusky, Ohio, in the Big Storm of 1913. [1]

DISPATCH BOAT #1 ■ Tug
Lake Michigan: This tug was reportedly destroyed by fire and sank two miles off the Chicago waterfront in April, 1935. [1]

DIXIE ■ Barge
Lake Erie: The unrigged barge DIXIE was reported to have foundered on December 4, 1964. Her wreckage still lies four miles off Ashtabula, Ohio. [1]

HIRAM R DIXON ▪ Wooden steam coaster of 329 t. and 149 ft., launched in 1883 at Mystic, CT
Lake Superior: Built on the east coast, the little steamer HIRAM R DIXON was brought to the Lakes to service the many small lumber ports flourishing in the 1880s. She was destroyed by fire at one such port, that of Michipicoten Island, Ontario, on August 18, 1903. No lives were lost in the accident. [4]

J W DOANE ▪ Merchant schooner of 617 t. and 180 ft., launched at Sturgeon Bay, WI in 1874
Lake Erie: Running without cargo, the schooner J W DOANE went out of control in a heavy storm when approaching the harbor at Buffalo. Big waves tossed the hapless ship on a breakwater, where she settled to the bottom. Her 8 crewmen were rescued from her rigging, but the vessel broke up on the same day, November 23, 1882. [2]

THOMAS DOBBIE ▪ Merchant schooner of 322 t. and 137 ft. launched as the schooner COMANCHE at Oswego, NY, in 1867
Lake Ontario: After a long career as a freight hauler, this schooner was abandoned after her hull was crushed by an early season ice floe. The accident occurred on December 3, 1904, at Deseronto, Ontario. [2]

ANNA DOBBINS ▪ Wooden tug
Lake Huron: The reefs surrounding the Charity Islands, which guard the mouth of Saginaw Bay, spelled the end for this tug when she foundered among them in 1886. [1]

DOLPHIN ▪ Merchant schooner, perhaps the 24 t. vessel built in 1817 at Sacket's Harbor, NY
Lake Ontario: No lives were lost, but this early schooner was a total loss when she was crushed by ice and sank at Pultneyville, New York, in 1818. [2]

DOLPHIN ▪ Merchant schooner
Lake Michigan: The schooner DOLPHIN was lost near Waugoschance Point, Michigan, in 1869. She suffered a collision with an unrecorded vessel in the narrow channel west of the point and sank. [1]

DOLPHIN ▪ Bulk freight schooner of 147 t.
Lake Huron: This small schooner was off Harbor Beach, Michigan, with a load of lumber when she foundered in a storm with all hands. Six lives were lost in the October 22, 1887, accident. [2]

DOMINION ▪ Sidewheel steamer of 117 ft. (about 175 t.), launched in 1867 at Wallaceburg, Ont.
Lake St. Clair: The small riverine steamer DOMINION was lost when she was destroyed by fire at her dock on the Thames River at Chatham, Ontario. The loss occurred in July of 1875. [1]

DOMINION ▪ Barge of 138 t. and 95 ft., launched as a steamer at Chatham, Ont., in 1890, rebuilt as barge in 1897
Lake St. Clair: The barge DOMINION was lost when she wrecked at Chatham, Ontario, on the Thames River, in March of 1898. [1]

DOMINION ▪ Wooden bulk freight steamer of 478 t. and 135 ft., launched at St. Catharine's, Ont., in 1868
Detroit River: On October 2, 1900, this elderly steamer caught fire and was destroyed at Sandwich, Ontario (now part of Windsor). She was declared a total loss, but her hull was recovered and returned to service as the barge CANADA. [3]

DON QUIXOTE ▪ Wooden passenger and package freight steamer of 80 t. launched in 1836 at Toledo, OH
Lake Huron: The small steamer DON QUIXOTE was lost on the lake in her very first year of operation, 1836. Unfortunately, no details of her demise were recorded. [2]

DONALDSON ▪ Bulk freight schooner-barge of 420 t. and 163 ft., launched at Tonawanda, NY, in 1866
Lake Erie: When this schooner began to leak in a storm on August 17, 1913, her tow vessel made a rush to Cleveland harbor in an attempt to save the ship. The action was in vain, for the DONALDSON sank just inside the entrance. She was considered to be too aged to salvage, and was left in place to rot. [3]

JAMES P DONALDSON ▪ Wooden lumber steamer of 521 t. and 185 ft., launched in 1880 at Marine City, MI
Lake Superior: A spring gale struck this vessel when she was exiting Thunder Bay, Ontario, with a full cargo of lumber. The old steamer's hull couldn't take the strain, and she split her seams and sank on May 6, 1923. [2]

DORMER #2 ▪ Freight barge of 82 t.
Lake Huron: This barge sank in the Saginaw River near Crow Island on July 7, 1940. Crow Island is just north of the site of the present Zilwaukee Bridge. [2]

GRACE DORMER ▪ Package and bulk freight propeller
Lake Michigan: The DORMER was a small steamer that had just loaded a cargo of fish at St. James, Beaver Island, when she caught fire. One crew member died in the July 3, 1872 blaze. The remains of the steamer were later recovered. [2]

DOROTHY MAY ■ 29 t. vessel of unreported type
Lake Erie: Caught in heavy weather on Oct. 2, 1941, the DOROTHY MAY sank 15 miles off Port Alma, Ont. [1]

E P DORR ■ Steam tug
Lake Huron: This tug was a well-known and popular vessel around Saginaw Bay. In 1856, she was lost there following a collision with an unreported vessel. [2]

E P DORR ■ Merchant schooner of 216 t.
Lake Erie: Seven lives were lost in the sinking of this schooner on November 15, 1881, when the vessel struck bottom on Tecumseh Reef, 20 miles east of Long Point, and was destroyed. [2]

G J DORR ■ Tow tug of 26 t. and 56 ft.
Lake Michigan: The towing vessel G J DORR was hauling two scows and was moving across Chicago harbor when she sank off South Chicago. The accident occurred in September of 1899. [2]

DOT ■ Bulk freight schooner-barge of 347 t., launched in 1866 as the schooner MARY MERRITT
Lake Superior: In tow of the steamer M M DRAKE (qv), the DOT was loaded with iron ore when she met with her fate on Aug. 25, 1883. The barge's seams opened and she began to sink quickly under the heavy burden of her cargo. The steamer took her crew off before the DOT sank, several miles off Grand Marais, MI. In 1881, as the MARY MERRITT, she had nearly been lost when she went ashore in a gale just six miles east of her final resting place. [2]

L R DOTY ■ Wooden bulk freight steamer of 2,056 t. and 291 ft., launched in 1893 at W Bay City, MI
Lake Michigan: The DOTY was only five years old on October 24, 1898, when she met with disaster. Bound for Chicago with a load of corn and the big schooner-barge OLIVE JEANETTE (qv) in tow, the steamer met with a real howler of a Lakes gale. Immediately in trouble, she cut her barge loose and tried to make it to shore. The OLIVE JEANETTE's crew were the last to see her until her wreckage washed up near Kenosha, Wisconsin. All seventeen hands were lost along with the big ship. [5+]

REUBEN DOUD ■ Package freight schooner of 145 ft., launched at Winneconne, WI, in 1873
Lake Ontario: One of only a handful of commercial vessels built at Winneconne, which is 40 miles by water from Lake Michigan, the REUBEN DOUD was lost on August 24, 1906. While entering the harbor at Toronto, she was dashed onto Ward's Island by a gale and was rapidly torn to pieces by big waves. [2]

M DOUSMAN ■ Merchant schooner of 157 t., launched in 1843 at Milwaukee
Lake Erie: The schooner M DOUSMAN was lost in 1852, when she sank off Dunkirk, New York. [1]

NANCY DOUSMAN ■ Merchant schooner
Lake Huron: An early loss occurring in the Straits of Mackinac was the schooner NANCY DOUSMAN. She foundered at an unrecorded position in 1834. [1]

DOVER ■ Sidewheel passenger steamer of 552 t. and 203 ft., built as the steamer FRANK E KIRBY and launched in 1890 at Detroit
Detroit River: The graceful sidewheeler DOVER was one of the most popular passenger vessels on the Lakes throughout her 42-year career. She was semi-retired and tied up at her dock at Ecorse, Michigan, when she caught fire and was destroyed on June 23, 1932. The sunken wreck was removed in 1939. [3]

FANNY DOWELL ■ 18 t. vessel of unreported type
Lake Erie: This small vessel, probably a packet or excursion boat, was lost on July 8, 1890. On that date, she reportedly sank two miles from Pelee Island. [1]

TOM DOWLING ■ Steam tug of 36 t. and 67 ft., launched in 1873 at Cleveland
Lake Michigan: The same fate that befell many working tugs with wooden hulls and wood or coal-stoked powerplants, settled upon the tug TOM DOWLING. The little vessel caught fire and burned to the waterline on August 17, 1908, at Ashland, Wisconsin. [2]

DAVID DOWS ■ Package and bulk freight schooner of 1,481 t. and 265 ft., launched in 1881 at Toledo
Lake Michigan: This famous five-masted sailing ship was the largest schooner in the world when she was launched, and equalled even the famous tea "clipper" ships in size and grace. She was still rigged as a schooner, but was working as a towed vessel when she met her end on November 25, 1889. The DOWS was under tow when she encountered a gale off Whiting, Indiana. The long wooden ship rode up on a series of big waves, broke her back and foundered. For part of her life, she was square-rigged on her foremast. [4]

M M DRAKE ■ Wooden bulk freight steamer of 1,102 t. and 201 ft., launched at Buffalo in 1882
Lake Superior: Many a steamer captain has been censured by landlubbers for failing to attempt to recover a barge lost in heavy weather. In fact, most schooner-barges carried enough sail to ride out a storm or even make port if necessary. The hazards of attempting to re-attach to a lost barge is illustrated in the case of the M M DRAKE. On October 2, 1901, the steamer lost her consort, the schooner-barge MICHIGAN (qv) in a strong gale off Ver-

milion Point, Michigan. In attempting to link up again, the two vessels were thrown together by huge waves. The two wooden hulls were crushed like eggshells, and both vessels quickly sank. Fortunately, other ships were standing by, and the DRAKE'S crew was rescued. The wreckage of the ship was located in 1978. [4]

DREADNAUGHT ■ Merchant schooner
Lake Huron: The schooner DREADNAUGHT was wrecked in September, 1886, when she collided with the tug CHENEY and sank off AuGres, Michigan, near the top of Saginaw Bay. One report says she was recovered, and she may be the same vessel as below. [2]

DREADNAUGHT ■ Merchant schooner, perhaps the 59 t., 66 ft. vessel built at Detroit in 1867
Lake Michigan: This schooner was lost in 1893 when she went ashore on rugged Seul Choix Point, on the east side of the Garden Peninsula, and broke up. [2]

DREDGE #1 ■ Dredge scow or barge
Lake Huron: The same characteristics that make a scow a perfect platform for dredging equipment—her broad beam, low freeboard, and flat bottom—make her very susceptible to capsizing or swamping in heavy weather. The dredge-scow called DREDGE #1 was in tow of her tug MAX #1, when she broke her towline and was immediately swamped. She sank off Bayfield, Ontario, in June of 1932. [2]

DREDGE #2 ■ Dredge barge of 403 t.
Lake Erie: One crewman died when this dredge barge was lost in a storm at an unreported location on the lake on December 13, 1907. [2]

DREDGE #8 ■ Dredge of 415 t.
Lake Superior: This work vessel went down in a storm off Hatton Island, Thunder Bay, Ontario. The barge sank just east of the island on December 9, 1909. [1]

DREDGE #906 ■ Dredge
Lake Michigan: Little detail is reported on the loss of this vessel, which sank six miles east of Milwaukee. [1]

CITY OF DRESDEN ■ Package freight steamer of 193 t. and 93 ft., launched in 1872 at Walkerville, Ont.
Lake Erie: During the era of Prohibition in the United States, fortunes were made and lost in smuggling liquor across the border from Canada. Vessels engaged in this illicit trade were as likely to be wrecked as any other. On November 18, 1922, the little old steamer CITY OF DRESDEN was carrying a load of illegal liquor when she was assailed by a Lake Erie gale and driven on the rocks on the south side of Long Point, near Port Rowan. She was noticed to be stranded and breaking up by two local women, who almost singlehandedly—it is said that others summoned to help rescued the steamer's cargo instead—brought all but one of the ship's crew ashore. [4]

JOSEPHINE DRESDEN ■ Bulk freight schooner of 84 t. and 95 ft., launched in 1852 at Michigan City, IN
Lake Michigan: Upbound and in ballast on November 27, 1907, the small "Grand Haven rigged" schooner JOSEPHINE DRESDEN encountered a typically violent fall gale near the upper end of the Lake, and was tossed ashore on North Manitou Island. Well-known photos of her show her partially dismasted and lying in the shallows with decks awash. Her crew was rescued before the old ship went completely to pieces. [4]

GEORGE C DREW ■ Merchant schooner
Lake Huron: Usually-gentle Saginaw Bay is guarded by the Charity Islands, friendly-looking landmarks strung across the top of the bay like knots in a spider's web. In foul weather the shoal water and reefs around the islands have snared a goodly number of ships, particularly in the days before a profusion of bouys and lighthouses marked the area. The schooner GEORGE C DREW was one of these unfortunate vessels, hung up on a reef and destroyed at Big Charity in 1866. [2]

DRILL BOAT #3 ■ Drill boat of 93 t.
Lake Ontario: This vessel, about which little detail is recorded, is reported to have foundered ten miles east of Toronto, near Scarborough, Ontario, on September 9, 1942. [1]

DRIVER ■ Bulk freight schooner-barge of 174 t. and 103 ft., launched as a schooner in 1856 at Milwaukee
Lake Michigan: This veteran lumber and coal carrier was downbound with a load of hardwood on August 30, 1901, when she met with disaster. A sudden squall struck and capsized her off South Manitou Island. The wreckage drifted ashore on the mainland near Pointe Aux Becs Scies (Point Betsie), Michigan. This was the schooner that came to the rescue of the steambarge H C AKELEY (qv) in 1883. [4]

DROMEDARY ■ Wooden propeller of 461 t. and 120 ft., launched in 1868 at Port Dalhousie, Ontario
Lake Ontario: Wooden steamers lying idle with their fires banked and often untended were highly susceptible to fires caused by an errant spark. Such was the fate of the steamer DROMEDARY, which burned at a wharf at Hamilton, Ontario, on November 8, 1882. [3]

JESSIE DRUMMOND ■ Merchant schooner of 432 t. and 142 ft., launched at St Catharine's, Ont., in 1864
Lake Ontario: The schooner JESSIE DRUMMOND was attempting to make the harbor at Cobourg, Ontario, when

she struck bottom. Before she could be released she was pounded to pieces by the gale. One source says all hands were lost in the December 2, 1902 accident. [5+]

DUDLEY ■ Dredge
Lake Huron: This dredge vessel reportedly foundered off Au Sable Point, near Oscoda, Michigan, in 1934. [1]

NELLIE A DUFF ■ Merchant schooner of 54 t. and 77 ft., launched in 1885 at Port Clinton, OH
Lake Erie: Laden with gravel, a heavy cargo that was prone to shift in heavy seas, the little NELLIE DUFF was trying to make port at Lorain, Ohio in a gale when she was lost. She lost the fight with the October 14, 1895, storm while still two miles out, and went down, taking three crewmen to the bottom with her. See schooner KATE WINSLOW for further information. [4]

LADY DUFFERIN ■ Schooner-barge of 300 t. and 135 ft.
Lake Huron: Battling a Georgian Bay storm in 1886, this schooner barge was lost from the tow of the steamer W B HALL. The helpless vessel was thrown ashore to break up on the point which still bears her name. There are reports of a ship of the same name lost or heavily damaged on Lake Superior in 1884. [3]

DULUTH ■ Dredge
Lake Superior: Vessels are not always safe from disaster just because they are lying quietly at dock. The dredge DULUTH was tied up at Duluth on October 12, 1918, when the lakehead city was swept by a forest fire. Part of the dock area, including the dredge, was completely destroyed. [2]

CITY OF DULUTH ■ Package freight steamer of 1,310 t. and 202 ft., launched in 1874 at Marine City, MI
Lake Michigan: Laden with a cargo of general merchandise, the steamer CITY OF DULUTH was making a late-season run when she was struck by a storm on January 26, 1898. She was driven ashore north of the harbor at St. Joseph, Michigan, where she broke up. [2]

GEORGE DUNBAR ■ Wooden bulk freight steamer of 238 t. and 134 ft., launched in 1867 at Allegan, MI
Lake Huron or *Lake Erie:* Conflicting reports place the loss of this small freighter in two widely separated locations on June 29, 1902. Several reports say that she was lost when she was damaged by a sudden squall on a run from Alpena to Port Huron, and sank with all seven hands. Other reliable reports state that she was sunk by a squall on Lake Erie. [5+]

DUNCAN CITY ■ Merchant schooner of 261 t. and 115 ft., launched in 1873 at Oswego, NY

Lake Huron: The two-master DUNCAN CITY was lost in the Frazier Bay area of the North Channel in 1888. Little detail is recorded. [2]

JOHN DUNCAN ■ Bulk freight steamer of 1,268 t. and 225 ft., launched in 1891 at Fort Howard, WI
Lake Huron: The freighter JOHN DUNCAN suffered a serious casualty near the lumber port of Harrisville, Michigan, in 1905. She sank just off the docks, but reports are unclear as to whether lives were lost or not. She was subsequently recovered, rebuilt and renamed HOWARD W, and was wrecked in the St. Lawrence River in 1919. [3]

MAGGIE DUNCAN ■ Merchant schooner
Lake Huron: Harrisville, Michigan, 20 miles north of Oscoda, was a major lumber-shipping point in the late 1800's. Several ships were lost off the Harrisville docks, exposed as they were to the weather and waves. The schooner NINA (qv), the steamer JOHN DUNCAN (qv) and this cargo carrier were just a few. The MAGGIE DUNCAN was wrecked just off the docks in 1895. [1]

DUNDEE ■ Bulk freight schooner-barge of 1,043 t. and 211 ft., launched in 1893 at W Bay City, MI
Lake Erie: Bound to the east end of the lake with a load of lumber, this schooner-barge was lost on September 11, 1900. One life was lost when the big ship was blasted by an autumnal storm and foundered well offshore and ten miles west of Cleveland. [4]

DUNDERBURG ■ Merchant schooner
Lake Huron: The shipping lane off Harbor Beach (formerly Sand Beach), Michigan, is often congested. In the last century the area was the confluence of shipping from Saginaw Bay and Harbor Beach as well as the traffic area for all up- and downbound freight. As a result, it has been the site of a number of collisions, including that of the DUNDERBURG. The three-masted schooner was carrying a cargo of corn in August of 1868, when her path merged with that of the steamer EMPIRE STATE. The schooner went down quickly a few miles from shore, with the loss of one of her crew members. [2]

DUNDURN ■ Bulk freight barge of 637 t. and 232 ft., launched in 1882 at Wyandotte as the break-bulk carrier FLINT & PERE MARQUETTE #2, lengthened 35 ft. and converted to a barge in 1906
Lake Erie: The barge DUNDURN was in tow of the steam tug HOME RULE (qv) when she was lost on July 15, 1919. Two of the barge's crew perished when she was swamped and foundered in a heavy storm just outside of the harbor at Ashtabula, Ohio. [3]

WILLIAM H DUNHAM ■ Lumber schooner of 185 t. and 116 ft., launched in 1873 at Eastmanville, MI
Lake Michigan: A veteran lumber carrier known up and down the Michigan shoreline, the schooner WILLIAM H DUNHAM was wrecked beyond repair on the last day of 1902. She went ashore in a storm and broke up near Duke's Creek. [2]

GEORGE L DUNLAP ■ Steamer
Lake Huron: The steamer GEORGE DUNLAP was damaged by ice and sank in Saginaw Bay, 14 miles from Bay City, Michigan, in 1880. [2]

JOHN DUNN ■ Merchant schooner of 320 t. and 138 ft., launched in 1874 as Oswego, NY
Lake Erie: Little detail has been reported on the loss of this schooner, but she was brand new when she sank on the lake in 1874. [1]

STUART H DUNN ■ Schooner-barge of 458 t. and 164 ft., launched as the schooner WILFRED R TAYLOR at Marysburgh, Ont., in 1877
Lake Ontario: Nearing the end of her useful life, the 43-year-old STUART H DUNN foundered at Port Dalhousie, Ontario, on July 4, 1920. She was recovered soon after, but was not returned to service. She was stripped of usable hardware and resunk in 1925. [3]

J DUVALL ■ Package and bulk freight schooner of 132 t. and 107 ft, launched in 1874 at Manitowoc, Wis. Three sources give three different accounts of the loss of this small schooner. Only one registered schooner on the lakes carried this name during this period.
Lake Michigan: The DUVALL was reported as driven ashore and wrecked on South Manitou Island, December 11, 1905. [1]
Lake St. Clair: A vessel of the same name is recorded as having collided with the whaleback JAMES B COLGATE (qv) and sunk near Harsen's Island on December 5, 1905. [1]
Lake Superior: A schooner of the same name is reported to have sunk on the lake in 1904. [2]

JAMES E. EAGLE ■ Wooden steam tug
Lake Huron: The tug EAGLE was reported as lost, a victim of fire, on Saginaw Bay in 1869. [1]

EAGLE ■ Gas screw of 13 t.
Lake Michigan: The harbor at South Haven, Michigan, saw the loss of this small vessel. She foundered there on April 5, 1947. [1]

EAGLE WING ■ Merchant schooner of 278 t.
Lake Erie: The schooner EAGLE WING was lost in April of 1878 when she struck a reef near Bar Point, which guards the Ontario side of the Detroit River mouth, and sank. [1]

HATTIE EARL ■ Merchant schooner of 101 t. and 95 ft., launched in 1869 at South Haven, MI
Lake Michigan: In the commercial boom that affected Lakes trade following the Civil War, dozens of small schooners like the HATTIE EARL were built to take advantage of the increased flow of goods to the west. These small craft were excellent for their purpose in good weather, but were apt to take tremendous punishment in almost any poor conditions. This schooner was swept ashore by a storm which occurred on April 5, 1889. She reportedly broke up on the beach one mile south of Kenosha, Wisconsin, but she was still shown in ship registers in 1892. [2]

EAST SAGINAW ■ Package freighter
Lake Huron: An unconfirmed report states that this propeller ship foundered near Harrisville, Michigan, in 1875. She may have been recovered and rebuilt as a bulk freighter, which was destroyed by fire in 1923. [1]

EASTLAND ■ Steel excursion steamer of 1,961 t. and 269 ft., launched in 1903 at Port Huron, MI
Lake Michigan: The tragic accident which befell the EASTLAND on July 24, 1915, was the cause of the greatest loss of life of any Great Lakes disaster. Always known as a "tender" boat, she was reportedly overloaded and topheavy after the boarding of more than 2,500 picnickers at her dock in the Chicago River. As she was pulling away, the big ship capsized, killing 835. She was recovered soon after the accident, but public outcry against her was much too great for her to be returned to passenger service. Her big superstructure was cut down and she was converted to the naval training vessel USS WILMETTE. See U C 97. [5+]

EASTNOR ■ Steam freighter of 101 t. and 92 ft., launched as the steamer CHARLES LEMCKE in 1909 at Lion's Head, Ont.
Lake Huron: Fire claimed the small steamer EASTNOR on November 18, 1933, while she was loading bunker coal at a dock at Wiarton, Ontario. [3]

EAU J ■ steamer
Lake Erie: This vessel was reported lost in an explosion which occurred off Pte Aux Pins, Ontario, on April 27, 1955. [1]

EBENEZER ■ Lumber schooner-barge of 115 t. and 99 ft., launched in 1847 at Buffalo as the schooner WATTS SHERMAN
Lake Michigan: An old vessel by any standards, the schooner-barge EBENEZER was no match for a fall storm, and was cast ashore on South Manitou Island on October 14, 1903. [2]

KATE ECCLES ■ Merchant schooner of 122 t. and 95 ft., launched at Deseronto, Ont., in 1877
Lake Ontario: Bound to Napanee, Ontario, with a cargo of coal, this little two-masted schooner foundered in a storm off Timber Island and was lost on November 28, 1922. [1]

ECLIPSE ■ Steam freighter
Lake Huron: Like the sun disappearing during a total eclipse, the steamer ECLIPSE simply "sailed away" in a November, 1874, storm. She was lost with all hands at an unknown position. [2]

ECLIPSE ■ Merchant schooner of 158 t.
Lake Michigan: In a freezing gale, the schooner ECLIPSE was cast aground on a rocky reef at Big Sable Point, on the Michigan shoreline. The ship sank quickly, but her crew were able to scramble up the rigging where they clung until rescued by the U.S. Lifesaving Service. Only one life was lost in the November 24, 1882 incident. [3]

ECLIPSE ■ Schooner of 49 t.
Lake Huron: This tiny schooner was reported to have "gone missing" with all hands at an unknown location on the lake. She disappeared on November 22, 1883. [2]

EDDIE S ■ Fishing tug of 45 ft.
Lake Superior: Good weather turned bad spelled the end for this fishing boat and two of her crew of three. The tug was lost off Grand Marais, Michigan, in a sudden squall which occurred on May 22, 1945. [2]

JOHN F EDDY ■ Wooden bulk freight barge of 1,678 t. and 259 ft., launched as a steamer in 1886 at Wyandotte, MI (one report says Saginaw)
Lake Erie: This barge was carrying a load of coal and was in tow of the tug CUSTODIAN when she met her demise on November 13, 1920. While in transit just off West Sister Island in heavy weather, the wooden vessel sprang a leak and sank in the channel. She was later dynamited as a hazard. [5]

NEWELL A EDDY ■ Schooner-barge of 1,270 t. and 242 ft., launched at W Bay City, MI, in 1890
Lake Huron: Only a few years after the completion of the the lighthouse at Spectacle Reef, west of Mackinac Island, this grain-carrying schooner-barge was driven ashore and wrecked there. The 86-foot lighthouse was one of the greatest marine construction projects of all time, but even the close proximity of such a magnificent structure cannot guarantee the safety of a barge which has broken her towline and had her meager sails blown out. All seven of the EDDY's crew perished in the April, 1893, disaster. The stern of the vessel washed up on Bois Blanc Island, a dozen miles to the southwest, a few days later. [5+]

WILLIAM EDENBORN ■ Steel bulk freight steamer of 8,000 t. and 478 ft., launched in 1900 at W Bay City, MI
Lake Superior: The rugged coast surrounding aptly-named Castle Danger, Minnesota, has beckoned many a fine ship to her end. The big steamer WILLIAM EDENBORN was light when she was pushed onto a stony reef at nearby Split Rock, by the giant November 28, 1905, storm. All but one of the crew evacuated the ship before she split in two. The vessel was recovered, but was too badly damaged to be returned to service, and was eventually sunk at Cleveland for a breakwater. [3]

JOHN EDWARD ■ Sloop of 11 t.
Lake Michigan: On November 9, 1876, this small carrier foundered close in to shore and five miles north of Saugatuck, Michigan. [1]

MARION EGAN ■ Merchant schooner
Lake Huron: The schooner MARION EGAN was lost off Thunder Bay Island, near Alpena, Michigan, as a result of damage sustained in a collision in 1875. [1]

JOHN EGGERS ■ Schooner-scow of 25 t. and 59 ft., launched in 1887 at Milwaukee, WI
Lake Michigan: This small sailing scow ended her career on Wind Point, near Racine, Wis., when she stranded there on May 26, 1906. Her one-man crew was saved. [2]

EGYPTIAN ■ Wooden propeller freighter of 1,430 t. and 232 ft., launched in 1873 at Black River, OH
Lake Huron: The steamer EGYPTIAN was lost 15 miles out of Alpena, Michigan, when she caught fire and was destroyed in 1897. This is the steamer that was equipped with the first fore-and-aft compound engine used on the Lakes. [4]

EIGHTH OHIO ■ Sidewheel passenger steamer of 122 t. and 121 ft., launched in 1867 at Sandusky, OH
Detroit River: This small wooden sidewheeler was reported to have been destroyed by fire at Windsor, Ontario, in 1877. [1]

EILEEN G ▪ Tug of 10 t.
Lake Superior: This tiny tug was lost near the Tunnel Islands when she sank on May 9, 1955. [1]

ELDORADO ▪ Merchant schooner of 489 t.
Lake Erie: The schooner ELDORADO is reported to have sunk just east of Presque Isle, near the mouth of the harbor at Erie, Pennsylvania, on November 20, 1880. [2]

ELEANOR ▪ 5 t. vessel of unreported type
Lake Ontario: On February 29, 1892, this diminutive vessel sank five miles north of Main Duck Island. [1]

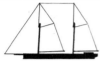

ELGIN ▪ Lumber schooner-barge of 330 t. and 139 ft., launched in 1874 at St. Catharine's, Ont.
Lake Superior: This schooner-barge was lost on October 29, 1906, when she was overtaken by a gale. The ELGIN swamped and was torn to pieces by big waves off Grand Marais, Michigan. [2]

LADY ELGIN ▪ Sidewheel passenger steamer of 1,037 t. and 252 ft., launched in 1851 at Buffalo
Lake Michigan: The sidewheeler LADY ELGIN was one of the largest vessels operating on the Lakes in 1860. She was the height of luxury and at the peak of her popularity when she was overcome by one of the worst tragedies in freshwater history. On the night of September 8, 1860 the steamer was near Winnetka, Illinois, with about 400 passengers and crew aboard when she was struck broadside, aft of her great paddlewheels, by the loaded lumber schooner AUGUSTA, which was making for Chicago under full sail. The crew of the schooner, naturally thinking they had received the worst of a collision with a steamer three times their size, turned the AUGUSTA to starboard and raced for Chicago as fast as the heavily damaged ship could move. But the big steamer was fatally holed and left on her own on the lonely lake. About a hundred of her passengers made it to shore in lifeboats or clinging to wreckage, but 297 souls were lost with the elegant LADY. The big steamer's wreckage was located by divers in 1989. [5+]

LORD ELGIN ▪ Sidewheel steamer of 116 ft., launched in 1845 at Oswego, NY as the steamer SYRACUSE
Lake Ontario: Though detailed reports are lacking, it is known that this sidewheeler was wrecked on Long Point, near the eastern end of the lake, in December of 1856. [1]

WILLIAM ELGIN ▪ Bulk freight schooner of 156 t.
Lake Ontario: The schooner WILLIAM ELGIN was 16 miles out of Oswego, New York, when she sprang a leak and sank on May 19, 1888. The vessel's crew survived the accident. [2]

ELI ▪ Merchant schooner
Lake Erie: Nine crewmen were lost when this schooner went down northeast of the harbor at Ashtabula, Ohio, on November 14, 1887. See also ELI BATES. [1]

ELITE ▪ Tug of 24 t.
Lake Huron: Jennie Island, in Georgian Bay, was the site of the loss of this tug in 1933. She was moored at her dock when she caught fire and was destroyed on the 23rd of September. [2]

ELIZA ▪ Bulk freight schooner of 30 t.
Lake Michigan: Three persons, probably her entire crew, were lost when this tiny sailing vessel foundered with her cargo of sand in July of 1890. Her position at the time of the accident is either unknown or unreported. [1]

ELIZA CAROLINE ▪ Merchant schooner of 33 t. and 44 ft., launched in 1851 at Sandusky, OH
Lake Erie: Another vessel lost at an unreported location is the schooner ELIZA CAROLINE, said to have gone ashore and broken up somewhere on Lake Erie in 1871. [1]

ELIZABETH ▪ Merchant schooner or schooner-scow, perhaps the 23 t. schooner-scow launched at Swan Creek, MI, in 1866
Lake Huron: The schooner ELIZABETH was reported to have foundered near Detour, Michigan, at one of the entrances to the St. Marys River. She was lost in a big storm in 1882. She had also been stranded on Georgian Bay in 1872, but was recovered. [2]

ELLEN ▪ Merchant schooner
Lake Huron: The ELLEN was one of the earliest schooner losses at Thunder Bay, on the Michigan coast. She was reportedly wrecked and sank there in 1856. [1]

ELLA ELLINWOOD or **ELLEN ELLENWOOD** ▪ Lumber schooner of 168 t. and 106 ft., launched in 1870 at E Saginaw, MI
Lake Huron: The loss of the schooner ELLA ELLINWOOD has been reported for September 21, 1901. She was carrying a load of sawn wood and bark when she was driven ashore by a gale and was pounded to pieces. The location of the wreck has been reported as either just south or 13-14 miles north of Milwaukee. [5]

ELLIOT ▪ Merchant schooner of 300 t.
Lake Erie: The schooner ELLIOT sank nine miles off Port Burwell, Ontario, on September 18, 1872. [1]

COLONEL ELLSWORTH ▪ Merchant schooner of 318 t. and 140 ft., launched in 1861 at Euclid, OH
Lake Michigan: This veteran schooner was travelling in ballast when she collided with the the schooner EMILY B MAXWELL (qv), and quickly sank. The accident occurred near Waugoschance Point in September of 1896. [2]

October 20, 1905

The year 1905 was a dreadful one for lakemen. At least three major storms tore up the Great Lakes, sending more than 50 ships to the bottom. But one particular storm, one particular day, in fact, outdid the others in violence and damage done.

We are shocked by the Big Storm of 1913 because of its' destruction of so many big, modern ships. The Big Blow of 1905 occurred at the end of November and was memorable for its' violence to steel vessels of all types.

But October 20, 1905, may have done more in one day to end the era of wooden ships (though the era of iron men has never ended) than all other storms combined. In October, most lake ships were still out. Though the storm season was beginning, most gales could be handled by prudence and seamanship. But on October 20, an incredible gale swept the Lakes clean. It was not the typical "three days to blow in and three days to blow out" storm, but a mammoth squall that struck the Lakes almost without warning. The big steel ships had little to fear from this gale, but smaller wooden vessels were in danger and did not even have time to run for shelter. For about 50 vessels it meant the end of the season, time for repairing broken equipment. At least 27 vessels, all wooden ships, did not return to port at all, and more than 50 lives were lost. The roll:

Schooner-barge ALTA, Steamer ARGO, Schooner COMMERCE, Steamer JOSEPH S FAY, Schooner GLEN CUYLER, Tug CYGNET, Schooner-barge FOSTER, Schooner-barge GALATEA, Schooner JOHN V JONES, Steamer KALIYUGA, Schooner KATAHDIN, Schooner LYDIA, Schooner KATE LYONS, Schooner-barge IVER LAWSON, Schooner-barge MAUTENEE, Schooner MINNEDOSA, Schooner NEILSEN, Schooner-barge NIRVANA, Tug JAY OCHS, Steamer OREGON, Schooner PRINCE, Schooner RHODES, Schooner SARAH E SHELDON, Steamer SIBERIA, Schooner-barge TASMANIA, Schooner VEGA, Schooner-barge YUKON

Largest vessels of various types lost on the lakes

1. Freighter: EDMUND FITZGERALD - 729 ft., 25,891 t. (1975)
2. Barge: MADEIRA - 436 ft., 5,039 t. (1905)
3. Tanker: JUPITER - 384 ft., 54,000 bbl (1990)
4. Passenger Steamer: NORONIC - 362 ft., 6905 t. (1949)
5. Sidewheel Steamer: WESTERN STATES - 350 ft., 3077 t. (1959)
6. Carferry: PERE MARQUETTE 18, 338 ft., 2993 t. (1910)
   MARQUETTE & BESSEMER #2 338 ft., 2534 t. (1909)
   MILWAUKEE 338 ft. 2933 t. (1929)
7. Schooner-Barge: PRETORIA - 338 t., 2790 ft. (1905)
8. Schooner: DAVID DOWS - 265 ft., 1,481 t. (1889)
9. Sandsucker: SAND MERCHANT - 252 ft., 1891 t. (1936)
10. Bark: CANADA - 199 ft., 758 t. (1855)
11. Coast Guard Vessel: MESQUITE - 180 ft., 1,025 t. (1989)
12. Yacht: GUNILDA - 177 ft., 385 t. (1911)

Largest schooner-barges lost on the lakes

1. PRETORIA - 338 ft., 2,790 t. Foundered in gale, Lake Superior, 1905.
2. SANTIAGO - 324 ft., 2,600 t. Foundered on Lake Huron, 1918.
3. CHICKAMAUGA - 322 ft., 2472 t. Foundered in gale, Lake Huron, 1919.
4. CHATTANOOGA - 308 ft. 2329 t. Stranded and wrecked, Lake Erie, 1925.
5. ABYSSINIA - 305 ft., 2037 t. Stranded and broke up in storm, Lake Erie, 1917.
6. ATHENS - 289 ft., 2073 t. Broke up and sank in storm, Lake Huron, 1917.
7. ARMENIA - 285 ft., 2040 t. Foundered in gale, Lake Erie, 1906.
8. ALGERIA - 285 ft., 2038 t. Foundered in gale, Lake Erie, 1906.
9. YUKON - 270 ft., 1602 t. Foundered in gale, Lake Erie, 1905.
10. MAGNETIC - 264 ft., 1676 t. Broke in half and sank in gale, 1917.

The most dangerous decade

Which period of Great Lakes history saw the largest number of shipwrecks? Below are the figures for the vessels listed in this book. Note that wrecks for which data has not been found are probably older, so that figures for the first half of the 19th Century may be low. The number of wrecks for each decade is somewhat in proportion to the number of vessel in use at the time.

TIME PERIOD	NUMBER OF WRECKS	PERCENT OF TOTAL
1600s	2	.1
1700s	4	.1
1800s	4	.1
1810s	18	.5
1820s	17	.5
1830s	33	.9
1840s	86	2.3
1850s	205	5.6
1860s	229	6.2
1870s	377	10.3
1880s	568	14.3
1890s	515	14.0
1900s	607	16.5
1910s	362	9.9
1920s	220	5.9
1930s	115	3.1
1940s	76	2.1
1950s	56	1.5
1960s	21	.6
1970s	18	.5
1980s	8	.2
1990s	2	1.0
Unknown	140	3.8
Total	**3683**	**100.0**

The stormy Great Lakes

The gales of November are almost legendary for the violence they wreak upon Great Lakes shipping. November is indeed the month when the greatest number of storm-related losses occur, and some of the most violent weather on record has happened in the eleventh month. But sailors are well aware that heavy seas and big wind can happens at any time of year. For several months in winter, the shriek of the north wind goes unanswered by any ship's whistle. In the summer months, storms and squalls come out of nowhere to send careless vessels to the bottom. But the really awful, magnificent weather occurs in spring and fall, when arctic and temperate air masses lock in mortal combat over possession of the Lakes. Below are approximate percentages of all storm-related shipping losses for the various months:

MONTH	PERCENT	MONTH	PERCENT
January	less than 1	July	3
February	less than 1	August	6
March	less than 1	September	12
April	4	October	24
May	8	November	32
June	3	December	6

LEM ELLSWORTH ■ Bulk freight schooner of 340 t. and 138 ft., launched in 1874 at Milwaukee
Lake Michigan: In May of 1894, the LEM ELLSWORTH was lost with seven of her crew when she sank two miles off Kenosha, Wisconsin. She was carrying a cargo of stone blocks at the time. [1]

ELLWOOD ■ Steamer
Lake Superior: The ELLWOOD sank in the harbor at Duluth, on November 28, 1905. [1]

ELMA ■ Lumber schooner-barge of 410 t. and 165 ft., launched at Marine City, MI, in 1873
Lake Superior: In tow of the steamer P H BIRCKHEAD (qv) with two other barges, this lumber-laden vessel was downbound on September 28, 1895, when disaster struck. Overtaken by a tremendous gale, the four vessels were separated off the Pictured Rocks, near Munising, Michigan. The ELMA's steering gear soon became disabled and the helpless ship was thrown into the shallows under towering Miner's Castle. One crewman died trying to carry a rope to shore, while another heroic sailor made it. He sat in the rocks all night in the storm holding on to the end of a rescue line. In the morning, the remaining crew were able to come ashore. The other three ships in the little fleet survived the storm, but the ELMA went to pieces where she lay. [5+]

C W ELPHICKE ■ Wooden bulk freighter of 2,059 t. and 273 ft., launched in 1889 at Trenton, MI
Lake Erie: One of largest of the many victims of treacherous Long Point was this big steamer. On October 21, 1913, she was driven hard aground by a heavy storm, broke in half, and sank. [3]

ELVA ■ Freight barge
Lake Huron: In 1954, this barge was destroyed by fire and was scuttled near Mackinac Island, Michigan. [1]

ELVINA ■ Bulk freight schooner-barge of 296 t. and 137 ft., launched in 1868 at Sacket's Harbor, NY
Lake Huron: Lost from the grasp of her tow steamer in a storm on October 31, 1901, the ELVINA was soon in serious trouble. Within a short span of time she had foundered off Michigan's Thunder Bay. One source gives October 12 as the date of the accident. [3]

GEORGE H ELY ■ Freight barge
Lake Huron: An 1882 storm swamped this barge, which sank near Detour, Michigan. [1]

GRACE ELY ■ Merchant schooner
Lake Superior: While in tow of the tug MYSTIC, this small schooner began to swamp due to poor stowage and trimming of her cargo. Before the situation could be corrected, the ship turned turtle, drowning one member of her crew. She was later recovered from the September, 1885, accident, which took place off Little Presque Isle, near Marquette, Michigan. [1]

S P ELY ■ Schooner-barge
Lake Superior: The ELY was approaching Two Harbors, Minnesota, in a gale when she reportedly went out of control and struck the harbor breakwall. She sank on October 29, 1896. [1]

EMBA ■ Bulk freight barge
Lake Michigan: According to one report, this coal-laden barge sank 9 miles off Milwaukee. No date is given for the loss. [1]

EMBURY ■ Wooden bulk freight steamer of 373 t. and 158 ft., launched at Gibraltar, MI, in 1869 as the steamer COLIN CAMPBELL
Lake Erie: The freighter EMBURY was a victim of a fire which destroyed her at Tonawanda, New York, on December 4, 1903. The hulk was abandoned to sink in the Niagara River. [1]

EMERALD ■ Sidewheel steamer of about 96 t. and 132 ft., launched in 1844 at Chippewa, Ont.
Lake St. Clair: This small sidewheeler was reported to have foundered on the lake in December of 1858. [1]

EMERALD ■ Freight barge
Lake Huron: The barge EMERALD was lost in 1880 when she sank on the Saginaw River and was not recovered. The wreck is reportedly still visible above water. [2]

EMERALD ■ Bulk freight schooner or brig of 287 ft., probably the vessel of this name launched at Saginaw, MI, in 1875
Lake Michigan: Five lives were lost when the coal-laden schooner was overwhelmed and destroyed by a gale off Kewaunee, Wisconsin. The vessel was wrecked on November 17, 1886. [1]

EMERALD ■ Bulk freight schooner-barge of 287 t. and 133 ft., launched at Bay City, MI, in 1869, as a sloop
Lake Ontario: A strong westerly gale struck this small schooner-barge on November 29, 1903. Loaded with coal, the vessel tried to ride out the storm at anchor under Scarborough Bluffs, near Toronto, but was overwhelmed and sank with all hands. [2]

EMERALD ■ Bulk freighter of 215 t. and 144 ft., launched at Algonac, MI, in 1863 as the sidewheel steamer D W POWERS
Lake Huron: On November 13, 1909, the steamer EMERALD was lost on reef-studded Thunder Bay Island, east of Alpena, Michigan. On that date the rabbit was driven ashore by a gale and broken up by big waves. [3]

EMERALD ■ Schooner of 145 ft., launched in 1872 at Port Colborne, Ont.
Lake Ontario: This 39-year-old schooner just "sailed away" and was lost on November 29, 1911. The coal-carrying vessel and her crew disappeared at an unknown position, and without a trace. [1]

W J EMERSON ■ Tug of 19 t., launched in 1910
Lake Superior: This small tug was lost when she foundered off Light Number 10, in the Fall of 1932. [1]

H A EMERY ■ Merchant schooner of 67 t. and 73 ft., launched at Bay City, MI, in 1887
Lake Huron: This tiny schooner was attempting to enter the anchorage at Harbor Beach, Michigan, on August 9, 1899, when she foundered just off the harbor entrance. She was laden with a cargo of lumber at the time. [3]

W Y EMERY ■ Bulk freight schooner of 154 t.
Lake Ontario: On September 26, 1899, the coal carrying W Y EMERY was lost when she sank off the mouth of Bear Creek, near Oswego, New York. [1]

EMEU or EMUE ■ Schooner of 234 t.
Lake Huron: The sinking of the EMEU occurred on May 3, 1888. On that date the sailing ship went down five miles off Grindstone City, Michigan, near Pte Aux Barques. [3]

EMILINE ■ Bulk freight schooner of 128 t.
Lake Michigan: This small schooner, laden with a load of bark, was driven ashore and lost 25 miles south of Bailey's Harbor, Wisconsin, on August 8, 1896. [1]

EMILY ■ Merchant schooner or schooner-scow
Lake St. Clair: The sail vessel EMILY was one of the earliest commercial losses on Lake St. Clair. She wrecked there with the loss of seven crew members on November 15, 1830. See also JULES LaPLANTE. [2]

EMILY ■ Bulk freight schooner
Lake Erie: This schooner was lost with all hands in November of 1842. In that stormy month she was in transit with a cargo of wheat when she was blown down by a gale, capsized and sank near Long Point. [1]

EMILY ■ Merchant schooner, perhaps the 69 t. vessel of this name launched at Milwaukee in 1853
Lake Huron: Georgian Bay was the area where Europeans first looked upon the inland seas in 1615. Almost since that time it has been a beehive of commerce, even though much of the shoreline is sparsely populated. It is also dotted with over 30,000 islands and innumerable reefs and shoals. No wonder that close to 200 vessels are recorded as having been lost there in the past two centuries. The schooner EMILY was typical, going about her business when struck by a fast-rising gale, driven into the shallows, and destroyed in 1858. [2]

EMILY AND ELIZA ■ Schooner-scow of 78 ft., launched in 1878 at Oak Harbor, OH
Lake Michigan: The schooner-scow EMILY AND ELIZA was lost near Sleeping Bear, in the Platte Bay, on September 9, 1910. [2]

EMMA ■ Merchant schooner, possibly the 169 t. vessel of this name launched at Milwaukee in 1853
Lake Huron: In 1869 the schooner EMMA was reported lost near Blue Point, at the south end of the lake. [1]

EMMA ■ Passenger and freight steamer of 146 t. and 89 ft., launched as a tug at Collingwood, Ont. in 1894, rebuilt and enlarged in 1901
Lake Erie: On July 3, 1912, the small steamer EMMA was destroyed on Georgian Bay by a fire. The accident occurred at Sister Rock, near Parry Sound, Ontario. [4]

EMPEROR ■ Steel bulk freight steamer of 7,031 t. and 525 ft., launched in 1911 at Collingwood, Ont.
Lake Superior: This big steamer's imperial name and size are ironic, since she was lost on Isle Royale on the night of June 4, 1947. Due to inattentiveness in navigation, the steel ship piled onto Canoe Rocks in calm weather, broke in two and quickly sank. Twelve men and women from her crew of 31 were lost when she took her plunge. The steamer is a well-known target for divers. [5+]

EMPIRE ■ Lumber bark of 350 t.
Lake Erie: The bark EMPIRE was the victim of a spring gale. On May 3, 1857, the ship was carrying a load of timbers and fighting the storm among the narrow channels of the Erie Islands when she went aground and quickly broke up at Marblehead, near Sandusky, Ohio. Though she was not far from shore, 11 of her 13 crew were lost before they could be rescued. [2]

EMPIRE ■ Propeller passenger and package freighter of 1,136 t. and 254 ft., built in Cleveland in 1844 as a sidewheeler
Lake Erie: The steamer EMPIRE was reportedly the first American-built vessel of over 1,000 gross tons displace-

ment. On October 26, 1870, she was struck by a viscious lake storm and stranded on Long Point. The old hull could not take the pounding, and she quickly broke up and was lost. [3]

EMPIRE STATE ■ Merchant schooner of 396 t., launched at St Catharine's, Ont., in 1862
Lake Huron: The schooner EMPIRE STATE was leaving the busy confines of Thunder Bay (Michigan) when she was struck by a gale raging on the open lake and foundered near North Point on November 8, 1877. One report gives the location of the accident as Lake Erie. [3]

EMPIRE STATE ■ Sidewheel passenger steamer of 380 t. and 157 ft., launched at New York, NY in 1863 as the steamer SYLVAN STREAM
Lake Ontario: This small wooden sidewheeler was lost in a June 25, 1903 fire. After a career of passenger service on the east coast and in the Thousand Islands area of the St. Lawrence River, she was laid up at a dock at Kingston, Ontario, in 1901. She was still there when she caught fire and was destroyed. [2]

EMPRESS ■ Sidewheel steamer, launched as the NEW ERA at Kingston, Ont., in 1849
Lake Ontario: This early sidewheeler was the victim of fire. She was destroyed at Kingston in March of 1868. [1]

BETHA ENDRESS ■ Steam tug
Lake Superior: Five lives were lost when this tug foundered in a storm off Whitefish Point on September 29, 1891. [2]

ORA ENDRESS ■ Passenger and package freight packet
Lake Superior: This little vessel capsized just offshore in Whitefish Bay in November, 1914. Happily, all those aboard were rescued by the Whitefish Point Lighthouse keeper. [2]

ENTERPRISE ■ Scow
Lake Huron: The Straits of Mackinac are the last resting place of this scow, which broke up and sank there in 1861. [1]

ENTERPRISE ■ Passenger and package freight propeller of 197 t. and 120 ft., launched in 1874 at Dresden, Ont.
Lake Huron: An exact number is not given, but reports say that many lives were lost in the accident which struck this vessel on November 20, 1883. She was sunk by a storm off Pte Aux Barques, but was later recovered. One report gives the location as "east end of Green Island." [3]

ENTERPRISE ■ Steam freighter of 915 t.
Lake Huron: North Point, which forms the top of Michigan's Thunder Bay, is surrounded by reefs and shallows, but ships transiting in and out of Alpena still have to pass dangerously close. Some, like the steamer ENTERPRISE,

don't quite make it. The vessel was fully loaded with a cargo of wheat when she struck bottom in heavy weather and foundered off the point on September 13, 1894. [3]

ENTERPRISE ■ Merchant schooner
Lake Huron: The "Lac du Hurones" (Lake of the Huron Indian nation) was unkind to vessels with the name ENTERPRISE. All four ships of that name that were lost on the Great Lakes met their end on Huron. This one foundered in Georgian Bay, at Barrie Island, in 1903. [1]

EQUATOR ■ Wooden steamer
Lake Michigan: In a heavy gale on November 18, 1869, this steam vessel was carrying a load of railroad ties when she piled into the shallows surrounding North Manitou Island. She sank up to her decks and was considered to be unsalvagable, but she was eventually refloated and pulled off in 1871. Her engine was recovered for use in the tug BISMARK, and, after extensive rebuilding her hull became the schooner-barge ELDORADO. [3]

EQUINOX ■ Wooden steamer, probably a 200 t., 100 ft. propeller
Lake Michigan: The position of this steamer at the time of her loss has not been reported, but it is said that 20 to 26 lives were lost when she foundered on September 10, 1875. [2]

ERIE ■ Wooden steamer of 147 t., probably a sidewheeler
Lake Erie: This ship was the first of at least seven ships with this name to be lost on the Lakes. On August 4, 1840, she was destroyed by a boiler explosion near Malden, Ontario. Loss of life is shown as either one or six. [2]

ERIE ■ Sidewheel passenger and package freight steamer of 497 t. and 176 ft., launched in 1837 at Detroit (one source says Erie, PA)
Lake Erie: One of the greatest losses of life ever recorded on the Lakes was the burning of the the passenger steamer ERIE. On August 9, 1841, the popular sidewheeler was cruising along the south shore of the lake with a full complement of passengers—mostly immigrants heading west to start a new life—when she was wracked by a teriffic explosion off Silver Creek, New York. In the conflagration that followed, between 100 and 175 passengers burned to death or drowned jumping overboard to avoid the fire. The vessel burned to the waterline and sank, and when the remains of her burned-out hull were raised years later, they reportedly contained over $200,000 in melted gold and silver specie. [5+]

ERIE ■ Wooden steamer
Lake Huron: This steamer was lost when she collided with an ice floe and sank off Port Huron, Michigan, in 1842. [1]

ERIE ■ Merchant schooner
Lake Michigan or *Erie:* A single, rather confusing report lists this schooner as lost in April of 1843 with seven of her crew. The report goes on to state that the accident occurred near Michigan City on Lake Erie, but research has failed to reveal such a place. The accident probably occurred on Lake Michigan. [1]

ERIE ■ Merchant schooner of 71 t. and 66 ft., launched in 1847 at Sandusky, OH
Lake Erie: This four-year-old schooner was reported lost in 1851, near Sandusky. [1]

ERIE ■ Scow of 23 t.
Position unreported: A listing of shipping disasters for 1902 shows this vessel as a total loss. [2]

ERIE ■ Dredge of 186 ft. launched in 1900
Lake Superior: A fire started by an errant spark from a welder's torch turned this dredge into an inferno. She was destroyed at Duluth on June 2, 1935. [2]

ERIE BELLE ■ Steam tug of 221 t. and 112 ft., launched in 1862 at Cleveland, OH as the tug HECTOR
Lake Huron: The large tug ERIE BELLE met a violent end at Kincardine (pronounced Kin-CAR-din), Ontario, in November of 1883. Four of her crew died, and the vessel was totally destroyed and sank following a boiler explosion. [2]

ERIE BELLE ■ Bulk freight schooner-barge of 128 ft. overall, launched in 1873 at Port Burwell, Ont.
Lake Ontario: An interesting footnote to this vessel's history is the fact that she was hidden from the Erie County, New York, sheriff's department for 16 years to prevent her confiscation. She returned to service in 1924. That same year she was lost when she sank in the Eastern Gap, in front of Toronto, Ontario. [2]

ERIE WAVE ■ Merchant schooner of 72 t. and 76 ft.
Lake Erie: The fatal accident that ended this schooner's career was her third major mishap. There are no details available on the first two, except that each cost one life. On October 10, 1889, she was thrown onto a sandy reef near the Houghton Sand Hills, west of Clear Creek, Ontario, and rolled over. Eight of her 10 crew were lost. One source gives the date as September 30. [3]

ERIN ■ Wooden package freight steamer of 651 t. and 174 ft., launched in 1881 at St Catharine's, Ont.
Lake St. Clair: This steamer was laden with a cargo of coal and was upbound when she collided with the big steel steamer JOHN B COWLE (qv) and quickly sank. She went down so quickly, in fact, that five of her crew were unable to escape in time, and were drowned. The accident occurred one mile south of Courtright, Ontario on May 31, 1906. The remains of the ERIN were later dynamited to clear the channel. [4]

ERINDALE ■ Sidewheel passenger and package freight steamer of 336 t. and 129 ft., launched at Sorel, Que. in 1866 as the large sidewheel tug METEOR
Lake Ontario: After 34 seasons working as a tug, the ERINDALE was in her sixth year as a passenger and freight carrier when she caught fire at her berth at Bowmanville, Ontario, and was destroyed. The accident occurred on August 9, 1906. [2]

ESCANABA ■ Wooden freighter, possibly the 1,160 t., 201 ft. vessel built at Gibraltar, MI, in 1881
Lake Huron: It was reported that this ship went missing at an unknown position on the lake in 1894. The report of totality of loss may be in error, as a vessel of the same name was stranded and recovered on the lake in the same year, and was rebuilt as the steamer BALTIMORE (qv). [2]

ESCORT ■ Tug
Lake Ontario: The tug ESCORT was lost in a passing error while overtaking the schooner-barge BENJ. HARRISON east of the mouth of the Niagara River. The tug cut under the bows of the unmaneuverable barge and was rammed on November 3, 1907. Three of the ESCORT's crew were lost in the incident. [1]

ESPERANCE ■ Schooner or sloop, built on Saginaw Bay in 1787
Lake Huron: This sail vessel was the first to be built in an area which was later to become one of the great shipbuilding centers of the Lakes. After more than 50 years of service, she sank in a freak Bay storm in 1842. [2]

ESPERANZA ■ Sloop of 11 t.
Lake Huron: This little one-sticker was lost to fire on July 30, 1907. She was in transit off Cape Croker, in the Georgian, when destroyed. [2]

ESPINDOLA ■ Bulk freight schooner of 54 t.
Lake Michigan: Coming into Chicago with a cargo of railroad ties on April 10, 1882, this little schooner was struck by a storm and quickly overwhelmed. She went to pieces one mile north of the waterfront, before she could be steered to shore. [1]

ESSEX ■ Sidewheel steamer of 141 t. and 81 ft., launched in 1860 at Windsor, Ont.
St. Clair River: The little sidewheeler ESSEX became a victim of fire in 1884. She was burned to the waterline at Sarnia, Ontario, and her hulk was abandoned. [2]

HATTIE A ESTELLE ■ Merchant schooner of 311 t. and 138 ft.
Lake Michigan: A westerly storm blew this schooner off course and onto a bar north of Manistee, Michigan. Three of the ship's crew died in the accident, which reportedly occurred on November 17, 1891 (one source says November, 1887). [3]

ETRURIA ■ Steel bulk freight steamer of 4,744 t. and 432 ft., launched in 1902 at W Bay City, MI
Lake Huron: The ETRURIA was a big ship for her time and was nearly new when she was lost on June 18, 1905. According to contemporary reports, she foundered off Presque Isle (Michigan) lighthouse, following a collision with another large steel freighter, the AMASA STONE. The two big ships were in a dense fog, and even though they could hear each other, neither knew the other's exact location until too late. [4]

HANNA ETTY ■ Merchant schooner of 60 t.
Lake Michigan: The schooner HANNA ETTY was forced ashore and demolished by a storm on August 26, 1880. She was carrying a load of wood and was just to the south of Sheboygan, Wisconsin, when the accident occurred. [1]

EUGENE ■ Schooner-scow of 40 t. and 64 ft., launched in 1865 at Fair Haven, MI
Lake Huron: On October 22, 1890, this little sail vessel, laden with oats and general merchandise, was struck by a vicious storm and blown on Port Austin Reef, on the northeast side of Saginaw Bay. She reportedly broke up in place. One source records a vessel of the same name as having been lost in the same spot in 1867. [3]

EUPHRATES ■ Steamer
Lake Erie: The steamer EUPHRATES was wrecked at the mouth of Sandusky Bay on July 3, 1862. Her machinery was later salvaged. [1]

EUREKA ■ Merchant sloop
Lake Huron: This single-mast vessel was reported a total loss in a mishap off Au Sable, Michigan, in 1869, perhaps in the great storm of that year. [1]

EUREKA ■ Sternwheel steamer of 214 t. and 240 ft. (including paddlewheel)
Lake Michigan: The paddle steamer EUREKA was one of the few sternwheelers to operate on the open lake. Caught by an equinoctial storm in October of 1873, she was thrown into shallow water and wrecked off Michigan City, Indiana. [1]

EUREKA ■ 152 t. vessel of unreported type
Lake Ontario: Pigeon Island, in the eastern end of the lake, is the final resting place of this vessel. She foundered just offshore on November 26, 1883. [1]

EUREKA ■ Bulk freight schooner-barge of 330 t. and 138 ft., launched in 1873 at Trenton, MI
Lake Superior: Loaded with a cargo of iron ore and part of a three-barge tow of the steamer PRENTICE, the small EUREKA was the victim of a teriffic northerly gale on October 20, 1886. The four vessels became disconnected and had to fend for themselves. While the other three eventually made it to port, the EUREKA was not seen

again until divers located her wreckage in 1983 off Vermilion Point, Michigan. All six of the barge's people were lost when she foundered. [5]

EUREKA ■ Lumber schooner-barge of 338 t. and 140 ft., launched in 1872 at Hamilton, Ont. as the propeller CANADA
Lake Huron: This schooner-barge was assailed by a fall storm on November 7, 1901 and sank somewhere between Tawas City and Port Huron. One crewman drowned before her tow steamer was able to put about and affect a rescue. After the surviving crewmen were taken off, the EUREKA was abandoned, but her below-decks cargo of lumber probably kept her partially afloat, as her wreckage washed up at Kincardine, Ontario, a few days later. [4]

EUROPE ■ Wooden propeller of 709 t. and 136 ft., launched at St. Catharine's, Ont., in 1870
Lake Erie: This vessel was almost totally destroyed by a fire which struck her in the Welland Canal in April of 1884. Her scorched hull was later rebuilt into a barge. [1]

EVA ■ Tug
Lake Huron: The tug EVA was reportedly burned at Lindsay Beach, in the North Channel north of Drummond Island, in 1881. [1]

EVELYN ■ 47 t. vessel of unreported type
Lake Huron: The eastern shore of Georgian Bay is spattered with as many as 30,000 islands and cays, and hundreds of inlets, fjords and points. Each bit of land emerging from the lake can grasp the unwary or unlucky, and thus dozens of vessels have been lost along this coast. The small carrier EVELYN was one of them, reportedly sunk at Byng Inlet on June 13, 1915. [1]

EVENING STAR ■ Steamer
Lake Huron: Not much is reported on the loss of this early Lake Huron steamer. It is said that she sank near Gravelly Shoal in upper Saginaw Bay, in 1841. [1]

EVENING STAR ■ Merchant schooner of 214 t. and 126 ft., launched in 1869 at Sheboygan, WI
Lake Michigan: This small schooner was destroyed after stranding near Chicago on May 18, 1894. [2]

EVENING STAR ■ Merchant schooner
Lake Huron: The second vessel of this name to be lost on the Lakes in 1894 was this schooner. She went down in Fisherman Bay, near Goderich, Ontario, on September 12. [1]

EVENING STAR ■ Fishing tug of 31 t. and 70 ft., launched in 1905 at Chicago as a passenger steamer
Lake Michigan: Commercial fishing craft routinely weather some of the worst the Lakes have to offer, so it must have been a powerful gale indeed that sent the EVENING STAR to the bottom off St. Joseph, Michigan, on November 13, 1911. [3]

JOHN EVENSON ■ Steamer of 33 t.
Lake Michigan: This tiny steam vessel was lost on the lake on June 5, 1895, costing the life of one crew member. [1]

EVERETT ■ Merchant schooner
Lake Erie: In 1857 the schooner EVERETT was lost when she went on a reef near Port Burwell, Ontario, and was wrecked. [1]

A E EVERETT ■ Steam propeller freighter, probably the A EVERETT of 1,058 t. and 212 ft., launched at Cleveland in 1880
Lake Huron: Caught in a field of grinding ice floes in April of 1895, the EVERETT was crushed and sank north of Pte Aux Barques, Michigan. [2]

MARY EVERETT ■ Merchant schooner of 126 ft. overall, launched in 1865 at Wallaceburg, Ont., as the schooner SEREPTA
Lake Ontario: The sail vessel MARY EVERETT was lost on November 18, 1903, when she sank at an unreported position on Lake Ontario. [1]

EVERGREEN ■ Merchant schooner of 68 t.
Lake Michigan: On April 16 of 1880, the schooner EVERGREEN was caught by a spring gale southeast of Milwaukee, was driven ashore, and broken up by the action of waves. [1]

EVERGREEN CITY ■ Merchant schooner
Lake Erie: Windblown Long Point juts 24 miles out into Lake Erie from the Canadian shore. Ships driven down the lake by the normal westerly storms have a good chance of finishing on the Point's southwestern coast. The EVERGREEN CITY was in just this situation on November 15, 1871, when she was thrown ashore on the point and wrecked. [2]

EXCELSIOR ■ Merchant schooner
Lake Erie: Several vessels have been wrecked on Claybanks Reef near Port Stanley, Ontario. This schooner was reported lost there in 1862. [1]

EXCELSIOR ■ Merchant schooner
Lake Huron: This schooner became a victim of fire on the busy Saginaw River in 1869. [1]

EXCELSIOR ■ Merchant bark of 374 t. and 156 ft., launched in 1865 at Buffalo
Lake Huron: The bark EXCELSIOR was reported to have foundered north of Thunder Bay Island, on the Michigan coast, on October 15, 1871. [1]

EXILE ■ Lumber schooner-barge of 387 t. and 152 ft., launched at Huron (Milan), OH, in 1867
Lake Michigan: After almost 50 years of service on the Lakes, the schooner-barge EXILE was destroyed when she broke her towline in a storm and went ashore near Sturgeon Bay, Wisconsin. The accident occurred on November 25, 1916. [4]

EXPERIMENT ■ Merchant schooner
Lake Michigan: The little schooner EXPERIMENT was lost about 1840 off St. Joseph, Michigan. Caught on the lake by a sudden storm, she broached to and capsized. The only survivors were a woman and her two children, who remained trapped in the air pocket under the upturned hull until their rescue the next day. [2]

EXPERIMENT ■ Barge of 400 t., launched in 1863 at Pigeon River, MI
Lake Huron: Details are lacking in the report of this vessel's loss off Lexington, Michigan, in 1869. [2]

EXPERIMENT ■ Merchant schooner of 49 t. and 65 ft., launched in 1854 at St. Joseph, MI
Lake Michigan: On September 12, 1902, this tiny schooner was wrecked by a storm in St. Joseph (Michigan) harbor, and was a total loss. [3]

EXPLORER ■ Merchant schooner
Lake Huron: Stokes Bay, on the Lake Huron side of the Saugeen (Bruce Peninsula), was the site of the loss of this sail vessel in 1883. Five crewmen perished. [1]

EXPRESS ■ Merchant schooner
Lake Michigan: The only available information on this accident states that she was lost following a collision with an unreported vessel in April, 1878. [1]

FAIR AMERICAN ■ Merchant schooner of 82 t. and 64 ft., launched at Oswego, NY, in 1804
Lake Ontario: This vessel had served as an armed schooner with Perry during the War of 1812. Converted to a merchant vessel after the war, she was wrecked off the Salmon River in October of 1818. [2]

N K FAIRBANKS ■ Wooden steamer of 980 t. and 205 ft.
Lake Huron: This large wooden vessel was lost in Potagannissing Bay, eight miles northeast of Detour light, in 1895. She was stranded in shallow water and before she could be released was destroyed by fire. The FAIRBANKS was reportedly heavily damaged by fire on Lake Erie ten years earlier. [3]

H S FAIRCHILD ■ Merchant schooner of 347 t. and 136 ft., launched in 1857 at Charlotte, NY
Lake Erie: Long Point is a dangerous place for ships, but often even avoiding it could be dangerous. The shipping lanes converge around the end of the point, and many vessels have collided there. The schooner FAIRCHILD was off the tip of the point in October of 1871, when she collided with the vessel HARVEST HOME, and quickly sank. [1]

FAIRPORT ■ Steamer (probably sidewheeler)
St. Clair River: Newspapers of the time reported the loss of this steamer off Algonac, Michigan. She caught fire and was totally destroyed on October 18, 1844. [1]

FALCON ■ Wooden bulk freight steamer of 865 t. and 174 ft., launched in 1881 at Marine City, MI as the steamer KATE BUTTIRONI
Lake Michigan: This freighter became a fall storm victim when she went ashore and was lost on South Fox Island, west of Charlexoix, Michigan. The vessel went to pieces in the November 7, 1909 blow, but her crew made it safely to the beach. [2]

ANNIE FALCONER ■ Package/bulk freight schooner of 175 t. and 114 ft., launched at Kingston, Ont., in 1867
Lake Ontario: After encountering a storm near Amherst Island (Ontario), this two-mast schooner swamped and sank off South Bay Point with a loss of one life. The loss occurred on November 12, 1904. [2]

FALLING WATERS ■ Wooden passenger steamer
Lake Erie: The steamer FALLING WATERS was reportedly destroyed by fire in 1875. [1]

FALMOUTH ■ Bulk freight schooner of 234 t.
Lake Erie: Laden with a cargo of wheat, this schooner was attempting to enter the harbor at Buffalo in a November 21, 1880 storm, when she struck a breakwater and sank. [1]

FAME ■ Merchant bark
Lake Huron: The bark FAME is reported to have foundered in 1854 off Goderich (pronounced God-rich), Ontario. [1]

FAME ■ Schooner
Lake Erie: The schooner FAME was struck by a lake squall, capsized and sank three miles off Monroe, Michigan, on August 31, 1858. [1]

FAME ■ Merchant bark of 428 t., reportedly of Swedish registry
Lake Huron: The little schooner FAME stranded and broke up on the beach near Presque Isle, Michigan, in

1882. According to one report, a lighthouse was built near the site from her timbers. Though both the Presque Isle lighthouse and the range lights predate this wreck by many years, this may refer to other structures associated with the light. [2]

FARMER'S DAUGHTER ■ Merchant schooner of 39 t. and 59 ft., launched in 1816 at Sandy Creek
Lake Ontario: Though the date is not reported, it is known that this early schooner went missing and was lost with all hands. [2]

JOSEPH P FARNAN ■ Bulk freight steam barge of 410 t. and 152 ft.
Lake Michigan: On July 20, 1889, this vessel was destroyed by fire offshore and sank near Benton Harbor, Michigan. One report says a steamer named JAMES P FARNUM was lost by stranding on the same date at the adjacent city of St. Joseph. [3]

RAY S FARR ■ Schooner
Lake Michigan: Local records show the loss of the schooner RAY S FARR on November 30, 1886. On that date the vessel was beset by a gale and foundered off South Manitou Island. [2]

C M FARRAR ■ Steam tug
Lake Huron: This towing vessel was destroyed by an explosion which occurred off Port Huron, Michigan, in 1873. [1]

FASHION ■ Steam freighter
Lake Huron: In 1856 this steamer was reported to have "sailed away," lost without a trace off Bayfield, Ontario. [1]

FAUSTIN ■ Propeller freighter of 256 t. and 123 ft., launched in 1882 at Port Dover, Ont. as the steamer E M FOSTER
Lake Erie: This steamer was reported by one source to have sunk off Bar Point, at the approach to the Detroit River, on September 4, 1912. Another reference says she was simply abandoned in the same year. [3]

FAVORITE ■ Gas screw packet of 11 t.
Lake Superior: The little packet FAVORITE was operating out of Marquette, Michigan, when she went off course and beached on the northeast shore of Presque Isle, a few miles northwest of town. She was broken up by waves following the accident, which occurred on May 29, 1947. [2]

FAWN ■ Wooden steamer of 50 ft.
Lake Michigan: This small lumber-laden steamer was transiting the Death's Door passage, at the mouth of Green Bay, when she foundered in a storm on August 8, 1888. [2]

T S FAXTON ▪ Wooden passenger steamer of 153 t. and 120 ft., launched in 1874 at Clayton, NY
St. Clair River: This little passenger steamer was destroyed by fire at Marine City, Michigan, on October 20, 1901. [2]

JOSEPH S FAY ▪ Wooden bulk freight steamer of 1,220 t. and 215 ft., launched in 1871 at Cleveland
Lake Huron: The heaving of a towbarge against its hawser during heavy weather creates almost unbelievable strain. When this tension becomes too much, the towline is usually the component that breaks. But, in the case of the JOSEPH S FAY, her schooner-barge, the D P RHODES, jerked the entire sternpost off the aft end of the steamer. By keeping her going full ahead, the FAY's crew was able to beach her at 40-mile Point, near Rogers City, Michigan, before she filled. The storm subsequently pounded the freighter to pieces on October 19, 1905. [5+]

FEARLESS ▪ 190 t. vessel of unreported type, probably the 190 t., 126 ft. schooner of this name built at Ferrysburg, MI
Lake Ontario: The FEARLESS was lost on November 14, 1875, when she stranded and broke up three miles east of the Toronto lighthouse. [2]

FEDORA ▪ Wooden bulk feight steamer of 1,848 t. and 282 ft., launched in 1889 at W Bay City, MI
Lake Superior: This big steamer was lost in a freakish fire which occurred on September 20, 1901. On that date she was set ablaze by an exploding lantern, and was totally destroyed. Her skipper had enough time to save her crew by beaching her near Michigan's Passage Island, but the ship burned to the waterline. [5+]

FERGUSON ▪ Barge or schooner-barge
Lake Huron: This unpowered vessel was lost in 1886 when she sank in Tawas Bay, just off East Tawas, Michigan. [1]

DAVID FERGUSON ▪ Lumber schooner of 223 t. and 130 ft., launched in 1853 at Port Huron, MI
The position of this vessel at the time of her loss is not recorded. In the fall of 1907, she was badly mauled and dismasted by a storm. The schooner made it to port, but the 54-year-old ship was considered too old and badly battered to be repaired. [2]

FERN ▪ Wrecking tug of 48 ft. and 65 t., launched in 1882 at Algonac, MI
Lake Superior: Salvage vessels were often at risk when going into shallow water to recover wrecked ships. The small salvage tug FERN was on station off Eagle River, Michigan, stripping the stranded propeller COLORADO (wrecked in 1898, qv), when a sudden storm blew up and drove her to the bottom. Five men died in the accident, which occurred on June 29, 1901. [4]

B F FERRIS ▪ Steam freighter of 168 t. and 124 ft., launched in 1870 at Sandusky, OH
Lake Huron: Victim of an 1891 fire, the steamer B F FERRIS was destroyed at Caseville, Michigan, on Saginaw Bay. She may have been recovered, as she was still listed in registry in 1892. [3]

E P FERRY ▪ Tug
Lake Superior: One of a number of serious tug fires that occurred at Duluth caused the demise of the E P FERRY at her winter mooring on January 28, 1900. [2]

MAJOR N H FERRY ▪ Merchant schooner of 171 t. and 117 ft., launched in 1867 at Ferrysburg, MI
Lake Ontario: On May 28, 1913, this elderly schooner was damaged beyond repair when she struck a pier in the Murray Canal, near the Bay of Quinte area, and sank. [2]

E FIE ▪ 35 t. vessel of unreported type
Lake Huron: The E FIE was a small vessel that went ashore in a westerly gale and was wrecked at Chantry Island, near Southampton, Ontario in 1877. [1]

A S FIELD ▪ Steam tug
Detroit River: All five crew were lost when the FIELD's boiler exploded and she was destroyed on the Fourth of July, 1860. [3]

D L FILER ▪ Bulk freight schooner-barge of 357 t. and 161 ft., built at Manistee, MI, in 1871
Lake Erie: Caught in the infamous "Black Friday Storm" of October 20-21, 1916, the FILER broke up near Bar Point while trying to make Detroit with her cargo of coal. Six of her seven crew members perished with her. [4]

MILLARD FILLMORE ▪ Merchant schooner of 139 ft., launched at Buffalo in 1856
Lake Huron: The schooner MILLARD FILLMORE sank off Rogers (now Rogers City), Michigan, in August of 1891. [3]

FINGLO ■ Propeller of 83 t. and 77 ft., launched at Port Stanley, Ont., in 1925
Lake Ontario: In June of 1941, this little prop was lost at Toronto when she caught fire and was destroyed in the harbor. [2]

GEORGE C FINNEY ■ Bulk freight schooner of 301 t. and 136 ft.
Lake Erie: Laden with a cargo of wheat, this schooner went down in a storm 16 miles off Port Maitland, Ontario, on October 22, 1891. Seven members of her crew perished when the vessel foundered. [2]

FIRIEN ■ Gas motor packet of 120 ft.
Lake Superior: On her trials after conversion from a steamer, this small passenger and package freight hauler caught fire off Knife River, near Duluth, and was destroyed on May 16, 1926. Her crew escaped the burning ship. [1]

WILLIAM FISH ■ Merchant brig
Lake Huron: The brig WILLIAM FISH was reported to have gone ashore and wrecked at the mouth of the Devil River, near Ossineke, Michigan, on the south coast of Thunder Bay, in 1869. [1]

JAMES FISK, Jr ■ Wooden bulk freight steamer of 1,096 t. and 216 ft., launched in 1870 at Buffalo
Lake St. Clair: St. Clair Flats is a low area of mud flats at the mouth of the St. Clair River, created by the deposition of millions of tons of silt from the big lakes to the north. It is laced with channels, and in 1906 the busy steamer channel was narrow and twisting (so convoluted. in fact, that sailors called it the "snake run"). In times of heavy traffic, vessels often had to lie to above or below the Flats and wait for other ships to pass through. A steamer suddenly at idle after days of travel was susceptible to fires caused by red-hot boilers. The wooden steamer JAMES FISK, Jr was in just such a situation on November 4, 1906. She caught fire, burned to the waterline and sank at the edge of the channel and north of the Flats. The wreck was removed in 1920. The channel has since been straightened and much of the flats area is now a wildlife refuge. [2]

EDWARD FISKE ■ Steam towing tug of 44 t. and 66 ft., launched in 1883 at Buffalo
Lake Superior: The tug EDWARD FISKE was the victim of a terrible fire which occurred at Duluth on September 27, 1893. Though almost completely destroyed and declared a total loss, the tug was rebuilt and returned to service. [3]

F FITCH ■ Package freight schooner of 13 t.
Lake Erie: This little sail vessel regularly plied the route between Michigan's "fruit belt" and Chicago. A storm on the lake drove the diminutive schooner ashore near Point Betsie, on August 28, 1898. The FITCH and her cargo of fruit were a total loss. [2]

E FITZGERALD ■ Bulk freight schooner of 298 t.
Lake Erie: On November 14, 1883, the schooner E FITZGERALD went down with all eight hands in a storm that was raging off Long Point. [1]

EDMUND FITZGERALD ■ Steel bulk freight steamer of 25,891 t. and 729 ft., launched in 1958 at River Rouge, MI
Lake Superior: Probably the most well-known of all Great Lakes wrecks, the "Big Fitz" was also the longest and most capacious vessel ever lost on the Lakes. On November 10, 1975 she was carrying a full load of taconite iron pellets, when the giant steel ship was literally torn apart, twisted in half by a mighty gale which assaulted her with 90 mph winds and 25-foot seas. Not one member of her crew of 29 survived to describe how a big, modern ship could succumb to the same forces that destroyed a thousand lesser vessels before her. The wreck is in deep water off Whitefish Point, and has been visited by remote control a number of times. An excellent model of the site is on display at the Great Lakes Historical Society Museum at Vermilion, Ohio. [5+]

FLANDE ■ Propeller freighter
Lake Huron: Victim of a collision with an unknown vessel, this steamer sank in 1897. [1]

FLEETWIND ■ Merchant schooner
Lake Ontario: This romantically-named schooner is simply reported as having been lost in a white squall. [1]

FLEETWING ■ Wooden ferry of 60 t.
Lake Erie: This little ferry vessel is reported to have burned and sank in the harbor at Conneaut, OH, in 1920. [1]

FLEETWING or **FLEET WING** ■ Bulk freight schooner of 350 t. and 136 ft., launched in 1867 at Manitowoc, WI
Lake Michigan: Laden with a cargo of barrel staves, the storm-wracked schooner FLEETWING failed to negotiate the narrow channel known as Death's Door, near the tip of Wisconsin's Door Peninsula. She went ashore in September of 1885, and was broken up by the action of waves. None of her crew were lost. [2]

KATE FLETCHER or **FLECHER** ■ Steam tug, possibly the 10 t. vessel built at Bay City, MI in 1868
Lake Huron: This tug was reported burned on the Saginaw River at Saginaw, Michigan, in 1877. [1]

FLIGHT ■ Merchant schooner
Lake Huron: Bois Blanc Island, a few minute's sail from Mackinac Island in the Straits of Mackinac, snared this schooner in 1865. She went aground there and was abandoned. [1]

FLINT ■ Vessel information unavailable
Lake Superior: A rather cryptic report shows this vessel as having burned and sunk on the lake in 1910. Perhaps this actually refers to the OSCAR T FLINT accident, below. [1]

FLINT & PERE MARQUETTE #1 ■ Wooden passenger and package freight steamer of 770 t. and 181 ft., launched at Detroit in 1882
Lake Michigan: A vessel with a ten foot draft and bucking ten foot waves, needs at least 25 feet of water to avoid kissing the bottom in a storm. This break-bulk carrier discovered a shallow spot in the harbor at Ludington, Michigan, on December 31, 1884. Filling with water and with her fires out, the F & P M #1 was thrown in the shallows. One crew member was drowned in the rescue effort. The ship herself, being almost new, was recovered at great expense to her owners. [2]

OSCAR T FLINT ■ Wooden steam freighter of 823 t. and 218 ft., launched in 1899 at St. Clair, MI
Lake Huron: The propeller OSCAR T FLINT was just underway out of Alpena with a load of limestone when she caught fire and was destroyed. She was run into shoal water near the mouth of Thunder Bay in a successful attempt to save her crew, but the ship's remains later slipped off into deeper water. The accident took place on November 25, 1909. [5]

SAM FLINT ■ Bulk freight schooner-barge of 499 t. and 168 ft., launched in 1868 at Toledo
Lake Huron: This schooner-barge was lost from tow in a heavy storm which she encountered on October 27, 1916. She was torn up by the big waves and sank in Mississagi Strait, at the northwest end of Manitoulin Island. [2]

FLORA ■ Sidewheel passenger and package freight steamer of 562 t. and 164 ft., launched in 1875 at Milwaukee
Lake Huron: Some vessels refuse to be scrapped. Even in recent times, several big vessels have sunk in the Atlantic while being towed to European shipyards for scrapping. The 37-year-old FLORA had made it to the breaker's yard in Chicago harbor, but caught fire on November 14, 1912, and was destroyed before dismantlement could begin. There were no casualties. [3]

FLORA ■ Fishing tug of 45 ft.
Lake Michigan: No date is given for the loss of this commercial fishing boat off the picturesque village of Northport, Michigan. She reportedly swamped in heavy weather and sank. [1]

FLORENCE ■ Propeller of 113 t. and 91 ft., launched in 1885 at Levis, Quebec
Lake Ontario: In November of 1933, this ship foundered near Timber Island, east of Picton, Ontario. [1]

FLORENCE or **FLORENCE B** ■ Passenger ferry of 30 t. and 31 ft., probably launched at Detroit in 1892
Detroit River: On March 16, 1933, this little ferryboat sank at the Michigan Central Railroad dock and was lost. [2]

FLORIDA ■ Package freight schooner
Lake Erie: Laden with a cargo of barrelled flour and pork, the schooner FLORIDA went ashore and was wrecked somewhere in the northeast part of the lake. She was lost in November of 1842. [1]

FLORIDA ■ Merchant schooner of 352 t.
Lake Erie: On August 21, 1882 this schooner sank near Mohawk Island, 12 miles east-southeast of Port Maitland, Ontario. [2]

FLORIDA ■ Bulk freight schooner of 299 t.
Lake Superior: One crewman perished when this schooner was forced ashore and wrecked at the mouth of Whetstone Brook, near Marquette, Michigan. She had been sheltering from a gale just off shore, but big seas caused her anchors to slip. She was carrying a cargo of coal at the time of the accident—November 17, 1886. [3]

FLORIDA ■ Steamer
Lake Michigan: The steamer FLORIDA is reported to have sunk off Leland, MI, in 1894. Other details are lacking. [1]

FLORIDA ■ Bulk freight propeller of 2,103 t. and 271 ft., launched in 1889 at Buffalo
Lake Huron: The steamer FLORIDA was one of the larger boats on the lakes at the time of her demise on May 20, 1897. She was unlucky enough to collide with an even bigger ship, the 281-foot steamer GEORGE W ROBY (qv), and sink off False Presque Isle, Michigan. [4]

FLORIDA ■ Wooden passenger steamer of 213 ft., launched at Wyandotte in 1883 as the steamer CITY OF MACKINAW (one source says she was built in 1892)
Detroit River: Slowly succumbing to old age, the steamer FLORIDA was tied to a layup dock awaiting her fate when she was struck by fire and burned on the Rouge River at Detroit. The June 27, 1932, blaze ended her

career as a commercial carrier, but her remains were renovated and used as a yacht club clubhouse in Chicago for a few years. [2]

GEORGE A FLOSS ▪ Fishing tug of 24 t. and 58 ft., launched at Buffalo in 1903. The position of the fishing craft GEORGE A FLOSS is not reported. The small vessel and the nine people aboard disappeared on April 7, 1909. [2]

ROSWELL P or **R P FLOWERS** ▪ Steam freighter, probably the 1,837 t., 273 ft. steamer built at W Bay City, MI, in 1887
Lake Michigan: This steamer was reported as wrecked on a reef near Waugoschance Point, at the western end of the Straits of Mackinac, in 1892. [2]

FLYING CLOUD ▪ Package freight schooner
Lake Michigan: Seven crew members were lost in the wreck of the schooner FLYING CLOUD, two miles northeast of Gary, Indiana. The sailing ship stranded offshore in November of 1857 and before her crew could be rescued, the seven froze to death. [1]

FLYING CLOUD ▪ Bulk freight schooner of 148 t.
Lake Ontario: This schooner went ashore and was wrecked at Red Creek, near Oswego, New York, on October 18, 1870. None of her crew were lost in the accident, but the vessel and her cargo of lumber were destroyed. [1]

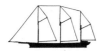

FLYING CLOUD ▪ Bulk freight schooner of 255 t. and 133 ft., launched at Clayton, New York, in 1854
Lake Michigan: Carrying a cargo of coal near the end of her 38th season, this schooner was caught by an October, 1892, storm. She was thrown on the rocks near Glen Arbor, Michigan, in the shadow of the Sleeping Bear, then broke up in place. [3]

F A FOLGER ▪ 26 t. vessel of unreported type
St. Clair River: This vessel was reportedly destroyed by a gale on the river in September of 1898. [1]

HENRY FOLGER ▪ Bulk freight schooner of 326 t.
Lake Ontario: On December 1, 1882, the schooner HENRY FOLGER, laden with coal, piled on the Salmon Point Reef, near Wellington, Ontario. She quickly broke up, carrying eight crewmen to their deaths. [1]

JAMES W FOLLETTE ▪ Wooden bulk freight steamer of 1,201 t. and 212 ft., launched in 1881 at Gibraltar, MI as the steamer JESSE H FARWELL
Lake Ontario: The freighter JAMES W FOLLETTE was muscling through a big spring storm on May 16, 1923, when she made a fateful mistake. The vessel slewed sideways into the troughs of the waves, where the heavy seas

were able to hit her flank with piledriver blows. In a short time the rudder was torn off the wooden ship. Water began rushing through the hole in her counter, and she was in trouble. Despite a tremendous effort by her crew to save her, the FOLLETTE filled and sank in the middle of the lake. [2]

FONTANA ▪ Bulk freight schooner-barge of 1,163 t. and 240 ft., launched in 1888 at St. Clair, MI
St. Clair River: This big schooner-barge was loaded with iron ore and in tow of the steamer KALIYUGA (qv) when she was lost on August 3, 1900. She struck the giant, 2,600-ton schooner-barge SANTIAGO (qv) and quickly sank, coming to rest with her fantail above water in one of the busiest shipping lanes in the world. She was dynamited several times to reduce her wreckage. [3]

COMMODORE FOOTE ▪ Merchant schooner of 254 t. and 112 ft., launched in 1862 at Oswego, NY
Lake Huron: The two-master COMMODORE FOOTE was lost in 1867 in midlake when she collided with an unnamed vessel and sank. [2]

CHRISTIAN FORBES ▪ Tug
Lake Huron: The tug CHRISTIAN FORBES became a victim of fire in the year 1895 when she caught fire and burned at Bay City, Michigan, near the mouth of the Saginaw River. [1]

KITTIE M FORBES ▪ Wooden bulk freight steamer of 986 t. and 209 ft., launched in 1883 at Bay City, MI
Lake St. Clair: May 21, 1902 was the date of the demise of this small propeller. She caught fire on the St. Clair Flats, burned to the waterline and sank in shallow water. Her machinery was salvaged and placed in the steamer WILLIAM B MORELEY. The FORBES was also heavily damaged in a drydock fire, in 1894. [3]

AUGUSTA FORD ▪ Lumber schooner of 184 t.
Lake Erie: While inbound with a cargo of lumber this small schooner was beset by wind-driven ice and was wrecked near the entrance to the harbor at Fairport, Ohio. The date was April 18, 1890. [2]

E M FORD ▪ Steel bulk freight steamer of 7000 t. and 428 ft., launched in 1898 at Cleveland as the steamer PRESQUE ISLE
Lake Michigan: The aged cement carrier E M FORD gave the phrase "sank like a brick" a whole new meaning. The 81-year-old ship was the victim of a gale which sank her at her dock in the harbor at Milwaukee on Christmas Eve,

1979. What makes her accident unique is that salvage divers had to chip thousands of tons of hardened cement out of her holds before they could raise the ship. The FORD was still operating in 1991. [1]

J C FORD ■ Wooden lumber steamer of 432 t. and 172 ft., launched in 1889 at Grand Haven, MI
Lake Huron: This steamer was lost on November 26, 1924. On that date, she caught fire and was destroyed near Little Trout Island, a few miles northeast of Detour, MI. [4]

FORELLE ■ Steel tug of 46 t. and 54 ft.
Lake Michigan: Five lives were lost when this tug sank seven miles southeast of Kenosha, Wisconsin, in 1923. [1]

FOREST ■ Merchant schooner
Lake Huron: The schooner FOREST was reported to have foundered off Kincardine, Ontario, in 1857. [1]

FOREST CITY ■ Wooden steam freighter
Lake Erie: This steamer was reported as totally destroyed by fire at Port Stanley, Ontario, on April 5, 1858 (also listed as 1856). No lives were lost in the incident. [2]

FOREST CITY ■ Wooden bulk freight steamer of 1,236 t. and 214 ft., launched in 1870 at Cleveland as a schooner-barge
Lake Huron: On June 5, 1904, this large steamer was reported wrecked at Bear's Rump, an island near Tobermory, Ontario. She struck the island hard in a dense fog and could not be released. [3]

FOREST KING ■ Merchant schooner
Lake Huron: Georgian Bay, big enough to be called the "sixth Great Lake," was the site of the loss of this schooner in 1869. Sometime in that year she was overtaken by a particularly violent storm and sank. [1]

FOREST QUEEN ■ 137 t. vessel of unreported type
Lake Ontario: The FOREST QUEEN was a victim of a stranding which occurred on the Bay of Quinte on November 26, 1886. She went ashore on Indian Point and was wrecked. [1]

FORESTER ■ Merchant schooner
Lake Huron or Michigan: The schooner FORESTER was reported to have gone down in the Straits of Mackinac in 1846. [1]

FORESTER ■ Merchant schooner of 350 t.
Lake Erie: This schooner was lost on September 18, 1872. She sank 19 miles off Port Burwell, Ontario. [1]

FORESTER ■ Steam freighter
Lake Huron: A single brief report states that this ship was lost off Port Sanilac, on the east side of Michigan's Thumb, in 1898. [1]

INGEBORG M FORREST ■ Merchant schooner of 174 t. and 122 ft., launched in 1871 at Fort Howard, WI
Lake Michigan: The small two-sticker INGEBORG FORREST went down in a spring gale near the entrance to the harbor at Pentwater, Michigan. She was lost on April 16, 1897. [3]

DANIEL G FORT ■ Merchant schooner of 340 t. and 137 ft., launched in 1869 at Tonawanda, NY
Lake Erie: Oswego, New York, is the site of the loss of this vessel on November 27, 1894. On that date, the FORT had approached the harbor in a storm and had been picked up by a local tug. But the cargoless schooner thrashed on the end of her towline until it broke, and she went on the rocks and sank near the harbor entrance. Her wreckage rubbed shoulders with that of the schooner BALTIC (qv), thrown ashore on the same spot three days earlier. [3]

FORTUNE ■ Merchant schooner
Lake Huron: The sail vessel FORTUNE was said to have "gone missing" on the lake in 1864. [1]

FORTUNE ■ Steam propeller of 233 t. and 110 ft., launched in 1876 at Fort Franks, Ont. One report says she was a schooner.
Lake Erie: On October 23, 1884, this vessel was wrecked when driven onto Long Point by a violent Lake Erie storm. [2]

FORWARD ■ Merchant schooner of 36 t.
Lake Michigan: The tiny schooner FORWARD foundered on Kewaunee Bay, Wisconsin, on May 30, 1910. No lives were lost in the incident. [1]

FORWARDER ■ Merchant schooner
Lake Huron: This sailing ship was lost well offshore from Kincardine, Ontario in 1864. [1]

FOSTER ■ Schooner-barge of 841 t., launched at Oshkosh, WI, in 1884
All that is reported about this vessel is that she was lost on October 20, 1905. [1]

A M FOSTER ■ Wooden propeller
Lake Huron: The steamer A M FOSTER foundered after a collision with an unrecorded vessel off Pte Aux Barques, Michigan, in 1888. See also schooner E M FOSTER and ANNIE M FOSTER. [3]

ANNA FOSTER ■ Merchant schooner
Lake Huron: Little is known of the loss of this schooner, wrecked in Georgian Bay in 1882. [1]

ANNIE M FOSTER ■ 77 t. vessel of unreported type
Lake Ontario: August 31, 1889, was the date of the loss of this vessel 20 miles northeast of Charlotte, New York (near Rochester), by collision with the vessel SIESTA. [1]

CHARLES FOSTER ■ Bulk freight schooner-barge of 997 t. and 227 ft., launched at Milan, OH, in 1877
Lake Erie: In tow of the steamer IRON DUKE, this barge was overtaken by a gale on December 9, 1900. She filled and sank off Presque Isle, Pennsylvania, with the loss of eight of her crew. [2]

D FOSTER ■ 48 t. vessel of unreported type
Lake Erie: On September 10, 1887, at Port Burwell, Ont., this carrier was destroyed by fire following a collision. [1]

D M FOSTER ■ Lumber schooner of 251 t., launched at Port Burwell, Ont., in 1863
Lake Ontario: While trying to enter the harbor at Oswego, New York in a storm, the lumber-laden FOSTER was lost from the tow of a harbor tug, struck the breakwater head-on and sank. The ship's crew were all rescued in the December 1, 1881, accident. [2]

DAVID FOSTER ■ Bulk freight barge of 447 t.
Lake Erie: The barge DAVID FOSTER was lost on November 9, 1936, when she foundered 18 miles from Presque Isle, on the Pennsylvania coast. [1]

E M FOSTER ■ Merchant schooner
Lake Huron: Pte Aux Barques claimed another victim in this schooner, which was driven ashore there in a storm which occurred on October 8, 1888. Note the similarities among the reports for the vessels A M FOSTER, ANNIE M FOSTER, and E M FOSTER. These may refer to one, two or three separate wrecks. [1]

I N FOSTER ■ Bulk freight schooner of 143 ft., launched in 1872 at Port Huron, MI
Lake Michigan: The schooner I N FOSTER foundered in the shallows surrounding Washington Island, off the tip of Wisconsin's Door Peninsula, on August 7, 1887. There may have been some loss of life in the accident, though the ship herself was later recovered and rebuilt as a steamer (scrapped 1928). [2]

SAMUEL H FOSTER ■ Lumber schooner-barge of 673 t. and 189 ft., launched in 1873 at Cleveland
Lake Superior: An early season gale-blizzard seized this vessel and hurled her ashore at Misery Bay, near the root of the "Rabbit's ear" (Keweenaw Peninsula). Her crew

reached safety following the October 6, 1906 grounding, but the old barge was torn to pieces by the storm. [2]

WILLIAM FOSTER ■ Merchant schooner
Lake Michigan: Little detail is recorded on the loss of this vessel to a white squall. [1]

FOSTORIA ■ Merchant schooner of 237 t. and 130 ft., launched in 1865 at Black River, OH
Lake Huron: Ice still floating on the lake on May 10, 1901, was the cause of the schooner FOSTORIA's demise. She struck hard and stove in her bows, sinking quickly near Port Huron, with the loss of two lives. She had also been seriously damaged in a grounding near Detour, Michigan, in 1874. [4]

FRANCE ■ Merchant bark
Lake Huron: Not much is known about this vessel except that she foundered near Goderich, Ontario, in 1854. [1]

FRANKLIN ■ Merchant schooner
Lake Erie: The early schooner FRANKLIN was lost one mile off the mouth of the Grand River at Fairport, Ohio. She foundered with all hands on October 20, 1820. [3]

BEN FRANKLIN ■ Merchant schooner
Lake Erie: This schooner was said to have gone aground and broken up in a November gale in 1842. She was reported ashore near the mouth of the Grand River, at the site of Fairport, Ohio. [1]

BEN FRANKLIN ■ Wooden propeller of 231 t. and 135 ft., launched in 1842 at Algonac, MI
Lake Huron: This steamer was an early victim of Thunder Bay Island, near Alpena, Michigan. The shallows around this island have been the final resting ground of at least 20 ships, and they claimed the FRANKLIN on October 8, 1850. [3]

LADY FRANKLIN ■ Merchant schooner of 302 t. and 137 ft., launched in 1861 at Chicago
Lake Huron: Railroad ties were much in demand in the burgeoning Midwest in the 1890s, and the schooner LADY FRANKLIN was carrying a load of them when she beached at Hammond Bay, near Cheboygan, MI, and broke up. The vessel was lost on September 30, 1895. [3]

W C FRANZ ■ Steel bulk freight steamer of 3,429 t. and 346 ft., launched in 1901 at Wyandotte, MI, as the steamer URANUS
Lake Huron: Four lives were lost when this big freight boat collided with the package freighter EDWARD E LOOMIS and sank. The accident occurred eight miles east of Thunder Bay Island on November 21, 1934. One source places her further to the southeast. [5+]

FRED & WILL ▪ Wooden steam tug
Lake Superior: This tug suffered a boiler explosion and sank off Sand Island, in the Apostles group, on October 14, 1878. Her crew of three was able to swim ashore following the incident. [1]

FREE STATE ▪ Propeller freighter of 959 t.
Lake Michigan: This steamer was reportedly carrying a valuable cargo when she struck the shallows near Gray's Reef, 2 miles west of Waugoschance Point, and was wrecked. The FREE STATE was lost in Sept. of 1871. [2]

FREE TRADE ▪ Tug of 66 ft.
Lake Superior: The tug FREE TRADE was reported as having been destroyed by fire at Duluth on November 1, 1890. One source gives the date as July 5. [2]

FREE TRADER ▪ Sidewheel passenger and freight steamer of 136 ft., launched in 1848 at Montreal
Lake Erie: The FREE TRADER became another victim of fire in the harbor at Port Stanley, Ont., in October of 1857. [1]

FREE TRADER ▪ Merchant schooner launched in 1829 at St. Ignace, MI
Lake Michigan: The graceful sail vessel FREE TRADER was reported ashore and destroyed in Manitou Passage, in 1835. Two sailors were lost in the accident. [1]

FREEDOM ▪ Merchant schooner
Lake Huron: Three lives were lost when this schooner capsized from unknown causes, 15 miles north of Fort Gratiot, at the lower end of the lake. [1]

B FREEMAN ▪ Merchant schooner
Lake Ontario: August 13, 1888, was the day of the loss of this sail vessel, which foundered off Oswego, NY. [1]

MARTHA FREEME ▪ Probably a schooner
Lake Erie: The FREEME piled on a reef near Port Burwell, Ontario, and was demolished in 1848. [1]

FREMONT ▪ Sidewheel passenger and package freight steamer of 95 t. and 114 ft., launched in 1851 at Sandusky, OH
Lake Erie: In 1858 this little steamer was lost when she was destroyed by fire at Plaster Bed, near Sandusky, Ohio. [1]

THOMAS FRIANT ▪ Wooden passenger and package freight steamer of 81 t. and 96 ft., launched in 1884 at Grand Haven, MI
Lake Superior: The crew of the Duluth-based steamer THOMAS FRIANT was earning some off-season money by taking visitors on a fishing trip on January 6, 1924. This is often a dangerous time of year due to heavy, shifting ice, and the FRIANT encountered moving floes near

Knife River, Minnesota. Her hull was cut and she sank, but, fortunately, with no loss of life. The old vessel had been nearly destroyed by fire at the Soo in 1908. [3]

FRONTENAC ▪ Trading and exploration brig of 40 t.
Lake Ontario: This ship was one of the first European-style ships to be lost anywhere on the Great Lakes. In 1679, she was dashed ashore at Cape Enrage, near the Niagara River mouth, and destroyed by the pounding of waves. She was probably carrying a cargo of furs and trade goods at the time. [1]

FRONTENAC ▪ Wooden sidewheel passenger and package freight steamer of 700 t. and 170 ft., launched at Ernestown (Kingston), Ont. in 1816
Lake Erie: The steamer FRONTENAC was the first steam-powered vessel on the Great Lakes. In September of 1827, she was set ablaze by an arsonist and destroyed near Niagara. Several lives were reportedly lost in the incident. [4]

FRONTENAC ▪ Merchant schooner
Lake Erie: In 1865 it was reported that this schooner went ashore near Port Burwell, Ontario, and was wrecked. [1]

FRONTENAC ▪ Propeller freighter of 111 t. and 89 ft., launched in 1901 at Garden Island, Ont.
Lake Ontario: The demise of the propeller FRONTENAC came on December 5, 1929, when she foundered near Simcoe Island, Ontario. [2]

FRONTENAC ▪ Steel bulk freight motor ship of 604 ft., launched in 1923 at River Rouge, MI
Lake Superior: At least five lost vessels have carried the illustrious name of FRONTENAC: a brig, a schooner, a sidewheeler, a propeller and this motor vessel, which was lost on November 22, 1979. On that date she struck a reef near Pellet Island, Minnesota, and was so heavily damaged that she was declared a total loss. She was eventually pulled off and towed away for scrapping. [2]

FRONTIER ▪ Sidewheel passenger and package freight steamer of 700 t. and 185 ft., launched in 1876 at Mill Point, Ont. as the steamer EMPRESS OF INDIA
Detroit River: This sidewheeler sank at Chatham, Ontario, in 1916, and was towed to Detroit for reconditioning. Shortly after being returned to service in 1918, she foundered off Detroit. The vessel was stripped and cut up for scrap. [2]

FRONTIER ■ Steam freighter of 120 ft., launched in 1902 at Buffalo
Lake Huron: The steamer FRONTIER foundered in the St. Marys River on July 19, 1937. The vessel was salvaged and returned to service, but two of her crew were lost beyond recovery. [2]

FRONTIER CITY ■ Merchant brig of 267 t. and 178 ft., built on the hull of the schooner CANTON at Oswego, NY, and launched in 1860
Lake Huron: The brig FRONTIER CITY was one of the many sail vessels driven onto the Canadian coast of Lake Huron by frequent westerly gales that occur in spring and fall. She was cast ashore near Kincardine and wrecked in the autumn of 1871. [3]

GEORGE M or **GEORGE S FROST** ■ Steam freighter
Lake Erie: A harbor fire claimed this steamer in September of 1879. She was destroyed at Erie, Pennsylvania, but with no loss of life. [2]

WALTER L FROST ■ Wooden steam package freighter of 1,322 t. and 235 ft., launched in 1883 at Wyandotte, MI
Lake Michigan: The areas surrounding the Manitou, Fox and Beaver Islands is very often fogbound in the spring and fall of the year, when the water temperature may be drastically different than that of the islands. Carrying a cargo of general merchandise, this freighter was off South Manitou and travelling in high winds and a dense fog when she piled on a rocky reef on November 4, 1903. Her crew members all made it safely to shore, but the vessel was too badly damaged to be recovered, and was left in place to break up. [5+]

EVRA FULLER ■ Lumber schooner of 229 t. and 132 ft., launched in 1873 at Fort Howard, WI, as the schooner LENA JOHNSON
Lake Michigan: While downbound with a cargo of lumber, the small schooner EVRA FULLER went on a reef near Racine, Wisconsin, and was destroyed. The accident happened in October of 1873. [3]

FULTON ■ Schooner-barge of 256 t., launched in 1854
Lake Erie: The schooner-barge FULTON was lost off Toledo, when she foundered on July 7, 1908. Luckily, all of her crew were rescued before she went under. [1]

E A FULTON ■ Merchant schooner of 287 t. and 137 ft. launched in 1863 at Toledo as the schooner A BOODY
Lake Huron or *Michigan:* The schooner FULTON was reported to have foundered in the Straits of Mackinac in 1859. No other details are available, except that she was probably recovered. [1]

ROBERT FULTON ■ Merchant steamer of 308 t., launched at Cleveland in 1835
Lake Erie: Some of the information on this early steam vessel's loss is disputed. By best reckoning, she was lost on October 25, 1844, when she went on the rocks 14 miles west of Dunkirk, New York, and went to pieces with the loss of four lives. 1842 is also given as the year, and one report has her lost on Lake Huron. [4]

FUR TRADER ■ Schooner of 40 t.
Lake Superior: One of the earlier commercial vessels lost on the Lakes was this small ship, owned by John Jacob Astor. In 1812 she was reported to have wrecked near Sault Ste. Marie. [2]

G L 37 ■ Scow of 242 t.
Lake Superior: This scow was reported to have been lost near the outlet the lake, just off Sault Ste. Marie, Michigan, on October 9, 1913. [1]

MOSES GAGE ■ Bulk freight schooner of 224 t. and 128 ft., launched in 1886 at Geneva, OH
Lake Michigan: On May 18, 1894, the schooner MOSES GAGE was inbound with a load of lumber when she stranded off Michigan City, Indiana. She later broke up in place. [3]

GALATEA ■ Bulk freight schooner-barge of 610 t. and 176 ft., launched in 1882 at W Bay City, MI
Lake Superior: The big schooner-barge GALATEA was in tow of the steamer L L BARTH and without cargo when disaster overtook her on October 20, 1905, in the form of one of the most powerful storms recorded to that time. The bucking ship broke her towline and was thrust stern-foremost on the beach near Grand Marais, Michigan. Her crew were able to climb ashore, with the help of the Lifesaving Service, but the barge was unsalvageable. See also NIRVANA. [4]

GALATEA ■ Merchant schooner
Lake Huron: A collision was the cause of the demise of this sail vessel off Harbor Beach, Michigan, in 1924, though further details are unavailable. [1]

CHARLES GALE ■ 23 t. vessel of unreported type
Lake Erie: A report states that this vessel was lost to fire off North Duck Island on August 27, 1913. [1]

S E GALE ■ Merchant brig
Lake Huron: This two-master was reported to have sunk following a collision with the steamer TELEGRAPH, in 1850. The name of this vessel may be a pun rather than the name of a person. [1]

STEVEN F or **S F GALE** ▪ Sail vessel of 266 t. (reported as bark, brig or schooner)
Lake Erie: The STEVEN F GALE was in transit with a cargo of mixed merchandise when she was lost off Fairport, Ohio, on November 28, 1866 (also given as 1876). These reports may represent two separate vessels. [3]

GALENA ▪ Wooden passenger and package freight propeller of 709 t. and 190 ft., launched in 1857 at Cleveland
Lake Huron: The loss of the GALENA apparently cost a significant number of lives, as she was known to be a passenger-carrier and was reported to have gone ashore and broken up with the loss of all hands on September 25, 1872. The tragedy occurred on the Thunder Bay side of North Point, when the ship was outbound from Alpena, Michigan, to Chicago. [3]

GALLATIN ▪ Merchant schooner of 422 t. and 138 ft., launched at Oswego, NY, in 1863
Lake Erie: This small two-mast schooner was lost in 1882, when she struck bottom and foundered off Point Pelee, which juts 12 miles straight out from the Ontario shore. [1]

GALLINIPPER ▪ Merchant schooner of 142 t., launched before 1847
Lake Michigan: A white squall claimed this sailing ship in 1851, but the exact location has not been reported. [2]

GAME ▪ Merchant schooner
Lake Huron: The schooner GAME was destroyed near Collingwood, Ontario, in an 1871 Georgian Bay storm. [1]

GARDEN CITY ▪ Sidewheel steamer of 450 t.
Lake Huron: In May of 1854, this steamboat was lost when she went on Martin Reef, in the Straits of Mackinac west of Detour, and was wrecked. Her machinery was eventually recovered. [2]

GARDEN CITY ▪ Wooden bulk freight steamer of 352 t. and 145 ft., launched in 1873 at Ogdensburg, NY
Lake Huron: This freighter became a victim of fire on October 10, 1902, when she burst into flame and was destroyed in Saginaw Bay, four miles from Bay City, Michigan. [3]

F B GARDNER ▪ Bulk freight schooner-barge of 402 t. and 177 ft., launched as a brig in 1855 at Sheboygan, WI, lengthened 60 ft. in 1877
Lake Huron: On September 15, 1904, the old schooner-barge F B GARDNER was in tow of the steamer D LEU-

TY (qv), when she caught fire. She burned to the water's edge off Port Sanilac, Michigan, and sank. [5]

NELLIE GARDNER ▪ Bulk freight schooner-barge of 565 t. and 178 ft., launched in 1873 at Marine City, MI
Lake Huron: The coal-laden schooner-barge NELLIE GARDNER was demolished by an October, 1883, storm. Thrashing about in big waves, she broke her towline and grounded on a reef near Scarecrow Island, in the southeast corner of Thunder Bay, Michigan, and went to pieces. Fortunately, her crew was rescued. [2]

J A GARFIELD ▪ Bulk freight schooner of 72 t., launched in 1880 at Sandusky, OH
Lake Erie: This tiny schooner was burdened with a cargo of stone when she foundered south of Pelee Island on October 29, 1887. [2]

GARGANTUA ▪ Schooner-barge or barge, perhaps the 381 t., 130 ft. vessel built in Marine City in 1919 on the hull of the uncompleted SEAFARER
Lake Huron: This barge was reported lost from her tow steamer, burned and sunk in Wingfield Basin, near Cabot Head light. The year is given as 1952. [2]

GARGANTUA ▪ Steam propeller of 1,490 t. and 240 ft., launched in 1882 at St. Clair, MI as the steamer D C WHITNEY (qv)
The propeller GARGANTUA is just reported as wrecked in 1912. Her hull was recovered and rebuilt as a barge. [1]

GARIBALDI ▪ Merchant schooner of 120 t., launched in 1854 at Chatham, Ont.
Lake Huron: Four lives were lost when the schooner GARIBALDI foundered in a Georgian Bay storm, in 1865. [2]

GARIBALDI ▪ 209 t. vessel, probably a schooner
Lake Ontario: This vessel was reported to have stranded and broken up at Weller's Beach, Ontario, on November 17, 1880. [1]

GARIBALDI ▪ Propeller steamer
Lake Huron: The steamer GARIBALDI was lost when she was struck by a Fall, 1880, gale at the lumber dock at the small timber town of Springport, Michigan (just south of Harrisville). She was driven ashore from the dock and broken up on the beach by big combers. [1]

GARIBALDI ▪ 164 t. vessel of unreported type
Lake Huron: This GARIBALDI was lost at Port Elgin, Ontario, when she was stranded five miles south of town on October 3, 1887. [1]

GARY D ▪ Tug of 18 t.
Lake Huron: Strawberry Island, in the North Channel, was the location of the fire that destroyed this small tug on August 5, 1958. She burned near the Strawberry Island lighthouse. [2]

GORDON GAUTHIER ■ Steam tug of 26 t., launched in 1885
Lake Superior: Port Arthur, part of what is now Thunder Bay, Ontario, was the site of the loss of the tug GORDON GAUTHIER. She was destroyed by fire on October 8, 1911. [2]

THOMAS GAWN ■ Freight barge of 550 t. and 176 ft., launched as a 3-mast schooner at Lorain, OH, in 1872
Detroit River: In one of the simplest types of shipping losses there is, the barge GAWN sprang a leak and sank at River Rouge, Michigan, on April 26, 1926. She had previously been sunk at Duluth (1903). [4]

JAMES GAYLEY ■ Steel bulk freight steamer of 4,777 t. and 416 ft., launched in 1902 at Cleveland
Lake Superior: On August 7, 1912, the big steel steamer JAMES GAYLEY became a victim of one of the least violent and most deadly weather conditions that seamen know. Laden with coal and groping her way in a dense fog, she was about 35 miles east of Manitou Island when the big freighter RENSSELAER loomed out of the mist and rammed her. A well-drilled crew had to abandon ship quickly, because the GAYLEY went to the bottom in a mere 16 minutes. [4]

GAZELLE ■ Paddle steamer (probably sidewheeler) of 422 t., launched at Newport (Marine City), MI, in 1856
Lake Superior: At least a dozen vessels have been lost at Eagle Harbor, Michigan, at the most northerly point on the Keweenaw. This paddle steamer was reportedly driven ashore and wrecked there on September 8, 1856 or '58. Her wreckage was removed in 1864. [2]

A GEBHART or **GEBHARDT** ■ Bulk freight schooner-barge of 354 t. and 145 ft., launched in 1869 at Marine City, MI
Lake Huron: The schooner-barge A GEBHART was loading a cargo of cedar posts at Drummond Island, Michigan, when she was discovered to be on fire. The June 4, 1909, blaze consumed the vessel quickly. [2]

GENERAL ■ Tug of 132 t. and 97 ft., launched in 1899 at W Bay City, MI
Lake Huron: This big tug was involved in a collision with the freighter ATHABASCA (qv) on November 30, 1910. Both vessels foundered following the crash, which occurred off Lonely Island, near the mouth of Georgian Bay. The GENERAL may have been recovered, as there is a report of a large tug of this name having burned on the lower St. Marys River in 1920 (also see below). [3]

GENERAL ■ Tug
Lake Huron: This tug is reported to have burned and sunk near Frying Pan Island, off Detour, Michigan, in April of 1930 (or 1920). May be same as tug above. [1]

GENESEE CHIEF ■ Merchant schooner of 275 t. and 142 ft., launched in 1873 at Cleveland
Lake Huron: The Straits of Mackinac are littered with the remains of ships lost there during more than 300 years of commerce. The schooner GENESEE CHIEF foundered in the South Channel, off Cheboygan, Michigan, in 1891. She may have been recovered. [2]

GENEVA ■ Schooner-scow
Lake Michigan: The schooner-scow GENEVA was wrecked one mile off the east shore of North Manitou Island, in 1859. The remains of her load of bricks reportedly marks her final resting place. [2]

GENEVA ■ Bulk freight steam barge of 741 t., launched in 1873 (possibly at Detroit)
Lake Superior: The new steamer GENEVA was downbound with a cargo of wheat on October 23, 1873 when she encountered a fall gale off Caribou Island. The stress of the heaving ship caused her propshaft to break, and the flailing propeller chewed a large hole in her stern. There was nothing left to do but abandon the ship to her fate, and she sank 15 miles off Caribou. [1]

CITY OF GENOA ■ Wooden bulk freight steamer of 2,109 t. and 301 ft., launched in 1892 at W Bay City, MI
Lake Huron: At the lower end of the lake, just off Sarnia, Ontario, this large steamer collided with an even bigger steel freighter, the W H GILBERT (qv). She sank quickly with her cargo of grain. The accident took place August 26, 1911. Coincidentally, the two vessels were built in rival Bay City shipyards and launched in the same year. The CITY OF GENOA was raised, but was not repairable. [2]

GEORGE ■ Bulk freight schooner of 790 t. and 203 ft., launched in 1873 at Manitowoc, WI
Lake Superior: Upbound with a cargo of coal, this big schooner was assaulted by a quick-rising gale on October 25, 1893. Her masts quickly blew out, rendering the GEORGE almost completely helpless, whereupon she was blown ashore at Pictured Rocks, near Munising, Michigan, and dismembered on the rocks. None of her crew were lost. [4]

GEORGE E ■ Tug of 28 t. and 66 ft., launched in 1892 at Indian River, MI
Lake Huron: The Les Cheneaux Islands, on the northern edge of the Straits of Mackinac, offer protection to the

towns of Cedarville and Hessel, Michigan. In earlier times, these were prosperous fishing and lumbering ports, and thus had their own local tugs to help in handling ships. The tug GEORGE E was based out of Cedarville when she caught fire and burned on October 30, 1909. [3]

F A GEORGER ■ Bulk freight schooner-barge of 825 t. and 200 ft., launched in 1874 at Tonawanda, NY
Lake Erie: This must have been a staunch vessel indeed, for she plied the Lakes for 66 seasons and then met her end only at the hands of one of the most powerful storms ever recorded, the "Armistice Day Storm" of November 11, 1940. In tow of the steamer JOHN B LYON (qv), she broke up and sank north of Girard, Pennsylvania. She had been abandoned for poor condition in 1926, but had later been reconditioned and put back into service. [3]

GEORGIAN ■ Steam freighter of 466 t. and 131 ft., launched in 1864 at Pt. McNicoll, Ont.
Lake Huron: The hazards of early season navigation are demonstrated by the loss of this wooden steamer, lost in May of 1884 when she was holed by wind-driven ice and sank in Georgian Bay. [2]

HOWARD S GERKEN ■ Steel sandsucker of 1,320 t. and 241 ft., launched as the steamer T P PHELEN in 1918 at Trois Rivieres, Que.
Lake Erie: On August 21, 1926, the sandsucker HOWARD S GERKEN had just finished loading a cargo of sand when she was struck by a gale. She foundered off Erie, Pennsylvania, with the loss of three lives. [3]

GERMAN FE or **GERMANIA** ■ Bulk freight steamer
Lake Michigan: This iron ore-laden steamer was reported ashore and broken up off Glencoe, Illinois, on November 25, 1905. [2]

GERMANIA ■ Sidewheel passenger and package freight steamer of 73 t. and 90 ft., launched in 1869 at Sandusky, OH
Lake Erie: The small sidewheeler GERMANIA was thrust ashore and destroyed on Cedar Point (near Sandusky, OH-in 1881. [1]

GERMANIC ■ Wooden passenger and package freight steamer of 1,014 t. and 196 ft., launched in Collingwood, Ont., in 1899
Lake Huron: The GERMANIC ended her career where she had begun it 18 years before, at Collingwood, Ontario. She was destroyed by fire at her winter berth on March 30, 1917, as she was preparing for the upcoming season. [3]

GERMANIC ■ Wooden propeller, reportedly of 959 nt. and 216 ft. (these dimensions fit the GERMANIC built at W Bay City in 1888, but that ship was burned on Georgian Bay in 1909—see RELIEVER)
St. Clair River: The propeller GERMANIC was lost to fire when she stranded and burned on Stag Island, near Corunna, Ontario, on November 4, 1914. [2]

GERTRUDE ■ Merchant schooner
Lake Michigan: The schooner GERTRUDE was reported as sunk by ice four miles west of Mackinaw City, Michigan, in 1868. [1]

GERTRUDE ■ Merchant schooner of 81 ft., launched in 1856 at Two Rivers, WI
Lake Michigan: This schooner was blown ashore and lost at Otter Creek, near Michigan's Sleeping Bear Point, on September 26, 1880. She was riding at anchor with a load of firewood and pitching heavily when her chains broke and she was thrown on the beach. One crewman drowned swimming to shore. [2]

GETWORK ■ Steam freighter
Lake Huron: The steamer GETWORK was lost in a fire which occurred at Collingwood, Ontario, in Georgian Bay, in 1917. [1]

GIANT ■ Tug, possibly the 10 t., 36 ft. vessel built at Buffalo in 1883
Lake Huron: During the heyday of the neighboring cities of Saginaw and Bay City, Michigan, as lumbering and shipbuilding centers, more than two-hundred fifty tugs operated on the Saginaw River. The congested waterway saw the loss of dozens of vessels, including the tug GIANT, which sank in the river in 1894. [1]

R J GIBB ■ Merchant schooner of 176 t. and 121 ft.
Lake Erie: The schooner R J GIBB was lost when she sank while riding at anchor off Bar Point, Ontario, in 1893. [1]

GIBRALTAR ■ 270 t. vessel of unrecorded type
Lake Huron: The GIBRALTAR was lost when she stranded off White Rock, Michigan (near Port Hope), on October 3, 1888, and presumably broke up. [1]

GIBSON ■ Merchant schooner of 327 t.
Lake Erie: On October 31, 1875, this schooner stranded in shoal water and was pounded to pieces at Port Burwell, Ontario. [1]

J C GIDLEY ■ Tug of 39 t.
Lake Huron: The J C GIDLEY was a tug that was lost to fire in the North Channel, at Sand Bay (near Meldrum Bay), on June 14, 1909. [2]

W H GILBERT ■ Steel steam freighter of 2,820 t. and 328 ft., launched in 1892 at W Bay City, MI
Lake Huron: Foggy weather in Thunder Bay, Michigan, was the primary cause of the loss of this big steamer on May 22, 1914. She was feeling her way through the mist when she collided with the 500-footer CALDERA off Thunder Bay Island and sank quickly. The wreck was located by divers in 1983. [5+]

W H GILCHER ■ Steel bulk freight steamer of 2,392 t. and 301 ft., launched in 1891 at Cleveland
Lake Michigan: The steamer W H GILCHER was less than two years old and in her prime when she was lost in a tremendous gale that drove her down on Oct. 1, 1892. The big steamer was loaded with coal at the time of her loss, the details of which are uncertain since all 21 of the GILCHER's crew went to the bottom with her. Some sources speculate that she collided with the big schooner OSTRICH (qv), lost in the same area on the same day. [5+]

EDWARD GILLEN ■ Tug of 56 t. and 68 ft., launched in 1891 at Buffalo
Lake Superior: The water in far northern Duluth-Superior harbor is icy almost all year long, and in spring warm spells, the temperature contrast between air and water causes thick clouds of fog to settle on the harbor. The tug GILLEN was groping her way through one of these on May 18, 1903, when her path crossed that of the steamer MAUNALOA and she was rammed. She quickly sank with the loss of one of her crew. [4]

EDWARD E GILLEN ■ Tug of 64 ft., launched in 1907
Lake Michigan: Modern tugs are periodically tested as to their rated performance and safety. The EDWARD E GILLEN was undergoing strain tests off Milwaukee on June 4, 1981, when she inexplicably capsized and sank. [2]

GILLEY ■ 81 t. vessel of unreported type
Lake Huron: On September 18, 1937, this vessel was reported to have stranded, a total loss, twelve miles up the beach from Goderich, Ontario. [1]

J C GILMORE ■ Merchant schooner
Lake Michigan: Pilot Island, in Green Bay, was the reported location for the loss of this schooner on November 2, 1892. She ran aground in a storm, but she may have been recovered. [2]

GILPHIE ■ Steam propeller of 35 t. and 75 ft., launched in 1884 at Lockeport, Nova Scotia as the steamer JOE
Lake Huron: The small steamer GILPHIE was destroyed by fire on July 22, 1909. She reportedly went aground at Whippoorwill Shore, near Lion's Head, Ontario, caught fire and was destroyed. [3]

GLAD TIDING ■ Vessel information unavailable
Lake Erie: October 26, 1870, was the date of the loss of this vessel. She reportedly sprang a leak and sank near Long Point. [1]

GLAD TIDINGS ■ Merchant schooner of 82 t. and 79 ft., launched in 1883 at Manitowoc, WI
Detroit River: Four seamen were drowned when the little schooner GLAD TIDINGS sank on the river on July 29, 1894. She was carrying a cargo of stone at the time of her demise. [2]

GLAD TIDINGS ■ Merchant schooner of 183 t. and 113 ft., launched in 1866 at Detroit
Lake Huron: Ice or storm damage was the cause of the loss of this schooner when she sank on the Hammond Bay side of 9-mile Point, near Cheboygan, Michigan. The ship went down on April 19, 1898. She was also reported sunk, but recovered on Green Bay in 1894. [4]

GLADIATOR ■ Merchant schooner of 141 t.
Lake Michigan: The exact position of this schooner at the time of her loss is either unknown or unreported. It is said that she sank with the loss of one life on July 4, 1890. She was laden with lumber at the time. [1]

GLADSTONE ■ Merchant schooner
Lake Huron: The schooner GLADSTONE was reportedly lost near Port Huron, in 1883. [1]

GLADSTONE ■ Wooden bulk freight steamer of 2,112 t. and 283 ft., launched at Cleveland in 1888
St. Clair River: In the winter of 1918, this steamer was tied up at her dock in the Pine River at St. Clair, Michigan, when the river developed an ice jam. The buildup of ice crushed the hull of the GLADSTONE and she sank, a total loss. Her remains were removed in 1923 to become a breakwater at Sarnia. [2]

GLENFINLAS ■ Wooden propeller freighter of 425 t. and 145 ft., launched at Port Dalhousie, Ont., in 1873 as the steamer CALABRIA
Lake Ontario: The steamer GLENFINLAS was close to her home port when she caught fire off St. Catharine's, Ont., and was destroyed. The loss occurred on Aug. 17, 1883. [2]

GLENIFFER ■ Bulk freight schooner-barge of 328 t. and 140 ft., launched in 1873 at Port Robinson, Ont.
St. Clair River: The schooner-barge GLENIFFER was lost to a collision on the river June 27, 1902. Two lives were lost when she met with the steamer ADMIRAL, went out of control, grounded and broke up in a seven m.p.h. current. [4]

GLENLYON ■ Steel bulk freight steamer of 2,818 t. and 328 ft., launched in 1893 at Bay City, Michigan, as the

steamer WILLIAM H GRATWICK
Lake Superior: On November 1, 1924, the big steel freighter GLENLYON was downbound with a cargo of wheat when she was beset by heavy winds and monster waves. She was making for shelter in Siskiwit Bay, Isle Royale, when she struck a shoal just off Menagerie Island. With big holes already torn in her bottom, the skipper scuttled her on the shoal (now called "Glenlyon Shoal"), in an effort to stabilize the ship and keep the waves from pounding her to pieces. He and his crew then abandoned her to await better weather. His efforts were in vain, though, as the ship broke up before she could be salvaged. [5+]

GLENORA ■ Package freight schooner
Lake Ontario: The schooner GLENORA was near Kingston, Ont., on Nov. 19, 1887, when she sank (probably from a storm), 2.5 miles west of Amherst Island. She was reported to have a quantity of gold and silver coinage aboard. [1]

GLENORCHY ■ Steel bulk freight steamer of 2,465 t. and 326 ft. overall, launched in 1902 at W Bay City, MI, as the steamer A E STEWART
Lake Huron: A bare two days before the destruction of her fleetmate GLENLYON (qv), this big freighter was wrecked off Harbor Beach, MI. On Oct. 29, 1924, she was gliding through a dense fog, when she collided with the steamer LEONARD B MILLER, and sank. No lives were lost. [4]

GLENSTRIVEN ■ Steel bulk freight steamer of 2,171 t. and 275 ft., launched in 1889 at Buffalo as the steamer AMERICA
Lake Huron: Another victim of fog was the steamer GLENSTRIVEN. She struck a reef near Cove Island, in Georgian Bay, on November 16, 1923, and was wrecked. The hulk was salvaged for scrap the next year. [3]

JOHN M GLIDDEN ■ Wooden bulk freight steamer of 1,323 t. and 222 ft., launched in 1879 at Cleveland, originally hog braced, later braces were removed
St. Clair River: The busy river, through which all traffic from Lakes Michigan, Huron and Superior had to pass to reach Erie and Ontario, was the site of many collisions. On October 9, 1903, this steamer was struck by the towed barge MAGNA and sank off Harsen's Island, where the river meets Lake St. Clair. The hulk was removed from the waterway in 1904. [4]

GLOBE ■ Merchant bark, probably the vessel of this name built at Buffalo in 1844
Lake Erie: In 1854 this sailing ship reportedly went on a reef near Port Burwell, Ontario, and was lost. [1]

GLOBE ■ Wooden propeller of 590 t. and 140 ft., probably built in Canada
Lake Superior: The propeller GLOBE was sunk on the Big Lake in 1860. [1]

GLOBE ■ Wooden propeller of 1,233 t. and 251 ft., launched in 1847 at Trenton, MI as the sidewheeler ODDFELLOW
Lake Erie: On November 6, 1860, the steamer GLOBE was docked at Buffalo and unloading when she was destroyed by an explosion. [1]

GLOBE ■ Wooden steamer
Lake Huron: This steamer was lost on Saginaw Bay when she was destroyed by fire in 1863. [3]

GLOBE ■ Oil screw
Lake Huron: This motor vessel foundered on Saginaw Bay on September 9, 1954, but details of both the vessel and her loss are lacking. [2]

GOGEBIC ■ Steam freighter, one source says she displaced 1,213 t., but she is probably the 1,681 t., 227 ft. boat of this name launched at W Bay City, MI, in 1887
Lake Superior: On June 13, 1919, this large steamer was reported to have stranded and broken up on Dead Man's Rock. The vessel was probably recovered following the accident. [2]

GOLD HUNTER ■ Merchant schooner of 271 t. built at Milwaukee in 1852
Lake Michigan: The schooner GOLD HUNTER was carrying a cargo of chinaware when she came ashore and broke up on the west side of Sleeping Bear Point, Michigan. The loss was recorded as occurring on November 11 or 12, 1852. She may have been recovered. [2]
Lake Huron: A vessel of the same name and tonnage was wrecked by a gale and sank ten miles north of Sturgeon Point, near Alcona, MI, on Nov. 6, 1879. She was bound L'Anse to Cleveland with her holds full of iron ore. [3]

GOLD HUNTER ■ 219 t. vessel of unreported type
Lake Huron: This vessel was stranded and lost at Cabot Head, on the Bay side of the Saugeen (Bruce Peninsula), on November 15, 1871. [1]

GOLDEN FISHER ■ 37 t. vessel of unreported type
Lake Huron: On June 5, 1943, the GOLDEN FISHER was destroyed by fire two miles offshore from Cape Hurd, near Tobermory, Ontario. [2]

GOLDEN FLEECE ■ Merchant schooner of 452 t. and 161 ft.
Lake Erie: The schooner GOLDEN FLEECE was driven onto the beach by a gale and broke up seven miles west of Dunkirk, NY, on Oct. 14, 1890 (one source says 1893). [3]

GOLDEN RULE ■ Merchant schooner
Lake Superior: Two lives were lost when this sailing vessel capsized on September 24, 1884. The ship herself may

have been recovered, as a schooner of this name operated on the lake until her abandonment in 1908. [2]

GOLDEN WEST ■ Merchant schooner
Lake Huron: An 1884 loss, the schooner GOLDEN WEST reportedly foundered near Snake Island, in Georgian Bay.[1]

L GOLDISH ■ Diesel passenger and freight packet of 40 t. and 65 ft. launched at Larsmont, MN, in 1913
Lake Michigan: This tiny motor vessel was lost to fire at Waukegan, Illinois in about 1930. She might have been little remembered except that her longtime skipper braved many a Lakes' gale in the little boat to rescue other seamen in distress. In all, 29 sailors owed their lives to the L GOLDISH and her crew. [3]

GOLIAH (not "Goliath") ■ Package and bulk freight propeller
Lake Huron: An early steamer disaster on Lake Huron was the loss of the freighter GOLIAH, along with 18 of those aboard her. On September 13, 1848, she was in transit off Lexington, Michigan, when sparks touched her cargo of general freight, bricks and 200 kegs of blasting powder. The ship was literally blown to pieces in the resulting blast. [4]

GOLSPIE ■ Wooden package freight steamer of 980 t. and 180 ft., launched in 1882 at W Bay City, MI, as the steamer OSCEOLA
Lake Superior: The steamer GOLSPIE ran ashore in Brule Bay (Ontario) at an unfortunate time of year. She stranded due to navigational error on December 4, 1906, with little damage. However, before she could be released the vessel was destroyed by a storm which tore her to pieces on the 7th. [5]

GOOD INTENT ■ Merchant schooner
Lake Erie: An early loss occurring near Dunkirk, New York, was this schooner, which was wrecked two miles northeast of the harbor in 1825. [2]

N P GOODELL ■ Merchant schooner of 224 t. and 119 ft., launched at Cleveland in 1864
Lake Huron: November 27, 1891, was the date of a heavy gale which overwhelmed the schooner N P GOODELL near "Yankee Reef," 35 miles northeast of Pointe Aux Barques, Michigan. [2]

R F GOODMAN ■ Steam tug of 23 t. and 51 ft., launched in 1882 at Buffalo
Lake Superior: Another of dozens of wooden steam tugs that fell victim to fires was the R F GOODMAN, which burned to the waterline when three miles off Lester Park, on August 16, 1898. [3]

WILLIAM GOODNOW ■ Wooden tug
Lake Huron: This tug was sunk as the result of a collision off Lexington, Michigan, on the east shore of the "thumb," in 1869. [1]

FRANK H GOODYEAR ■ Steel bulk freight steamer of 4,815 t. and 436 ft., launched in 1902 at Lorain, OH
Lake Huron: The exact number of lives reported lost when the GOODYEAR went down varies from 16 to 23. On May 23, 1910, the big steamer—one of the largest in operation at that time—was groping her way through dense fog above Pointe Aux Barques, Michigan. Suddenly the steamer JAMES B WOOD slid out of the gloom and the two vessels collided. The heavily damaged WOOD staggered backwards from the blow, while the FRANK H GOODYEAR sank in less than four minutes. She reportedly had a luxury rail car installed on deck for the personal use of her owner. [5+]

D A GORDON ■ Wooden bulk freight steamer of 148 t. and 115 ft., launched in 1902 at Wallaceburg, ON
Lake St. Clair: On April 20, 1909, this freighter caught fire and burned to almost total destruction offshore near Wallaceburg, Ontario. Her hull was subsequently rebuilt as a barge. [3]

R J GORDON ■ Steam freighter of 187 t. and 103 ft., launched in 1881 at Marine City, MI
Lake Michigan: No lives were lost, but the small steamer R J GORDON was completely destroyed in a fire which occurred at Chicago on September 28, 1899. [2]

GOSHAWK ■ Lumber schooner-barge of 550 t. and 180 ft., launched in 1866 at Cleveland
Lake Huron: This old ship's hull could not take the battering given it by a summer storm which occurred on June 16, 1920. The pounding of the waves outside and shifting of her lumber cargo caused her seams to open and she sank four miles off Tawas Point. [4]

GOTHAM ■ Steel fish tug of 65 ft., built in 1940 at Saugatuck, MI
Lake Michigan: This commercial fisher, thought to be nearly unsinkable because of her steel construction, went down in a gale with all five hands while returning to port. She sank on December 11, 1943, north of Saugatuck. The GOTHAM was raised in 1944 and rebuilt as a harbor tug. [1]

GOUDREAU ■ Steel bulk freight steamer of 2,298 t. and 301 ft., launched in 1889 at Cleveland as the steamer PONTIAC
Lake Huron: The steel steamer GOUDREAU was destroyed by a storm that assailed her on November 23, 1917. She was holding her own against the mountainous waves and gale winds until her rudder was ripped off by a huge sea. Helpless, she was thrown onto the south shore of Lyal Island, in Stokes Bay (Ontario) and wrecked. She later slipped off into deep water. [5]

E F GOULD ■ Steam freighter or perhaps the 262 t., 157 ft. schooner of this name built at Carrollton, MI, in 1875.
Lake Huron: This steamer was reported to have wrecked near Oscoda, Michigan, in 1898. [1]

JAY GOULD ■ Wooden bulk freight steamer of 997 t. and 214 ft., launched at Buffalo in 1869
Lake Erie: The old wooden freighter JAY GOULD was pressed into service in spite of her aged condition by the needs of a wartime economy. Laden with a cargo of coal and towing a barge, she fought the heavy seas of a June 17, 1918 storm until her seams opened and she sank in Pelee Passage. This ship was reportedly equipped with the first marine compound engine ever used on the Lakes. [5+]

GRACE ■ Steam yacht of 7 t., working as a lumber camp supply vessel
Lake Superior: This small craft was lost on October 13, 1882, when she ran ashore near Whitefish Point, with her load of camp supplies. Two of those aboard died in the accident, but the vessel itself was eventually recovered. [1]

GRACE AMELIA ■ Merchant schooner of 45 t. and 60 ft., launched in 1836 at Sandusky, OH The schooner GRACE AMELIA was simply reported as wrecked in 1851. [1]

GRACE M ■ Schooner or tug of 12 t. and 45 ft.
Lake Erie: Two lives were lost when this vessel was rammed and sunk off the Middle Islands in 1915. The second vessel involved in the collision was identified as either the steamer VIGILANT or the Canadian Coast Guard Cutter WIGILAND. [2]

GEORGE A GRAHAM ■ Steel bulk freight steamer of 2,410 t. and 308 ft., launched as the steamer MARINA at Chicago in 1892
Lake Huron: On October 17, 1917, this big ship was driven ashore by a gale and wrecked on the rugged west coast of Manitoulin Island, near fjord-like South Bay. She was abandoned in place. [5+]

JENNIE GRAHAM ■ Merchant bark of 362 t. and 146 ft., launched at St. Catharine's, Ont. in 1871
Lake Huron: Three of this bark's ten crew drowned when she was blown down by a squall and capsized, 40 miles north of Port Huron, Michigan. She was recovered after the 1872 accident. [3]
Lake Huron: In April of 1880, the JENNIE GRAHAM was near Great Duck Island, off the western side of Manitoulin, when she stranded on a submerged boulder, slipped off and sank. The place where she struck is still known as "Jennie Graham Rock". [2]

NISBET GRAMMAR ■ Steel bulk freight steamer of 1,267 t. and 233 ft., launched in 1923 at Birkenhead, Eng.
Lake Ontario: One of the largest vessels to be sunk in Lake Ontario was the steamer NISBET GRAMMAR. Bound for Montreal with a cargo of grain on May 31, 1926, she encountered a dense fog. Off Thirty-mile Point, New York, she collided with the steel steamer DALWARNIC, a ship of about the same size. She sank quickly in deep water, but the DALWARNIC stood by to rescue her crew. [4]

G J GRAMMER ■ Steel passenger and freight steamer of 4,471 t. and 418 ft., launched in 1902 at W Superior, WI
Lake Huron: The big steamer G J GRAMMER was involved in two major accidents in a little over a year. On July 14, 1912, she collided with the steamer NORTHERN QUEEN in a dense fog, near Corsich Shoals. Though heavily damaged, she was recovered and repaired, only to be sunk again in the harbor at Lorain, Ohio, on November 11, 1913, during the Big Storm that claimed such a huge toll of ships and men. Again she was recovered and repaired, and served many more years. [5]

GRANADA ■ Merchant schooner
Lake Huron or *Michigan:* The schooner GRANADA was reported as struck down by an 1875 storm in the Straits of Mackinac. [1]

GRANADA ■ Lumber schooner of 270 t.
Lake Michigan: The lumber-laden schooner GRANADA was wrecked, and two of her crewmen were lost, when she was driven ashore by a gale and broke up near Port Sherman, two miles north of Muskegon, Michigan. The ship was destroyed on October 17, 1880. [2]

GRANADA ■ Bulk freight schooner
Lake Superior: Laden with a heavy cargo of iron ore, this schooner was discovered to be leaking and was run aground in Murray Bay, on Grand Island, Michigan, to prevent her sinking. She eventually slipped off into deeper water. The accident occurred in about 1886. [1]

CITY OF GRAND RAPIDS ▪ Wooden passenger and package freight steamer of 335 t. and 122 ft., launched in 1879 at Grand Haven, MI
Lake Huron: On October 29, 1907, this small ship was discovered to be afire at her dock at Tobermory, Ontario. She drifted free and sank in the arm of the harbor known as "Big Tub". An inquiry into the loss revealed that the fire was deliberately set. [5]

GRAND TRAVERSE ▪ Bulk freight steam barge of 869 t. and 181 ft., launched in 1879 at Marine City, MI, as the steamer MORELY
Lake Erie: The steam barge GRAND TRAVERSE was lost on October 20, 1896, as the result of a collision. While in transit near Colchester Shoals, she struck the propeller LIVINGSTON and sank. [2]

GRAND TURK ▪ Lumber schooner of 130 ft., launched in 1854 at Irving, NY
Lake Michigan: This well-travelled schooner had plied the Atlantic for two years before returning to the Lakes, where she met her end on November 17, 1869. On that date she broke her anchor chains and drifted ashore near Leland, Michigan, with the loss of one crewman. She was carrying a cargo of wood at the time. [1]

WILLIAM GRANDY ▪ Schooner-barge of 464 t. and 165 ft., launched in 1867 at Cleveland
Lake Erie: No lives were lost when this schooner-barge was destroyed by fire at Cleveland on August 28, 1906. [2]

GRANGER ▪ Merchant schooner of 366 t. and 155 ft., launched in 1874 at Two Rivers, WI
Lake Michigan: Seul Choix Point, jutting out from the belly of Michigan's Upper Peninsula, snagged this passing schooner in 1896. The GRANGER was reported as a total wreck after she grounded there. [2]

GRANITE STATE ▪ Passenger and package freight propeller, launched in Cleveland in 1852
Lake Michigan: This early propeller was lost on a reef south of Sturgeon Bay, Wisconsin. She stranded there on October 3, 1881 in a storm and quickly went to pieces. [2]

JOHN GRANT ▪ Merchant schooner of 93 t., launched in 1832 on the Genessee R., NY
Lake Erie: In May of 1845, this little schooner capsized and sank off Erie, Pennsylvania. [1]

KITTY GRANT ▪ Bulk freight schooner of 75 t., launched in 1853 at Milwaukee
Lake Michigan: Four lives were lost when the tiny schooner KITTY GRANT lost her battle with a storm and foundered on October 8, 1884. She went down 20 miles from Little Sable Point, on the Michigan shore. [1]

GENERAL GRANT ▪ Sidewheel passenger and freight steamer of 153 t. and 110 t., launched in 1864 at Sandusky, OH
Detroit River: The steamer GENERAL GRANT was burnt to a shell at Detroit in 1876. Her hull was preserved for possible rebuilding until 1880, then abandoned. [1]

U S GRANT ▪ Merchant schooner of 81 t.
Lake Michigan: This small schooner sank off Grand Haven, Michigan's, north pier on November 11, 1881. [1]

GRANTHAM ▪ Bulk freight schooner-barge of 146 ft. over-all, launched in 1873 at Port Robinson, Ont.
Lake Ontario: On July 6, 1913, the schooner-barge GRANTHAM sank off the Salmon River, in the Bay of Quinte area, while assisting in lightering the stranded steamer A E AMES. [2]

WILLIAM T GRAVES ▪ Bulk freight barge of 1,075 t.
Lake Superior or *Lake Michigan:* This schooner-barge was loaded with corn when driven ashore in a gale on October 31, 1885. Her position at the time is in some doubt, as one reporter says she went on Manitou Island, off the northern Lake Superior shore, while the other states she grounded on North Manitou Island, Lake Michigan. [2]

GREAT WESTERN ▪ Wooden sidewheel passenger and freight steamer of 780 t., launched at Huron, OH, in 1838
Lake Huron: No lives were lost when this big passenger vessel was destroyed by fire while tied to a wharf at Detroit in September of 1839. She may have been recovered and rebuilt. [2]

GRECIAN ▪ Steel bulk freight steamer of 2,348 t. and 296 ft., launched in 1891 at Cleveland
Lake Huron: On June 7, 1906, this large steamer went aground near Detour, Michigan, and suffered severe hull damage. Salvagers removed her cargo and refloated her a few days later. Taken in tow of the steamer SIR HENRY BESSEMER for the trip to drydock in Detroit, she started taking on water and sank off Thunder Bay on June 15. No lives were lost in either incident. [5]

CITY OF GREEN BAY ■ Bulk freight schooner of 346 t. and 145 ft.
Lake Michigan: The schooner CITY OF GREEN BAY was the victim of a gale that struck her on October 3, 1887. She was dashed ashore at Evergreen Point, near South Haven, MI, and went to pieces in short order, killing six of her seven crew. She was carrying a cargo of stone at the time. One report says a schooner of this name foundered in the Straits of Mackinac, near Epoufette, MI, also in 1887 and also with the loss of six lives. [4]

CITY OF GREEN BAY ■ Passenger and package freight propeller of 208 t. and 131 ft., launched in 1866 at Fort Howard, WI, as the sidewheel steamer M C HAWLEY (converted to prop in 1889). One source says she was built in 1880
Lake Huron: On August 19, 1909 this ship was reported to have burned and sunk in Saginaw Bay. The specific location is given as Whistler's Point, though this may be Whitestone Point. [5]

G R or **C R GREEN** ■ Steam tug of 18 t. and 48 ft., launched in 1874 at Milwaukee
Lake Huron: This little vessel was lost off the lighthouse at Detour, Michigan, near the entrance to the St. Marys River. She foundered there on June 7, 1915, but none of her crew were lost. [3]

M T GREENE ■ Wooden bulk freight steamer of 524 t. and 155 ft., launched in 1887 at Gibraltar, MI
Lake Erie: This small wooden freighter was destroyed by fire near Bridgeburg, Ontario, on the Niagara River, on March 18, 1928, after a long career. She was also listed as lost on Lake Huron in 1894, but this report appears to be somewhat exaggerated. [4]

GRACE GREENWOOD ■ Bulk freight schooner
Lake Michigan: Laden with a cargo of iron ore, the schooner GREENWOOD foundered near the north pier at St. Joseph, Michigan, on October 5, 1876. [1]

JOHN GREGORY ■ Steam tug of 75 t. and 80 ft., launched at Milwaukee in 1878
Lake Erie: The busy port of Cleveland lists a number of vessel losses within its congested confines. No specific reason is given for the sinking of this tug on November 13, 1904, near the harbor entrance. [2]

GREY EAGLE ■ Merchant schooner of 287 t. and 167 ft.
Lake Superior: Treacherous Whitefish Point claimed this schooner on July 17, 1869, when she grounded there and broke up. [1]

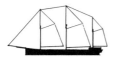

GRACE G GRIBBIE ■ Bulk freight schooner-barge of 298 t. and 141 ft., launched as the schooner CHEENY AMES at Youngstown, NY, in 1873
Lake Erie: At the beginning of her 29th season, this schooner barge was punctured by an ice floe off Point Pelee and sank. Three lives were loss in the accident, which took place on April 26, 1902. [3]

GRIFFIN ■ Steam freighter, possibly the 1,856 t., 256 ft. iron or steel steamer of this name launched in 1891 at Cleveland
Lake Superior: Some lives may have been lost when this freighter sank near Point Iroquois (Michigan), near the Soo, on June 3, 1899. On a foggy night, the vessel was rammed by the steamer WAWATAM and went down rapidly. [2]

GRIFFIN (anglicized version of the French **LE GRIFON**) ■ Armed brig of 50-60 t. and about 60 ft., launched at Niagara in 1679 (possibly most of her timber was cut and fitted at Montreal and carried to Niagara for assembly). She is often referred to as a barque.
Lake Huron: Generally considered to be the first European-style vessel on the Upper Great Lakes, the GRIFFIN carried the explorer LaSalle and his party to Green Bay on her maiden voyage. Loaded to the gun-whales with furs, she left on the return trip with a crew of six in the fall of 1679 and was never heard from again. Many claims as to her last resting place have been made. One interesting one: early settlers in the Tawas, Michigan, area reported the bones of a very old ship, claimed to be the GRIFFIN, in Lake Solitude, behind the town. Locations with the most supporting evidence are in upper Georgian Bay. [5 +]

G R GRIFFIN ■ Steam freighter
Lake Erie: Laden with a cargo of valuable copper bars, the steamer G R GRIFFIN foundered two miles north of Lorain, Ohio, after being struck by a gale on June 6, 1896. [2]

G P GRIFFITH ■ Wooden passenger steamer of 587 t., launched in 1847 at Maumee, OH
Lake Erie: One of the worst disasters in Great Lakes history, in terms of loss of life, was the burning of the steamer G P GRIFFITH on the night of June 17, 1850. The passenger vessel was off the Chagrin River, 20 miles east of Cleveland, and crowded with sleeping immigrants and their belongings, when a fire was discovered in her hold. She was immediately turned for shore in an effort to make the beach before flames consumed the ship and her occupants. But with the engines pushing the GRIFFITH full

ahead, the blaze was fanned to even greater fury, and the steamer was completely enveloped in flame before she could reach shore. It is estimated that 250 to 295 hopeful immigrants lost their lives, burned or drowned escaping the fire. [5+]

W C GRISWOLD ■ Merchant schooner of 354 t., launched in 1854 at Vermilion, OH
Lake Superior: All six of the W C GRISWOLD's crew died when the schooner was destroyed by a gale off Whitefish Point. She was loaded with a cargo of grain when the November 27, 1872, accident occurred. [3]

MICHAEL GROH ■ Bulk freight steam barge of 290 t. and 142 ft., launched in 1867 at Cleveland
Lake Superior: On November 22, 1895, the steamer MICHAEL GROH was downbound with a cargo of lumber when she was overtaken by a northerly gale. She held her own for awhile, but soon her fires were doused by storm water that found its way to the engineering spaces. With her engine out, the ship was helpless. She was blown ashore and destroyed at Pictured Rocks, near Munising, Michigan. Fortunately, all crewmen escaped with their lives. [2]

GROTON ■ Merchant schooner
Lake Michigan: The schooner GROTON was bucking heavy seas when she collided with the brig ROSCIUS and sank on November 25, 1875. She was rounding Waugoschance Point, where the channel narrows and turns south for the Inside Passage, between the Beavers and the Michigan shore, when the collision occurred. No lives were lost, but the ship and her cargo of coal were not recoverable. [2]

GROTON ■ Merchant schooner of 352 t.
Lake Erie: One of the hundreds of victims of November storms was the schooner GROTON, which foundered 2.5 miles west by southwest of the harbor at Buffalo. She went down on November 24, 1882. [1]

GROTON ■ Bulk freight schooner of 630 t. and 136 ft.
Lake Erie: Sometimes even the greatest prudence on the part of a skipper is no warranty against disaster. The schooner GROTON was waiting out a storm riding at anchor rather than attempt to enter the harbor at Talbot, Ontario. She had a cargo of coal aboard when the November 11, 1897, storm filled her and she sank. [1]

CRISS GROVER ■ Merchant schooner of 133 t. and 89 ft., launched in 1878 at Lorain, OH
Lake Superior: The schooner CRISS GROVER was destroyed by an October, 1899 gale when she was blown ashore near Split Rock, Minnesota. A ship of the same name was reported wrecked near AuSable, Michigan, in 1880. [3]

HERMAN GUENTHER ■ Barge
Lake Huron: This barge was wrecked on Thunder Bay in 1890. [1]

GUERIERRE ■ Merchant schooner of 75 t.
Lake Erie: The tiny schooner GUERIERRE was one of the earliest losses in the approaches to the Detroit River. She capsized and sank off Bar Point on May 29, 1832, costing five sailors their lives. [1]

GUIDE ■ Steamer (perhaps a tug) of 48 t. and 64 ft., launched in 1884 at Massena, NY
Lake Ontario: On May 14, 1895, the steamer GUIDE was sunk off the harbor entrance at Oswego, New York. [2]

GUIDING STAR ■ Merchant schooner of 619 t.
Lake Erie: Port Maitland, Ontario, was the site of the loss of this schooner on July 17, 1870. She was blown to pieces by an explosion of unknown origin. [1]

GUIDING STAR ■ Bulk freight schooner of 324 t.
Lake Michigan: The coal-carrying schooner GUIDING STAR was lost when she was sent ashore north of Milwaukee by a November 6, 1883. Subsequent wave action destroyed the ship. [1]

GUILLOTINE ■ Merchant schooner of 358 t.
Lake Huron: Reports say that this schooner was lost near Middle Island, north of Michigan's Thunder Bay, in April on 1881. [2]

GULNAIR ■ Merchant schooner
Lake Huron: The islands guarding the northern reaches of Thunder Bay, Michigan, captured another victim in this schooner, which reportedly went ashore and was wrecked on North Point in 1890. [1]

GUNILDA ■ Luxury steam yacht of 385 t. and 177 ft., launched in 1897 in Scotland
Lake Superior: The opulent white yacht GUNILDA was lost when her owner refused the advice of a salvager trying to rescue her. She had grated up on a rock pinnacle called Mc Garvey Shoal, near Rossport, Ontario, and was teetering on the brink of disaster when salvagers arrived. The recommendation was to lash barges to her flanks before pulling her off the rock, but her owner said to just yank her straight off (he had also refused the services of a local pilot before entering the area). One brief tug and the graceful GUNILDA rolled off the pinnacle and sank in deep water. No lives were lost in the August 11, 1911, incident, but a diver was lost while exploring the wreck in 1970. Valuable personal possessions and appointments are reportedly still on board. [5]

E GUNNELL ■ Propeller of 688 t.
Lake Michigan: In December of 1912, this steamer was reportedly stranded in a storm and bashed to pieces by waves near Michigan City, Indiana. [1]

L MAY GUTHRIE ▪ Merchant schooner of 137 t. and 102 ft., launched in 1874 at Conneaut, OH
Lake Michigan: A brief report says simply that this schooner was lost on the lake in 1894. [2]

H B ▪ Bulk freight schooner-barge of 541 t. and 176 ft. overall, launched in 1890 at Montreal
Lake Ontario: The schooner-barge H B was in transit off Main Duck Island with a cargo of coal when she broke loose from her tow steamer in a storm and went on a reef. She was broken up, a total loss, following the October 12 (or 17), 1912, accident. [2]

H 24 ▪ 154 t. vessel of unreported type, reputedly launched at W Bay City, Michigan, in 1889 (probably under a different name)
Lake Huron: This ship was near the harbor at Kincardine, Ontario, when she foundered on July 3, 1913. [1]

ALICE HACKETT ▪ Merchant schooner of 60 t.
Lake Huron: It is reported that the crew of this early schooner suffered from too much celebration after receiving pay for cargo delivered, and ran the ship hard aground on Fitzwilliam Island, at the mouth of Georgian Bay, where she broke up. The date was November 4, 1828. [2]

BOB HACKETT ▪ Wooden propeller of about 55 t. and 92 ft., launched in 1868 at Amherstberg, Ont.
Detroit River: The steamer BOB HACKETT was lost in September of 1885 when she foundered after a collision with an unreported vessel. [1]

R J HACKETT ▪ Wooden bulk freight steamer of 1,129 t. and 211 ft., launched in 1869 at Cleveland (one reliable source says Detroit)
Lake Michigan: On November 12, 1906, this steamer ran aground on Whaleback Shoal, near the Cedar River, in Green Bay. Before she could work loose, she caught fire and burned to the waterline. The remains later slipped into deeper water and sank. All 14 of her crew escaped the blazing ship. The R J HACKETT delivered the first load of iron ore to Cleveland in 1871. [5+]

ERIE L HACKLEY ▪ Wooden steam coaster of 55 t. and 79 ft., launched in 1882 at Muskegon, MI
Lake Michigan: This small but well-known steamer was traversing Little Bay De Noc, off Menominee, Michigan, when she was simply overwhelmed by an October 3, 1903, gale. The little HACKLEY went down with a cargo of general freight and with the loss of 11 of her 19 crew and passengers. The wreck was located in 1980. [5+]

E B HALE ▪ Propeller freighter of 1,186 t. and 218 ft., launched at Cleveland in 1874
Lake Huron: Struck by a gale on October 9, 1897, this steamer was whipped about by strong weather until her cargo of steel billets shifted and she foundered. Even though the sinking occurred almost 25 miles off Harrisville, Michigan, lucky chance brought the steamer NEBRASKA to the scene in time to rescue the HALE's crew from a lonely death. [5+]

FRED B HALL ▪ Tug of 15 t. and 50 ft., launched in 1883 at Erie, PA
Lake Superior: The miniscule tug FRED B HALL sank after being damaged by ice on April 15, 1909. She went down near Susie Island. [3]

JAMES H HALL ▪ Merchant schooner of 100 t. and 92 ft., launched in 1885 at Manitowoc, WI
Lake Huron: The schooner JAMES H HALL was reported as lost off the marshy mouth of the Thunder Bay River, just south of Alpena, Michigan, on November 7, 1916. [1]

JESSIE HALL ▪ Wooden propeller of 57 t. and 84 ft., launched in 1867 at Buffalo
Lake Superior: A truly aged ship by Lakes standards, the little steamer JESSE HALL was finishing her 69th season when she met with disaster, foundering near Thunder Bay, Ontario, in October of 1936. [1]

JOHN E HALL ▪ Wooden bulk freight steamer of 343 t. and 139 ft., launched in 1889 at Manitowoc, WI
Lake Ontario: Late season travel on the big lakes is always risky. This steamer was trying to deliver a last cargo of coal when she and her tow barge JOHN R NOYES (qv) were caught by a blizzard-gale on December 14, 1902. Immediately hard-pressed, the HALL cut her charge loose and tried to make it to shelter, but the storm swamped her north of Main Duck Island and she sank with the loss of all nine hands. [4]

MINNIE HALL ▪ Wooden steam tug of 42 t. and 68 ft., launched in 1869 at St. Catharine's, Ont.
Lake Huron: The tug MINNIE HALL met her end on July 2, 1902, when she caught fire and was destroyed at Byng Inlet, on Georgian Bay's convoluted eastern shore. [2]

R HALLARAN ▪ Bulk freight schooner-barge of of 698 t. and 189 ft., launched in 1889 at Toledo as a bark
Lake Superior: Bound for the Soo with her holds full of iron ore, the schooner-barge R HALLARAN sprang a leak on May 2, 1900. Incoming water simply overcame the capacity of her pumps to throw it back overboard, and the vessel sank near Stannard Rock, 35 miles off the shore of Michigan's Upper Peninsula. Fortunately, her tow steamer M M DRAKE (qv) was standing by to take her crew aboard. [4]

HALSTEAD ■ Schooner-barge of 496 t. and 171 ft., launched in 1873 at Little Sturgeon Bay, WI
Lake Michigan: In the terrible, much-publicized loss of ten big steel steamers in the "Big Storm" of November 11-14, 1913, the HALSTEAD is often overlooked. Caught asea when the grandfather of gales swept across Lake Michigan, the barge went down with all hands on the 11th (one source says no lives were lost). She was later recovered from the bottom near Washington Island. [4]

HAMILTON or **GENERAL HAMILTON** ■ Armed schooner of 76 t. and 112 ft., launched in 1809 at Oswego, NY as the merchantman DIANA
Lake Ontario: A War of 1812 veteran, this schooner and her fellow warship SCOURGE (qv) were anchored off the mouth of the Niagara River when they were blasted by a summer storm. The August 8, 1813 blow sent both ships to the bottom. The exact number of lives lost when the HAMILTON went down is not known, but it is said that many sailors and marines stationed aboard were lost. The wreckage was rediscovered by sonar in 1975, explored by camera in 1980 and was the subject of an experimental satellite television show in 1990. [3]

LILLY HAMILTON ■ Merchant schooner of 320 t.
Lake Michigan: This ship is said to have foundered at an unreported position in October of 1885. [1]

HAMILTONIAN ■ Sidewheel excursion steamer of 482 t. and 144 ft., launched in 1897 at Levis, Que. as the steamer CHAMPION
Lake Ontario: This popular little steamer was lost on August 30, 1952, when she caught fire and was destroyed at her namesake city of Hamilton, Ontario. No lives were lost. [3]

NELLIE HAMMOND ■ Bulk freight schooner of 48 t. and 69 ft., launched in 1877 at De Pere, WI
Lake Michigan: The schooner NELLIE HAMMOND was carrying a load of wood slabs when she encountered a storm and sank just off shore near the entrance to White Lake, ten miles north of Muskegon, Michigan. She was lost on October 8, 1897. [2]

HAMONIC ■ Steel passenger steamer of 5,269 t. and 350 ft., launched at Collingwood, Ont., in 1909
Lake Huron: One of the largest passenger vessels ever lost on the Lakes, the HAMONIC was destroyed by fire at her dock at Point Edward, near Sarnia, Ontario. She burned to a shell on July 17, 1945, but with no loss of life. The ship had been a popular lake cruiser for 36 seasons. [5]

C C HAND ■ Wooden bulk freight steamer of 2,122 t. and 265 ft., launched at Cleveland in 1890 as the steamer R E SHUCK
Lake Michigan: Big Summer Island, off the tip of Michigan's Garden Peninsula, was the site of the demise of this big steamer. On October 7, 1913, the vessel caught fire there and was destroyed. The ship and her cargo of coal were a total loss. [2]

GEORGE R HAND ■ Steam tug of 34 t. and 60 ft., launched at Buffalo in 1881
Lake Superior: The little tug GEORGE R HAND was engaged in salvage operations over the wreck of the big passenger steamer ALGOMA (qv), which had hit the rocks and sunk the year before, when she herself was blown ashore by a storm and wrecked. The tug wound up on the beach at Little Schooner Island, just off the southeast shore of Isle Royale, on August 9, 1886. Though thought to be a total loss, she was later recovered. [3]

HANDY BOY ■ Bulk freight steam barge of 285 t. and 105 ft., probably the vessel of this name launched at Mt. Clemens , MI, in 1883
Lake Erie: Laden with a cargo of lime, this vessel was cruising up the south shore of the lake when she caught fire on August 4, 1888, and was run to the beach to save her crew. She burned to ruins on the shore near Huron, Ohio. [1]

AUGUSTUS HANDY ■ Vessel information unavailable
Lake Huron: This vessel was recorded as wrecked on Spectacle Reef, east of Mackinac Island, Michigan, in 1861. [1]

T P HANDY ■ Merchant schooner
Lake Michigan: The T P HANDY was carrying a full load of wagon wheels when she reportedly stranded and broke up near Kenosha, Wisconsin, in 1860. [1]

D R HANNA ■ Steel bulk freight steamer of 7,023 t. and 532 ft. launched in 1906 at Lorain, OH
Lake Huron: One of the largest vessels ever lost on the Lakes went down off Thunder Bay Light, near Alpena, Michigan. Carrying a cargo of grain, the downbound steamer D R HANNA collided with the big freighter QUINCY A SHAW, capsized, and foundered. Her sinking, on May 16, 1919, was the largest monetary loss in Lakes history up to that time, but fortunately, the HANNA's crew was rescued by the SHAW. [5]

HOWARD M HANNA, Jr ■ Steel bulk freight steamer of 8,500 t. and 500 ft., launched at Cleveland in 1908
Lake Huron: The huge HOWARD M HANNA, Jr., was "the one that got away" for the Big Storm of November, 1913. She was laden with coal when she was struck by one of the most violent bouts of Lakes weather in recorded history. She was literally thrown onto Port Austin Reef, in the upper reaches of Saginaw Bay, on the eleventh. The big freighter was immediately declared to be a total loss, but salvagers were able to take her off the rocks in one of the most expensive salvage operations up to that time. No lives were lost in the accident, and the ship sailed for many profitable seasons, until she was finally scrapped in the early 1980s. [5+]

LEONARD HANNA ■ Merchant schooner of 680 t. and 190 ft.
Lake Michigan: On October 20, 1889, the schooner LEONARD HANNA is reported to have foundered near the northwest side of South Fox Island, after striking bottom in a dense fog. One source states that she was lost on Lake Superior. [3]

W R HANNA ■ Merchant schooner of 103 t. and 86 ft., launched in 1857 at Sandusky, OH
Lake Michigan: Victim of a violent local white squall, this schooner capsized and sank off Milwaukee in 1870. [2]

PERRY HANNA ■ Vessel information unavailable
Lake Michigan: The PERRY HANNA ran aground near Jacksonport, Wisconsin, in a gale that occurred on October 15, 1880. She was pounded to pieces before she could be released. [1]

ANNA O HANSEN or **HANSON** ■ Lumber schooner of 185 t. and 113 ft., launched in 1869 at DePere, WI
Lake Michigan: In Lakes commerce, the cargoes brought to market on the earliest date following the spring break-up of ice ususally demanded and received the highest prices. The schooner HANSEN apparently tried to begin her final season too early. She was lost on March 30, 1902, when she was pushed ashore and wrecked by moving ice near Manistee, Michigan. [3]

HARBINGER ■ Steamer, possibly the 133 t., 97 ft. vessel built in Nova Scotia in 1901 and seized by the U.S. as a rumrunner in 1922
Lake Erie: A report simply says that the HARBINGER was destroyed by fire on December 9, 1928. [1]

HAROLD ■ Bulk freight schooner-barge of 718 t. and 190

ft., launched in 1891 at W Bay City, MI
Lake Huron: The schooner-barge HAROLD was a victim of fire, lost at Spragge, Ontario, in the North Channel, on November 18, 1915. A second reliable source says the loss was on July 14, 1915, at Nesterville, Ontario. [3]

JOHN HARPER ■ Wooden bulk freight steamer of 1,951 t. and 298 ft., launched in 1890 at W Bay City, MI
Detroit River: September 29, 1914, was the date of the loss of this steamer. She suffered a devastating fire which completely gutted her and put her out of service for good. [2]

HARRIET ANN ■ Merchant schooner, probably the 115 t. vessel built at Sheboygan, WI, in 1856
Lake Huron: The schooner HARRIET ANN is reported to have sunk off Ninemile Point, in the eastern Straits of Mackinac, in 1859. [1]

HARRIET B ■ Barge of 1,938 t. and 298 ft., launched as the carferry SHENANGO #2 at Toledo in 1895
Lake Superior: The barge HARRIET B was known around the lake ports as a hard-luck ship, even in her former life as a carferry. She suffered many accidents and mishaps, but her end finally came on May 3, 1922, when she was rammed in a fog by the big steamer QUINCY A SHAW and sank off Two Harbors, Minnesota. [3]

J C HARRISON ■ Merchant schooner
Lake Huron: The schooner J C HARRISON was reported lost off Oscoda, Michigan, in the year 1885. [1]

HARSEN ■ Sandsucker-barge of 561 t. and 157 ft. overall, launched as a bulk freight barge at Duluth in 1916
Lake Erie: This sandsucker was in transit when she capsized and sank in Pelee Passage on September 4, 1926. She was on the bottom in shallow water, so close to the channel that she was removed and resunk in October. The vessel was one of the few wooden ships ever built of fir and pine, rather than hardwoods. [2]

ASA HART ■ Merchant schooner
Lake Huron: The ASA HART foundered in midlake in an 1869 gale that reportedly destroyed a large number of Lakes ships. [2]

HARRIET A HART ■ Wooden passenger and package freight steamer of 554 t. and 178 ft., launched in 1889 at Saugatuck, MI as the steamer R C REID

Lake Superior or *Huron:* The steamer HARRIET A HART was lost on June 15, 1905, when she caught fire, burned to the waterline and sank. No lives were lost in the incident, but historians don't agree on her position at the time of the wreck, shown variously as Whitefish Point or at either end of the St. Marys River. [4]

JUDGE HART ■ Steel bulk freight steamer of 1,729 t. and 253 ft., launched in 1923 at Cowes, England
Lake Superior: A well-meaning rescue attempt caused the loss of this grain-laden steamer on November 28, 1942. The downbound vessel struck and was impaled on a boulder in Ashburton Bay, on the North Shore. No lives were lost and she seemed to be in little trouble, but an attempt to pull her off the rock ended in disaster when she rapidly filled and sank. [2]

HARTFORD ■ Merchant schooner of 323 t. and 137 ft., launched in 1873 at Gibraltar, MI
Lake Ontario: Mexico Bay, near Oswego, New York, was the site of the loss of the schooner HARTFORD on October 11, 1894. She was carrying a cargo of wheat when she sank with the loss of seven of her crew. [2]

J H HARTZELL ■ Bulk freight schooner of 253 t.
Lake Michigan: Loaded with a cargo of iron ore, this schooner foundered on October 16, 1880, one mile south of Frankfort, Michigan. One life was lost when she went down. [1]

HARVEST QUEEN ■ Merchant schooner
Lake Huron: Presque Isle is a bulbous pensinsula (the name means "peninsular island") that erupts from the shoreline south of Rogers City, Michigan. Its productive limestone quarries, located near the edge of the lake, have meant heavy vessel traffic for the area, and with that, the inevitable ship losses. The HARVEST QUEEN became a victim when she foundered just offshore in 1880. [2]

J M HARVEY ■ Gas screw of 22 t. and 55 ft., launched in 1896 at Chicago
Lake Michigan: This small vessel was lost on November 23, 1908, when she stranded and was wrecked at Sheboygan, Wisconsin. No lives were lost in the incident. [1]

LIZZIE HARVEY ■ Barge of 426 t.
Lake Erie: The loss of this sulphur-laden barge may be related to the sinking of three other barges in the same area, nine days earlier (see BETTY HEDGER). The HARVEY went down off Barcelona, New York, on November 11, 1937. [2]

HARWICH ■ Merchant schooner
Lake Huron: In 1858 this sailing ship was reported to have gone down with all seven hands, just above False Presque Isle (Michigan shore, near Presque Isle). [1]

WILLIAM M HATCH ■ Propeller of 73 t.
Lake Erie: On October 3, 1935, the WILLIAM M HATCH reportedly foundered, 12 miles off Point Aux Pins, Ontario. [1]

HATTIE ■ Steam screw of 66 t. launched in 1882
St. Clair River: The small steamer HATTIE was destroyed at her dock at Courtright, Ontario by a fire which occurred January 14, 1906. All four of those aboard escaped. [1]

HAVANA ■ Merchant schooner of 306 t. and 135 ft., launched in 1871 at Oswego, NY
Lake Michigan: Three of this two-master's seven crew died when the schooner foundered a mile off the beach, north of St. Joseph, Michigan. The HAVANA was carrying iron ore at the time of the loss, on October 3, 1887. [3]

HAVRE ■ Merchant schooner of 150 t. launched in 1836 on Ohio's Grand River
Lake Huron: The schooner HAVRE was sunk in 1845, off Middle Island, north of Thunder Bay (Michigan). [2]

R K HAWLEY ■ Steam tug of 27 t. and 53 ft., launched in 1873 at Cleveland
Lake Erie: Perhaps this tug was already disabled when she sank off Lorain, Ohio, in December of 1899. Reports say that she was under tow at the time of her sinking. [2]

DAN HAYES ■ Bulk freight schooner of 146 t. and 112 ft., launched in 1868 at Fairport, OH
Lake Michigan: The little schooner DAN HAYES sank 12 miles out of Milwaukee on August 3, 1898. She was carrying a cargo of bark at the time. [3]

KATE HAYES ■ Merchant schooner
Lake Huron: Prior to the 1870 construction of the lighthouse on Spectacle Reef (in the center of the eastern approach to the Straits of Mackinac), sailors dreaded finding its hidden teeth with the hulls of their ships. The schooner KATE HAYES did just that in 1856, bursting in her planking and going down on the shoal. Her loss was cited as one of the justifications for the building of the 86-foot light. [3]

A D HAYWARD ■ Wooden bulk freight steamer of 305 t. and 138 ft., launched in 1887 at Manitowoc, WI
Lake Huron: On April 11, 1911, the HAYWARD was caught in an ice floe near Harbor Beach, Michigan, was crushed, and foundered. [3]

A L HAZELTON ■ Merchant schooner
Lake Erie: This sailing ship was reported as having been sunk by a white squall, but details are lacking. [1]

JOSEPH HEALD ■ Steamer of 49 t. and 66 ft., launched in 1873 at Perrysburg, OH
Lake Michigan: Details are lacking on the reason for the loss of this steamer, which reportedly sank on White Lake, near Montague, Michigan, on September 20, 1894. [2]

G P HEATH ■ Bulk freight steam barge of 135 t. and 96 ft.
Lake Michigan: The steamer G P HEATH was destroyed by a fire which began in her cargo of hay and consumed the entire ship in May of 1889. One life was lost in the conflagration, which occurred off Sheboygan, Wis. [2]

CHARLES HEBARD ■ Wooden lumber hooker of 763 t. and 184 ft., launched in 1888 at Detroit
Lake Superior: The steamer HEBARD was downbound with a load of lumber and was towing three barges when she was hit by a gale on November 29, 1902. The ship cut her barges loose to save themselves before she was cast upon the rocks at Point Maimanse, Ont., and destroyed. [4]

HECTOR ■ Merchant schooner of 38 t. and 50 ft., launched in 1884 at Bay City, MI
Lake Huron: The tiny schooner HECTOR foundered in Saginaw Bay in the year 1903. [2]

BETTY HEDGER ■ Barge of 460 t.
Lake Erie: On November 2, 1937, this barge sank off Barcelona, New York, perhaps in the same incident that claimed the barges AMERICAN SCOUT and AMERICAN SAILOR. [1]

R R HEFFERD ■ Steam tug
Lake Erie: The harbor at Buffalo, New York, was the site of the loss of the tug R R HEFFERD in June of 1875. Three lives were lost when the vessel suffered a boiler explosion, then burned to the waterline. [1]

HELEN ■ Merchant schooner of 120 t. and 90 ft.
Lake Michigan: The schooner HELEN was thrust aground by a gale on November 18, 1886, three miles north of Muskegon, Michigan. Though she was stranded only a hundred yards offshore, seven (one source says three) of her crew drowned before they could make it to the beach. [2]

HELEN B ■ Tug of 11 t.
Lake Huron: A tiny vessel like the HELEN B is quickly at the mercy of a big storm. The tug was reportedly lost in a 1936 blow, off Georgian Bay's Gull Island. [2]

HELEN C ■ Wooden bulk freight steamer of 622 t. and 186 ft., launched in 1874 at Chatham, Ont. and the passenger and package freight steamer QUEBEC
Lake Huron: The steamer HELEN C had a long and checkered career on the Lakes as both a passenger steamer and a bulk freighter. As the Canadian steamer

QUEBEC, she was heavily damaged in a stranding on Magnetic Reef, in the Georgian, in 1878, and foundered on the St. Marys River in 1885. Again she was raised and renamed F E SPINNER. As the bulk freighter HELEN C, she sank for good in a storm in Thunder Bay near Alpena, Michigan, on October 14, 1922. [4]

E HENDERSON ■ Merchant schooner of 105 t., launched in 1845 at Milwaukee
Lake Michigan: This small sailing ship was reported as lost off Waukegan, Illinois, in 1861. [1]

HENNEPIN ■ Self-unloading wooden bulk freight steamer of 1,372 t. and 208 ft., launched in 1888 at Milwaukee as the steamer GEORGE H DYER
Lake Michigan: The 39-year-old steamer HENNEPIN was sunk by a storm on August 18, 1927. Her remains lie a few miles off South Haven, Michigan. [2]

PATRICK HENRY ■ Steamer of 35 t.
Lake Erie: This little steamer was without cargo and traversing in front of Vermilion, Ohio, when she sank near the lighthouse on August 12, 1887. One person was lost in the accident. [1]

HERALD ■ Propeller steamer of 73 t. and 92 ft., launched as the steamer JENNIE BRISCOE at Detroit in 1870
Lake Erie: Two disparate dates are given for the loss of this little steamer, which sank one mile off Port Stanley, Ontario. One source reports 1883 as the year, while another reference says she was lost on April 15, 1876. [2]

GEORGE HERBERT ■ Freight scow of 362 t., launched in 1902 at Duluth
Lake Superior: The "Big Blow of 1905" was responsible for the loss of this cargo vessel near Two Islands, on the North Shore. Some lakemen claim this was the most violent, if not the most monetarily damaging, storm in the recorded history of the Lakes. The GEORGE HERBERT was in tow of the tug GILETTE, en route to lighten the stranded gas screw FAVORITE on November 28, when she broke loose and was blown aground. Three of the vessel's 12 crewmen lost their lives when she went to pieces on the rocks. [5+]

HERCULES ■ Merchant schooner of 60 t.
Lake Michigan: On October 3, 1818, the schooner HERCULES was wrecked by a gale on the beach at the mouth of the Calumet River, near the present site of Chicago. All six hands were lost in the accident, drowned and then their bodies devoured by wild animals. One source says that this ship was the first decked vessel wrecked on Lake Michigan. [4]

HERCULES ■ Barge (or perhaps the 120 t. scow built at Detroit in 1854)
Lake Huron: This tow vessel was reportedly lost in midlake in 1870. [2]

HERCULES ■ Wooden sidewheel steamer of 331 t. and 122 ft., launched in 1857 at Garden Island, Ont.
Lake Ontario: Sources don't state whether the fire that destroyed this steamer at the shipyard at Garden Island was accidental or not. The ship burned in December of 1871. [1]

HERCULES ■ Merchant schooner of 90 t. and 80 ft.
Lake Michigan: The schooner HERCULES was carrying a load of bark when she encountered a violent summer storm and was wrecked on June 14, 1886. She capsized near shore and was wrecked off Sheboygan, Wisconsin. [2]

HERCULES ■ Merchant schooner of 240 t.
Lake Huron: This schooner was wrecked only 100 ft. from the lighthouse at Michael's Bay, on the lake side of Manitoulin Island. She was lost in November of 1892. [2]

HERCULES ■ Dredge of 559 t., launched in 1904 at Detroit
Lake Huron: The dredge HERCULES sank north of Tawas light, near Au Sable, Michigan, in 1932. [2]

PAT HERNER ■ Merchant schooner of 125 ft.
Lake Michigan: The harbor at Michigan City, Indiana was the site of the loss of the schooner PAT HERNER to fire in the year 1854. [1]

HERO ■ Sidewheel passenger and package freight steamer of 200 t. and 138 ft., launched in 1878 at Sorel, Que.
Lake Ontario: Belleville, Ontario, was the site of the destruction of this steamer on June 19, 1901. She was ravaged by fire at her dock, a blaze that one source says was started by a stroke of lightning. No lives were lost. [2]

HERRING KING ■ Fishing tug
Lake Superior: This fishing boat was destroyed by fire off-shore near Sand Island when a backfiring engine set her ablaze. One of her two crewmen was lost in the September 20, 1917 accident, and the other was rescued by the tiny packet L GOLDISH (qv). [2]

HESPER ■ Wooden bulk freight steamer of 2,105 t. and 250 ft., launched at Cleveland in 1890
Lake Superior: A particularly violent spring storm destroyed this large freighter on May 3, 1905. Winds reported at 60 mph blew her on a reef near Silver Bay, Minnesota, where she broke in half, then slid into deep water. Fortunately, no lives were lost. [3]

HERMAN H HETTLER ■ Wooden bulk freight steamer of 789 t. and 210 ft., launched in 1890 at W Bay City, MI as the steamer WALTER VAIL
Lake Superior: The HETTLER was laden with a cargo of table salt when she encountered a typical November storm in 1926. She was headed for the shelter of Grand Island, near Munising, Michigan, when she struck a reef along the island's west side and was destroyed on the 23rd. All of her crew escaped before the steamer broke up. [5+]

HIAWATHA ■ 518 t. vessel of unreported type
Lake Ontario: September 20, 1917, was the last day for this ship, which foundered eight miles off Yorkshire Island, in the Ducks group. [1]

HIAWATHA ■ Propeller steamer of 163 t. and 93 ft., launched in 1874 at Dresden, Ont.
Lake Huron: It was reported that the steamer HIAWATHA was beached and abandoned in the North Channel in 1924. A second source states that the vessel was abandoned in 1940. [2]

W B HIBBARD ■ Merchant schooner
Lake Huron: The schooner W B HIBBARD was said to have stranded and then broken up near Southampton, Ontario, in 1867. [1]

HIBERNIA ■ 120 t. vessel of unreported type
Lake Ontario: In November of 1878, this ship foundered in a storm near Amherst Island, opposite Bath, Ont. [2]

HIBOU ■ Passenger and package freight motor ship of 559 t. and 122 ft., launched in 1907 at Toronto as the steamer ALICE
Lake Huron: Inquiry following the loss of the HIBOU on November 21, 1936, blamed the loss on improper loading of her cargo of flour and general merchandise, combined with heavy weather. She foundered four miles out of Owen Sound, Ontario, near Squaw Point. Seven of the 17 aboard her died in the sinking. She was raised in 1942 and sold foreign, finally sinking off Chile in 1953. She was originally built as a quarantine vessel. [5]

HICKORY STICK ■ Dredge-barge of 260 t.
Lake Erie: The dredge HICKORY STICK foundered in a gale which struck her off Avon Point, east of Cleveland, on November 29, 1958. [2]

C HICKOX ■ Wooden bulk freight steamer of 208 t. and 130 ft., launched at Lorain, OH, in 1873
Lake Ontario: Main Duck Island, near the east end of the Lake, claimed this freighter on December 2, 1906. On that date, while carrying a cargo of coal, she ran aground there, caught fire, and was destroyed. [4]

LEN HIGBY ■ Merchant schooner of 52 t. and 83 ft., launched in 1865 at Sheboygan, WI
Lake Michigan: The little two-master LEN HIGBY was bested by an October, 1898, storm. She foundered off Frankfort, Michigan, with no loss of life. [2]

HIGHLANDER ■ Wooden sidewheel steamer of 320 t. and 171 ft., launched in 1850 at Montreal
Lake Ontario: The steamer HIGHLANDER was destroyed by fire at Garden Island, Ontario, in December of 1871. [1]

CHARLES B HILL ▪ Wooden passenger and package freighter of 1,731 t. and 252 ft., launched as the steamer DELAWARE in 1878 at Cleveland
Lake Erie: A victim of the shoal water surrounding Long Point, this big ship was stranded on the south side on November 22, 1906. The HILL broke up before she could be released. [4]

FLORA M HILL ▪ Iron passenger and package freight steamer of 623 t. and 130 ft., launched in 1874 at Philadelphia, PA
Lake Michigan: After a long career on the Lakes, the steamer FLORA M HILL met her fate in the harbor at Chicago. On March 11, 1912, the vessel was caught in an ice floe, crushed, and sunk. She was reportedly carrying a cargo of brass automobile headlamps when she was lost. [2]

JOHN H HILL ▪ Merchant schooner of 90 t.
Lake Erie: Burdened with a heavy cargo of limestone, the schooner JOHN H HILL sank near the entrance to the harbor at Fairport, Ohio, on June 22, 1885. [1]

MARIA HILLIARD ▪ Merchant schooner of 175 t., built before 1847
Lake Michigan: The MARIA HILLIARD was attemping to thread her way through the reef-studded area known as Death's Door, off the tip of Wisconsin's Door Peninsula, when she struck a bar and was wrecked. The year of her loss was 1856. [2]

HINCKLEY ▪ Wooden bulk freight steamer of 350 t. and 119 ft. overall, launched in 1901 at Chaumont, NY
Lake Ontario: One of the last wooden freighters to be built, the HINCKLEY was lost on July 29, 1929. She had run aground and broken up near Stony Point (New York). [1]

CHARLES HINCKLEY ▪ Wooden barge
Lake Huron: This barge was reported to have foundered in midlake in 1886. [1]

FRANCIS HINTON ▪ Wooden bulk freight steamer of 397 t. and 164 ft., launched in 1889 at Manitowoc, WI
Lake Michigan: Laden with a cargo of lumber, the steamer FRANCIS HINTON stranded in a storm and broke up off Two Rivers, Wisconsin, on November 16, 1909. All 11 of her crew survived the accident. [4]

HIPPOCAMPUS ▪ Merchant steamer
Lake Michigan: Little is known of the loss of this ship in 1868, except that she foundered on September 8 with the loss of 25 lives. [1]

SAMUEL HODGE ▪ Steam freighter of 587 t. and 149 ft., launched at Detroit in 1881
Lake Ontario: Reports simply say that the SAMUEL HODGE was lost on July 5, 1896. [2]

KITTIE HOIGHT ▪ Merchant schooner
Lake Huron: The schooner KITTIE HOIGHT was reportedly in mid-lake when she caught fire and was destroyed in September of 1899. [2]

HOLIDAY ▪ Gas screw passenger vessel of 10 t. and 47 ft., launched in 1906 at Chicago
Lake Michigan: Nobody was aboard this little passenger boat when she caught fire and was destroyed while docked at Holland, Michigan, on September 19, 1908. [1]

GRACE HOLLAND ▪ Bulk freight schooner-barge of 629 t. and 189 ft., launched in 1880 at Marine City, MI
Lake Huron: Schooner-barges, even though they could usually sail under their own canvas if the need arose, were sometimes dragged to their dooms by their towing vessels. The GRACE HOLLAND was wrecked on Wheeler's Reef, near False Detour passage, when her steamer, the CREAM CITY (qv), went ashore in fog and the old schooner was pulled into disaster with her. The accident took place on July 1, 1918. [4]

JOSEPH HOLLAND ▪ Schooner (or perhaps the 157 t. schooner-barge of this name built at Bay City, MI, in 1867)
Lake Huron: Three lives were lost when this sail vessel was lost in midlake in 1870. [1]

ROBERT HOLLAND ▪ Wooden propeller freighter of 423 t. and 156 ft., launched in 1872 at Marine City, MI
Lake Michigan: The propeller ROBERT HOLLAND ended her days at Sturgeon Bay, Wisconsin, when she was destroyed by fire on May 11, 1915. She had suffered a previous serious accident when she collided with the steamer LAKE ERIE and sank in 1881. [3]

JOHN HOLLISTER ▪ Steam freighter
Lake Huron: All that is reported about this vessel is that she foundered on the lake sometime in the 19th Century. [1]

HOLMES ▪ Merchant schooner
Lake Huron: The schooner HOLMES was stranded and lost in 1887 on Middle Island Reef, southeast of Rockport, Michigan. [1]

GEORGE W HOLT ■ Bulk freight schooner of 266 t.
Lake Huron or *Ontario:* Carrying a cargo of iron ore, this schooner was reportedly lost on July 19, 1880. Both reports of her demise give Port Austin Reef as her location, but one says Lake Huron (Saginaw Bay), while the other claims Lake Ontario. [2]

E D HOLTON ■ Wooden steamer of 25 t. and 58 ft., launched in 1874 at Milwaukee
Lake Superior: The small steamer E D HOLTON was destroyed by fire at Houghton, Michigan, halfway up the ship canal which crosses the Keeweenaw Peninsula, on August 31, 1927. [2]

HOME RULE ■ Steam tug of 81 t. and 75 ft., launched in 1890 at Thorold, Ont.
Lake Erie: The hazards of tugboat operations were demonstrated by the accident that befell the HOME RULE on December 6, 1924. The tug was trying to tow the 6,600-ton steamer MIDLAND PRINCE into Port Colborne, Ontario, in a gale, when the big freighter swung out of control and pushed the smaller vessel into a reef, crushing and sinking her. [2]

WILLIAM HOME ■ Merchant schooner of 305 t. and 141 ft., launched in 1871 at Clayton, NY
Lake Michigan: Six crewmen drowned when the schooner WILLIAM HOME foundered in a storm, three mile off Seul Choix Point (Michigan). The sailing ship was lost on September 25, 1894. [3]

HOPE ■ Passenger and freight sloop
Lake Huron: Lost in 1804, this is one of the earliest recorded commercial vessels wrecked above Detroit. She went down near St. Joseph Island, at the western end of the North Channel. [1]

HOPE ■ Merchant schooner, perhaps the 26 t. vessel built in 1843 at Sandusky
Lake Huron: Georgian Bay claimed this schooner for her own in 1858. The ship was lost in a Bay squall. [1]

HOPE ■ Merchant schooner
Lake Huron: An 1867 squall took this schooner to the bottom, in the middle of the lake. [1]

AGNES HOPE ■ Lumber schooner of 220 t., launched at Hamilton, Ont., in 1869
Lake Ontario: Reports state that this carrier opened her seams to the Lake and sank near Oswego, New York, in a November 7, 1884 storm. Her crew was rescued. [2]

J A HOPE ■ Merchant schooner
Lake Erie: The schooner J A HOPE was wrecked on a reef, a total loss, near Port Burwell, Ontario, in 1858. [1]

A L HOPKINS ■ Wooden bulk freight steamer of 639 t. and 186 ft., launched in 1888 at Marine City, MI

Lake Superior: On October 3, 1911, the steamer A L HOPKINS was overtaken by a heavy fall gale off Ontonagon, Michigan. Heavily laden with lumber, her seams opened and she sank. [2]

CHARLES HORN ■ Wooden bulk freight steamer of 1,206 t. and 217 ft., launched as the steamer MARION at Sheboygan, WI, in 1889
Lake Ontario: This freighter caught fire while underway off Point Petre, Ontario, on May 16, 1926. Her crew escaped, but the HORN and her cargo of grain were totally destroyed. [1]

MOLLY T HORNER ■ Merchant schooner of 160 t.
Lake Huron: Scarecrow Island is a sparsely treed dot of land at the southern end of Michigan's Thunder Bay. Today it is part of a National Wildlife Refuge, as well as a marker for the schooner MOLLY T HORNER, which sank nearby in 1906. Her crew made it to shore near Hardwood Point, two miles away. [3]

HORNET ■ Merchant schooner (coaster) of 40 t. and 60 ft., launched in 1861 at Two Rivers, WI
Lake Michigan: The tiny schooner HORNET was light when she was thrown ashore by a gale to break up in Good Harbor Bay, near the lumber (now resort) town of Petoskey, Michigan. She was wrecked in November of 1870. [3]

J S HORRO ■ Propeller of 4,760 t.
Detroit River: This vessel is somewhat of an enigma. Reported sunk off Peche Island on April 13, 1937, little else can be found about her (unusual for so large a vessel). [1]

ADELAIDE or ANNA HORTON ■ Propeller freighter of 91 t. and 107 ft., launched in 1871 at Goderich, Ont.
Lake Huron: The steamer HORTON was almost brand new when she was lost off Kincardine, Ontario, in October of 1871. All crew members were rescued before the ship foundered well offshore. [2]

LEWIS HOTCHKISS ■ Propeller freighter of 1,001 t.
Lake Huron: On September 5, 1891, this steamer foundered due west of Goderich, Ontario, 25 miles from shore. No other details are recorded. [2]

H HOUGHTEN ■ Wooden bulk freight steamer of 210 t. and 126 ft., launched in 1889 at W Bay City, MI
Lake St. Clair: Two lives were lost when the H HOUGHTEN was sunk with her cargo of stone, at the lower end of the lake, near Detroit, on September 9, 1902. The ship

was later raised and returned to service. She was converted to a sandsucker in 1920. [3]

St. Clair River: The sandsucker H HOUGHTEN was destroyed when she caught fire and burned to a total loss in the Snyebora Channel, seven miles below Algonac, Michigan, on November 20, 1926. [4]

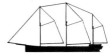

GEORGE G HOUGHTON ■ Package and bulk freight schooner of 332 t. and 137 ft., launched in 1873 at Milwaukee

Lake Erie: This three-master was lost off Bar Point, on the Ontario side of the the Detroit River mouth, on September 10, 1907. In an early fall blow she simply opened her seams and sank. The wreck was removed from its resting place in 1908. [2]

HOWARD ■ Wooden steamer of 195 t. and 115 ft., launched in 1864 at Wilmington, Delaware

Lake Superior: On June 13, 1921, the small steamer HOWARD was destroyed by fire after stranding on Victoria Island, off Cloud Bay, Ont. (a few miles south of Thunder Bay). According to one source, she was the oldest vessel operating on Lake Superior at the time of her loss. [3]

HATTIE HOWARD ■ Lumber schooner of 256 t., launched in 1868 at Port Huron, MI

Lake Ontario: The schooner HATTIE HOWARD was inbound with her cargo of lumber when she was ripped by a gale on November 16, 1878. She was blown ashore near the lighthouse at Oswego, New York and broke up in place. [2]

HENRY HOWARD ■ Bulk freight steam barge of 261 t.

St. Clair River: Harsen's Island, where the St. Clair River empties into Lake St. Clair, was the site of the loss of this small steamer on September 10, 1884. She caught fire while in transit and was beached on the island, where she burned herself out. [1]

R S HOWARD ■ 77 ft. vessel of unreported type, launched in 1856 at Dunnville, Ont.

Lake Ontario: The R S HOWARD sank on the lake in 1868 or 69. [1]

THOMAS HOWLAND ■ Merchant schooner

Lake Michigan: Sometime in the 1870s, the schooner THOMAS HOWLAND was entering St. James harbor, Beaver Island, Michigan, when she began to sink. Spotting the vessel in distress, the local lightkeeper launched a boat to rescue her crew, but was lost himself in the attempt. The HOWLAND sank before reaching shore and there is no report on the fate of her crew. [1]

BELA HUBBARD ■ Merchant schooner

Lake Huron: The schooner BELA HUBBARD was lost in the 1850s when she capsized and sank off Thunder Bay Island (Michigan). Future iron magnate Peter White was part of the HUBBARD's crew at the time. [2]

HENRY HUBBARD ■ Merchant schooner

Lake Huron: In 1845 the schooner HENRY HUBBARD capsized and went down with all hands in the middle of the lake. [1]

R B HUBBARD ■ Merchant schooner of 137 t. and 90 ft., launched in 1857 at Sandusky, OH

Lake Erie: It was reported that this schooner sank at Cleveland in 1862. [1]

H S HUBBLE ■ Propeller freighter of 365 t. and 142 ft.

Lake Michigan: The steamer H S HUBBLE was lost in November of 1888, when she exploded and burned offshore. The accident destroyed the ship 20 miles east by northeast of Poverty Island light, near the mouth of Little Bay De Noc. [1]

L M HUBLEY ■ Merchant schooner

Lake Michigan: The only information on this vessel is that it was sunk in a white squall. [1]

HUDSON ■ Steel package freight steamer of 2,294 t. and 288 ft., launched in 1888 at Wyandotte

Lake Michigan: This steamer's fore-and-aft tandem stacks, green and grey color scheme, and graceful lines made her one of the handsomest, most distinctive freighters on the Lakes. On September 16, 1901, she was downbound with a cargo of wheat and flax when she encountered a terrific gale. Sometime during the storm her cargo probably shifted and she capsized and went down with all 25 hands. Her remains lie somewhere off Eagle River, Michigan, near the tip of the Keweenaw. [5+]

BRUCE HUDSON ■ Steamer

Lake Michigan: Four crewmen were lost when this steamer exploded at Chicago on July 27, 1943. [1]

MARY ANN HULBERT ■ Schooner-barge of 82 t. (one source says 62)

Lake Superior: The schooner-barge MARY ANN HULBERT was fighting a heavy storm with her tow steamer KINCARDINE (qv), when she was overwhelmed and foundered off St. Ignace Island, about 40 miles northeast of Thunder Bay, Ontario. Both vessels were in ballast (without cargo) at the time. Reports say that 20 people were lost when she sank, making the December 14, 1883, loss the worst sailing ship disaster in the history of the Big Lake. [3]

HUMBOLDT ■ Schooner-scow of 103 t. and 87 ft., launched in 1857 at Sandusky, OH

Lake Michigan: This flat-bottomed sailing vessel was lost in 1868 when she sank at Chicago. [2]

THOMAS HUME ■ Merchant schooner

Lake Michigan: The big schooner THOMAS HUME is one of those ghost ships that just sailed away one day and failed to report at any living port. She was without cargo and travelling the Chicago-Muskegon course when she just "went missing" with all six hands on May 21, 1891. [4]

HUMKO ■ Oil screw of 128 t.
Lake Michigan: The motor vessel HUMKO was lost on July 22, 1956 (one source says 1856, but this is probably an error), off Two Rivers Point, Wisconsin. She caught fire and burned until she sank. [2]

GEORGE M HUMPHREY ■ Steel bulk freight steamer of 8,004 t.
Lake Huron: No lives were lost when the HUMPHREY sank, but her recovery was one of the most expensive salvage operations up to that time. The ship sank on June 15, 1943, in the Straits of Mackinac, following a collision with the 5,500 ton steamer D M CLEMSON (qv). She was sold for scrap in the mid-1980s. [5+]

HUNTER ■ Merchant schooner (perhaps the schooner-barge of 173 t., built at Milan, OH, in 1854)
Lake Huron: This sail vessel was reportedly driven ashore to break up near Harrisville, Michigan, in 1872. [2]

HUNTER ■ Wooden steam coaster of 224 t. and 134 ft., launched at Philadelphia, PA, in 1877
Lake Superior: This small coaster had served the communities along the Michigan shore of Lake Superior for several years until October 4, 1904. On that date she stranded in the harbor at Grand Marais and, before she could be refloated, caught fire and burned to the waterline. No lives were lost. [3]

ELVIRA HUNTER ■ Merchant schooner
Lake Huron: The schooner ELVIRA HUNTER foundered far from sight of land in 1895. [1]

CHARLES H HURD ■ Merchant schooner
Lake Michigan: Only one of her ten crew survived when the schooner CHARLES H HURD sprang a leak and quickly sank in a gale. The loss occurred off South Manitou Island on September 22, 1871. [1]

JOSEPH L HURD ■ Wooden lumber hooker of 759 t. and 171 ft., launched in 1869 at Detroit
Lake Michigan: One crewman lost his life when this steamer went down near the tiny islet of Skillagalee, between the Beavers and the mainland. She sank following a collision with the steamer CAYUGA (qv) on May 10, 1895. She was recovered and returned to service. Originally the vessel had large arched braces (hog braces) along her sides, but these were removed during this rebuild. [2]
Lake Michigan: The JOSEPH L HURD was lost for good

when she was heavily damaged by fire at her dock at Sturgeon Bay, Wisconsin, on July 6, 1913. At first she was thought to be repairable, but was finally towed out into Green Bay and scuttled in September. [2]

CHAUNCEY HURLBUT ■ Wooden package freight steamer of 1,009 t. and 185 ft., launched at St. Clair, MI, in 1873
Lake Superior: This old steamer, laden with a heavy cargo of stamp sand, was beset by a terrific gale on September 6, 1908. The worn hull could not take the strain, and began to leak badly. To save her crew and prevent the ship's sinking, her skipper beached her near Vermilion Point, Michigan. Lifesavers took the 14 crewmen off, but the storm-driven combers soon pounded the ship to pieces. The HURLBUT had also been heavily damaged in a fire in 1889. [5+]

HURON ■ Wooden steamer, probably the 140 t. vessel built at Newport (now Marine City), MI, in 1839
Lake Huron: The steamer HURON was reported to have been lost on Port Austin Reef, in upper Saginaw Bay, in 1861. [1]

HURON ■ 25 t. vessel of unreported type
Lake Huron: In October of 1871, the little HURON stranded in Georgian Bay, on the eastern shore of the Bruce Peninsula, and was lost. [1]

HURON CITY ■ Bulk freight steam barge of 369 t. and 168 ft., launched in 1867 at Sandusky, OH
Detroit River: This vessel met her end as the result of a shipboard fire that occurred at Sandwich, Ontario (now part of Windsor), in 1917, and totally destroyed her. [1]

HURONTON ■ Steel bulk freight steamer of 1,945 t. and 238 ft., launched in 1898 at Lorain, OH as the steamer HURON
Lake Superior: The combination of heavy ship traffic and treacherous weather makes the area around Whitefish Point a veritable "graveyard of ships." Dense fog was abroad when the HURONTON was passing through on her way north on October 11, 1922. Suddenly her path crossed that of the 4,700 ton steel steamer CETUS. The larger ship rammed the HURONTON broadside and it was apparent from the outset that the vessel was doomed. Quick thinking on the part of the CETUS' skipper saved the lives of the other's crew. Keeping his engines running ahead, he kept his ship firmly in the giant rent in the HURONTON, until the stricken vessel's crew could scramble aboard. As soon as he backed his vessel out of the hole, the HURONTON took her plunge, but all of her crew had been saved. [5+]

HURRICAINE ■ Merchant schooner
Lake Michigan: The name of this vessel is sadly ironic, considering her loss at the hands of a storm on November 23, 1860. She sailed off into heavy weather and was never heard from again, vanishing in the storm with all hands. [1]

C L HUTCHINSON ■ Merchant schooner, probably the 341 t. ship of this name built at Milwaukee in 1846
Lake Erie: The schooner HUTCHINSON was lost while fighting her way through a storm to the harbor at Port Colborne, Ontario. She lost the fight and sank just southwest of the harbor entrance on October 3, 1887. [4]

JOHN M HUTCHINSON ■ Bulk freight schooner-barge of 980 t. and 225 ft., launched in 1873 at Cleveland
Lake Superior: This big schooner-barge was in tow of the steamer CALEDONIA in a storm when she just opened her seams to the lake and sank off Fourteen Mile Point, northeast of Ontonagon, Michigan. The HUTCHINSON went down on August 17, 1905. [3]

H HYDE ■ Scow
Lake Huron: The freight-carrying scow H HYDE was another victim of Pte Aux Barques, Michigan. She sank off the point in 1883. [1]

HYDRUS ■ Steel bulk freight steamer of 7,000 t. and 436 ft., launched in 1903 at Lorain, OH, as the steamer R E SHUCK
Lake Huron: The Big Storm of November 11-14, 1913, is proof that man should never become complacent over his supposed conquest of nature. The HYDRUS was just one of ten big, modern steel freighters that were destroyed by this storm. Winds in the area of the HYDRUS that night were reported to be gusting at 90 mph, and the waves were some of the largest ever seen on the Lakes. One can picture the stout ship, too heavy with her load of iron ore to climb the giant seas, battling her way through them toward the shelter of the St. Clair River. But the vessel was finally simply overwhelmed, sinking on the 11th off Lexington, Michigan, and taking all 28 of her crew with her. [5+]

ICEBERG ■ Merchant brig
Lake Ontario: No date is given for the loss of this little ship with all hands. According to one source, she just sailed away and never reported to her next port-of-call. [1]

ICEBIRD ■ Vessel information unavailable
Lake Ontario: It is possible that the report for this ship and the one for the ICEBERG refer to the same incident. In the fall of 1861, the ICEBIRD is said to have collided with another ship, and was sunk with the loss of all aboard. [1]

IDA ■ Lumber schooner of 169 t. and 121 ft., launched at Milwaukee in 1865
Lake Michigan: At harvest time, ships normally engaged in the lumber and bulk freight trades often earned extra money by carrying cargoes of fruits and vegetables. The lumber schooner IDA was hauling a load of potatoes to Chicago when she was smacked by a gale on September 29, 1908. The little ship capsized and sank 12 miles off Frankfort, Michigan, but another vessel that was passing the scene was able to rescue all of her crew. [4]

IDA & MARY ■ Scow or schooner-scow
Lake Huron: This vessel was reported lost on Sturgeon Point, a few miles north of Harrisville, Michigan, in 1872. [1]

IDAHO ■ Wooden package freight steamer of 1,100 t. and 220 ft., launched in 1863 at Cleveland
Lake Erie: The freighter IDAHO was carrying a cargo of Christmas supplies on November 5, 1897, when she was hit by a tremendous gale off Long Point. She sank four miles from shore, carrying 19 of her 21 crew to their deaths. Like many of her contemporaries, this ship carried a tall mast forward that was capable of carrying enough sail to assist her engines or move her in case of engine failure. This mast now figured in one of the most magnificent rescues in the annals of Lakes heroism. As the ship settled to the bottom, the tip of her mast was left above the water, and to this tiny stick the two remaining men now clung in desperation, and continued to do so for almost 12 frigid hours. Then, by merest chance, the big steel bulk freighter MARIPOSA spotted the two, and swung in to block the wind and waves for the rescue attempt. Several tries showed that the weather was too violent and the men too frozen for boats to be launched or lines to be cast. In what must be one of the greatest feats of ship-handling of all time, the MARIPOSA's skipper brought the big steamer up so close to the mast that her crewmen could reach out and pry the survivors' frozen fingers from their perch. As lakers are wont to do, the steamer then just carried on to report the loss of the IDAHO at her next port. [5+]

IDAHO ■ Merchant schooner, built in Milan, OH
Lake Erie: The schooner IDAHO sank in the lower locks of the old Welland Canal, but the date is not reported. [1]

IDLE HOUR ■ Wooden passenger steamer of 148 ft., launched in 1893 at Buffalo
Lake Erie: The excursion steamer IDLE HOUR had just been put up for the winter at her berth on Grand Island,

in the Niagara River, when she caught fire and was destroyed. The accident occurred on December 8, 1901. [1]

ILLINOIS ■ Propeller freighter of 752 t. and 182 ft., launched in 1837 at Detroit
Lake Erie: In June of 1865 the steamer ILLINOIS was sunk off Point Pelee light following a collision. She had been rammed by the steamer DEAN RICHMOND. [1]

ILLINOIS ■ Barge, former steamer built before 1855
Lake Huron: This vessel reportedly foundered well offshore in 1869. [3]

IMPERIAL ■ Merchant schooner
Lake Huron: In 1889 the schooner IMPERIAL was lost when she capsized and sank in a storm that struck her in Georgian Bay. [1]

INDEPENDENCE ■ Merchant schooner of 17 t. and 46 ft., launched in 1818 at Sandusky or Dansbury, OH
Lake Erie: The tiny schooner INDEPENDENCE was still brand-new and carrying a cargo of general merchandise, when she capsized and went down with all hands in October of 1818. Her wreckage lies somewhere off Black River (Lorain), Ohio. [3]

INDEPENDENCE ■ Steam propeller of 162 t. and 119 ft., launched in 1845 at Chicago
Lake Superior: The historic vessel INDEPENDENCE was the first steamer on Lake Superior, having carried the necessary equipment for her own portage around the St. Marys Rapids. The process of dragging her around the rapids took seven weeks during the winter of 1845-6. She was lost on the lake, just above those same rapids, when she suffered a boiler explosion and sank on November 22, 1853. Four lives were lost in the disaster. Parts of the vessel were recovered in 1933. [4]

INDIA ■ Wooden bulk freight steamer of 976 t. and 216 ft., launched in 1899 at Garden Island, Ont.
Lake Huron: On September 5, 1928, the steamer INDIA caught fire, burned to the water, and sank off West Mary Island, in upper Georgian Bay, near Little Current. [5]

INDIAN ■ Wooden steamer of 320 t. and 137 ft., launched in 1853 at Buffalo as the steamer CITY OF HAMILTON
Lake Ontario: Another victim of fire was this small steamer that was destroyed at Kingston, Ontario, on October 26, 1885. [4]

INDIAN ■ Fishing tug of 26 t. and 48 ft.
Lake Michigan: The great Armistice Day Storm of November 11, 1940, drove this tug to the bottom. She went down with her crew of five off South Haven, Michigan, and was one of two fishing boats to be lost that day in the same area (see RICHARD H). [2]

INDIAN BELLE ■ Schooner
Lake Huron: Details are lacking on the loss of this schooner in Georgian Bay, near Giant's Tomb Island. She was apparently stranded and not recovered. [1]

INDIANA ■ Wooden passenger and package freight steamer, perhaps the 534 t. vessel launched at Toledo in 1841
Lake Erie: A report says that this vessel struck a snag and sank in Maumee Bay, near Toledo, in 1845. Compare this with the report below. [1]

INDIANA ■ Wooden steam freighter of 434 t.
Lake Erie: After hitting an obstruction, the steamer INDIANA caught fire and burned to a total loss off Conneaut, Ohio. The accident occurred on December 5, 1848, with no loss of life. [2]

INDIANA ■ Bulk freight propeller of 350 t. and 146 ft., launched in 1848 at Vermilion, OH
Lake Superior: On June 6, 1858, the steamer INDIANA was downbound with a cargo of iron ore when she blew a propeller seal. The water coming in around her propshaft was much more than her pumps could handle, and she foundered off Crisp Point (Michigan). Her machinery was recovered in 1978-9 and now rests in the Smithsonian. [4]

INDUSTRY ■ Merchant schooner of 30 t.
Lake Michigan: The schooner INDUSTRY was without cargo and in transit just off South Haven, Michigan, when she capsized and sank with the loss of three lives. The foundering happened on June 1, 1882. [2]

INDUSTRY ■ Barge of 203 t.
Lake Michigan: The barge INDUSTRY was reported to have foundered off Lansing Shoal, north of the Beaver Islands, on October 6, 1953. [2]

INKERMAN ■ Wooden steam freighter, launched in 1855 at Kingston, Ontario
Lake Ontario: A disastrous boiler explosion and fire ended this steamer's short career and cost the lives of all of her crew. She sank following the 1856 explosion, which occurred in the harbor at Toronto. [2]

INKERMANN ■ Minesweeper of 630 t. and 145 ft., launched in 1918 at Ft. William, Ont.
Lake Superior: The INKERMANN was one of a number of minesweepers that were built at Ft. William for the French Navy during World War I. This ship, along with her sisters CERISOLES (qv) and SEBASTOPOL, set out for delivery in France in November of 1918. Only the SEBASTOPOL even made the Soo. Somewhere along the icy route, the two other ships met with disaster, probably sunk by a gale that swept the area on the 24th. No sure evidence of them was ever found. Each carried a crew of 38. [5]

INTER OCEAN ■ Steam freighter of 148 t. and 74 ft., launched at Collingwood, Ont., in 1888
St Clair River: The small steamer INTER OCEAN, was lost, a victim of fire, at Sarnia, Ont., in October of 1892. [4]

INTERLAKEN ■ Construction schooner-barge of 567 t. and 170 ft., launched in 1893 at Algonac, MI
Lake Michigan: This aged schooner-barge had served for many years in the freight business before being converted to a construction barge. She was off White Lake, Michigan, when she was hit by a heavy storm which opened her seams. She sank in 1936. [3]

INTERNATIONAL ■ Steam ferry of 474 t. and 160 ft., launched in 1853 at Chippawa, Ont.
Lake Erie: This wooden ferry was lost to fire during a blizzard which hit her at her dock in Buffalo on December 3, 1854. She burned to a total loss. [2]

INTERNATIONAL ■ Wooden steam carferry of 1,121 t. and 226 ft., launched in 1857 at Buffalo
Lake Erie: One of the earliest carferries on the Great Lakes, the oddly-shaped INTERNATIONAL had a degree of success carrying railroad rolling stock across Lake Erie and the Niagara River. On February 2, 1874, she was lost to fire, possibly set by an arsonist, at Fort Erie, Ontario, opposite Buffalo. [2]

INTERNATIONAL ■ Wooden steam freighter of 144 t. and 81 ft., launched in 1889 at Buffalo
Lake Superior: On November 2, 1913, the freighter INTERNATIONAL was lying at her dock at White City, Michigan, on the Portage Ship Canal, when she caught fire and was destroyed. [3]

INVINCIBLE ■ Trade and exploration schooner of 20 to 100 t., launched in 1802
Lake Superior: The schooner INVINCIBLE was one of the earliest ships to succumb to Whitefish Point. She was driven ashore there and broke up on November 14, 1816. None of her crew were lost when she wrecked. [4]

IONA ■ Wooden bulk freight steamer of 157 t. and 136 ft., launched in 1892 at Trenton, Ont.
Lake Ontario: This small steamer was in transit with a cargo of coal when she caught fire off Stony Point, New York (near Oswego), and was destroyed on May 23, 1912. One source says that she was scuttled on the lake in 1902. [4]

IONIA ■ 52 t. vessel of unreported type
Lake Ontario: Another victim of fire was the little IONIA, which burned at Port Metcalfe, on July 11, 1881. [1]

IOSCO ■ Wooden bulk freight steamer of 2,051 t. and 291 ft., launched in 1891 at Bay City, MI
Lake Superior: Lake Superior is said to keep lost sailors in its icy grasp, never giving them up to those who may search the beaches for signs of their passing. So it is sometimes with ships as well, even large ones like the steamer IOSCO. The freighter was downbound on September 2, 1905, with a load of iron ore and the similarly-laden schooner-barge OLIVE JEANETTE (qv) in tow. Perhaps her skipper thought it was too early in the year for one of the killer storms that stalk the Lakes in the fall. If so, he was wrong. For somewhere near the Keweenaw Peninsula, a heavy gale rose up to claim the IOSCO, her 19-man crew, and the OLIVE JEANETTE, sending them all to the bottom without a trace. [5+]

IOWA ■ Wooden bulk freight propeller of 796 t. and 202 ft., launched at Manitowoc, WI, in 1896 as the steamer MENOMINEE
Lake Michigan: Many ships' crews have been surprised at the sneaking ways the Lakes have of removing a vessel from the rolls. The IOWA's people thought to take advantage of a midwinter thaw to move a cargo of machinery from Chicago on February 4, 1915. While she was still in the harbor, she was captured by ice as the temperature returned to normal and the lake quickly froze over. The relentless pressure of ice crushed her hull and she sank, though her passengers and crew were able to disembark and walk to shore. [3]

R L IRELAND ■ Steel bulk freight steamer of 4,470 t. and 416 ft., launched at Chicago in 1903
Lake Superior: The big steel steamer R L IRELAND had a short life as a bulk carrier. She was heavily damaged in a stranding in the fall of 1906, but quick salvage work kept her from becoming a victim of winter ice. The lake gods will not be denied, however, and while the vessel was being towed in for repairs, she was struck by a gale and lost from her tow vessel. She went on the rocks in the Apostles Islands on December 10, with the loss of one of her salvage crew. The big IRELAND was eventually cut up for scrap in place, but her pilothouse, at least, had a long career, serving as an information booth at Superior, Wisconsin. [3]

IRENE ■ Fishing tug
Lake Michigan: In 1956, it was reported that this fishing craft had exploded and sunk one mile south of the Chicago Coast Guard Station. [1]

IRON AGE ■ Wooden bulk freight steamer of 1,114 t. and 226 ft., launched in 1880 at Wyandotte, MI
Lake Erie: No lives were lost when the IRON AGE caught fire, burned to the waterline and sank in the steamer channel on June 4, 1909. She went down off Bar Point, at the southern entrance to the Detroit River, and later had to be dynamited to remove her hulk. [3]

IRON CHIEF ■ Wooden bulk freight steamer of 1,154 t. and 212 ft., launched as a schooner-barge at Wyandotte, MI, in 1881
Lake Huron: One of a small number of vessels to be converted from sail to steam, the IRON CHIEF ended her career on October 4, 1904. She foundered in heavy weather, six miles off Pte Aux Barques, Michigan. [5]

IRON CITY ■ Bulk freight barge of 648 t. and 187 ft., launched as the schooner DANIEL E BAILEY at Toledo in 1874
St. Clair River: A collision spelled the end for this venerable ship. On May 13, 1913, she collided with the steamer THOMAS F COLE in the busy channel off Algonac, Michigan, and sank near Russel Island. [2]

IRONSIDES ■ Wooden passenger and package freight propeller of 1,123 t. and 233 ft., launched in 1864 at Cleveland
Lake Michigan: Eighteen of the 35 aboard this vessel were lost when she was driven onto the Grand Haven Bar by a storm and was broken up by the hammering of waves. The vessel and her cargo of general merchandise were a total loss in the September 15, 1873 accident. [4]

IRONTON ■ Merchant schooner of 786 t. and 191 ft., launched at Buffalo in 1873
Lake Huron: The big schooner IRONTON was in ballast when she sank near Presque Isle, Michigan. On September 26, 1894, she suffered a fatal collision with the vessel (probably steamer) OHIO, and went down with five of her crew. [4]

IROQUOIS ■ Merchant bark
Lake Huron: A wreck for which little information is reported is the bark IROQUOIS, which was lost in the North Channel in 1864. [1]

IROQUOIS ■ Wooden passenger/package freight steamer and tug of 152 t. and 112 ft., launched in 1902 at Wiarton, Ont.
Lake Huron: The steamer IROQUOIS was lost on October 24, 1908 (one source says 1906). On that date, she caught

fire and was destroyed off Spanish Mills (now Spanish), Ontario, in the North Channel. Her burned-out hull finally sank in McBean Channel. [3]

LEWIS C IRWIN ■ Merchant schooner
Lake Michigan: The schooner LEWIS C IRWIN was reported as sunk by a white squall (a short-lived, violent wind that came out of a clear sky and calm air). [1]

ISABELLA ■ Merchant schooner
Lake Huron: This schooner was lost in mid-lake in 1864. [1]

ISABELLA ■ Bulk freight schooner of 50 t.
Lake Ontario: All that remains of the schooner ISABELLA and her cargo of iron ore lies off the entrance to the harbor at Charlotte, New York, (near Rochester), where she sank on September 10, 1890. [1]

ISABELLA H ■ Wooden bulk freight steamer of 161 t. and 101 ft., launched at Grand Haven, MI, in 1887 as the passenger and freight steamer McCORMICK
Lake Ontario: Operating in her home waters near Oswego, New York, and carrying a cargo of stone, this aged steamer encountered heavy seas that were just too much for her old hull and pumps. She swamped and sank off Oswego on September 28, 1925. [2]

ISHPEMING ■ Bulk freight schooner-barge of 418 t. and 157 ft., launched in 1872 at Detroit
Lake Huron: On November 29, 1903, the schooner-barge ISHPEMING went ashore and was wrecked on Black River Island, near Black River, Michigan, south of Thunder Bay. Carrying loads of coal, she and her tow steamer were both having a hard time at the hands of a storm. The barge was finally cast off and was driven ashore, where she broke up. [4]

ISLAND CITY ■ Lumber schooner of 55 t. and 81 ft., launched in 1865 at St. Clair, MI
Lake Michigan: The little schooner ISLAND CITY was carrying her usual cargo of wood when she foundered 14 miles offshore near Milwaukee on April 8, 1894. Two lives were lost in the wreckage. [2]

ISLAND QUEEN ■ Merchant schooner
Lake Michigan: In 1859 the schooner ISLAND QUEEN sank west of the Straits of Mackinac, off Waugoschance Point. [1]

ISLAND QUEEN ■ Passenger and package freight propeller of 129 t. and 98 ft., launched in 1905 at Toronto
Lake Ontario: The little steamer ISLAND QUEEN was destroyed by fire at Toronto in March of 1918. [1]

ISLE ROYALE ■ Passenger and package freight steamer of 55 t. and 91 ft., launched in 1879 at Port Huron, MI, as the steamer AGNES
Lake Superior: This little steamer was lost off the shores of her namesake, the wild and beautiful Isle Royale, on July 26, 1885. She struck bottom in a moderate blow and sank in shallow water. No lives were lost in the accident. [2]

ISLET PRINCE ■ Passenger and package freight steamer of 245 t. and 105 ft., launched in 1902 at Manitowoc, WI as the steamer MARIPOSA (later BON AMI). Vessel data also given as 142 t. and 118 ft., launched in 1894 at Saugatuck, MI
Lake Huron: The port of Southampton, Ontario is guarded by Chantry Island, which partially blocks its entrance. Several vessels, hoping to find the docks, have found the island's shores instead. The little steamer ISLET PRINCE went aground on Chantry on July 17, 1938, caught fire and was destroyed. She was later recovered for scrap. [4]

ISOLDE ■ Wooden steam freighter of 2,140 t. and 298 ft.
Lake Erie: The wooden steamer ISOLDE was under tow on April 27, 1933, when her lines parted and she was driven to the shallows and wrecked. She went aground two miles east of Erie, Pennsylvania, and 400 yards offshore. [1]

ITASCA ■ Steam freighter
Lake Huron: The freighter ITASCA was reported lost off Lexington, Michigan, in 1895. [1]

ITHACA ■ Lumber schooner of 144 t.
Lake Michigan: Laden with her normal cargo of lumber, the sailing ship ITHACA struck a reef and sank near the north pier at St. Joseph, Michigan, on November 2, 1879, while trying to dock. [2]

ANDREW JACKSON ■ Lumber schooner of 198 t. and 126 ft., launched at Grand Haven, MI, in 1874
Lake Huron: The JACKSON was a two-stick schooner that was driven aground at Pte Aux Barques, Michigan, and broke up. The loss occurred on September 7, 1901. [3]

JAMAICA ■ Merchant schooner
Lake Huron: No position is given for the loss of the schooner JAMAICA, reported knocked down, capsized and quickly sunk by a white squall on June 18, 1872. All of the ship's crew were rescued by the passing schooner STARLIGHT. The JAMAICA had been in a very similar accident at the same spot the previous year. [3]

JAMAICA ■ Bulk freight schooner of 390 t.
Lake Michigan: The schooner JAMAICA was laden with a cargo of coal when she went ashore and broke up eight miles north of Evanston, Illinois. The ship was lost on August 2, 1885. [2]

WILLIAM JAMIESON ■ Bulk freight schooner of 143 t. and 100 ft., launched in 1878 at Deseronto, Ont.
Lake Ontario: A spring storm was too much for the old hull of this schooner. On May 15, 1923, she began to leak heavily in a strong blow, was abandoned and sank off Amherst Island, with her load of coal. All of the old vessel's crew made it to shore safely. She was one of the last working schooners on the Lakes when lost. [2]

JAPAN ■ Bulk freight schooner of 182 t.
Lake Michigan: The schooner JAPAN was reportedly carrying a cargo of liquor when she sank in Garret Bay of Green Bay in October of 1885. [1]

MARY JARECKI ■ Wooden bulk freight steam barge of 645 t. and 200 ft., launched in 1871 at Toledo
Lake Superior: Downbound with a load of iron ore, the steamer MARY JARECKI was intercepted by Au Sable Point, near Grand Marais, Michigan. On July 4, 1883, she lost her way in one of the heavy fogs that frequent the area, and ran into the shallows on the west side of the point. The ship was later broken up by waves. [2]

JEAN ■ Steam tug of 15 t. and 49 ft., launched in 1889 at Buffalo
Detroit River: The tiny steam tug JEAN was destroyed by fire in December of 1910, when she was in the river off Amherstburg, Ontario. [2]

JEFFERSON ■ Package and passenger schooner
Lake Erie: This schooner is mentioned many times in old records of Lake Erie commerce. She was carrying a few passengers, plus a cargo of meat, salt, and general merchandise, when she was driven ashore near Buffalo and demolished by a gale. At least nine people died in the November 18, 1842, disaster. [1]

J H JEFFERY ■ Steam tug
Lake Superior: The small tug J H JEFFERY was reported destroyed by fire at Duluth on October 1, 1892. This may be the same vessel as below. [1]

JOHN H JEFFERY, Jr ■ Steam tug of 12 t. and 42 ft., launched at Duluth in 1892
Lake Superior: The frequent forest fires that were a byproduct of the lumbering era in the Great Lakes Basin, caused the loss of a number of commercial ships. Most went aground or collided when blinded by fire smoke, but a few, like the tug JEFFERY, were just unlucky enough to be tied to the dock in a laketown ravished by fire. The

little tug was destroyed at her dock at Duluth on October 12, 1918, when burned. [2]

EDWARD H JENKS ▪ Wooden bulk freight steamer of 150 t. and 98 ft., launched in 1882 at Port Dover, Ont. as the steamer E M FOSTER
Detroit River: Three lives were lost when the steamer EDWARD H JENKS sank following a collision with the 1,000 ton steamer GEORGE W MORELEY on September 1, 1891. The wreck's position near Ballard Reef constituted no hazard to shipping, so she was left in place, ballasted by the cargo of rocks which she was carrying at the time of the accident. In 1912 she was raised in hopes of returning her to service, but she was too badly damaged, and was abandoned. [5]

J M JENKS ▪ Steel passenger and package freight steamer of 4,644 t. and 414 ft., launched in 1902 at Lorain, OH
Lake Huron: The big freighter J M JENKS was one of the large, modern vessels heavily damaged in the Big Storm of November, 1913. She was wrecked on the 12th by huge waves encountered a few miles north of Midland, Ontario, in lower Georgian Bay. Though the ship lived to sail another day, the cost of her repairs was enormous. She was eventually scrapped, as the steamer RALPH S CAULKINS, in 1963. [4]

JENNIE AND ANNIE ▪ Bulk freight schooner of 255 t. and 137 ft., launched in 1863 at Buffalo
Lake Michigan: Laden with a cargo of grain, the JENNIE AND ANNIE was driven ashore by a gale on November 13, 1872. Six or seven of her crew of ten died when the schooner went to pieces north under Empire Bluffs, nine miles south of Sleeping Bear Point (Michigan). [2]

A H JENNIE ▪ Wooden bulk freight steamer of 197 t. and 119 ft., launched in 1882 at Port Rowan, ON
Lake Ontario: Caught in a heavy storm on November 21, 1900, this ship swamped and sank off Pickering, Ontario. She had just been rebuilt the previous year. [2]

JENNIFER ▪ Steel bulk freight steamer of 210 ft., built as the steamer LORNA P, from the halves of two sister ships
Lake Michigan: Though none of her crew was lost, the steamer JENNIFER went to the bottom on December 1, 1974. She reportedly sank in a storm 30 miles northeast of Milwaukee when her cargo of steel plates shifted. [2]

GORDON JERRY ▪ Wooden bulk freight steamer of 124 t. and 102 ft., launched in 1874 at Port Burwell, Ont. as the schooner GRACE AMELIA. One source says she was U.S. built.
Lake Ontario: The little rabbit GORDON JERRY went aground on Ward Island, off Toronto, in the fall of 1905.

She was abandoned as not worth salvaging and was destroyed by fire on October 10, 1906. [2]

JERSEY CITY ▪ Steam freighter, launched in 1855
Lake Erie: Seventeen of the 22 souls aboard the steamer JERSEY CITY, were lost when she went aground in a gale, near the tip of Long Point. The ship was wrecked on November 24, 1860. [1]

JERSEY CITY ▪ Vessel information unavailable
Lake Erie: In November of 1890 this JERSEY CITY was reported to have "gone missing" with all hands. This report and the one above may refer to the same wreck. [1]

JESKA ▪ Bulk freight composite steamer of 308 t. and 108 ft., launched in 1909 at Kingston, Ont.
Lake Ontario: The small steamer JESKA foundered in a storm on October 7, 1926. She filled and went down ten miles off Fair Haven, New York, southeast of Oswego. [3]

JESSIE ▪ Merchant schooner of 250 t.
Lake Ontario: On October 31, 1870, the schooner JESSIE stranded and broke up with the loss of all hands. She was lost on Salmon Point, Ontario. [2]

JESSIE ▪ Merchant schooner
Lake Huron: Bois Blanc Island, set in the Straits of Mackinac like a cork blowing out of the bottled-up Lake Michigan, was the site of the loss of this schooner in 1890. The JESSIE reportedly stranded on the island and went to pieces in a storm. [1]

JOHN JEWETT ▪ Merchant schooner of 103 t. and 92 ft., launched in 1866 at Vermilion, OH
Lake Huron: On October 18, 1898, the schooner JOHN JEWETT foundered in upper Lake Huron, eight miles off Hammond Bay, on the Michigan shore. [3]

H N JEX ▪ Wooden bulk freight steamer of 441 t. and 170 ft., launched as the passenger and package freight steamer LAWRENCE at Cleveland in 1868
Lake Ontario: The steamer H N JEX was carrying a cargo of coal when she was struck by heavy wind and rainstorm, sprang a leak, and sank. She went down on August 16, 1921, ten miles southeast of Point Petre, Ontario. This wreck has also been reported under a previous name of the same vessel, FRONTENAC. [4]

JOE ▪ Package freight propeller of 38 t. and 80 ft., launched in 1889 at Grand Haven
Lake Michigan: At harvest time, the eastern shoreline of Lake Michigan was alive with small vessels rushing fruits and vegetables to market from Michigan's fruit belt. Unfortunately, this stormy time of year also claimed many of

these same ships. On September 17, 1903, the little steamer JOE was carrying a load of fruit off Holland, Michigan, when she was overcome by a storm and pushed ashore to break up near the entrance to Black Lake. [3]

JOHN MARK ■ Bulk freight schooner-barge of 299 t. and 142 ft., launched in 1870 at Trenton, MI
Lake Erie: The schooner-barge JOHN MARK was lost on October 23, 1903, when she filled and sank off Kelley's Island, Ontario. [2]

WILLIAM JOHN ■ 100 t. vessel of unreported type
Lake Ontario: In November of 1872 the WILLIAM JOHN foundered ten miles from Oswego, New York. [1]

C M JOHNSON ■ Merchant schooner of 258 t. and 138 ft.
Lake Erie: This schooner was reported to have sunk off the mouth of the Detroit River near Amherstburg, Ontario, on October 16, 1895. [1]

CHARLES H JOHNSON ■ Merchant schooner of 332 t. and 137 ft., launched in 1870 at Marine City, MI
Lake Michigan: The schooner CHARLES H JOHNSON was a storm victim lost in September of 1895. She was heading for shelter behind St. Helena Island, in the western Straits of Mackinac, when she sank near the town of Gros Cap. [2]

HATTIE JOHNSON ■ Merchant schooner
Lake Huron: In 1868, the schooner HATTIE JOHNSON was reported to have struck bottom and sunk on Goose Island Shoal, in the Les Cheneaux group, at the extreme northern end of the lake. [1]

HATTIE L JOHNSON ■ Freight barge of 227 t.
Lake Ontario: The barge HATTIE L JOHNSON sank off the entrance to the harbor at Oswego, New York, on October 3, 1885. [1]

HENRY J JOHNSON ■ Wooden bulk freight steamer of 1,947 t. and 273 ft., launched in 1888 at Cleveland
Lake Huron: The Straits of Mackinac are noted among sailors for their dense fogs. The steamer HENRY J JOHNSON was proceeding in such a fog on July 24, 1902, when she collided with the steamer FRED PABST and sank off Spectacle Reef, nine miles east of Bois Blanc Island. [4]

J F JOHNSON ■ Package freight steamer
Lake Michigan: Laden with a cargo of general merchandise, the steamer J F JOHNSON was reported to have gone ashore near South Haven, Michigan, in a storm which occurred on November 25, 1891. She probably broke up in place. [1]

JOHN T JOHNSON ■ Lumber schooner-barge of 448 t. and 171 ft., launched in 1873 at Huron, OH
Lake Huron: November 28, 1904, was the last day for the schooner-barge JOHN T JOHNSON. She was downbound with a load of lumber when she ran into a heavy storm and was thrown ashore on North Point of Thunder Bay, Michigan. No lives were lost in the incident. The vessel was also reported heavily damaged in a Lake Erie accident in 1883. [5]

K R JOHNSON ■ Merchant schooner
Lake Erie: A storm victim in 1854, this schooner was carrying a load of wheat when she went down with all hands near Fairport, Ohio. [1]

L B JOHNSON ■ Steam tug of 43 t. and 61 ft., launched in 1868 at Chicago
Lake Erie: On May 2, 1907, the small tug L B JOHNSON sprang a leak and was purposely beached near Fairport, Ohio. She was a total loss. [2]

LAURA JOHNSON ■ Bulk freight schooner of 34 t.
Lake Michigan: The tiny schooner LAURA JOHNSON was burdened with a load of gravel when she foundered on July 17, 1890, eight miles north of Racine, Wisconsin. [1]

LEVI JOHNSON ■ Steam tug
Lake Huron: Four lives were lost when this tug exploded and burned on the Saginaw River in 1867. [1]

SOLON H JOHNSON ■ Steamer of 129 t.
Lake Michigan: On November 24, 1887, a fall storm cast this small, lumber-carrying steamer ashore near Washington Island, Wisconsin. [1]

WILLARD JOHNSON ■ Merchant schooner
Lake Huron: The schooner WILLARD JOHNSON was reported to have foundered off Pte Aux Barques, Michigan, in 1865. [1]

JOHNSWOOD ■ Merchant schooner
Lake Huron: No date is given for the loss of this schooner, stranded in the shallows of Scammon Cove, on the south shore of Drummond Island. [1]

JOLIET ■ Steel bulk freight steamer of 1,921 t. and 266 ft., launched in 1890 at Cleveland
St. Clair River: The JOLIET was lying peacefully at her dock, one mile south of Sarnia, Ontario, when she was rammed by the steamer HENRY PHIPPS, and sank on September 22, 1911. The wreck was removed in 1963. [4]

Some pleasure craft lost on the lakes

Information acquired incidentally to main research. Parenthetical abbreviations are for each of the Great Lakes.

AMERICA - 6 t sloop stranded and broke up near Michigan City, IN, 1905 (M)

BLACK HAWK - 22 t gas screw foundered off Charlevoix, MI, 1939 (M)

BUCCANEER - 54 t houseboat sank in Green Bay, 1981 (M)

CELT - Sank south of Siskiwit Harbor, 1889 (S)

CHERUB - Burned and sank in Saginaw River, 1974 (H)

CRUISER - Small vessel lost off Chapel Rock, MN, 1890 (S)

GLORIANA - Big yacht burned at Grand Marais, MI, 1909 (S)

GRACE - 7 t steam screw ashore and wrecked, Whitefish Pt, 1882 (S)

GUNILDA - Very large luxury yacht, see text

HALF MOON - 38 ft racing sloop capsized in Green Bay and sank, 1946, 5 of 6 died (M)

KEOSAGAS - Steam screw burned at mouth of Saginaw River, 1916 (H)

KIMBERLY I - Foundered 17 mi off Rogers City, MI, crew rescued by M/V ROGER M KEYES (H)

LEO - yacht or packet, see text

LORELEI - 27 ft racing sloop disappeared during race near Indiana Shoals, 1965, 4 lost (M)

LURLINE - yacht or commercial vessel, see text

MABLE W - 17 t, 45 ft gas screw collided with steamer GEORGE N ORR and sank off Chicago, 1908 (M)

MARGARET - Destroyed by fire at Essexville, MI, 1924 (H)

MARGUERITE - Sail yacht capsized in storm, Keweenaw Pt.,1901 (S)

NAIAD - 17 t gas screw foundered off Au Sable, MI, 1911 (H)

NORTH WEST - 66 t gas screw lost off Harbor Beach, MI, 1945 (H)

NYMPH - 47 t, 87 ft yacht lost near Point Abino, 1901 (E)

OUTDOORSMAN IV - 36 ft gas screw collided with another yacht in fog and sank 20 miles off Saugatuck, MI, 1980 (M)

PANZOLA II - 49 t yacht or commercial vessel, see text

RESTLESS - 7 t sloop foundered off Rocky River, OH, 1908 (E)

RIPPLE - 10 t sloop wrecked w of lighthouse at Lyal Island, 1905 (H)

ROBERTA - 71 ft steam screw burned near W Sister Island, --- (E)

ROSINCO - Gas screw struck snag and lost off Racine, WI, 1923 (M

SEA MAR III - 32 ft gas screw sank between Chicago and Holland, MI, after apparent engine failure, 1980, 4 lost (M)

SIRENE - Schooner exploded and burned off Niagara Bar, 1946 (O)

TITANIA - Iron steamer, possibly a yacht. See text.

TOPAZ VII - 23 t oil screw burned near Rogers City, 1941 (H)

VENCEDOR-18 t, 50 ft sloop went ashore and wrecked near Charlevoix, MI, 1911 (M)

VITA - 69 t, 86 ft yacht lost off Yeo Island, Geo. Bay, 1910 (H)

WANDERER - 11 t yacht sank in Lake Erie, 1892 (E)

WANEKA - 22 t, 51 ft oil screw burned, St Clair Flats, 1908 (O)

UNIDENTIFIED VESSELS:

Cabin cruiser cut between tug SACHEM and tow, rammed and sunk, 1975, 4 died (E)

New 45 ft sloop ashore and wrecked at Hamlin Beach, 1981 (O)

Mackinaw sailboat sank in squall, Grand Isl., 3 teens died, 1859 (S)

Fishing boat sank in squall, Munising West Channel, 3 died, 1959 (S)

Sailboat lost in gale off Grand Marais, MI, 1 died, 1903 (S)

Fishing boat swamped in heavy seas, 5 Mile Point, 1975 (S)

Which lake?

Which of the Great Lakes is the most dangerous to ships? Using the data gathered for this book as a base, the old contention that Lake Huron is the "graveyard of ships" seems to be valid. The total number for each lake, plus the Lake St. Clair complex, appear at right.

LAKE	NUMBER OF WRECKS	PERCENT OF TOTAL
Huron	1212	33.0
Michigan	772	21.0
Erie	710	19.3
Superior	503	13.7
Ontario	340	9.3
St. Clair complex	91	2.5
Unknown	45	1.2
TOTAL	**3673**	**100.0**

Largest freighters lost on the lakes

1. EDMUND FITZGERALD - 729 ft, 25,891 t. Broke up and sank in storm on Superior in 1975.
2. CARL D BRADLEY - 640 ft.,10,028 t. Sank in storm on Michigan in 1958.
3. CEDARVILLE - 604 ft., 14,000 t. Sank following collision with Norwegian freighter in Straits of Mackinac, 1965.
4. DANIEL J MORRELL - 587 ft., 7,239 t. Broke in half and sank on Huron in gale, 1966.
5. WILLIAM C MORELAND - 580 ft., 10,000 t. Grounded and broke in half in storm on Superior, 1910.
6. JAMES C CARRUTHERS - 550 ft., 9,500 t. Sank on Huron in giant waves of Big Storm of 1913.
7. CHARLES S PRICE - 524 ft., 10,000 t. Capsized and sank on Huron in Big Storm of 1913.
8. CHESTER A CONGDON - 532 ft., 6,530 t. Went aground in fog on Superior, later broke up, 1918.
9. EMPEROR - 525 ft., 7,031 t. Struck rocks and sank on Superior in storm, 1947.
10. ISAAC M SCOTT - 504 ft., 6,372 t. Capsized and sank on Huron in Big Storm of 1913.

Largest passenger and passenger/freight steamers lost on the lakes

1. NORONIC - 362 ft., 6,905 t. Destroyed by fire at her dock at Toronto, Erie, 1949.
2. HAMONIC - 350 ft., 7,160 t. Destroyed in dock fire at Sarnia, Ontario in 1945.
3. WESTERN STATES - 350 ft., 3,077 t. Gutted by fire at her moorings at Tawas City, Michigan, Lake Huron, 1959.
4. CITY OF BUFFALO - 340 ft., 2940 t. Destroyed by fire at winter moorings at Cleveland, Lake Erie, 1938.
5. NORTHWEST - 305 ft., 4244 t. Destroyed by fire at her dock at Buffalo, Lake Erie, 1911.
6. ALGOMA - 262 ft., 1,733 t. Blown aground and broken up by storm on Superior, 1885.
7. GEORGE M COX - 259 ft., 1,792 t. Went on rocks on Superior and slipped into deep water, 1933.
8. SARONIC - 252 ft., 1,961 t. Grounded, caught fire and destroyed in Georgian Bay, Huron, 1926.
9. MONARCH - 240 ft., 2,017 t. Went hard aground and broke up on Superior, 1906.
10. TASHMOO -303 ft., 1,344 t. Struck submerged object in Detroit River, ran to dock and sank in shallow water, 1936.

Largest sailing ships lost on the lakes

1. DAVID DOWS - 265 ft., 1,481 t. Schooner. Broke back and foundered in gale, Lake Michigan, 1889.
2. WAHNAPITAE - 260 ft., 1,432 t. Schooner. Struck breakwater and foundered in gale, Lake Erie, 1890 (may have been barge at the time).
3. MINNEDOSA - 245 ft., 1,041 t. Schooner. Foundered in gale, Lake Huron, 1905.
4. MONTPELIER - 1,290 t. Schooner. Foundered, Lake Michigan, 1878.
5. NORTHWEST - 235 ft., 1,017 t. Schooner. Stranded and broke up in storm, Straits of Mackinac, 1894.
6. J H RUTTER - 212 ft., 1,200 t. Schooner. Stranded and broke up in gale, Lake Michigan, 1878.
7. CHURCHILL - 202 ft., 1,010 t. Schooner. Foundered, Lake Michigan, 1898.
8. POLYNESIA - 204 ft., 979 t. Schooner. Foundered in gale, Lake Michigan, 1887.
9. OUR SON - 182 ft., 1000 t. Schooner. Foundered in gale, Lake Michigan, 1930.
10. CANADA - 199 ft., 758 t. Bark. Lost on Lake Erie, 1855.

Unusual shipwreck sisters

1. Two sets of sister ships, the bulk steamers ARGUS and HYDRUS, and the ore boats CHARLES S PRICE and ISAAC M SCOTT, sank in the same storm, November 8-12, 1913.

2. The steamer PEWABIC rammed her own sister ship METEOR and sank with the loss of up to 100 lives, in 1865.

3. Three schooners owned by the Duff family sank on the same date, at exactly two-year intervals. The ships were the C B BENSON (October 14, 1893), the NELLIE DUFF (October 14, 1895), and the KATE WINSLOW (October 14, 1897).

4. The sister ships ARMENIA and ALGERIA sank within 40 miles of each other on the same day, May 9, 1906.

5. Only three vessels lost on the Lakes were named after people with the surname "Stone," and all three were lost on October 12th; the WILLIAM STONE in 1901, the ELLA G STONE in 1918 and the GEORGE STONE in 1919.

JOLLY INEZ ▪ Turret steamer of 1,827 t. and 253 ft., launched at Sunderland, England in 1896 as the steamer TURRET CHIEF (qv)
Lake Huron: The JOLLY INEZ was stranded on a reef near Saddle Bag Island, on November 16, 1927. She was heavily damaged, and this spelled the end of her career as a commercial steamer. Following the accident, her engines were removed and she was converted to the barge SALVOR (qv). [3]

JONAS ▪ Merchant schooner
Lake Huron: The schooner JONAS was lost in 1898 as the result of a collision on Georgian Bay. [1]

B B JONES ▪ Tug
Lake Huron: Seven crewmen were lost when this tug exploded at her dock at Port Huron, Michigan, on May 26, 1871. [2]

B F JONES ▪ Steel bulk freight steamer of 8,500 t. and 540 ft, launched in 1906 at Ecorse, MI.
The accident that ended the career of the big ore boat B F JONES occurred on August 21, 1955. On that date she suffered a collision and was damaged beyond repair. [1]

ELIZABETH JONES ▪ Bulk freight schooner of 636 t.
Lake Michigan: This "jackass-rigged" two master was carrying a load of sand when she was wrecked on November 11, 1883. The ship was driven ashore by a storm, coming to rest on Racine Reef, two miles south of Racine, and breaking up in place. [2]

FANNY L JONES ▪ Bulk freight schooner of 112 t., launched in 1867 at Lorain, OH
Lake Erie: The Lakes' fickle weather patterns are most predictable in the summer, when alternating periods of calm and moderately rough water can be expected. Occasionally though, a heavy gale blows its way into July or August. One vessel surprised by a big summer storm was the schooner FANNY L JONES. Loaded with a cargo of stone, she was sunk by a tremendous gale off Avon Point, Ohio, on August 11, 1890. One of her crew went down with the ship. [2]

GEORGE H JONES ▪ 48 t. vessel of unreported type
Lake Huron: Parry Sound, Ontario, in the Georgian Bay, was the site of the destruction of this ship by fire on October 4, 1917. [1]

HARRY R JONES ▪ Steel bulk freight steamer of 5,531 t. and 468 ft., launched in 1903 at Superior, WI, as the passenger steamer D G KERR
Detroit River: Even with the most modern radar and navigational aids, big vessels still sometimes run aground, especially in congested areas like the Detroit River. In November of 1958, this big old freighter struck bottom off Detroit. Though she was quickly refloated, the HARRY R JONES was so severely damaged that she was never returned to service. [1]

J H JONES ▪ Passenger steamer of 208 t. and 109 ft., built as a tug at Goderich, Ont., in 1888
Lake Huron: Georgian Bay is large enough to be whipped into as big a storm as is seen on any of the "other" lakes. A tragic example is the loss of the little steamer J H JONES, which was caught by a northerly storm and driven down on November 22, 1906. Waves built up over 65 miles of open Bay water sank her east of Cape Croker, with the loss of all 26 aboard. Several sources give 1896 as the year of her loss. [5 +]

JOHN V JONES ▪ Bulk freight schooner of 200 t. and 125 ft., launched in 1876 at Manitowoc, WI
Lake Michigan: One more storm in a year of storms caused the loss of this lumber-carrying schooner on October 20, 1905. Two of the JOHN V JONES' crew died when the schooner foundered close in to shore, near Harrington Beach, on the Wisconsin side. The ship was later recovered and returned to service. Reports that she went down on Huron with all hands on the same date are erroneous. [5]

WILLIAM JONES ▪ Merchant schooner of 154 t.
Lake Michigan: A storm raging at the time was the probable reason for the loss of the schooner WILLIAM JONES, sunk at the mouth of the Manistee, Michigan, harbor, on November 22, 1890. [1]

JORDAN BOYS ▪ Barge of 405 t.
Lake Erie: The barge JORDAN BOYS reportedly went down in the harbor at Buffalo on May 4, 1945. [1]

JOSEPH ▪ Barge or schooner-barge of 293 t., launched in 1867 at Bay City, Michigan
Lake Huron: This barge was lost near the shore town of Caseville, Michigan, in northern Saginaw Bay, in 1885. [2]

JOSEPH H ▪ Tug of 31 t.
Lake Erie: A freak accident caused the destruction of this tug on December 6, 1924. The JOSEPH H was maneuvering the 6,600 ton freighter MIDLAND PRINCE off Port Colborne, Ont., when the big steamer went out of control and crushed the tug against a reef, demolishing her. [2]

JOSEPHINE ▪ Merchant brig
Lake Erie: In 1855 the brig JOSEPHINE was driven on a reef off Port Burwell, Ontario, by a white squall and destroyed. [1]

JOSEPHINE ■ Merchant schooner
Lake Superior: This small schooner was reported to have gone aground on Michigan Island, in the Apostles, and wrecked in early November of 1877. [1]

JOSEPHINE ■ Steamer of 146 t.
Lake Michigan: This small steamer sank a short distance north of Milwaukee on April 14, 1888. [1]

JOSEPHINE ■ Steam barge of 36 t. and 66 ft., launched at Sandusky, OH, in 1879
Lake Erie: The little JOSEPHINE was destroyed by fire at Johnson Island, near Sandusky, in 1893. [1]

JAMES F JOY ■ Mechant schooner of 553 t. and 175 ft
Lake Erie: Laden with a cargo of iron ore, the schooner JAMES F JOY was stranded on a city beach at Ashtabula, Ohio, by an October 23, 1887, storm. She subsequently was broken up by wave action, but all of her crew made it to shore safely. [4]

JOYLAND ■ Wooden sandsucker of 1,531 t. and 242 ft. launched in 1884 at Wyandotte as the passenger and package freight steamer WILLIAM A HASKELL
Lake Huron: The big wooden steamer JOYLAND went aground on Burnt Island, behind Manitoulin, in 1926. The the estimated cost of a salvage operation was more than the old vessel was worth, and she was left in place. She was just rotting away when she caught fire and was consumed in the fall of 1930. [4]

JULIA ■ Merchant schooner
Lake Ontario: On November 25, 1877, the schooner JULIA sank in a storm, near the lighthouse at Point Petre. [1]

JULIA ■ Merchant schooner of 25 t. and 50 ft., launched at Sandusky, OH, in 1881
Lake Huron: This tiny schooner was reported ashore and wrecked near Harbor Beach, Michigan, in 1890 (one source: 1896). [2]

JULIA ■ 108 t. vessel of unreported type
Lake Ontario: Wolfe Island, near Kingston, Ontario, was the site of the loss of this vessel. She was destroyed by fire there on February 25, 1895. [1]

JULIA ■ Bulk freight schooner-barge of 47 t. and 71 ft., launched in 1888 at Fort Howard, WI
Lake Michigan: On September 2, 1905, the schooner-barge JULIA was stranded and wrecked near Cedar Ford River, on the Michigan coast near Menominee. [2]

JUNIOR ■ Sandsucker barge of 142 ft. overall, launched in 1902 at Sturgeon Bay, WI
Lake Erie: The barge JUNIOR was lost near Cleveland on May 9, 1915. In tow of the tug FRANK E BARNES, she struck a breakwall in the harbor, capsized, and sank, drowning four of her crew. [3]

JUNO ■ Propeller freighter of 288 t. and 140 ft., launched in 1885 at Wallaceburg, Ont.
Lake Ontario: This small steamer was lost in November of 1912, when she foundered and was abandoned near Cobourg, Ontario. [1]

JUPITER ■ Bulk freight schooner-barge of 400 t.
Lake Superior: Beset by a howling arctic gale, the iron-ore laden schooner-barge JUPITER was in tow of the steamer JOHN A DIX, and was holding her own until her towline parted. She was then driven ashore near Vermilion Point, on Michigan's upper peninsula, and quickly destroyed by the storm-built combers. All hands (7 or 8) died in the November 27, 1872 wreck. [3]

JUPITER ■ Lumber schooner of 253 t. and 138 ft., launched in 1857 at Irving, NY
Lake Huron: On September 15, 1901, the schooner JUPITER went down in a heavy gale, south of Alpena, Michigan. Three or four of her crew were lost with the ship. [4]

JUPITER ■ Motor tanker of 384 ft. and 54,000 bbl capacity, launched in 1976 at Jennings, LA
Lake Huron: One man perished and several more were injured on September 16, 1990, when the diesel-engined tanker JUPITER exploded and burned on the Saginaw River. She was unloading at a dock at Bay City, Michigan, with one million gallons of gasoline aboard, when something caused the vessel to shift, breaking her hoses and setting off sparks that ignited the explosion. Flames from the burning vessel were visible for at least five miles, and smoke for more than 40. The vessel's inner hull was reportedly melted from the fire, which burned for almost two days. Ironically, the JUPITER had been used in a local emergency-preparedness drill the previous week and this probably kept damage and loss of life to a minimum. [5+]

JURA ■ Lumber schooner-barge of 227 t. and 129 ft., launched in 1862 at Milan, OH
Lake Michigan: Prudence is not always the best remedy when a sailing ship finds herself battling a Lake Michigan gale. The old schooner-barge JURA was trying to find shelter in the lee of the Beaver Islands, when she fetched up on a reef near Cross Village, Michigan, and was destroyed. The 49-year-old vessel grounded on October 4, 1911, and was destroyed by the pounding of big waves. [3]

KAKABEKA ■ Steam propeller of 113 t. and 75 ft., launched in 1885 at Toronto
Lake Superior: On December 12, 1895, the steamer KAKABEKA broke away from her dock at Sand Island, in the Apostles group, and sank. [2]

KALAMAZOO ▪ Wooden steam freighter of 288 t. and 115 ft., launched in 1888 at Saugatuck, Michigan
Lake Michigan: The large "rabbit" KALAMAZOO was on the Chicago-Saugatuck route on May 25, 1892, when she collided with the steamer PILGRIM in a passing error. The PILGRIM immediately took the other ship's crew aboard and took the slowly sinking KALAMAZOO in tow, in an attempt to save her. For six hours the freighter was towed with her decks awash before she finally sank while still well out in the lake. [2]

CITY OF KALAMAZOO ▪ Wooden passenger and package freight steamer of 729 t. and 162 ft., launched in 1892 at South Haven, MI
Lake Michigan: The "eleventh hour" rescue never came for the steamer CITY OF KALAMAZOO. She caught fire and was destroyed at her dock at Manistee, Michigan, on November 11, 1911 (11/11/11). [2]

KALIYUGA ▪ Wooden bulk freight steamer of 1,941 t. and 270 ft., launched in 1887 at St. Clair, MI
Lake Huron: This bulk carrier was loaded with iron ore for a Lake Erie steelmill when she was lost on October 20, 1905, with all 17 hands. The KALIYUGA is one of the "Flying Dutchmen" of the Lakes. Like that legendary ship, she just sailed away, vanishing from all knowledge of mere men. Just like the Dutchman, she is sometimes said to be seen nosing wraithlike through the Thunder Bay fog, trying to find her way through the shoals to Alpena, and her mournful whistle can still be heard above the crash of storm waves. She was last seen off Presque Isle, Michigan, and is probably on the bottom somewhere off Thunder Bay. [5+]

KALKASKA ▪ Wooden steam sandsucker of 679 t. and 190 ft., launched at St. Clair, MI, in 1884 as a freighter
St. Clair River: The old sandsucker KALKASKA was destroyed by fire off Marine City, Michigan, on September 15, 1932. Though she did not sink, her burned-out hulk was only suitable for scrapping. [3]

KALOOLAH ▪ Sidewheel passenger and freight steamer of 443 t. and 188 ft., launched in 1853 at Buffalo
Lake Huron: Succumbing to a summer storm, the sidewheeler KALOOLAH was forced ashore near Goderich, Ontario, in August of 1862. She broke up on the beach. [4]

KAMINISTIQUIA ▪ Wooden passenger and package freight steamer of 106 t. and 109 ft., launched as the steamer IMPERIAL in 1886 at Toronto
Lake Superior: This little steamboat was destroyed by fire at Port Arthur (now Thunder Bay), Ontario, near the namesake Kaministiquia River, on August 21, 1910. She burned to the waterline. She was almost destroyed by fire at the same spot in 1906. [2]

KAMLOOPS ▪ Steel package freight canaller of 2,402 t. and 250 ft., launched in 1924 on the Tees Estuary, England
Lake Superior: Until recently the steamer KAMLOOPS was the subject of one of the ghost stories about lost ships that still roam the Lakes decades after sailing away. The KAMLOOPS went missing in a tremendous gale on December 7, 1927, with a cargo of general freight and a crew of 22. She disappeared so completely that virtually nothing was known of her loss until she was accidentally discovered on the bottom near Isle Royale, off Twelve O'Clock Point, Isle Royale, in 1977. Perhaps the spirits of her 22 drowned crewmen keep the ghost stories alive, for at least one diver has died on the wreck since its discovery. [5+]

KANSAS ▪ Wooden passenger and package freight steamer of 200 ft. overall, launched at Cleveland in 1884 as the steamer CHAMPLAIN
Lake Michigan: The steamer KANSAS had terrible luck when it came to fire. She had suffered at least two major fires before the one that finally did her in came on October 27, 1924, at Manistee, Michigan. [2]

E KANTER ▪ Schooner-barge of 245 t. and 133 ft., launched in 1862 at Newport (Marine City), MI, as a schooner
Lake Michigan: On November 26, 1872, the schooner E KANTER was driven ashore two miles from Leland, Michigan, and went to pieces. Her fittings and her cargo of railroad ties were recovered, but the vessel was a total loss. [2]

R KANTERS ▪ Merchant schooner of 164 t. and 112 ft., launched as the schooner S ANDERSON at Manitowoc, WI, in 1873
Lake Michigan: Plum Island is one of a number of isles that form a chain across the entrance to Green Bay. The schooner R KANTERS was lost three miles off the island when she sank on May 29, 1896. [2]

KASOTA ■ Bulk freight steam barge of 1,660 t. and 247 ft. overall, launched in 1884 at Cleveland
Detroit River: One crewman lost his life when the steamer KASOTA went down following a collision off Ecorse, MI. On July 17, 1890, she was carrying a load of iron ore when she was rammed and sunk by the passenger steamer CITY OF DETROIT II. She was subsequently recovered and rebuilt as the steamer A A PARKER (qv). [3]

KATAHDIN ■ Merchant schooner
Lake Huron: The schooner KATAHDIN was reported lost on the lake in 1862. [1]

KATAHDIN ■ Propeller freighter, possibly the 1,381 t. vessel built at Bay City, MI, in 1895
Lake Huron: The stormy year 1905 saw the loss of this ship, reportedly wrecked in a big storm on October 20. [1]

KATHLEEN ■ Steam propeller of 110 t. and 84 ft., launched at Toronto in 1886
Lake Ontario: The steamer KATHLEEN served the Toronto area until she was destroyed by fire in March of 1918. [1]

A C KEATING ■ Bulk freight schooner-barge of 326 t. and 138 ft., launched in 1874 at Trenton, MI
Lake Superior: In a strong gale on November 8, 1900, the barge KEATING's towing steamer developed trouble and left her riding at anchor at Coppermine Point, Ont. But her anchors could not hold against the big greybeards and she was torn loose and thrown on the rocks, where she quickly broke up. Her crew made it to shore safely, but the ship and her cargo of pulpwood were a total loss. [4]

KEEPSAKE ■ Barge
Lake Huron: The barge KEEPSAKE was said to have foundered far out in the lake in 1905. [1]

KEEPSAKE ■ Merchant schooner of 45 t. and 50 ft.
Lake Erie: The small sailing ship KEEPSAKE foundered ten miles off Marblehead Point, near Sandusky, Ohio, on August 12, 1911. [3]

KEEPSAKE ■ Merchant schooner of 287 t. and 133 ft., launched in 1867 at Newport (Marine City), MI
Lake Erie: On September 17, 1898, this schooner foundered in a storm with all hands. Although the exact location of her loss is not known, her masts and rigging were found floating six miles north of Ashtabula, Ohio. [2]

KEEWEENAH ■ Merchant schooner
Lake Huron: In 1889 the schooner KEEWEENAH was reported lost by sinking in the Neebish Rapids area of the St. Marys River. [1]

IDA KEITH ■ Bulk freight schooner-barge of 490 t. and 163 ft., launched in 1873 at Saugatuck, MI, as a schooner
Lake Erie: 1922 was a disastrous year for the schooner-barge IDA KEITH. In January she caught fire at her dock

at Sandusky, Ohio. Before it was decided what the old vessel's ultimate fate might be, another fire completed her destruction on July 17. The schooner had been a well-known vessel around lake ports before her demise. [3]

WILLIAM G KEITH ■ Merchant schooner of 211 t., launched in 1869 at Port Huron, MI
Lake Erie: The schooner WILLIAM G KEITH was completing her second year of operation when she was seized by a gale and flung ashore on Long Point. She was totally destroyed in the October 31, 1870 wreck. [3]

WILLIE or **WILLIAM KELLER** ■ Merchant schooner
Lake Huron: The schooner WILLIE KELLER sank off Au Sable Point, near Oscoda, Michigan, following a collision. The loss occurred in 1888. [2]

KELLEY ISLAND ■ Steam sandsucker
Lake Erie: Nine men drowned when the sandsucker KELLEY ISLAND capsized and sank off Point Pelee, on May 2, 1925. Inquiry showed that she was lost due to an error in stowing her sand-gathering equipment, allowing a probing finger of the lake to rush in through an open port. The vessel sank in shallow water and was later recovered. [3]

EDWARD KELLEY ■ Bulk freight schooner-barge of 737 t. and 196 ft., launched in 1874 at Port Huron
Lake Erie: A November gale destroyed the schooner-barge EDWARD KELLEY at Port Colborne, Ontario. On November 25, 1911, the barge was torn from the grasp of her tow vessel and driven on the breakwater, where she broke up. [3]

A T KELLY ■ 26 t. vessel of unreported type
St. Clair River: This small carrier was destroyed by fire near Wallaceburg, Ontario, on November 14, 1885. [1]

KATE KELLY ■ Bulk freight schooner of 257 t. and 126 ft., launched in 1867 at Tonawanda, NY
Lake Michigan: A spring equinoctial gale destroyed this three-masted schooner near Racine, Wisconsin, on May 14, 1895. She was hauling a load of railroad ties when she was sunk off Wind Point Light. All seven of her crew went down with their ship. [3]

KENOSHA ■ Package and bulk freight propeller
St. Clair River: The large propeller KENOSHA was destroyed by fire on October 26, 1864. On that date she was tied to a dock at Sarnia, Ontario, when she caught fire from unknown causes. The blaze soon burnt through her hawsers and sent the blazing steamboat drifting down the river, where she imperiled a number of other ships and caused much consternation before she finally sank a few miles downstream. [2]

KENOSHA ■ Steel passenger and package freight steamer of 135 ft. overall, launched as a tug in 1919 at Sturgeon Bay, WI
Lake Michigan: This small steamer had just been "put away" for the winter when she caught fire at her layup dock in Milwaukee. She burned to the hull on December 5, 1935. [1]

KENT ■ Sidewheel passenger and package freight steamer of 180 t. and 122 ft., launched in 1839 at Chatham, Ont.
Lake Erie: This steamboat was making her way around Point Pelee on the night of August 12, 1845, when she collided with the steamer LONDON (qv,1858). She sank off the tip of the point, drowning ten of the 87 people charged to her care. [4]

HENRY A KENT ■ Bulk freight schooner-barge of 722 t. and 174 ft., launched at Detroit in 1873
Lake Superior: Lake buffs will remember the famous photo of the big HENRY A KENT and her fellow barge MOONLIGHT (qv) sitting high and dry on a beach near Marquette, Michigan, in 1895 (see CHARLES J KERSHAW). She was rescued from that sandy perch, but was lost for good a bare two years later, on September 18, 1897. Carrying a full cargo of iron ore, she was driven down and sunk by a gale near Stannard Rock, site of the Great Lakes' most isolated lighthouse. All of her crew were rescued before the ship disappeared forever. [4]

KENTUCKIAN ■ Merchant schooner
Lake Ontario: The name of the schooner and the lake of her demise are the only bits of infomation available on the KENTUCKIAN. [1]

CHARLES J KERSHAW ■ Wooden bulk freight steamer of 1,324 t. and 223 ft., launched in 1874 at Bangor (Bay City), MI
Lake Superior: The KERSHAW, with two schooner-barges in tow, was fighting a storm to make Marquette harbor when she struck Chocolay Reef hard, lost power and settled to the bottom near shore, dragging the barges into the shallows with her. Her crew made it to shore safely, but the ship was broken up by the pounding surf. Her two barges, the MOONLIGHT (qv) and the HENRY A KENT (qv) were cast high up on the beach, but were later recovered. [5+]

KETCHUM ■ Merchant schooner of 188 t. and 122 ft., launched in 1855 at Huron, OH
Lake Michigan: Around the beginning of May, 1867, the

KETCHUM was struck by a white squall and capsized. The vessel was later found upside-down with her yawlboat still in place, and her crew was presumed lost. [2]
Lake Michigan: The schooner KETCHUM was blown ashore near Gill's Pier, north of Leland, Michigan, on October 31, 1883. Waves demolished the vessel quickly and she was abandoned. [1]

V H KETCHUM or **KETCHAM** ■ Bulk freight schooner-barge of 1,669 t. and 223 ft., launched as a steamer in 1874 at Marine City, MI
Lake Superior: The schooner-barge V H KETCHUM was lost on Parisienne Island, just northwest of the Soo, in 1905. Two of her nine crew were lost when she ran aground, then caught fire and was destroyed on September 16. The KETCHUM was downbound with iron ore when the accident occurred. Her anchor and chain are on the grounds of Lake Superior State College at Sault Ste. Marie, Michigan. [5]

KEUKA ■ Merchant schooner
Lake Michigan: This schooner was reported to have sunk 2.5 miles off the entrance to the harbor at Charlevoix, Michigan, but the date is not given. She may have been recovered. [2]

KEWANNE ■ Merchant schooner
Lake Huron: The early schooner KEWANNE was thrust ashore near Port Huron by a gale in May of 1840. She broke up with the loss of one of her crew. [1]

KEWEENAW ■ Bulk freight schooner of 493 t. and 205 ft., launched in 1866 at Marine City (Newport), MI
Lake Superior: The lakeport town of Grand Marais, Michigan, has a fine natural harbor that has offered protection for storm-tossed ships for many decades. But a storm coming directly out of the north will drive right through the mouth of the bay, and these northerlies are usually "humdingers". On November 8, 1901, the schooner KEWEENAW was sunk right in the harbor by a northerly gale. She was probably recovered following the accident. [2]

J C KEYES ■ Wooden steam tug of 19 t.
Lake Superior: This small vessel was struck by a storm, pitched on the beach and wrecked on November 7, 1874. [1]

M O KEYES ■ Bulk freight schooner of 41 t.
Lake Erie: On October 8, 1884, the schooner M O KEYES was sunk east of Marblehead (Ohio). She was carrying a cargo of stone, probably just loaded at the nearby Quarry Docks. [1]

KEYSTONE ■ Steel tug of 94 t. and 82 ft., launched at Buffalo in 1891
Lake Superior: No lives were lost, but the tug KEYSTONE was almost totally destroyed by a fire which swept her at her dock at Ashland, Wisconsin, on November 19, 1901. She was later rebuilt at a cost almost equal to her value. [2]

KEYSTONE STATE ■ Sidewheel passenger and package freight steamer of 1,354 t. and 279 ft., launched in 1849 at Buffalo
Lake Huron: A large vessel for her time, the KEYSTONE STATE was also a well-known carrier that plied the lakeshore ports of Erie, Huron, and Michigan. On November 10, 1861, she was carrying passengers and a load of hardware (according to one source, she had gold in her safe as well) on a scheduled trip from Detroit to Milwaukee when she met disaster. She was struck by a heavy November storm and foundered offshore from Port Austin, Michigan. All 33 of those aboard perished. The ship's wreckage washed ashore at Pointe Aux Barques. [5]

KEYSTORM ■ Steel bulk freight canaller of 1,673 t. and 250 ft., launched in 1909 at Wallsend, England
Lake Ontario: The steel canaller KEYSTORM foundered at the head of the St. Lawrence River on October 26, 1912. No lives were lost when she struck a reef off Scow Island, near Kingston, Ontario, and foundered. The wreck was located in 1958. [3]

JOSEPHINE KIDD ■ Propeller freighter of 49 t.
Lake Ontario: The small freighter JOSEPHINE KIDD was destroyed by fire on November 4, 1882, four miles from Big Bay, in the Bay of Quinte area. The loss was also reported from Lake Huron in the same year. [2]

KILLARNEY ■ Tug of 96 t., built on the East Coast
Lake Erie: This tug sank on September 12, 1974, 20 miles off Fairport Harbor, Ohio, without loss of life. [1]

S H KIMBALL ■ Schooner-barge of 319 t. and 138 ft., launched in 1864 at Vermilion, OH
Lake Huron: Few details are available to explain the accident that spelled the end for the schooner-barge S H KIMBALL. In May of 1895 she collided with her own towing steamer, the GEORGE STONE (qv) and sank three miles northwest of Pointe Aux Barques, Michigan. The STONE presumably picked up the barge's crew, as all were reported rescued. The vessel was light at the time. [3]

W C KIMBALL ■ Merchant schooner of 33 t.
Lake Michigan: The tiny schooner W C KIMBALL foundered near Point Betsie, on Michigan's west coast, on May 8, 1891. [1]

KINCARDINE ■ Package and bulk freight propeller of 199 t. and 107 ft., launched in 1871 at Port Dalhousie, Ont.
Lake Huron: There are a number of conflicting reports on the demise of this steamer in Georgian Bay. She probably stranded and broke up off Cabot Head in November of 1892, though the French River is also given as the location, and 1888 as the year. [5]

KING SISTERS ■ Merchant schooner of 400 t.
Lake Erie: On October 19, 1884, the schooner KING SISTERS stranded and broke up on Gull Island Shoal. She was a total loss. [2]

A B KING ■ Schooner-barge of 594 t. and 177 ft., launched as the schooner TEUTONIA at Marine City, MI, in 1881
Lake Huron: Off Harbor Beach, Michigan, the KING stranded and broke up in a summer gale on August 11, 1928. [2]

C G KING ■ Bulk freight schooner-barge of 457 t. and 163 ft., built at S Saginaw, MI, in 1870
Lake Erie: One of the all-too-frequent November gales drove the schooner-barge C G KING ashore near Lorain, Ohio in 1913, on the 14th. The ship was abandoned as unsalvageable and later broke up. [1]

CHARLES A KING ■ Merchant schooner of 316 t. and 140 ft., launched in 1863 at Cleveland
Lake Huron: Two widely disparate dates are given for the loss of this ore-carrying schooner off Pte Aux Barques. One says she foundered off the point in September of 1918, the other gives 1895 as the year. Apparently, no lives were lost in the accident. [3]

F J KING ■ Merchant schooner
Lake Michigan: The schooner F J KING was lost on September 15, 1886, when she foundered three miles off Rawley Bay, on the Wisconsin shore. [1]

GEORGE KING ■ Wooden bulk freight steamer of 533 t. and 176 ft., launched in 1874 at Marine City, MI
Lake Erie: This freighter was lost, the victim of fire, in the harbor at Buffalo on September 20, 1926. [1]

JAMES C KING ■ Package and bulk freight schooner of 512 t. and 175 ft., launched as a bark in 1867 at E Saginaw, MI

Lake Huron: A November 29, 1901, gale struck down this graceful schooner when she was blown ashore and destroyed near Tobermory, Ontario, at the tip of the Bruce Peninsula. [3]

JENNIE P KING ■ Merchant schooner
Lake Erie: No location is given, but reports say that the schooner JENNIE P KING was stranded and destroyed with the loss of 14 lives on June 4, 1866. [1]

R B KING ■ Merchant schooner of 83 t.
Lake Michigan: Two lives were lost when this schooner sank in the harbor at Muskegon, Michigan, on November 7, 1885. [1]

KINGFISHER ■ Bulk freight schooner-barge of 517 t. and 165 ft., launched in 1867 at Cleveland
Lake Erie: The schooner KINGFISHER encountered an exceedingly violent storm off Cleveland and sank on October 5, 1905. [2]

THOMAS KINGSFORD ■ Merchant schooner
Lake Michigan: This schooner fell victim to ice in 1877. While in transit off Waugoschance Point, northeast of the Beavers, her hull was cut by a floe and she sank. [1]

KINGSTON ■ Iron sidewheel passenger and package freight steamer of 344 t. and 176 ft. launched at Montreal in 1855
Lake Ontario: The iron-hulled steamboat KINGSTON had 125 passengers and crew aboard when she caught fire and was beached on Grenadier Island, at the eastern end of the lake. Miraculously for those times, only two persons lost their lives in the conflagration. The ship burned to an empty shell, was rebuilt as the BAVARIAN (qv), burned again in 1873, was again rebuilt and served until she was finally broken up in 1930, after her hull had given 75 years of use on the Lakes. [2]

KINSMAN INDEPENDENT ■ Steel bulk freighter of 629 ft. and 18,500 t., launched in 1952 as the ERNEST R BREECH
Lake Superior: The large bulk carrier KINSMAN INDEPENDENT ran aground on rocks just south of Isle Royale on November 24, 1990. As of February 1991, it was believed that her extensive hull damage would necessitate scrapping of the ship. [2]

KIOWA ■ Steel bulk freight steamer of 2,309 t. and 251 ft, launched in 1920 at Wyandotte, MI
Lake Superior: The KIOWA was blasted by a tremendous fall gale on November 30, 1929. The shifting of her unstable cargo of flax seed made her unmanageable, and she went on an Au Sable Reef, several miles west of Grand Marais, Michigan. Five lives were lost, but the other 16

crewmen were saved in a courageous rescue effort. Though it is not agreed upon who actually did the rescuing, local fishermen probably deserve the credit. The ship went to pieces in place. [4]

S R KIRBY ■ Bulk freight composite steamer of 2,338 t. and 294 ft., launched in 1890 at Wyandotte, MI
Lake Superior: This iron and wood vessel was the largest composite steamer ever built on the Lakes, but she was no match for the spring blizzard-gale that ended her career on May 8, 1916. She was carrying a load of iron ore when the power of the storm became too much for her engines and she began to be pushed to shore. While trying to avoid dreaded Sawtooth Reef, near the top of the Keweenaw Peninsula, she broke her back in the big waves, then drifted to the reef and sank. 20 of her 22 crew perished in the freezing storm. [5+]

GILBERT KNAPP ■ Merchant schooner of 120 ft., launched in 1854 at Racine, WI (built as a 100 ft. two-master, lengthened in 1871)
Lake Michigan: This sail vessel had just taken on cargo and was trying to ride out a gale before departing, when she slipped her anchors and was driven ashore near Sholda Creek, close by the Sleeping Bear. Crashing waves wrecked the vessel following the September 6, 1896 grounding. [1]

KNIGHT TEMPLAR ■ Package and bulk freight schooner of 290 t. and 136 ft., launched in 1865 at Osewgo, NY
Lake Huron: This schooner with the dashing name finished her 40-year career smashed to kindling near Alpena, Michigan. On December 16, 1905, she was overwhelmed by a storm and cast into the shallows, where she was abandoned and later went to pieces. [2]

KREETAN ■ Gas screw of 15 t.
Lake Michigan: On November 15, 1939, the small motor vessel KREETAN was lost when she was one mile south of Grand Haven, Michigan. She was reportely crushed between two scows and sank. [1]

DAN KUNTZ or **KUNZ** ■ Wooden propeller freighter of 99 t. and 102 ft., launched in 1888 at Sandusky, OH
Lake Erie: This little steamer was stranded and totally wrecked near Cleveland on June 5, 1909. [2]

La FRENIER ■ Merchant schooner of 514 t. and 157 ft.
Lake Michigan: On November 7, 1886, the schooner La FRENIER struck Hog Island Shoal, in the Beaver Islands, and was lost. [3]

La PETITE ■ Merchant schooner
Lake Huron: The La PETITE was reported lost on the lake in 1871. [1]

La PETITE ■ Lumber schooner of 172 t. and 119 ft., launched in 1866 at Port Huron, MI
Lake Michigan: The schooner La PETITE was carrying wood slabs and a consignment of crockery when a heavy gale swept in on her on September 7, 1903. She was off Sturgeon Bay, Wisconsin, when she sprang a leak and found herself in deep trouble. The tug SYDNEY SMITH somehow got her in tow, but the tall ship capsized and sank before she could be brought to shore. Fortunately, no lives were lost in the foundering. [3]

LAC La BELLE ■ Wooden package and bulk freight steamer
Lake Superior: A single, cryptic report says that this ship, which had been carrying a cargo of treaty goods, was found on the beach by the steamer IRON CITY in 1865. There was no word on the fate of her crew or of her condition. This and the vessel below may be the same. [1]

LAC La BELLE ■ Wooden passenger and package freight steamer of 872 t. and 218 ft., launched in 1864 and rebuilt as a 1,187 tonner in 1869
St. Clair River: On November 23, 1866, the LAC La BELLE was carrying package freight and barrels of copper, silver, and iron ore when she was rammed by the steamer MILWAUKEE and sunk. She went down so quickly following the collision that two men were trapped below decks and drowned. She was recovered at great cost in 1869 and rebuilt. [2]
Lake Michigan: The LAC La BELLE was carrying a load of grain when she opened her seams in a gale and sank 20 miles off Racine, Wisconsin. Eight (maybe only 6) of her crew died in the October 13, 1872, accident. [2]

LACKAWANNA ■ Steel steam freighter of 2,015 t. and 260 ft., launched in 1880 at Cleveland
Lake Erie: For such a large vessel, information on the LACKAWANNA is strangely unavailable. Reports say that she went down on October 27, 1906 or 1909 north of Cleveland after a collision with a pier or vessel, but other records state that the only ship of this name and size was still operational until 1930. [3]

LADY OF THE LAKE ■ Merchant schooner of 230 t., launched in 1813 at Sacket's Harbor, NY as an 89 t. warship
Lake Ontario: This vessel was a former five-gun armed schooner that operated with the American Great Lakes Navy during the War of 1812. After the war she was converted to a merchant ship and served until she sank off Oswego, New York, in December of 1826. [2]

LADY OF THE LAKE ■ Merchant schooner
Lake Ontario: No lives were lost when the LADY OF THE LAKE went aground near Oak Orchard, New York, and was pounded to pieces by waves in August of 1847. [1]

LADY OF THE LAKE ■ Wooden propeller freighter of 326 t., built before 1847
Lake Erie: Two persons perished when this steamer exploded in March of 1859. [2]

LADY OF THE LAKE ■ Wooden steamer
Lake Superior: In 1869 the steamer LADY OF THE LAKE was destroyed by fire off Whetstone Brook, near Marquette, Michigan. [1]

LADY OF THE LAKE ■ Steamer of 2,504 t.
Lake Huron: This big steamer was reported to have sunk following a collision off Christian Island, near Penetanguishene, Ontario, on November 30, 1911. The vessel appears on neither U.S. nor Canadian ship records. [2]

FRANK LaFARGE ■ Merchant schooner
Lake Huron: The schooner FRANK LaFARGE was reported to have stranded and broken up in 1901 in Thunder Bay, on the Michigan coast. [1]

LAFAYETTE ■ Steel bulk freight steamer of 5,113 t. and 454 ft., launched in 1900 at Lorain, OH
Lake Superior: The giant freighter LAFAYETTE seemed to be the victim of a conspiracy to wreck her on November 29, 1905. She was fighting a terrible gale that was blowing in from the northeast when she was rammed by her towbarge, the 5,000 ton steel MANILA (qv). Rendered helpless, she was then thrown against the cliffs of Encampment Island, near Two Harbors, Minnesota, where she broke in half. The almost new steamer was quickly reduced to shambles. Her forward part was torn to pieces while her crew huddled in the battered after end. After the storm, the remainder of the vessel was towed away for scrap, with only her engine being salvageable. Miraculously, only one life was lost. [5+]

LAKE BREEZE ■ Wooden steamer of 301 t. and 122 ft., launched in 1868 at Toledo (one source says she was a schooner)
Lake Ontario: This vessel was destroyed by fire at a dock at Leamington, Ontario, on November 26, 1878. [2]

LAKE ERIE ■ Wooden steam canaller of 414 t. and 136 ft., launched in 1873 at St Catharine's, Ont.
Lake Michigan: On November 24, 1881, the steamer LAKE ERIE was underway when she met and collided with the steamer NORTHERN QUEEN and sank off Poverty Island, in the chain of islands that guards the mouth of Green Bay. One source gives Pointe Aux Barques as the location, which probably refers to the point of that name several miles to the northwest of Poverty Island. [5]

LAKELAND ■ Steel or iron package freight steamer and automobile carrier of 1,878 t. and 280 ft. (301 overall), launched at Cleveland in 1887 as the bulk freighter CAMBRIA
Lake Huron: The LAKELAND was a significant vessel in Lakes history. Not only was she the first Lakes vessel of over 300 ft., but she was the first ship to be powered by a triple expansion engine, which was the preferred powerplant on lakers for many years. The LAKELAND was carrying a cargo of new automobiles when she struck a reef, began to leak, then foundered off Sturgeon Bay, Wisconsin. She went down in a storm on December 4, 1924. In 1979, a 1924 Rowan automobile was salvaged from her deck. [5+]

LAKETON ■ Steam package freighter
Lake Superior: The LAKETON was laden with a cargo of lumber camp supplies on November 8, 1888, when she sank in heavy weather, five miles northeast of Grand Marais, Michigan. [2]

H A LAMARS ■ Merchant schooner of 88 t.
Lake Erie: The schooner H A LAMARS, laden with a cargo of wood, was reportedly lost to a white squall near Fairport, Ohio. No date is given. [2]

L L LAMB ■ Schooner-barge of 253 t. and 126 ft., launched in 1869 at Erie, PA
Lake Erie: Burdened with a cargo of stone, the barge L L LAMB foundered in heavy seas off Fairport, Ohio, on August 16, 1902. [3]

R T LAMBERT ■ Merchant schooner of 54 t. and 50 ft., launched in 1873 at Sebewaing, MI
Lake Huron: This little schooner was brand new when she was lost near the top of Saginaw Bay, off Caseville, Michigan, in 1873. [1]

LAMBTON ■ Lighthouse tender of 323 t. and 108 ft., launched in 1909 at Sorel, Que.
Lake Superior: The Canadian lighthouse tender LAMBTON was packed with gear and carrying relief keepers and crews to several Lake Superior lighthouses when she disappeared in a spring gale. She is thought to have gone down somewhere between Caribou Island and Whitefish Bay on April 19, 1922. Twenty-two men perished when the sturdy little ship sailed away. [5]

LAMBTON ■ Steel bulk freight steamer of 1,866 t. and 252 ft., launched in 1921 at Port Arthur, Ont. as the steamer GLENAFTON
Lake Superior: Two of the 20 men aboard the freighter LAMBTON were drowned when the steamer was driven ashore on Parisienne Island, northwest of the Soo, and heavily damaged on December 8, 1927. The ship was carrying grain at the time, and was recovered the next year and converted to a barge. [5+]

GEORGE LAMONT ■ Steam tug of 5 t.
Lake Michigan: This miniscule tow vessel was lost on March 14, 1880, off Pentwater, Michigan. She was one of the competitors in a tug race when a gale struck and overwhelmed the little vessel, causing her to sink with the loss of three of her crew. She had been sunk previously, on Lake Erie in 1877. [2]

LANCASTER ■ Barge
Lake Huron: In 1907 the barge LANCASTER was lost in Bayfield Sound, on the east side of Georgian Bay. [1]

LANGELL BOYS ■ Wooden bulk freight steamer of 387 t. and 151 ft., launched in 1890 at St. Clair, MI
Lake Huron: While travelling in ballast down the western side of the lake, the steamer LANGELL BOYS caught fire and was destroyed. The accident occurred near Au Sable Point, six miles south of Au Sable, Michigan, on June 13, 1931. No lives were lost in the accident. [3]

SIMON LANGELL ■ Wooden bulk freight steamer of 845 t. and 195 ft., launched in 1886 at St. Clair, MI
Lake Ontario or Huron: Stories conflict as to the location of the loss of the SIMON LANGELL. The fire that destroyed the 50-year-old ship occurred on November 23, 1936, but sources disagree as to whether the site was Kingston, Ontario (at the outlet of Lake Ontario) or Sarnia, Ontario (at the outlet of Lake Huron). The burned-out hulk was later scuttled. [4]

LANGHAM ■ Wooden bulk freight steamer of 1,810 t. and 281 ft., launched as the steamer TOM ADAMS in 1888 at W Bay City, MI
Lake Superior: All of the freighter LANGHAM's crew escaped when the vessel caught fire, burned to the waterline and sank on October 24, 1910. The blaze occurred while the steamer was sheltering in Michigan's Bete Grise Bay. The vessel and her cargo of coal were a total loss. [3]

JULES La PLANTE or **JULIE PLANTE** ■ Schooner-scow or scow
Lake St. Clair: This vessel is fictitious, but perhaps the tale of her loss reflects a real incident. A traditional French-accented poem that was entitled "The Wreck of the Jules LaPlante" was popular in foc'sles and wharfside taverns in the mid-19th Century. It described the loss of the wood carrying schooner-scow on the lake in a sudden storm. In the poem, only one person survives the disaster. Later, the poem was sold in modified form, describing the ship as the JULIE PLANTE. The incident in the poem is similar in many ways to the loss of the schooner-scow EMILY (qv) in 1830. [2]

LARK ■ Bulk freight schooner of 138 ft., launched in 1855 at Cleveland
Lake Michigan: The wreckage of this schooner is still visible from shore, even though she stranded and broke up on November 10, 1872. She lies near the mouth of the Carp River, close to Leland, Michigan. [2]

JULIA LARSEN ■ Merchant schooner of 60 t. and 70 ft., launched in 1874 at Manitowoc, WI
Lake Huron: The small schooner JULIA LARSEN was stranded and became a total loss on the southeast corner of Thunder Bay Island, on the Michigan coast. She was wrecked in 1912. [3]

LAURA BELLE ■ Merchant schooner of 269 t. and 138 ft., launched in 1870 at W Bay City, MI
Lake Superior: Carrying a cargo of coal. the schooner LAURA BELLE sank off Shot Point, east of Marquette, Michigan, on September 7, 1883. One life was lost in the foundering. She previously had been heavily damaged in a grounding in Waiska Bay, near the Soo, in 1879. [3]

LAURINA ■ Bulk freight schooner of 55 t. and 72 ft., launched in 1872 at Chicago
Lake Michigan: On April 20, 1893, the schooner LAURINA foundered with her cargo of lumber near Milwaukee. [2]

LIZZIE A LAW ■ Bulk freight schooner-barge of 747 t. and 196 ft., launched in 1875 at Port Huron, MI
Lake Superior: On October 19, 1908, the schooner-barge LIZZIE A LAW was in tow of the steamer L EDWARD HINES, when she was struck by a gale. The big, coal-laden vessel soon broke her towline and was driven ashore on Traverse Island, off the east side of the Keweenaw Peninsula, where she was pounded to pieces by waves. The crew members took to her lifeboat, and were saved. [4]

LAWRENCE ■ Merchant schooner of 284 t., launched in 1847 at Milwaukee
Lake Michigan: This schooner was lost in the Straits of Mackinac in 1850, when she was cut by ice and sank near St. Helena Island. [2]

LAWRENCE ■ Steam passenger and package freighter of 447 t. and 135 ft., launched in 1868 at Cleveland
Lake Michigan: The steamer LAWRENCE was wrecked in November of 1898, when she was blown ashore by a gale and wrecked on Point Betsie, on the Michigan side. One person died in the accident. [2]

A W LAWRENCE ■ Wooden passenger and package freight steamer of 48 t.
Lake Michigan: On October 30, 1888, this small steamer foundered in heavy weather off Milwaukee with a loss of four lives. She was in ballast at the time. [1]

IVER LAWSON ■ Bulk freight schooner-barge of 149 t. and 116 ft., launched in 1869 at Chicago
Lake Michigan: Horseshoe Bay, in Green Bay, was where the loss of the IVER LAWSON occurred. The schooner-barge stranded there on October 19, 1905, and was later broken up by wave action. [2]

CLARENCE LeBEAU ■ Wooden steam package freighter of 439 t. and 142 ft., launched in 1893 at Saugatuck as the steamer CITY OF HOLLAND
Lake Erie: The crane-equipped package freighter CLARENCE LeBEAU was destroyed at her dock—a victim of fire—at Toledo, Ohio. She burned on July 11, 1922. [2]

Le BLANC HENRI ■ Merchant bark
Lake Ontario: It's possible that the bark Le BLANC HENRI has a small fortune in coins aboard. She was reported to have foundered off Wolfe Island, near Kingston, Ontario, on June 17, 1864. [1]

LEAFIELD ■ Steel bulk freight steamer of 1,454 t. and 248 ft., in 1892 at Sunderland, England
Lake Superior: While the greatest damage from the Big Storm of 1913 was done in lower Lake Huron, the ferocious gale vented its wrath on all five of the Lakes in succession. The LEAFIELD was carrying a cargo of railroad ties and equipment to Fort William, at the lakehead, when the worst of the monster storm hit her on November 8. Though she was only a score or so miles from her destination, she could not make enough headway to get her through the big greybeards to safety. The vessel was finally driven aground on Angus Island, 14 miles from Thunder Bay. After ripping up her bottom plates, the big

waves pushed her into deep water, where she still lies. All 18 of the LEAFIELD's crew accompanied their vessel to the bottom. [5+]

LEANDER ■ Merchant schooner
Lake Michigan: In 1857 the schooner LEANDER foundered and was lost near Gros Cap, on the northern shore of the Straits of Mackinac. [1]

FREDERICK A LEE ■ Steam tug of 33 t.
Lake Huron: The tug FREDERICK A LEE was lost with all five hands off Pointe Aux Barques, Michigan, on November 13, 1936. It is speculated that her boilers exploded and she went down quickly. [5]

JOHN LEE, Sr ■ Steam tug of 61 t. and 52 ft., launched in 1888, at Wallaceburg, Ont.
Lake Huron: In August of 1913 the tug JOHN LEE, Sr, caught fire and was destroyed at a dock at Port McNicoll, Ontario, in Georgian Bay. [3]

LAURA H LEE ■ Tug of 81 t.
Lake Huron: A fire destroyed this tug on October 23, 1929, while she was sitting at her dock at Meldrum Bay, on the North Channel side of Manitoulin Island. [2]

OLIVE LEE ■ Merchant bark of 432 t. and 160 ft., launched in 1845 at Chippewa, Ont. as the steamer CANADIAN
Lake Huron: The bark OLIVE LEE was wrecked in a storm in November of 1857. Her remains ended up near Old Mackinac Point, just east of the site of the present Mackinac Bridge. [2]

LEHIGH ■ Steam freighter
Lake Huron: This steamer reportedly sank following a collision in heavy weather in 1914. There is no report of her position at the time of the accident, and the vessel was probably recovered. [1]

LELAND ■ Wooden bulk freight steamer of 366 t. and 148 ft., launched in 1873 at New Jerusalem, OH
Lake Erie: A fire was the cause of the demise of the LELAND on December 7, 1910. The ship was destroyed at Huron, Ohio. She may also have been severely damaged in an 1888 fire. [5]

LEO ■ Steam launch
Lake Erie: The LEO had set out from Rocky River, Ohio, for a pleasure cruise on September 25, 1889 with nine persons aboard. Before she returned home, the little vessel was struck by a heavy squall during which she was rocked by an explosion and sank. Tragically, all those on board perished. [2]

FLORENCE LESTER ■ Lumber schooner-barge of of 265 t. and 135 ft.
Lake Michigan: The schooner-barge FLORENCE LESTER and her cargo of lumber were lost on October

1, 1889, when the ship was blown ashore and wrecked near Manistee, Michigan. [1]

T G LESTER ■ Lumber schooner of 257 t. and 141 ft., launched in 1868 at E. Saginaw, MI
Lake Erie: Wooden ships that set forth on the Lakes before the winter ice was off were always in jeopardy. On March 30, 1908, the schooner T G LESTER gambled against the ice and lost, striking a floe and quickly sinking at an undisclosed position. [2]

D LEUTY ■ Wooden bulk freight steamer of 647 t. and 179 ft., built at Lorain, OH, in 1882
Lake Superior: No lives were lost, but the LEUTY was totally destroyed in an accident that occurred on October 31, 1911. The ship was without cargo and near Marquette when she stranded in a blinding snowstorm. Big waves that followed literally ripped the vessel apart. Not much of the LEUTY remained, but her after deckhouse was used for a summer cottage nearby until 1965. [5]

LEVIATHAN ■ Merchant schooner of 91 t.
Lake Erie: This vessel was driven ashore in a storm on the "clay banks" area near Port Burwell, Ontario, on October 5, 1870. She was a total loss. [2]

LEVIATHAN ■ Wooden tug or towing steamer of 232 t. and 136 ft., launched in 1857 at Buffalo
Lake Huron: The big tug LEVIATHAN was lost at Cheboygan, Michigan, on November 21, 1891. She caught fire and burned to the waterline. [2]

LEWIE ■ Merchant schooner of 11 t. and 39 ft., launched in 1884 at Duluth
Lake Superior: The lake gods have no mercy on a tiny wooden vessel like the LEWIE. On September 2, 1904, she foundered off Two Harbors, Minnesota. Neither of her two crewmen were lost. [2]

SAM LEWIS ■ Propeller freighter of 102 t., launched at Detroit in 1861
Lake Huron: The SAM LEWIS was another victim of the rugged shoreline of Georgian Bay. On November 12, 1871, she was stranded and lost on Cape Croker, on the Bruce Peninsula. [3]

LEXINGTON ■ Merchant schooner of 53 t.
Lake Erie: Point Mouillee, at the extreme western end of the lake, beckoned this schooner to her death on November 19, 1846. She foundered four miles offshore with the loss of 13 lives. The LEXINGTON was reportedly carrying a cargo of barrelled whiskey at the time. One source gives the Lake Erie Islands as the location. [5]

LIBBY ■ Merchant schooner
Lake Superior: The small schooner LIBBY was pulled away from her dock at Marquette by a November 24, 1877 storm. The vessel was thrown ashore and dashed to pieces, a total loss. [1]

LIBERTY ■ Wooden package and bulk freight steamer of 85 t. and 97 ft., launched in 1889 at Fort Howard, WI
Lake Superior: In 1919 the steamer LIBERTY was destroyed by fire at Grand Marais, Minnesota. [2]

LIGHTSHIP #82 ■ Lightship of 187 t. and 80 ft., launched in 1912 at Muskegon, MI
Lake Erie: This vessel was popularly known as the "Buffalo," since this was painted on her sides in large letters. During the Big Storm of 1913, the brave little ship stayed on station off Buffalo while giant steamers all over the lakes were being torn apart or sunk by the gale. But on the 12th of November, the small ship could take no more. She suddenly sank, taking all six of her crew with her. Though her wreckage was difficult to locate, she was later recovered and returned to service as a tender. [5+]

CHARLES W LIKEN ■ Wooden packet of 37 t. and 63 ft., launched at W Bay City in 1880
Lake Huron: This little vessel was a total loss to fire when she burned on the Saginaw River at Bay City, Michigan. The accident took place on August 13, 1905. [2]

J C or JOHN C LIKEN ■ Propeller freighter, probably the 79 t., 90 ft. vessel launched at Sebewaing, MI, in 1873
Lake Huron: The steamer J C LIKEN was reportedly lost on May 2, 1890, when she foundered in a gale on Hammond Bay, in the northwest part of the lake. She was carrying a cargo of general freight at the time. [3]

LILLIE E ■ Bulk freight schooner of 182 t.
Lake Michigan: Both Manistee and Milwaukee are given as sites for the accident that destroyed this schooner. On May 21, 1883, in a howling gale, she struck a bar off one of those harbors (probably Milwaukee), then limped away to sink near the beach. The U.S. Lifesaving Service rescued all of her crew. She was carrying a cargo of oats at the time of her demise. [2]

JOHN LILLIE ■ Scow of 96 t., built before 1847
Lake Michigan: The scow JOHN LILLIE was reported wrecked off Grand Haven, Michigan, in 1870. [1]

LILLY MAY ■ Merchant schooner of 301 t. and 150 ft., launched in 1867 at Algonac, MI
Detroit River: The schooner LILLY MAY went down off Detroit on May 16, 1905. She was abandoned as a total loss. [2]

LILY ■ Schooner-scow of 29 t. and 58 ft., launched in 1858 at Sandusky
Lake Erie: This schooner-scow was reported as lost near Vermilion, Ohio, in 1862. [1]

LINA ■ Steamer of 106 t. and 88 ft., launched in 1866 at Montreal
Lake Ontario: Trenton, Ont., was the site of the loss of the steamer LINA. She was lost to fire in July of 1868. [1]

LINCOLN ■ Bulk freight steam barge of 375 t. and 131 ft., launched in 1872 at St Catharine's, Ont.
Lake Huron: On October 19, 1887, the steamer LINCOLN was carrying a cargo of railroad ties when she encountered a storm and was forced ashore and wrecked at Little Pike Bay, near the Fishing Islands. Most reports end there. However, two reliable sources report that the vessel was rebuilt and returned to service as the LILLIE SMITH, and later as the MARY BATTLE. She had a long career, finally sinking in the Atlantic, off the Gaspé, in 1922. [7]

A LINCOLN ■ Merchant schooner
Lake Huron: This schooner was reported to have been driven ashore and lost at Au Sable, Michigan (near Oscoda) in 1872. [1]

JENNY LIND ■ Bulk freight schooner of 111 t.
Lake Michigan: The schooner JENNY LIND met her fate south of the Chicago waterfront on May 21, 1883. Four crew members died when the vessel capsized and sank. [2]

LINDEN ■ Wooden bulk freight steamer of 894 t. and 206 ft., launched in 1895 at Port Huron, MI
Lake Huron: The handsome steamer LINDEN was lost in Tawas Bay, on the Michigan coast, on November 28, 1923. She caught fire at her dock at Tawas City, drifted out into the bay, and sank. Her remains were salvaged for their scrap value in 1930. She had also been sunk in a mishap near Sarnia in 1911. [5]

WILLIAM R LINN ■ Steel bulk freight steamer of 4,328 t. and 420 ft., launched in 1898 at Chicago
Lake Huron: Fighting a November 4, 1918 storm just north of Point Edward, at the base of the lake, the big steamer WILLIAM R LINN swamped and foundered well offshore. An expensive salvage operation recovered her, even though she had been declared lost. She was later converted to a tanker. [2]

LISGAR ■ Merchant schooner of 323 t.
Lake Huron: Cove Island, just north of Tobermory, Ontario, saw the loss of the schooner LISGAR, on September 3, 1899. She went aground and was wrecked. [2]

LITTLE EASTERN ■ Steam tug of 32 t., launched in 1859 at Detroit
Lake Huron: This small tug was lost on the Saginaw River, when she collided with the steamer FOX and sank on June 29, 1861. [2]

LITTLE BELT ■ Armed schooner of 96 t., launched on Lake Erie in 1813
Lake Erie: The LITTLE BELT was a three-gun Royal Navy gunboat that served near the end of the War of 1812. She burned at Black Rock, in 1813, either by accident or by arson. [1]

LITTLE GEORGY ■ Merchant schooner of 52 t. and 81 ft., launched in 1870 at Sheboygan, WI
Lake Huron: The small sail vessel LITTLE GEORGY was lost in the Straits of Mackinac when she foundered in a storm in 1912. [2]

LITTLE NELL ■ Steam freighter
Lake Huron: This steamer exploded and was lost on the Saginaw River, at Saginaw, in 1862. [1]

LITTLE WESTERN ■ Wooden steam freighter of 60 t., launched in 1834 at Chatham, Ont.
Lake Erie: This steam vessel was reported destroyed by fire on the lake in 1842. [2]

LITTLE WISSAHICKON ■ Bulk freight schooner-barge of 377 t. and 146 ft.
Lake Erie: Three men lost their lives when the barge LITTLE WISSAHICKON was lost from the tow of her steamer, the DONALDSON, in a storm. She filled and sank 22 miles south of Rondeau Point, on July 10, 1896. The barge was carrying a load of coal at the time of the tragedy. [2]

LIVE YANKEE ■ Merchant schooner of 212 t.
Lake Michigan: A mild winter tempted this schooner to test the lake in January of 1867. She did not live to regret the mistake. She stranded and broke up one mile off Beaver Island. [2]

LIVELY ■ Merchant schooner
Lake Huron: The schooner LIVELY was reported to have foundered of Harbor Beach, Michigan, in 1878. [1]

P B LOCKE ■ Bulk freight schooner-barge of 285 t. and 135 ft., launched in 1873 at Toledo, OH
Lake Ontario: This little schooner-barge was in tow of the steamer JUNO when she was caught in a storm and sank three miles offshore near Port Hope, Ontario. The loss happened on November 1, 1912. [2]

C B LOCKWOOD ■ Wooden bulk freight steamer of 2,323 t. and 293 ft., launched at Cleveland in 1890
Lake Erie: The big freighter C B LOCKWOOD went down in a fall storm, taking ten of her crew and her cargo of wheat with her. The accident occurred on October 13, 1902, off Fairport, Ohio. [5+]

LODI ■ Merchant schooner
Lake Erie: The schooner LODI was reported driven ashore and demolished by a gale on November 20, 1838. [1]

LODI ■ Merchant schooner
Lake Huron: This sail vessel was lost following a collision with the steamer CHATAUQUA in 1842. The schooner's remains lie somewhere off Sturgeon Point, north of Harrisville, MI. This may be the same LODI as above. [1]

LONDON ■ Armed brig
Lake Ontario (probably): The LONDON was a British warship that was lost in armed combat with the French in 1756 (Seven Year's War). [1]

LONDON ■ Type uncertain, but probably propeller, launched at Cobourg, Ont., in 1843
Lake Ontario: This vessel was reported lost on the lake in 1858. [1]

LONDON ■ Bulk freight barge of 263 t.
Lake Ontario: This barge was without cargo when she was ripped away from her towing vessel, the tug FERRIS, and thrown ashore near Oswego, New York. The windstorm which caused the damage occurred on October 2, 1886. [1]

CITY OF LONDON ■ Steam freighter of 307 t. and 145 ft., launched in 1865 at St. Catharine's, Ont.
Lake Huron: The steamer CITY OF LONDON was destroyed on Georgian Bay's remote Collins Inlet on September 20, 1874 (some sources say 1875). She was destroyed by fire. [4]

CITY OF LONDON ■ Wooden bulk freight steamer of 2,005 t. and 297 ft., launched in 1891 at W Bay City, MI
Lake Erie: The main shipping channels up and down Lake Erie converge and are compressed where they must pass between Point Pelee and Pelee Island. The unfortunate result is that many collisions have occurred at that point. The steamer CITY OF LONDON was victim of such an accident on September 30, 1913. She was downbound with a load of wheat when she crossed paths with the steel steamer JOSEPH S MORROW, was rammed and sank just south of Point Pelee. She was later dynamited as a navigational hazard. [3]

LONE STAR ■ Lumber schooner of 21 t.
Lake Erie: The lumber-carrying schooner LONE STAR is reported to have gone ashore at the Quarry Docks, near Sandusky, Ohio. She was lost on September 26, 1892. [1]

JOHN J LONG ■ Tug of 201 t. and 98 ft., launched in 1894 at Collingwood, Ont.
Lake Huron: The big tug JOHN J LONG was operating at Meldrum Bay, in the North Channel, when she caught fire and was destroyed. The accident happened in September of 1901. [2]

LOOKOUT ■ Merchant schooner of 226 t. and 127 ft., launched in 1855 at Buffalo
Lake Michigan: A spring storm struck the old schooner LOOKOUT on April 29, 1897, and caused her to sink north of the harbor at Two Rivers, Wisconsin. One source says she was lost in December of the same year. [3]

B R LOOMIS ■ Vessel information unreported
Lake Huron: All but one of the crew of the B R LOOMIS were lost when this vessel foundered in midlake in 1872. [1]

EDWARD E LOOMIS ■ Steam freighter
Lake Huron: The LOOMIS was reported ashore and wrecked at Harrisville, Michigan, in 1934, but no details are available. See also W C FRANZ. [1]

JARVIS LORD ■ Wooden propeller freighter of 178 ft., launched in 1872 at Marine City, MI
Lake Michigan: Following a collision with a schooner in July of 1885, the steamer JARVIS LORD was inspected and declared seaworthy. However, on August 17 the LORD was bound for Chicago with a load of iron ore when she was discovered to have developed a serious leak. Her crew quickly abandoned her, and she sank in deep water in the Manitou Passage, east of the Manitou Islands. [2]

LOTHAIR ■ Bulk freight steam barge of 413 t. and 130 ft., launched in 1872 at St. Catharine's, Ont.
Detroit River: The steam barge LOTHAIR was lying at her dock at Windsor, Ontario, when she caught fire and burned to her hull in January of 1893. Though the LOTHAIR was thought to be a total loss, her hull was used as the basis for rebuilding as an unrigged barge. [3]

LOUISA ■ Barge of 323 t.
Lake Huron: On November 13, 1890, the barge LOUISA and her consort, the steamer BRUNO (qv), were beset by a heavy gale. The steamer piled in on Magnetic Reef, near Cockburn Island, and the hapless LOUISA was dragged in after. Both vessels foundered on the reef. [2]

LOUISE ■ Merchant schooner of 39 t. and 60 ft., launched in 1874 at W Bay City, MI. The position of the little LOUISE when she met her fate is not disclosed, but the schooner was reported as a total loss in 1902. [1]

LOUISE ■ Gas screw of 11 t.
Lake St. Clair: The little motor vessel LOUISE was sunk on the Detroit waterfront, near the site of "Chickenbone Reef," on March 22, 1946. (The term Chickenbone Reef was used derisively to refer to the supposed reef formed by the dinner waste from naval reserve vessels tied up at the foot of Woodward Avenue in Detroit for decades on end.) [1]

LOUISIANA ■ Wooden bulk freight steamer of 1,753 t. and 267 ft., launched in 1887 at Marine City, MI
Lake Michigan: Though no lives were lost, the wooden steamer LOUISIANA was a significant loss in the Big Storm of 1913. On November 10, the cargoless vessel was being tossed and beaten so heavily by the storm that she anchored in Washington Harbor, on Washington Island, at the tip of Wisconsin's Door Peninsula. Sometime during the early morning of the 11th, the battered vessel caught fire and was completely destroyed. [5+]

LOUISVILLE ■ Wooden steam freighter of 366 t. and 140 ft.
Lake Michigan: The steamer LOUISVILLE was a victim of fire in September of 1857. She burned and sank near Calumet, Illinois, with no loss of life. [2]

LOWELL ■ Merchant brig
Lake Huron: The small sailing vessel LOWELL was reported lost near Cove Island, in the mouth of Georgian Bay, in 1871. [1]

LOWELL ■ Propeller freighter of 344 t. and 136 ft., launched in 1865 at Cleveland
Lake Huron: The steamer LOWELL had just emerged from the St. Clair River when she caught fire and was destroyed, a short distance offshore from Port Huron, Michigan. She burned in 1893. [2]

LUCERNE ■ Merchant schooner of 728 t. and 195 ft.
Lake Superior: Laden with a cargo of iron ore, the graceful schooner LUCERNE was outbound, a short distance from Ashland, Wisconsin, when she foundered near Chequamegon Point. All 10 hands were lost when the ship went down on November 17, 1886. [2]

LUCILLE ■ Propeller of 136 t.
Lake Erie: The small propeller LUCILLE is reported to have foundered one mile east of Turtle Island light, near Toledo, in August of 1906. [1]

LUCKNOW ■ Wooden steam freighter of 256 t. and 120 ft. launched as the steam tug WILLIAM H PRINGLE (qv) at Saginaw, MI, in 1871
Lake Huron: The Georgian Bay port of Midland, Ontario, was the site of the loss of this aged steamer. The LUCKNOW was destroyed by fire there in December of 1935. [2]

LUCKPORT ■ Wooden steam freighter of 231 t. and 126 ft., launched in 1880 at Hamilton, Ont. as the steamer 170 ft. propeller ST MAGNUS (qv), shortened 44 ft after an 1895 fire
Lake Huron: The wooden steamer LUCKPORT was totally destroyed by fire at Midland, Ontario, in lower Georgian Bay, in December of 1934. [3]

LUCKY ▪ Scow of 109 t.
Lake Huron: This scow was stranded on Cordwood Point, a few miles east of Cheboygan, Michigan, and wrecked. The vessel grounded on September 22, 1951 (or '57). [2]

LURLINE ▪ Steam yacht and sometime cargo carrier of 66 t. and 79 ft., launched in 1888 at Windsor, Ont.
Lake Huron: Taking a late-season trip up the coast from Windsor in October of 1907, the lovely yacht/cargo vessel LURLINE was wrecked and lost off Goderich, Ont. [2]

LYCOMING ▪ Wooden bulk freight steamer of 1,609 t. and 251 ft., launched in 1880 at W Bay City, MI as a package freighter
Lake Erie: The freighter LYCOMING became a victim of fire on October 21, 1910, when she was destroyed at her berth at Rondeau, Ontario. She was one of a small number of hog-braced bulk freighters on the Lakes. [4]

LYDIA ▪ Package and bulk freight schooner of 83 t. and 80 ft., launched in 1874 at Manitowoc, WI
Lake Huron: The little schooner LYDIA could not stand up to one of the several gales that struck the Lakes in 1905. She was lost far out on the lake on October 20. [3]

LYDIA ▪ Fishing tug of 54 t. and 47 ft.
Lake Superior: Commercial fishing craft are among the most seaworthy of vessels, for they often must venture out when even the large steamers would stop to ponder. Therefore it was a violent gale indeed that turned the fishing tug LYDIA bottom-up and sank her, just off the entrance to the harbor at Grand Marais, Michigan. All five fishermen aboard died in the November 25, 1932 sinking. [2]

MARY ANN LYDON ▪ Merchant schooner of 117 t., launched in 1874 at Port Burwell, Ont.
Lake Ontario: The position of the schooner LYDON at the time of her loss is not reported, but the vessel was destroyed somewhere along the south shore of the lake in a storm which hit her on October 14, 1912. [1]

JOHN B LYON ▪ Wooden bulk freight steamer of 1,710 t. and 250 ft., launched in 1881 at Cleveland
Lake Erie: As violent as Great Lakes storms can be, they are localized disturbances when compared to the vast hurricanes that harry the Gulf of Mexico and other parts of the earth's surface. In September of 1900, one of the largest hurricanes ever recorded nearly flattened the gulf port of Galveston, Texas, costing over 6,000 lives. As this "Galveston Hurricane" swept up the Mississipi Valley and into the Great Lakes Basin, it lost some of its fury, but it was still powerful enough to tear the big steamer JOHN B LYON apart and sink her off North Girard, Pennsylvania, on September 11. Eleven of the sixteen crewmen of the LYON were drowned in the maelstrom. [4]

NELLIE LYON ▪ Wooden sandsucker barge of 316 t. and 145 ft., launched in 1880 at S Rockwood, MI, launched as the barge H C SPRAGUE, converted to a powered freighter in 1906, then back to a barge in 1910
St. Clair River: The wooden barge NELLIE LYON was lost on April 9, 1911, when she burned near Algonac, Michigan. [3]

DANIEL LYONS ▪ Merchant schooner
Lake Michigan: This schooner, the DANIEL LYONS, was lost in October of 1878, when she sank following a collision. [1]

KATE LYONS ▪ Lumber schooner of 201 t. and 122 ft., launched in 1867 at Black River, OH
Lake Michigan: Big storms stalked the Lakes all through the fall of 1905. At least three major gales and several minor ones ended the careers of more than 75 vessels. The small lumber schooner KATE LYONS succumbed to the October 20th storm. All four of her crew died (though one source says all were rescued) when the vessel stranded on a bar and quickly went to pieces near Holland, Michigan. [5+]

W S LYONS ▪ Merchant schooner
Lake Michigan: The area between the Beaver Islands and the Michigan shore is carpeted with reefs, islets and shallow areas. Even today, there are no fewer than five working lighthouses in this small area. White Shoals, northwest of Waugoschance Island, is one of the more dangerous spots and has captured a number of vessels, including the schooner W S LYONS, which piled into the reef and was lost in 1871. [1]

LYRIC ▪ Steam tug of 11 t. and 33 ft., launched in 1887 at Buffalo
Lake Superior: A major port for iron ore, lumber, and wheat at the turn of the century, it was no wonder the harbor at Duluth was the site of so many collisions. On August 25, 1898, two of the dozens of busy harbor tugs, the LYRIC and the G EMERSON, collided. The diminutive LYRIC was rammed amidships by the much larger EMERSON, and quickly sank. [2]

MACEDONIAN ▪ Merchant schooner
Lake Erie: The early schooner MACEDONIAN was abroad in the island-flecked western end of Lake Erie when she struck the west side of East Sister Island and sank near shore. At the time of the accident, October 23, 1829, there were still only a relatively small number of

ships plying the Lakes, so her crew was fortunate that they were picked up by the passing schooner MINERVA. [1]

LYDIA MACK ■ 4 t. vessel of unreported type
Lake Erie: The tiny LYDIA MACK was reported to have foundered off Port Stanley, Ontario, on October 3, 1877. [1]

MACK JEAN ■ Propeller steamer of 146 t. and 83 ft., launched in 1898 at Manitowoc, WI, as the steamer C W ENDRESS
Lake Erie: Fire destroyed the MACK JEAN in port at Kingsville, Ontario, in August of 1927. [1]

MACKINAC ■ Scow of 238 t.
Lake Michigan: The scow MACKINAC was carrying a load of lumber when she foundered in a storm off Muskegon, Michigan, on November 16, 1893. [2]

MACKINAW ■ Propeller freighter, probably the 142 t. vessel built at Detroit in 1866
Lake Huron: The freighter MACKINAW was destroyed by fire offshore near Black River, Michigan, south of Thunder Bay. The vessel burned in 1890. [2]

SILVANUS J MACY ■ Wooden bulk freight steamer of 752 t. and 165 ft., launched in 1881 at Marine City, MI
Lake Erie: The SILVANUS J MACY was upbound with a cargo of coal on the night of November 23, 1902. She had been shouldering her way through a heavy gale all day, but was finally overwhelmed when she was well offshore, abeam of Port Burwell, Ontario. She went down with all hands, 14 men. [5+]

LIZZIE MADDEN ■ Wooden bulk freight steamer of 690 t. and 175 ft., launched at Detroit in 1887 as the steamer CHENANGO (qv)
Lake Huron: The LIZZIE MADDEN was a well-known vessel in the Saginaw-Bay City area of Michigan. Residents were saddened on November 22, 1907, by the news that the steamer, with a load of lumber from Saginaw, had caught fire near Point Lookout, some miles up the beach, and burned to a shell. Her remains drifted out to end up on the beach on the south side of Big Charity Island. [4]

MADELINE ■ Merchant schooner of 20 t. and 40 ft., launched in 1837 at Lorain, OH
Lake Superior: In 1839, the Lake Superior area was still mostly uncharted and without regular lines of communication. It is no wonder that there are conflicting reports of the loss of the tiny schooner MADELINE in that year. She was reportedly wrecked either on the south shore of Isle Royale, at Minnesota Point, or on the shore of the island in the Apostles now known as Madeline Island. [4]

MADIERA ■ 322 t. vessel of unreported type
Lake Erie: The MADIERA was lost on October 3, 1887, when she stranded on Long Point and broke up. [1]

MADIERA ■ Steel schooner-barge of 5,039 t. and 436 ft., launched at South Chicago in 1900
Lake Superior: Technically a schooner-barge, it is doubtful if this huge vessel could have made much headway on her own with her tiny masts and sails. She was even unmanageable to her tow vessel, the big steamer WILLIAM EDENBORN (qv), when the two were caught in a powerful storm that struck the western end of the lake on November 29, 1905. The MADIERA piled ashore near Split Rock, Minnesota, and broke up. One of the big vessel's 11 crewmen lost his life in the accident. [5]

CITY OF MADISON ■ Wooden propeller freighter of 395 t. and 134 ft., launched in 1857 at Buffalo
Lake Michigan: This wooden steamer was reportedly without cargo when she caught fire and was destroyed on August 17, 1877. [1]

MAGANETTAWAN ■ Passenger and package freight propeller of 187 t. and 100 ft., launched in 1877 at Byng Inlet
Lake Huron: On July 15, 1896, the steamer MAGANETTAWAN went on a bar near Byng Inlet, Ontario, and was wrecked. [4]

MAGELLAN ■ Bulk freight schooner of 350 t.
Lake Michigan: Carrying a cargo of corn, the schooner MAGELLAN went missing somewhere off the southern Wisconsin coast (possibly near Two Rivers), on November 9, 1877. All eight of the sailing ship's crew were lost with her. One source says she was lost on Lake Superior. [3]

MAGGIE ■ Scow
Lake Huron: The scow MAGGIE went ashore near Goderich, Ontario, and was wrecked in 1871. [1]

MAGGIE ■ Bulk freight schooner-barge
Lake Huron: The schooner-barge MAGGIE was in tow of the steamer EMBERLY, when she broke her towline in a storm. With her heavy cargo of ore she could not come up to meet the waves, and was just pounded until her seams opened and she sank off Presque Isle, Michigan. The exact date of her loss is not reported, but it occurred around the year 1918. [1]

MAGIC ■ Merchant schooner
Lake Huron: The schooner MAGIC was reported to have sunk in Saginaw Bay in 1861. She may have been recovered. [1]

MAGNETIC ■ Bulk freight schooner-barge of 1,676 t. and 264 ft., launched in 1882 at Cleveland
Lake Erie: It has been said that 250 feet was the approximate length limit for wooden vessels not equipped with special bracing to keep them from "hogging" (drooping at the ends), and eventually breaking. The theory was tested by several large schooner-barges and schooners, and a number of them failed (see DAVID DOWS, ATHENS). The MAGNETIC was in tow of the steamer E M BREITUNG and loaded with iron ore when the two vessels encountered a moderate blow on August 25, 1917. The big schooner-barge rode up on a wave, broke her back, and sank 19 miles west of Long Point. [3]

J H MAGRUDER ■ Merchant schooner of 137 t. and 114 ft., launched in 1869 at Toussaint, Ohio
Lake Huron: Downbound with her cargo of lumber in September of 1895, the schooner J H MAGRUDER went onto the beach and broke up a few miles south of Sturgeon Point, near Harrisville, Michigan. [4]

MAIA ■ Self-unloading steel barge of 3,804 t. and 376 ft., launched in 1898 at Chicago
Lake Superior: A big gale which struck Lake Superior on November 29, 1905, almost proved to be the undoing of the big barge MAIA. She was torn away from her tow steamer and cast ashore near Split Rock, Minnesota, where she was heavily battered by waves. She was quickly declared a total loss. Too quickly, perhaps, because she was later salvaged and returned to service and was not finally retired until 1962. [4]

MAID OF THE MIST ■ Merchant schooner launched at Buffalo in 1854
Lake Huron: In 1878 this schooner was reported as lost on Ninemile Point, in the South Channel of the Straits of Mackinac. [2]

MAID-OF-THE-MIST ■ Excursion steamer of 62 t. and 71 ft., launched in 1885 at Niagara Falls, Ont. and
MAID-OF-THE-MIST #2 ■ Excursion steamer of 80 t. and 76 ft., launched in 1892 at Niagara Falls, NY
Lake Ontario: These two little propellers thrilled thousands by challenging the spray and eddying currents below thundering Niagara Falls. After long careers, they were both destroyed in the same fire in April of 1955, at Niagara Falls, Ontario. [2]

MAIME ■ Scow or schooner-scow
Lake Huron: The MAIME reportedly foundered a short distance offshore at Pte Aux Barques, MI, in 1858. [1]

MAINE ■ Propeller freighter of 332 t. and 132 ft., launched in 1862 at Buffalo
Lake Superior: The steamer MAINE sank in 1906, just off the lower entry to the Portage Ship Canal. This is probably the same vessel as listed below. [2]

MAINE ■ Wooden bulk freight steamer of 138 ft. overall, launched in 1862 at Buffalo
St. Clair River: The steamer MAINE seemed destined to meet her end by fire. After being heavily damaged by blazes in 1880 and 1898 (not to mention the possible sinking listed above), she caught fire and was destroyed for good at Marine City, Michigan, on July 11, 1911. [2]

MAINE or **MAIME** ■ Bulk freight schooner of 153 t.
Lake Michigan: On October 23, 1887, the schooner MAINE sank at the mouth of the harbor at Milwaukee. Her cargo of railroad ties reputedly washed up on beaches all over the lake for months afterwards. [3]

MAITLAND ■ Bark of 134 ft.
Lake Michigan: The four-masted bark MAITLAND was lost near Waugoschance Point, in the northeast corner of the lake, as the result of a bizarre three-way collision between her and schooners MEARS (qv) and GOLDEN HARVEST. The accident occurred in June of 1871. [2]

ALEX MAITLAND ■ Steamer
Lake Huron: Little detail is reported about this steam vessel that was destroyed by fire near Port Huron, Michigan, in 1924. [2]

THOMAS MAITLAND ■ Wooden steamer of 107 t. and 90 ft., launched in 1899 at Owen Sound, Ont.
Lake Superior: The fate of this steamer was gravely in doubt after she was devastated by fire at Port Arthur, Ontario, on May 9, 1927. Though it took more than a year to begin work, she was rebuilt and returned to service for another 20 years. [3]

MAJESTIC ■ Wooden passenger and package freight propeller of 1,578 t. and 209 ft., launched in 1895 at Collingwood, Ont.
St. Clair River: On the night of December 15, 1915, the steamer MAJESTIC caught fire at her moorings at Point Edward, Ontario. She burned through her mooring lines and was set adrift on the river, imperiling docks, warehouses and other boats. She finally sank several miles downstream, below Sarnia. [4]

MAJESTIC ■ Propeller freighter of 1,985 t. and 291 ft., launched in 1889 at W Bay City, MI
Lake Erie: The big steamer MAJESTIC was a September 19, 1907 loss. On that date, she caught fire while in transit, burned and sank, twelve miles west of Long Point. [2]

MAJOR ■ Wooden bulk freight steamer of 1,864 t. and 293 ft., launched in 1889 at W Bay City, MI, as the steamer JOHN MITCHELL
Lake Superior: This wooden freighter was the final victim of the Big Storm of 1913. On November 13, after the monster storm had done its damage all over the Lakes, it gave a flick of its tail and struck the MAJOR. Still encountering heavy waves after five days, the 24-year-old vessel sprang a leak and began to fill off Whitefish Bay. Her crew hastily abandoned the seemingly doomed old freighter. In the general pessimism concerning shipping losses that followed the storm, she was quickly declared a total loss, but was later found still afloat, was recovered, and served on until converted to a floating drydock in 1920. [5+]

MALAKOFF ■ Steamer of 172 ft., launched in 1842 at Montreal as the steamer NORTH AMERICA (may have been a schooner)
Lake Huron: The steamer MALAKOFF foundered well offshore from Goderich, Ontario, in November of 1857. [2]

MANASOO ■ Steel passenger steamer and cattle carrier of 529 t. and 178 ft., launched in 1889 at Glasgow, Scotland, as the steamer MACASSA
Lake Huron: The MANASOO was in transit across Georgian Bay with her holds full of cattle, and breasting a heavy gale in the early morning hours of September 15, 1928. At the heighth of the tempest the steamer's live cargo shifted, causing the ship to turn turtle and sink. Sixteen of the 21 persons aboard lost their lives in the accident. It is said that those cattle that didn't make it to shore alive stocked the winter larder of many a local home. [4]

EDWARD J MANEY ■ Steamer
Lake Superior: Twenty-one people perished when the steamer EDWARD J MANEY, bucking a May 8, 1916, storm, broke in two and sank near Duluth. [2]

MANHATTAN ■ Merchant brig of 140 t.
Lake Erie: The brig MANHATTAN was reported to have gone aground and broken up at Point Abino, halfway between Port Colborne, Ontario, and Buffalo. She was carrying a cargo of general merchandise when she was lost in November of 1838. [2]

MANHATTAN ■ Wooden passenger and package freight steamer of 319 t. and 149 ft. launched in 1847 at Cleveland
Lake Superior: The MANHATTAN was carrying passengers and cargo of general freight when she was driven ashore by a gale on September 1, 1859. She was attempting to enter the harbor at Grand Marais, Michigan, for

shelter when she struck a bar. Local reports say that her wreckage partially blocked the mouth of the harbor for almost 20 years. In an interesting footnote, a local trapper wrote to his supplier in 1861 that he had scavenged the hulk to obtain grooved siding to make a window sash for his cabin. [4]

MANHATTAN ■ Wooden bulk freight steamer of 1,545 t. and 252 ft., launched in 1887 at Wyandotte, MI
Lake Superior: The approach to Munising, Michigan, harbor is guarded by Grand Island, which has a channel on each side. The East Channel, leading to Pictured Rocks and, eventually, Sault Ste. Marie, was the site of the loss of the wheat-laden freighter MANHATTAN, on October 26, 1903. A gale driving right down the throat of the channel forced the ship onto the rocky shore, where she caught fire and was destroyed before she could be released. [5+]

MANISTEE ■ Wooden passenger and package freight steamer of 677 t. and 184 ft., launched in 1867 at Cleveland
Lake Superior: The wooden propeller MANISTEE had a cargo of mixed freight, plus her usual crew and a manifest of passengers totalling 23 people, when she steamed over the horizon and out of knowlege on November 15, 1883. She went down with all hands in a gale somewhere west of the Keweenaw Peninsula, leaving the beaches on the east side strewn with her tragic artifacts. [5+]

MANISTEE ■ Wooden passenger and package freight steamer of 843 t. and 202 ft., launched as the steamer LORA in 1882 at Benton Harbor, MI (built at 616 t. and 161 ft., lengthened in 1890)
Lake Michigan: Even ships that are sitting idle can sometimes come to a premature end. The steamer MANISTEE was resting at her winter berth at Ferrysburg (near Grand Haven), Michigan, on January 28, 1914, when she caught fire and was destroyed. She was a total loss. [3]

MANITOBA ■ Steam propeller of 100 t. and 74 ft., launched in 1870 at Chatham, Ont.
Lake Erie: In October of 1883, the steamer MANITOBA caught fire and was destroyed at Chatham, Ontario. [1]

MANITOBA ■ Steamer of 524 t. and 173 ft., launched at Port Robinson, Ont., in 1871
Detroit River: The steamer MANITOBA caught fire at Sandwich, Ontario (now part of Windsor), and was destroyed in 1903. [1]

MANITOU ■ Lumber schooner of 333 t. and 146 ft., launched in 1873 at Port Dalhousie, Ont.
Lake Erie: Caught in a storm on November 4, 1905, the schooner MANITOU was lost off Scotch Bonnet Light, at the eastern end of the lake. Her hull simply failed and the vessel sank. [2]

MANITOULIN ■ Wooden passenger and package freight propeller of 422 t. and 162 ft. overall, launched in 1880 at Owen Sound, Ont.
Lake Huron: The steamer MANITOULIN was carring a general cargo and was crossing Georgian Bay when she was discovered to be afire. In a desperate effort to save her passengers and crew, her skipper turned the blazing steamboat toward shore. She was beached near Manitowaning, Ontario, where she burned to the hull. The run to the shore was only partially successful. Estimates of the number of lives lost run from 11 to 23. The vessel herself was recovered and rebuilt as the steamer ATLANTIC (qv). The loss occurred on May 19, 1882. [5+]

MANITOWOC ■ Lumber schooner of 507 t. and 210 ft., launched in 1868 at Manitowoc, WI
Lake Michigan: The lumber schooner MANITOWOC was reported as wrecked on North Manitou Island, off Michigan's western shore, on November 10, 1900. [2]

MANZANILLA ■ Lumber schooner of 400 t. and 137 ft.
Lake Erie: The MANZANILLA was carrying her usual load of lumber eastward when she was waylaid by a storm on October 13, 1887. The ship was forced ashore at Van Buren Point, six miles west of Dunkirk, New York, and battered to pieces by waves. [2]

MAPLE LEAF ■ Merchant schooner, launched in 1872 at Bayfield, WI
Lake Superior: A November, 1882 gale drove this sail vessel ashore near the mouth of Minnesota's Iron River. Her crew managed to escape before the schooner broke up in place. She had been wrecked and declared lost in 1872, but was subsequently recovered. [3]

MAPLE LEAF ■ Bulk freight schooner of 87 t.
Lake Michigan: The schooner MAPLE LEAF was out trying to deliver her load of lumber in a big gale which struck the Lakes November 19-22, 1879. She never made her scheduled port, having foundered off Grand Haven, Michigan, on the 19th. [2]

MAPLE LEAF ■ Lumber schooner of 135 t.
Lake Erie: This schooner had almost made it to Buffalo with her cargo of lumber when she was overcome by a November gale and sank off the harbor entrance. The MAPLE LEAF was lost on November 13, 1883. [1]

MAPLEDAWN ■ Steel bulk freight steamer of 3,100 t. and 350 ft., launched in 1890 at Cleveland as the steamer MANOLA, lengthened by 100 ft. in 1923
Lake Huron: As the MANOLA, she was cut in half in 1918 to allow her to be towed down the St. Lawrence for reassembly on salt water. The forward half was lost en route in Lake Ontario (off Main Duck Island). This vessel was spliced onto the stern half in 1920, hence the odd profile. On November 30, 1924, the steel steamer MAPLEDAWN, loaded with a cargo of barley, sailed into a blizzard that was molesting Georgian Bay ports. Blinded by snow and disoriented by heavy waves, she ran hard aground on Christian Island, near Penetanguishene, Ontario, and stuck fast. Though her cargo was offloaded, the only way to remove the ship was to cut her up for scrap, right where she sat. [5+]

MAPLEGROVE ■ Bulk freight steamer of 1,177 t. and 208 ft., launched in 1889 at Marine City, MI, as the steamer CHEROKEE
Lake Erie: The freighter MAPLEGROVE had worn her name for less than a year when she foundered (cause unreported) in the Welland Canal on July 11, 1920. She was quickly removed as a navigational hazard, but her career as a steamer was over. She was converted to a barge (one source says steamer) in 1922. [3]

MAPLEGULF ■ Wooden bulk freight steamer of 639 t. and 170 ft., launched in 1889 at Marine City, MI, as the steamer PAWNEE
Lake Ontario: Some ships seem intent on the destruction of their crew, while others appear to make heroic efforts to save them. On November 15, 1920, the freighter MAPLEGULF was near Kingston, Ontario, and battling a heavy storm when the unthinkable happened. The steamer rode up on a big sea and cracked in the center. The MAPLEGULF refused to succumb to the weather, and finally made it to Kingston. The old girl had brought her men home to port for the last time, for her wounds were fatal and she was sent to the shipbreaker's yard for final disposition. [3]

MAPLEHURST ■ Steel bulk freight steamer of 1,297 t. and 235 ft., launched in 1892 at Chicago as the steamer CADILLAC
Lake Superior: One of four of Canada Steamship Line's "Maple" ships to come to grief in the early '20s, (see MAPLEDAWN, MAPLEGROVE, MAPLEGULF), the MAPLEHURST was lost on December 1, 1922. Loaded with a cargo of coal, the freighter was holding her own against a fall gale. But as she neared the Portage Ship

Canal, her engine failed, and the proud ship became a helpless pawn of the storm. Without steerage, she quickly fell sideways into the wave troughs and, inevitably, capsized and sank. Eleven of her 20 crew perished when she went under. [5]

JOHN P MARCH ■ Merchant schooner of 146 ft., launched in 1864 at Vermilion, OH as a bark
Lake Michigan: The schooner JOHN P MARSH was caught in a fall storm on October 30, 1878. Blown to the limits of control, the schooner struck rocks off Good Harbor, Michigan, near Sleeping Bear Point, and went to pieces. Four of her eight crew perished in the accident. [1]

MARENGO ■ Bulk freight schooner-barge of 648 ft. and 189 t., launched in 1873 at Milwaukee
Lake Erie: Ontario's Morgan Point, west of Port Colborne, was the location of the loss of the schooner-barge MARENGO, on October 12, 1912. On that date, she was wrenched from the tow of the steamer LLOYD S PORTER (qv), and thrown on the beach to break up near the point. [3]

MARGARET MARY ■ Merchant schooner of 89 t., built before 1847
Lake Michigan: A report states that the schooner MARGARET MARY was wrecked on the lake in 1854

MARGRETTA ■ Steam tug of 18 t. and 52 ft., launched in 1892 at Ashtabula, OH
Lake Huron: The little tug MARGRETTA was lost in 1907 when she caught fire and was destroyed off Grindstone City, Michigan, a few miles east of Pte Aux Barques. [2]

MARIA ■ Merchant schooner
Lake Huron or Michigan: In 1841, this schooner was lost in the Straits of Mackinac, when she foundered near Nine Mile Point. [1]

MARINE CITY ■ Passenger and package freight steamer of 696 t.
Lake Huron: On August 30, 1880, the steamer MARINE CITY, carrying a load of shingles and fish, caught fire off Alcona, Michigan, a few miles north of Harrisville. She was seen to be in distress from Harrisville, whereupon two tugs, the VULCAN and the GRAYLING, rushed to her rescue. The tugs were able to save a number of those aboard, but ten to 20 people were still lost in the accident. The MARINE CITY burned and sank two miles from shore. According to local reports, the ship's boiler was still visible above the water in the 1950s. [4]

MARINE CITY ■ Lumber schooner of 338 t. and 147 ft., launched in 1866 at Marine City, MI
Lake Huron: Four lives were lost in the foundering of this schooner, which reportedly went down in heavy seas off Goderich, Ontario, on November 11, 1901. [5]

MARINER ■ Merchant schooner of 96 t. and 75 ft., launched in 1824 at Sandusky, OH
Lake Michigan: The little schooner MARINER was reported wrecked at Chicago in 1852. [1]

MARINETTE or **MARIONETTE** ■ Bulk freight schooner of 559 t. and 176 ft.
Lake Michigan: On November 19, 1886, this sail vessel, her crew of seven, and her cargo of lumber were lost far out in the lake. She went down southeast of Fairport, Michigan, in a three-day fall gale. [2]

MARJON S or **MARION S** ■ Tug of 5 t.
Lake Erie: Three lives were lost when this tiny tug exploded and burned a few miles west of Port Burwell, Ontario, on April 29, 1943. [2]

MAROLD II ■ Passenger and package freight ferry of 165 t. and 129 ft., launched in 1889 (or 1909) at Boston, as the yacht LA BELLE
Lake Michigan: The ferry MAROLD II was in the service of Beaver Island, shuttling cargoes back and forth for several years before her demise on January 1, 1937. In the fall of 1936, the big tanker J OSWALD BOYD had run aground on Simmons Reef, a few miles northwest of St. James, Beaver Island. The BOYD was carrying almost a million gallons of gasoline and, though a significant amount had been siphoned off by locals and salvagers, most of the fuel still remained. The MAROLD was removing the gas in an organized manner, but on January 1, something went wrong. The tanker, and the MAROLD with her, were enveloped by a terrific explosion and a fire that was visible for miles on the lake. When it finally died out, little was left of the BOYD, and only tiny fragments of the ferry could be found. She and her crew of five had virtually disappeared in the conflagration. The MAROLD had once been the private yacht of pioneer automaker Alexander Winton, and had served as a subchaser in World War I. [3]

MARQUETTE ■ Merchant schooner
Lake Huron or Michigan: The schooner MARQUETTE was reported sunk in the Straits of Mackinac in 1870. One source reports that some life was lost in the accident. She was later raised and may be one of the vessels shown below. [2]

MARQUETTE ■ Bulk freight schooner of 400 t. and 138 ft.
Lake Superior: The schooner MARQUETTE was laden with iron ore when she went aground in the west channel of the approach to Munising, Michigan, on November 14, 1872. All of her crew were safe and though an initial salvage attempt failed, it was hoped (as with many other vessels before and since) that the MARQUETTE could be refloated in the spring. By April, storms and ice had reduced her to a shambles. [2]

MARQUETTE ■ Barge
Lake Huron: The barge MARQUETTE was reported sunk in the Saginaw River at Essexville, Michigan, in 1924. [1]

MARQUETTE ■ Wooden bulk freight steamer of 1,343 t. and 235 ft., launched at Cleveland in 1881 as the steamer REPUBLIC
Lake Superior: The numerous Apostles Islands, off the northern Wisconsin shore, have been the final resting place of a number of ships attempting to come into Duluth or Ashland, Wisconsin. The large wooden freighter MARQUETTE was overwhelmed by a storm that battered and beat her on October 15, 1903. After long hours of struggle, the ship finally just broke up and foundered just east of the Apostles. Fortunately, her crew were able to abandon ship before she went down. [4]

MARQUETTE & BESSEMER No. 2 ■ Steel steam carferry of 2,514 t. and 338 ft., launched in 1905 at Cleveland
Lake Erie: The big carferry MARQUETTE & BESSEMER No. 2 was built to operate year-round, in defiance of winter storms and ice. Her powerful engines and reinforced hull made her one of the most seaworthy vessels on the Lakes. She left Conneaut, Ohio, on the evening of December 8, 1909, with 32 coal hopper-cars, on her usual cross-lake route to Port Stanley, Ontario. Sometime during the night the lake had its revenge on the big ship, smacking her with an explosive blizzard and gale and taking her down with all 36 aboard. Her whistle had been heard and her lights seen along both shores during the night, as she vainly searched for a safe port. [5+]

MARQUIS ■ Merchant schooner of 424 t.
Lake Huron: On November 12, 1892 (one source says 1880), this schooner was lost offshore from Harbor Beach, Michigan. [2]

MARS ■ Lumber schooner of 126 ft. overall, launched in 1872 at Toledo, OH
Lake Michigan: South Fox Island is the in the center of a chain of islands that extend along the northeastern shore of the lake. Each of these verdant islands have intercepted its share of ships seeking ports or blown off course by the frequent westerly gales. The two-masted schooner MARS was thrust ashore on South Fox by just such a gale on November 19, 1903. The relentless action of storm waves pounded her to pieces after the stranding. [2]

CAROLINE MARSH ■ Bulk freight schooner of 320 t., launched at Port Hope, MI, in 1852

Lake Ontario: Loaded with coal and unable to negotiate the harbor entrance at Oswego, New York in a gale, the MARSH was picked up by a harbor tug to be towed in. However, she broke her towline and was driven ashore, where she broke up in place. No lives were lost in the November 3, 1890 accident, but the ship was a total loss. [2]

GEORGE A MARSH ■ Bulk freight schooner of 220 t. and 135 ft., launched in 1882 at Kingston, Ont.
Lake Ontario: On August 8, 1917, the schooner GEORGE A MARSH was bound for her home port of Kingston with a cargo of coal when she was hit by a following gale and sank off Amherst Island. Twelve persons, probably her entire crew and then some, perished when she foundered. [3]

PHINEAS S MARSH ■ Bulk freight schooner of 543 t. and 177 ft., launched in 1867 at Black River, OH
Lake Superior: Laden with a full cargo of limestone blocks, the schooner PHINEAS S MARSH was blown to shore and dashed to pieces by a storm on August 26, 1896. She hit the shallows near Crisp Point, and her people took to the rigging as she went down. The U.S. Lifesaving Service's local crew, in a magnificent effort, rescued them all before the ship went to pieces. [4]

J D MARSHALL ■ Wooden bulk freight steam barge of 532 t. and 154 ft., launched in 1891 at South Haven, MI
Lake Michigan: The J D MARSHALL was carrying holds full of iron "pigs" (unrefined ingots), when she ran into trouble on June 11, 1911. The normal rolling of the ship caused her cargo to shift, and she turned turtle and sank off Michigan City, Indiana. Most of the crew were able to escape, but four lost their lives. [3]

A E MARSILLIOT ■ Merchant schooner
Lake Erie: Reported only as having sunk in a white squall, other details are lacking concerning this wreck. [2]

MARTHA ■ Fishing tug of 19 t.
Lake Michigan: The MARTHA's entire crew of four drowned when the fishing boat capsized and sank near Michigan City, Indiana, in December of 1933. [1]

MARTHO ■ Barge of 2,815 t.
St. Clair River: On September 5, 1928, the barge MARTHO was reported wrecked at the lower end of Stag Island, near Corunna, Ontario. [1]

MARTIAN ■ Steam freighter of 2,010 t. and 360 ft., launched in 1901 at Wyandotte, MI, as the steamer MARS
Lake Superior: The steamer MARTIAN was lost at Hare Island on December 9, 1927, when she went ashore and was wrecked. She was later recovered, but there is some confusion over whether she was ever returned to service. She lay idle for several years, and was then scrapped in 1937. [3]

C C MARTIN ■ Tug of 45 t.
Lake Huron: On August 21, 1911, this tug foundered at Key Harbor, in Georgian Bay. One source gives the same date and location, but shows 1870 as the year, while another states that she burned to the waterline at Sandusky, Ohio, on September 16, 1911. [3]

D R or **J S MARTIN** ■ Package and bulk freight schooner of 326 t. and 137 ft., launched at Cleveland in 1857
Lake Huron: On November 3, 1904, this veteran sailing ship was reported wrecked on Devil's Island, in Georgian Bay. [3]

J B MARTIN ■ Merchant schooner
Lake Huron: The schooner J B MARTIN was reported as lost on the lake with all hands in the year 1869. [1]

JESSIE MARTIN ■ Lumber schooner of 42 t. and 68 ft., launched in 1881 at Muskegon, MI
Lake Michigan: An unusually powerful summer gale wrecked the schooner JESSIE MARTIN on August 20, 1908. The ship was carrying a load of lumber when she stranded and broke up near Ludington, Michigan. [4]

JOHN MARTIN ■ Steam tug, possibly the 20 t., 57 ft. tug of this name built at Algonac, MI, in 1871
Lake Huron: The tug JOHN MARTIN was lost in a wild Georgian Bay storm in the year 1890. [2]

JOHN MARTIN ■ Bulk freight schooner-barge of 937 t. and 220 ft., launched in 1873 at Cleveland
Lake Huron: Laden with a cargo of iron ore, this tow barge foundered off Fort Gratiot, at the extreme southern end of the lake, as the result of a collision with the big steel bulk freighter YUMA. The accident occurred on September 22, 1900, and four lives were lost when the MARTIN went down. [4]

MARIA MARTIN ■ Merchant schooner of 568 t. and 175 ft., launched in 1866 at Cleveland
Detroit River: In November of 1906 the veteran schooner MARIA MARTIN apparently decided to go off exploring on her own. She slipped her moorings in a strong wind and drifted down the river. She finally stranded and was reported to be a total loss. There is some evidence that she was recovered, but not returned to service. [3]

MARY MARTINI ■ Steam packet of 96 t. and 85 ft., launched in 1877 at W Bay City, MI
Lake Superior: The little packet MARY MARTINI was wrecked on December 23, 1885. In fair weather, the little steamer went aground on Brule Point, near Grand Marais, Minnesota and was destroyed. [2]

S K MARTIN ■ Wooden bulk freight steamer of 303 t. and 153 ft., launched in 1883 at Benton Harbor, MI as the steamer CITY OF ST JOSEPH
Lake Erie: October 12, 1912, was the final day of operation for the steamer S K MARTIN. On that date she was in transit off Harbor Creek, New York, when she sprang a leak that was too large for her pumps to handle, and sank. Her crew had time to launch the ship's yawl and made it to shore. [3]

W J MARTIN ■ Propeller of 75 ft.
Lake Huron: The small propeller W J MARTIN was reportedly stranded and burned in Long Bay of Georgian Bay in 1905. [1]

SELDEN E MARVIN ■ Lumber schooner-barge of 618 t. and 177 ft., launched in 1882 at Marine City, MI
Lake Superior: One of the biggest storms ever recorded on Lake Superior destroyed the SELDEN E MARVIN on November 19, 1914. Laden with a cargo of lumber, the MARVIN and her fellow barge ANNIE F PETERSON (qv) were in tow of the lumber hooker C F CURTIS (qv), when the screaming gale struck. The three vessels were immediately blinded by snow and wind-driven spray and soon they became separated, each living out its final hours in its own separate drama. The SELDEN E MARVIN had the most mysterious end. Apparently she was ripped apart by the combination of waves and wind. Wreckage of the shattered ship was strewn all along the beach near Crisp Point, east of Grand Marais, Michigan, but none of the bodies of her crew were ever found. [5+]

SYLVANUS MARVIN ■ Merchant schooner of 73 t., built before 1847
Lake Michigan: This small schooner took nine sailors to their final rest when she was lost off Grand Haven, Michigan, in 1851. [1]

MARY ■ Merchant schooner of 40 t.
Lake Huron: The little schooner MARY met her end when she was driven ashore and wrecked near Goderich, Ontario. The loss was reported for the fall of 1844, though one source says 1836. [3]

MARY ■ Tug or fishing tug of 50 t. and 70 ft., launched in 1876 at Milwaukee
Lake Michigan: A November gale at the extreme southern end of the lake ended the career of this tug in 1910. She reportedly foundered in the storm, 18 miles southwest of South Chicago. [2]

MARY & LUCY ■ Schooner-barge of 112 t. and 91 ft., launched in 1855 at Cleveland
Lake Huron: Chantry Island, which guards the harbor at Southampton, Ontario, from westerly Huron storms, has snagged a number of vessels as well. The schooner-barge MARY & LUCY was thrust ashore there in November of 1879, and wrecked by the bashing of the waves that followed. [4]

MARY ANN ■ Steam tug
Lake Huron: Two lives were lost when this tug went down in an 1883 Georgian Bay storm. [1]

MARY HATTIE ■ Merchant schooner of 174 t.
Lake Huron: The schooner MARY HATTIE was carrying a cargo of telegraph poles when she was sent ashore by big waves and wrecked near White Rock Point, four miles north of Forestville, Michigan (at the village of White Rock). She was lost in 1888. [1]

MARY JANE ■ Merchant bark of 345 t. and 136 ft.
Lake Erie: Long Point Cut, near Port Rowan, Ontario, was the site of the loss of this bark on November 19, 1881. The MARY JANE was laden with telegraph poles when she was cast ashore by a storm. She later broke up. [2]

MARY NAN ■ Bulk freight schooner of 136 t.
Lake Michigan: The schooner MARY NAN was reported to have sunk off the harbor entrance at Grand Haven, Michigan, On October 30, 1883. She was burdened with a cargo of lumber at the time. [1]

MARY OF DETROIT ■ Merchant schooner
Lake Erie: All hands were lost when this sail vessel wrecked in the harbor at Cleveland. On October 17, 1870, the schooner struck a pier in a gale and went to pieces before a rescue could be accomplished. [1]

MARYSVILLE ■ Crane-equipped wooden bulk freight steamer of 567 t. and 160 ft., launched in 1864 at Green Bay, WI, as the steamer NORMANDIE
St. Clair River: The steamer MARYSVILLE was tied up near the mouth of the Belle River, at Marine City, Michigan, when she caught fire and was destroyed. Her burned-out shell sank at the mouth of the river after the fire, which took place on June 25, 1928. [3]

GOVERNOR MASON ■ Steamer, probably a passenger and package freight vessel
Lake Michigan: A spring storm destroyed the early steamer GOVERNOR MASON on May 3, 1840. She was blown ashore and broken up by the gale near the mouth of Michigan's Muskegon River. [1]

JANE MASON ■ Merchant schooner
Lake Huron: This schooner was reported stranded and lost off Oscoda, Michigan, in 1889. [1]

L G MASON ■ Steam freighter
Lake Huron: The steamer L G MASON was destroyed by fire and sank at Bay City, Michigan, in the Saginaw River, in 1890. [2]

NELLIE MASON ■ Lumber schooner-barge of 554 t. and 181 ft., launched in 1882 at Saginaw, MI
Lake Erie: None of the six crewmen aboard were lost when the schooner-barge NELLIE MASON was wrecked on November 13, 1905. While attempting to enter the harbor at Cleveland, the ship stranded on a breakwall. Before her cargo of coal could be removed and she could be refloated, several big gales moved in and battered her to pieces. It was the MASON's second major accident, having stranded and burned on Observation Point, near Alpena, Michigan, in 1887. [5]

R P MASON ■ Merchant schooner of 122 ft. overall, launched in 1867 at Grand Haven, MI
Lake Michigan: It was reported in 1917 that the old schooner R P MASON had gone down in a storm after swamping on June 20. [1]

MASSASOIT ■ Bulk freight schooner-barge of 842 t. and 189 ft., launched in 1874 at Gibraltar, MI, as the schooner JESSE H LINN
Lake Erie: The schooner-barge MASSASOIT was lost on November 25, 1904, when she stranded on a reef in the Niagara River (near the waterworks), and was wrecked. The 30-year-old ship was light at the time (thus could not be lightened) and it was considerd uneconomical to salvage her, so she was abandoned. [3]

MASSILON ■ Merchant schooner
Lake Huron: This schooner was reported to have foundered north of Pte Aux Barques, Michigan, in 1876. [1]

JOSEPH G MASTEN ■ Bulk freight schooner of 621 t. and 186 ft., launched in 1867 at Cleveland
Lake Michigan: On December 4, 1897, the coal-carrying

schooner JOSEPH G MASTEN was blown ashore and wrecked, just north of Two Rivers, Wisconsin. [2]

MATAAFA ■ Steel bulk freight steamer of 4,840 t. and 430 ft., launched in 1899 at Lorain, OH, as the steamer PENNSYLVANIA
Lake Superior: The big gale that struck Lake Superior at the end of November, 1905, provided one of the most dramatic and tragic losses in Lakes annals. The MATAAFA had departed Duluth on the 27th with a cargo of iron ore and the barge JAMES NASMYTH. She was only a few leagues out when she was struck by the toughest gale to blast the Big Lake in decades. After struggling for hours against it, she turned back and made a run for Duluth. It was obvious to the skipper that the barge would be impossible to maneuver back into the harbor, so the NASMYTH was left at anchor a few miles out while the steamer tried to go it alone. As a freezing crowd gathered on the shore to cheer her on, the MATAAFA made her run at the harbor. However, huge waves and fate intervened to foil the attempt. Her machinery failed at the climactic moment, and the vessel was hurled on the breakwater and broken in two, isolating the forward and after crews. The storm turned back repeated rescue attempts, and the nine men aft froze to death within sight of the crowd. The men trapped forward almost suffered the same fate, but the persevering lifesavers finally brought them to shore. Considering the severity of the damage, it was incredible the MATAAFA was recovered, reassembled and returned to the trade. [5+]

MATERIAL SERVICE ■ Steel bulk freight motor vessel of 246 ft., launched in 1929 at Sturgeon Bay, WI
Lake Michigan: The big motor vessel MATERIAL SERVICE was carrying a load of sand when she was caught by a wild gale off South Chicago. She sank off the lighthouse on July 29, 1936, dragging 15 of her 22 crewmen to their deaths with her. [5]

SAMUEL MATHER ■ Wooden steam freighter of 1,576 t. and 246 ft., launched in 1887 at Cleveland
Lake Superior: Whitefish Bay is one of those spots on the Great Lakes that is often shrouded in fog. This, combined with the heavy traffic in the area, has contrived to cause a significant number of collisions. The big wooden steamer SAMUEL MATHER was cutting her way through the soup on November 22, 1891, when she was rammed and sunk by the package freighter BRAZIL. Her crew were able to abandon the wheat-laden MATHER before she went down off Point Iroquois, on the southern shore. The wreck was located in 1978, and is reported to be very well-preserved. [3]

MATILDA ■ Barge
Lake Huron: The barge MATILDA was reported lost on the lake in a storm, in 1886. [1]

MATOA ■ Steel bulk freight steamer of 2,311 t. and 290 ft., launched in 1890 at Cleveland
Lake Huron: This big steamer was upbound with a cargo of coal when she found herself in the middle of one of the greatest storms of the century. On November 11, 1913, the Big Storm of 1913 hit her with such fury that the powerful freighter was rendered helpless. She was tossed onto Port Austin Reef, near the mouth of Saginaw Bay, and severely damaged. In a sense she was lucky indeed, for on the same day, within a few miles of where she sat high, if not dry, several larger, newer and even more powerful vessels were sunk in deep water with all hands. The MATOA's crew sat out the storm unharmed. At first declared a total loss, the vessel was recovered the next year at great cost. [5+]

MATTAWAN ■ Steam freighter of 348 t. and 143 ft., launched in 1874 at Montreal
Lake Huron: In Oct. of 1888, the steamer MATTAWAN was lost when she either stranded or foundered southeast of Forestville, MI, near the southern end of the lake. [2]

MAUD L ■ 33 t. vessel of unreported type
Lake Huron: This boat was reported as destroyed by fire at Vail's Point, on December 13, 1915. [1]

MAUD S ■ Steam tug of 34 t. and 68 ft., launched in 1881 at Bay City, MI
Lake Huron: In 1888 the tug MAUD S was lost to unknown causes near Cheboygan, Michigan. [1]

MAUMEE VALLEY ■ Package and bulk freight schooner of 213 t. and 127 ft., launched in 1868 at Perrysburg, OH
Lake Erie: The schooner MAUMEE VALLEY was bound north with her holds full of coal when she sailed into a storm on November 22, 1900. She was never heard from again. The little vessel and her crew of seven are thought to lie in the vicinity of Pelee Island. [5]

MAUTENEE ■ Lumber schooner-barge of 647 t. and 200 ft., launched in 1873 at Trenton, MI
Lake Ontario: The Oct. 20, 1905 storm that did so much damage and sank so many vessel on the Lakes, caught the schooner-barge MAUTENEE near Ripley, NY. She was torn loose from her tow steamer and cast ashore, where her crew was able to abandon her. Waves from this and following storms tore the derelict to pieces. One source says she was lost near Picton, Ont. [4]

MAXWELL ▪ Merchant schooner
Lake Huron: The schooner MAXWELL was reported as lost offshore from Goderich, Ontario, in 1886. [1]

MAXWELL A ▪ Steam propeller of 98 t. and 80 ft., launched in 1891 at Bay City, MI as a fishing tug
Lake Erie: This small vessel was lost in a fire that destroyed her at Port Burwell, Ontario, in 1915. [2]

A C MAXWELL ▪ Package and bulk freight schooner of 469 t. and 166 ft. overall, launched in 1870 (one source says 1890) at E Saginaw, MI
Lake Huron: The schooner A C MAXWELL sank following a collision with the steamer R W IRELAND in the St. Marys River below the Soo on November 5, 1908, and was abandoned in place. [3]

EMILY B MAXWELL ▪ Bulk freight schooner-barge of 360 t. and 148 ft., launched in 1881 at Manitowoc, WI
Lake Erie: The full gale that destroyed the schooner-barge EMILY B MAXWELL occurred on August 31, 1909. On that date, the vessel was heaved up against the breakwater at Cleveland, then pounded to pieces. [3]

WILLIAM MAXWELL ▪ Fishing tug of 43 t. and 67 ft., launched in 1883 at Chicago
Lake Huron: This little tug was stranded and demolished on Thunder Bay Reef, on Thunder Bay. The vessel was lost September 15, 1908. [2]

MAY QUEEN ▪ Sidewheel passenger and package freight steamer of 694 t., launched in 1853, at Trenton, MI
Lake Michigan: This steamer made regularly scheduled runs between Cleveland and Lake Michigan ports. She was lost when she stranded near Sheboygan, Wisconsin, on September 17, 1865. All of her crew and passengers escaped before the vessel caught fire and burned to the waterline. [2]

POLLY M MAYERS ▪ Merchant schooner of 328 t.
Lake Ontario: On November 24, 1890, the schooner POLLY MAYERS sank six miles east of Scotch Bonnet Light, southeast of Brighton, Ontario. [1]

E A MAYES ▪ Package and bulk freight schooner-barge
Lake Superior: Ice on Lake Superior is still a force to be reckoned with in May. On the 10th of that month, in 1884, the schooner-barge E A MAYES struck an ice floe off Grand Island, near Munising, Michigan. She quickly sank, but her crew was able to abandon in time. The MAYES was carrying a load of stove coal. [1]

MAYFLOWER ▪ Wooden passenger and package freight steamer of 1,354 t., launched in 1848 at Detroit
Lake Erie: A large vessel for its day, the steamer MAYFLOWER was still no match for a floating sheet of ice. She was traversing Pelee Passage in a fog on December 11 of 1851, when she rammed an ice floe and sank off Point Pelee. Reports do not say if lives were lost in the accident. [2]

MAYFLOWER ▪ Merchant brig
Lake Huron: This small two-master foundered in a squall in 1867. [1]

MAYFLOWER ▪ Merchant schooner of 230 t.
Lake Superior: Lovely Madeline Island, which anchors the Apostles group, was the site of the loss of the schooner MAYFLOWER on June 2, 1891. She foundered from unreported causes on the south end of the island, near LaPorte, Wisconsin. [1]

MAYFLOWER ▪ Merchant steamer
Lake Huron: In 1900, a vessel named MAYFLOWER was reported destroyed by fire in Georgian Bay, near the old naval town of Penetanguishene, Ontario. [1]

NELLIE MAYS or MAYO ▪ Steam tug of 35 t., launched in 1868 at Saginaw, MI
Lake Huron: These reports may refer to one or two vessels, or a pair of separate incidents. The NELLIE MAYS was reported to have burned at Saginaw, Michigan, in 1870, and a tug called the NELLIE MAYO was destroyed by fire at the same spot in 1887. [2]

MAZEPPA ▪ Wooden steam freighter, launched in 1850 at Bath, Ontario as the steamer FARMER
Lake Huron: In November of 1856, the steamer MAZEPPA was said to have wrecked at Southampton, Ontario, on the west side of the Saugeen (Bruce Peninsula). [2]

JAMES McBRIDE ▪ Merchant brig of 121 ft., launched in 1848 at Irving, NY
Lake Michigan: The schooner JAMES McBRIDE was the earliest vessel to carry a cargo directly from the West Indies to Chicago. Her career ended on October 19, 1857, when she was forced ashore and wrecked by a storm near Sleeping Bear Point, Michigan. [1]

A J McBRIER ▪ Steam freighter of 111 t. and 95 ft., launched in 1885 at Wilson, NY
Lake Huron: The propeller A J McBRIER was lost, the victim of fire, at an unreported position on Georgian Bay, in 1906. [1]

FRED McBRIER ▪ Wooden steam freighter of 355 t. and 161 ft., launched in 1881 at Bay City, MI
Lake Huron: The FRED McBRIER was lost in a collision in October of 1890. She was travelling in the area of Waugoschance Point, at the western end of the Straits of Mackinac, when she was rammed by the steamer PROGRESS and sank, seven miles east of the point. [3]

McCLELLAN ▪ Merchant schooner
Lake Huron: Four lives were lost when the schooner McCLELLAN foundered far out in the lake in 1883. [1]

B B McCOLL ▪ Propeller freighter of 1,023 t. and 210 ft., launched at Chatham, England, in 1915 as the steamer PULOE BRANI
Lake Erie: This British-registered steamer became a victim of fire when she burned at a dock at Buffalo, on July 27, 1928. [2]

McCONNELL ▪ Scow
Lake Erie: The scow McCONNELL sank near the entrance to the harbor at Erie, Pennsylvania, on November 24, 1898. [1]

ANTHONY McCUE ▪ Canal barge of of 418 t. and 114 ft.
Lake Erie: The canal boat McCUE was lost when she broke away from the steamer BARRYTON and stranded two miles east of Dunkirk, New York, on November 8, 1925. [1]

McDERMOTT ▪ Barge
Lake Huron: This barge was lost at the northeast end of Thunder Bay, on the Michigan coast. She was reportedly blown ashore and wrecked 75 yards north of the lighthouse, in 1902. [1]

CHARLES A McDONALD ▪ Tug
Lake Huron: The tug McDONALD is reported to have been destroyed by fire on the Saginaw River, in 1894. [1]

J H McDONALD ▪ Tug of 28 t.
Lake Huron: The small tug J H McDONALD was tied to a wharf at Southampton, Ontario, when she caught fire and was destroyed on January 11, 1934. [2]

JOHN A McDONALD ▪ 326 t. vessel of unknown type
Lake Ontario: Salt Point, near Presqu'ile, Ontario, saw the loss of this vessel on November 17, 1872. She was driven onto the point by a westerly storm, struck bottom and sank. This could be the steamer built at Garden Island, Ontario, in 1862, but if so, she was recovered. [1]

ROBERT McDONALD ▪ Propeller freighter of 97 t. and 96 ft., launched in 1890 at Picton, Ont. as a barge
Lake Ontario: The steamer ROBERT McDONALD sank in the harbor at Picton, Ontario, in 1919. [1]

D E McFARLAND ▪ 16 t. vessel of unreported type
Lake Erie: This vessel foundered west of Port Colborne, Ontario, at Morgan Point, on August 8, 1880. [1]

JOHN A McGEAN ▪ Steel bulk freight steamer of 7,500 t. and 452 ft., launched in 1908 at Lorain, OH
Lake Huron: In 1913, big steel steamers like the McGEAN were the epitome of the shipbuilder's art. Few people thought that these sturdy vessels had anything to fear from mere lake gales. The JOHN A McGEAN was only one of the ten giant freighters that sailed out into the

maelstrom on November 11, and were never seen at another port. The big vessel was riding low with a cargo of coal and a crew of 28 when she was last seen breasting big waves off the Tawases, on the Michigan shore. She was lost until her wreckage was finally discovered in 1985. [5+]

NELLIE McGILVRAY ▪ Schooner-barge of 427 t., launched in 1870 at Black Rock, NY
Lake Superior: This schooner-barge was lost in the Portage Ship Canal, which crosses the Keweenaw Peninsula and saves shippers 80 or 90 miles on the Duluth-Soo run. She was reported stranded and a total loss on August 28, 1882. She was also wrecked but recovered on Lake Erie in 1874. [2]

J G or **J W McGRATH** ▪ Merchant schooner of 279 t. and 104 ft., launched in 1870 at St. Catharine's, Ont.
Lake Erie: The schooner McGRATH foundered well out in the lake, 20 miles off Long Point, on October 28, 1878. [2]

MARY A McGREGOR ▪ Wooden bulk freight steamer of 711 t. and 192 ft. overall, launched in 1889 at Grand Haven, MI
Lake Huron: Magnetic Shoal, in Georgian Bay seems able to draw unwary ships in, for several have left their bones there. On August 28, 1920, the steamer MARY A McGREGOR grounded there and, before she could be released, caught fire and was destroyed. She and her cargo of salt were lost, but her crew was safe. [5]

McKAY ▪ Bulk freight schooner
Lake Michigan: The schooner McKAY had brought her cargo of lumber right into Chicago harbor when she foundered in a November, 1856 storm. [2]

JOHN H McKERCHEY ▪ Steel sandsucker and freighter of 506 t. and 169 ft., launched in 1906 at Ecorse, MI
Lake Erie: One of the McKERCHEY's 20-man crew was lost when the old vessel foundered in the harbor at Lorain, Ohio, on October 15, 1950. Sources conflict as to the cause of her sinking, and the date as well. [4]

P E or **P R McKERRAL** ▪ Propeller steamer of 136 t. and 97 ft., launched in 1869 at Wallaceburg, Ont.
Lake Huron: A victim of fire, this wooden steamer burned at Collingwood, Ontario, in September of 1878. [2]

MARY E McLACHLAN ▪ Bulk freight schooner-barge of 1,394 t. and 251 ft., launched in 1893 at Bay City, MI
Lake Superior: Nipigon Bay, on the north shore of the lake, was the site of the loss of the MARY E McLACHLAN on November 7, 1921. She sank in a storm. [1]

J LOOMIS McLAREN ■ Lumber schooner of 287 ft. and 132 ft. launched in 1882 at Manitowoc, WI
Lake Michigan: The McLAREN, her cargo of lumber, and one member of her crew were lost on May 18, 1894, when the schooner foundered, 4.5 miles north of downtown Chicago. [3]

ANDREW A McLEAN ■ Wooden tug of 23 t. and 50 ft., launched at W Bay City, MI, in 1890
Lake Huron: This small tug was reported to have foundered southeast of Tawas City, in upper Saginaw Bay, in 1916. [1]

JANE McLEOD ■ Merchant schooner of 230 t. and 125 ft. overall, launched in 1868 at St. Catharine's, Ont.
Lake Erie: The JANE McLEOD was reported wrecked near Niagara in 1891. She had experienced a near-fatal accident in Georgian Bay the previous year, being stranded and heavily damaged. She was later recovered, but left her name behind on "McLeod" Island. [4]

SYDNEY C McLOUTH ■ Wooden steam package freighter of 2,220 t. and 267 ft., launched in 1890 at Buffalo
Lake Michigan: This large wooden steamer was destroyed by fire off Peshtigo, Wisconsin, near Marinette, on June 28, 1912. [2]

JOHN A McPHAIL ■ Steel passenger and automobile motor ferry
Lake Huron: In May of 1964, the small ferry JOHN A McPHAIL was being towed to Georgian Bay for refitting. She was chained to the similar ferry JAMES W CURRAN (qv), when the CURRAN was struck by a tornado and sunk. Though otherwise undamaged, the McPHAIL was dragged to the bottom with her partner. The ships went down in deep water, several miles north of Pointe Aux Barques, Michigan. [1]

BELLE McPHEE ■ Merchant schooner of 121 t., launched at Owen Sound, Ont., in 1850
Lake Huron: The schooner BELLE McPHEE was reported to have gone on the rocks and wrecked on May 7, 1876, near Thornbury, Ontario, west of Collingwood. [3]

PATRICIA McQUEEN ■ 19 t. vessel of unreported type
Detroit River: This small vessel reportedly sank in the Livingstone Channel, near the lighthouse (off Belle Isle), on April 3, 1956. [1]

MAGGIE McRAE ■ Merchant bark of 314 t. and 139 ft., launched in 1872 at Port Dalhousie, Ont.

Lake Superior: Late season ice was the reason for the loss of the bark MAGGIE McRAE, on May 30, 1888 (one report says June 4). She had just left port and was running off Thunder Cape Light when she encountered an ice field, stove in her bow planking, and sank. Her crew managed to escape before the ship went down. [4]

WILLIAM F McRAE ■ Tug
Lake Huron: This tug was reportedly lost on the lake in 1895, but her position is not noted. [1]

MARY McVIE ■ Propeller freighter of 208 t.
Lake Huron: The little steamer MARY McVIE foundered in 1878, at Walker Point, on the south side of Manitoulin Island, near South Baymouth. [1]

CITY OF MEAFORD ■ Passenger and package freight steamer of 328 t. and 111 ft., launched as the steamer SEAMAN at Meaford, Ontario, in 1906
Lake Huron: This little steamer, which was used mainly as a Georgian Bay "coaster" was destroyed by fire at her dock at Collingwood, Ontario, on May 18, 1919. [3]

MEARS ■ Bulk freight schooner-barge of 430 t. and 172 ft., built as a schooner
Lake Huron: One life was lost when the schooner-barge MEARS stranded and broke up, ten miles north of Au Sable, MI. The vessel was lost on November 27, 1889. [3]

MECHANIC ■ Mechant brig
Lake Michigan: The brig MECHANIC was reported as lost with all hands at an unknown position in 1871. [1]

MEDBURY ■ 226 t. vessel of unreported type
Lake Ontario: The MEDBURY was the victim of a collision. In the crowded shipping lane above Four Mile Point, a few miles below Niagara, the ship collided with an unknown vessel and sank on November 6, 1872. [1]

MEDITERRANEAN ■ Merchant schooner of 239 t., 123 ft.
Lake Michigan: On October 2, 1891, the schooner MEDITERRANEAN foundered, two miles south of the harbor at Sheboygan, Wisconsin. [2]

ADA MEDORA ■ Lumber schooner of 290 t. and 137 ft., launched in 1867 at Gibraltar, MI
Lake Erie: Caught in a gale while near Buffalo, the MEDORA was blown ashore on October 6, 1906. She broke up in place before she could be released. [3]

LEWIS MEEKER ■ Merchant schooner
Lake Huron: This sailing vessel foundered with all hands in 1872. She lies on the bottom somewhere off Middle Island, north of Alpena, Michigan. [1]

MELBOURNE ■ Wooden passenger and package freight steamer of 540 t. and 185 ft. overall, launched in 1873 at Port Dalhousie, Ont. as the steamer ALMA MUNRO
Lake Ontario: Reports on this vessel vary somewhat as to her fate. One says she was almost totally destroyed in a fire on September 19, 1905, at the northeast entrance to the Murray Canal, while others state that she was in operation until 1914, under the name JOHN R, then scrapped. She is also reported to have been converted to a barge late in her career, and scrapped in 1918. [3]

MELBOURNE ■ Steamer
Lake Huron: The steamer MELBOURNE was reported to have sunk in the Saginaw River, at Bay City, in 1918. She may have been scuttled in lieu of scrapping, and may even be the MELBOURNE/JOHN R above. [1]

MARIA MELVIN ■ Steam tug
Lake Ontario: Tug crews considered it routine to rush to the aid of vessels in distress, and their efforts were usually unsung. Once in a while a tug was lost in a rescue attempt. On August 20, 1870, the schooner NORWEGIAN (qv) was seen to be in deep trouble in a storm off Oswego, New York. In best tugboat tradition, the MARIA MELVIN came steaming hurriedly through the spray to try to take her in tow. The gale was too much even for the staunch tug, and she was blown ashore and wrecked. The NORWEGIAN survived the incident. [1]

ADDIE MEMBERY ■ Lumber schooner of 42 t.
Lake Ontario: Trying to enter the harbor at Oswego, New York, in a storm on October 29, 1885, the schooner ADDIE MEMBERY struck the breakwater and was blown ashore and dashed to pieces. [2]

MENDOTA ■ Steamer
Lake Michigan: Only sketchy references to the loss of the MENDOTA on September 10, 1875, seem to exist. Reports say only that she went down on the lake with 12 of her crew lost. [2]

MENEKAUNEE ■ Bulk freight schooner of 588 t., 172 ft.
Lake Michigan: Seven to ten crew members died when the schooner MENEKAUNEE foundered several miles off Fairport, Michigan, at the tip of the Garden Peninsula. The ship was carrying a cargo of lumber when she went down on November 19, 1886. [2]

MENTOR ■ Steam tug of 29 t. and 54 ft., launched in 1868 at Cleveland
Lake Superior: The veteran tug MENTOR was unlucky enough to be tied to a dock at Duluth when a forest fire swept the area on October 12, 1918, destroying much of the waterfront, and the little tug as well. See also ELLA G STONE. [2]

MENTOR ■ Steam tug of 22 t. and 52 ft., launched in 1882 at Saugatuck, MI, as the tug HATTIE A FOX
Lake Michigan: On July 14, 1908, this little tug sank south of Chicago. [3]

MERCER ■ Merchant schooner
Lake Huron: This schooner was reported lost on the lake in the year 1869. The precise location is not reported. [1]

MERCHANT ■ Merchant schooner
Lake Erie: In November of 1842, the schooner MERCHANT went ashore near Fairport, Ohio, and was wrecked. Two men perished in the accident. [1]

MERCHANT ■ Passenger and package freight brig or schooner of 74 t.
Lake Superior: The brig MERCHANT was a vessel of historic note. One of the first ships to engage in the copper trade, she was hauled around the Soo Rapids on skids in the winter of 1845-6. On June 13, 1847, she had her holds filled with freight and a full manifest of passengers when she was struck by a gale near Munising, MI. Said to be overloaded at the time, she was last seen off Grand Island. At least 15 people disappeared with her. [5+]

MERCHANT ■ Merchant schooner
Lake Huron: Five lives were ended when the schooner MERCHANT was wrecked on Pte Aux Barques, Michigan, in 1849. [1]

MERCHANT ■ Iron steam freighter of 750 t. and 200 ft., launched in 1862 at Buffalo
Lake Michigan: The steamer MERCHANT was reported to have stranded on Racine Reef, Near Racine, Wisconsin, in October of 1875. Before she could be refloated, she caught fire and was destroyed. The MERCHANT was a milestone vessel, the first iron cargo ship on the Lakes. [4]

MERCURY ■ Lumber schooner of 230 t. probably the 121 ft. vessel of this name launched at New Jerusalem, OH, in 1871
Lake Michigan: The three-masted schooner MERCURY was hauling a cargo of pine planking down the lake when she was driven ashore near Pentwater, Michigan by a November 10, 1879, storm. The action of waves finished the job of destroying her. [3]

MERCURY ■ Bulk freight schooner
Lake Michigan: This schooner was pulling into Chicago with her usual lumber cargo when she sank off the Chicago River light. Details of the May 18, 1894 accident are not given. [1]

MERIDA ▪ Steel bulk freight steamer of 3,261 t. and 360 ft., launched in 1893 at W Bay City, MI
Lake Erie: A somewhat localized but very violent storm roiled the center of Lake Erie on October 20-22, 1916, and at least two large vessels succumbed to its wrath. The big steamer MERIDA was loaded almost to the gunwhales with a cargo of iron ore when she sailed into it on the 20th. When the storm had passed, the steamer was gone, sunk about 40 miles southeast of Long Point (above Barcelona, New York). The vessel's crew of 24 went to the bottom with her, so the details of her passing are not known. See also JAMES B COLGATE. [5+]

E G MERRICK ▪ Merchant schooner
Lake Erie: The schooner E G MERRICK was reported stranded and lost near Vermilion, Ohio, in October of 1851. [1]

M F MERRICK ▪ Merchant schooner of 295 t. and 137 ft.
Lake Huron: Five crewmen drowned when the M F MERRICK was lost in a collision off Presque Isle, Michigan, on May 17, 1889. She was well offshore when she was struck by the steamer R P RANEY (perhaps RUFUS P RANNEY) and sank. [3]

JOHN B MERRILL ▪ Merchant schooner of 640 t. and 189 ft., launched in 1873 at Milwaukee
Lake Huron: The schooner JOHN B MERRILL encountered a strong gale off Drummond Island, Michigan, in 1892. She was simply overwhelmed by the storm, breaking up and sinking in the big waves. Her crew successfully abandoned her before she came apart. [4]

C H MERRITT ▪ Steam propeller freighter of 122 t. and 85 ft., launched in 1883 at Chatham, Ont.
All that is known about the loss of the MERRITT is that she was sunk in 1902. [1]

THOMAS R MERRITT ▪ Merchant schooner of 700 t. and 141 ft., launched in 1874 at Port Dalhousie, Ont.
Lake Ontario: No lives were lost, but the MERRITT was totally destroyed after she was driven ashore by a gale near Fair Haven, New York. The vessel was in ballast at the time of the September 12, 1900 accident. [3]

H F MERRY ▪ Merchant schooner of 170 t. and 121 ft., launched as a schooner-barge in 1868 at Sandusky, OH
Lake Erie: Two unidentifiable locations are given for the loss of this small schooner on November 15, 1883. She was blown ashore and wrecked near either Silver Creek, Pennsylvania, or Silver Island, New York. The actual location is probably off Silver Creek, New York. She was carrying a cargo of wheat at the time of her demise. [3]

MESQUITE WB305 ▪ U S Coast Guard buoy tender (motor vessel) of 1,025 t. and 180 ft., launched in 1943 at Duluth
Lake Superior: On December 4, 1989, the buoy tender MESQUITE was doing her annual late fall duty of picking up navigational markers along the rugged northern Keweenaw Peninsula coast. She struck a rock ledge off Keweenaw Point and settled on the rocks. Immediate salvage attempts were unsuccessful. Within two months, the tender had been declared a total loss due to damage caused by storm waves and ice. The next spring she was stripped, and in July of 1990, she was carried offshore by a wrecking vessel and lowered to the bottom, to become the center of a new underwater preserve. The MESQUITE had served in the Pacific in World War II. [5+]

MESSENGER ▪ Steam freighter
Lake Huron: In 1890 the steamer MESSENGER was destroyed by fire and lost off Rogers City, Michigan. [1]

METAMORA ▪ Steam tug of 239 t. and 115 ft., launched at Cleveland in 1864
Lake Huron: The big old tug METAMORA had served in Georgian Bay for many years before her loss on September 29, 1907. On that fateful day she caught fire and was destroyed at Shawanaga (Sha-WA-na-ga) Bay, near Parry Sound, Ontario. [4]

METEOR ▪ Merchant schooner of 956 t.
Lake Erie: This big schooner was lost near Put-in-Bay, in the Erie Islands, in November of 1871. She was bucking the big waves of a fall storm when she stove in her bottom planking and foundered. [1]

METEOR ▪ Passenger and package freight steamer
Detroit River: On June 7 of 1873 the steamer METEOR was tied to a dock at Detroit when a nearby warehouse caught fire. In those days of wooden structures and horse-drawn fire engines, the warehouse, dock and the METEOR were consumed before effective help arrived. The were no casualties among the steamer's crew. [2]

METEOR ▪ Steam freighter
Lake Huron: This steamer was reported to have been lost on the Spanish River, in the North Channel, in 1883. [1]

METEOR ▪ Whaleback bulk freight steamer of 2,759 t. and 366 ft., launched in 1896 at W Superior, WI as the steamer FRANK ROCKEFELLER
Lake Superior: The whaleback steamer METEOR had served for 73 years and was the last remaining vessel of this type on the Lakes when she ran aground and was damaged near Marquette, Michigan, in 1969. Though she

was salvaged, it was the end of her career as a merchant vessel. The story has a happy ending, though, as the METEOR was purchased by an historical society and now resides as a museum ship at the port of her birth, Superior, Wisconsin. [4]

METROPOLE ■ Wooden bulk freight steamer of 188 t. and 100 ft., launched as the steamer SAKIR SHEPARD in 1883 at Huron, OH
Lake Huron: The steamer METROPOLE was carrying a cargo of wooden staves when she was lost north of Port Austin, Michigan, just west of Pointe Aux Barques. She was holding her own against a big gale when one of the storm-driven greybeards ripped out her rudder, sending her out of control and allowing the lake to rush into her holds. She sank a short time later. The loss occurred on August 8, 1903. She had also been heavily damaged in a fire in 1898. [4]

METROPOLIS ■ Merchant schooner of 246 t. and 125 ft.
Lake Michigan: Laden with a cargo of iron fittings and lumber, the steamer METROPOLIS foundered in a storm, three miles off the Old Mission Peninsula, in Grand Traverse Bay, on the northwest Michigan coast. The ship went down in November of 1886. [1]

METROPOLIS ■ Sidewheel passenger steamer of 425 t. and 168 ft., launched in 1868 at Trenton, MI
Lake Erie: While docked at her regular berth at Toledo, Ohio, the popular old steamer METROPOLIS caught fire and was destroyed on June 13, 1902. [4]

F A MEYER ■ Wooden bulk freight steamer of 1,739 t. and 256 ft., launched as the steamer J EMORY OWEN in 1888 at Detroit
Lake Erie: There were no casualties except for the F A MEYER herself in a December 18, 1909, accident. On that date the steamer was off Port Colborne, Ontario, when she was caught in an ice floe. The irresistible pressure of ice crushed the freighter's hull and she sank. This accident is also reported to have happened in 1910. [3]

MIAMI ■ Bulk freight steam barge of 288 t. and 131 ft., launched in 1888 at Marine City, MI
Lake Huron: Thunder Bay, Michigan, was the site of the blaze that destroyed this little freighter on August 6, 1924. Fortunately, all of the steamer's crew escaped. [5]

C MICHELSON ■ Lumber schooner of 137 t. and 102 ft., launched in 1867 at White Lake, MI
Lake Michigan: This small two-master was in upper Green Bay, a few miles south of Escanaba, Michigan, when she was overwhelmed by a storm and foundered. The loss took place on October 30, 1901. [3]

MICHIGAN ■ Merchant brig
Lake Huron: The two-masted sail vessel MICHIGAN was wrecked on a reef at Pte Aux Barques, Michigan, in 1870. [1]

MICHIGAN ■ Iron propeller freighter of 1,921 t. and 209 ft., launched in 1883 at Detroit
Lake Michigan: The iron-hulled vessels that came off the ways in the mid-to-late 19th Century quickly gained a reputation as icebreakers. Perhaps the skipper of the steamer MICHIGAN took this too much for granted when he took his vessel out to the aid of the steamer ONEIDA, stranded and threatened by ice near Grand Haven, Michigan. The lake was still too icy on March 20, 1885 for even the sturdy hull of the MICHIGAN. She was holed and sunk. [5+]

MICHIGAN ■ Freight barge of 1,344 t. and 265 ft., launched in 1873 at Sandwich, Ont., as a carferry
Lake Superior: The lovely and impressive dunes of Grand Sable Banks, east of the Pictured Rocks, overlook the site of the September 22, 1893, loss of the barge MICHIGAN. She foundered just east of Point Sable in a storm. [2]

MICHIGAN ■ Schooner-barge of 1,056 t. and 213 ft., launched at Detroit in 1874
Lake Superior: Towing vessels often got into deadly trouble when coming to the aid of their wounded charges, and sometimes they caused more problems than they solved. On stormy October 2, 1901, the veteran barge MICHIGAN sprang a leak and began to fill off Vermilion Point, on the Michigan coast. In a valiant attempt to take the schooner-barge's crew off, her tow steamer, the M M DRAKE, tried to pull in close along her flanks. Instead, a big wave threw the two wooden vessels together, and both hulls were crushed. Steamer and schooner sank together, with the loss of one of the MICHIGAN's crew. [4]

MICHIGAN ■ Steel bulk freight barge of 1,730 t. and 296 ft., launched as a carferry in 1890 at W Bay City, MI
Lake Huron: The MICHIGAN served for 34 years as a rail car ferry before being converted to a barge in 1924. Her odd lines made her a well-known fixture around Georgian Bay until her demise on November 14, 1943. On that date she was driven by a storm onto Lottie Wolf Shoal, near Hope Island, broke in half, and sank. No casualties were reported. [5]

MICHIGAN CENTRAL ■ Steel bulk freight barge of 1,522 t. and 263 ft., launched at Wyandotte, MI, as a carferry in 1884
Lake Huron: Another of several large carferries that ended their days as barges on Georgian Bay, the MICHIGAN CENTRAL was carrying a load of stone when she was lost on October 27, 1926. She went down in a storm near the False Detour Channel entrance, west of Cockburn Island. [4]

MICHIGAN CITY ■ Scow of 500 t., built as a propeller
Lake Michigan: The scow MICHIGAN CITY was lost when she foundered seven miles off her namesake, Michigan City, Indiana, on October 5, 1889. [1]

STATE OF MICHIGAN ■ Wooden passenger and package freight steamer of 736 t. and 175 ft., launched in 1875 at Manitowoc, WI, as the steamer DE PERE
Lake Michigan: A rather bizarre mechanical problem caused the loss of this wooden ship off the mouth of Michigan's White River, north of Muskegon. On October 18, 1901, she was several miles offshore when she threw a piston rod from her big engine. The offending piece went into the lake, right through the bottom of the ship. She sank quickly, though good weather allowed boats to be launched, and all aboard made it to shore safely. [3]

MICHIPICOTEN ■ Wooden passenger and package freight steamer of 511 t. and 117 ft., launched as the tug E K ROBERTS at Wyandotte, MI, in 1883
Lake Huron: This veteran steamer was destroyed by fire at Cook's Dock, west of Bayfield Sound on Manitoulin Island. She burned on October 10, 1927. [4]

MIDLAND CITY ■ Wooden motor freighter of 580 t. and 153 ft., launched in 1871 at Kingston, Ont. as the side-wheel steamer MAUD
Lake Huron: This ship served under four different names for an almost incredible (for a wooden ship) 84 years. She was finally destroyed by fire at Midland, Ontario, in 1955, and her remains were abandoned on the Rye River. [2]

MIDLAND ROVER ■ 354 t. vessel of unreported type
Lake Ontario: This ship (probably a schooner) stranded and broke up in Toronto Bay on December 7, 1882. [1]

CITY OF MIDLAND ■ Wooden bulk freight steamer of 665 t. and 188 ft., launched in 1890 at Owen Sound, Ont.
Lake Huron: Lying at her moorings at Collingwood, Ont., and fitting out for the coming season, the steamer CITY OF MIDLAND caught fire and was destroyed on March 17, 1916. [4]

MIDNIGHT ■ Merchant schooner of 288 t.
Lake Huron: Laden with a cargo of lumber, this schooner was driven onto Au Sable Point, near Oscoda, Michigan, by an unusual southeast gale. Once on shore, she was torn completely apart by the November 27, 1889 storm. [4]

C A MIESEL or MEISEL ■ Cargo barge
Lake Huron: This carrier was reported stranded and lost near Lakeport, MI, a few miles north of Port Huron, in 1870. [1]

C G MIESEL ■ 132 t. vessel of unreported type
Detroit River: The C G MIESEL was lost in a collision in the narrow shipping lane off Bois Blanc Island (Bob-Lo) in the lower river and sank on August 10, 1870. [1]

MILAN ■ Merchant schooner, probably the 196 t., 121 ft. schooner launched at Milan, OH, in 1862
Lake Superior: The MILAN was reported to have been lost in a destructive gale in October of 1869, off Whitefish Point. However, she may have been recovered and rebuilt as the schooner JESSIE L BOYCE (qv). [2]

MILDER ■ 45 t. vessel of unreported type
Lake Erie: This little vessel was reported to have stranded at Fish Point (Pelee Island) and been destroyed by waves. [1]

MILDRED ■ Steam tug
Lake Huron: A heavy storm that struck the Alpena, Michigan area in 1872 drove this tug down in Thunder Bay. [1]

ALBERT MILLER ■ Bulk freight propeller of 284 t.
Lake Michigan: Two conflicting reports are offered for the loss of this propeller in 1882. One says she was lost to fire at an unknown position on Lake Michigan on August 20, while the other states that the loss was near Oscoda, Michigan, on Lake Huron. [2]

E H MILLER ■ Steam tug of 42 ft. and 60 t., launched in 1874 at Saginaw, MI
Lake Huron: The E H MILLER was reported abandoned on Thunder Bay at Alpena in 1920, athough it is not clear whether this was due to an accident or not. [2]

E M MILLER ■ Steam tug
Lake Huron: This tug was said to have been destroyed by fire on the Saginaw River at Saginaw on April 11, 1874 (one source says January). This could be the same vessel as above. [2]

GRACE MILLER ■ Steam tug
Lake Huron: In 1875 the tug GRACE MILLER sank in a full gale which struck her on Thunder Bay (Michigan). [1]

JANE MILLER ■ Wooden steam coaster of 210 t. and 78 ft., launched in 1878 at Little Current, Ont.
Lake Huron: The little steamer JANE MILLER made a good living shuttling cargo and passengers among the small ports along the inside of the Bruce Peninsula. On November 26, 1881, she departed Meaford, Ontario, into the teeth of a vicious gale. She was bound for Wiarton with a load of general freight and 30 people aboard. The MILLER was never seen again. She is thought to have gone down off the mouth of Colpoy's Bay. [4]

LAURA MILLER ■ Merchant schooner of 56 t. and 75 ft., launched in 1886 at Chicago
Lake Michigan: This tiny schooner was reported to have sunk off the entrance to the harbor at Grand Haven, Michigan, on November 2, 1894. [2]

DAVID W MILLS ■ Wooden bulk freight steamer of 1,200 t. and 220 ft., launched in 1874 at Cleveland as the steamer SPARTA
Lake Ontario: Ford Shoal, off Oswego, New York, is the final resting place of this steamer. She struck bottom there and was held fast on August 11, 1919. Later storms tore her to pieces. [2]

HAMILTON J MILLS ■ Bulk freight barge of 509 t., launched in 1881 at Buffalo
Lake Ontario: The position of the HAMILTON J MILLS at the time of her demise is not reported, but it is known that she was carrying coal at when she sank on August 29, 1892. Three crew members perished with her. [2]

M I MILLS or **MILLIS** ■ Steam tug of 7 t.
Lake Huron: One of the smallest commercial vessels on the Lakes, the tug M I MILLS was lost in May of 1873, off Sand (now Harbor) Beach, Michigan. She sank as the result of a collision. [2]

MARY MILLS ■ Wooden bulk freight steamer of 119 t. and 113 ft., launched in 1872 at Vicksburg, MI
Lake Michigan: The small freighter MARY MILLS was destroyed by fire in the harbor at Sturgeon Bay, Wisconsin, on December 11, 1900. [2]

NELSON or **N MILLS** ■ Bulk freight steamer of 391 t. and 164 ft., launched in 1870 at Vicksburg, MI
St. Clair River: Two lives were lost when this steamer sank off McGregor Point on Sept. 6, 1906, following a collision with the steamer MILWAUKEE. Fourteen crewmen were saved. She was also reported as beached and heavily damaged in the Straits of Mackinac in 1892. [3]

MILTON ■ Bulk freight schooner of 131 t.
Lake Michigan: Five crewmen drowned when this little sailing ship, laden with a cargo of wood, foundered off Two Rivers Point, on the Wisconsin shore. The MILTON went down on September 8, 1885. [1]

JOE MILTON ■ Steam tug of 93 t. and 93 ft., launched in 1891 at Port Stanley, Ont.
Lake Huron: On June 13, 1904, the tug JOE MILTON caught fire and was destroyed at Papoose Island, north of Midland, Ontario. [2]

MILWAUKEE ■ Steam freighter
Lake Huron or Michigan: In 1859 it was reported that the steamer MILWAUKEE had collided with the schooner J H TIFFANY (qv) and sunk in the Straits of Mackinac. The TIFFANY was lost as well. [1]

MILWAUKEE ■ Sidewheel passenger and package freight steamer of 1,039 t. and 239 ft., launched in 1859 at Buffalo
Lake Michigan: The Grand Haven Bar, to one side of the harbor entrance at Grand Haven, Michigan, has snagged a number of unwary lakes vessels. The large wooden steamer MILWAUKEE ran aground there and broke up in 1868. Fortunately, no lives were lost in the accident. [1]

MILWAUKEE ■ 352 t. vessel of unreported type
Lake Ontario: This vessel was reported to have sunk on November 10, 1883, among the Duck Islands. [1]

MILWAUKEE ■ Wooden steamer of 277 t.
Lake Michigan: On July 8, 1886, the steamer MILWAUKEE sank following a collision suffered a few miles off Grand Haven, Michigan. One life was lost. [1]

MILWAUKEE ■ Steel steam carferry of 2,933 t. and 338 ft., launched at Cleveland in 1903 as the carferry M M & N NUMBER 1
Lake Michigan: The carferry MILWAUKEE was one of the largest ships ever to disappear on Lake Michigan. Carferries of this size were built to run all year, with powerful engines and reinforced hulls. Thus, it was considered routine when she sailed off into a gale on October 21, 1929 with 27 loaded railroad cars and 52 souls aboard. Somewhere between Milwaukee and Grand Haven, Michigan, the big steel vessel just "sailed through a crack in the lake" on the 22nd. It is theorized that her railcars came loose in the huge waves and rolled off her stern, carrying her protective "seagate" with them and leaving her exposed to the worst the following storm had to offer. The wreck was located in 1972. [5+]

MILWAUKEE BELLE ■ Merchant schooner of 368 t. and 133 ft., launched at Milwaukee in 1854
Lake Michigan: A terrific westerly storm caught up with this schooner north of the Beaver Islands on November 18, 1886. Reports say that she was quickly dismasted and rendered helpless. The relentless gale shoved her all the

way into the Straits to a position south of Brevoort (now Brevort) Michigan, a distance of almost 40 miles, before she sank. [2]

CITY OF MILWAUKEE ■ Merchant schooner
Lake Huron: The schooner CITY OF MILWAUKEE was lost in 1875, when she foundered above Port Sanilac, on the Michigan shore. [1]

MILWAUKIE ■ Sidewheel passenger and freight steamer of 401 t. and 172 ft., launched in 1837 on the Niagara River
Lake Michigan: The expression "so close, and yet so far" has applied to many vessels that hit the bottom close to land, but were so beset by storm conditions that her people could not make it to the shore. So it was with the early steamboat MILWAUKIE. She was blown to within a few hundred yards of the beach near the mouth of the Kalamazoo River by an icy gale that struck her on November 20, 1842. In calm weather, it would have been a trivial matter for the 15 aboard to row or even walk ashore. But in the bitter cold wind and giant waves, nine people froze to death on the steamer before they could be rescued. The vessel was carrying a cargo of flour and wine at the time. [3]

ANNA C MINCH ■ Steel bulk freight steamer of 2,880 t. and 380 ft., launched at Cleveland in 1903
Lake Michigan: In the extremely violent Armistice Day Storm of November 11, 1940, the big steel freighter ANNA C MINCH, her crew of 24, and her cargo of coal disappeared without a trace off Pentwater, Michigan. Historians have speculated that she had collided with another big steamer, the WILLIAM B DAVOCK (qv) but current evidence suggests that she was simply overwhelmed by a record fall gale and foundered. [5+]

CHARLES P MINCH ■ Merchant schooner of 408 t. and 155 ft., launched in 1867 at Vermilion, OH
Lake Huron: Tecumseh Cove, on the eastern side of Cove Island, near Tobermory, Ontario, was the site of the loss of the CHARLES P MINCH. The schooner sank there in October of 1898. [3]

PHILIP MINCH ■ Wooden bulk freight steamer of 1,988 t. and 275 ft., launched in 1888 at Cleveland
Lake Erie: The MINCH was a victim of an offshore fire on November 20, 1904. She was almost completely destroyed, then sank approximately 10 miles southwest of Southeast Shoal. The wreck was dynamited as a navigational hazard in 1906. One source places her closer to Marblehead. [3]

SOPHIA MINCH ■ Merchant schooner of 130 ft., launched in 1840 at Vermilion, OH
Lake Erie: The saga of the SOPHIA MINCH is a classic example of the dramatic Great Lakes shipwreck. Disabled by a fall gale on October 30, 1883, she was unable to negotiate the harbor entrance at Cleveland. The veteran schooner dropped anchor outside and ran up her distress signals. Two sturdy harbor tugs rushed out into the gale and threw lines to the schooner in an attempt to tow her in, but the MINCH sank before she made it to still water. Her desperate crew climbed her rigging as the MINCH went down. Their situation seemed hopeless, until the surfmen of the U.S. Lifesaving Service came battling their way through the storm in their oar-powered surfboat and plucked them off, without the loss of a single life. Heavily damaged and thought to be unsalvageable, the SOPHIA MINCH was later raised and rebuilt as a schooner-barge. She served until scrapped in 1927. [3]

JOHN MINER or **MINOR** ■ Package and bulk freight schooner of 273 t. and 134 t., launched in 1866 at Detroit
Lake Huron: This schooner was still another victim of the dangerous waters surrounding Pointe Aux Barques, Michigan. On October 19, 1902, she was thrown into the boulder-studded shallows west of the point. She went to pieces within a few hours of her stranding. In a confusing piece of geography, the MINER's wreckage is said to be located two miles east of the lighthouse, yet west of the point, even though the Pte Aux Barques light is actually located on Bald Eagle Point, approximately eight miles east of Pte Aux Barques itself. [5]

J T MINER ■ Merchant schooner
Lake Huron: The picturesque village of Caseville, Michigan, is located on the beach a few miles to the west of Pointe Aux Barques. The area between this town and the Charity Islands has a shallow and uneven bottom, which is only about 20 feet in depth at its deepest. In the schooner days, small commercial vessels making their way to Saginaw or Bay City would try to save a few hours by traversing the Charity Passage. In fair weather they were safe enough, but in one of the quick-rising storms that plague the area, a laden ship dropping into a wave trough was quite likely to kiss the rocky bottom. So it was with the J T MINER. She struck bottom in an 1877 storm, drifted into the shallows and was torn apart by wave action. [2]

MINERAL STATE ■ Bulk freight schooner of 294 t. and 137 ft., launched at Detroit in 1872
Lake Erie: Loaded with a cargo of coal, the schooner MINERAL STATE went on a reef near Port Stanley, Ont.,

and was pounded to pieces by waves. The vessel was lost on October 30, 1902. [4]

MINGOE ■ Lumber schooner-barge of 210 ft. overall, launched in 1893 at Marine City, MI
Lake Superior: The desolate Huron Islands are located a few miles off a sparsely-inhabited shore of Michigan's upper peninsula. They are today part of a National Widlife Refuge. The gulls and gamebirds share the waters around the islands with the wreckage of the schooner-barge MINGOE. The old vessel encountered a storm near there on May 24, 1908, sprang a leak and sank, killing three of her crew. Some historians speculate that she struck an ice floe. [3]

MINNEAPOLIS ■ Propeller freighter, probably of 1,072 t. and 226 ft., launched in 1873 at Marine City, MI, but one source describes her as a 1,550 t., 300 footer
Lake Michigan: In 1894 this steamer was reported to have struck bottom near Mc Gulpin Point, a mile west of the Mackinac Bridge site. She reportedly broke in half, then went to pieces and then sank at a point almost directly under the bridge. [4]

MINNEDOSA ■ Bulk freight schooner of 1,041 t. and 245 ft., launched in 1890 at Kingston, Ont.
Lake Huron: A large and impressive four-masted schooner, the MINNEDOSA spent much of her life being used as a towbarge, though she was still rigged for full sail until the end. In a big gale which wiped the Lakes clean of ships on October 20, 1905, the ship broke away from her towing steamer, the 1,900 ton WESTMOUNT. The WESTMOUNT soon lost sight of her charge, and somewhere off Harbor Beach, Michigan, the giant MINNEDOSA sank with all nine hands. [5]

MINNEHAHA ■ Bulk freight schooner, probably the 75 t., 75 ft. vessel of this name built at Cheboygan, MI, in 1875
Lake Michigan: Six lives (most likely her entire crew) were lost when this little schooner stranded and went to pieces on October 14, 1893, off Frankfort, Michigan. [3]

MINNEHAHA ■ Merchant schooner of 75 t.
An undated report shows the schooner MINNEHAHA as sunk off Sheboygan, Wisconsin with a cargo of wood. This may be the same vessel as above. [1]

MINNEHAHA ■ Merchant schooner of 59 t. and 71 ft., launched in 1872 at Manitowoc, WI
Lake Michigan: Records say that this tiny schooner sank off Whiting, Indiana, in July of 1905. [2]

MINNEHAHA ■ 22 t. vessel of unreported type
Lake Huron: The loss of this vessel was reported on Georgian Bay for October 11, 1909, She stranded on the east side of the bay and was wrecked. [1]

MINNESOTA ■ Wooden bulk freight steamer of 1,138 t. and 206 ft., launched in 1880 at Milwaukee
St Clair River: On November 18, 1903 (also reported as 1909), this wood-hulled bulk freighter caught fire off the village of Walpole Island, near the mouth of the river. While still ablaze, she drifted three miles, to a point opposite Sans Souci, Michigan, and sank. [3]

MINNESOTA ■ Schooner
Lake Huron: This vessel was reported as sunk in mid-lake in 1905. The record is probably a mistranscription of the wreck of the MINNEDOSA (qv). [1]

MINNIE ■ 90 ft. vessel of unreported type
Lake Ontario: Salt Point, near Presq'isle, Ontario, was the site of the loss of this vessel. On November 2, 1877, she sank one mile east of the point. [1]

JULIA MINOR or **MINER** ■ Merchant schooner of 44 t. and 61 ft., launched in 1867 at Detroit
Lake Huron: Historians are unsure of the year of the loss of this tiny schooner. She went down east-southeast of Pointe Aux Barques light, probably in the year 1902. There may be some confusion between this vessel and the JOHN MINER (qv). [4]

J S MINOR ■ Vessel information unavailable
Lake Huron: A stranding near Kincardine, Ontario, ended this vessel's career on October 15, 1871. [1]

E MINT ■ Package freight schooner
Lake Michigan: The schooner MINT was said to have stranded and broken up south of the entrance to the Calumet, Illinois, harbor, in 1850. [1]

MIRANDA ■ Merchant schooner
Lake Huron: Port Austin reef claimed another when the schooner MIRANDA wrecked there in 1871. [1]

C F MISCHLER ■ Steam screw tug of 18 t. and 51 ft., launched in 1868 at Ashtabula, OH
Lake Erie: One of the dozens of disastrous tug fires the Lakes have seen destroyed this little vessel on October 28, 1915. No lives were lost when she burned at Erie, Pennsylvania. [2]

MISSOULA ■ Wooden bulk freight steamer of 1,926 t. and 272 ft., launched in 1887 at Cleveland
Lake Superior: The wheat-laden steamer MISSOULA was battling a gale off Whitefish Point on November 22, 1895, when she broke her driveshaft. Steamers sometimes had this problem in big seas when the vessel would ride down the backside of a big wave and her screw would come out of the water. The engine would then over-revolve, and if it was not braked, even a well-made shaft could twist off when the prop bit back into the water. This was the case

with the MISSOULA. The broken shaft meant that the vessel lost her steerageway and was cast to the mercy of the storm. November storms on Superior are notoriously merciless and, after drifting for a full day, the vessel was overwhelmed and sank. Luckily, her crew was able to abandon ship, but had to drift 30 miles in an open boat before landfall. [5]

MISSOURI ■ Vessel information unreported, but possibly the 612 t. passenger and package freight propeller (originally a sidewheeler) built at Erie, PA, in 1840
Lake Erie: This steamer was reported stranded and then pounded to matchsticks and scrap iron by a gale that struck her on October 26, 1870. She hit the beach near Port Burwell, Ontario. [1]

BELLE MITCHELL ■ Bulk freight schooner, 304 t. and 136 ft.
Lake Erie: The MITCHELL was carrying a cargo of wheat eastward on October 14, 1886, when she was overtaken by a gale and foundered 22 miles off Long Point. Eight of her crew were lost along with the ship. [2]

JOHN MITCHELL ■ Steel bulk freight steamer of 7,500 t. and 420 ft., launched in 1907 at St. Clair, MI
Lake Superior: In 1911 the MITCHELL was almost brand new and was one of the largest vessels on the Lakes. In view of her size, she had little to worry about in the case of a collision, unless the other was a boat almost as large. The steamer was downbound in a Whitefish Point fog with wheat on July 10, 1911, when her path crossed that of the steamer WILLIAM HENRY MACK. As luck would have it, the MACK was heavily laden with coal, making the two vessels close to the same weight. The MITCHELL was rammed broadside, and even though the MACK tried to plug the wound with her mangled bow, the JOHN MITCHELL sank in only seven minutes. Quick action saved most of the big ship's crew, but three of the 34 aboard were still lost. The wreck was located upside-down on the bottom in 1972. [5]

C G MIXER ■ Merchant schooner of 294 t. and 130 ft., launched at Hudson, NY, in 1867
Lake Michigan: The MIXER was coming in to Calumet, Illinois, with a cargo of railroad ties when she was lost 1.5 miles off the harbor entrance. The loss occurred on May 18, 1894. [2]

MIZTEC ■ Bulk freight schooner-barge of 777 t. and 194 ft., launched in 1890 at Marine City, MI
Lake Superior: Often it seemed to superstitious sailors that a vessel was destined to die on a specific rock or stretch of beach. Sometimes there appeared to be hard evidence to back that up. The barge MIZTEC struck bottom

and stranded off Vermilion Point, ten miles west of Whitefish, in the fall on 1919. She was quickly rescued and returned to service, before the gales could get at her. Rebuilt and back in service in 1920, the vessel suffered a similar accident at almost the same spot. Again she was pulled off the rocks and reconditioned. On one of her first trips of the 1921 season, on May 15, the barge was in tow of the steamer ZILLAH (qv) and breasting a terrific gale when the siren of Vermilion Point beckoned again. The salt-carrying schooner broke her towline and foundered off the point where she had kissed the bottom twice before. Seven unwilling men, the schooner's entire crew, shared her destiny. The remains of the barge were located in 1983. [4]

MOCKING BIRD ■ Steam tug, probably the 72 t., 67 ft. vessel built at Bay City, MI in 1885
Lake Huron: The small lumber harbor at Cheboygan, MI, saw the loss of this tug to fire in the year 1890. [2]

GEORGE M MOFFAT ■ Wooden steam freighter of 135 ft., launched in 1853 at Chatham, Ont.
Lake Huron: The steamer GEORGE M MOFFAT was reported lost on Raby Head, west of Bowmanville, Ontario, in a gale. The date of the accident is given as December 13, 1864. Reports of this disaster occurring on Lake Huron are in error. [3]

FRANK MOFFATT ■ Steam tug of 123 t.
Lake Huron: Five lives were lost and the FRANK MOFFAT's career came to an abrupt end when she was destroyed in an explosion on November 1, 1885. The big tug was off Port Huron, Michigan, at the time. She was reported sunk in a collision in the same area in 1873. [3]

KATE MOFFATT ■ Steam tug
Lake Huron: The tug KATE MOFFATT was lost at Presque Isle, Michigan, when she burned in 1885. [1]

MOHAWK ■ Armed schooner
Lake Ontario: This warship was sunk during combat with the French fleet in 1756 (Seven Years' War). [1]

MOHAWK ■ Schooner of 99 ft., launched at Kingston, Ont., in 1842 as a sidewheel steam gunboat of the Royal Navy
Lake Huron: The MOHAWK was a schooner that foundered with all hands in 1868 or '70. She reportedly went down off Pointe Aux Barques, Michigan. [4]

MOHAWK ■ Vessel information unreported
Lake Ontario: A vessel called MOHAWK was reported to have foundered on the lake with all hands, but the date is not given. [1]

MOHEGAN ■ Merchant brig
Lake Huron: This little vessel sank in a storm off Pte Aux Barques, Michigan, in 1870. [1]

ANNIE MOILES ■ Salvage tug of 72 t. and 86 ft., launched at Bay City, MI, in 1867
St. Clair River: Owned by the famous Reid Towing Company of Sarnia, the tug ANNIE MOILES capsized and sank in the "whirlpool" formed where Lake Huron empties into the river. All seven of the tug's crew perished in the 1904 accident. Tom Reid himself dove on the wreck to prepare her for salvage, and encountered part of her crew that was still on board. [3]
Detroit River: The end came for the (now aged) tug when she suffered a collison and sank off Detroit in May, 1922. [3]

MOJAVE ■ Bark or schooner of 137 ft. overall, launched in 1864 at Detroit
Lake Michigan: Some journalists of the time said that the loss of the schooner MOJAVE was an example of justice served. The crew of the schooner was, almost to a man, the same group that was handling the ill-starred schooner AUGUSTA on the fateful day in 1860 when she rammed and sunk the passenger steamer LADY ELGIN (qv). Though the AUGUSTA crew was officially cleared of any blame in the matter, they were held responsible by an angry public. In September of 1864, the MOJAVE set sail on the lake, left port in fine weather, and was never heard from again, nor was any wreckage ever found. Perhaps her humble bones lie somewhere in the vicinity of those of the palatial LADY ELGIN. [4]

MOLLIE ■ Scow
Lake Huron: This unpowered vessel was reported sunk at Sarnia in 1881. [1]

GILBERT MOLLISON ■ Merchant schooner of 318 t. and 138 ft., launched in 1857 at Oswego, NY
Lake Michigan: Laden with a cargo of corn, the small two-sticker GILBERT MOLLISON went missing with all hands on October 27, 1873. The vessel was last seen off the Manitou Islands. [5]

MONA ■ Merchant schooner of 102 t.
Lake Huron: A commercial schooner of this size carries a crew of four to six. This was the approximate number of sailors that perished when the MONA was lost off Pointe Aux Barques, Michigan, on September 10, 1887. [2]

MONARCH ■ Sidewheel package freight steamer of 174 ft., launched in 1856 at Sorel, Que.
Lake Ontario: This proud new steamer was winding up her first season, making one of her last scheduled trips of 1856 laden with a cargo of fish and general merchandise. She encountered a powerful storm and blizzard conditions when approaching Toronto, and her skipper was unable to see the entrance to the harbor. Instead of pulling into the safe harbor, the sidewheeler struck ground at Gibraltar Point and was wrecked by the gale-driven waves that followed. Fortunately, all aboard were able to evacuate the vessel safely. [1]

MONARCH ■ Passenger and package freight steamer of 2,017 t. and 240 ft, launched in 1890 at Sarnia, Ont.
Lake Superior: Downbound with a load of wheat and general freight. The MONARCH was making her last run of the season from Port Arthur (Thunder Bay), Ontario, on December 6, 1906. Though she had left in fair weather, by the time she reached the vicinity of Isle Royale there was a full-blown blizzard and gale in progress. Groping her way through the blinding snow, the steamer almost made it around the northern end of the island, but struck Blake Point hard, shoving her prow right up into the woods. Wave action quickly began to tear the vessel up, but her proximity to land made it possible for all but one of the 61 passengers and crew to climb down to dry land. They survived four days in a freezing North Country blizzard until help arrived. Divers who have visited the MONARCH since she was located in 1978 say the remnants of the steamer still lie on the bottom below the spot she struck. [5+]

MONARCH ■ Gas packet of 42 ft.
Lake Superior: The little packet vessel MONARCH was reportedly destroyed by fire in the harbor at Grand Marais, Michigan, on October 6, 1913. No lives were lost. [1]

MONARCH OF THE GLEN ■ Merchant schooner of 24 t. and 42 ft., launched in 1861 at Sandusky, OH
Lake Erie: Five crewmen died when this tiny schooner capsized and went down off Marblehead, north of Sandusky, Ohio. The accident occurred on November 5, 1862. [2]

MONGUAGON ■ Bulk freight schooner-barge of 301 t. and 136 ft. launched in 1874 at Trenton, MI
Detroit River: This 36-year-old sail vessel was reported to have simply opened her seams and sunk on the river on July 2, 1911. [2]

MONITOR ■ Merchant schooner
Lake Michigan: The schooner MONITOR was wrecked in 1883 on Seul Choix Point, on the eastern shore of Michigan's Garden Peninsula. [1]

MONITOR ■ Lighter
Lake Superior: Five lives were lost when the lighter MONITOR was sunk near Point Iroquois, on the south side of Whitefish Bay, in September of 1898. [1]

MONKSHAVEN ■ Bulk freight turret steamer of 2,097 t. and 249 ft., launched in 1882 at South Shields, England.

Lake Superior: This three-island steamer was lost on November 28, 1905, when she was blown out of control by a monstrous gale and struck the rocky coast of Angus Island, near Thunder Cape, Ontario. No lives were lost, but the steel freighter was almost totally destroyed. She was pulled off the reef for scrap in 1906, but sank on the way to the breakers. [5+]

MONOHANSETT ■ Wooden bulk freight propeller of 572 t. and 162 ft., launched in 1872 at Gibraltar, Michigan, as the steamer IRA H OWEN
Lake Huron: On November 23, 1907, the MONOHANSETT was inbound with her cargo of coal when she caught fire near the north arc of Thunder Bay, Michigan. Visible from Alpena, eight miles away, the steamer burned and sank 1/2 mile west of the Thunder Bay Island Light. [5]

MONROVIA ■ Steel package and bulk freight steamer of 6,700 t. and 430 ft., launched in 1943 in Scotland
Lake Huron: This "saltie" was a truly international vessel. Built in Scotland and Liberian-flagged, she carried a Greek crew—and wound up on the bottom near Alpena, Michigan. On June 25, 1959, the big steamer was moving through a thick fog near the top of Thunder Bay when she collided with the freighter ROYALTON. She went down off Thunder Bay Island, but all hands were rescued. The vessel and her cargo of steel were considered too deep to salvage. [5]

MONSON ■ Merchant schooner
Lake Erie: The schooner MONSON reportedly foundered near Port Hope, Ontario, in 1851. [1]

MONSOON ■ Bulk freight schooner of 132 t.
Lake Michigan: Somewhere along the route between Chicago and Grand Haven, the schooner MONSOON was struck by a storm and foundered with all six hands. She went missing in November of 1881. [1]

MONT BLANC ■ Bulk freight schooner of 288 t. and 137 ft., launched in 1867 at Clayton, NY
Lake Erie: This sail vessel foundered in a storm off Bar Point, on the Ontario shore, on October 21, 1901. [2]

MONTANA ■ Bulk freight schooner of 346 t.
Lake Huron: Carrying a load of iron ore down the coast, the schooner MONTANA was lost north of Middle Island, below Presque Isle, Michigan, on November 2, 1890. Her crew was rescued. [2]

MONTANA ■ Wooden steam package freighter of 1,535 t. and 236 ft., launched in 1872 at Port Huron, MI
Lake Huron: On September 6, 1914, this braced package freighter caught fire and was destroyed offshore from Thunder Bay Island, about five miles from the lighthouse. None of her crew were injured in the accident. Her cargo at the time was probably lumber. [3]

MONTAUK ■ Bulk freight schooner of 332 t.
Lake Michigan: The schooner MONTAUK foundered north of Pickard's Dock, North Manitou Island, on November 24, 1882. [1]

MONTCALM ■ Bulk freight schooner
Lake Erie: This ship was reportedly lost on Lapp Point, when she went aground there and was wrecked on November 19, 1891. [1]

MONTEAGLE ■ Wooden bulk freight steamer of 1,273 t. and 213 ft., launched in 1884 at Buffalo
Lake Huron: The St. Marys River channel, connecting Sault Ste. Marie with Lake Huron, passes though a number of significant lakes. The steamer MONTEAGLE was creeping through one of these, Lake Muniscong, when she caught fire on September 22, 1909. The blaze, as they often do on wooden ships, quickly spread out of control, and the freighter's crew was forced to abandon her. She burned to total destruction and sank, and her remains still lie where she went down. [5]

MONTEZUMA ■ Merchant brig
Lake Huron: This little square-rigger was lost in a collision with an unreported vessel above Pointe Aux Barques, Michigan, in the year 1871. [1]

MONTGOMERY ■ Passenger and package freight steamer of 204 ft., launched in 1856 at Newport (Marine City), MI
Lake Huron: This steamer was destroyed by fire of Point Edward, at the extreme lower end of the lake, in June of 1878. Her hull was recovered and rebuilt as the vessel below. [3]

MONTGOMERY ■ Bulk freight schooner-barge of 709 t. and 204 ft., launched in 1856 at Newport, (Marine City) MI as a passenger/freight steamer, converted to a schooner in 1879
Lake Superior: This ancient vessel, which had served for 45 years as a steamer, schooner and schooner-barge, finally met her fate off Michigan's Crisp Point on October 19, 1901. She was in tow of the steamer LELAND when struck by a gale. Her towline suddenly parted, and, though a valiant effort was made to re-connect, it was soon

apparent that the lumber laden barge would strike a bar just offshore. The LELAND stood by and picked up the MONTGOMERY's crew just before she went aground. She was pounded to pieces in place. [5]

MONTICELLO ■ Wooden sidewheel passenger and package freight steamer of 364 t. launched in 1848 at Fairport, OH
Lake Superior: In 1851 there were few steamers operating on Lake Superior, since each one had to be either built above the Soo rapids, or hauled around them on skids (the Soo locks did not open until 1855). Therefore, it is interesting that, in August of 1851, the MONTICELLO collided with another steamer, the MANHATTAN (qv). Though inspection of the vessel's hull revealed no significant damage, the steamer foundered off the Keweenaw Peninsula in a relatively moderate storm on September 25. [3]

MONTICELLO ■ Lumber schooner of 316 t. and 142 ft., launched in 1870 at Detroit
Lake Huron: This schooner was driven ashore and broken up in a gale which destroyed her on August 16, 1904. The MONTICELLO was carrying a cargo of sand when she came ashore at Port Crescent, Michigan, near the tip of the "thumb." Port Crescent is now a ghost town. [3]

MONTMORENCY ■ Bulk freight schooner-barge of 299 t. and 136 ft., launched in 1866 at Clayton, NY on the burnt-out hull of the schooner SOVEREIGN OF THE SEAS (qv)
Lake Huron: This schooner-barge may have been under her own sail when she became lost in a fog and stranded in the shallows to the west of the Charity Islands, in the mouth of Saginaw Bay. She was wrecked on May 19, 1901. The wreck is still visible to those who dare to challenge this reefy area. [4]

MONTPELIER ■ Merchant schooner of 1,290 t., may be erroneous tonnage, very few schooners of this large size were built
Lake Michigan: The schooner MONTPELIER was reported sunk off Grand Haven, Michigan, on November 1, 1878. Though there is no record of her recovery, this could be the same ship as below. [1]

MONTPELIER ■ Package and bulk freight schooner of 290 t. and 138 ft., launched in 1866 at Clayton, NY
Detroit River: The strength and condition of a vessel's hull has as much to do with whether it stays afloat as does stress of weather or accidents. This small carrier had been in the water for more than fifty years when she was lost due to hull failure. On August 11, 1907, she was transiting the river and was off Belle Isle, near Detroit, when

she just began to leak beyond the capacity of her pumps. Her crew abandoned ship, and she sank. [2]

CITY OF MONTREAL ■ Steam freighter of 662 t. and 138 ft., launched in 1871 at Chatham, Ont.
Lake Superior: The steamer CITY OF MONTREAL probably sank near Michipicoten Island from unknown causes on October 24, 1888. One life was lost when she went down. Sources are not much in agreement about this wreck. She is also described as a schooner, and one report gives the location of her loss as the Portage Ship Canal. [3]

MOONLIGHT ■ Bulk freight schooner-barge of 777 t. and 206 ft., launched at Milwaukee in 1874 as a schooner
Lake Superior: On September 17, 1903, this schooner-barge foundered off Michigan Island, in the Apostles group. While in tow of the wooden twin-stack steamer VOLUNTEER on that date, she was deep-laden with iron ore and bucking a tremendous storm. Sometime during the day, the strain on her towline became too much, and she was set adrift. Probably knowing the futility of trying to get the big barge back in tow, the skipper of the VOLUNTEER took the barge's crew aboard and made for port. The old ship sank soon after. [5]

H D MOORE ■ Lumber schooner of 143 t. and 103 ft., launched in 1874 at Saugatuck, MI
Lake Michigan: Storm-beset vessels in northern Lake Michigan often sought refuge in the almost-circular harbor at South Manitou Island. However, the little bay was not always a paragon of safety. The small schooner H D MOORE came struggling into the harbor during a gale on September 10, 1907. She struck a rocky area on the south side of the bay, settled to the bottom in shallow water, and was destroyed by the repeated assaults of waves. [3]

JOHN MOORE ■ 322 t. vessel of unreported type
Lake Ontario: The JOHN MOORE reportedly was lost about six miles southeast of Toronto on April 21, 1940. [1]

SMITH MOORE ■ Wooden steam barge of 1,191 t. and 223 ft., launched in 1883 at Cleveland
Lake Superior: No lives were lost, but the steamer SMITH MOORE went to the bottom off the northeast of Grand Island, near Munising, Michigan, in an accident which occurred on July 13, 1889. Bound from Marquette with her holds piled with iron ore, the freighter was running in a dense fog when she was rammed by the similarly-sized steamer JAMES PICKANDS. The PICKANDS never stopped and, though she remained afloat for some

time, the MOORE was fatally damaged. After the fog lifted, her distress signals brought the freighter M M DRAKE to her assistance. The MOORE's crew was taken off and the steamer herself taken in tow, but she sank on her approach to Munising. [3]

T M MOORE ■ Tug of 52 ft.
Lake Erie: On December 22, 1898, the tug T M MOORE was destroyed northwest of Put-in-Bay, on Rattlesnake Island, when she stranded, then burned. [1]

W A MOORE ■ Steam tug
Lake Huron: The tug W A MOORE sank in a Saginaw Bay squall in the year 1871. [1]

MORANIA #130 ■ Steel fuel-tanker barge of 230 ft.
Lake Erie: Two men aboard this barge died a firey death when she was rammed by the bulk freighter PENOBSCOT (qv) on October 29, 1951. She was in tow of the tug DAUNTLESS –12 (qv) when the collision occurred in the harbor at Buffalo. Her 800,000 gallons of gasoline exploded, destroying both tug and barge, and seriously damaging the PENOBSCOT. [3]

FRANCISCO MORAZON ■ Steel package and bulk freight steamer of 900 t.
Lake Michigan: The finest in charts and the latest in navigational gear is no guarantee that a vessel won't find the rocks in one of the Lakes' fits of weather. On November 24, 1960, the Liberian-flagged MORAZON was bound for Chicago when she was struck by a sudden blizzard and lost her way. She finally found land on the west side of South Manitou Island. She struck the rocks there and sank just offshore. Most of the wreck still protrudes from the water and is an attraction for island hikers. [5]

WILLIAM C MORELAND ■ Steel bulk freight steamer of 8,800 t. and 580 ft., launched in 1910 at Lorain, OH
Lake Superior: This giant ore boat was brand new and just finishing up her first season of operation when she was overtaken by disaster. On October 18 of 1910, the big steamer was approaching Eagle Harbor, Michigan, near the top of the Keweenaw Peninsula, when she struck treacherous Sawtooth Reef. Her stern stuck fast, but the forward half of the ship quickly filled with water. Thus unbalanced, the steamer broke in half. The bow sank in deep water, while the after portion remained firmly in the rocks. With brand-new engines and equipment, the remaining segment of the ship was a valuable piece of hardware, and was salvaged in 1912 and towed to Lake Erie. At Lorain a new forward portion was attached and the vessel became the freighter CHAS. J HUTCHINSON, one of very few vessels that could be termed "half a shipwreck". [5]

MOREY ■ Steam tug
Lake Ontario: This harbor tug was lost in a valiant but futile attempt to rescue the schooner WAYNE (qv) from the breakwall at Oswego, New York. On December 5, 1877, the schooner struck the outer edge of the breakwall and began to sink. The MOREY charged out to assist, but in attempting to get a line on the endangered vessel, she was thrown against the breakwater herself, and went to pieces. [2]

J P MORGAN, Jr. ■ Steel bulk freight steamer of 7,521 t. and 580 ft., launched in 1910 at Lorain, OH
Lake Superior: In a rare type of accident, the big freighter J P MORGAN, Jr. suffered a collision with the steamer CRETE. The two vessels met almost perfectly "bows-on" near the Keweenaw Peninsula on June 23, 1948. Though neither vessel sank, both were extensively damaged, and two men were crushed in the foc'sle of the MORGAN. [3]

GEORGE W MORELY ■ Wooden bulk feight steamer of 1,046 t. and 192 ft., launched in 1888 at W Bay City, MI
Lake Michigan: On December 5, 1897, the steamer GEORGE W MORELY, loaded with coal, exploded and burned off Evanston, Illinois. She sank several miles offshore. [3]

MORNING LIGHT ■ Bulk freight schooner of 236 t.
Lake Michigan: In November of 1882, the schooner MORNING LIGHT was carrying her usual cargo of lumber when she sank after a collision with an unreported vessel. She was lost off the Claybanks area, near the town of Stony Lake, Michigan. [2]

MORNING STAR ■ Merchant schooner of 31 t. and 44 ft., launched in 1825 at Sandusky, OH
Lake Erie: The tiny schooner MORNING STAR was reported to have capsized and sunk off Conneaut, Ohio, in 1844. [1]

MORNING STAR ■ Wooden sidewheel passenger and package freight steamer of 1,075 t. and 243 ft., launched in 1863 at Detroit
Lake Erie: This sidewheeler was carrying a cargo of iron bars and glass on June 21, 1868, when she met with a tragedy ten miles off Lorain, Ohio. All 23 people aboard the MORNING STAR drowned when she collided with the schooner (or bark) COURTLANDT (qv) and quickly sank. One source claims she was in tow at the time of the accident. Some estimates of those lost run as high as 45. [5]

MORNING STAR ■ Merchant schooner of 498 t.
Lake Erie: The schooner MORNING STAR was carrying a cargo of wheat when she foundered in a storm off Port Burwell, Ontario. Seven of her crew died when the ship went down on November 4, 1880. [1]

MORNING STAR ■ Merchant schooner of 205 t. and 118 ft., launched in 1868 at Sheboygan, WI
Lake Michigan: Reports do not give the date of this accident, but it is known that the schooner stranded and broke up near Michigan City, Indiana. [2]

DANIEL J MORRELL ■ Steel bulk freight steamer of 7,237 t. and 587 ft., launched in 1906 at W Bay City, MI
Lake Huron: Even the great steel freighters are sometimes no match for an angry Great Lakes gale. This huge bulk carrier encountered a tremendous storm north of Port Austin, Michigan, on November 29, 1966. The big ship was fighting waves of 25 feet or more. According to the report of her one surviving crewman, the long ship rode up on the crest of a giant sea and broke in two. The bow portion sank quickly, but the amputated stern portion plowed on until she lost steam and sank. When the big ore boat went down, about 25 miles north of Port Austin, Michigan, she took 28 men to the bottom with her. She was light at the time of the accident. [5 +]

F MORRELL ■ Merchant schooner of 369 t. and 144 ft.
Lake Superior: Little is known about this shipwreck except that the vessel was lost off Sand Point in 1874. No lives were lost. [3]

MORRIS ■ Merchant schooner
Lake Huron: The schooner MORRIS was reported to have foundered off Port Austin, Michigan, in the year 1887. [1]

ANNE F MORSE ■ Merchant schooner of 32 t. and 61 ft., launched at Muskegon, MI, in 1881
Lake Michigan: On a short trip between South Haven and Whitehall, Michigan, this tiny schooner and her cargo of wood just disappeared. One person (this may have been her entire crew) was lost in the May 19, 1904, accident. [3]

FRED A MORSE ■ Merchant schooner of 592 t. and 182 ft., launched in 1871 at Vermilion, OH
Lake Huron: The crowded waters near Thunder Bay Island were the scene of many collisions when Alpena was a bustling lumber port in the latter part of the 19th Century. On June 27, 1892, the schooner FRED A MORSE suffered a collision with an unnamed vessel and sank southeast of the island. [2]

JAY C MORSE ■ Tug and excursion vessel of about 75 ft
Lake Superior: Between towing jobs, the tug JAY C MORSE took small numbers of passengers on short sightseeing trips. During one of these jaunts, on July 17, 1867, the vessel struck a rock near Marquette and punctured her hull. Her skipper spun her around and raced for shore, but the vessel sank just short, with the loss of one of those aboard. She was subsequently raised and returned to service. [2]

Lake Superior: The JAY C MORSE foundered for a second time—and this time for good—in 1889. She was approaching the Portage Ship Canal when she struck rocks offshore and sank. [1]

J D MORTON ■ Wooden steam freighter
Lake Huron: This steamer was reported lost in a storm on Thunder Bay, on the Michigan shore, in the year 1853. [1]

MINNIE MORTON ■ Steam tug
Lake Huron: The tug MINNIE MORTON went down in the Straits of Mackinac, near Bois Blanc Island, in 1881. [1]

SYLVIA MORTON ■ Vessel information unavailable
Lake Huron: A single brief report says that this schooner was lost somewhere on the lake in 1887. [1]

RICHARD MORWOOD or **MOREWOOD** ■ Schooner-barge of 268 t., launched in 1856 at Port Dover, Ont.
Lake Superior: The schooner-barge RICHARD MORWOOD was upbound with a cargo of barrelled stove oil when she was caught in a storm off Munising, Michigan. Separated from her tow vessel and with her sails ripped out, she drifted for some time before striking bottom and sinking off Grand Island, close enough to shore for her crew to be rescued. Her cargo was recovered immediately, but the vessel, which had been delared a total loss, was not refloated until two years later in 1879. [4]

MOSES AND ELIAS ■ Merchant schooner
Lake Erie: In November of 1851, the schooner MOSES AND ELIAS was carrying a cargo of general merchandise when she stranded and was lost off Middle Bass Island. [1]

AMARETTA MOSHER ■ Lumber schooner of 300 t. and 139 ft. overall, launched at Ashtabula, OH, in 1867
Lake Erie: The two-masted AMARETTA MOSHER was declared a total loss after being blown on Starve Island Reef, near Port Clinton, OH, and wrecked in a storm on November 29, 1902. She was laden with coal at the time. [3]

A H MOSS ■ Merchant schooner
Lake Huron: This sailing ship was lost at an unrecorded position in 1887. [1]

J O MOSS ■ Merchant schooner of 198 t. and 96 ft., launched in 1863 at Sandusky, OH
Lake Michigan: The unfortunate schooner J O MOSS had been battered by a big gale on November 23, 1882. She was anchored in relatively calm weather and was licking her wounds, when a northwest squall struck her. The schooner's anchors would not hold, and the vessel was blown into the shallows near Big Sable Point to break up. A crew from the U.S. Lifesaving Service rescued five men from her rigging, but a sixth was lost overboard. [2]

LADY MOULTON ■ 79 t. vessel of unreported type
Lake Ontario: The LADY MOULTON is recorded as having foundered off Point Petre in May of 1880. [1]

CITY OF MT CLEMENS ■ Steam propeller of 102 t. and 95 ft., launched in 1880 at Mt. Clemens, MI
Lake St. Clair: This little propeller is reported to have foundered on the lake in November of 1908. [1]

MOUNTAINEER ■ Merchant schooner of 43 t.
Lake Erie: Port Glasgow, Ont., is a small village to the northeast of Point Aux Pins. With its back to the west wind, the town has seen few shipwrecks over the years. However, on July 31, 1882, a southeasterly gale blew the schooner MOUNTAINEER ashore near the city. Though she was only mildly damaged initially, heavy seas that followed pounded the vessel to pieces. The sailing ship had also been heavily damaged in a grounding on Georgian Bay in 1869. [2]

OLIVER MOWAT ■ Bulk freight schooner of 341 t. and 116 ft. overall, launched in 1873 at Millhaven, Ont.
Lake Ontario: This small three-master was bound for Oswego, New York, with a cargo of coal when she met with disaster in the form of the 1,700 ton steamer KEYWEST. The schooner was gliding through the Duck Islands on the night of September 21, 1921, when she was run down and sunk by the bulk freighter. Five of her crew perished in the accident. [2]

JAMES MOWATT ■ Bulk freight schooner-barge of 523 t. and 166 ft., launched in 1884 at Milwaukee
Lake Huron: Collisions between vessels were not the only crashes that brought ships to untimely ends. On October 10, 1919, the JAMES MOWATT rammed a stone jetty at Alpena, Michigan, and sank. She was loaded with lumber at the time. [3]

GEORGE M MOWBRAY ■ Merchant schooner of 40 t.
Lake Erie: This little ship was toting one of the most dangerous cargoes a boat could carry at the time of her loss. On November 10, 1880, the schooner was caught in a storm and sunk a few miles off Presque Isle (Erie), PA. In her holds was a carefully-packed cargo of nitroglycerine. Fortunately, salvagers gingerly removed the explosive before it could turn an incident into a disaster. [2]

ISAAC MUNSON ■ Merchant schooner
Lake Huron: This sail vessel was reported to have touched the rocky bottom and foundered in an 1888 storm. She went down off Caseville, MI, in lower Saginaw Bay. [2]

MUNSTER ■ Scow of 316 t.
Lake Huron: The scow MUNSTER is said to have foundered on December 6, 1936, off Harbor Beach, Michigan. She sank well offshore. [1]

MURIEL W ■ Wooden bulk freight steamer of 1,093 t. and 210 ft., launched in 1886 at Milwaukee as the steamer VERONICA
Lake Ontario: This big steamer was lost near Port Weller, Ontario, on August 11, 1919. She reportedly struck a sunken crib and sank. [2]

H P MURRAY ■ Vessel information unavailable
Lake Erie: This vessel was another victim of the narrow Pelee Passage. On October 4, 1877, the H P MURRAY went ashore near Pelee Island light, and was broken up by wave action. [1]

ELLA MURTON ■ Crane-equipped bulk freight schooner of 125 ft. overall, launched in 1875 at Deseronto, Ont.
Lake Huron: South Bay, which reaches up into Manitoulin Island like a Norwegian fjord, was the site of the loss of this schooner. On November 3, 1903, the MURTON stranded near the mouth of the bay and was wrecked. [1]

MUSCALLONGE ■ Steam propeller of 360 t. and 128 ft., launched in 1896 at Port Huron, MI
Lake Ontario: The small steamer MUSCALLONGE (sic) was reported wrecked near Port Weller, Ont., in August of 1936. [1]

MUSIC ■ Tug of 92 t. and 93 ft., launched in 1892 at South Haven, MI
Lake Michigan: This small tug caught fire and was destroyed on the north side of Portage Lake (north of Manistee, MI). She met her end in September of 1899. [2]

MUSKEGON ■ Sidewheel steamer of 618 t. and 193 ft., launched in 1871 at Manitowoc, WI
Lake Michigan: This sidewheeler was one of the few commercial vessels ever to be lost on dry land. After 25 years of service, she was brought to Milwaukee for a rebuild. On September 22, 1896, she was up on blocks in the drydock when several of her supports slipped. She fell only a few feet, but her tremendous weight was enough to destroy her wooden hull. When work was resumed on the steamer, it was to dismantle her. [2]

MUSKEGON ■ Steel or composite sidewheel passenger and package freight steamer of 1,149 t. and 230 ft., launched in 1881 at Detroit as the steamer CITY OF MILWAUKEE
Lake Michigan: This steamer suffered a tragic accident in the harbor of her namesake city of Muskegon, MI. On September 22, 1919, she was attempting to enter her harbor in a terrific westerly gale. At a critical moment she went out of control and rammed the pierhead, putting a huge hole in her bows and causing her to sink quickly.

Twenty-nine people perished, most trapped belowdecks as she sank. The ship is often seen in the literature under the erroneous name "City of Muskegon." [5+]

MUSKEGON ■ Wooden steam sandsucker of 1,199 t. and 211 ft., launched in 1872 at Cleveland as the passenger and package freighter PEERLESS
Lake Michigan: This combination sandsucker and bulk freighter was destroyed at Michigan City, Indiana, on October 6, 1910. She was moored to a dock and was unloading when she caught fire and was completely demolished. [3]

MYLES ■ 929 t. vessel of unreported type, may be the 1,211 t., 175 ft. steamer of this name built in 1882 at Hamilton, Ont.
Lake Ontario: The steamer MYLES was reported to have gone aground on Murray Shoal, near Brighton, Ontario, on November 2, 1886. Though she was said to have been lost, if she is the vessel described above, she was recovered and later became the steamer CATARACT. [2]

MYOSOTIS ■ Bulk freight schooner of 332 t. and 137 ft.
Lake Michigan: On November 11, 1887, the schooner MYOSOTIS foundered on a reef near the mouth of the harbor at St. Joseph, Michigan, at the south end of the lake. She was totally wrecked and thus was abandoned to break up. [2]

MYRON ■ Gas passenger and package freight launch of 42 ft.
Lake Superior: This little packet boat was destroyed by fire and sank at Lipe's Dock on October 6, 1913. [1]

MYRON ■ Wooden lumber hooker of 676 t. and 186 ft., launched in 1888 at Grand Haven, MI, as the steamer MARK HOPKINS
Lake Superior: When downbound with a load of lumber and the schooner-barge MIZTEC (qv) in tow, this steamer was blasted by a vicious northwest gale. The veteran lumber hooker began to leak profusely, and by the time she reached the vicinity of Whitefish Point, it was apparent that she was going to go down. The barge was cut loose and the MYRON's crew made ready to abandon ship. However, huge waves and a howling wind made it impossible to launch a boat, even though the big steamer ADRIATIC had placed herself to windward of the stricken ship. Three rescue attempts were made by the local unit of the U.S. Lifesaving Service, but to no avail. Within sight of the lifesavers and the other vessels, the old MYRON took her plunge. Only one of her 18 crew survived the Nov. 22, 1919 accident. The wreck was located in 1972. [5+]

MYRTIE ■ Merchant schooner of 25 t.
Lake Erie: Horseshoe Reef has been snagging unwary ships ever since the nearby City of Buffalo was founded. On November 2, 1907, the little schooner MYRTIE stranded there and was broken up in place. [1]

MYRTLE ■ Merchant schooner of 207 t. and 118 ft., launched in 1857 at Milan, OH
Lake Michigan: Vessels on the open lake in heavy weather are usually safer than those attempting to enter the narrow confines of harbors and maneuver in the same conditions. The schooner MYRTLE had battled a storm all day on May 18, 1894, in an attempt to bring her cargo of lumber to Chicago. As she was approaching the waterfront area, she dropped in a wave trough and hit bottom. Before her crew could escape, the schooner went to pieces, and all hands were lost with her. [5]

MYRTLE ■ Steam tug of 50 t. and 57 ft., launched in 1877 at St. Catharine's, Ont. No location is given for the fire that destroyed this vessel in the winter of 1891. [1]

MYSTERY ■ Package and bulk freight steamer of 3,578 t.
Lake Huron: On August 31, 1911, this steamer was reported as destroyed by fire at Georgian Bay's White Cloud Island. No further information is given, and the ship may have been recovered. [2]

MYSTERY ■ 37 t. vessel of unreported type
Lake Superior: This little vessel was reportedly destroyed by fire on the east side of Sawyer Bay on October 11, 1927. [1]

MYSTIC ■ Steam tug, probably the 121 t. vessel built at Detroit in 1870
Lake Huron: The tug MYSTIC foundered in the North Channel, near Cockburn Island, in 1878. [1]

MYSTIC ■ Steamer of 68 t. and 81 ft., launched at Detroit in 1870
Lake Superior: On September 27, 1893, the little steamer MYSTIC caught fire and burned to the water's edge in Tahquamenon Bay of Whitefish Bay. No lives were lost. [4]

N ELLEN M ■ 17 t. vessel of unreported type
Lake Huron: The small vessel N ELLEN M was destroyed by fire at Cabot Head, in Georgian Bay, on August 6, 1949. [1]

NA-MA-PUK ■ Steam packet of 24 t., launched in 1899
Lake Superior: This little steamer was lost when she foundered off Sable Island, Minnesota, on August 28, 1909. No lives were lost in the incident. [1]

NAGAHO ■ Wooden bulk freight steamer of 1,438 t. and 194 ft., launched in 1888 at Mt. Clemens, MI, as the schooner-barge F R BUELL
Lake Ontario: The big old steamer NAGAHO was struck by a heavy westerly gale on October 27, 1922. Though the vessel was almost in sinking condition, she limped back to a point near Port Collins, Ontario, and sank in shallow water. In November it was decided that it would be too expensive to repair the veteran ship, and she was abandoned in place. [2]

NAHANT ■ Wooden package and bulk feight steamer of 909 t. and 213 ft., launched in 1873 at Detroit
Lake Michigan: The freighter NAHANT was docked at Escanaba, Michigan, in Little Bay de Noc, at the north end of Green Bay, when she caught fire at dock. Hampered by below-zero temperatures, firefighters were unable to douse the blaze, and the vessel burned to the water with the loss of one of her crew on Nov. 29, 1897. [3]

NAIAD ■ Steamer
Lake Huron: Little is known of the loss of this steamer off Pte Aux Barques, Michigan. She reportedly sank off the point in 1892 with some loss of life, but was probably recovered. [2]

NAIAD ■ Merchant schooner of 312 t. and 146 ft., launched in 1863 at Huron, OH
Lake Michigan: Two men perished in the accident that befell this lumber schooner in July of 1895. She was off Charlevoix, Michigan, when she was struck by a sudden squall which dismasted her and tore up her equipment. The two seamen were carried over the side by rigging. Somehow the NAIAD stayed afloat, and was rescued and later returned to service. [3]

NAIAD ■ Vessel information unavailable
Lake Huron: This vessel, which could be either one of the two listed above or some other ship, was reported to have foundered off Au Sable Point, near Oscoda, Michigan, on October 22, 1911. [2]

H.M.S. NANCY ■ Merchant schooner launched in 1789 at Detroit as a naval support vessel and gunboat
Lake Huron: This little schooner burned and sank at "Nancy" Island, in Georgian Bay, on August 14, 1814. Parts of the vessel have been recovered and now form part of a museum at Collingwood, Ontario. [3]

NAOMI ■ Merchant bark
Lake Ontario: At least two crew members were lost when the bark NAOMI went down in a storm in 1869. [1]

NAOMI ■ Iron steam freighter of 1,182 t. and 203 ft., launched in 1881 at Wyandotte, MI, as the steamer WISCONSIN
Lake Michigan: The steamer NAOMI was running offshore from Grand Haven, Michigan, when she was discovered to be afire. In the blaze that followed, seven of her crew perished. The fire was finally brought under control, but the ship was almost an empty shell. The fire occurred on May 21, 1907, and the NAOMI was completely rebuilt the next year. [4]

CITY OF NAPLES ■ Steam freighter, possibly the 2,109 t., 301 ft. carrier built at W Bay City, MI, in 1892. See also FRANK O'CONNOR.
Lake Huron: This steamer was reported wrecked offshore from Presque Isle, Michigan, in 1892. [2]

NAPOLEAN ■ Steamer
Lake Huron: The steamer NAPOLEAN (sic) was lost in 1857, when she was reported to have foundered off the Saugeen (Bruce) Peninsula. [1]

NARRAGANSET ■ Merchant schooner
Lake Huron: This schooner is said to have been lost in Hammond Bay, near Cheboygan, MI, in 1872. She may have been recovered and be the same vessel as below. [1]

NARRAGANSETT ■ Bulk freight schooner of 317 t. and 139 ft., launched in 1861 at Cleveland
Lake Huron: The lumber-laden schooner NARRAGANSETT was downbound off Port Sanilac, Michigan, and buffeted by heavy weather when her 40-year-old hull simply sprang a leak, the vessel became waterlogged and sank. She went down on May 13, 1901. [3]

NASHUA ■ Wooden lumber hooker of 298 t. and 134 ft., launched in 1868 at Cleveland as a passenger and package freight steamer
Lake Huron: Bound for Toledo with a cargo of lumber, the little wooden steamer NASHUA was lost near Bayfield, Ontario, near the south end of the lake. On October 4, 1892, she was struck by a terrific gale, capsized and sank with all hands. Fourteen perished in the tragedy. [5+]

NASSAU ■ Bulk freight schooner of 315 t. and 137 ft., launched in 1872 at Oswego, NY
Lake Erie: Lost at an unreported position, the schooner NASSAU was carrying a cargo of wheat when she met her fate on October 14, 1898. One person died as a result of the accident. [2]

NAUTILLUS ■ Merchant sloop of 24 t. and 42 ft., launched in 1816 at Sandusky
Lake Erie: The early sail vessel NAUTILLUS was reportedly capsized by a storm which struck her above Erie, Pennsylvania, on September 18, 1817. One sailor lost his life in the accident, but the NAUTILLUS was recovered. [2]
Lake Michigan: The little ship met her end when she was wrecked by an 1854 storm off Chicago. [1]

NAUTILUS ■ Steam tug of 39 t. and 88 ft., launched in 1886 at Poughkeepsie, NY
Lake Superior: The little tug NAUTILUS was reportedly destroyed by fire at Bark Bay on August 14, 1892. [2]

NAVAJO ■ Wooden bulk freight steamer of 164 t. and 111 ft., launched in 1895 at Kingston, Ont. as the steamer KING BEN

Lake Ontario: This little bulk freighter stranded on the south side of Main Duck Island in a December 6, 1914, storm. No lives were lost, but the boat was totally destroyed. [3]

NAVARINO ■ Steam freighter of 761 t., launched in 1871 at Manitowoc, WI
Lake Michigan: The owners of the steamer NAVARINO must have looked forward to their new vessel having a long and profitable career as she sat out at her dock at Chicago on October 9, 1871. No one would have forseen that on that day the City of Chicago would be largely razed by an enormous fire and that the shining new NAVARINO, as well as her docks and warehouses, would be completely destroyed. [2]

NEEBING ■ Steel sandsucker and bulk freighter of 908 t. and 193 ft., launched in 1892 at Toledo as the JOHN B KETCHUM, Jr
Lake Superior: The steamer NEEBING was the first steel-hulled vessel built especially for the lumber trade. In her latter years she had become a sandsucker, with a huge crane installed on her deck, and was engaged in hauling a load of lakebottom gravel when she was lost. On September 24, 1937, the steamer foundered 800 yards off Eagle's Nest Point, in the North Shore's Nipigon Strait, with the loss of five of her 14 crew. [5+]

NEECHEE ■ Merchant schooner
Lake Huron: In 1863 the schooner NEECHEE was wrecked on the shores of Russel Island, just west of Tobermory, Ontario. [1]

G M NEELON ■ Bulk freight schooner-barge of 410 t. and 139 ft., launched in 1873 at Port Dalhousie, Ont. as a schooner
Lake Superior: The G M NEELON was lost in an icy gale in November of 1897. In high seas she broke her towline and was driven on Gull Rock, off the very tip of the Keweenaw Peninsula. The vessel went to pieces quickly, but all of her people were rescued. [2]

M C NEFF ■ Wooden lumber hooker of 276 t. and 137 ft., launched in 1888 at Oshkosh, WI
Lake Superior: The steamer M C NEFF was unloading a cargo on the St. Louis River, at Duluth, when she caught fire and was destroyed on Sept. 20, 1909. Fortunately, all her crew were able to escape in time to avoid the blaze. [3]

S NEFF ■ Steam freighter of 129 t. and 128 ft., launched in 1882 at Oshkosh, WI
Lake Erie: On August 11, 1892, the steamer S NEFF was caught in a summer blow and driven on the breakwater at Cleveland. A gaping hole in her side allowed her to sink quickly. She was later partially salvaged. [2]

SIDNEY O NEFF ■ Wooden bulk freight steamer of 346 t. and 160 ft., launched as a schooner in 1890 at Manitowoc, WI
Lake Michigan: In June of 1940, the SIDNEY O NEFF's 50-year-old wooden hull sprang a leak and she sank near the mouth of the Menominee River, at Menominee, MI. [5]

NEGAUNEE ■ Bulk freight schooner-barge of 640 t. and 195 ft., launched in 1867 at Vermilion, OH
Lake Erie: Although her exact position is not recorded, the barge NEGAUNEE is known to have gone on a reef on the 27th of September, 1906, and sustained serious damage. On the 30th, before plans to remove her could be formed, the vessel slipped off her perch and sank in deep water. She was the tow of the steamer CITY OF CLEVELAND at the time of the accident. [3]

NEILSEN ■ Merchant schooner
Lake Huron: The schooner NEILSEN was reported lost on the lake in the big gale of October 20, 1905. [2]

CHRISTINE NEILSEN ■ Merchant schooner of 295 t.
Lake Michigan: This schooner was wrecked on a reef near Bailey's Harbor, Wisconsin, on the lake side of the Door Peninsula, in October of 1884. [1]

ELSIE NELL ■ Steam tug of 41 t. and 62 ft., launched at Sturgeon Bay, WI
Lake Huron: The small tug ELSIE NELL was destroyed by fire at Drummond Island, off the eastern tip of Michigan's upper peninsula in 1936. [2]

NELLIE TERESA ■ 98 t. vessel of unreported type
Lake Ontario: In May of 1884 the NELLIE TERESA was wrecked by a gale at her pier at Port Hope, Ontario. [1]

NELSON ■ Bulk freight schooner-barge of 766 t. and 136 ft., launched in 1866 at Milwaukee as a schooner
Lake Superior: Seven of this schooner-barge's eight man crew died as a result of her sinking on May 13, 1899. Deep-laden with a cargo of coal, the barge was in tow of the steamer ALEX FOLSOM (qv) when she was beset by a spring gale. The force of the storm broke her towline and then tore the vessel apart, sinking her off Grand Marais, Michigan. [3]

O M NELSON ■ Merchant schooner of 167 t.
Lake Michigan: On June 4, 1889, the small schooner O M NELSON was reported to have sunk near Plum Island, in Wisconsin's Porte de Mortes passage. [1]

NEMESIS ■ Merchant schooner
Lake Huron: Bayfield, Ontario, on the province's western shore, was the closest town to the site of the 1883 loss of the schooner NEMESIS. [1]

NEPTUNE ■ Merchant schooner
Lake Ontario: This early schooner's loss was typical of the hundreds of like accidents that were to follow. On December 23, 1840, the NEPTUNE was caught by a gale and blown into the shallows. Once she was helpless, storm-driven combers rushed in to finish the job, literally pounding the vessel to pieces. Nineteen of the 20 persons aboard perished in the disaster. The location is given as Point Sable. [2]

NESHOTO ■ Merchant schooner
Lake Huron: Sturgeon Point, north of Harrisville, Michigan, saw the loss of this schooner, which foundered near there in 1872. Five sailors died when she went down. [1]

NESHOTO ■ Wooden steam freighter of 2,255 t. and 284 ft., launched in 1889 at Cleveland
Lake Superior: One of several vessels which were blinded and ultimately destroyed by the smoke from forest fires was this steamer. On September 27, 1908, the NESHOTO was downbound with her holds full of iron ore when she sailed into a big plume of smoke from a fire to the southwest. Unable to get her bearings, the boat steamed right up into the shallows near Crisp Point, on the Michigan shore. No lives were lost, and the steamer was thought to be recoverable, but a storm that struck a few days later tore her limb from limb, a total loss. [5+]

N J NESSEN ■ Wooden bulk freight steamer of 368 t. and 150 ft., launched in 1880 at Lorain, OH as the steamer H LOUELLA WORTHINGTON
Lake Erie: The steamer NESSEN was lost on October 22, 1929. She was hit by a heavy gale that drove her ashore in Pigeon Bay, near Leamington, Ontario. The constant strain of waves pulling and pushing at her sides, and her heavy, unstable load of scrap iron, caused the steamer to break in half and sink. Although she is often reported to have gone down with all hands, not a life was lost in the incident. The NESSEN was also sunk in shallow water in 1919, and a famous photo shows her with her decks awash and her sister ship at her side. [5+]

GEORGE NESTER ■ Lumber schooner-barge of 790 t. and 207 ft., launched in 1887 (or 1882) at Baraga, MI
Lake Superior: The Huron Islands are directly north of the "rabbit's hump" section of Michigan's upper peninsula. They lie near the path of vessels going to and from upper peninsula, and have intercepted a number of boats using that route. The GEORGE NESTER was fighting through a terrible spring blizzard-gale with her tow-steamer SCHOOLCRAFT on April 30, 1909, when disaster struck. The heaving barge broke her towline and was cast ashore on the Hurons, where she was shattered by the repeated blows of the rocky shore. All seven men aboard the NESTER perished in the frigid conditions when the ship broke up. [5]

NEVADA ■ Steam freighter, perhaps the 186 ft. vessel built in 1882 at Saginaw, MI
Lake Michigan: No lives were lost when the steamer NEVADA went down in 1890. A reliable source says she was lost off Two Rivers, Wisconsin, but others say she foundered at St. Joseph, Michigan, or off Bois Blanc Island, in the Straits of Mackinac. [3]

OLLIE NEVILLE ■ Merchant schooner of 70 t., launched in 1887
Lake Erie: This little vessel was destroyed, but all three of her crew managed to escape when she foundered off Ripley, New York, on January 3, 1905. [1]

NEW BRUNSWICK ■ Merchant schooner of 400 t. and 128 ft., launched in 1847 at St. Catharine's, Ont.
Lake Erie: This schooner was well-known in her time as the first vessel to haul grain directly from Chicago to Europe, and she has even made news as late as 1985. She was carrying a cargo of valuable black walnut timber when she was struck by a gale on August 26, 1858. Her cargo shifted as she was passing abreast of Pelee Island and she turned turtle and sank, killing five of the nine people on board. In 1985, part of her cargo was recovered, and proved to be in excellent condition and still usable despite 127 years at the lake bottom. [5]

NEW CONNECTICUT ■ Merchant schooner
Lake Erie: The schooner NEW CONNECTICUT sprang a leak and capsized off the present site of Portland, New York, in the fall of 1833. Her crew abandoned ship and was saved. The wreck would have been much like dozens of others of that ilk, but it received a lot of extra attention because one woman passenger, believed drowned when the vessel went over, survived for five days under her upturned hull. [2]

NEW DOMINION ■ Merchant schooner of 154 t., launched in 1867 at Port Dalhousie, Ont.
Lake Erie: The position of this schooner at the time of her loss was not reported, but the NEW DOMINION foundered on October 26, 1884, with the loss of six lives. [2]

NEW HAMPSHIRE ■ Merchant schooner of 94 t.
Lake Huron: The small schooner NEW HAMPSHIRE was an October 21, 1885 loss when she foundered four miles north of the lighthouse at Sturgeon Point, on the Michigan side. This vessel was also heavily damaged in a stranding near Marblehead, Lake Erie, in 1879. [3]

NEW LISBON ■ Merchant schooner
Lake Erie: Definite information as to whether this schooner was lost in her 1871 accident is not available, but it is known that she was blown down by a white squall near Fairport, OH. [1]

NEW ORLEANS ■ Sidewheel passenger and package freighter of 610 t., launched in 1844 at Detroit
Lake Huron: The sidewheeler NEW ORLEANS went aground at Thunder Bay, Michigan and became a total loss. The date of the accident is given as June 11, 1849, though the year is the subject of some debate. [2]

NEW ORLEANS ■ Wooden bulk freight steamer of 1,457 t. and 231 ft., launched in 1885 at Marine City, MI
Lake Huron: As might be expected, the wooden steamer NEW ORLEANS came out second best in a collision with the 4,500 ton steel bulk freighter WILLIAM R LINN (qv), on June 30, 1906. Both ships were battling a heavy summer storm when the accident occurred off Thunder Bay Island, near Alpena, Michigan. The LINN stood by and picked up the NEW ORLEANS' people without loss. [4]

NEW YORK ■ Wooden propeller freighter of 704 t., launched in 1856 at Buffalo
Lake Huron: The freighter NEW YORK was carrying a load of lumber on October 14, 1876, when she encountered a northerly gale and sank well offshore, abeam of Forester, Michigan. In 1989 her wreckage was discovered in 25 fathoms of water, and plans were being made to salvage her unusual (for a laker) oscillating engine. [3]

NEW YORK ■ Wooden steam package freighter of 1,921 t. and 269 ft., launched in 1879 at Buffalo
Lake Huron: The exact location of the loss of this steamer is spotted at various points around Thunder Bay, Michigan. On October 1, 1910, the freighter was caught in a vicious storm and began to take on water in the area. Thanks to good fortune and the heavy traffic around the area at that time, her distress signals were spotted by the big steamer MATAAFA (qv), which was able to "run interference," maneuvering to windward of the stricken vessel to flatten the seas and cut the wind. In this way the crew of the NEW YORK were able to launch a boat, and were rescued before the she broke up and went down. The location of the wreck is given as: 30 miles off North Point; a few miles from Thunder Bay Island; near South Point; or in the center of the mouth of the bay. [5+]

CITY OF NEW YORK ■ Wooden bulk freight steamer of 395 t. and 136 ft., launched as a passenger and freight steamer in 1863 at Cleveland

Lake Ontario: Ships of the advanced age of the CITY OF NEW YORK were fine in calm water. But when battered by big waves the old hulls were likely to just open their seams and let the lake in, particularly when they were heavily laden, as was this 48-year-old vessel on November 25, 1921. The coal-carrying steamer had never had a rebuild, and was a ripe target for a November gale, and when one struck her off Main Duck Island, she didn't last long. There is some confusion about the date (also given as 1910 and November, 1919) and the location (also reported as nearer Oswego) of this accident. [5]

NEWARK ■ Merchant schooner
Lake Huron: This schooner was reportedly lost in a storm that struck the lake in 1864. Her location is not reported. [1]

NEWAYGO ■ Lumber steamer of 906 t. and 196 ft., launched in 1890 at Marine City
Lake Huron: Blinded by a November blizzard-gale, the steamer NEWAYGO missed the channel above Tobermory, Ontario, and went aground. Big waves from this and succeeding storms tore her to pieces before she could be released. The date of her stranding was November 17, 1903. [4]

NEWBURGH ■ Propeller freighter of 1,299 t. and 216 ft., launched in 1871 at Buffalo as the steamer WILLIAM M TWEED
Lake Erie: The NEWBURGH is one of dozens of vessels claimed to have "valuable" cargoes aboard, but whose greatest value is probably historic, no matter what her cargo. She was reported aground and destroyed ten miles west of the Long Point lighthouse. The wreck occurred on November 19, 1892. [1]

J B NEWLAND ■ Merchant schooner of 158 t. and 112 ft., launched in 1870 at Manitowoc, WI
Lake Michigan: When two of a vessel's most feared foes combine forces, the ship has little chance of survival. While negotiating the confined area east of South Manitou Island, the schooner J B NEWLAND encountered a combination of heavy fog and large seas. Blinded, she was driven aground on September 8, 1910. Fortunately, no lives were lost in the accident. [1]

NEWSBOY ■ Bulk freight schooner-barge of 413 t. and 152 ft., launched as a bark at Bay City, MI, in 1862
Lake Michigan: The schooner-barge NEWSBOY was reported ashore and wrecked at Rock Island, Wisconsin, on November 21, 1891. This may be the same vessel that collided with the E B ALLEN in 1871. [2]

U S S NIAGARA ■ Armed brig of 480 t., launched in 1813 at Presque Isle, PA (Erie)
Lake Erie: This historic vessel was the flagship of Commodore Perry's victorious fleet at the Battle of Put-in-Bay in the War of 1812. She sank out of sheer neglect in

Misery Bay, near Erie, Pennsylvania, in about 1833. She was raised in 1913, still in remarkably good condition, and was rebuilt for the centennial of the famous battle. She now rides at anchor at Erie. [5+]

NIAGARA ■ Sidewheel passenger and package freight steamer of 1,099 t. and 255 ft., launched in 1845 at Buffalo
Lake Michigan: The disastrous loss of the passenger vessel NIAGARA is, unfortunately, the subject of several reports which conflict in major details. The big steamer caught fire offshore near Sheboygan, Wisconsin, on September 24, 1856. As is often the case, a desperate skipper turned her for shore and made a mad dash for the shallows in hopes of saving her people. The breeze generated by the ship running "full ahead" only fanned the flames to quicker destruction, and the steamer foundered a few miles short of her goal. Casualty estimates vary from about 50 to as many as 170 lost. [5]

NIAGARA ■ Bulk freight schooner-barge of 764 t. and 205 ft., launched in 1873 at Barcelona, NY
Lake Superior: Iron ore is generally a stable cargo, and skippers liked to carry it, because it generally stayed low in the hull. Sometimes, however, a particularly big storm could cause the opposite effect. On September 7, 1887, the schooner-barge NIAGARA was battling a gale off Vermilion Point, on the Michigan coast, when she got sideways to the line of the heaving seas. The ship heeled over far enough for her cargo to slide up her inside, causing the ship to roll down on her beam ends and sink, drowning all nine of her crew. The wreckage of the NIAGARA was located in 1972. [3]

NIAGARA ■ Bulk freight steamer of 458 t. and 144 ft., launched in 1875 at St. Catharine's, Ont.
Lake Erie: This steamer was downbound with a mixed cargo of lumber and pig iron when she was beset by a tremendous storm off Long Point. She went down on December 5, 1899, with the loss of 12 lives. [5+]

NIAGARA ■ Freight tug of 276 t. and 139 ft., launched in 1872 at Detroit
Lake Superior: Fog bedeviled this big tug until she went ashore on Knife Island and was destroyed. She was lost on June 4, 1904. Her crew made it safely to shore. [3]

NIAGARA ■ Wooden barge of 396 t. and 159 ft., launched at Glasgow, Scotland in 1856 as the sidewheel passenger steamer DRUID and converted to a propeller in 1894 and barge in 1914
Lake Superior: This vessel was a visible tribute to the skills of Scots shipbuilders. When she finally foundered in Thunder Bay, Ontario in October of 1936, the hull was more than 80 years old. [1]

I W NICHOLAS ■ Steel bulk freight steamer (one source says passenger and package freighter) of 2,624 t. and 328 ft., launched in 1894 at Cleveland
Lake Huron: Two weeks after she weathered the Big Storm of 1913, this large steamer was hauling a cargo of flax when she stranded in a storm on the shores of Thunder Bay, Michigan. She was declared a total loss, but her steel hull would not give up so easily. The NICHOLAS was recovered and, after extensive repairs (shortened 68 ft.), she sailed again as the freighter INLAND, and was not scrapped until 1937. [4]

A P NICHOLS ■ Merchant schooner
Lake Michigan: On October 28, 1892, the NICHOLS went on the rocks at Pilot Island, Green Bay, and was destroyed. The schooner's crew, however, was rescued by the local lightkeeper. One source gives the date of the accident as November 9, 1872. [3]

ELIZABETH A NICHOLSON ■ Bulk freight schooner of 722 t. and 188 ft., launched in 1872 at Port Huron, MI
Lake Michigan: This schooner almost finished her career "on the rocks," seven miles north of Evanston, Illinois. She was driven aground with her cargo of coal on November 26, 1895, and supposed to be a total loss, but some clever salvage work and a very expensive repair job put her back to work. [3]

JOHN M NICOL ■ Wooden package freight steamer of 2,126 t. and 263 ft., launched in 1889 at W Bay City, MI
Lake Michigan: Just as vessels going south into Green Bay must navigate the treacherous "Death's Door," ships bound for the the more northerly bay ports of Escanaba and Menominee need to thread their way through the Summer Islands. One that didn't make it was the large package freighter JOHN M NICOL. She piled ashore on Big Summer, off the tip of the Garden Peninsula, on December 13, 1906, and was a total loss. Fortunately, none of her crew was injured. [2]

EMMA L NIELSEN ■ Bulk freight schooner-barge of 90 t. and 98 ft., launched in 1883 at Manitowoc, WI as a schooner
Lake Huron: The schooner-barge EMMA L NIELSEN was upbound light from Saginaw on the night of June 26, 1911, when she was struck down. Twelve miles east of Tawas Bay the vessel was rammed and sunk by the big steel steamer WYANDOTTE, plowing through to Lake Erie with a full load of ore. The little NIELSEN went down quickly, but the fate of her crew is not reported. Presumably, her tow steamer and the WYANDOTTE were standing by to pick them up. [4]

LENA M NIELSEN ■ Lumber schooner of 86 t.
Lake Michigan: The LENA M NIELSEN was toting her usual cargo of lumber when she was snatched up by a November storm and tossed ashore near the village of Lakeside, Michigan, a few miles north of New Buffalo. She was declared a total loss following the November 10, 1898 accident (one source gives the date as 1878). [2]

NIGHTINGALE ■ Merchant schooner
Lake Huron: In 1869 the schooner NIGHTINGALE was reported to have sunk in the Straits of Mackinac, near dreaded Spectacle Reef. [1]

NIKO ■ Wooden bulk freight steamer of 1,039 t. and 189 ft., launched in 1889 at Trenton
Lake Michigan: No lives were lost in the sinking of this bulk freighter on November 2, 1924. The NIKO was caught in a storm in northern Lake Michigan and foundered near Garden Island, in the Beavers. Her crew managed to escape. [4]

NILE ■ Steam freighter, probably the 650 t. vessel built at Detroit in 1843
Lake Michigan: This early steamer was destroyed, the victim of fire, in the harbor at Milwaukee on September 6, 1850. She may have been rebuilt and is the same vessel as below. [2]

NILE ■ Steam freighter
Detroit River: On May 21, 1864, the freighter NILE was lost to the type of accident that a steamer's engine crew feared most, a boiler explosion. She was sitting at her dock at Detroit when her powerplant burst violently, killing eight of those on board and destroying the ship. [2]

ALEX. NIMICK ■ Wooden bulk freight steamer of 1,968 t. and 298 ft., launched at W Bay City, MI, in 1890
Lake Superior: Westerly storms often increase in violence on the surface when they are compressed into the funnel at the east end of the lake, above Sault Ste. Marie. On September 20, 1907, after lying in the lee of Whitefish Point for a day, the coal-laden NIMICK pulled out onto the open lake for her run to Duluth. She was immediately assaulted by waves and wind of tremendous proportions. Before the big ship could turn and run for shelter, she was driven on a bar and broken up. Six of her crew of 17 perished when she went to pieces, but the remainder somehow made it to shore in the one undamaged lifeboat. [5+]

C K NIMS ■ Merchant schooner or bark of 700 t.
Lake Erie: The NIMS was lost during an informal race with the giant five-masted schooner DAVID DOWS (qv) in 1881. The NIMS' skipper had challenged and was slightly in the lead, but when the competitors were abreast of Pelee Island, the smaller ship—the NIMS was only half the displacement of the DOWS—cut under the bows of the big schooner and was run down and sunk. One source places the accident at Bar Point. [3]

NINA ■ Merchant schooner
Lake Huron: This vessel was reported sunk in a storm off Harrisville, Michigan, in 1875. [1]

NIPIGON ■ Merchant schooner
Lake Huron: In the 19th Century this schooner touched bottom in a storm, stove in her planking and sank in the Straits of Mackinac, south of Bois Blanc Island. Though called "South Channel" today, older maps refer to this area as "Nipigon Strait," perhaps in honor of this schooner. [2]

NIRVANA ■ Lumber schooner-barge of 611 t. and 169 ft., launched in 1890 at W Bay City, MI
Lake Superior: The barge NIRVANA was light and therefore subject to severe buffeting, even from a mild blow. Unfortunately, the vessel was attempting to dock at Grand Marais, Michigan, on October 20, 1905, in one of the biggest storms of the century. She was being assisted by her tow vessel, the steamer L L BARTH, when she was thrown against a pier and fatally holed. Her crew scrambled to safety just before she sank. [3]

BENJAMIN NOBLE ■ Crane-equipped steel bulk freighter of 1,481 t. and 239 ft., launched in 1909 at Wyandotte, MI
Lake Superior: After attempting (unsuccessfully) to negotiate the harbor entrance at Duluth in a wild gale on April 27, 1914, the steamer BENJAMIN NOBLE turned back towards Two Harbors, Minnesota for shelter. Somewhere along that course the big freighter went down with all hands, for she was never seen again. Twenty-one crew members perished when the ship was lost. She was reportedly overloaded with steel rails at the time of her loss. [5+]

NOMAD ■ Merchant schooner
Lake Huron: The schooner NOMAD was lost in 1871 near Presque Isle, Michigan. [1]

NONPARIEL ■ Merchant schooner
Lake Huron: The NONPARIEL was a schooner that was reported stranded on Middle Island Reef, a mile southwest of Middle Island, Michigan, in 1866. [2]

NOQUEBAY ■ Lumber schooner-barge of 685 t. and 205 ft., launched in 1872 at Trenton, MI, as a schooner
Lake Superior: Stockton Island, in the Apostles group (north of the Wisconsin coast), saw the loss of this lumber-carrying vessel on October 5, 1905. She stranded in a gale in Presque Isle Bay, caught fire and was destroyed. [4]

NORDMEER ■ Steel package and bulk freighter of 8,683 t. and 470 ft., launched in 1954 at Flensburg, Germany
Lake Huron: Probably the largest saltie to be lost on the Lakes was the graceful, German-registered NORDMEER.

The big freighter was carrying a cargo of stainless steel wire to Chicago when she misread a marker bouy in fine weather on November 19, 1966, and tore her bottom out on a shoal a few miles north of Thunder Bay Island (near Alpena, Michigan). At first she was thought to be an easy salvage job, since she was just sitting on the bottom with waves lapping at her main deck. A northern lakes storm on the 28th put an end to such optimism, suddenly lifting the steamer up and cracking her in half on the reef like an egg. Her crew, which had stayed on board, had to be rescued by helicopter. Though the NORDMEER's valuable cargo was mostly salvaged, the big ship was abandoned to the elements, and boaters may still approach the large section of her superstructure that shows above the water. [5+]

NORFOLK ▪ Sidewheel passenger and package freight steamer of 80 ft. and about 70 t., launched in 1868 at Port Rowan, Ont.
Lake Ontario: This little steamer was reportedly destroyed by fire at Napanee, Ontario, in April of 1877. [1]

NORLOND ▪ Wooden passenger and package freight steamer of 522 t. and 152 ft. (lengthened from original 126 ft.), launched in 1890 at Manitowoc, WI as the steamer EUGENE C HART
Lake Michigan: This small steamer was fighting a storm off Milwaukee when she sprang a fatal leak on November 13, 1922. She came about when it was apparent that her pumps could not handle the incoming water, and raced for shore. The vessel sank about two miles short of the harbor. [3]

NORMAN ▪ Steam propeller of 153 t. and 98 ft., launched in 1872 at Opinicon Lake, Ont.
Lake Ontario: This little steamer was away from her home on the Rideau Canal when she caught fire and was destroyed in Pryner Cove, in the Bay of Quinte area. The steamer was lost on November 30, 1883. [1]

NORMAN ▪ Steel bulk freight steamer of 2,304 t. and 296 ft., launched in 1890 at Cleveland
Lake Huron: Three lives were lost on May 30, 1895, when this big freighter sank northeast of Middle Island, off Rockport, Michigan. She was without cargo when she collided with the wooden steamer JACK (see BOTHNIA) and went down quickly. [5]

NORONIC ▪ Steel passenger steamer of 6,905 t. and 362 ft., launched at Port Arthur, Ont. in 1913
Lake Ontario: One of the largest of the Lakes passenger ships helped to bring the era of liners on the Lakes to a close on a tragic note. Docked overnight at Toronto on September 17, 1949, the big steamer caught fire. Before all of her passengers could be awakened and evacuated, the big steamship was completely engulfed in flame. 119 of those on board died and the lovely NORONIC was burned to a shell. [5]

NORRIS ▪ Merchant schooner
Lake Huron: The schooner NORRIS is reported to have foundered on the lake in 1887. [1]

NORTH CAROLINA ▪ Motor tug of 81 ft.
Lake Erie: No detail is provided in the loss of this tug, which sank off Fairport Harbor, Ohio, on December 9, 1968. Her position is also given as 1.5 miles off the harbor entrance at Mentor. [2]

NORTH HAMPTON ▪ Merchant brig of 242 t. and 119 ft., launched in 1847 at Sandusky, OH
Lake Huron: This two-master is one of dozens of vessels lost within sight of Thunder Bay Island (Michigan). She foundered off the island in 1854. [2]

NORTH SHORE ▪ Wooden steam coaster of 115 ft. overall, launched as the small passenger and package freighter BON AMI at Saugatuck, MI, in 1890
Lake Michigan: A tragedy may sometimes be the only way for a vessel to convince her owners that she is past her time. After a long career in the passenger and freight trade, this steamer was abandoned due to poor condition in 1929. But by 1930 she was back in harness again, pressed into service hauling fruit up and down the Michigan and Wisconsin coasts. On September 26 of that year, she was carrying 10,000 baskets of fruit to Milwaukee when she was overtaken by a fall gale. She was last seen north of Racine, and probably foundered, with her crew of six or seven, somewhere near Milwaukee. [4]

NORTH STAR ▪ Sidewheel passenger and package freight steamer of 1,106 t. and 274 ft, launched in 1854 at Cleveland
Lake Erie: The NORTH STAR was burned to the waterline in a fire which took her at Cleveland on February 20, 1862. She was destroyed while tied to her dock. [2]

NORTH STAR ▪ Merchant schooner of 160 t.
Lake Ontario: The NORTH STAR was reported as having foundered near Stony Island, north of Oswego, New York, in 1886. [1]

NORTH STAR ▪ Steel package freight steamer of 2,476 t. and 300 ft., launched in 1889 at Cleveland

Lake Huron: On November 25, 1908, this big package freighter went down off Port Sanilac, Michigan. She had collided with the steel freighter NORTHERN QUEEN and broken in two. The vessel and her cargo of shingles and wheat went to the bottom quickly. At the time of building she was identical to her fleetmates NORTH WIND (qv) and NORTHERN QUEEN (qv, not the same vessel she collided with). [5+]

NORTH STAR ■ Merchant schooner
Lake Erie: No date is given for the loss of this schooner, which was sunk by a white squall. [2]

NORTH WEST ■ Sidewheel steamer
Lake Michigan: This steamer was destroyed by fire near Ajax Island, in Green Bay, in 1875. [1]

NORTH WIND ■ Steel bulk freight steamer of 2,476 t. and 300 ft., launched in 1888 at Cleveland as a package freighter (see also NORTH STAR, NORTHERN QUEEN)
Lake Huron: Clapperton Island, near the east end of the North Channel, was the site of the demise of this big freighter on July 1, 1926. She went on the rocks in a fog and sank. [5+]

NORTHERN BELLE ■ Merchant schooner
Lake Michigan: This schooner was lost southwest of Skillagalee, near the northeast side of the lake, in 1873. [1]

NORTHERN BELLE ■ Merchant schooner of 40 t.
Lake Superior: The schooner NORTHERN BELLE was reported abandoned (though it is not clear whether this was due to an accident) at Malone Bay, Isle Royale, in 1885. [1]

NORTHERN BELLE ■ Passenger and package freight steamer of 514 t. and 129 ft., launched in 1875 at Marine City as the steamer GLADYS
Lake Huron: This small steamer was destroyed by fire on November 6, 1898. She burned at Byng Inlet, on the eastern shore of Georgian Bay. [5+]

NORTHERN BELLE ■ Propeller passenger and packet boat of 40 t. and 76 ft., launched in 1878 at Ionia, MI (on the Grand River, about 70 miles by water from Lake Michigan)
Lake Superior: On August 10, 1902, this little steamer was reported as a total loss, from unknown causes and at an unreported position. [3]

NORTHERN INDIANA ■ Passenger and package freight steamer (probably sidewheeler)
Lake Erie: Probably as a reflection of how common fatal accidents were on the Lakes in those days, there is little specific information on the loss of this steamer. She reportedly burned on the lake on July 17, 1856, with the loss of 30 to 56 lives. [1]

NORTHERN LIGHT ■ Merchant bark
Lake Erie: The bark NORTHERN LIGHT was reported wrecked on a reef off Port Burwell, Ontario, in 1862. [1]

NORTHERN LIGHT ■ Freight barge
Lake Huron: In 1881 the barge NORTHERN LIGHT was destroyed by fire at her dock at Harrisville, Michigan. She had been heavily damaged in a stranding the previous year. [2]

NORTHERN QUEEN ■ Merchant schooner
Lake Michigan: This schooner sank on November 24, 1881, following a collision with the vessel LAKE ERIE. She went to the bottom near Poverty Island, six miles south of Fairport, Michigan. [1]

NORTHERN QUEEN ■ Steel package freight steamer of 2,476 t. and 300 ft., launched in 1889 at Cleveland
Lake Huron: In the general frenzy following the Big Storm of 1913, this big steamer was supposed to be a total loss. She had been driven ashore at Kettle Point, on the Ontario side near the lower end of the lake, on November 11. Cooler heads later decided to try and remove her, and the vessel was freed and returned to service, later going to salt water. She was cut up for scrap in 1925. She was the sister ship of NORTH STAR (qv) and NORTH WIND (qv). [4]

NORTHERN STAR ■ Vessel information unavailable
Lake Huron: In 1856 the NORTHERN STAR sank following a collision with the vessel ONTONAGON. [1]

NORTHERNER ■ Sidewheel passenger and package freight steamer of 514 t.
Lake Huron: Reportedly laden with a cargo of whiskey, the steamer NORTHERNER sank on April 16, 1856. On that date she collided with the steamer FOREST QUEEN off Port Huron, Michigan. The vessel broke in half and sank, but not before all but 12 of her 142 passengers and crew were rescued. [5]

NORTHERNER ■ Lumber schooner
Lake Michigan: This schooner was lost near Port Washington, Wisconsin, when she became waterlogged and sank in 1868. [1]

NORTHERNER ■ Wooden steam freighter of 1,391 t. and 220 ft., launched in 1871 at Marine City, MI
Lake Superior: On December 7, 1892, this steamer was docked at L'anse, Michigan, when she was overtaken by disaster. The vessel caught fire and, despite efforts to extinguish it from shore, the blaze soon reached her hold full of barrelled oil. Once it reached that cargo, it became uncontrollable, destroying not only the ship, but the dock and nearby warehouse as well. [2]

NORTHMAN ▪ Vessel information unavailable
Lake Ontario: This vessel was reported to have foundered with all hands in a gale that struck her off Port Credit, Ontario. The ship was lost in 1861. [1]

NORTHUMBERLAND ▪ Propeller passenger and package freight steamer of 1,255 t. and 220 ft., launched in 1891 at Newcastle, England
Lake Ontario: This steamer was lost after a career of 58 years on the Lakes. In June of 1949 she caught fire at her dock at Port Dalhousie, Ontario, and was destroyed. [2]

NORTHWEST ▪ Merchant schooner of 1,017 t. and 233 ft., launched in 1873 at Bangor, MI as the schooner ALEXANDER B MOORE
Lake Michigan: This big schooner was hauling a load of corn when she encountered a storm in the Straits of Mackinac in April of 1894 (one source says 1898). She was reported wrecked and sunk by big waves at Big Stone Bay, on the lower peninsula coast. [3]

NORTHWEST ▪ Merchant schooner of 7 t., 40 ft., launched in 1879 at Sand Beach, MI
Lake Huron: Probably among the smallest registered commercial vessels ever to ply the Lakes, this tiny schooner was reported aground and lost in East Moran Bay, at St. Ignace, MI. She stranded and broke up in October of 1905. [1]

NORTHWEST ▪ Steel passenger steamer of 4,244 t. and 385 ft., launched in 1894 at Cleveland
Lake Erie: This magnificent passenger vessel was destroyed by fire at her dock in Buffalo on June 3, 1911. No lives were lost in the initial accident, but as her forward half was being towed away for rebuilding, it sank on Lake Ontario, drowning the two men aboard. [3]

HENRY NORTON ▪ Merchant schooner of 151 t. built brfore 1847
Lake Michigan: The schooner HENRY NORTON was reported wrecked on Pilot Island in 1863. [1]

KATE NORTON ▪ Merchant schooner, launched in 1863 (one reference says 1859) at Milan, OH
Lake Erie: In her first season of operation, perhaps on her maiden voyage, the schooner KATE NORTON went down with all hands near Long Point. [2]

NORWAY ▪ Package and bulk freight schooner, perhaps the 143 ft. vessel of this name built at Garden Island, Ont., in 1873
Lake Ontario: The schooner NORWAY was bearing a cargo of timber when she was caught in a westerly gale in the fall of 1882. The icy storm, built up over almost the entire length of the lake, swept the schooner ashore on the False Duck Islands, near Prince Edward Point. Her entire crew perished in the wet and cold, but the vessel herself was later recovered. [2]

NORWEGIAN ▪ Package and bulk freight schooner of 390 t., launched in 1856 at Three Mile Bay, NY
Lake Ontario: On October 18, 1870, the schooner NORWEGIAN was blown ashore and wrecked near Oswego, New York. Though the vessel was a total loss, all hands survived the accident. [1]

WILLIAM NOTTINGHAM ▪ Steel bulk freight steamer of 4,324 t. and 377 ft., launched in 1902 at Buffalo
Lake Superior: The saga of the big grain boat WILLIAM NOTTINGHAM is the classic example of the struggle that men must make against the elements. The great storm that ground the Lakes under its heel in the second week of November, 1913, created a sensation with the stories of the big steel ships lost on lower Lake Huron. Meanwhile, Lake Superior had been the scene of a drama of its own. Almost as soon as the WILLIAM NOTTINGHAM left her western terminal with her cargo of grain, the steel ship had to wage a battle with the big gale. The steamer needed so much power to hold her own against wind and wave—alternately running before the wind, then turning to breast the waves—that she used up her entire stock of bunker coal, normally enough to take her to Lake Erie, before she had made the Soo. With steam failing, the life of the ship depended upon some source of fuel, and soon the ship had been denuded of furniture, wooden trim and all other burnables that were part of her fittings. Then her coal-passers and firemen began hauling up the cargo of Minnesota wheat and shovelling it into her dwindling boiler fires. Alas, their efforts were in vain. The makeshift fuel did not give off enough heat to keep steam up, and on the 11th, the ship was finally tossed on a reef near Sandy Island, where she was damaged beyond repair. Three of the NOTTINGHAM's crew lost their lives, while the boat stayed on the reef until she was later cut up for scrap. [3]

NOVADOC ▪ Steel bulk freight steamer of 1,153 t. and 235 ft., launched in 1928 at Wallsend, England
Lake Michigan: This canal-sized steamer was a major victim of the dreadful Armistice Day Storm of November, 1940, that vented much of its wrath on Lake Michigan. The NOVADOC carried a cargo of powdered coke on her final run, and as she made her way north along the Michigan coast, the big greybeards elbowed her closer and closer to the shore. Despite the efforts of her crew to keep her out of the shallows, she was finally pushed on a reef near Pentwater, Michigan, on the 11th. For two days and nights, her stranded crew huddled within hailing distance of shore as the merciless storm tore the ship apart under them. Two men were washed overboard and drowned. On the morning of the 13th, while the storm was still snarling at their door, the NOVADOC's people were overjoyed to see the little fishing tug THREE BROTHERS steaming

through the liquid mountains to their rescue. The 17 remaining crewmen were brought on board with great effort. The THREE BROTHERS' crew were later cited for bravery, while the NOVADOC went to pieces where she lay. [5+]

JOHN R NOYES ■ Bulk freight schooner-barge of 315 t. and 136 ft., launched in 1872 at Algonac, MI
Lake Ontario: A gale which struck the lake in December of 1902 spelled the end for this barge, and her towing steamer as well. She was in mid-lake and under the tow of the 343 ton wooden steamer JOHN E HALL (qv), when the two were struck by a wicked westerly gale. After a day-long struggle and in a sinking condition, the HALL cut the barge loose to fend for herself. For two lonely, wave-tossed days the old sail vessel drifted to the east, before she finally went ashore to break up on Salmon Point, Ontario, on the 15th. No lives were lost on board the NOYES, but the HALL had gone down with all hands on the previous day. [2]

NUCLEUS ■ Bulk freight bark of 310 t., launched in 1848 at Milwaukee
Lake Superior: The bark NUCLEUS was downbound with iron ore when she was sunk off Whitefish Point in 1869. One source says some lives were lost in the sinking. [2]

NUMBER 83 ■ Scow of 365 t.
Lake Huron: On October 26, 1941, the scow NUMBER 83 was lost when she foundered four miles offshore near Thunder Bay Island, on the Michigan shore. [1]

NYACK ■ Passenger and package freight steamer of 1,188 t., and 220 ft., launched in 1878 at Buffalo
Lake Michigan: Muskegon, MI, harbor was the winter lay-up port for many Lake Michigan steamers and carferries in the early part of this century. On December 30, 1915, the NYACK was preparing for winter at her dock when she caught fire and was burned to almost total destruction. Her hull was later converted to a barge. [2]

FRANK O'CONNOR ■ Wooden bulk freight steamer of 2,109 t. and 301 ft., launched in 1891 at W Bay City, MI, as the steamer CITY OF NAPLES
Lake Michigan: The freighter FRANK O'CONNOR was carrying a cargo of coal to Milwaukee when she was discovered to be on fire off Cana Island, near the tip of the Door Peninsula (Wisconsin). The wooden vessel burned rapidly, but quick action on the part of the Cana Island lightkeeper who immediately launched a boat and pulled for the ship with his helper, saved the crew. The vessel burned to the waterline and sank on Oct. 2, 1919. [2]

WALTER H OADES ■ Merchant schooner of 500 t. and 170 ft., launched at Detroit
Lake Erie: Sailors have the reputation of being a superstitious lot. The WALTER S OADES often had a difficult time securing a crew since she had been dubbed "the unluckiest boat on the Lakes." She had been involved in dozens of mishaps before the final disaster that did her in on August 20, 1888. The vessel was two miles from Southeast Shoal light (also known as "the Dummy"), on the night of August 20, 1888, when she collided with the schooner R HALLARAN (qv) and sank. She was upbound with coal at the time. [3]

OAKWOOD ■ Wooden steam freighter of 2,051 t. and 298 ft., launched in 1891 at W Bay City, MI as the steamer CITY OF BERLIN
Lake Erie: This bulk freighter came to a sad end at Buffalo in 1925. On June 8, the cargoless ship was tossed aground at Miller's Point in heavy weather and was badly damaged. A Toronto salvager refloated her and towed her into Buffalo for evaluation. While she was laid up there she was destroyed in an accidental fire. One source gives 1929 for the year. [3]

OCEAN ■ Merchant schooner of 121 t., launched in 1843 at Cleveland
Lake Ontario: The schooner OCEAN was reported to have been destroyed by fire at Port Dalhousie, Ontario, in October of 1854. [1]

OCEAN ■ Merchant brig
Lake Huron: This small square-rigger was lost in an 1865 storm at an unreported location. [1]

OCEAN ■ Merchant schooner
Lake Huron: This schooner was lost off Tawas (now Tawas City) Michigan, when she foundered in Tawas Bay in 1873. [1]

OCEAN ■ Wooden passenger and package freight propeller of 454 t. and 157 ft., launched in 1872 at Port Dalhousie, Ont.
Lake Ontario: In November of 1904, the steamer OCEAN was destroyed by fire at Port Dalhousie, Ont. No lives were lost, but the vessel's life as a steamer was over. She was recovered and reconstructed as the barge HELENA. [4]

OCEAN WAVE ■ Sidewheel passenger and package freight steamer of 174 ft., launched in 1852 at Montreal
Lake Ontario: It seems paradoxical that wooden ships surrounded by a seemingly infinite quantity of water could become be so susceptible to fire, but vessels were well-sealed against the weather and could be tinder-dry, especially inside. They were also often painted with flammable paints or treated with flammable waterproofing materials. Many cargoes were themselves combustible or were packed in flammable ambrosia or sawdust. The steamer OCEAN WAVE had a boatload of passengers and her usual cargo of mixed freight on April 30, 1853, when a fire began in her main cargo hold. Before plans could

be made to fight the blaze or even abandon ship, the steamer was a veritable torch. She was almost entirely consumed in about ten minutes, according to witnesses, and 33 of the 57 aboard perished in the flames or drowned. The loss occurred off the Duck Islands. [3]

OCEAN WAVE ■ Bulk freight schooner of 100 t., launched in 1868 at Picton, Ont.
Lake Ontario: The specifics of many accidents are known in great detail from accounts of survivors or historians who have reconstructed them. Other stories, such as the tale of the OCEAN WAVE, are entirely guesswork. It is not known from what port she originated or to which she was bound, but the vessel was discovered capsized and drifting 15 miles off Oswego, New York, on November 11, 1890. The schooner's yawl and her crew were missing from the vessel, but no trace of them was ever found and they are presumed to have drowned. [2]

JAY OCHS ■ Steam tug of 18 t. and 53 ft., launched in 1888 at Huron, OH
Lake Huron: A big gale in 1905 was more than a match for this tiny tug. On October 20, the JAY OCHS was overwhelmed by the storm and foundered 3.5 miles southwest of Middle Island, south of Rogers City, Michigan. [2]

ODD FELLOW ■ Merchant brig
Lake Huron: The brig ODD FELLOW foundered in a storm that drove her down three miles from Mackinaw City, Michigan. The vessel was lost in 1854. [1]

ODEN ■ Scow of 96 t. and 88 ft., launched in 1888 at Fon du Lac, WI, as a steam barge
Lake Superior: This former steamer ended her career when she foundered off Superior, Wisconsin, on July 8, 1907. [2]

OGARITA ■ Bulk freight schooner of 604 t. and 174 ft., launched in 1864 at Conneaut, OH
Lake Huron: On October 25, 1905, the big schooner OGARITA was laden with a cargo of coal when she caught fire, burned to the water and sank, 15 miles off Thunder Bay Island, Michigan. The ship's crew were able to save themselves from the inferno, which was later determined to have been caused by spontaneous combustion of her cargo. [3]

MARTHA OGDEN ■ Sidewheel passenger and package freight steamer of 150 t. and 74 ft., launched in 1825 at Sackett's Harbor, NY
Lake Ontario: One of the earliest steam vessels on the Great Lakes, the MARTHA OGDEN was lost after only a few seasons of navigation, and but a few miles from her place of launch. On November 12, 1832, the paddlewheel steamer was driven ashore near Stony Point by a storm, and broken apart by rampant waves. Though she was carrying passengers and her usual crew, no lives were lost. [3]

OGEMAW ■ Steamer
Lake Michigan: The steamer OGEMAW was reportedly lost on December 4, 1891, when she foundered on Drisco Shoal, in Green Bay. [1]

OGEMAW ■ Wooden bulk freight steamer of 171 ft. overall, launched in 1881 at St. Clair, MI
Lake St. Clair: Grande Pointe, on the eastern shore of the lake was the site of the loss of the old OGEMAW on December 3, 1922. She reportely went aground 1.5 miles south of the little town, caught fire and was destroyed. [2]

E W OGLEBAY ■ Steel bulk freight steamer of 3,666 t. and 375 ft., launched in 1896 at W Bay City, MI
Lake Superior: Sail yachtsmen are well aware of the amount of force a strong wind can exert against a few dozen square yards of rigged canvas. A large ship without cargo and riding high in the water can expose tens of thousands of square feet of slab sides and superstructure to winds that may reach 70 miles per hour or better in a storm. The E W OGLEBAY, for example, probably had a quarter acre of her flank exposed to the gale which hit her on December 8, 1927. Try as she might, the big empty steamer could not make it into the harbor at Marquette. She was tossed ashore by the waves at Shot Point, a few miles to the east, where she stayed until she caught fire and was virtually destroyed. Two years later her scorched hull was dragged off the point and towed to Drummond Island, where it was sunk for use as a dock footing. [4]

OHIO ■ Wooden passenger and freight steamer of 187 t., launched in 1830, possibly in the Sandusky, OH, area
Lake Erie: This little steamer was reported to have sunk in 1837, but no details are available. [2]

OHIO ■ Passenger and package freight propeller, probably the 583 t. steamer of this name launched in 1847 at Ohio City, OH
Lake Erie: The steamer OHIO was off Long Point on November 6, 1859, when she was rocked by an explosion. She quickly sank, but 15 of the 17 aboard were able to abandon ship before the vessel went down. [2]

OHIO ■ Propeller freighter, either of two vessels: A 1,102 t., 203 ft. steamer launched in 1875 at Huron, OH, or a 210 t., 132 ft steamer built at Toledo in 1890 (both have been reported as this ship)
Lake Huron: In 1894, the steamer OHIO was lost north of Presque Isle, Michigan, as the result of a collision with an unidentified vessel. [2]

OHIO ■ Motor tug
Lake Erie: The tug OHIO was lost at Kelley's Island, as a result of a towing accident. She was manuevering the big steamer WILLIAM H WHITE in tight quarters when a wind caused the vessel to swing around and crush the tug against a dock. The OHIO was a total loss, but her crew escaped. [1]

STATE OF OHIO ■ Passenger and package freight steamer of 917 t. and 225 ft., launched in 1880 at Wyandotte as the steamer CITY OF CLEVELAND
Lake Erie: One or two lives were lost when this veteran steamer was destroyed by fire at her dock at Cleveland on May 20, 1924. Her hull was recovered and converted to a barge, which in turn sank in the harbor at Lorain, Ohio, on December 17, 1929. [4]

OKENZA or **OKONRA** ■ Tug of 52 t. and 60 ft.
Lake Huron: This tug was lost to fire at the docks at Wiarton, Ontario, (Georgian Bay) on September 5, 1878. [2]

OLD CONCORD ■ Barge of 457 t., launched at Detroit in 1855 as a steamer
Lake Huron: This old vessel reportedly foundered off Lion's Head, Georgian Bay, in an 1888 storm. [3]

OLGA ■ Schooner-barge of 305 t. and 137 ft., launched in 1881 at Manitowoc, WI as a schooner
Lake Huron: The schooner-barge OLGA was caught in one of the big storms of 1905. On the 26th of November she was torn loose from her towing steamer in mid-lake, and it was soon apparent to the crew that she would sink. They abandoned her in the yawl and were later picked up by a passing steamer. The OLGA, however, was not ready to sink just yet. She floated on the lake for several days and made herself a hazard to shipping until she finally went ashore a few miles north of Goderich, Ontario, and was destroyed by waves. [4]

OLIVE BRANCH ■ Merchant sloop of 20 t., launched in 1816 at Henderson, NY
Lake Erie: When she was lost, the OLIVE BRANCH was reportedly carrying a cargo of copper ore and whiskey, though there may be some doubt of a copper cargo at this early date. In October of 1831 she sank near the mouth of the Grand River (site of Fairport, Ohio). [2]

OLIVE BRANCH ■ 160 t. vessel of unreported type
Lake Ontario: On November 14, 1875, this vessel stranded and broke up two miles below Toronto. It is barely possible that she is the same vessel as below, after rebuilding. [1]

OLIVE BRANCH ■ 121 t. vessel of unreported type
Lake Ontario: This small vessel was reported as having foundered among the Duck Islands in 1880. [1]

OLIVE JEANETTE ■ Lumber schooner-barge of 1,271 t. and

242 ft., launched as a schooner in 1890 at W Bay City, MI
Lake Superior: A powerful gale that tore across the Big Lake on September 2, 1905, proved to be too much for this huge schooner-barge and her tow steamer, the bulk freighter IOSCO (qv). The pair were deep-laden with iron ore and battling giant waves off the Keweenaw Peninsula when they were simply overwhelmed. The OLIVE JEANETTE broke up at sea and went down with all seven hands. She was a long and graceful four-master, one of the largest wooden vessels of this type ever built. [5+]

OLIVER ■ Steamer
Lake Erie: Carrying a cargo of stone, the OLIVER sank east of the harbor at Lorain, Ohio, in 1906. [1]

OLIVIA ■ Merchant brig
Lake Ontario: No detailed information is available on this small sailing ship, which was reportedly lost to a white squall. [1]

MARGARET OLWILL ■ Wooden steam freighter of 925 t. and 177 ft., launched in 1887 at Cleveland
Lake Erie: June and July gales on the Lakes are usually puny when compared to vast cyclonic storms that sweep the area in the spring and fall. Still, a strong summer storm can rise quickly and catch a vessel unawares. Many a fine ship has been killed by fitful summer weather, and the steamer MARGARET OLWILL is a good example. Laden with a cargo of stone for an eastern port, she capsized and sank in a storm that struck her off Kelley's Island. She went down on June 28, 1899, with the loss of seven of her eleven crew. [5]

OMAR PASHA ■ Propeller freighter built in 1854 at Buffalo
Lake Michigan: The OMAR PASHA was an example of a vessel that simply "went missing." Perhaps her officers were lulled by the fact that she was a fine new ship and did not believe her to be intimidated by storms. At any rate, she sailed out into a November gale in 1855, and was never heard from again. Neither crew nor wreckage was ever identified. [3]

ONAWA ■ Gas screw of 17 t.
Lake Huron: The little vessel ONAWA was destroyed by fire at Cheboygan, Michigan, on October 6, 1954. [2]

ONEIDA ■ Sidewheel passenger and package freight steamer of 227 t.
Lake Ontario: On November 19, 1842, this sidewheeler sprang a leak and was run ashore near Sackett's Harbor, New York, to save her cargo and people. She was reported a total loss. [2]

ONEIDA ■ Steamer of 345 t.
Lake Erie: Nineteen lives were snuffed out when the steamer ONEIDA was lost in a gale on November 11, 1852. She ostensibly capsized in a gale and sank off Barcelona, New York. [4]

ONEIDA ■ Merchant schooner of 201 t. and 134 ft., launched in 1857 at Ashtabula, OH
Lake Michigan: No date is given for the loss of this vessel, reportedly sunk with all hands in a gale. [2]

ONEIDA ■ Steam freighter of 887 t. and 200 ft., launched in 1862 at Buffalo
Lake Erie: The date for the loss of the ONEIDA is not given, but she was still in operation in 1892. She was reportedly destroyed by fire. [2]

ONEIDA CHIEF ■ Merchant schooner
Lake Huron: Loaded with a cargo of pig iron for Cleveland, the schooner ONEIDA CHIEF was cast into the shallows of Au Sable Point, near Au Sable, MI, in May, 1868. No lives were lost, but the ship went to pieces where she was. [2]

ONGIARA ■ Propeller freighter of 98 t. and 91 ft., launched at Toronto in 1885 as the steamer QUEEN CITY
Lake Ontario: In October of 1918, the little steamer ONGIARA was wrecked at Bowmanville, Ontario. [1]

ONOKO ■ Iron bulk freight steamer of 2,164 t. and 299 ft., launched in 1882 at Cleveland
Lake Superior: The steamer ONOKO was a well-known vessel on the upper lakes, one which held many cargo records. Her illustrious career ended September 15, 1915, near Duluth. On that date the sturdy vessel was breasting big waves and holding her own when disaster struck off Knife Island. Her boiler exploded and the vessel lost power. With no steerageway she was at the mercy of the storm and she was soon overwhelmed and sank. Fortunately, no lives were lost in the accident. [5+]

ONONDAGO ■ Bulk freight schooner-barge of 142 ft. overall, launched in 1870 at Garden Island, Ont.
Lake Ontario: The schooner-barge ONONDAGO was lost on November 5, 1907, in the shallow area near Stony Point, Ontario, (possibly Stony Point, New York). She sprang a leak and sank and was deemed not worth the cost of recovery. [1]

ONTARIO ■ Armed sloop warship
Lake Ontario: The loss of this Royal Navy vessel is clouded by a number of conflicting reports. She must have been large for a single-mast ship, as it was reported between 200 and 350 soldiers and sailors were lost when she went down in mid-lake in a blizzard-gale. The date of the accident is given as either November 1, 1780, or November 23, 1783. One report states that she had a quantity of gold and silver aboard as well. [2]

ONTARIO ■ Propeller steamer of 176 ft., launched in 1851 at Sorel, Que.

Lake Ontario: This steamer was wrecked somewhere on the lake in November of 1857. She was later recovered and rebuilt as a schooner. [1]

ONTARIO ■ Merchant brig
Lake Michigan: The brig ONTARIO was lost in 1858 when she sank in Green Bay, near the western end of the Sturgeon Bay Ship Canal. She was carrying a cargo of general freight at the time. [1]

ONTARIO ■ 79 t. vessel of unreported type
Lake Ontario: On September 10, 1881, the little ONTARIO is simply reported to have foundered, 15 miles off Point Petre (Ontario). [1]

ONTARIO ■ Steam tug
Lake Huron: This tug caught fire and was destroyed off Port Huron, Michigan, in 1883. [1]

ONTARIO ■ Propeller freighter of 150 t. and 104 ft., launched in 1871 at Wolfe Island, Ont.
Lake Ontario: The steamer ONTARIO was lost in August of 1885 when she was destroyed by fire at Toronto. [1]

ONTARIO ■ Wooden passenger and freight steamer of 1,338 t. and 181 ft., launched in 1874 at Chatham, Ont.
Lake Superior: On August 10, 1899, this big steamer went hard aground on the shore of Battle Island, near Rossport, Ontario, and was destroyed by waves. [4]

ONTARIO ■ Merchant schooner of 165 ft., perhaps the same ship as the 1851-built vessel above
Lake Huron: This schooner was lost in October of 1907 at Southampton, Ontario. In that month she was driven on the breakwater while attempting to enter the harbor, and was dashed to pieces. [2]

ONTARIO ■ Steel pulpwood barge of 1,668 t. and 297 ft., launched as a carferry in 1890 at Owen Sound, Ont.
Lake Superior: After 34 years of service as a carferry, the big ONTARIO was converted to a barge in 1924. In tow of the steam tug BUTTERFIELD and laden with her usual cargo of pulpwood, the vessel foundered in a storm on October 13, 1927. She went down east of Outer Island, in the Apostles archipelago. [5]

ONTONAGON ■ Merchant schooner
Lake Superior: The ONTONAGON was a small schooner that was sunk by a white squall near Sault Ste. Marie in 1870. [2]

ONWARD ■ Merchant schooner of 132 ft., launched in 1855 at Sacket's Harbor, NY
Lake Michigan: This two-masted sailing ship was lost on September 21, 1885, when she was blown ashore from the dock at Gills' Pier, north of Leland, Michigan. She was later broken up by the action of waves. [1]

ONWARD ■ Tug
Lake Michigan: In 1892 the tug ONWARD was reported stranded and lost in the southeast corner of Grand Traverse Bay. [1]

OPHIR ■ Tug of 8 t.
Lake Huron: The diminutive tug OPHIR ended her career at Parry Sound, Ontario, on the east side of Georgian Bay, when she caught fire and was destroyed. The fateful day was May 27, 1919. [2]

OREGON ■ Steamer
Detroit River: The disastrous loss of this steamer came on April 20, 1865. Twelve persons died when the OREGON exploded and sank abeam of Detroit. [1]

OREGON ■ Steam freighter
Lake Huron: Sometime in 1886 the steamer OREGON was navigating the Straits of Mackinac in a fog when she collided with an unnamed vessel and sank near Bois Blanc Island. One source says this accident occurred on Lake Erie. [2]

OREGON ■ Merchant schooner of 46 t. and 64 ft., launched in 1880 at Pine River, MI
The position of the wreck of the schooner OREGON is not given, but she was one of a large number of sailing vessels destroyed in the great storm of October 20, 1905. [2]

OREGON ■ Wooden lumber hooker of 974 t. and 197 ft., launched in 1892 at W Bay City, MI
Lake Huron: The combination of storm and fire was a fairly common method of destruction of Great Lakes vessels. A ship driven ashore would often jolt to a stop, throwing everything, including lanterns, woodstoves and even glowing lumps of coal from her boiler fires, out on her wooden decks. Once ablaze, a lumber-carrying vessel such as the OREGON stood little chance of survival. A summer storm drove her aground on a reef near Thessalon, Ontario, in the North Channel, on August 23, 1908. The sailors aboard her were faced with the unenviable choice of staying with the blazing ship, or abandoning her for the crashing seas around her. It turned out to be no choice at all, as all 15 of the OREGON's crew perished. [5+]

ORIENT ■ Wooden steam tug of 37 t. and 62 ft., launched in 1874 at Buffalo
Lake Erie: On October 4, 1887, the small tug ORIENT added her bones to those of the score or more other vessels that have sunk in the Pelee Passage. All hands joined her in her last plunge. [2]

ORIENTAL ■ Propeller freighter
Lake Michigan: In 1859 the steamer ORIENTAL was reported aground and broken up in the shallows surrounding Skillagallee Shoal, east of the Beaver Islands. [1]

ORIENTAL ■ 328 t. vessel of unreported type
Lake Ontario: Seven lives were lost when this vessel foundered two miles off Port Dalhousie, Ontario, on October 23, 1887. [1]

ORINOCO ■ Wooden bulk freight steamer of 2,226 t. and 297 ft., launched in 1898 at W Bay City, MI
Lake Superior: The freighter ORINOCO was laden with a cargo of pulpwood and towing the barge CHIEFTAIN when she was lost in a heavy gale in the early morning hours of May 18, 1924. The steamer cut her barge loose, then foundered six miles off Agawa Bay, north and west of the Soo. Most of her crew was rescued, but five lost their lives. [5]

ORIOLE ■ Merchant schooner of 323 t. and 141 ft.
Lake Superior: The three-mast schooner ORIOLE carried a cargo of iron ore, and apparently several passengers as well, when she sailed out into the Lake Superior fog on August 9, 1892. She was near Grand Island, off Munising, Michigan, when she was run down and sunk by the aged sidewheeler ILLINOIS. Those aboard the ILLINOIS thought that their vessel was in immediate danger of sinking, and so made for Munising without stopping. Her sharp bow had cut the schooner in two, and the ORIOLE went down in the icy water with only one survivor of the 13 persons on board. [3]

ORION ■ Merchant schooner
Lake Michigan: The accident that finished this schooner was her second major one in five years. In 1856, she had kissed the bottom near Pointe Aux Barques, Michigan, and sunk in shallow water. Extensive rebuilding at Saginaw put her back in service, but in 1861 she sank for good at St. Joseph, Michigan. [2]

ORION ■ Sidewheel passenger and freight steamer of 495 t. and 185 ft., launched in 1866 at Manitowoc, WI
Lake Michigan: Part of the reason that propeller steamers were able to push paddlewheel vessels off the Lakes was illustrated by the loss of the ORION on October 16, 1870. She was fighting a huge gale coming in from astern, and attempting to negotiate the harbor entrance at Grand Haven, Michigan, at the same time. As the giant seas would lift the ship, her big wheels would come out of the water and flail at the air, and the ship would go out of control. She finally struck a bar and jammed fast, becoming fodder for the driving breakers and going to pieces quickly. No lives were lost in the accident. [3]

ORION ■ 240 t. vessel of unreported type
Lake Erie: This ORION was lost on August 31, 1872, when she foundered off Long Point. [1]

ORION ■ Bulk freight steam barge of 392 t. and 167 ft., launched in 1872 at Welland, Ont. as the steamer ISAAC MAY
Lake Ontario: The steamer ORION was reported lost on the lake in 1907, at an unreported position. As the ISAAC MAY, she had been nearly destroyed by fire in 1890. [4]

ORONTES ■ Freight barge
Lake Huron: In 1883, the barge ORONTES was lost when she grounded and sank on Point Edward, at the base of the lake. [1]

ORPHAN BOY ■ Package and bulk freight bark or schooner of 365 t. and 144 ft., launched in 1862 at Lorain, OH
Lake Michigan: Although Lakes schooners were generally seaworthy vessels, they could be easily outmatched by weather if their skippers or owners sent them out to face the big fall storms. The ORPHAN BOY was making a late run with lumber on December 5, 1885, when she was attacked by a violent, but seasonal, storm. She was literally picked up and hurled ashore on Michigan's Big Sable Point, where she immediately went to pieces. The 12 seamen aboard would surely have regretted challenging the storm gods of the Chippewa, had they lived. [3]

T H ORTON ■ Barge of 262 t. and 173 ft., launched in 1873 at Buffalo
Lake Erie: On July 14, 1889, this barge reportedly sank at Marblehead, north of Sandusky. She may have been recovered, as she was still listed in registry in 1892. [2]

OSBORNE ■ Merchant bark, built in 1867
Lake Erie: The bark OSBORNE was stranded and given up for lost on Cassidy's Reef, two miles from Port Colborne, Ontario. She was wrecked on November 3, 1873 or '74. [2]

JOHN M OSBORNE ■ Bulk freight steam barge of 891 t. and 178 ft., launched in 1882 at Marine City, MI
Lake Superior: The pervasive fog that so often reduces visiblity to zero in eastern Lake Superior, claimed another victim in the steamer JOHN M OSBORNE. On July 27, 1884, the OSBORNE was downbound with iron ore and two barges in tow. She was picking her way through the heavy soup when she was rammed by the 1,700 t. steel passenger and freight steamer ALBERTA. The two vessels stayed jammed together long enough for most of the OSBORNE's crew to make it aboard the other steamer, but three or possibly four went down with her when she dove for the bottom. One passenger from the ALBERTA was also lost in a brave rescue attempt. The wreck was located in 1984 off Whitefish Point, where she had lain for 100 years. [5+]

OSCEOLA ■ Merchant brig
Lake Erie: Four lives were lost when this little sail vessel was driven ashore and wrecked by a gale in 1846. The accident happened near Silver Creek, New York, just five years after the passenger steamer ERIE burned near the same spot, in the worst Lakes disaster up to that time. The OSCEOLA had had the distinction of having carried the first load of grain directly from Chicago to the East. [2]

OSCEOLA ■ Propeller freighter of 980 t. and 183 ft., launched in 1882 at W Bay City, MI
Lake Huron: This steamer was driven on a reef at Flat Rock Point, near Grindstone City, Michigan. She was wrecked and sunk on November 7, 1887 (or 1888). See also GOLSPIE. [3]

OSCODA ■ Wooden lumber hooker of 529 t. and 175 ft., launched in 1878 at St. Clair, MI
Lake Michigan: On November 8, 1914, the steamer OSCODA was bound for Chicago with a load of lumber and two schooner-barges in tow, when she was driven on an offshore reef near Epoufette, Michigan, by a gale. Her barges, the A C TUXBURY and the ALICE B NORRIS had been released before the OSCODA struck, and now rode heavily at anchor while the steamer's crew made a frantic effort to launch a boat. A concerted, cooperative effort by all three crews and several local bystanders saved the sailors from the deck of the ship. During a later salvage attempt, the steamer rolled off the bar and sank. Her wreckage is still on the bottom, but the barges were none the worse for wear, and were picked up by a passing steamer and delivered to their destination shortly after the accident. [5+]

OSPRAY ■ Merchant schooner
Lake Ontario: On October 7, 1858, this schooner was destroyed in the harbor at Oswego, New York, when she was blown against a pier by a sudden squall, and went to pieces. Three sailors perished in the accident. [1]

OSPREY ■ Sidewheel steamer of 966 t. and 175 ft., launched in 1863 at Sorel, Que.
Lake Ontario: The sidewheeler OSPREY was destroyed in harbor at Hamilton, Ontario. She caught fire and burned down to the lake in 1878. [1]

OSPREY ■ Tug of 26 t.
Lake Huron: On October 5, 1895, the little tug OSPREY was reportedly destroyed by fire at Cedar Point, Georgian Bay. [2]

OSPREY ■ Fishing tug of 56 t. and 62 ft.
Lake Superior: Fire claimed this fisherman on April 13, 1915. She was destroyed at Stony Point. [2]

OSSIFRAGE ■ Wooden passenger and package freight steamer of 433 t. and 123 ft., launched in 1886 at W Bay City, MI

Lake Huron: The propeller steamer OSSIFRAGE foundered off Sturgeon Point, Michigan, near Harrisville, in 1900. At first she was declared unrecoverable, but salvagers were later able to raise her. She was rebuilt and went to salt water, where she sank in the Northumberland Strait in 1919. [3]

OSTRICH ▪ Lumber schooner of 279 t. and 139 ft., launched in 1886 at Buffalo
Lake Michigan: A very violent storm struck lower (i.e. northern) Lake Michigan on October 1, 1892, and caused the loss of the OSTRICH and all of her crew of 6. The schooner was without cargo and must have taken a terrific buffeting before she went down off the Manitou Islands. The big steamer W H GILCHER (qv) was lost at the same time in roughly the same area, and some historians speculate that the two collided in the wild seas. [5+]

OSWEGATCHIE ▪ Propeller freighter of 350 t. and 135 ft.
Lake Huron: Though the steamer OSWEGATCHIE and her two or even three barges were a significant loss when they were wrecked in a gale off Sturgeon Point, Michigan, little is known about the wrecks. The accident occurred on November 21, 1891. [3]

OSWEGO ▪ Steam freighter
Lake Erie: Five lives were lost when this steamer stranded and broke up somewhere on the lake in October of 1867. [1]

OTEGO ▪ Steam freighter of 334 t. and 139 ft., launched in 1874 at Port Robinson, Ont. as the steamer CITY OF ST. CATHARINES
Lake Michigan: On October 17, 1895, the steamer OTEGO foundered off Green Bay, Wisconsin, from unknown causes. The vessel was in ballast at the time, and one life was lost in the incident. [3]

OTTAWA ▪ Merchant schooner
Lake Erie: The schooner OTTAWA stranded and went to pieces on a reef near Port Burwell, Ontario, in 1848. [1]

OTTAWA ▪ Sidewheel steamer built in 1840 at Trois Rivieres, Que.
Lake Ontario: In 1851 this sidewheeler was wrecked near Kingston, Ontario. [1]

OTTAWA ▪ Merchant schooner
Lake Huron: This schooner was reported sunk off Sarnia, Ontario, as the result of a collision. The accident occurred in 1875. [1]

OTTAWA ▪ Steel package freight steamer of 2,431 t. and 256 ft., launched in 1900 at Toronto
Lake Superior: The big freighter OTTAWA was downbound with a cargo of wheat when disaster caught up with her on November 15, 1909. Blinded and battered by a terrific blizzard-gale, the steamer took on a strong list when her cargo shifted, then struck a rocky reef near Passage Island, off the northeast tip of Isle Royale. The OTTAWA's crew gave up the fight to save her and abandoned ship in the lifeboat, while the giant waves sent the big steamer to the bottom, stern foremost. After watching their home slide beneath the waves, the crewmen had a 16-hour pull through the gale in the open boat to safety. [5+]

OTTAWA ▪ Salvage tug of 610 t. and 151 ft., launched in 1881 at Chicago as the steamer BOSCOBEL
Lake Superior: The second vessel of this name to be destroyed on Lake Superior in November of 1909 was the big tug OTTAWA, lost on the 29th. One of the best-equipped salvage vessels on the Lakes, the tug was riding at anchor in Frog Bay, near Red Cliff, Wisconsin (a few miles from Bayfield), when she caught fire and burned to the waterline. Though all of her crew escaped harm, the loss of the $50,000 tug and equipment was the most costly tug loss in Superior history. [4]

OTTAWA ▪ Wooden passenger and package freight steamer of 94 t. and 106 ft., launched at Saugatuck in 1884 as the steamer A B TAYLOR
Lake Ontario: This little steamer was destroyed by fire at her dock at Cape Vincent, New York, at the head of the St. Lawrence River. She was declared a total loss following the December 14, 1910, accident. She had also suffered a serious fire at Grand Haven, MI, in 1901. [4]

OTTAWA ▪ Lumber schooner of 163 t. and 113 ft., launched in 1874 at Grand Haven, MI
Lake Michigan: Five crewmen were lost when the two-stick schooner OTTAWA foundered in a severe storm just off Sturgeon Bay, Michigan. The accident occurred on October 13, 1911. [3]

OTTER ▪ Merchant schooner of 45 t., built in 1813
Lake Superior: The schooner OTTER was one of the first commercial vessels used on Lake Superior. She engaged in trade with the Indian tribes and supply to missionaries and trappers. In 1828 the vessel was returning to the Soo with a cargo of furs when she was struck by a gale. She sank with all hands off the Grand Sable Banks, several miles west of the site of Grand Marais, Michigan. A vessel of the same name was reported destroyed trying to run the St. Marys Rapids (Sault de Ste. Marie) in 1823. [3]

OTTER ▪ Bulk freight schooner of 265 t. and 105 ft., launched in 1863 at Freeport, OH
Lake Michigan: On October 10, 1895, this schooner was carrying a cargo of wood when she was driven ashore by a gale and broke up, 12 miles north of the ship canal, near Sturgeon Bay, Wisconsin. One source reports a ship of the same name lost at Sturgeon Point, Lake Erie, on the same date. [4]

OUR SON ▪ Bulk freight schooner of 1,000 t. and 182 ft., launched in 1875 at Lorain, OH
Lake Michigan: In 1930 there were only a very few working schooners left on the lakes. In fact, the aged three-master OUR SON had once been converted to a schooner-barge, then back to a schooner again. On September 26 of her 55th year, OUR SON, laden with pulpwood and a score of miles off Sheboygan, Wisconsin, found herself in deep trouble. A fall gale was sweeping out of the west, the aged sails had been ripped out, and the old hull could no longer take the strain. Huge waves made the launching of her yawl impossible, and the windjammer's crew had about given up hope. Then, miraculously, a small, off-course steamer, the wooden bulk freighter WILLIAM NELSON, happened upon the OUR SON and her frantic crew. After several tries, the little steamer worked her way to windward of the stricken ship and took her crew off, just a few moments before the gallant old schooner bowed to a few last waves and went down. [5+]

J H OUTHWAITE ▪ Wooden bulk freight steamer of 1,304 t., and 224 ft., launched in 1886 at Cleveland
Lake Huron: Two of the biggest storms of the century occurred within a month of each other in 1905. The October 20th gale took down at least 28 vessels, but while the Big Blow of November 28 through 30 sank fewer ships, it destroyed a number of the big steamers that were the Lakes' pride and joy. Lake Superior bore the brunt of the storm, which reportedly pushed 80 mile-per-hour winds across the lake for three solid days. But on Lake Huron, the big steamer J H OUTHWAITE was destroyed just as permanently when she was thrown ashore on Point Nipigon, near Cheboygan, Michigan, on the 28th. Before any action could be taken to save her, the steamer caught fire and burned to rubble. [4]

OWEN ▪ Propeller steamer of 68 t. and 61 ft., launched in 1881 at Detroit
Lake Ontario: Gull Shoal, near Long Point, in the Bay of Quinte area, was the final resting place for this tiny steamer. She went ashore there on October 12, 1902, and was damaged to the point of total loss. [4]

OWEN ▪ Tug
Lake Huron: The tug OWEN was reported destroyed by fire at Tawas City, Michigan, in 1921. [1]

CITY OF OWEN SOUND ▪ Propeller freighter of 1,093 t. and 172 ft., launched in 1875 at Owen Sound, Ont.
Lake Huron: Two widely disparate locations are given for the major accident suffered by this steamer on October 24, 1887. Some sources say she was wrecked on Clapperton Island, in the North Channel, while others give Bear's Rump, near Tobermory, Ont. as the location. In any case,

the steamer was thought to be a total loss, but was in the end recovered. Her name was later changed to SATURN (qv), and under that name she was lost in 1901. [5]

GEORGE B OWEN ▪ Bulk freight schooner-barge of 744 t. and 196 ft. overall, launched in 1893 at W Bay City, MI
Detroit River: The schooner-barge GEORGE B OWEN was upbound and deep-laden with coal when she swamped and sank off Grosse Ile, Michigan, on October 1, 1926. Her cargo was salvaged. [1]

IRA H OWEN ▪ Steel bulk freight steamer of 1,753 t. and 262 ft., launched in 1887 at Cleveland
Lake Superior: One of a number of big vessels lost in the Big Blow of 1905, the barley-carrying steamer IRA H OWEN was lost on November 28. The tremendous storm, with some of the highest-velocity winds ever recorded on the Lakes, broke the vessel up offshore and sank her near Outer Island, at the north end of the Apostles group. Oddly, though most other references say she went down with all 19 hands, a U.S. Lifesaving Service report states that no lives were lost. [5+]

JOHN OWEN ▪ Steamer of 250 t., launched in 1843 at Detroit
Lake Huron: This steamer was reported destroyed by fire at Port Huron, Michigan, in 1860. [2]

JOHN OWEN ▪ Composite bulk freight steamer of 2,127 t. and 281 ft., launched in 1889 at Wyandotte, MI
Lake Superior: A westerly fall gale was more than a match for this steamer's iron-and-wood hull. On November 13, 1919, the OWEN was beset by huge waves that tore her to pieces and sent her to the bottom northeast of the Manitou Islands, along the North Shore. She took all 23 of her crew to the lakebed and her cargo of barley as well. [5+]

OXFORD ▪ Steamer of 90 ft. launched in 1853 at Buffalo
Lake Huron: In the fall of 1855, this little steamer was wrecked in the Fishing Islands, in Smith Bay of Manitoulin. [2]

OXFORD ▪ Merchant brig
Lake Erie: Five lives were lost when the brig OXFORD collided with the propeller CATARACT and sank in 1856. [2]

OZAUKEE ▪ Passenger and package freight paddle steamer, launched in 1857 at Port Washington, WI
Lake Superior: The steamer OZAUKEE was towing a log raft when she foundered with no loss of life near Ashland, Wisconsin, on May 27, 1884. In an earlier accident, she had been almost completely destroyed by fire in 1870. [3]

P W D 114 ■ Barge of 103 t.
Lake Ontario: This utility barge sank in a storm on October 24, 1919. She went down 11 miles east-northeast of Hamilton, Ontario, near Oakville. [1]

P W D 117 ■ Barge of 507 t.
Lake Erie: This vessel foundered in the harbor at Port Stanley, Ontario, on May 29, 1952. [2]

PACIFIC ■ Wooden steam tug of 69 ft.
Lake Superior: Three lives were lost when the boiler of this little tug exploded on August 20, 1884. The vessel was destroyed near Ashland, Wisconsin. [1]

PACIFIC ■ Bulk freight steam barge of 766 t. and 187 ft., launched in 1864 at Cleveland
Lake Superior: No lives were lost, but the steamer PACIFIC was totally dismantled by a gale that forced her ashore on November 16, 1887. The ship hit the shallows near Deer Park, in a largely uninhabited (even today) area of Michigan's upper peninsula. She was shipping a load of lumber at the time. [3]

PACIFIC ■ Propeller freighter of 624 t. and 179 ft., launched in 1883 at Owen Sound, Ont.
Lake Huron: The PACIFIC was docked at Collingwood, Ontario, when she was discovered to be on fire on November 3, 1898. Despite the efforts of those on shore, the steamer burned to a shell. She was later towed several miles out into Georgian Bay and scuttled. [5+]

CHARLES B PACKARD ■ Wooden bulk freight steamer of 1,054 t. and 190 ft., launched as the steamer ELFIN MERE at W Bay City, MI, in 1887
Lake Erie: While struggling through the Pelee Passage on a stormy night, the steamer PACKARD is reported to have struck the wreckage of the large schooner ARMENIA (qv), sunk four months earlier. The big freighter went down near Southeast Shoal on September 16, 1906. [5]

JOHN A PAIGE ■ Steam tug of 52 t. and 74 ft., launched in 1881 at Green Bay, WI
Lake Superior: The tug JOHN A PAIGE was maneuvering a log raft off the Siskowit River, Wisconsin, on September 6, 1892, when she caught fire and was destroyed, possibly due to overheating. Toward the end of the lumber era, rafts were often used to move large masses of sawlogs over relatively short distances, although there are records of rafts being moved hundreds of miles and even one story of a raft being purposely run down the St. Marys Rapids. A log raft consisted of a large ring of big logs chained together end to end. The circle thus formed would be filled with timbertrees and the whole mass taken in tow by one or more tugs. Needless to say, rafts were highly unmaneuverable and were almost impossible to handle in even slightly rough weather. [3]

JOSEPH PAIGE ■ Package and bulk freight schooner-barge of 625 t. and 190 ft., launched in 1872 at Milwaukee
Lake Superior: The JOSEPH PAIGE was downbound with a load of iron ore and in tow of the steamer H B TUTTLE when she was struck by a north gale. A heavily-laden vessel such as she would jerk against her towline unmercifully under such conditions. The tow cable was actually just strong enough to break when conditions got really bad (wooden ships towing with steel cable had been known to have their sterns ripped off by a madly plunging barge). On the night of December 1, 1897, the PAIGE broke her cable off Vermilion Point, Michigan. Even though she immediately set sail, there was no hope in such a storm as this, and the barge was driven onto a bar a few hundred yards off shore. Fortunately, a sharp-eyed member of the U.S. Lifesaving Service on beach patrol spotted the ship and by dawn the Vermilion Point crew were poised to launch their boats into to the surf, even though the storm had worsened during the night. The courageous and well-trained Lifesavers managed to rescue the PAIGE's crew of eight men and one woman, even though one of their boats was smashed in the process. The barge lasted only a short time after the rescue. She was smashed to pieces by the furious breakers. [4]

S B PAIGE ■ Merchant schooner of 47 t. and 79 ft., launched in 1863 at Oshkosh, WI
Lake Michigan: In September of 1907, the little schooner S B PAIGE was reported to have foundered off Sturgeon Bay, Wisconsin, in Green Bay. [2]

GEN. H E PAINE or **GENE H PAINE** ■ Steam tug of 248 t.
Lake Michigan: The large tug GEN. H E PAINE was destroyed on November 19, 1875. On that date she struck a submerged crib near Grand Haven, Michigan, went to pieces and sank. [2]

PAL ■ Gas screw of 17 t.
Lake Michigan: On November 18, 1947, this little motor vessel foundered in a gale which struck her off Pentwater, Michigan. [1]

PALMBAY ■ Wooden bulk freight steamer of 905 t. and 236 ft., launched in 1891 at Milwaukee as the steamer PUEBLO
Lake Ontario: The aging steamer PALMBAY had been laid up at a dock at Kingston, Ontario, while her owners decided her fate. The decision was made for them on November 19, 1926, when the vessel caught fire and burned to the hull. The hulk remained in place until towed out to a point opposite Portsmouth and scuttled in 1937. [3]

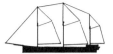

E B PALMER ■ Merchant schooner of 277 t. and 138 ft., launched in 1875 at Welland, Ont. as RICHARD MORWOOD

Lake Huron: The schooner E B PALMER became the victim of a fall storm on November 13, 1892, when she foundered off Middle Island without loss of life. One source places the wreck further south, off North Point Reef. [4]

JULIA PALMER ■ Sidewheel steamer of 300 t., launched in 1836 at Buffalo

Lake Superior: Early steamers such as the PALMER were woefully inefficient in the use of fuel. A vessel of this size could burn a hundred cords of wood going from one end of the Lake to the other. Fueling stations all along the coast kept the long-haul steamers from having to use all their cargo space for fuel. In a storm such as the one that the JULIA PALMER found herself in in about 1850, a vessel could be trapped on the vast lake, unable to land to take on fuel, and expending what she had at a fearful rate in fighting the gale. The PALMER was in just this situation, burning her woodwork and cabin walls in an effort to keep steam up. In the end she lost the fight. Her fires went out and she drifted for nearly two weeks before going ashore west of Whitefish Point. [1]

JULIA PALMER ■ Merchant schooner of 280 t.

Lake Superior: In 1889, the schooner JULIA PALMER ran aground near Duluth and was destroyed. [1]

THOMAS W PALMER ■ Composite bulk freight steamer of 2,134 t. and 281 ft., launched in 1889 at Wyandotte, MI

Lake Superior: When the air is warming up for spring and the lake water is still cold enough to be speckled with sheets of ice, terrifically dense fogs make shipping slow to a crawl. Shipmasters sometimes bent the rules on speed under these conditions in order to keep their schedules, particularly if they were far from land. On May 16, 1905, the fog set up a collision between two large vessels, the THOMAS PALMER and the steel steamer HARVARD. The HARVARD rammed the PALMER almost amidships with such force that the wood and iron vessel was cut practically in two. While the two ships were still forming a "T" on the lake, the PALMER's crew clambered aboard the other ship. When the HARVARD backed away, the PALMER went to the bottom like a brick. The accident occurred off Stannard Rock, a pinnacle 55 miles north of Marquette and about 25 miles from the nearest land. [3]

PALMETTO ■ Merchant schooner

Lake Huron: In 1865 the schooner PALMETTO was reported to have sunk following a collision in mid-lake. [1]

FRANCIS or **FRANCES PALMS** ■ Merchant schooner of 560 t. and 172 ft.

Lake Michigan: On November 12, 1889, the FRANCIS PALMS went hard aground on a reef near the Beaver Islands and was pounded to pieces by a gale. Sources disagree on which reef, either Simmons or Gray's. [3]

PANAMA ■ Wooden bulk freight steamer of 2,044 t. and 275 ft., launched in 1888 at Trenton, MI, as the steamer JOHN CRAIG

Lake Superior: Seaworthy vessels are built to work in big waves, bending and twisting to absorb the stress of weather, rather than break. This flexibility can take its toll on the ship's hull. The PANAMA was loaded with coal, towing the schooner-barge MATANZAS, and doing fine against a November 21, 1906, gale when she was discovered to be leaking badly off Ontonagon, Michigan. Seeing that her pumps could not handle the inflow, her skipper released the towbarge and rapidly changed course to make a run for the beach. The ship made it to shore a few miles from town. Her crew was safe, but the PANAMA was battered to pieces by weather before she could be rescued. This was the vessel's second serious mishap. In 1903, as the JOHN CRAIG, she had suffered heavy damage in another accident. [5]

PANTHER ■ Wooden bulk freight steamer of 1,684 t. and 237 ft., launched in 1890 at W Bay City, MI

Lake Superior: Laden with a cargo of wheat, the steamer PANTHER was a victim of fog off Whitefish Point on June 17, 1916. In a particularly dense soup, she was rammed by the steel steamer JAMES J HILL and sunk. As in a number of other accidents of this type, the HILL was kept in the hole in the other's flank until the PANTHER's crew could climb aboard, then backed away, allowing the wooden vessel to sink. The wreck was discovered in 1975. The PANTHER had also been sunk near the Beaver Islands in 1910. [5+]

PANZOLA II ■ Gas screw of 49 t.

Lake Michigan: On October 5, 1957, the little motor vessel PANZOLA II was destroyed by fire at Whitehall, Michigan, on White Lake. She may have been a yacht. [1]

PARAGON ■ Merchant schooner

St. Clair River: The schooner PARAGON was reported destroyed at Sarnia, Ontario, in 1868. [1]

PARANA ■ Merchant bark

Lake Huron: The sailing vessel PARANA finished her career at the bottom of Saginaw Bay. She foundered in a heavy storm in 1863. [1]

PARISIEN ■ Vessel information unreported

Lake Huron: This ship was reported lost on the lake near Goderich, Ontario, in 1890. [1]

T F PARK ▪ Sidewheel passenger and package freight steamer of 450 t. and 170 ft., launched as the steamer PLOUGHBOY at Chatham, Ont. in 1851
Detroit River: While docked at Detroit following one of her many cross-river runs on June 3, 1870, the T F PARK caught fire and burned to the water's edge. [3]

A A PARKER ▪ Wooden bulk freighter of 1,660 t. and 247 ft., launched as the steamer KASOTA (qv) at Cleveland in 1884
Lake Superior: On September 19, 1903, with a full load of iron ore, the steamer A A PARKER encountered a terrible storm just after passing Munising, Michigan. When she was seen to be in great distress off Grand Marais, the U.S. Lifesaving Service launched their boats and took the steamer's 17-man crew off her decks, a few moments before she foundered. [5+]

B W PARKER ▪ Bulk freight schooner-barge of 1,476 t. and 256 ft., launched in 1890 at Gibraltar, MI
Lake Erie: A severe storm swept the lake on November 13, 1905, and carried this big vessel to her doom. Swamped by big waves, she went down off Cleveland. Fortunately, her crew had time to escape before she sank. [2]

CHARLES W PARKER ▪ Towing tug of 36 t.
Lake Michigan: Two different dates are given for the loss of this tug two miles north of Chicago. Both reports say that she was destroyed by a boiler explosion while underway, with the loss of four lives, but one gives September 22, 1879, the other October 4, 1891 as the date. [2]

CLARA PARKER ▪ Bulk freight schooner of 424 t.
Lake Michigan: The account of the loss of the CLARA PARKER is one of those magnificent tales that color much of Great Lakes lore. On November 13, 1883, a small boy was riding his horse on the storm-lashed bluff above the mouth of the Pigeon River. Looking out to the wild lake, he saw a schooner, the CLARA PARKER, a few hundred yards from shore, and obviously in serious trouble. As the ship went down, the boy wheeled his steed around and took off at a gallop for the U.S. Lifesaving Station at Grand Haven, seven miles to the north. The surfmen returned with their equipment a few hours later to find the wave-battered sailing ship sitting on the bottom with her reeling masts and spars above the water, and with her crewmen desperately clinging to them. The lifesavers hastily launched their boat and brought the frozen and exhausted sailors to shore without a single casualty. The boy was praised as a hero for some time after. The PARKER had been headed for Chicago with a cargo of corn at the time of the accident. [3]

GEORGE W PARKER ▪ Wooden steam sandsucker of 112 ft. overall, launched in 1903 at Marine City, MI as the steamer L G POWELL
St. Clair River: No lives were lost, but the PARKER was totally destroyed in a fire that struck her six miles south of Algonac, Michigan, on May 8, 1929. She sank in the channel, but her crew escaped in the ship's yawl. [1]

O E PARKS ▪ Lumber motor vessel of 391 t. and 134 ft., launched as a steamer at Saugatuck in 1891, converted to a barge, then a diesel M/V
Lake Huron: This small ship had a hold and deckload of lumber when she went down on May 3, 1929. Struck by an extremely violent, localized storm, she foundered off Thunder Bay Island, near Alpena. [5]

CHARLES STEWART PARNELL ▪ Wooden bulk freight steamer of 1,740 t. and 256 ft., launched at Wyandotte, MI, in 1888
Lake Michigan: The freighter CHARLES STEWART PARNELL was traversing the channel off Squaw Island, in the Beavers group, when she caught fire and was destroyed on November 29, 1905. The burnt-out hull later sank. [3]

CITY OF PARRY SOUND ▪ Wooden package freight steamer of 491 t. and 130 ft., launched in 1889 as the steamer FAVOURITE at Meaford, Ont.
Lake Huron: The little coaster CITY OF PARRY SOUND was lost on October 9, 1900, when she was destroyed by fire at Collingwood, Ontario, in the Georgian. [4]

JOHN S PARSONS ▪ Package and bulk freight schooner-barge of 115 t. and 93 ft., launched in 1891 at Chaumont, NY
Lake Ontario: The small schooner-barge JOHN S PARSONS was caught in a gale while in tow of the steamer FRANK D PHELPS when she was lost on November 24, 1913. The three-masted vessel swamped in heavy seas and foundered off Fair Haven, New York, a few miles from Oswego. [4]

THOMAS PARSONS ■ Merchant schooner of 350 t. and 135 ft., launched in 1868 at Charlotte, NY
Lake Erie: Fairport, Ohio (now Fairport Harbor), was the site of the loss of this sailing ship in 1891. She reportedly sank a few miles offshore. The PARSONS had suffered an earlier sinking at Sarnia, Ontario, in 1882. [2]

PASADENA ■ Bulk freight barge of 2,076 t. and 250 ft., launched in 1889 at Cleveland as a steamer
Lake Superior: The big barge PASADENA was lost near the upper entry to the Keweenaw Waterway. On October 8, 1906, she was loaded with a cargo of coal and in tow of the steamer GLADSTONE (qv), when her towline broke in a gale. She was thrown against a pier, sank and went to pieces with the loss of two lives among the ten crew aboard. [5]

PASSAIC ■ Steamer of 654 t. and 196 ft., launched in 1862 at Buffalo
Lake Erie: This steamer was reported to have been lost within a mile of shore near Dunkirk, New York, on November 1, 1891. [2]

A D PATCHIN ■ Sidewheel passenger and freight steamer, launched in 1846 at Truago (now Trenton), MI
Lake Michigan: Skillagallee Reef ("Skillagallee" is the way the local Irish fishermen pronounced the original French name "Isle Aux Galets". "Skillagallee" was at the time a type of thin gruel, used in England to feed prisoners.) claimed the sidewheeler A D PATCHIN, when she ran ashore there and was wrecked in 1853. The steamer broke up in the shadow of the lighthouse that had been finished just the year before. Skillagalee Reef is located east of the Beaver Islands. [1]

PATHFINDER ■ Steam tug of 38 t. and 69 ft., launched in Chicago in 1863 as the steamer J A CRAWFORD
Lake Superior: The tug PATHFINDER was lost on September 1, 1895, when she collided with another tug, the MEDINA, and sank near Duluth. One of the PATHFINDER's crewmen died in the accident. [3]

H C PATTER or **POTTER** ■ Schooner or steamer, maybe the steamer HENRY C POTTER, built at Bay City, MI, in 1868
Lake Huron: The combination of a fall gale and the dangerous Pointe Aux Barques area spelled the end for the H C PATTER on November 21, 1891. She foundered three miles northeast of the point. [2]

GRACE PATTERSON ■ Bulk freight steamer of 111 t.
Lake Michigan: March 15, 1882, was the last day for the steamer GRACE PATTERSON. Carrying a cargo of lumber and lath, she went hard aground on Two Rivers Point, on the Wisconsin shore, caught fire and was destroyed. There was no loss of life. One source gives Lake Superior as the location. [3]

JOHN H PAULEY ■ Wooden bulk freight steamer of 184 t. and 116 ft., launched in 1884 at Oswego, NY as the steamer THOMPSON KINGSFORD
St. Clair River: Destruction by fire was the fate of this little freighter. She caught fire at Marine City, Michigan, on August 10, 1906, and burned to the water. Her crew escaped unharmed. [2]

PAULINA ■ Merchant schooner
Lake Erie: One of the earlier Erie shipwrecks involved the loss of this schooner. She struck bottom and was wrecked near the mouth of the Grand River, on the Ohio coast in November, 1818. [1]

WILLIAM PEACOCK ■ Wooden sidewheel passenger and package freight steamer of 120 t., launched in 1829 at Barcelona, NY
Lake Erie: The small steamer WILLIAM PEACOCK had the dubious distinction of being the first steamer on Lake Erie to be destroyed in a boiler explosion. On September 17, 1830, she was lying tied to her wharf at Buffalo when a violent explosion ripped her boiler and steam piping apart and set the ship ablaze. Several men in her engineering spaces were scalded to death, and a number of passengers perished in the fire. Estimates of the death toll range from 15 to 30. [4]

PEARL ■ Merchant schooner
Lake Erie: This schooner was lost in 1855 when she wrecked on East Sister Reef, on the western end of the lake. This accident was also reported as having occurred in Georgian Bay. [2]

PEARL ■ Scow
Lake Superior: The scow (possibly schooner-scow) PEARL was reported to have been wrecked near Whitefish Point, in 1882. [1]

EDWARD S PEASE ■ Wooden bulk freight steamer of 716 t. and 168 ft., launched in 1873 at Hamilton, Ont., as the passenger steamer CALIFORNIA (qv)
Lake Huron: This vessel's career as a working steamer came to an end on November 24, 1904, when she caught fire while unloading and was burned to a shell. No lives were lost in the accident at Collingwood, Ontario, and the burned-out hull was later converted to a barge. [5+]

PECK ■ Barge, may be the 366 t., 154 ft. vessel W L PECK, launched in 1873 at Carrollton, MI
Lake Huron: In 1885, the PECK foundered offshore near Harbor Beach, Michigan. [1]

PEG ■ Steam tug
Lake Huron: One of the many tug accidents to occur in the North Channel, the tug PEG was wrecked on Cockburn Island in 1878. [1]

PELICAN ■ Bulk freight schooner of 813 t. and 205 ft.
Lake Erie: Vessels the size of the schooner PELICAN are usually safer riding out a storm at anchor than trying to negotiate a narrow harbor entrance in big waves. On May 16, 1893, this ship was anchored a short distance off Ashtabula in a spring gale when disaster struck. Perhaps her heavy cargo of iron ore caused her to slide up a big wave, then dive for the bottom on the downward drop. In any case, the vessel sank with the loss of four. [1]

JAMES H PELLETT ■ Steel barge of 346 t. and 179 ft. overall, launched in 1905 at Buffalo
Lake Erie: On July 2, 1943, the barge JAMES H PELLETT was lost when she foundered in the harbor at Cleveland. [2]

DORCAS PENDELL ■ Bulk freight schooner-barge of 407 t. and 148 ft., launched in 1884 at E Saginaw, MI
Lake Huron: The aging DORCAS PENDELL was already in poor condition when she was put on the shoreline near Harbor Beach, Michigan, to prevent her sinking in a 1913 storm. Before her owners could decide on her final disposition, the ship caught fire on July 6, 1914, and was destroyed. [3]

J P PENFIELD ■ Merchant schooner
Lake Huron: The schooner PENFIELD was lost at an unreported position on the lake in 1870. [1]

PENINSULA ■ Propeller freighter of 355 t. and 154 ft., launched in 1849 at Vickers Landing
Lake Superior: On November 15, 1854, the steamer PENINSULA was lost on dreaded Sawtooth Reef, near Eagle River, Michigan, on the Keweenaw Peninsula. The ship was fighting a gale when she broke her propeller shaft and was driven onto the reef, where she went to pieces. No lives were lost. [4]

WILLIAM PENN ■ Merchant schooner
Lake Ontario: This schooner sank on the lake in a white squall. [1]

PENOBSCOT ■ Wooden steam sandsucker of 257 t. and 131 ft., launched as a schooner in 1881 at Manitowoc, WI
St. Clair River: The PENOBSCOT went down on the river off Marine City, Michigan, following a collision. The accident occurred on August 19, 1925. Although the vessel was sitting in relatively shallow water, she was deemed too seriously damaged to repair, and was abandoned. [3]

PENOBSCOT ■ Steel bulk freight steamer of 5,200 t. and 445 ft., launched in 1895 at W Bay City, MI
Lake Erie: This big steamer figured prominently in an accident that killed 11 men in the harbor at Buffalo on October 29, 1951. On that date, the path of the PENOBSCOT intersected that of the tug DAUNTLESS #12 (qv) and her tanker-barge MORANIA #130 (qv). The steamer struck the gasoline-laden barge, which exploded and burned fiercely. The fire killed two of the 29 aboard the PENOBSCOT. The steamer was extensively rebuilt following the accident, and was not retired until 1963. [4]

PENSAUKEE ■ Tug of 34 t. and 52 ft.
Lake Erie: This tug was working the barge AURORA in Cleveland harbor when the barge swung out of control and crushed the PENSAUKEE against a dock, sinking her. The accident happened on June 5, 1902. [1]

PENTLAND ■ Wooden bulk freight steamer of 200 ft. overall, launched in 1894 at Grand Haven, MI
Lake Erie: The steamer PENTLAND's career ended in 1928, when she rammed a breakwall at Port Colborne, Ontario, and was damaged beyond repair. [1]

PEORIA ■ Lumber schooner (may have been a either a steamer or a schooner converted from a steamer) of 172 t. and 112 ft., launched in 1854 at Black River, OH
Lake Michigan: Carrying her normal cargo of lumber, the old schooner PEORIA was blown ashore by a storm and wrecked. The ship was lost near Bailey's Harbor, Wisconsin on November 12, 1901. [4]

PERE MARQUETTE 3 ■ Wooden passenger and package freight steamer (break-bulk) of 924 t. and 190 ft., launched in 1887 at Wyandotte, MI, as the steamer FLINT & PERE MARQUETTE #3
Lake Michigan: This carrier was built specifically to move passengers and cargo across Lake Michigan for the railroad. Since the work was necessary all year long, the steamer had a reinforced ice-breaking hull. The winter of 1919-20 was, however, much more than her designers had allowed for. At the end of April in 1920, the steamer became trapped in an ice field off Ludington, Michigan. The ice thickened around her until she was solidly frozen in. Then, on the 7th of March, a shift in the wind caused her hull to be crushed. Her crew calmly disembarked onto the ice and walked to the big carferry PERE MARQUETTE

18 (qv), standing by in open water. The railroad was able to salvage almost everything aboard her of value before the ice thawed and she went down. [5+]

PERE MARQUETTE 4 ■ Wooden passenger and package freight steamer (break-bulk) of 941 t. and 186 ft., launched in 1888 at Wyandotte, MI as the steamer FLINT & PERE MARQUETTE #4
Lake Michigan: Another of the break-bulk ships designed to carry cargoes across the lake from one set of rail cars to another on the other side, the PERE MARQUETTE 4, was lost On May 15, 1923. On that date, she was making her usual run from Ludington to Milwaukee when she suffered a nearly bows-on collision with the large steel carferry PERE MARQUETTE 17. No lives were lost, and the vessel was taken into tow and brought into Milwaukee, but was soon declared a total loss. The hulk was sold to a local yacht club, which used it for a clubhouse until 1936. [3]

PERE MARQUETTE 8 ■ Wooden passenger and package freight steamer (break-bulk) of 185 ft. overall, launched at South Haven, Michigan, in 1888 as the steamer H W WILLIAMS
Lake Michigan: The break-bulk carrier PERE MARQUETTE 8 was lost at Manistee, Michigan, on October 27, 1927. She caught fire and was destroyed at her winter moorings. [2]

PERE MARQUETTE 18 ■ Steel carferry of 2,993 t. and 338 ft., launched in 1902 at Cleveland
Lake Michigan: Most open-lake carferries were equipped with a sea-gate, which closed behind her main deck and prevented following seas from climbing on board. As an economy measure, the big ferry PERE MARQUETTE was not so equipped. On September 8, 1910, the steamer was coming across the lake in a big westerly gale when giant waves washing over the stern smashed her hatchways, opening them to the assault of the lake. She filled from the stern and sank in mid-lake, carrying 25 of the 62 aboard to the bottom with her. She was carrying a deck-full of railroad cars at the time of her loss. [4]

HATTIE B PEREUE ■ Wooden lumber hooker of 193 t. and 123 ft., launched in 1881 at South Haven, MI
Lake Michigan: The HATTIE B PEREUE was entering the harbor at Holland, MI, in a storm when she struck a bar and began to sink. Clear thinking by her wheels-man saved her crew from possible disaster when he turned

the vessel into the breakwater, where the men were able to leap from the ship, with no loss of life. The PEREUE settled to the bottom and went to pieces, pounded apart by waves. The loss occurred on October 15, 1902. [4]

FRANK PEREW ■ Bulk freight schooner-barge of of 524 t. and 174 ft., launched in 1867 at Cleveland
Lake Superior: Six of the seven men aboard the FRANK PEREW died in an accident which occurred on September 29, 1891. In a howling gale, the coal-laden schooner-barge snapped her towline and was swamped in a gale off Vermilion Point, Michigan. The crew took to her yawl and rowed 13 miles to the east, only to have the small boat overturn in the surf on Parisienne Island, drowning all but one. [4]

PERRY & COMPANY ■ Bulk freight steam barge of 100 t.
Lake Superior: On November 18, 1900, the steamer PERRY & COMPANY swamped in a gale and foundered three miles east of Grand Marais, Michigan. Five lives were lost in the disaster. [2]

COMMODORE PERRY ■ Wooden steam freighter of 352 t., launched in 1834 at Perrysburg, OH
Lake Erie: Six people died in the explosion and fire aboard the steamer COMMODORE PERRY on July 21, 1835. The almost-new steamer was wrecked in the harbor at Buffalo. [2]

COMMODORE PERRY ■ Cutter
Lake Huron: In 1877 this small vessel was lost when she wrecked on Sturgeon Point, near Harrisville, Michigan. [1]

DANIEL D PERRY ■ Scow of 286 t.
Lake Erie: On August 24, 1916, the scow DANIEL D PERRY stranded and was wrecked at the north end of Strawberry Island, near Buffalo. [1]

OLIVER H PERRY ■ Wooden sidewheel passenger and package freight steamer of 148 t. and 122 ft., launched in 1869 at Sandusky, OH
Lake Erie: The handsome passenger steamer OLIVER H PERRY was launched with much fanfare at Sandusky on August 13, 1869. On the 5th of September, she was tied to her wharf in the same city when she caught fire and burned to the waterline. [1]

THEODORE PERRY ■ Bulk freight schooner-barge of 262 t.
Lake Erie: This small schooner-barge was in transit in a relatively mild blow when she dropped into the trough of a wave and hit the bottom. The mass of the ship and her coal cargo was enough to open her seams, and she quickly sank, with the loss of five lives. She went down fifteen miles east of Rondeau Point (Pte Aux Pins), on the Ontario shore, July 22, 1887. [2]

PERSEVERANCE ■ Merchant schooner, perhaps the 140 t. vessel built at Niagara in 1855
Lake Huron or Michigan: In 1864, this vessel was lost in the Straits of Mackinac following a collision with the vessel GRAY EAGLE. [2]

PERSEVERANCE ■ Propeller freighter of 750 t. and 173 ft., launched in 1864 at Port Dalhousie, Ont.
Lake Ontario: The steamer PERSEVERANCE was lost near Oswego, New York, when she was destroyed by fire in October of 1868. [2]

PERSIAN ■ Merchant schooner
Lake Huron: All hands—ten sailors—were lost when this schooner foundered following a collision with the schooner E B ALLEN (qv) in September of 1868. The PERSIAN sank near 40-mile Point (so-called because it is 40 miles southeast of Old Mackinac Point and 40 miles nothwest of Thunder Bay). She was carrying a load of wheat at the time. Ironically, the E B ALLEN was herself lost in a collision three years later. [3]

PERSIAN ■ Propeller of 1,630 t.
Lake Erie: An offshore fire destroyed the steamer PERSIAN on August 23, 1875. She was carrying a cargo of grain when she caught fire ten miles east of Long Point, burned to the waterline and sank. [1]

PESHTIGO ■ Merchant bark
Lake Huron: The position of the PESHTIGO at time of her loss is not reported, but she was said to have gone down in 1898 following a collision with the schooner ST ANDREWS. Compare this report with the one for the ST ANDREW. [1]

PESHTIGO ■ Wooden lumber hooker of 817 t. and 203 ft., launched in 1869 at Trenton, MI
Lake Huron: The lumber hooker PESHTIGO was laden with her normal cargo when she was beset by a heavy fall gale in the Straits of Mackinac on October 24, 1908. Unable to make the narrow channel between Mackinac Island and Round Island, she struck bottom near the latter, broke up, and foundered. Fortunately, no lives were lost in the accident. [3]

PESHTIGO ■ Lumber schooner-barge of 633 t. and 201 ft., launched in 1889 at Milwaukee
Lake Huron: One of the heavy fall-like gales that sometimes occur in late summer struck the schooner-barge PESHTIGO as she was downbound with close to a million board-feet of lumber on August 11, 1928. She broke away from her towing steamer and was blown in to within a quarter mile of shore off Harbor Beach, Michigan, where she broke up in place. [2]

E T PETERS ■ Merchant schooner of 130 t.
Lake Erie: In a storm which struck on November 17, 1877, the schooner E T PETERS was driven off course, stranded and pounded to pieces at the mouth of the harbor at Port Colborne, Ontario. [1]

R G PETERS ■ Steam barge of 386 t.
Lake Michigan: The lake alone knows the location of the remains of the steamer R G PETERS and the 14 persons who were with her on December 1, 1882. On that date, she was travelling the normal course between Racine and Milwaukee when she simply sailed off the map. No wreckage or sightings of the vanished ship ever shed light upon her final whereabouts. [2]

ANNIE M PETERSON ■ Lumber schooner-barge of 691 t. and 190 ft., launched at Green Bay, WI, in 1874
Lake Superior: This big schooner-barge was lost with all nine hands and a lumber cargo on November 19, 1914. She was struck by a tremendous gale, lost from the tow of the steamer C F CURTIS (qv), torn to pieces and sunk by heavy seas off the mouth of the Two-Hearted River. See also SELDEN E MARVIN. [5+]

PETOSKEY ■ Wooden passenger and package freight steamer of 771 t. and 171 ft., launched in 1880 at Manitowoc, WI
Lake Michigan: The steamer PETOSKEY had already finished her 45 year career and was at a scrapyard at Sturgeon Bay, Wisconsin, awaiting final disposition when she was destroyed in an accidental fire. The blaze occurred on December 5, 1935, and involved several other vessels as well. [4]

PETREL ■ Bulk freight schooner of 151 t.
Lake Michigan: Laden with a cargo of lumber, the schooner PETREL was just leaving the harbor at Sheboygan, Wisconsin, when she foundered on October 17, 1883. [1]

PEWABIC ■ Wooden passenger and package freight propeller of 997 t. and 200 ft., launched in 1867 at Cleveland
Lake Huron: The PEWABIC had a full manifest of passengers and a hold full of high-grade upper peninsula copper when she met with disaster on the evening of August 9, 1865. It was fine summer weather when the downbound PEWABIC attempted to pass her upbound sister ship METEOR, and no one knows just what happened to cause the two vessels to collide seven miles off Alpena, Michigan, but the METEOR rammed far into the side of the unfortunate PEWABIC, and the latter quickly sank. She went down so rapidly that between 75 and 100 passengers and crew went down with her, even though the METEOR stood by for awhile (she was in a sinking condition herself) to pick up survivors. Her valuable copper cargo has been mostly salvaged, but at least five divers have added their ghosts to those below in an attempt to reclaim the treasure. [5+]

PEWAUKEE ■ Bulk freight steamer of 319 t. and 141 ft., launched in 1873 at Port Burwell, Ont. as the bark TWO FRIENDS (qv)
Lake Michigan: A fire that occured at Sturgeon Bay, Wisconsin, on October 10, 1907, destroyed the steamer PEWAUKEE at her dock. The vessel had sunk in the same general area when she was a sailing ship in 1890, but was recovered and rebuilt as this steamer. [2]

GUIDO PFISTER ■ Merchant schooner of 694 t. and 198 ft.
Lake Superior: The schooner GUIDO PFISTER was destroyed in an unusual accident at the mouth of the Duluth Ship Canal on October 10, 1885. She was coasting into position behind a tug when her towline was lost by the tug and the schooner serenely glided onto the rocks. She was abandoned in place and her rotting hull was later covered over with fill. [1]

PFOHL ■ Wooden bulk freight steamer of 760 t. and 203 ft., launched in 1868 at Marine City, Michigan, as the passenger and freight steamer ST PAUL
Lake Huron: On May 20, 1905, the steamer PFOHL was running off Goderich, Ontario, when she caught fire, burned and sank. [3]

PHANTOM ■ Merchant schooner
Lake Superior: This small schooner was reported to have gone ashore and wrecked near the mouth of the Bad River (Wisconsin) on June 1, 1878. [1]

W B PHELPS ■ Merchant schooner of 137 ft., launched in 1873 at Sacket's Harbor, NY
Lake Michigan: While shipwreck annals are full of stories about men who were plucked from their ship's rigging and saved from death, there are probably an equal number of wrecks in which lonely, frozen men were lost when help never arrived. The W B PHELPS had her sails blown out and was driven ashore near Glen Arbor, Michigan, near the Sleeping Bear Dunes area. Typical of many Lakes disasters, the vessel struck an offshore bar and went to the bottom. Also typical was the crewmens' desperate scramble up the ratlines to keep from being sucked down when the hull went under. The men spent many hours in the freezing gale, praying for deliverance and, one by one, freezing to death. The last two haggard survivors were finally rescued by local residents who discovered the ship, then launched a tiny rowboat into the ferocious gale and pulled them from the rigging. The PHELPS later broke up in place, losing her cargo of beer into the lake. The accident took place on November 19, 1879. [2]

PHILADELPHIA ■ Iron propeller freighter of 1,464 t. and 236 ft., launched in 1868 at Buffalo
Lake Huron: Between 16 and 24 people died when the coal-laden steam freighter PHILADELPHIA collided with the steel steamer ALBANY (qv) in a fog and sank off Pte Aux Barques, Michigan. The accident occurred on November 7, 1893. [5]

PHILADELPHIA ■ Propeller freighter of 148 t. and 90 ft., launched in 1867 at Stromness, Ont. as the steamer JESSIE
Lake Superior: This little steamer was reported wrecked at N. Gros Cap, Ontario. The accident happened in October of 1907. [1]

PHILIP ■ Tug
Lake Huron: The tug PHILIP was destroyed by fire at Detour, Michigan, in 1933. [1]

PHILIP M ■ Merchant schooner
Lake Ontario: On May 17, 1889, the schooner PHILIP M was reported to have foundered off Port Weller, Ont. [1]

PHOENIX ■ Wooden passenger and package freight propeller of 350 t. and 155 ft., launched in 1846 at Cleveland
Lake Michigan: When one thinks of Lakes' contribution to the growth of the United States and Canada, the tendency is to picture long ships full of iron ore or grain, or the three-masted windjammers piled high with deckloads of lumber. But without a doubt, the most significant consignment carried aboard freshwater vessels was human. Hundreds of thousands of settlers from the east and immigrants from across the Atlantic sailed to new homes in Wisconsin or Illinois or western Ontario on board the fleets of lakes steamboats such as the PHOENIX. On the night of November 21, 1847, the steamer was making her final run of the season with almost 250 Dutch immigrants on the passenger manifest, and a hold packed with household goods. Somewhere off Sheboygan, Wisconsin, the ship caught fire, probably from an overheated boiler, and went up like a torch. As was usual for the times, the lifeboats would hold only a pitiful few, and almost 200 men, women and children, hopeful for a new life in the New World, spent the rest of eternity on the bottom of the lake. The ship was rumored to have had a large amount of personal wealth in the form of coinage in her safe when she was lost. [5+]

PHOENIX ■ Tug
Lake Ontario: The tug PHOENIX reportedly burned and sank on the north shore of the lake in 1863. [1]

PHOENIX ■ Barge, possibly the 151 t. vessel of this name built in 1858 at Milan, OH
Lake Erie: The barge PHOENIX sank in a sudden squall somewhere on the lake in 1864. [2]

PHOENIX ▪ Tug
Detroit River: No date is given for the loss of this tug to fire near Detroit. [1]

JAMES PICKANDS ▪ Wooden bulk freight steamer of 1,546 t. and 233 ft., launched in 1886 at Cleveland
Lake Superior: Sawtooth Reef, as its name implies, was deadly to unwary wooden vessels that plied the northern shores of the Keweenaw. This big steamer, carrying a load of iron ore on September 22, 1894, struck the reef off Eagle River, and ran hard up on the rocks. A storm which followed pushed her off her perch and she sank in deep water. [3]

PICTON ▪ Sidewheel steamer or propeller of 490 t. and 158 ft., launched in 1870 at Mill Point, Ont.
Lake Erie: On September 22, 1882, the steamer PICTON was driven ashore by a storm. She grounded three miles east of Rondeau Point (Ontario), lighthouse and broke up in place. [2]

PICTON ▪ Bulk freight schooner of 160 t. and 106 ft., launched in 1877 at Picton, Ont.
Lake Ontario: All six of the sailors aboard the schooner PICTON perished with their ship when she sank in a summer gale in the middle of the lake. The loss occurred on June 29, 1900. [2]

PICTON ▪ Sidewheel passenger and package freight steamer of 1,203 t. and 175 ft., launched in 1870 at Montreal as the steamer CORSICAN
Lake Ontario: In September of 1907, the sidewheeler PICTON was destroyed by fire at her dock at Toronto. [1]

A C PIERCE ▪ Merchant steamer of 36 t., launched in 1887
Lake Michigan: The little steamer A C PIERCE was lost in a storm that struck her on August 15, 1915. She stranded on the shore of South Fox Island and was wrecked, a total loss. All of her crew escaped without injury. [1]

MARY E PIERCE ▪ Steam tug of 20 t. and 48 ft., launched in 1871 at Buffalo
Lake Huron: This tiny utility vessel was lost on February 13, 1906, when she went aground near Au Sable, Michigan, and was destroyed. Both of her crewmen escaped the wreck. [2]

A N PIKE ▪ 22 t. vessel of unreported type
Lake St. Clair: This little boat caught fire and was destroyed just down the Thames River from Chatham, Ontario, on January 3, 1879. [1]

PILE DRIVER ▪ Barge
Lake Superior: On July 15, 1892, this vessel sank in or near Muskallonge Lake, near Deer Park, Michigan. [2]

PILGRIM ▪ Wooden passenger and package freight steamer of 300 t. and 119 ft., launched in 1888 at Saugatuck, MI
Lake Huron: An early-season run ended in disaster when the steamer PILGRIM struck an ice floe and began to sink on April 29, 1907. She was beached near Fort Gratiot, Michigan, and broke up or was dismantled in place. [3]

PILOT ▪ Schooner-scow, reported as two different vessels, a 60-tonner built in 1845 at Milwaukee or a 40 t., 63-footer launched in 1847 at Sandusky
Lake Michigan: This small vessel was reportedly sunk off Chicago in 1857 or '58. These reports may refer to two ships of the same name. [3]

PILOT ▪ Merchant schooner of 17 t. and 40 ft. launched in 1886 at Essexville, MI
Lake Huron: This tiny schooner sank following a collision suffered near Caseville, Michigan, in 1896. [2]

PILOT ▪ Tug of 48 t.
Lake Huron: This unregistered tug was destroyed by fire on the Moon River, south of Parry Sound, Ontario, on September 11, 1910. [2]

PINCUSVILLE ▪ Scow launched in 1873 at Oak Harbor, OH, as a sidewheel steamer
Lake Erie: In 1881 this former steamer was lost when she sank near Sandusky, Ohio. [1]

PINE LAKE ▪ Wooden steam sandsucker of 238 t. and 135 ft., launched in 1881 at Mt. Clemens, MI, as the steam freighter R McDONALD
Detroit River: The sandsucker PINE LAKE went down in the steamer channel abreast of Belle Isle on October 21, 1912. Two lives were lost when she sank following a collision with the 1,200 ton wooden steamer FLEETWOOD. The wreckage was later dynamited to clear the channel. The ship had been nearly destroyed by fire at Cross Village, Michigan, in 1893, when she was called IDA M TORRENT. [4]

ELLEN PINE ▪ Merchant schooner
Lake Michigan: No detail is given on the loss of this schooner, sunk in a white squall. [1]

PINTA ▪ 36 t. vessel of unknown type
Lake Ontario: The PINTA was reported to have foundered five miles northeast of Oakville, Ontario, near Toronto, on November 20, 1879. [1]

PIONEER ▪ Bulk freight schooner of 190 t.
Lake Ontario: The loss of the schooner PIONEER is somewhat of a mystery. According to contemporary records, she foundered off Presq'ile, Ontario, in good weather and

for no apparent reason. The ship went down in 1875 with her cargo of coal, but with no loss of life. A schooner of the same name was sunk in Lake Huron on June 12, 1871, and may be the same vessel. [3]

PITTSBURG ■ Sidewheel passenger and package freight steamer of 1,349 t. and 223 ft., launched in 1871 at Port Robinson, Ont. as the steamer MANITOBA
Detroit River: This steamer was destroyed at Sandwich, Ontario (now part of Windsor), on August 13, 1903. She was tied to her dock when she caught fire and burned to a total loss. [5]

PLANET ■ Steamer
Lake Superior: Little seems to be known about the loss of the steamer PLANET, except that she was reported to have gone down near Eagle River, Michigan, on the Keweenaw Peninsula, in August of 1862. Reports state that 35 lives were lost in the accident. [2]

PLANET ■ Bulk freight steam barge of 1,153 t. and 257 ft.
Lake Michigan: The large steamer PLANET sank off Two Rivers, Wisconsin, in November of 1872. Seven lives were lost when she went down. [1]

JOHN PLANKINTON ■ Wooden bulk freight steamer of 1,821 t. and 280 ft., launched in 1889 at W Bay City, MI
Detroit River: Considering the heavy traffic moving up and down the Detroit River, and the busy cross-grain ferry traffic, it is almost surprising that more accidents of the type that befell the JOHN PLANKINTON have not occurred. On May 9, 1917, the big steamer collided with the carferry DETROIT off Windsor and sank quickly. Her major machinery was later recovered, but salvagers could not refloat the hulk, and she was leveled by explosives. [5]

PLATINA ■ Merchant schooner of 91 t. and 70 ft., launched in 1834 at Sandusky, OH
Lake Huron: The schooner PLATINA went ashore and was wrecked somewhere on the lake in 1848. [1]

PLOVER ■ Bulk freight schooner of 390 t., launched in 1857 at Milan, OH
Lake Superior: Carrying a load of grain to a lower lakes port, the schooner PLOVER stranded and went to pieces near Whitefish Point. The ship was wrecked on October 12, 1871, but, fortunately, her crew escaped from harm. They were at first reported as lost, but arrived at the Soo in the ship's yawl two days later. [2]

C H PLUMMER ■ Bulk freight schooner-barge of 219 t. and 117 ft., launched in 1888 at Sandusky, OH
Lake Erie: The brand-new schooner-barge C H PLUMMER caught fire at Kelley's Island and was destroyed in 1888. [1]

PLYMOUTH ■ Lumber schooner
Lake Superior: The schooner PLYMOUTH was lost between Grand Marais, Michigan, and Crisp Point, when she foundered in a gale on October 24, 1888. [2]

PLYMOUTH ■ Bulk freight schooner-barge of 727 t. and 213 ft., launched in 1854 at Ohio City, OH, as a steamer
Lake Michigan: As a steamer, this vessel had been wrecked near Marquette, Michigan, in an 1887 gale and had been declared a total loss. Entrepreneurs, however, had her salvaged and converted to this barge. Near the beginning of the Big Storm of 1913, the PLYMOUTH was in tow of the tug JAMES H MARTIN, and with a cargo of cedar posts, when the two vessels were set upon by the first big waves of the storm. After struggling against the violent weather for a day and a half, the tug was in a bad way, and her crew thought she was in danger of sinking. She left the PLYMOUTH in the lee of St. Martin's Island, off the tip of Michigan's Garden Peninsula, while she ran for a harbor and temporary repairs. When she returned several days later, the barge had disappeared. The only tangible evidence of the PLYMOUTH and her nine crewmen that was found was a "note in a bottle" which said the tug had "left us and never even said good-bye!" [5 +]

PLYMOUTH ROCK ■ Merchant schooner of 107 ft., launched in 1862 at Oswego, NY
Detroit River: This little two-master was destroyed by a fire which struck her while she was tied to a dock at Detroit. The accident happened in 1884. [1]

POINT ABINO ■ Wooden bulk freight steamer of 204 t. and 112 ft., launched in 1872 at Buffalo
Lake St. Clair: The little POINT ABINO was wrecked on November 14, 1905. On that date, she was stranded and wrecked in the St. Clair Flats Canal, (known as the "snake run" because of its convoluted course) where she sank. Her wreckage lies near that of the steamer NELSON MILLS (qv). [4]

POLYNESIA ■ Merchant schooner of 979 t. and 204 ft., launched in 1885 at W Bay City, MI
Lake Michigan: The big schooner POLYNESIA foundered off Sheboygan, Wisconsin, in a storm which struck her on October 23, 1887. [2]

PONTIAC ■ Wooden steamer
Lake Huron: This wooden vessel was lost on the St. Marys River on July 11, 1891. She was just below the Soo when she turned in front of the big passenger steamer ATHABASCA, was rammed, and sank. [2]

CITY OF PORT HURON ■ Wooden freight or passenger and package freight steamer
Lake Huron: This steamer was reported to have foundered off Lexington, Michigan, in 1876. [1]

E M PORTCH ■ Merchant schooner of 306 t.
Lake Huron: The many shallow spots and reefs to the north of Cheboygan, Michigan, have claimed a good number of ships. The schooner E M PORTCH was heaving and plunging up and down in big waves when she struck bottom and sank near the town on March 27, 1882. [2]

JOHN F or **JOHN A PORTER** ■ Merchant schooner
Lake Erie: On June 9 of 1846 or '47, the schooner JOHN PORTER rammed the steamer CHESAPEAKE (qv) off Conneaut, Ohio. She ran for the beach in a much-damaged condition, but sank a few hundred yards offshore. She may have been recovered and may be the vessel below. [3]

JOHN F PORTER ■ Merchant schooner of 116 t. and 88 ft., launched as the passenger steamer CINCINNATI in 1836 at Sandusky, OH
Lake Michigan: This vessel was reported wrecked near Milwaukee in 1855. [1]

LLOYD S PORTER ■ Wooden lumber hooker of 380 t. and 170 ft., launched in 1893 at Port Huron, MI
Lake Ontario: On May 17, 1917, the LLOYD S PORTER was burned to a shell at a dock near Fair Haven, New York. The burned-out hull was later taken out in the lake and scuttled. [4]

PORTLAND ■ Merchant schooner
Lake Huron: The schooner PORTLAND was lost in 1867. She reportedly stranded and broke up at False Presque Isle, north of Alpena, Michigan. [1]

PORTSMOUTH ■ Wooden bulk freight propeller of 674 t. and 176 ft., launched in 1852 at Buffalo
Lake Huron: The steamer PORTSMOUTH was downbound with a cargo of pig iron when she was caught in a gale and driven ashore. She went aground on Middle Island Reef, north of Thunder Bay Island, Michigan, then caught fire and was destroyed. The loss occurred on November 10, 1867. The ship's crew was able to escape. [5]

POST BOY ■ Package freight schooner
Lake Michigan: The schooner POST BOY was victim of her own volatile cargo in 1841. She was at Buffington Harbor, near the south end of the lake, when her cargo of general merchandise and kegs of gunpowder exploded and the vessel was destroyed. Ten lives were lost in this violent accident. [1]

POST BOY ■ Wooden steamer of 123 t. and 73 ft., launched in 1888 at W Bay City, MI
Lake Michigan: A harbor fire at Holland, Michigan destroyed this little vessel on August 8, 1905. Neither of her two crewmen were injured. [2]

POTOMAC ■ Merchant schooner of 388 t., launched in 1842 at Cape Vincent, NY
Lake Michigan: This large two-masted schooner was nearing the end of her career in 1883, when she grounded and wrecked north of Frankfort, Michigan. [2]

AGNES L POTTER ■ Bulk freight schooner-barge of 279 t. and 134 ft., launched as a schooner at St. Clair, MI, in 1870
Lake Erie: While in tow off Cleveland on August 28, 1906, the three-master AGNES L POTTER caught fire and was destroyed. [2]

PRAIRIE STATE ■ Steamer
Lake Huron or Michigan: The steamer PRAIRIE was reported lost in the Straits of Mackinac, Michigan, in an 1860 storm. [1]

PRAIRIE STATE ■ Barge
Lake Huron: The barge PRAIRIE STATE went ashore and was destroyed near Sand Beach, Michigan, in 1879. [1]

PASCAL P PRATT ■ Wooden bulk freight steamer of 1,927 t. and 286 ft., launched in 1888 at Cleveland
Lake Erie: This large steamer was a victim of fire on November 18, 1908. While in transit off Long Point she burst into flame and was turned to make a run to shore in an attempt to save her people. She came up near the beach about a mile from the Long Point lighthouse, where her crew was able to make it to shore. The PRATT burned to a total loss. [3]

PREMIER ■ Wooden passenger and package freight steamer of 331 t. and 130 ft., launched in 1888 at Hamilton, Ont. as the steamer GREYHOUND
Lake Huron: Bruce Mines, Ontario, in the North Channel, was the site of the demise of the steamer PREMIER. On November 13, 1920, the aging passenger and freight vessel caught fire at her dock and was destroyed. [2]

GEORGE PRESLEY ■ Wooden bulk freight steamer of 1,963 t. and 285 ft., launched in 1889 at Cleveland
Lake Michigan: The steamer GEORGE PRESLEY burned

to a total loss at Washington Harbor, Wisconsin. On June 26, 1905, the iron ore laden vessel was groping her way through a fog when she ran aground, caught fire, and was destroyed. All 15 of her crew escaped unharmed, and the vessel was later recovered, but only for scrapping. [3]

PRESTO ▪ Merchant schooner of 184 t. and 111 ft., launched in 1857 at Huron, MI
Lake Huron: This small steamer broke up and sank in a storm in the anchorage at Harbor Beach, Michigan. The ship was lost on October 16, 1895. [3]

PRESTON ▪ Wooden steamer of 472 t. and 154 ft. launched in 1891 at Green Bay, WI
Lake Superior: The steamer PRESTON was burdened with a cargo of lumber and had just departed Fort William, Ontario, when she was discovered to be leaking badly. Her crew quickly abandoned ship—perhaps too quickly, as the PRESTON was later found still afloat, apparently bouyed up by her cargo. The June 29, 1901, incident would have been amusing had not one seaman died in the scramble to escape the ship. [3]

PRESTON'S STORE BOAT ▪ Propeller vessel of 28 t.
Lake Huron: This little vessel was used to transport groceries and other supplies among the many islands of southeastern Georgian Bay. On August 10, 1934, she was going about her business when she suddenly exploded and sank west of Minnicognashene Island and north of Sawlog Bay, Ontario. Lives were presumably lost in the accident, but sources are unsure of how many. [2]

MAUD PRESTON ▪ Propeller steamer of 175 t. and 109 ft.
Lake Erie: On May 20, 1898, this wooden propeller was destroyed by a fire on Maumee Bay, at Toledo. [1]

PRETORIA ▪ Bulk freight schooner-barge of 2,790 t. and 338 ft., launched in 1900 at W Bay City, MI
Lake Superior: This vessel was one of the largest sail-powered ships as well as one of the biggest wooden vessels ever used on the Lakes, with double the displacement of the big five-mast schooner DAVID DOWS (qv). On September 2, 1905, the PRETORIA was in tow of the steamer VENEZUELA and carrying a cargo of iron ore when the two were attacked by a fall storm near the Apostle Islands. The VENEZUELA was significantly smaller than the big barge and underpowered for the task of managing her in heavy weather. The PRETORIA broke her towrope and, with her huge bulk and pathetically small sails, she was at the mercy of wind and wave. She foundered off Outer Island with the loss of five of her 11 crewmen. [5+]

CHARLES S PRICE ▪ Steel bulk freight steamer of 10,000 t. and 524 ft., built at Lorain, OH, in 1910

Lake Huron: One of the ten big steel steamers that were lost with all hands during the Big Storm of 1913, the PRICE was a sister ship of the ISAAC M SCOTT (qv), that went down the same day, November 11. Vessels reaching Port Huron during the latter part of the storm reported sighting the upturned hull of a large steel ship floating a few miles to the north. So many vessels were overdue in the storm that for awhile it was a mystery as to what vessel it could be. Divers finally went down and read the name CHARLES S PRICE off her bow on the 16th. The PRICE was upbound with a cargo of coal when she rolled over in gigantic seas and was lost with her crew of 28. The position of the wreck is known. See steamer REGINA for additional information. [5+]

PRIDE ▪ Merchant schooner of 70 t. and 64 ft., launched in 1849 at Sandusky, OH
Lake Michigan: The little schooner PRIDE was lost in November of 1905 (one source says '01) when she failed to find the Death's Door Passage (near Washington Island) and went ashore in a gale. She later broke up in place. [3]

JOHN PRIDGEON, Jr ▪ Wooden lumber hooker of 1,212 t. and 221 ft., launched in 1875 at Detroit
Lake Erie: Lake sailors sometimes say they fear Lake Erie storms the most. Because of its east-west orientation and relatively shallow depth, the lake can be whipped into a frenzy in very short order. Waves can come at irregular intervals and vary greatly in size. They can even curl and break far out in the lake. The JOHN PRIDGEON, Jr. was struck by one of these violent westerly gales on September 8, 1909. She did not even struggle for very long before she slipped sideways into the dreaded troughs between the waves, capsized and sank. The accident happened 14 miles off Cleveland. Since no sources mention any loss of life, it may be surmised that her crew escaped. [5+]

PRINCE ▪ Steamer
Lake Huron: Little detail is reported on the loss of this vessel, said to have filled and sunk somewhere on the lake in the big gale of October 20, 1905. [2]

PRINCE EDWARD ▪ Steamer of 170 t., launched in 1868 at St. Catharine's Ont.
Lake Huron: The small steamer PRINCE EDWARD was the victim of a storm on November 21, 1870. She was trying to negotiate the passage through the mouth of Georgian Bay when she ran aground near Cove Island Light and went to pieces. [2]

PRINCE EDWARD ▪ Sidewheel passenger and package freight steamer of 97 t. and 81 ft.
Lake Ontario: This little sidewheeler was lost to a fire at Belleville, Ontario, in June of 1884. [1]

PRINCE OF WALES ▪ Merchant schooner
Lake Huron: In 1835 this schooner went down on the lake, somewhere near Detour, Michigan. [1]

F H PRINCE ■ Wooden package freight steamer of 2,047 t. and 245 ft., launched in 1890 at Wyandotte, MI
Lake Erie: No lives were lost when this steamboat was driven ashore on Kelley's Island on November 14, 1911 (also given as August 8). Following the grounding, she caught fire and was destroyed. [3]

PRINCESS CHARLOTTE ■ Vessel information unavailable
Lake Ontario: The PRINCESS CHARLOTTE is reported to have "sailed through a crack in the lake," gone missing with all hands. No other information is available. [1]

PRINCESS PALMS ■ Merchant schooner
Lake Michigan: Simmons Reef, at the northern extremity of the Beaver Island group, has snagged many a ship, including the schooner PRINCESS PALMS. The schooner struck bottom and foundered off the reef on November 12, 1889. [1]

PRINCETON ■ Propeller freighter
Lake Erie: The steamer PRINCETON was carrying a cargo of agricultural implements when she was blown aground and wrecked near Van Buren Point, New York, in 1854. [1]

PRINDIVILLE ■ Propeller freighter
Lake Huron: This vessel was reported to have gone ashore near Oscoda, Michigan, in 1882, and been broken up by the action of waves. [1]

PRINDOC ■ Steel bulk freight steamer of 3,871 t. and 356 ft., launched in 1901 at W Bay City, MI, as the steamer GILCHRIST
Lake Superior: Isle Royale has proven to be one of the most dangerous areas on the Great Lakes. It sits like a large and evil reptile astride the steamer routes to the grain and ore ports on Ontario's Thunder Bay. Ships moving to and from the Soo must detour around the island, adding a significant amount of time over a straight course. For this reason, there has always been a shipping bottleneck at each end of the island, as vessels attempted the shortest possible routes. At the north end the channel runs through the narrow strait between the main island and little Passage Island, a scant three miles away. Subtract the shallows on either side and allow a little searoom, and ships are left with a lane only a few hundred yards wide to handle vessels moving in both directions. It is a tribute to the lakemen's navigational skills that the bottom of the passage is not a graveyard of ships. Still, adverse conditions have led to wrecks such as the loss of the PRINDOC on June 1, 1943. The big steamer was downbound with grain in a heavy fog when she collided with the almost equally large steel steamer BATTLEFORD. The PRINDOC sank quickly in almost 600 feet of water, but

with no loss of life, as the BATTLEFORD stood by to pick up her crew. [5]

JOHN C PRINGLE ■ Merchant schooner of 474 t. launched in 1880 at Detroit
Lake Huron: No date is given for the loss of the schooner JOHN C PRINGLE. She was lost at Big Trout Island, in Potaganissing Bay, just north of Detour Passage. [1]

MARY PRINGLE ■ Propeller freighter of 204 t. and 121 ft. launched in 1867 at Trenton, MI
Lake Huron: The small steamer MARY PRINGLE was destroyed by fire on the lake just north of Port Huron, Michigan, in 1893. [2]

ROBERT C PRINGLE ■ Steam tug of 143 t. and 101 ft., launched as the passenger steamer CHEQUAMEGON at Manitowoc, WI, in 1903
Lake Michigan: This odd little tug became waterlogged and sank off Manitowoc, Wisconsin, on July 19, 1922. [2]

WALTER R PRINGLE ■ Steam tug of 252 t. and 98 ft., launched in 1890 at Cleveland as the ferry SUPERIOR, also served as a package freighter for 12 years
St. Clair River: This small vessel was discovered to be afire while navigating the river on May 6, 1922. She was beached on Stag Island and subsequently destroyed by the flames. [2]

WILLIAM H PRINGLE ■ Tug of 219 ft. and 120 t., launched in 1871 at Saginaw, MI
Lake Huron: This large tug was destroyed by fire off Port Huron, Michigan, in 1877. Though she was thought to be a total loss, her hull and engines were recovered and used to rebuild her as the steamer INTERNATIONAL and later LUCKNOW (qv).

PRINS WILLEM V ■ Motor package freighter of 1,567 t. and 258 ft., built in Europe
Lake Michigan: The Dutch-registered motor ship PRINS WILLEM V was the victim of a collision which occurred on the night of October 14, 1954. The vessel was approximately four miles off Milwaukee, carrying a cargo of general merchandise consisting largely of television tubes, when she collided with a tug-barge combination and sank. No lives were lost. At one time her owners planned to refloat her and tow her back to Europe for repairs. [3]

PROGRESS ■ Wooden steam freighter of 1,596 t. and 255 ft., launched in 1880 at Milwaukee
Lake Michigan: The steamer PROGRESS was the victim of a storm that struck her on November 24, 1905. On that date, she stranded in Green Bay and suffered heavy damage. None of her crew were lost, but the ship's cargo-hauling days were over. Her hull was recovered the next year and converted to a construction barge. [2]

PROTECTION ▪ Steam tug
Lake Michigan: This tug was aiding a vessel in distress when she met an untimely end on November 14, 1883. She was towing the disabled schooner ARAB (qv) in a gale, when her propeller fouled the towline. The PROTECTION was then helpless and was driven onto a reef near Holland, Michigan, with both crews aboard. U.S. Lifesaving Service men rescued all but one of the tug's people, but the PROTECTION herself broke up in place. [2]

PROTECTION ▪ Wooden bulk freight steamer of 111 ft., launched in 1888 at Sault Ste. Marie, MI, originally 91 t. and 76 ft.
Lake Erie: Six crewmen perished when this small steamer filled and sank in a storm off Cedar Point, near Sandusky, Ohio. The ship was lost in November of 1923. [3]

PROVINCE ▪ Crane-equipped barge of 580 t. and 166 ft. overall, launched in 1911 at Ft. William, Ont.
St. Clair River: This odd-looking barge sank on the river on September 28, 1923, after capsizing while under tow. Three lives were lost in the accident. The barge was later recovered for scrap. [3]

PROVOST ▪ Merchant schooner
Lake Huron: This sailing ship was reported lost on the lake in 1887. [1]

PRUSSIA ▪ Propeller freighter of 458 t. and 138 ft., launched in 1873 at St. Catharine's, Ont.
Lake Superior or Huron: The steamer PRUSSIA was underway on September 12, 1885, when she was discovered to be afire. Her crew fought the blaze for awhile, then abandoned ship. The PRUSSIA burned to the waterline and sank. Four reports are split evenly on the position of the steamer at the time of her loss. Two say she was destroyed near Bayfield, Ontario, in Georgian Bay, while the others say she was lost near Bayfield, Wisconsin. The former seems slightly more plausible, since she was a Canadian vessel. [4]

PULASKI ▪ Bulk freight schooner of 349 t. and 136 ft., launched in 1873 at Port Huron, MI
Lake Michigan: This schooner was trying to ride a gale out at anchor in Good Harbor Bay, in the northeastern part of the lake, when her anchors lost purchase and she was blown onto a reef. Surfmen from the U.S. Lifesaving Service rescued her crew before the tall ship went to pieces. The accident occurred on October 3, 1887. Some sources say she was lost on Grosse Point, north of Mackinac Island. [3]

JIM PULLARD or **PULLAR** ▪ Wooden steam coaster of 39 t. and 62 ft., launched in 1864 at Sault Ste. Marie, MI
Lake Michigan: A fire destroyed this little steamer at Dog Island, near Sturgeon Bay, Wisconsin. The vessel sank as a result of the October 15, 1909 blaze. [4]

PUP ▪ Steam tug of 13 t. and 45 ft., launched in 1894 at Saugatuck, MI
Lake Michigan: No lives were lost when this tiny vessel foundered off Plum Island, in the mouth of Green Bay, on July 19, 1915. [2]

QUAIL ▪ Sidewheel passenger and package freight steamer of 34 t. and 77 ft., launched in 1868 at Chatham, Ont.
Lake Ontario: Most fires that caused the destruction of Great Lakes ships were either accidental or were used in lieu of scrapping. A few, such as that which destroyed the steamer QUAIL, were the work of arsonists. In March of 1873 the steamer was in the Bay of Quinte when a fire was set aboard her and she burned to the water. [1]

QUEEN CHARLOTTE ▪ Sidewheel passenger and package freight steamer of 150 ft., launched in 1816 or '18 at Finkle's Point (Kingston), Ont.
Lake Ontario: This little sidewheeler was lost in 1837 when she stranded in Cataraqui Bay, a few miles west of Kingston, Ont. and broke up. [2]

QUEEN CITY ▪ Sidewheel passenger and package freight steamer, launched in 1842 at Oswego, NY, as the steamer LADY OF THE LAKE
Lake Ontario: Fire was the cause of this steamer's demise on January 2, 1855. She was destroyed by a blaze at her dock at Toronto. [2]

QUEEN CITY ▪ Barge of 906 t. and 242 ft., launched in 1848 at Buffalo as a steamer
Lake Huron: In 1863, the barge QUEEN CITY was wrecked and sank on Pointe Aux Barques, Michigan. [2].

QUEEN CITY ▪ Sidewheel passenger and package freight steamer of 127 t. and 118 ft., launched in 1856 at Oshkosh, Wisconsin
The only information available on the loss of this ship is the date of her demise, November 22, 1875. [1]

QUEEN CITY ▪ Merchant schooner of 675 t. and 183 ft., launched in 1873 at Bay City, MI
Lake Michigan: The Beaver Island archipelago has a long and fascinating history, including a stint as the only declared kingdom on the continent. Its history includes French Trappers, Mormon farmers, Irish fishermen, rumors of piracy and a significant number of shipwrecks. The big schooner QUEEN CITY was wrecked in a storm on September 23, 1895, when she was driven on Hog Island Reef, northeast of Saint James, and destroyed. She was burdened with a cargo of coal at the time. [5]

QUEEN OF THE LAKES ▪ Steam freighter of 637 t. and 185 ft., launched in 1855 at Black River, OH

Lake Superior: No lives were lost, but the steamer QUEEN OF THE LAKES was burned to total destruction on June 12, 1869. She caught fire at her dock at Marquette after loading a cargo of pig iron, and was pushed away from the waterfront by a local tug. She burned up and sank a few hundred yards offshore. [4]

QUEEN OF THE LAKES ■ Iron sidewheel passenger and package freight steamer of 153 t. and 108 ft., launched in 1872 at Wyandotte, MI
Lake Michigan: An offshore blaze caused the loss of this vessel on September 18, 1898. She caught fire and was destroyed off South Manitou Island. [3]

QUEEN OF THE LAKES ■ Bulk freight schooner of 190 t. and 135 ft., launched as the ROBERT TAYLOR in 1858 at Portsmouth, Ont.
Lake Ontario: The old schooner QUEEN OF THE LAKES was destroyed by stress of weather in November 28, 1906. She was off Sodus Bay, on the New York shore when she was struck by high winds. The 48-year-old hull could not withstand the tension and sprang a leak and sank. [3]

QUEEN OF THE LAKES ■ Merchant schooner
Lake Ontario: The large schooner QUEEN OF THE LAKES was reportedly wrecked in a storm that struck her in December of 1919. [2]

QUEEN OF THE WEST ■ Sidewheel steamer of 146 t., launched in 1851 at Oswego, NY
Lake Ontario: In July of 1853 this steamer was destroyed by fire at Hamilton, Ontario. [1]

QUEEN OF THE WEST ■ Bulk freight steam barge of 876 t. and 215 ft., launched in 1881 at Bay City, MI
Lake Erie: The QUEEN OF THE WEST was the subject of a somewhat unusual rescue, ten miles northwest of Fairport, Ohio. On August 20, 1903, she was carrying a cargo of iron ore in a mild blow when she sprang a fatal leak in the after portion of the hull and was in danger of sinking. Her skipper discovered that if he kept her running full ahead, the leak was slowed. When a rescue craft finally arrived, it had to take the steamer's crew off while she was still moving at top speed. One man died in the transfer, and as the water rising in her hull reached the QUEEN's fires, she lost power, slowed to a stop and sank. [5+]

QUINTE ■ Wooden passenger and package freight steamer of 331 t. and 138 ft., launched in 1871 at Quebec as the steamer BEAUHARNOIS
Lake Ontario: On October 23, 1889, the steamer QUINTE was destroyed by a fire on Grassy Point, near Deseronto, Ontario. When discovered to be ablaze well offshore, the steamer made a wild run to the beach. She arrived in time to save most of her crew, but four perished in the accident. [3]

QUITO ■ Wooden bulk freight steamer of 1,395 t. and 215 ft., launched in 1873 at Bangor, MI (now part of Bay City) as the steamer DAVID BALLENTINE
Lake Erie: Laden with a cargo of iron ore, this freighter had travelled two thirds of the length of the Great Lakes, only to be destroyed at the very mouth of the harbor for which she was bound. On November 23, 1902, she was driven on the breakwater at Lorain, Ohio, by a storm. She broke up in place. [5]

LUCY RAAB ■ Merchant schooner
Lake Huron: In 1862 this sailing vessel was reported to have run hard aground on a reef near Middle Island, on the Michigan shore, and sunk. [1]

JOHN RABER ■ Merchant schooner of 224 t. and 116 ft., launched in 1848 at Cleveland as the schooner GENERAL WORTH
Lake Michigan: Travelling in ballast, the schooner JOHN RABER foundered on September 30, 1895 at an unreported position. One crewmember died as she went down. [2]

RACER ■ Merchant brig
Lake Huron: Hammond Bay, at the eastern end of the Straits of Mackinac, was the site of the loss of this sailing ship in 1869. She stranded in shallow water and broke up. [1]

RACINE ■ Propeller or schooner of 150 t.
Lake Erie: Eight seamen lost their lives in the 1849 wreck of the RACINE. The ship was probably lost in a wild gale off Rondeau Point, though one source says she was destroyed by fire. [2]

RACINE ■ Merchant schooner of 168 t. and 106 ft. launched in 1844 at Cleveland
Lake Huron: The schooner RACINE was downbound with a cargo of lumber when she was lost on Whiskey Harbor Reef, northwest of Port Hope, Michigan. The ship sank on July 3, 1892. [3]

RACINE ■ Scow
Lake Michigan: Laden with a cargo of stone, the scow RACINE was lost on August 19, 1893, when she sank near the harbor entrance at Two Rivers, Wisconsin. [1]

RADIANT ■ Merchant schooner
Lake Erie: All that is known about this wreck is that she was lost on the lake with all ten hands. [1]

R H RAE ■ Merchant bark of 344 t. and 137 ft., launched in 1857 at St. Catharine's, Ont.
Lake Ontario: The crew of this three-master managed to escape when the ship capsized and sank in a white squall on August 3, 1858. [3]

RAINBOW ■ Merchant schooner
Lake Erie: In August of 1837, the schooner RAINBOW stranded and was lost near Put-in-Bay, on South Bass Island. [1]

RAINBOW ■ Lumber schooner of 257 t. and 125 ft., launched in 1855 at Buffalo
Lake Michigan: This schooner went down off Chicago, seven miles out from the mouth of the Chicago River on May 18, 1894. [3]

RAINBOW ■ Tug of 16 t. and 53 ft.
Detroit River: June 10, 1927, was the date of the destruction of this tug by fire. She was discovered to be ablaze and was beached on Peche Island, where she burned down to the sand. [1]

RALEIGH ■ Merchant schooner
Lake Huron: In 1869 this schooner was lost at Portage Bay, on the north side of Manitoulin Island. [1]

RALEIGH ■ Wooden bulk freight steamer of 1,205 t. and 227 ft., launched in 1871 at Cleveland
Lake Erie: One of the worst disasters that can befall a storm-distressed vessel is to lose her rudder. Without this means of steering, a ship would be at the mercy of wind and wave, unable to veer away from hazards or even head into the weather. The steamer RALEIGH broke her rudder in a storm that set upon her on November 30, 1911. With her control gone, the vessel drifted helplessly ashore five miles east of Port Colborne, Ontario, and was destroyed by the pounding of waves. [4]

P J RALPH ■ Wooden bulk freight steamer of 965 t. and 211 ft., launched in 1889 at Marine City, MI
Lake Michigan: Laden with a cargo of lumber, the old steamer P J RALPH was struck by a storm on September 8, 1924. She was driven aground on the west side of South Manitou Island, where she broke up in place. [5]

JANE RALSTON ■ Lumber schooner of 261 t. and 137 ft., launched in 1866 at Gibraltar, MI
Lake Erie: The schooner JANE RALSTON was lost on July 21, 1910, on the western end of the lake. She sprang a leak, became waterlogged, and sank. Raised and towed into Sandusky for assessment, it was decided that the old hull was too far gone to repair economically, and the vessel was abandoned. [3]

RAMBLER ■ Vessel information unavailable
Lake Ontario: One rather sketchy report describes the RAMBLER as having "gone missing" on the lake with all hands. [1]

GEORGE F RAND ■ Propeller
Detroit River: On April 3, 1935, the steamer GEORGE F RAND ran aground on Peche Island, on the channel side. She was thought to be a routine, straight-off pull, but when the tug PATRIARCH began to drag her off, the RAND capsized and sank. She was laden with a cargo of limestone at the time of her demise. [1]

H RAND ■ Lumber schooner of 124 t. and 110 ft., launched in 1856 at Manitowoc, WI
Lake Michigan: Four lives were lost in the disaster which also destroyed the H RAND. On May 24, 1901, the schooner was off Manitowoc, Wisconsin, when she capsized and sank. [3]

JOHN RANDALL ■ Wooden bulk freight steamer of 194 t. and 104 ft., launched in 1905 at Kingston, Ont.
Lake Ontario: A terrific gale that swept the whole length of the lake caught this coal-carrying steamer unawares near Main Duck Island on November 17, 1920. The ship was simply overwhelmed, and broke up and sank. Her crew was able to abandon in the lifeboat and make their way to Main Duck. Their troubles were not over, however, as they had to survive freezing, windy conditions for more than a week before they were rescued. [2]

RAPHAEL ■ Freight barge
Lake Erie: The RAPHAEL was in tow of the tug SUPERIOR and carrying a cargo of steel goods when she was lost on July 12, 1966. The vessel sank when her cargo shifted and she heeled over too far. She went down 25 miles off Fairport Harbor, Ohio. One source says all crewmen were saved from the sinking vessel, while the other states that 26 persons died (this seems excessive, for a barge). [2]

RAPID CITY ■ 39 t. vessel of unreported type
Lake Ontario: This vessel foundered eight miles off Toronto on August 31, 1917. [1]

RAPPAHANNOCK ■ Wooden bulk freight steamer of 2,380 t. and 307 ft., launched in 1895 at W Bay City, MI
Lake Superior: Hard-pressed by a gale that struck her on July 25, 1911, this steamer struggled to shore to keep from sinking. Although the maneuver put her on the beach near Jackfish Point and saved her crew, the steamer was still lost, pounded to pieces by high waves. [2]

E W RATHBURNE ■ Merchant schooner, 200 t. and 149 ft.
Lake Huron: The schooner E W RATHBURNE went down in an October 9, 1886, gale, offshore from Goderich, Ontario. Her crew was able to make it to shore safely. [3]

ANNIE C RAYNOR ■ Merchant schooner
Lake Huron: This schooner grounded on Middle Island (northeast of Alpena, Michigan) and broke up, in 1863. [1]

WILLIAM RAYNOR ■ Merchant schooner
Lake Huron: The schooner WILLIAM RAYNOR reportedly foundered off Lexington, Michigan, in 1883. [1]

RAZEL BROS. ■ Fishing tug of 30 ft.
Lake Michigan: The little fishing tug RAZEL BROS. was sunk when she was either run down by or swamped by the wake of the big Yugoslav package freighter JABLONICA. Three died when the vessel sank off Charlevoix, Michigan, on August 20, 1986. [3]

REBECCA ■ Merchant schooner
Lake Huron: In 1872 the schooner REBECCA sank while under tow off Alabaster, Michigan. She was being towed down the lake for repairs from the site of an earlier wreck she suffered near Detour, Michigan. [1]

REBEL ■ Tug
Lake Superior: On October 25, 1898, this tug was lost off Two Harbors, Minnesota, when she sprang a leak in a gale and sank. [1]

RECORD ■ Steel steam tug of 59 t. and 68 ft., launched in 1884 at Cleveland
Lake Superior: The tug RECORD was involved in three separate fatal collisions in Duluth-Superior harbor in a four year period. On June 2, 1898, she was rammed and sunk by the steamer R L FULTON with the loss of three lives. On October 8, 1899, she was sunk again after being rammed by the steamer JAS. B NEILSON, this time with one life lost. Her final accident was on November 7, 1902, when she was run down by the steamer BRANSFORD, again with one life lost. The tug still lies on the bottom of the harbor from the last accident. [4]

RECOVERY ■ Sailing vessel (probably a schooner) of 90 t. launched in 1812
Lake Superior: The tall ship RECOVERY was reported wrecked and broken up on the beach near Fort William, Ontario, in 1820. [1]

RED BOTTOM ■ Mechant schooner
Lake Huron: In 1876 this schooner foundered on a reef near Middle Island, on the northwest shore of the lake. [1]

RED CLOUD ■ Tug
Lake Erie: This tug was lost on September 3 or 4 of 1899 when she was caught in a gale, thrown on a reef and broken in half near Cedar Point, Ohio. [2]

RED WHITE & BLUE ■ Merchant schooner of 447 t. and 157 ft., launched in 1863 at Madison Dock, OH
Lake Michigan: Whaleback Shoal, in Green Bay, was the final resting place of the schooner RED WHITE & BLUE when she stranded and broke up there in October of 1895. [2]

REDBIRD ■ Scow of 39 t.
Lake Erie: No date is given for the sinking of this vessel 12 miles northeast of Fairport Harbor, Ohio. [1]

C E REDFERN ■ Bulk freight motor ship of 680 t. and 190 ft., launched as a schooner at W Bay City, MI, in 1890
Lake Michigan: While outbound with a load of pulpwood, this motor vessel foundered in a heavy gale. The September 19, 1937, accident happened four miles off Point Betsie, near Frankfort, Michigan. The crew was rescued by the carferry ANN ARBOR #4. This and the reported Lake Huron wreck "Redfern," are probably one and the same. [5]

ELIZA J REDFORD ■ Steam tug of 35 t. and 59 ft., launched in 1881 at Oswego, NY
Lake Ontario: The tug ELIZA J REDFORD was lost at Oswego on November 16, 1893. She was trying to leave the harbor to rescue a distressed schooner in a blinding snowstorm, but lost her way and rammed a pier. The vessel then just exploded and sank. Somehow, only one life was lost, even though the tug was totally destroyed. [2]

CHARLES REED ■ Steam tug of 44 t. and 68 ft., launched in 1868 at Sandusky
Lake Erie: In 1922 this tug was destroyed by fire at Erie, Pennsylvania. [1]

FRANK REED ■ Tug
Lake Huron: November of 1899 saw the loss of this tug, wrecked near Barrie Island in the North Channel. [2]

JAMES H REED ■ Steel bulk freight steamer of 7,500 t. and 440 ft., launched in 1903 at Wyandotte, MI
Lake Erie: Fog was the culprit in the loss of this veteran freighter on April 27, 1944. She was approximately 20 miles north of Conneaut, Ohio, off Long Point, and was carrying a cargo of ore and stone when she met her end. Her path intersected that of the 550 foot steel steamer ASHCROFT and the two vessels collided, with the REED being struck broadside. The REED sank so quickly that 12 of her 35 crewmen were trapped below and drowned as she went down. She sank in relatively shallow water and it was later necessary to dynamite her as an obstruction. [5+]

KITTY or **ERMA B REEVES** ■ Merchant schooner
Lake Huron: Tawas Bay has been used as a harbor of refuge for as long as sailing vessels have been plying the Lakes. On November 7, 1870, the KITTY REEVES, down-bound with a load of high-grade copper ore, came around the point and dropped anchor in hopes of riding out a gale. However, she was blown down by high winds and foundered a few miles offshore. Her crew took to her boat, but they disappeared to those on shore and were presumed lost. The men, however were blown along by the gale, and after two days of rowing, fetched up on Point Lookout, 15 miles to the south. A number of expeditions have gone after the REEVES' valuable cargo, with varying degrees of success. [4]

REGINA ■ Merchant schooner of 118 t. and 75 ft.
Lake Huron: On October 22, 1881, this small schooner was lost in Georgian Bay. She was carrying a cargo of salt when she was overwhelmed by a storm and sank near the Cove Island lighthouse. [4]

REGINA ■ Steel bulk freight steamer of 2,957 t. and 269 ft., launched in Dumbarton, Scotland, in 1907
Lake Huron: The Big Storm of November, 1913, had swept into the lower end of the lake on the 9th, paralyzing Port Huron and other lake towns with huge snowdrifts and 70 to 80 mph winds. By the night of the 10th-11th, the lake had been whipped into a maelstrom of mountainous waves and blinding snow, and a number of large steamboats were in jeopardy. The smallest steamer that had ventured out into the area was the canal-sized freighter REGINA, carrying a load of steel pipe. Almost new, the sturdy Scots-built vessel had no reason to believe that she would be unduly troubled by the gale. But sometime during the night the "grandfather storm" proved her wrong. She went down with all 20 hands, a few miles off Harbor Beach, Michigan. Exactly what happened can only be surmised. She probably met up with the doomed steamer CHARLES S PRICE (qv)—or her wreckage—and then struggled on into the gale. Or perhaps the REGINA sank, and then the PRICE encountered her floating crew. In any case, when the wreckage of ships and crews were being sadly tallied, crewmen from the PRICE were found to have wandered ashore wearing life vests from the lost REGINA. The wreckage of the ship was located by divers in 1985. [5+]

REGULATOR ■ Merchant schooner of 121 t.
Lake Michigan: Carrying a load of general merchandise, the schooner REGULATOR was stranded and broken up, probably by a storm, in November of 1883. The accident occurred near St. Joseph, Michigan, and one life was lost. [1]

JAMES REID ■ Screw tug of 115 t. and 87 ft., launched in 1863 at Sandusky, OH, as the steamer GENERAL BURNSIDE
Lake Michigan: In 1887, this tug was reported lost to fire at Sturgeon Bay, but a more specific description of this location is not given. [1]

JAMES REID ■ Propeller freighter of 123 t. and 117 ft., launched in 1875 at Wilmington, DE as the steamer PROTECTOR
Lake Huron: The loss of this small steamer occurred at Byng Inlet, in Georgian Bay, on August 21, 1917. She reportedly foundered, though the cause in not given. [4]

KATE REID ■ Steam tug
Lake Huron: The KATE REID was destroyed by fire at Saginaw, Michigan, on the Saginaw River, in 1873. [1]

R P REIDENBACH ■ Tug
Lake Erie: This tug capsized and sank in the harbor at Ashtabula, Ohio, on October 28, 1929 (1939 is also given), with the loss of two lives. [2]

REINDEER ■ Sidewheel passenger and package freight steamer
Lake Michigan: An early Lake Michigan disaster about which little is known is the loss of the sidewheeler REINDEER on October 21, 1842. The steamer was carrying a cargo of flour, wheat and tallow when she sank. She foundered off Big Sable Point with the loss of 21 passengers and crew. The location is also given as Au Sable Point, on Lake Huron. [3]

REINDEER ■ Propeller of 136 ft., launched in 1848 at Portsmouth, Ont. as the steamer COMMERCE (qv)
Lake Michigan: In November of 1857, this steamer was said to have gone down on Lake Michigan. [1]

REINDEER ■ Merchant schooner, probably the 191 t., 111 ft. vessel of this name launched in 1860 at Clayton, NY
Lake Huron: A specific year is not given for the loss of the REINDEER at Port Huron, but she reportedly sank at her dock in the late 1800s. [2]

REINDEER ■ Bulk freight schooner of 43 t. probably the vessel of this size and name launched in 1853 at Fairport, OH
Lake Michigan: This little schooner sank offshore from Lincoln Park, Illinois, on November 3, 1879. [2]

REINDEER ■ Barge
Lake Huron: The barge REINDEER sank off 40-mile Point, above Rogers (now Rogers City), Michigan, in 1895. She reportedly foundered in a northeast gale. [1]

REINDEER ■ Merchant schooner of 450 t.
Lake Erie: In May of 1895 the schooner REINDEER, running in ballast, was reported in trouble and abandoned to sink off Cleveland. [1]

REINDEER ■ Vessel information unavailable
Lake Ontario: A single report states that this vessel went missing on the lake, with all hands. [1]

WILLIAM A REISS ■ Steel bulk freight steamer of 450 ft. overall, launched as the steamer FRANK H PEAVY in 1901 at Lorain, OH
Lake Michigan: A gale caused the demise of this big steamer in a more indirect way than is usually the case. The REISS was carrying a cargo of coal when she grounded in a moderate gale off the south pier at Sheboygan, WI. Her cargo was lightered, but the vessel, which was nearing the end of her useful life, was scrapped and cut up in place. The date of the grounding was Nov. 14, 1934. [2]

RELIABLE ■ Bulk freight schooner-barge of 84 t. and 91 ft., launched in 1870 at Detroit
Lake Michigan: The RELIABLE was carrying her usual cargo of sand when she encountered a dense fog and heavy seas off the Wisconsin shore in August of 1913. Her cargo may have shifted, or she might have turned sideways to the high waves, but she capsized and sank 2.5 miles southeast of Milwaukee. [3]

RELIANCE ■ Supply vessel and tug of 124 ft. and 311 t., launched in 1892 at Collingwood, Ont.
Lake Superior: The RELIANCE was transporting supplies, passengers, and a group of lumberjacks along a remote part of the Ontario shore of the lake when she went aground on Lizard Island on December 15, 1922. The 34 persons aboard were trapped on the little vessel in an arctic gale with temperatures plunging as low as -18° F. Four people died before a rescue could be accomplished. One source says the RELIANCE was recovered, although she drops off Canadian registry at this point. [3]

RELIEF ■ Tug
Lake Huron: The tug RELIEF was reported destroyed by fire on the Saginaw River in 1867. [1]

RELIEVER ■ Wooden bulk freight steamer of 1,131 t. and 216 ft., launched in 1888 at W Bay City, MI as the steamer GERMANIC
Lake Huron: On November 3, 1906, the freighter RELIEVER stranded on Methodist Point (south of Giant's Tomb Island), caught fire and was destroyed. [4]

REMORA ■ Propeller freighter of 184 t. and 100 ft., launched in 1883 at Detroit
Lake Huron: The REMORA was battling a storm in the Straits of Mackinac in 1892 when she caught fire, burned and sank off St. Ignace, Michigan. [3]

WILLIAM P REND ■ Wooden bulk freight barge of 2,323 t. and 287 ft., launched in 1888 at W Bay City, MI as the steamer GEORGE G HADLEY
Lake Huron: The big barge WILLIAM P REND had just picked up a load of limestone and was downbound on October 2, 1917, when she was driven aground near Alpena, Michigan. No lives were lost, but the REND was dismantled where she sat by the destructive action of waves. [5+]

RESOLUTE ■ Barge
Lake Erie: An early season storm caused the loss of this barge and two members of her crew. The RESOLUTE foundered off Long Point on March 14, 1887. [1]

RESTLESS ■ Sloop of 7 t. and 31 ft., launched in 1889 at Cleveland
Lake Erie: This tiny sail vessel was reported to have foundered off Rocky River, Ohio, with no loss of life on July 30, 1908. [2]

RESUMPTION ■ Lumber schooner of 294 t. and 143 ft., launched in 1879 at Milwaukee
Lake Michigan: The combination of big waves and a dangerous channel spelled the end for this ship on November 7, 1914. Carrying a cargo of lumber, the outbound schooner RESUMPTION was fighting heavy seas when she struck bottom and stranded on Plum Island, in the Death's Door Passage. She was subsequently broken up by waves. [3]

REUTAN ■ Steam freighter
Lake Michigan: In 1886, this steamer was reported to have stranded and been broken up somewhere on the northern part of the lake. [1]

REVELRY ■ Sloop (former yacht?)
Lake Huron: The single mast sail vessel REVELRY was reportedly sunk off Rogers City, Michigan, in 1975. [1]

GEORGE E REYNOLDS ■ Steam freighter
Lake Huron: Fire destroyed the steamer GEORGE E REYNOLDS at Bay City, Michigan, on the Saginaw River, in 1872. [1]

RHINE ■ Gas screw packet of 12 t. and 39 ft., launched in 1904 at Manitowoc, WI
Lake Michigan: A late-season run ended in disaster for this little vessel and her four-man crew. The little packet foundered in a storm off Frankfort, Michigan, on December 26, 1904, with all hands. [2]

RHODES ■ Merchant schooner
Lake Huron: Another of the nearly 30 vessels lost in the October 20, 1905 storm, was the schooner RHODES. She went down well offshore at an unrecorded position. [2]

ROBERT R RHODES ■ Wooden bulk freight steamer of 1,576 t. and 246 ft., launched in 1887 at Cleveland
Lake Ontario: The steamer ROBERT R RHODES was at a ripe age when she had her fatal accident in 1921. She was ready for either rebuilding or scrapping. On October 24, the steamer was transitting the Welland Canal when she struck a bridge and sank. The vessel was damaged beyond economical repair, and was towed to a beach on the New York shore of Lake Ontario and scuttled as an anti-erosion measure. [3]

JOHN RICE ■ Merchant schooner of 153 t. and 107 ft., launched in 1860 at Newport (Marine City), MI
Lake Huron: The small schooner JOHN RICE foundered in a storm off Thunder Bay Island., near the Michigan shore, in July of 1893. [3]

R N RICE ■ Freight barge of 1,096 t. and 247 ft., launched in 1866 at Detroit as a sidewheel passenger steamer
Lake Michigan: This vessel was an elegant and popular passenger steamer on Lake Erie until a fire ended her glory days in 1877. Reduced to a barge, she worked all over the Lakes until she met her end on a beach four miles north of Holland, Michigan. On October 3, 1888, she became waterlogged in a storm, drifted ashore and was abandoned. The sketch shows her as she looked as a steamer. [4]

A J RICH ■ Merchant schooner
Lake Huron: In 1864, the schooner A J RICH went ashore and was wrecked near Kincardine, Ontario. [2]

C RICH ■ Bulk freight schooner-scow of 40 t., built at Fairport, OH, in 1853
Lake Erie: A November 9, 1879, storm pushed this shallow-draft vessel ashore near Marblehead, above Sandusky, Ohio. The little schooner-scow was pounded to pieces on the beach. One source gives 1897 as the date of this accident. [3]

RICHARD H ■ Fishing tug of 19 t.
Lake Michigan: One of two commercial fishing vessels lost near the south end of the lake in the 1940 Armistice Day Storm, the RICHARD H sailed out of South Haven, Michigan, on November 11, and was never seen again. Three men perished when the vessel was lost. See also INDIAN. [3]

HENRY C RICHARDS ■ Merchant schooner of 700 t. and 189 ft., launched in 1873 at Manitowoc
Lake Michigan: On October 6, 1895, the schooner HENRY C RICHARDS foundered at an unreported position on the lake. [3]

J S RICHARDS ■ Merchant schooner of 273 t. and 137 ft., launched in 1869 at Conneaut, OH
Detroit River: This small carrier was moving her cargo of pig iron down the river on August 1, 1900, when she sank from unknown causes. Two of her crew were killed when she went down. The schooner was later recovered. [2]

MAY RICHARDS ■ Bulk freight schooner-barge of 511 t. and 161 ft., launched in 1881 at Manitowoc, WI
Lake Erie: The end came for this schooner on North Bass Island on October 6, 1906. On that date she stranded and went to pieces, a total loss. Her people all survived the accident. [2]

RICHARDSON ■ Bulk freight schooner of 162 t., launched in 1866 at Kingston, Ont.
Lake Ontario: Bouys and markers are often taken for granted by the weekend sailor. The necessity of them to commercial ships is demonstrated by the loss of the schooner RICHARDSON. On October 5, 1881, the little vessel was trying to enter the harbor at Oswego, New York, when she lost her bearings due to a failed marker light. The wooden vessel rammed a pier head-on, broke up and sank. Fortunately there was no loss of life. [2]

W C RICHARDSON ■ Steel bulk freight steamer of 3,818 t. and 324 ft., launched in 1902 at Cleveland
Lake Erie: Five of the 19 persons aboard the steamer W C RICHARDSON on December 9, 1909, did not survive her fatal accident. She was carrying a cargo of flax in an apalling storm when she ran hard up on Waverly Shoal, near Buffalo. Before anything could be done about her situation, waves pivoted her off the edge of the reef and she capsized and sank. [5+]

C V RICHMOND ■ Tug
Lake Huron: No specific position is given for the loss of this tug—said to have sunk well offshore—in 1868. [1]

DEAN RICHMOND ■ Merchant schooner built at Cleveland
Lake Michigan: Not much is known about the loss of this two-masted ship except that she was driven ashore in a gale and broken up before 1855. Possibly she was recovered later. [2]

DEAN RICHMOND ■ Merchant schooner
Lake Superior: One man died when the DEAN RICHMOND caught fire, burned and sank near Sault Ste. Marie in 1871. [2]

DEAN RICHMOND ■ Propeller passenger and package freighter of 1,432 t. and 238 ft., launched in 1864 at Cleveland
Lake Erie: Carrying a cargo of zinc ingots, the steamer DEAN RICHMOND went to pieces offshore and sank in a gale. She went down off Dunkirk, New York, on October 14, 1893. All 15 to 23 of her crew were lost with the big ship. [5]

DEAN RICHMOND ■ Sidewheel steamer of 1,400 t.
Lake Huron: This rather cryptic report says that the sidewheeler DEAN RICHMOND burned and was beached in the St. Marys River, below the Soo. [1]

KATE RICHMOND ■ Merchant schooner
Lake Huron: In 1885, this schooner sank northeast of Lexington, Michigan. [1]

RISING SUN ■ Wooden passenger and freight steamer of 477 t. and 140 ft., launched in 1884 at Detroit as the steamer MINNIE M
Lake Michigan: This steamer was said to be the only large vessel on the lakes ever to be owned and operated by a religious sect. It was managed by the House of David group out of Benton Harbor. On October 29, 1917, the steamer was hauling a cargo of lumber and live trees when she was attacked by a violent storm near the northern end of the lake, and was driven aground south of Pyramid Point (Michigan). No lives were lost. The RISING SUN was broken up in place by the action of waves, but it is said that her wreckage can still be seen from the bluff above the site. [5+]

H W RITCHIE ■ Wooden bulk freight steamer of 447 t. and 161 ft., launched in 1880 at Grand Haven, MI as the steamer STEVEN C HALL
Lake Superior: September 27, 1921, was the date of the loss of this steamer to fire at the northwest end of the lake. The RITCHIE was docked in the harbor at Port Arthur, Ontario, when she was destroyed. No one was aboard her at the time of her loss. The steamer's wreckage was recovered in 1961. As the HALL, she had stranded with serious damage at Sand Beach, Michigan, in 1884. [5+]

RIVERSIDE ■ Merchant schooner of 278 t. and 133 ft., launched in 1870 at Oswego, NY
Lake Ontario: Reports say that this vessel was carrying a cargo of limestone when she was lost on the lake in 1893. No loss of life was reported officially, but some say five men perished in the accident. A vessel of the same name was listed as wrecked in upper Lake Michigan in 1887, and may be the same RIVERSIDE. [4]

ROAMER ■ Trolling boat of 30 ft.
Lake Superior: One man died of nine aboard this fishing vessel when she swamped and sank in a sudden squall in the Munising West Channel on July 3, 1949. [1]

ROAMER ■ Fishing tug of 42 ft.
Lake Superior: On July 9, 1975, the fishing vessel ROAMER was destroyed in a boathouse fire at Port Wing, Wisconsin. [1]

ROANOAKE ■ Merchant schooner of 161 t. and 92 ft., launched in 1843 at Euclid, OH
Lake Huron: The little sailing ship ROANOAKE was lost on October 27, 1866, when she was blown down and sunk by high winds in Thunder Bay, near Alpena, Michigan. [2]

ROANOAKE ■ Wooden steamer of 1,070 t. and 218 ft., launched in 1867 at Cleveland
Lake Superior: No lives were lost, but the steamer ROANOAKE was completely destroyed in an offshore fire which occurred on August 7, 1894. The ship burned and sank in fine weather, off 14-mile Point, northeast of Ontonagon, Michigan. [4]

ROB ROY ■ Merchant schooner-barge of 470 t. and 144 ft., launched in 1847 at Acton, OH
Lake Erie: The ROB ROY was wrecked and sunk in a storm four miles off Erie, Pennsylvania, on September 17, 1912. [2]

ROBERT K ■ Tug of 39 t.
Lake Huron: The Georgian Bay port of Tobermory, Ontario, was the site of the loss of this tug on June 23, 1935. She reportedly caught fire at her dock and burned through her hawsers to drift away and sink on nearby rocks. [3]

ROBERVAL ■ Steel bulk freight steamer of 157 t. and 128 ft., launched in 1907 at Toronto
Lake Ontario: On September 25, 1916, the small steel steamer ROBERVAL was lost 12 miles off Oswego, New York, when she was simply dismantled by a storm and sank. [3]

MARY ROBINSON ▪ Propeller
Lake Michigan: No date is given for the loss of this steamer seven miles off Michigan City, Indiana, when she burned and sank. [1]

GEORGE W ROBY ▪ Bulk freight barge of 1,843 t. and 281 ft., launched in 1889 at W Bay City, MI, as a steamer
St. Marys River: The GEORGE W ROBY had been heavily damaged by a fire the year before her fatal accident, and had been converted to a barge upon rebuilding. She was moving up the river with her holds full of coal on November 14, 1906, when her volatile cargo caught fire. The ship was totally destroyed and sank near Lime Kiln Crossing. The sketch shows her as a steamer. The location of the accident is also reported as the Detroit River. [2]

ROCHESTER ▪ Freight barge of 472 t., launched in 1837 at Richmond City (near Fairport), OH, as a sidewheel steamer
Lake Erie: In November of 1852 the barge ROCHESTER sank eight miles east of North Girard, PA. Seven of her crew perished in the accident. [1]

ROCK QUEEN ▪ Steamer of 94 t.
Lake Huron: Two reports show a 100-year variance concerning the date of the loss of this little steamer near Port Sanilac. She was driven on the rocks ten miles north of town by a storm, and was fatally holed. One reference says she went down on November 18, 1956, while the other gives 1856 as the year. [2]

ROCKAWAY ▪ Merchant schooner
Lake Huron: The schooner ROCKAWAY was lost offshore from Goderich, Ontario, in the year 1858. [1]

ROCKAWAY ▪ Merchant schooner of 164 t. and 106 ft., launched in 1866 at Oswego, NY
Lake Michigan: A November gale destroyed this small schooner off South Haven, Michigan, in 1891. She was carrying lumber when she broke up and sank in heavy seas on the 18th. [3]

ROCKAWAY ▪ Fishing tug (net boat)
Lake Superior: All four of this fisher's crew died when the ROCKAWAY was lost off Grand Marais, Michigan, on July 3, 1945. She went down in a sudden and very violent northwest squall. [3]

ROCKET ▪ Merchant schooner, launched in 1856 at Buffalo
Lake Huron: A collision ended the career of this schooner in 1860. She was sunk north of Pte Aux Barques, MI. [2]

L R ROCKWELL ▪ Merchant schooner of 115 t., launched before 1847
Lake Michigan: The schooner L R ROCKWELL was reported to have been wrecked near Muskegon, Michigan, In 1855. [1]

HENRY RODNEY ▪ Merchant brig of 295 t.
Lake Ontario: One man died when this small square-rigger foundered three miles east of Charlotte, New York (near Rochester). She was laden with a cargo of limestone and wood lath when she went down on October 24, 1879. [1]

E A ROE ▪ Merchant schooner
Lake Ontario: Braddock Point, northwest of Rochester, New York, snagged this schooner on October 18, 1899, when she struck bottom there and foundered in a storm. She may have been recovered and rebuilt. [2]

MARQUIS ROEN ▪ Small steamer built about 1928
Lake Huron: The little steamer MARQUIS ROEN had a short career, then burned on the Saginaw River at Bay City, Michigan, in 1932. Plans were made to rebuild her, but they never came to anything, and the vessel just rotted away on the banks of the river. [2]

ALIDA JANE ROGERS ▪ Merchant schooner of 340 t. and 138 ft., launched in 1862 at Charlotte, NY (one source says Madison, OH)
Lake Michigan: The Old Mission Peninsula bisects lovely Grand Traverse Bay, on lower Michigan's northwest corner. This schooner was lost on a reef 4.5 miles off the tip of the peninsula in October of 1898. The ROGERS is sometimes called just ALIDA JANE. [3]

GEORGE ROGERS ▪ Steam tug of 64 t. and 77 ft., launched in 1889 at Toledo
Lake Michigan: The tug GEORGE ROGERS was reportedly destroyed by fire and sank south of the Grand Traverse Light, near Cat Head Point, in August of 1913. [2]

ROLAND ▪ Bulk freight steam barge of 124 t. and 108 ft., launched in 1885 at Sandusky, OH
Lake Erie: The small "rabbit" ROLAND was reported to have foundered off Green Island, in 1892. [1]

ROME ▪ Wooden package freight steamer of 1,847 t. and 265 ft., launched in 1879 at Cleveland as the steamer CHICAGO
Lake Huron: This big freighter was operating in her first year under new owners when she caught fire on the St. Marys River, burned and sank near Lime Island, east of Raber, Michigan. The ship was lost on November 17, 1909. [3]

CITY OF ROME ■ Wooden bulk freight steamer of 1,908 t. and 268 ft. launched in 1881 at Cleveland
Lake Erie: On May 6, 1914, the steamer CITY OF ROME was without cargo and moving along the south shore of the lake above Ripley, New York, when she caught fire and was destroyed. She sank close to shore, and it is said that her machinery is still visible just below the surface. [4]

RUSSEL ROQUE ■ Tug of 27 t.
Lake Huron: The tug RUSSEL ROQUE caught fire at Gore Bay, on the north side of Manitoulin Island, and was destroyed on August 16, 1931. [2]

ROSA BELLE ■ Merchant schooner of 132 t. and 100 ft., launched in 1863 at Milwaukee
Lake Michigan: In a somewhat mysterious accident, the little two-master ROSA BELLE was found floating upside-down in the middle of the lake in 1875 by a ferry steamer. Her crew of 10 were missing, and no evidence was found of what may have happened to her. She was towed in and returned to service. [3]
Lake Michigan: There was no mystery about the final demise of the ROSA BELLE. Again in the middle of the lake, the schooner was set upon by a gale and sank with all hands on October 20, 1921. She may be the only vessel in Lakes history ever to lose two entire crews. [3]

ROSE ■ Merchant schooner
Lake Huron: The schooner ROSE was reported lost on Georgian Bay in 1851. [1]

ROSE ■ Propeller of 121 t. and 104 ft., launched in 1869 at Kingston, Ont.
This small prop was recorded as lost to fire in 1887, but no details are available. [1]

ROSEDALE ■ Steamer
Lake Huron: The Charity Islands, in northern Saginaw Bay, were the site of the wreck of this steamer in 1897. She may have been recovered. [1]

ELLA ROSS ■ Sidewheel steamer of 228 t. and 99 ft., launched at Montreal in 1873 under another name (unknown)
Lake Huron: A fire at her dock caused the end of this small sidewheeler in June of 1912. She was destroyed at Parry Sound, Ontario, in eastern Georgian Bay. [2]

LEWIS ROSS ■ Merchant schooner of 212 t.
Lake Erie: On September 19, 1889, the LEWIS ROSS was struck by a storm and pushed ashore near Rondeau, Ontario, harbor. She later fell off into deep water and was lost. [2]

MYRTIE M ROSS ■ Wooden bulk freight steamer of 128 t. and 113 ft., launched in 1890 at South Haven, MI
Lake St. Clair: The little steamer MYRTIE M ROSS sprang a leak, became waterlogged, and sank near Gull Island in 1913. [3]

A ROSSITER ■ Propeller freighter of 200 ft., built prior to 1847
Lake Michigan: This early steamer is reported to have been lost on the lake in 1855, but her position is unknown. [1]

ROTARIAN ■ Sidewheel excursion steamer of 422 t. and 149 ft., launched in 1889 at Sandusky, OH as the steamer A WEHRLE, Jr.
Lake Michigan: There is some confusion about the ultimate demise of this well-known vessel. According to some sources, she was scrapped in 1929, but others say that she sank or was scuttled 12 miles off Chicago in September of 1931 or 1932. [4]

W H ROUNDS ■ Package and bulk freight schooner of 308 t. and 138 ft., launched in 1875 at Tonawanda, NY
Lake Huron: Black River Reef is located about eight miles north of Harrisville, Michigan, and a half mile offshore. On May 2, 1905, when the W H ROUNDS stranded on the reef and broke up, it was a largely uninhabited area, and it took some time for news of the wreck to reach the ship's owners. Today the area is part of State and National Forests, is still sparsely populated, and the wreckage of the ROUNDS still lies below the reef. One source says this ship was lost in the November 9-12 storm of the same year. [4]

ROVER ■ Merchant sloop of 7 t. and 36 ft., launched in 1897 at Alexandria Bay, NY
Lake Ontario: This tiny vessel was stranded and wrecked on Galoo Island, near the eastern end of the lake, on November 19, 1915. [2]

ROY ■ Tug of 88 t. and 79 ft.
Lake Erie: The wooden hull of this large tug was cut by ice in 1895 and she sank 1.5 miles east of Stony Point, at the extreme western end of the lake. [1]

E P ROYCE ■ Merchant schooner of 249 t. and 124 ft., built in 1873 at Sac Bay, Michigan
Lake Michigan: In November of 1893 this schooner stranded on a reef near Cana Island, Wisconsin, and was lost in a gale. [1]

J S RUBY ■ Propeller steamer of 128 t. and 107 ft., launched in 1888 at Fair Haven, MI
St. Clair River: The small steamer J S RUBY caught fire and went aground on Stag Island, where she burned to a total loss on November 10, 1891. [2]

GRACE A RUELLE ■ Packet steamer of 13 t. and 39 ft., launched at Buffalo in 1897 as the steam launch JOHN NICE
Lake Huron: One person died when the tiny GRACE A RUELLE was lost near Port Austin, Michigan, on July 29, 1899. [2]

JENNIE RUMBALL ■ Merchant schooner
Lake Huron: In 1882 the schooner JENNIE RUMBALL foundered well offshore from Goderich, Ontario. [1]

H E RUNNELS ■ Wooden bulk freight steamer of 889 t. and 178 ft., launched in 1893 at Port Huron, MI
Lake Superior: The steamer H E RUNNELS was bound for the Keweenaw with a cargo of coal when she had to pull in for shelter at Grand Marais, Michigan. When her skipper thought the gale had calmed a little, the steamer tried to continue her journey. But huge waves from a northeast storm drove her on a bar near the mouth of the harbor, and soon she was in real trouble, being slapped broadsides by tremendous seas. Local Coast Guard Lifesavers were hampered in their rescue attempts by the icy gale, which rendered both men and equipment inoperative. Finally, with the help of local fishermen and seamen from a Coast Guard subchaser sheltering nearby, the RUNNELS' crew was rescued from certain death by a magnificent combination of training and heroism on the part of the makeshift lifesaving crew. A half hour after they were all safely ashore, the steamer went to pieces. The accident occurred on November 14, 1919. [5+]

RURAL ■ Merchant schooner
Lake Huron: This schooner was lost on a reef near Caseville, Michigan, at the top of Saginaw Bay, when she stranded and broke up in 1873. [1]

RUSSELL ■ Merchant schooner
Lake Huron: Three lives were lost when this sail vessel sank in the St. Marys River following an 1882 collision with an unknown vessel. [1]

JOSEPH L RUSSELL ■ Tug of 200 t. and 121 ft., launched in 1888 at Windsor, Ont. as the passenger and freight steamer LAKESIDE
Lake Ontario: The the big tugboat JOSEPH L RUSSELL was lost on November 15, 1929. On that date, she was off Colborne, Ontario, when she was overwhelmed by a storm and foundered. [3]

ROY K RUSSEL ■ Iron tanker barge of 216 ft., launched as the 1,235 t. passenger steamer JAPAN in 1871 at Buffalo
Lake Ontario: 1934 was both happy and sad for the barge ROY K RUSSELL. It was happy because the vessel was operating on the Lakes for her 63rd year, but sad because 1934 was the year this proud old ship, operating as a tanker-barge, was to suffer an explosion and fire that retired her for good. She was one of the famous "Lake Triplets," three luxurious and almost identical passenger steamers named CHINA, JAPAN and INDIA. The JAPAN operated for almost 60 years as a passenger steamer before being converted to a barge in 1927. After the 1934 fire, her hull was still in good enough condition to be salvaged for its scrap value. [4]

RUSSIA ■ Bulk freight schooner of 133 t.
Lake Huron: The small schooner RUSSIA was sunk off the piers at Presque Isle, Michigan, on November 18, 1889. [1]

RUSSIA ■ Iron package freight steamer of 1,501 t. and 232 ft., launched in 1872 at Buffalo
Lake Huron: The steamer RUSSIA has been reported as carrying a valuable cargo when she was lost near Detour, Michigan, on April 30, 1909. On that date she was shouldering through a ferocious storm when her iron hull fractured and the vessel sank. Although most sources say all of her crew were rescued, at least two researchers say 13 were lost. A report of a vessel of the same name going down in the same area in 1860 is probably in error. [5+]

RUTH B ■ 31 t. vessel of unreported type
Lake St. Clair: On December 5, 1937, this little vessel struck a bridge on the Thames River below Chatham, Ontario, and sank. [1]

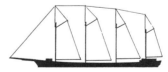

J H RUTTER ■ Bulk freight schooner of 1,200 t. and 212 ft., launched in 1873 at Marine City, MI
Lake Michigan: One of the largest sailing vessels ever to be used on the Great Lakes, this tall ship had a rather short career. On November 1 of 1878, the big four-master was bound for Chicago with her holds full of grain when she was blasted by a tremendous westerly gale. Her sails were quickly blown out and the ship was driven aground near Ludington, Michigan. With her bottom torn out, the

schooner rapidly sank up to her decks, while her crew clambered into the rigging. With the RUTTER going to pieces under them, the 44 men of the crew seemed to face inevitable doom at the hands of the lake. The local people who had accumulated to see the big schooner were not about to let the sailors die, and a rescue was hurriedly organized and bravely executed. Before it was over, all of the crewmen had been taken off by small boat. The giant J H RUTTER, however, was completely destroyed by the action of storm waves. [4]

RYAN ■ Steam freighter
Lake Huron: This steamer was lost in a gale which sent her ashore on Thunder Bay Island, near Alpena, Michigan. She was wrecked on June 12, 1890. [2]

A G RYAN ■ 111 t. vessel of unreported type
Lake Erie: Detailed information is lacking on this vessel, which reportedly sank in the Bay of Quinte on September 24, 1886. [1]

CHARLES C RYAN ■ Steam freighter of 491 t.
Lake Huron: In 1890, this steamer sank 20 miles off Pointe Aux Barques, Michigan, with her cargo of ice. One life was lost in the foundering, which occurred on June 7. One source gives 1875 as the year of this accident. [2]

CHARLES N RYAN ■ Merchant schooner of 412 ft. and 163 ft., launched in 1873 at Sandusky, OH
Lake Michigan: The schooner CHARLES N RYAN was lost when she sank north of the harbor entrance at Ludington, Michigan, on April 18, 1887. All of her crew escaped to safety. [3]

GENEVIEVE RYAN ■ Barge of 418 t.
Lake Erie: No date is given for the loss of this barge, which foundered between Erie, Pennsylvania, and Ashtabula, Ohio. [1]

SACHEM ■ Wooden steam sandsucker of 739 t. and 187 ft., launched in 1889 at Grand Haven
St. Clair River: On October 8 (one source says March 23), 1928, the sandsucker SACHEM was destroyed by fire near Port Lambton, Ontario. [3]

SACHEM ■ Steel tug of 100 t. and 71 ft., launched in 1907 at Buffalo as the tug JOHN KELDERHOUSE
Lake Erie: The reason for the loss of the sturdy tug SACHEM has never been determined with certainty. On December 18, 1950, the tug sank in fair weather some miles off Dunkirk, New York. Not one of the 12 sailors aboard lived to explain why she went down, but when she was recovered the following year, she was still in nearly perfect condition. The tug was reconditioned and was still in service, working out of Cleveland, in 1990. [3]

SACRAMENTO ■ Wooden bulk freight steamer of 2,380 t. and 307 ft., launched in 1895 at W Bay City, MI
Lake Huron: The big steamer SACRAMENTO was thought to be a total loss after she struck Port Austin Reef, in northeastern Saginaw Bay, and foundered on May 5, 1917. She went down near the lighthouse, but was later recovered and returned to service. [5]

SADDLEBAG ■ Vessel information unavailable
Lake Huron: No date is given for the loss of this vessel by stranding, six miles west of Detour, Michigan. [1]

SAGAMORE ■ Whaleback bulk freight barge of 1,601 t. and 308 ft., launched in 1892 at W Superior, WI
Lake Superior: When fully laden with a massive cargo such as iron ore, the whaleback steamers and barges had only a scant few feet of freeboard. According to their designer, this made the vessels more stable in all but the heaviest seas. It also made them difficult to see in adverse conditions. The barge SAGAMORE was riding at anchor off Point Iroquois, and waiting out fog when disaster struck. Deep-laden with iron ore, the barge offered a low profile, and her strong "tumblehome" (slope from the sides to the deck), meant that there was not even the slap of waves against her hull to warn of her presence. Out of the mist came the 300-foot steamer NORTHERN QUEEN, striking the SAGAMORE broadside and sending her to the bottom so quickly that three men were unable to escape before she went down. The accident occurred on July 29, 1901, and the wreck of the big barge was located in 1962. [5+]

SAGAMORE ■ Tug of 14 t.
Lake Huron: This small tug foundered five miles offshore near Harbor Beach, Michigan, on December 8, 1936. [2]

HENRY W or **H W SAGE** ■ Lumber schooner of 848 t. and 203 ft., launched in 1875 at Bangor (now part of Bay City), MI
St. Clair River: One life was reportedly lost when this big schooner sank on the river on July 29, 1900. [3]

SAGINAW ■ Barge of 508 t. and 198 ft., launched in 1866 at Marine City, MI as a schooner
Lake Huron: In 1905 the old barge SAGINAW was lost near Port Huron, when she was destroyed by fire. [2]

SAILOR BOY ■ Bulk freight schooner of 76 t.
Lake Michigan: The SAILOR BOY was loaded with a cargo of wood when she sank near Milwaukee on May 21, 1883. She went down two miles south of the harbor entrance. [1]

SAILOR BOY ■ Wooden steam freighter of 162 t. and 91 ft., launched in 1891 at W Bay City, MI
Lake Superior: The small wooden steamer SAILOR BOY was lost to fire on May 12, 1923. She burned at a dock on Wright's Point, in the Portage Ship Canal, near Hancock, Michigan. [3]

ST ALBANS ■ Passenger and package freight propeller
Lake Michigan: In January of 1881, this little steamer was sunk by ice eight miles east by northeast of Milwaukee. She had been one of the many small ships of this type that had shuttled between Lake Erie and Lake Michigan ports. [2]

ST ANDREW ■ Merchant schooner of 426 t.
Lake Huron: This sailing ship was lost in a collision with the steamer PESHTIGO. She went down off Cheboygan, Michigan, in the eastern Straits of Mackinac, in June of 1878. [2]

ST ANDREW ■ Wooden bulk freight propeller of 1,114 t. and 192 ft., launched in 1885 at St. Catharine's, Ont. as the steamer W B HALL
Lake Superior: No lives were lost, but the ST ANDREW disappeared into deep water following an accident which occurred on September 21, 1900. The steamer struck a rock ledge near Bachand Island, near the south end of Nipigon Strait, and severely damaged her hull. Before she could be recovered, the big vessel slid off the ledge and sank in the strait. [4]

ST ANDREW or **ST ANDREWS** ■ Merchant schooner of 202 t.
Lake Erie: In 1882, the small schooner ST ANDREW went down near Long Point. No cause is given for the sinking, which occurred about ten miles offshore, south of Big Creek, Ontario. [2]

ST ANTHONY ■ Merchant schooner
Lake Huron: This schooner was lost offshore from Goderich, Ontario, in 1856. [1]

CITY OF ST CATHARINE'S ■ Wooden propeller steamer of 606 t. and 139 ft., launched in 1874 at Port Robinson, Ont.
Lake Huron: In July of 1880, the steamer CITY OF ST CATHARINE'S foundered in a storm off Sand Beach, Michigan. She was thought to be a total loss by her owners, but was later recovered and rebuilt as the steamer OTEGO (qv). [2]

ST CLAIR ■ Sidewheel passenger and package freight steamer of 210 t. and 140 ft., launched in 1843 at Detroit
No detail is available, but there is some evidence that this steamer was lost to an accident on August 5, 1850. [1]

ST CLAIR ■ Small schooner-barge, possibly the 35 t. vessel built at Swan Creek (Detroit), MI, in 1845
Lake Huron: The schooner-barge ST CLAIR was reported sunk off Pte Aux Barques, Michigan, in 1855. This may

be an erroneous reporting of the 1888 wreck of a schooner-barge of the same name (see below). [1]

ST CLAIR ■ Passenger and package freight steamer of 316 t., launched in 1866 at Algonac, MI
Lake Superior: The steamer ST CLAIR was carrying a cargo of cattle and general merchandise when she was lost on July 9, 1876. She is reported to have caught fire off 14-mile Point, near Ontonagon, Michigan, and burned to the water. Twenty-six of the 31 people aboard her died, most perishing from exposure in the icy Lake Superior waters. One source gives 1879 as the year. [3]

ST CLAIR ■ Bulk freight schooner-barge, 450 t. and 156 ft.
Lake Huron: The schooner-barge ST CLAIR sank near the docks at Harbor Beach, Michigan, on October 1, 1888. Five of her crew were killed when she went down. The vessel was lightered of her cargo of coal and towed out into the lake and resunk. [4]

ST IGNACE ■ Scow of 238 t.
Lake Michigan: One life was lost when this vessel sank with her cargo of bricks on November 9, 1879. [1]

ST IGNACE ■ Wrecking steamer of 1,199 t. and 216 ft., launched in 1889 at Detroit
Lake Superior: This big wrecker was lost on August 30, 1916, when she was destroyed by fire in the harbor at Port Arthur (now part of Thunder Bay), Ontario. [3]

ST JOSEPH ■ Wooden steam tug of 70 t.
Lake Huron: This small tug was lost on Georgian Bay on November 8, 1875, when she foundered near Chantry Island, just off Southampton, Ontario. [2]

ST JOSEPH ■ 85 t. vessel of unreported type
Lake St. Clair: This vessel was said to have foundered in Lake St. Clair in a storm which struck her on November 30, 1884. [1]

CITY OF ST JOSEPH ■ Steel bulk freight barge of 1,439 t. and 254 ft., launched in 1890 at W Bay City, MI, as the sidewheel passenger steamer CITY OF CHICAGO
Lake Superior: This veteran vessel was in the tow of the tug JOHN ROEN and carrying her usual cargo of pulpwood, when she was beset by a storm. Mountainous seas caused her to break her towline, and the big vessel was thrown helplessly ashore near Eagle Harbor, Michigan, where she went to pieces. One life was lost in the accident, which took place on September 21, 1942. [2]

ST LAWRENCE ■ Merchant schooner of 140 t.
Lake Ontario: The small schooner ST LAWRENCE capsized and sank in a storm that blew her down near Oak Orchard, New York, in August of 1838. No lives were lost in the incident. [1]

ST LAWRENCE ▪ Bulk freight steamer of 1,437 t. and 239 ft., launched in 1890 at Marine City, MI
Lake Michigan: This large bulk freighter was lost on November 25, 1898, when she was driven aground and wrecked. A storm pushed her into the shallows near Point Betsie, two miles south of the lighthouse. [3]

ST LAWRENCE ▪ Merchant schooner of 281 t. and 137 ft., launched in 1863 at Cleveland
Lake Erie: On November 22, 1900, this sailing vessel was lost near Lorain, Ohio, when she was stranded in a storm and broke up. She was carrying a cargo of coal at the time of the accident. [3]

ST LOUIS ▪ Wooden sidewheel passenger and package freight steamer of 618 t. and 190 ft., launched in 1844 at Perrysburg, OH
Lake Erie: This steamer was lost off Kelley's Island, north of Sandusky, Ohio, in November of 1852. She capsized and sank two miles off shore. According to one report, she was carrying railroad cars when she went down. [4]

ST LOUIS ▪ Merchant schooner of 334 t. and 128 ft., launched in 1877 at St. Catharine's, Ont.
Lake Ontario: The canal-sized schooner ST LOUIS was lost on May 26, 1926, when she was destroyed by fire at her dock at Kingston, Ontario (perhaps in lieu of scrapping). She was one of the last operating sailing ships on the lakes when she burned. [2]

ST MAGNUS ▪ Wooden passenger and package freight steamer of 853 t. and 180 ft., launched in 1880 at Hamilton, Ont.
Lake Erie: The ST MAGNUS suffered several serious accidents in her career. The only fatal one was a double wreck which occurred on September 5, 1899. While loading a cargo of wire and pig iron at a dock at Cuyahoga, Ohio, the steamer turned turtle and sank in shallow water. One man died in the capsizing. The vessel was raised and towed to a drydock, where she caught fire and was almost destroyed while being repaired. She then had to be completely rebuilt and was reduced in length 44 ft. The steamer ended her days by burning at Midland, Ontario, under the somewhat ironic name of LUCKPORT (qv). [3]

ST MARY ▪ Wooden steam tug of 64 ft., launched in 1857 at Buffalo
Lake Michigan: On December 1, 1885, the tug ST MARY was destroyed by fire offshore from Glen Haven, Michigan. [1]

ST NICHOLAS ▪ Wooden bulk freight propeller of 136 ft., launched in 1853 at Cape Vincent, NY
Lake Michigan: This steamer was laden with a cargo of wheat when she ran into serious danger in Sleeping Bear Bay. Struck by a storm, the vessel became waterlogged and was put on the beach, where she was broken up by the action of waves. The accident occurred on November 23, 1857. [1]

ST PETER ▪ Merchant schooner of 290 t. and 136 ft., launched in 1873 at Toledo
Lake Ontario: An October 27, 1898 storm sent the ST PETER to the bottom five miles northwest of Sodus, New York. Eight of the nine sailors in her crew were lost in the sinking. Much of her remains were salvaged in 1971 and now form the basis for a museum. [3]

STE MARIES ▪ Passenger and package freight steamer 132 ft., launched in 1883 at Detroit (one source gives her gross tonnage as 1,357)
Lake Huron: The small propeller STE MARIES was sunk in 1888, four miles southeast of Sturgeon Point, Michigan, a few miles from Harrisville. [2]

SALINA ▪ Bulk freight schooner of 212 t. and 130 ft., launched in 1866 at Marine City, MI
Lake Huron: The schooner SALINA was reportedly rammed and sunk on the Saginaw River in 1895. She was hit by the large schooner LIZZIE A LAW (qv) and went down quickly. [2]

SALVOR ▪ Steam packet of 212 t. and 105 ft., launched in 1861 at Detroit as the tug GEORGE H PARKER
Lake Huron: In September of 1918, the little steamer SALVOR was lost when she foundered off Manitoulin Island. [3]

SALVOR ▪ Steel bulk freight barge of 1,140 t. and 253 ft., launched in 1896 at Sunderland, England as the steamer TURRET CHIEF (qv)
Lake Michigan: The the barge SALVOR was carrying a cargo of stone and a crew of five when she was lost on September 26, 1930. The steel vessel was in tow of the tug FITZGERALD when the two were struck by a wild lake gale. The SALVOR broke her towline and sank north of Muskegon, Michigan, with all hands. See also JOLLY INEZ. [5+]

SAMANA ■ Bulk freight schooner of 287 t. and 136 ft., launched in 1873 at Oswego, NY
Lake Erie: The SAMANA had a cargo of coal on board when she sank in the harbor at Cleveland on October 29, 1892. There is no record of her recovery. [3]

SAMOA ■ Wooden bulk freight steamer of 1,096 t. and 206 ft., launched in 1880 at Wyandotte, MI, as the steamer THOMAS W PALMER
Lake Superior: A freakish accident destroyed this ship on Torch Lake on September 21, 1909. Torch Lake is along the Portage Ship Canal, which allowed vessels to cross the peninsula and bypass the long trip around the tip of the "rabbit's ear." On the date mentioned, the SAMOA had taken refuge on the lake from an approaching electrical storm. Her attempt was in vain, for during the storm the steamer was struck by lightning, caught fire and burned to the waterline. All of her crew made it safely to shore. [5]

SAMPSON ■ Merchant schooner, possibly the 400 t., 140 ft. schooner of this name launched at St. Catharine's, Ont., in 1874
Lake Erie: The SAMPSON was lost on November 15, 1888 at the north end of Pelee Island. On that date she was cut by early ice, took on water and foundered. [2]

SAMSON ■ Barge
Lake Huron: The barge SAMSON was reported burned offshore and lost in 1879. [1]

SAN JACINTO ■ 265 t. vessel of unreported type
Lake Huron: South Baymouth, Ontario, is at the southern end of picturesque Manitoulin Island. On November 12, 1881, the SAN JACINTO foundered near the town, probably as the result of a gale. [1]

SAND MERCHANT ■ Steel steam sandsucker of 1,891 t. and 252 ft., launched in 1927 at Collingwood, Ont.
Lake Erie: A terrific gale swept the length of Lake Erie on October 17, 1936, and the steamer SAND MERCHANT was unfortunate enough to be right in the path of it. Probably topheavy with her intricate jumble of deck gear and sandsucking equipment, the vessel capsized and sank in big waves. She went down with 19 of her 26 crewmen, off Avon Point, several miles west of Cleveland. [5+]

WILLIAM SANDERSON ■ Merchant schooner of 307 t. and 136 ft., launched in 1853 at Oswego, NY
Lake Michigan: Residents who lived along the beach near Empire, Michigan, in the northeast corner of the lower peninsula, were startled to find the tangled wreckage of the SANDERSON washed up on the beach following a November 25, 1874, storm. Her crew, probably consisting of seven to ten men, was never found. [1]

SANDUSKY ■ Merchant bark of 377 t. and 198 ft., launched in 1834 at Sandusky, OH as a sidewheel passenger steamer
Lake Erie: The SANDUSKY was somewhat unique in that she was built as a sidewheeler, and later converted to a full-rigged sailing vessel. As a steamer, she caught fire at her dock at Buffalo Creek, near Buffalo, New York, on February 23, 1843. She burned to the hull, but was salvaged and rebuilt as a bark of the same name. [3]
Lake Erie: In October of 1848, the bark SANDUSKY was lost east of Long Point in a storm. [2]

SANDUSKY ■ Merchant bark of 226 t. and 110 ft., launched in 1848 at Sandusky, OH
Lake Huron: Seven lives were lost in 1856, when the bark SANDUSKY sank in a storm in the Straits of Mackinac. [3]

SANDUSKY ■ Merchant steamer
Lake Erie: This steamer was wrecked somewhere on the lake in October of 1857 when she was destroyed by fire. No lives were lost. [1]

CITY OF SANDUSKY ■ Sidewheel passenger and package freight steamer of 365 t. and 177 ft., launched in 1866 at Sandusky, OH
Lake Erie: Port Stanley, Ontario, was the site of the loss of this steamer to a fire on March 24, 1876. She reportedly had a valuable cargo on board when she sank following the blaze. [4]

CITY OF SANDUSKY ■ Steamer of 414 t. and 162 ft., launched in 1868 at Detroit
Lake Huron: The steamer CITY OF SANDUSKY is reported to have sunk far out in the lake in 1895. [2]

SANDY PAT ■ Fishing tug
Lake Erie: Two lives were lost when this fishing vessel sank on November 3, 1969. There is some confusion over the location of the accident. She sank either off Erie, Pennsylvania, or Erieau, Ontario. [2]

SANTIAGO ■ Bulk freight schooner-barge of 2,600 t. and 324 ft., launched in 1899 at W Bay City, MI
Lake Huron: This giant schooner-barge was one of several very large wooden vessels of this type built at Bay City. She was lost only about 50 miles from where she was built. The barge was loaded with a cargo of iron ore when she was lost from her tow steamer, the JOHN F MORROW. She swamped and sank just off Pte Aux Barques, on September 10, 1918. Fortunately, none of her crew were lost in the accident. [4]

SAPPHO ▪ Wooden passenger ferry of 224 t. and 107 ft., launched in 1883 at Wyandotte, MI
Detroit River: This little ferry made many thousands of trips across the Detroit River in her 46 years of operation between Detroit and Windsor, before coming to an ignominious end. On February 21, 1929, the little vessel caught fire and burned to the waterline at her winter dock at Ecorse, Michigan. She was neither repaired nor replaced, as the Ambassador Bridge, linking the two cities, was completed the following summer. [5]

SARATOGA ▪ Vessel of unknown type, launched in 1846
Lake Erie: The SARATOGA was reported to have been wrecked on the lake in 1854. [1]

SARDINIA ▪ Merchant schooner of 137 ft., launched in 1860 at Detroit
Lake Michigan: This schooner was carrying a cargo of salt in November of 1874, when she was lost. The SARDINIA stranded on Cathead Point, near the tip of the Leelanau Peninsula, and was broken up in place by a storm that followed. [1]

SARNIA ▪ Wooden steamer of 58 t., launched in 1901
Lake Superior: The bane of the wooden steamboat, fire, destroyed this small steamer in the harbor at Port Arthur, Ont. She burned on Nov. 30, 1929, with no loss of life. [1]

SARNIADOC ▪ Steamer of 1,160 t.
Lake Ontario: On November 30, 1929, the SARNIADOC was reported stranded and broken up on Main Duck Island. Reports of her loss may be exaggerations, as the only ship of this name and size on record lasted until 1942. [1]

SARNIAN ▪ Bulk freight steamer of 2,584 t. and 321 ft., launched in 1895 at Cleveland as the steamer CHILI
Lake Superior: Laden with a cargo of barley, the steamer SARNIAN was bound for Toronto on December 10, 1943, when she was blasted by a violent storm east of the Keweenaw Peninsula. Driven off course by mountainous seas, the vessel went on a reef at Pointe Isabelle, near Baraga, Michigan. She soon broke in half and began to go to pieces, but before she could dissemble completely, the Coast Guard arrived and removed her crew. The hulk was recovered for scrap in 1944. [4]

SARNOR ▪ Wooden bulk freight steamer of 1,152 t. and 219 ft., launched in 1888 at W Bay City, MI, as the steamer BRITTANIC
Lake Ontario: On March 15, 1926, this freighter was destroyed by fire in the harbor at Kingston, Ontario. [3]

SARONIC ▪ Passenger and package freight steamer of 1,961 t. and 252 ft., launched in 1882 at Sarnia, Ont., as the steamer UNITED EMPIRE
Lake Huron: The old passenger steamer SARONIC ended her days as a powered ship on the rocks around Cockburn Island, at the north end of the lake. She grounded there on August 21, 1926, and was burned to a shell by the fire which followed. Her hull was later recovered and rebuilt as the barge W L KENNEDY. An engraving of this vessel appeared on the 1907-08 Canadian dollar bill. [3]

SASCO ▪ Merchant schooner of 281 t.
Lake Erie: On November 17, 1879, the schooner SASCO was reported to have sunk, one half mile west of Fairport, Ohio. She was light at the time of the loss. [1]

SASSACUS ▪ Bulk freight schooner of 109 t. and 95 ft., launched in 1867 at Oswego, NY
Lake Michigan: The lumber and bulk freight schooner SASSACUS was carrying a cargo of wood when she foundered in a storm on October 8, 1893. She went down two miles north of the east entrance to the Sturgeon Bay Ship Canal. [3]

SATTELITE ▪ Towing steamer of 233 t., launched in 1864 at Cleveland
Lake Superior: Vessels of this type carried little cargo themselves, but were equipped to tow a number of barges for long distances. The SATTELITE was lugging a five-barge tow when she struck a deadhead (floating log) west of Whitefish Point and sank. The accident took place on June 21, 1879, with no loss of life. [2]

SATURN ▪ Bulk freight schooner-barge of 400 t.
Lake Superior: Downbound with a cargo of iron ore, the SATURN and her sister, the schooner-barge JUPITER (qv) were in tow of the steamer JOHN A DIX, when the little fleet was set upon by a raging storm. The two heavy barges thrashed about until they broke their tow cables. The SATURN was driven aground just west of Whitefish Point, where she quickly broke up, drowning her entire crew of seven (some sources say eight), on November 27, 1872. [5+]

SATURN ▪ Bulk freight steam barge of 571 t. and 172 ft., launched in 1875 at Owen Sound, Ont, as the steamer CITY OF OWEN SOUND
Lake Huron: The bulk freighter SATURN foundered in a westerly storm that struck her on September 17, 1901. She went down north of Southampton, Ontario. [5+]

WILLIAM F SAUBER ■ Wooden bulk freight steamer of 2,053 t. and 291 ft., launched in 1891 at W Bay City, MI
Lake Superior: Struck by a heavy gale on October 26, 1903, the big steamer WILLIAM F SAUBER's wooden hull could not take the strain of heavy weather on her iron ore-filled hull. Her seams opened off Whitefish Point and the steamer sank with the loss of two of her 17 crewmen. [5+]

SAUCY JIM ■ Wooden steam tug of 93 t. and 83 ft., launched in 1887 at Penetang, Ont.
Lake Huron: The fate of so many wooden tugs befell the SAUCY JIM as she was tied to a wharf at Christian Island, northwest of Midland, Ontario. The tug caught fire and was destroyed on November 18, 1910. [4]

SAVELAND ■ Lumber schooner-barge of 689 t. and 195 ft., launched in 1873 at Milwaukee
Lake Superior: Grand Marais, Michigan, has a fine natural harbor, that protects vessels from all heavy weather except that which comes directly from the north. It was a northerly storm that tore this vessel away from the steamer GETTYSBURG and tossed her against some pilings, where her hull was punctured and she sank. She was laden with a cargo of lumber on the day of the accident—October 22, 1903. [5+]

GEORGE P SAVIDGE or **SAVAGE** ■ Steam tug of 20 t. and 54 ft., launched in 1881 at Grand Haven, MI
Lake Superior: St. Louis Bay, near Duluth, was the site of the loss of this tug on June 1, 1893. She burned and sank in the small bay, but her crew made it safely to shore. [3]

HUNTER SAVIDGE ■ Merchant schooner of 152 t. and 117 ft., launched in 1879 at Grand Haven, MI
Lake Huron: This two-mast schooner was in ballast at the time of her loss on August 20, 1899. She was northeast of Pte Aux Barques, Michigan, when she was struck by a white squall or a tornado, capsized and quickly sank. Five lives were lost, including the captain's wife, and it is reported that the skipper patrolled the beaches of Michigan's Thumb for many months, hoping that she would come ashore. [5]

J D SAWYER ■ Merchant schooner
Lake Erie: On October 20, 1891, the schooner J D SAWYER is said to have sunk off Lorain, Ohio. She may be the same vessel as reported below. [1]

JAMES D SAWYER ■ Merchant schooner
Lake Michigan: In 1893 this vessel was traversing the western end of the Straits of Mackinac when she was struck by a white squall and drifted ashore. She touched land at Seul Choix Point, where she broke up. [2]

PHILETUS SAWYER ■ Wooden lumber hooker of 450 t. and 152 ft., launched in 1884 at Green Bay, WI
Lake Erie: Toledo, Ohio, was the site of the loss of this small lumber steamer, which was destroyed by fire on July 11, 1923. Several sources say she went down as a result of a collision on the Detroit River instead. [5]

W H SAWYER ■ Wooden bulk freight steamer of 746 t. and 201 ft., launched in 1890 at W Bay City, MI
Lake Huron: On September 20. 1928, the bulk freighter W H SAWYER stranded in a storm with her towbarge PESHTIGO (qv), and broke up. The accident occurred within sight of the lighthouse at Harbor Beach, Michigan. [4]

SAXON ■ 42 t. vessel of unreported type
Lake Erie: On November 10, 1871, the little SAXON went aground on the south side of Long Point and broke up due to the action of storm waves. [1]

SAYMO ■ Tug of 116 t. and 78 ft., launched in 1904 at Meaford, Ont., as the tug J D HAMMILL
Lake Huron: A Georgian Bay tug loss occurred on November 11, 1935, when the tug SAYMO was wrecked or foundered near Club Island, off southern Manitoulin. [3]

J YOUNG SCAMMON or **SCANNON** ■ Merchant brig or schooner
Lake Michigan: This sail vessel had a serious accident in August, 1840, in which two lives were lost. She was recovered from that wreck, but her end came on June 8, 1854, when she was driven on the rocky shore of South Manitou Island by a storm. She stranded so close to shore that her crew was able to use a broken spar for a bridge to the beach, and escaped, hardly getting their feet wet. The SCAMMON, on the other hand, went to pieces in place. [4]

JESSIE SCARTH ■ Bulk freight schooner
Lake Michigan: The SCARTH was carrying a cargo of corn when she was struck by a strong westerly gale on October 4, 1887. The ship was driven ashore on North Manitou Island, where she broke up under the pounding of storm waves. [1]

FERDINAND SCHLESINGER ■ Wooden bulk freight steamer of 2,607 t. and 305 ft., launched in 1891 at Milwaukee
Lake Superior: No lives were lost when this large vessel went down in a wild area of the lake on May 26, 1919. The steamer was upbound with a cargo of coal when she

sprang a leak in heavy waves and sank southeast of Passage Island, near Isle Royale. The crew had fought the incoming water for hours and had finally resigned themselves to abandoning the ship for the icy lake, when the big passenger steamer ASSINIBOIA happened along and rescued all. [5+]

SCHOOLCRAFT ▪ Wooden bulk freight steamer of 745 t. and 180 ft., launched in 1884 at Trenton, MI
Lake Ontario: On December 3, 1920, this old ship was lost on Wolfe Island, near Kingston, Ontario, when she caught fire and was destroyed. She is often reported to have been lost in an earlier serious accident in the harbor at Grand Marais, Michigan, when she foundered in a gale in 1901, but she had been recovered from that incident. [5]

JOHN SCHUETTE ▪ Bulk freight schooner of 270 t. and 137 ft., launched in 1875 at Two Rivers, WI
Detroit River: This little schooner suffered a common type of accident that ended many ships' active careers on this busy waterway. On July 2, 1909, the JOHN SCHUETTE foundered after a collision with the steamer ALFRED MITCHELL. She went down off Ecorse, MI, with no loss of life. The wreck partially obstructed the shipping lane and thus was dragged ashore by winch and abandoned. [4]

SCHUYKILL ▪ Merchant schooner of 472 t.
Lake Superior: No lives were reported lost when this vessel went down off the Portage Ship Canal on Oct. 5, 1889. [1]

SCOBELL ▪ Wooden steam sandsucker
Lake Erie: Little is recorded on the loss of this vessel in the early 1930s. She apparently sprank a leak well offshore and made a run for Cleveland. The sandsucker eventually made it to a dock on the Cuyahoga River, where she capsized and sank. [1]

SCOTIA ▪ Iron steamer of 1,502 t. and 231 ft., launched in 1873 at Buffalo
Lake Superior: The SCOTIA was wrecked on a reef off the tip of Keweenaw Point. On October 24, 1884, she struck ground and was torn to pieces by wave action. Her propeller was later salvaged and is on display at Fort Wilkins State Park, at Copper Harbor, Michigan. [2]

SCOTIA ▪ Vessel information unavailable
Lake Michigan: This SCOTIA was reported to have sunk off Pentwater, Michigan, in 1940. [1]

SCOTIADOC ▪ Steel bulk freight steamer of 4,635 t. and 416 ft., launched in 1904 at Cleveland as the steamer MARTIN MULLEN

Lake Superior: June 21, 1953, was the date of the loss of this big steamer off Thunder Bay, Ontario. She was outbound from the port in a heavy fog when she was rammed by the steamer BURLINGTON and sank, carrying one of her 29 crewmen and her cargo of wheat to the bottom with her. [5+]

SCOTLAND ▪ Merchant schooner (possibly steamer built at Toronto in 1847)
Lake Erie: The SCOTLAND was victim of the shallows off the region of high bluffs known as "Claybanks," near Port Stanley, Ontario. The ship stranded and broke up in 1848. [2]

SCOTT ▪ Wooden steamer of 240 t., launched in 1839 at Huron, OH
Lake St. Clair: In October of 1848, this steamer was involved in a collision with the schooner STAR and went down on the lake. [1]

GENERAL SCOTT ▪ Wooden steamer
Lake Huron: Ice breaking up in the spring thaw and moving out of the Saginaw River wrecked this small steamer. The ship's hull was sliced by the grinding sheets and she filled and sank on March 21, 1853. [1]

ISAAC M SCOTT ▪ Steel bulk freight steamer of 6,372 t. and 504 ft., launched in 1909 at Lorain, OH
Lake Huron: The giant, almost-new bulk freighter ISAAC M SCOTT was the sister ship of the ill-fated CHARLES S PRICE. The two big vessels went down in the same monster gale, the Big Storm of 1913. The SCOTT was upbound with her holds filled with coal when the worst of the weather struck her two-thirds of the way up the lake on the 9th. It is not known exactly what happened, but the big ship probably was struck broadsides by enormous seas and capsized, drowning all 28 of her crew and sinking seven miles northest of Thunder Bay Island, on the Michigan shore. Until her upside-down wreckage was discovered in 1976, it was thought that the vessel had been lost much closer to the Canadian side. [5+]

JAMES SCOTT ▪ 30 t. vessel of unreported type
Lake Erie: In November of 1882, this small vessel was reported to have stranded near Long Point, and gone to pieces. [1]

THOMAS A SCOTT ▪ Steamer
All that can be found about this steamer is that she foundered on November 18, 1869. [1]

THOMAS A SCOTT ▪ Bulk freight schooner-barge of 1,159 t.
Lake Michigan: A storm was raging on October 29, 1880, and this vessel was riding it out at anchor a mile off Milwaukee. The steamer AVON, trying to make her way into the shelter of the harbor, rammed the corn-laden SCOTT and sank her. [2]

THOMAS R SCOTT ■ Wooden bulk freight steamer of 240 t. and 136 ft., launched in 1887 at Grand Haven, MI
Lake Huron: This Georgian Bay accident occurred on September 2, 1914, when this small freighter foundered off Cabot Head, on the eastern side of the Bruce Peninsula. [5+]

SCOURGE ■ Armed schooner of 45 t. and 110 ft., launched in 1811, near Niagara as the Royal Navy schooner LORD NELSON
Lake Ontario: This small warship was anchored off the mouth of the Niagara River with her fleetmate HAMILTON (qv), when the two vessels were sunk by a storm. They went down on August 8, 1813, the SCOURGE with the loss of about 40 lives. She had been captured from the Royal Navy during the War of 1812 and was a subject of a live underwater television exploration in 1990. [3]

H M SCOVE ■ Merchant schooner of 305 t. and 138 ft., launched in 1873 at Manitowoc, WI
Lake Michigan: In November of 1891, the schooner H M SCOVE foundered just off Pilot Island, in the Death's Door Passage, at the mouth of Green Bay. [3]

DAVID SCOVILLE ■ Wooden steam tug of 25 t.
St. Clair River: The small steam tug DAVID SCOVILLE was lost on October 20, 1879, when she caught fire and was destroyed at a wharf at Sarnia, Ontario. [2]

PHILO SCOVILLE ■ Merchant schooner of 139 ft.
Lake Huron: The schooner PHILO SCOVILLE was victim of an October, 1889 storm which drove her ashore and wrecked her on Russel Island, near Tobermory, Ontario. [2]

SCOW #1 ■ Scow
Lake Michigan: This towed vessel was reported to have sunk at the foot of Wisconsin Street in Milwaukee harbor on September 22, 1895, and was not recovered. [1]

SCOW #2 ■ Scow
Lake Michigan: This vessel sunk near the entrance to the harbor at Two Rivers, Wisconsin, on October 19, 1896. [1]

SCOW #2 ■ Scow
Lake Michigan: On November 20, 1900, the scow called, prosaically, SCOW #2, sank near the east entrance to the Sturgeon Bay Ship Canal. [1]

SEA BIRD ■ Merchant schooner of 38 t. and 54 ft., launched in 1848 at Sandusky, OH
Lake Erie: This tiny schooner was sunk off the mouth of Ohio's Black River in 1850. [1]

SEA BIRD ■ Merchant schooner of 140 t.
Lake Michigan: Six sailors were lost when the schooner SEA BIRD sailed off the known map on July 21, 1883. Neither crew nor ship was ever heard from again. [1]

SEA GULL ■ Schooner-barge built in 1864
Lake Huron: This vessel has an interesting history, having plied the New York-Africa trade route for several years during her career. In 1888, she was on the Lakes and serving as a barge when she caught fire at the docks at Tawas City, Michigan, and was destroyed. [2]

SEA GULL ■ Steam tug, probably the 119 t. vessel built at Bay City, MI, in 1878
Lake Huron: The large tug SEA GULL was lost on Saginaw Bay when she collided with an unnamed vessel and sank off Linwood, Michigan, in 1889. [2]

SEA GULL ■ Propeller steamer of 289 t.
Lake Huron: One life was lost when the propeller SEA GULL was destroyed by fire at Tawas City, Michigan, on July 5, 1890. She was reportedly carrying a cargo of ice at the time. See also 1888 wreck above. [2]

SEA GULL ■ Steam tug of 75 t. and 103 ft., launched in 1868 at Portsmouth, MI
Lake Huron: Another tug fire destroyed this tow vessel in 1893. She was off Bois Blanc Island, in the Straits of Mackinac, when she burned and sank. [2]

SEA HORSE ■ Merchant schooner of 42 t.
Lake Huron: On October 17, 1871, the small schooner SEA HORSE stranded and was lost on Fitzwilliam Island, in the mouth of Georgian Bay. [2]

SEA LION ■ Bulk freight schooner of 65 t. and 71 ft., launched in 1884 at Nicolet, WI
Lake Michigan: A stranding which took place on September 23, 1894, was the final story on this ship. She went aground about ten miles south of Manistee, Michigan, and was wrecked. [2]

SEA QUEEN ■ Tug
Lake Huron: The tug SEA QUEEN was destroyed by fire at Meldrum Bay, in the North Channel, in 1932. [1]

SEA STAR ■ Bulk freight schooner of 95 t.
Lake Michigan: A fall storm which struck this schooner on November 5, 1886, cast the SEA STAR ashore about nine miles south of the east entrance of the Sturgeon Bay Ship Canal. The vessel had been carrying a cargo of wood at the time, and was a total loss from the accident. [1]

SEABIRD ■ Sidewheel passenger and package freight steamer of 638 t. and 191 ft., launched in 1859 at Newport, MI

Lake Michigan: The tragic story of this steamer has come to be known as the "SEABIRD disaster." On the night of April 9, 1868, a landlubber porter on board the wooden ship threw a bucket of glowing stove ashes to windward. The sun-baked upperworks of ships of this era were usually tinder-dry, naked wood and caulked with flammable pine pitch or tar. When the porter's embers blew back on the deck, the ship quickly turned from a peaceful evening cruiser to a flaming torch. Passengers—she was carrying a full manifest—could not be awakened fast enough to save them, nor were there enough boats or life jackets for all. All but two of the 102 passengers and crew burned to death on the ship, drowned jumping overboard, or perished from exposure in the icy Lake Michigan water of early spring. The tragedy occurred off Waukegan, Illinois. [5+]

SEABREEZE ■ Steam screw of 87 t.
Detroit River: This small steamer was reported lost off Sugar Island, near the southern tip of Grosse Ile, on December 3, 1946. [2]

SEAMAN ■ Package and bulk freight schooner-scow of 181 t. and 120 ft., launched in 1848 at Nicolet, WI
Lake Michigan: The SEAMAN was the oldest working sail vessel afloat at the time of her demise on November 15, 1908. It is somehow appropriate for a sailing ship with 60 years of experience to go down fighting the wind. This large schooner-scow was carrying a load of wood slabs and potatoes when she was struck by a mighty gale and cast ashore near Death's Door. The ship was probably no longer worth salvaging, and was left to break up in place. [2]

A SEAMAN ■ Tug of 52 t. and 69 ft., launched in 1873
Lake Superior: This little tug foundered suddenly near Michipicoten Island on September 5, 1906. [2]

SEARCH LIGHT ■ Fishing tug of 9 t. and 40 ft., launched in 1899 at W Bay City, MI
Lake Huron: This small fisher was returning to port with her catch when she foundered near Harbor Beach, Michigan, on April 23, 1907, with the loss of all six crewmen. It is interesting that no trace of the vessel was found until some wreckage and a body washed ashore six years later, during the Big Storm of 1913. [4]

L SEATON ■ Merchant schooner of 233 t. and 121 ft., launched in 1872 at Henderson, NY
Lake Huron: Laden with a cargo of railroad ties, this small schooner went aground near Pointe Aux Barques, Michigan, in November of 1892, and was destroyed. [4]

SEATTLE ■ Wooden bulk freight schooner of 166 t. overall, launched in 1892 at Oscoda, MI
Lake Huron: On November 12, 1903, this steamer stranded in a storm and was broken up on Georgian Bay. [2]

J S SEAVERNS ■ Bulk freight steam barge of 173 t., launched as the sidewheel steam tug JOHN P WARD
Lake Superior: Although this vessel got herself in trouble by running aground on a reef near Michipicoten Island in May of 1884, she was actually lost during the salvage attempt. After being pulled off her perch by a salvage tug, the vessel foundered in deep water. [1]

SECRET ■ Propeller freighter of 629 t.
Lake Huron: On October 13, 1911, the steamer SECRET was lost at Star Shoal, in Georgian Bay, when she caught fire and was destroyed. One source says a vessel of the same name burned at the same spot in 1871. [3]

SELT ■ Schooner-scow of 101 ft., launched in 1864 at Sheboygan, WI
Lake Michigan: The schooner-scow SELT had just taken on a cargo of railroad ties at a dock at Leland, Michigan, when she was struck by a powerful storm. Big waves began to batter the vessel against the pilings and so she was beached to prevent her breaking up. The action went for naught, as the small sailing vessel merely went to pieces on shore instead. The accident took place on October 20, 1888. [1]

SENATOR ■ Steel auto-carrying steamer of 4,048 t. and 410 ft., launched in 1896 at Wyandotte, MI
Lake Michigan: This large automobile carrier was one of several such ships to be lost on the Lakes in the '20s (see CITY OF BANGOR). The SENATOR was loaded with 240 Nash autos when she was lost on October 31, 1929, off Port Washington, Wisconsin. Groping her way through a heavy fog, the big steamer was rammed by the steamer MARQUETTE and sank rapidly. Ten of the 29 sailors aboard were lost when she went down. She had been previously listed as a wreck after sinking in the St. Marys River in 1909. [4]

SERVIA ■ Wooden bulk freight steamer of 1,425 t. and 242 ft., launched in 1888 at W Bay City, MI
Lake Superior: The steamer SERVIA was struck by a series of disasters on April 27, 1898, that turned her from a proud ship into a charred hulk on the bottom of the lake. The vessel was offshore from Whitefish Point when she caught fire. While her crew were fighting the blaze, a gale blew in, fanning the flames and making it almost impossible for the firefighters to stand on the heaving deck. After the crewmen had given up and abandoned ship, the steamer rolled over and sank, spilling her cargo of corn on the bottom of the lake. [5]

SEVERN ■ Schooner-barge launched in 1872 at Welland, Ont. as a steamer
Lake Huron: This schooner-barge was light and in tow of the steamer AFRICA (qv) when she was overtaken by a storm on Georgian Bay. She soon became too much for the small steamer to handle, and was released from tow.

The SEVERN was not able to set enough sail to overcome the storm, and was driven on a reef off Cove Island, where she went to pieces. The ship was lost on October 4, 1905. The AFRICA fared even worse, going down with all hands a few miles away. [4]

SEVONA ■ Steel bulk freight steamer of 4,800 t. and 372 ft., launched in 1890 at Bay City, MI, as the steamer EMILY P WEED
Lake Superior: The large steel bulk freighter SEVONA was lost near Bayfield, Wisconsin, on September 2, 1905. Caught in the talons of a tremendous gale, she broke in half close inshore. The after part of the vessel grounded on a reef near Sand Island, while the forward section sank in deep water. The crew, split into two groups, tried to make their way to shore separately. The after crew made it safely to shore while the skipper and six others who were for'ard were lost when their yawl capsized. The ship had been cut in two and lengthened 72 feet before coming out that spring. [5+]

R A SEYMOUR ■ Steam freighter of 92 t., launched in 1876 at New Baltimore, MI as the steamer LEWIS GILBERT
Lake Michigan: This small steamboat was lost when she sank off Port Washington, Wisconsin, in 1889. [2]

WILLIAM SEYMOUR ■ Steam freighter of 245 t. and 87 ft., launched in 1870 at Goderich, Ont.
Lake Huron: The little steamer WILLIAM SEYMOUR foundered near Lonely Island, due east of South Baymouth, Ontario, on October 9, 1877. [3]

SHAMROCK ■ Fishing tug
Lake Superior: Fishing tugs have often risked collision by working their lines and nets close to the heavily-trafficked area north of the Soo. This little vessel was lost in the area on the night of September 5, 1905, when she was rammed and sunk by the freighter W C RICHARDSON (qv). Two fishermen lost their lives in the accident. [2]

SHAMROCK ■ Wooden passenger and package freight steamer of 403 t. and 146 ft., launched in 1875 at St. Clair, MI, as the schooner-barge JOHN W HANNAFORD
Lake Huron: All 12 of this veteran steamer's crew made it safely to shore when the vessel foundered off the mouth of the Thunder Bay River, south of the town of Alpena, on June 26, 1905. [4]

SHANDON ■ Merchant schooner of 330 t.
Lake Huron: On October 27, 1884, this schooner was reported to have been lost in Wingfield Basin, near Cabot Head (Ontario). [2]

SHANNON ■ Merchant schooner
Lake Huron: The schooner SHANNON was reported foundered on Georgian Bay in 1870. [1]

SHANNON ■ Bulk freight schooner of 69 t.
Lake Ontario: No lives were lost when this little sail vessel sprang a leak on June 20, 1874, and went down 15 miles off Oswego, New York. [2]

J E SHAW ■ Merchant schooner
Lake Michigan: St. Helena Island, just west of the present Mackinaw Bridge, was the site of the loss of this schooner when she foundered in a storm in 1856. [2]

JOHN SHAW ■ Bulk freight schooner of 928 t. and 205 ft., launched in 1885 at W Bay City, MI
Lake Huron: The big schooner JOHN SHAW went on a reef near Au Sable Point in 1894, and was wrecked. [3]

O SHAW ■ Bulk freight schooner of 40 t. and 67 ft., launched in 1867 at South Haven, MI
Lake Michigan: Carrying a cargo of sawdust, the little schooner O SHAW sank on August 9, 1904, off Calumet, Illinois, at the extreme southwest corner of the lake. [2]

SHAWMUT ■ Barge of 250 t., launched in 1889
Lake Erie: The SHAWMUT was under tow in the harbor at Buffalo when she collided with the steamer AMERICA and sank on November 1, 1909. Both of the two men on board escaped before she sank. [1]

SHAWNEE ■ Bulk freight schooner-barge of 571 t. and 185 ft., launched in 1873 at Gibraltar, MI
Lake Erie: The schooner-barge SHAWNEE was lost near Cleveland on May 16, 1911, when she was driven on a rocky bar by a storm and went to pieces. She was laden with a cargo of coal at the time of the accident. [3]

CITY OF SHEBOYGAN ■ Lumber schooner of 260 t. and 135 ft., launched in 1871 at Sheboygan, WI
Lake Ontario: This schooner was carrying a hold full of the mineral feldspar when she sank in heavy seas, a few hundred yards off Amherst Island, west of Kingston, Ont. Several valiant rescue attempts by local people failed, and five of the vessel's crew died when the ship went to pieces. The disaster occurred on September 25, 1915. [4]

C J SHEFFIELD ■ Steel steam freighter of 1,700 t. and 259 ft., launched in 1887
Lake Superior: This new vessel was lost on June 19, 1889, when she was rammed broadsides in fog by the steel freighter NORTH STAR while running in ballast on Whitefish Bay. The NORTH STAR kept her engines running ahead to keep her prow in the hole while all of the

SHEFFIELD's crew clambered aboard. When the NORTH STAR backed away, her victim quickly sank. Compare this report with the one for CHARLES J SHEFFIELD. [3]

CHARLES J SHEFFIELD ■ Wooden package freight steamer
Lake Superior: This package freighter is reported to have sunk following a collision in the Keweenaw Waterway (Portage Ship Canal) on June 15, 1890, while carrying a cargo of kerosene. Possibly the same ship and accident as reported for C J SHEFFIELD. [2]

SARAH E SHELDON ■ Wooden bulk freight steamer of 907 t. and 193 ft., launched in 1872 at Black River, OH
Lake Erie: Two of 14 crewmen were killed when this steamer struck a reef near Lake Breeze, Ohio, and broke up 600 feet offshore. The loss occurred during the big gale of October 20, 1905. [4]

THOMAS P SHELDON ■ Merchant schooner of 669 t. and 194 ft., launched in 1871 at Bay City, MI
Lake Huron: In August of 1901, the schooner THOMAS P SHELDON was in tow when she sank northeast of Au Sable Point, near Oscoda, Michigan. She collided with her tow vessel, the steamer WAVERLY (qv), and was fatally holed. [3]

SHENANGO #1 ■ Wooden carferry of 1,938 t. and 282 ft., launched in 1895 at Toledo, OH
Lake Erie: Railroad carferries were generally expected to run year-round, and in most cases, they did. A colder-than-average winter, however, could play hob with these schedules, and sometimes even destroy a ship. The SHENANGO #1 was frozen into the ice off Conneaut, Ohio, in early January of 1904. She lay trapped with rolling stock aboard and fires banked for almost nine weeks. Then, just as the ice began to show signs of releasing its iron grip, the vessel caught fire and was destroyed. One crewman died in the blaze, which took place on March 11, 1904. [4]

L B SHEPARD ■ Mechant schooner, possibly the 214 t., 114 ft. vessel of this name launched at Buffalo in 1855
The SHEPARD is known to have been capsized by a white squall in the ninteenth century. [1]

SHEPHERD II ■ Tug
Lake Huron: In 1980 the tug SHEPHERD II was wrecked on a reef at Lyal Island, near Stokes Bay, Ontario. [1]

SHERIDAN ■ Barge, might be the schooner-barge PHIL SHERIDAN built at Bay City, MI
Lake Huron: This vessel reportedly went on the beach near Lexington, Michigan, in a storm and was wrecked in 1866. [1]

BELLE or **BELL SHERIDAN** ■ Merchant schooner of 265 t. and 135 ft., launched in 1852 at Oswego, NY
Lake Ontario: All but one of this schooner's crew were lost when she foundered in a huge storm on Weller's Bay, near Consecon, Ontario, on November 7, 1880. [2]

JIM SHERIFFS ■ Bulk freight steamer of 841 t. and 123 ft., launched in 1883 at Milwaukee
Lake Michigan: November 25, 1895 was the date that the steamer JIM SHERIFFS was driven ashore and wrecked by a gale. She went on the rocks near Summer Island, south of Michigan's Garden Peninsula, with the loss of one crewman. Though heavily damaged, she was recovered and rebuilt as the steamer JAMES DEMPSEY (qv). [2]

GRACE SHERMAN ■ Merchant schooner of 73 t.
Lake Erie: The little schooner GRACE SHERMAN was lost on October 8, 1875, when she stranded and was destroyed one mile east of the docks at Port Burwell, Ontario. [1]

P C SHERMAN ■ Merchant bark
Lake Erie: Seven men went down with this sailing ship on March 14, 1888. She sank in the icy spring waters off Long Point. [1]

ANNIE or **ANNE SHERWOOD** ■ Lumber schooner of 622 t. and 184 ft., launched at Fairport, OH, in 1866
Lake Superior: Laden with lumber and bound for Chicago, the schooner ANNIE SHERWOOD was caught by a violent storm on October 14, 1893. She was blown ashore to break up near Deer Park, Michigan, with two of her crew. She had suffered a previous serious accident, on Lake Erie in 1872. [4]

NELLIE SHERWOOD ■ Merchant schooner
Lake Huron: The sailing ship NELLIE SHERWOOD went down with all hands, five men, in September of 1882. The schooner was lost off Cabot Head, in western Georgian Bay. [2]

SHICKLUNA ■ Propeller freighter, probably the vessel of this name built in 1866 at St. Catharine's Ont.
Lake Huron: In 1883, this steamer foundered near Algoma Mills, Ontario, in the North Channel. [1]

L SHICKLUNA ■ Propeller freighter of 445 t. and 135 ft., launched in 1870 at St. Catharine's, Ont.
Lake Erie: The freighter L SHICKLUNA, built to the specifications of the old Welland Canal, was lost five miles east of Long Point on April 28, 1897. She reportedly foundered as a result of a collision. [2]

ADELLA SHORES ▪ Wooden lumber hooker of 734 t. and 195 ft., launched in 1894 at Gibraltar, MI
Lake Superior: The fate of this well-known steamer is one of the great mysteries of the Big Lake. She sailed into a heavy gale on May 1, 1909, with a crew of 14 and a cargo of salt, and was never heard from again. The ADELLA SHORES is thought to have been overwhelmed and sunk somewhere off Whitefish Point. [5+]

JAMES H SHRIGLEY ▪ Wooden bulk freight steamer of 534 t. and 172 ft., launched in 1881 at Milwaukee
Lake Ontario: On August 18, 1920, the SHRIGLEY foundered in a storm off Charlotte, New York, with a cargo of coal. Before the steamer sank, her crew was plucked off the vessel by the Coast Guard. The SHRIGLEY had been out on the lower part of Lake Huron in the big gale of 1913, and survived when many other larger and newer ships were destroyed in the area. [4]

ADAM SHUMAN ▪ Barge
Lake Erie: While in tow of the steamer BARRYTON, this barge broke in half in big waves and sank off Erie, Pennsylvania, on November 5, 1926. [1]

WILLIAM SHUPE ▪ Merchant schooner of 240 t. and 129 ft., launched in 1862 at Milan, OH
Lake Huron: Four crewmen perished when this schooner sank just north of Port Huron. She was carrying a cargo of lumber when she went down in a spring storm on May 19, 1894. [5]

SIBERIA ▪ Wooden bulk freight steamer of 1,618 t. and 272 ft., launched in 1882 at W Bay City, MI
Lake Erie: The October 20, 1905, blow swept down Lake Erie with teriffic force, almost wiping the lake clean of ships. The large steamer SIBERIA encountered towering seas and soon began to leak from their pounding, twisting punishment. She was turned toward Long Point and was successfully driven up on Bluff Bar, where her crew could escape, and, it was hoped, the steamer could wait out the gale. It was not to be. Before the storm ended, the waves had torn the big vessel to pieces where she lay. [5+]

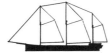

GENERAL FRANZ SIGEL ▪ Package and bulk freight schooner, 316 t. and 137 ft., launched in 1863 at Black River, OH
Lake Erie: As wooden vessels would become more and more aged, it would become less and less economical to repair them after accidents. On July 8, 1903 the 40-year-old schooner GENERAL FRANZ SIGEL filled and sank in shallow water from unknown causes. She went down near the lighthouse at Monroe, Michigan, and even though she appeared to be in a good position to be salvaged, she was abandoned to the lake. [3]

SIGNAL ▪ Propeller steamer of 94 t. and 82 ft., launched in 1896 at Collingwood, Ont.
Lake Huron: Midland, Ontario, is one of the oldest communities on the Upper Lakes. Long an area of Indian settlement, the Jesuits founded a mission there in 1639. The town was later a British military base and then a center of Georgian Bay commerce. In its heyday, dozens of ships operated out of the port, and a good number were lost in accidents. The small steamer SIGNAL was destroyed by fire at a Midland dock in 1905. [3]

SILVER CLOUD ▪ Merchant schooner of 97 t. and 79 ft., launched in 1869 at Sheboygan, WI
Lake Michigan: A white squall which occurred off Port Washington, WI, sank this little schooner. She was carrying a cargo of wood when she went down on July 7, 1891. [3]

SILVER LAKE ▪ Schooner-scow of 111 t. and 95 ft., launched in 1889 at Little Point Sauble, MI
Lake Michigan: One sailor died when this small, lumber carrying sailing ship was run down by a Pere Marquette Railroad carferry on May 28, 1900. The accident occurred off Manitowoc, Wisconsin. [3]

SILVER SPRAY ▪ Wooden steam freighter of 142 t. and 134 ft., launched in 1864 at Port Dalhousie, Ont.
Lake Huron: In March of each year, thousands of vessels all over the Great Lakes begin "fitting out" for the coming season. This process included minor repairs, painting, stocking supply lockers, testing equipment, and generally preparing the ship for the season ahead. For a few ships, fitting out meant disaster. The SILVER SPRAY was getting her coat of paint when she suddenly burst into flames and was quickly destroyed on March 29, 1878. The vessel was ruined at her dock at Owen Sound, Ontario. [5]

SILVER SPRAY ▪ Fishing tug of 40 t. and 83 ft., launched in 1889 at Buffalo, NY, as a passenger steamer
Lake Erie: The large fishing tug SILVER SPRAY went down off the entrance to the harbor at Cleveland. All nine of her crew perished with their boat on April 15, 1911. [4]

SILVER SPRAY ▪ Wooden passenger and package freight steamer of 95 t. and 109 ft., launched in 1894 at Ludington, MI, as the steamer BLOOMER GIRL
Lake Michigan: Three persons lost their lives when the little steamer SILVER SPRAY was nearly destroyed in September of 1914. She ran on Morgan Shoal, in Chicago harbor, then caught fire and was destroyed. The vessel was later recovered and completely rebuilt, and was not scrapped until 1925. [3]

SIMCOE ■ Steam freighter of 431 t. and 136 ft., launched in 1872 at Chatham, Ont., as the steamer MARY R ROBERTSON
Lake Huron: On November 24, 1880, this steamer was blasted by a gale and foundered with the loss of 16 of the 21 people aboard. She went down in Providence Bay on Manitoulin Island, on a spit of land that is known today as Simcoe Point. [5]

SIMLA ■ Wooden bulk freight steamer of 1,028 t. and 221 ft., launched in 1901 at Garden Island, Ont.
Lake Ontario: In 1926 the steamer SIMLA was destroyed by fire at her layup dock at Portsmouth, Ontario. The burned out hulk remained at the dock until she was towed out into the lake and scuttled in September of the following year. [2]

ROUSE SIMMONS ■ Package and bulk freight schooner of 245 t. and 130 ft., launched in 1869 at Milwaukee
Lake Michigan: The saga of the schooner ROUSE SIMMONS, the famous "Christmas tree ship" is a familiar one to Lakes buffs. For many years the SIMMONS had capped her season by making her final run to Chicago with her holds and decks packed with Christmas trees from Michigan's upper peninsula. In late November of 1913, the ship left Manistique, Michigan, loaded to the gunwales with her fragrant cargo. She sailed out into the teeth of a deadly westerly gale-blizzard, while most other lakers were making for shelter. The little ship struggled down the Wisconsin shore until, on the 26th, she was overwhelmed by the gale and foundered off Kewaunee, Wisconsin. All 17 sailors aboard the SIMMONS failed to make it home for Christmas that year. The wreck was believed to have been located in 1989. [5+]

WILLIAM H SIMONS ■ Barge of 471 t. and 114 ft., launched in 1919 at Kingston, NY
Lake Huron: An offshore fire destroyed this tow vessel on September 16, 1933. She was lost southwest of Thunder Bay Island, near Alpena, Michigan. [2]

LUCIA A SIMPSON ■ Merchant schooner of 227 t. and 127 ft., launched in 1875 at Manitowoc, WI
Lake Michigan: This schooner is well-known to historians and lovers of Lakes lore as one of the last remaining full-rigged sailing vessels on the inland seas. The schooner had finished her 60th season when she was destroyed by fire at her layup dock at Sturgeon Bay, Wisconsin, on December 5, 1935. The loss of this veteran ship must have brought a tear to the eye of many a gale-hardened lake sailor. [4]

SINGAPORE ■ Package and bulk freight schooner of 186 t. and 111 ft., launched in 1878 at Kingston, Ont.
Lake Huron: While attempting to ride out a storm at anchor off Kincardine, Ontario, on September 15, 1904, the SINGAPORE's anchors were torn loose from the bottom and the ship cast ashore south of the town. She was damaged beyond repair on the beach. She had also suffered a serious sinking accident near Marblehead, on Lake Erie, in 1898, but was recovered. [4]

SISKAWIT or **SISKOWIT** ■ Merchant schooner of 50 t., launched at LaPointe in 1840
Lake Superior: The small schooner SISKAWIT was engaged largely in the North Country's lucrative fur trade until she was lost on Christmas Day, 1849. She was wrecked just offshore near the mouth of the Chocolay River, southeast of Marquette. [4]

SISKIWIT ■ Steam tug
Lake Superior: In the fall of 1879, the tug SISKIWIT went hard aground on a reef near Grand Marais, Minnesota. One of the 30 people aboard her died during a rescue attempt, in which her rescuer, the tug AMETHYST, was almost destroyed as well. The SISKIWIT was later recovered. [2]

SITKA ■ Wooden bulk freight steamer of 1,740 t. and 272 ft., launched in 1887 at W Bay City
Lake Superior: This bulk freighter was laden with iron ore when she was driven aground in a gale on Au Sable Point, a few miles west of Grand Marais, Michigan. All of her crew were able to make it to shore, but the vessel fell apart and sank in the pounding waves. The accident occurred on October 4, 1904. [5+]

EDWARD E SKEELE ■ Merchant schooner of 214 t. and 123 ft., launched in 1856 at Manitowoc as the schooner PAULINE
Lake Huron: This small schooner had one of the longest working lives of any wooden vessel built on the Lakes. The were only a handful of schooners still engaged in lake trade when the SKEELE met her end on September 25, 1921, near the end of her 65th season. On that date, she was caught by a storm and tossed on a reef at Julia Bay, on Manitoulin Island, and destroyed. She later slipped into deep water. The remains of the ship were located in 1986. [3]

R J SKIDMORE ▪ Schooner-scow of 92 ft., launched in 1856 at Trenton, Michigan
Lake Michigan: During the Great Lakes lumbering era, many docks were built at seemingly random spots along the lakeshore. The main criteria for these little wharves seems to have been their proximity to standing timber. Many offered little shelter for the ships that needed to use them, and some were built in such shoal water that only the shallowest draft vessels could use them. Schooner-scows were the perfect vessels for this type of situation, but were still at the mercy of the vagaries of weather. The R J SKIDMORE had pulled away from Gill's Dock, north of Leland, Michigan, to keep from being beaten to death against the pilings. She dropped anchor a few hundred yards away and was attempting to ride out the gale, when her anchors slipped or her chains parted and she was driven ashore. She went to pieces near the beach on September 21, 1885. [2]

THOMAS B SKINNER ▪ Merchant schooner of 195 t.
Lake Michigan: On November 23, 1882, this lumber-laden schooner was reported lost near Grand Haven, Michigan. [1]

SLIGO ▪ Bulk freight schooner-barge of 284 t. and 142 ft., launched in 1860 at St. Catharine's, Ont.
Lake Ontario: Laden with a cargo of stone, this barge struck bottom on September 5, 1918, and sank near the west end of Toronto Island, off Toronto. She had also been heavily damaged in a wreck on Lake Huron in 1880. [3]

GEORGE B SLOAN ▪ Merchant schooner of of 353 t. and 139 ft., launched in 1873 at Oswego, NY
Lake Ontario: A 60 mph gale set upon this schooner on October 30, 1885. Riding high without cargo, the sail vessel was practically helpless before the powerful winds, and was driven on the breakwater at Oswego, where she broke up. One life was lost in the accident. [2]

SMITH ▪ Steam propeller of 218 t. and 120 ft., launched in 1881 at Buffalo
Lake Erie: The veteran steamer SMITH was lost on October 24, 1930. On that date she foundered in a storm, four miles off Long Point. [3]

SMITH & POST ▪ Schooner of 212 t. and 117 ft., launched in 1866 at Oakville, Ont.
Lake Erie: The schooner SMITH & POST had been leased by a private firm and converted for temporary duty as a lightship on Southeast Shoal. On August 18, 1901, the vessel was anchored on station when she caught fire, and with a quantity of highly-flammable illuminating oils on board, she was completely destroyed and sank before much could be done to save her. [3]

ABRAM SMITH ▪ Merchant schooner of 372 t. and 153 ft. overall, launched at Algonac, MI, in 1892
Lake Huron: This middle-sized schooner was pushed ashore on Great Duck Island by a gale on October 8, 1906. She was subsequently broken up by wave action. [2]

ANNA SMITH ▪ Bulk freight steam barge of 939 t. and 178 ft.
Lake Huron: This coal-carrying steamboat foundered in a heavy, late-season gale nine miles from the lighthouse at Cheboygan, Michigan, at the eastern end of the Straits of Mackinac. One life was lost in the November 27, 1889 accident. [4]

ELLA or **ELLA M SMITH** ▪ Steam tug, probably the 152 t., 88 ft. vessel launched in 1876 at Algonac, MI
Lake Huron: This large tug was reportedly sunk in the French River, just off Georgian Bay, in 1895. [1]

FLORENCE M SMITH ▪ Merchant schooner of 60 t. and 71 ft., launched in 1884 at Charlevoix, MI
Lake Michigan: In November of 1897, the schooner FLORENCE SMITH collided with a pier at South Haven, Michigan, in a storm and foundered. [2]

GOV. SMITH ▪ Wooden package freight steamer of 2,045 t. and 240 ft., launched in 1889 at Wyandotte, MI
Lake Huron: The steamer GOV. SMITH added her bones to the many lying off Pointe Aux Barques, Michigan, on August 19, 1906. The steamer collided with the much larger steel steamer URANUS (see W C FRANZ) and sank about ten miles north of the point. The URANUS was not seriously damaged, and stayed on the scene to pick up the crewmen of the lost steamer. [4]

H P SMITH ▪ Wooden steam tug
Lake Huron: The steam tug H P SMITH became a victim of fire when she burned and sank on the Saginaw River in 1872. [1]

HENRY B SMITH ▪ Steel bulk freight steamer of 6,631 t. and 565 ft., launched in 1906 at Cleveland
Lake Superior: Much of the wrath of the 1913 Big Storm seemed to be concentrated on Lake Huron, judging by the number of steamers destroyed there on Nov. 11. Far to the north, a similar fate had befallen the giant freighter HENRY B SMITH on the previous day. While downbound with a full cargo of iron ore, the big ore boat went missing with all hands, somewhere to the north of Marquette, Mich. 25 sailors were lost when the SMITH disappeared in one of the mightiest storms of the century. [5+]

HURLBUT or **HURLBURT W SMITH** ■ Steel bulk freight steamer of 4,662 t. and 414 ft., launched in 1903 at Lorain, OH, as a passenger steamer
Lake Huron: In August of 1958, the HURLBUT W SMITH went on the rocks near Little Current, Ontario, at the neck of Manitoulin Island and was so heavily damaged that she was abandoned. [3]

J A SMITH ■ Merchant schooner
Lake Huron: In 1887 this little schooner was reported to have sunk off Station Point, in the Straits of Mackinac. [1]

JESSIE SMITH ■ Merchant schooner of 117 t.
The SMITH was reported lost in 1848, but no detail was given. [1]

JOE SMITH ■ Propeller freighter of 145 t. and 82 ft., launched in 1907 at Superior, WI
Lake Superior: The small steamer JOE SMITH was reported lost to fire at Amethyst Harbor, Ont., in May of 1926. [1]

PETER SMITH ■ Steamer of 23 t.
Lake Erie: Three lives were lost when the tiny steamer PETER SMITH suffered a boiler explosion and sank off Vermilion, Ohio on April 6, 1884. [1]

SARAH M SMITH ■ Wooden steam tug of 45 t. and 75 ft., launched in 1882 at W Bay City, MI
Lake Superior: No lives were lost, but the the tug SARAH SMITH was destroyed when she caught fire, burned and sank on August 18, 1908. The vessel was lost just off Minnesota Point, near Duluth. [4]

SIDNEY E SMITH ■ Steel bulk freight steamer of 2,293 t. and 242 ft., launched in 1900 at Cleveland as the steamer WILLIAM P PALMER
Lake Erie: The bulk freighter SIDNEY E SMITH was destroyed when she went aground near Fairport Harbor, Ohio. She was shoved onto the beach by a heavy storm on November 17, 1936, and though the SMITH was later released, she was unable to be repaired economically, and was scrapped. No lives were lost in the accident, and her cargo of coal was later recovered. [2]

SIDNEY E SMITH, Jr ■ Steel bulk freight steamer of 5,712 t. and 480 ft., launched in 1906 at Wyandotte, MI as the steamer W K BIXBY

Lake Huron: The big ore boat SIDNEY E SMITH, Jr, was lost on June 5, 1972, near Port Huron, MI. On that date she was upbound light when she collided with the steamer PARKER EVANS, broke in half, and sank. No lives were lost. [4]

SOPHIA SMITH ■ Barge
Lake Huron: In 1874 this barge was lost on the lake, but details of the accident are lacking. [1]

THOMAS H SMITH ■ Tug of 130 ft.
Lake Michigan: This big tug was about five miles northeast of Racine, Wisconsin, when she collided with the steamer ARTHUR ORR and began to sink. When the cold lake water struck her hot boiler, the latter exploded violently, destroying the tug. The accident occurred in November of 1883. [2]

KITTIE SMOKE ■ Steam tug
Lake Huron: The tug KITTIE SMOKE burned to a total loss at the mouth of the Saginaw River in 1889. [2]

SNOW DROP ■ Merchant schooner of 190 t.
Lake Michigan: The schooner SNOW DROP was carrying a cargo of cedar posts when she was lost on April 30, 1892. The vessel stranded on North Point, near Milwaukee, and was destroyed. [2]

SNOWBIRD ■ Merchant schooner of 82 t., launched in 1862 at Presque Isle
Lake Ontario: The SNOWBIRD was inbound to Oswego, New York, with a cargo of lumber when she ran into a typical November gale. Unable to negotiate the harbor entrance, she signaled for a harbor tug to tow her in. The tug WHEELER responded, put a line on the schooner and began the tow, but the SNOWBIRD broke her towline and was driven ashore. Before she broke up, her crew was rescued by the U.S. Lifesaving Service. The accident occurred on November 12, 1880. [2]

SON & HEIR ■ Merchant schooner
Lake Huron: This schooner foundered on Georgian Bay in 1869 and was reported to be a total loss. [1]

ROSA SONSMITH ■ Merchant schooner of 766 t. and 181 ft., launched in 1882 at Saginaw, MI
Lake Erie: On November 5, 1900, the schooner ROSA SONSMITH was driven aground by a storm and broken up near Ashtabula, Ohio. She was laden with iron ore at the time. [3]

SOPHIA ■ Merchant schooner of 50 t.
Lake Huron: Club Island, northeast of the mouth of Georgian Bay, was the site of the loss of this little schooner. She was reportedly wrecked there on July 18, 1854. [2]

SOUTH AMERICAN ■ Package and bulk freight schooner of 100 t., launched in 1841 at Vermilion, OH
Lake Erie: In the last century, Lake Erie sailors often spoke of the ghost of this little schooner. Laden with a cargo of salt, the tall ship went missing, perhaps in a squall, somewhere along the course from Buffalo to Toledo. Long after the October 15, 1843 accident, sailors sometimes reported seeing her two-masted form slipping through the evening mist like a wraith, still manned by her ghostly crew of six. [3]

SOUTH HAVEN ■ Merchant schooner of 120 t. and 99 ft.
Lake Michigan: The small schooner SOUTH HAVEN went ashore in a storm on November 18, 1886, and was wrecked. She beached at Port Sheldon, Michigan, near Muskegon. [2]

SOUTH SHORE ■ Wooden steam coaster of 73 t. and 84 ft., launched in 1889
Lake Superior: The little steamer SOUTH SHORE was lost in a gale on November 24, 1912. Laden with a cargo of general freight, she split her seams in mountainous seas and sank west of Grand Marais, Michigan. All of her crew and her few passengers made it to shore safely. [2]

SOUTHERNER ■ Sidewheel passenger steamer of 550 t.
Lake Erie: This sidewheeler was stranded and lost somewhere on the lake in 1853. [1]

SOUTHAMPTON ■ Lumber schooner of 140 ft. overall, launched in 1861 at Garden Island, NY
Lake Huron: The schooner SOUTHAMPTON was pushed ashore and destroyed in Sarnia Bay, just north of the top of the St. Clair River. She was wrecked on October 28, 1904. Her remains were later removed. [2]

SOUTHEASTERN ■ Wooden carferry of 395 t. and 182 ft., launched at Montreal in 1880
Lake Ontario: A devastating fire struck this railroad ferry in June of 1897, burning off her upperworks and damaging her hull. She burned at Prescott, Ontario, and was thought to be a total loss. Her hull was still sound, however, and the ferry was recovered and completely rebuilt as the carferry INTERNATIONAL. [2]

SOUTHWESTERN ■ Merchant schooner
Lake Huron: In 1850, the schooner SOUTHWESTERN was lost in a collision near Pte Aux Barques, Michigan. [1]

SOUVENIR ■ Bulk freight schooner
Lake Michigan: Six lives were lost when the schooner SOUVENIR ran onto a bar near Ludington, Michigan, in a storm. Following the November 26, 1872, stranding, the vessel went to pieces. She was carrying a cargo of shingles at the time of the accident. [1]

SOVEREIGN ■ Steam freighter of 387 t. and 139 ft., launched in 1873 at St. Catharine's, Ont., as a barge
Lake Superior: This little freighter sank in an October 25, 1891, gale. She went down to the southwest of Lamb Island Light. There is some disagreement over the number of lives lost, some saying none, while others believe six crewmen died. [4]

SOVEREIGN OF THE SEAS ■ Merchant schooner of 135 t., launched in 1853
This vessel was almost completely destroyed by fire in 1865, probably on Lake Huron. Her ruined hull was used to build the schooner-barge MONTMORENCY (qv). [1]

CHARLES SPADEMAN ■ Bulk freight schooner-barge of 306 t. and 134 ft., launched in 1873 at Marine City, MI
Lake Erie: This sail-equipped barge, used primarily in the lumber trade, was lost on Dec. 10, 1909. She was holed by an ice floe and sank a few miles southwest of Put-in-Bay. [3]

GUY SPANGLER ■ Merchant schooner
Lake Michigan: The small schooner GUY SPANGLER was reported to have gone ashore and broken up near Glen Arbor, Michigan, in about 1876, while downbound with a cargo of grain. [1]

KYLE SPANGLER ■ Merchant schooner of 350 t. and 131 ft., launched in 1856 at Black River, OH
Lake Huron: On November 7, 1860, the schooner KYLE SPANGLER foundered from unknown causes south of Middle Island, on the northwest shore of the lake. [2]

SPARTA ■ Steel bulk freight steamer of 4,301 t. and 380 ft., launched in 1902 at Lorain, OH, as the steamer FRANK W HART
Lake Superior: Just a week before the deadly Armistice Day Storm of 1940 wrought so much destruction on Lake Michigan, the steamer SPARTA was destroyed by another big gale on Lake Superior. Deep-laden with a cargo of iron ore, the freighter was overwhelmed by the gale on November 5, and went aground on Mosquito Beach, 14 miles from Munising, Michigan. No lives were lost, and the SPARTA was pulled off the beach, but it was discovered that her back was broken, and she was cut up for scrap. [3]

SPARTAN ■ Sidewheel steamer
Lake Superior: This vessel stranded and was wrecked on remote Caribou Island, 22 miles south of Michipicoten Island, in June of 1883. She may have been recovered. [2]

J M SPAULDING ■ Merchant schooner of 72 t. and 88 ft., launched in 1875 at Manhattan, OH
Lake Huron: This small schooner was stranded and lost in the big blow of November 28, 1905. She went hard aground above Fort Gratiot, at the base of the lake. [2]

M B SPAULDING ■ Merchant schooner
Lake Huron: The schooner M B SPAULDING caught fire offshore and was destroyed off Forester, Michigan, in 1860. [1]

F V SPECHT ■ 55 t. vessel of unreported type
Detroit River: On October 24, 1888, the small F V SPECHT sank two miles below Windsor, Ontario. [1]

SPECULAR ■ Wooden bulk freight steamer of 1,741 t. and 263 ft., launched in 1882 at Cleveland
Lake Erie: The narrow Pelee Passage claimed this vessel on August 22, 1900. At the height of the shipping season, the SPECULAR collided with the wooden steamer DENVER, and sank a few miles west of Southeast Shoal. [4]

SPEED ■ Bulk freight schooner of 104 t.
Lake Michigan: Carrying a cargo of lumber, this small schooner foundered a quarter mile off Racine, Wisconsin, on April 18, 1883. Compare this report with the one below. [1]

SPEED ■ Schooner-scow of 40 t. and 59 ft., launched in 1866 at Detroit
Lake Michigan: In November of 1894, the little schooner-scow SPEED reportedly foundered off Racine, Wisconsin. [1]

SPEEDY ■ Merchant schooner launched in 1776 at Kingston, Ontario
Lake Ontario: An early Lakes disaster on Lake Ontario was the loss of this schooner on October 8, 1804. The veteran sailing ship lost a battle with a gale/blizzard and sank off Presqu'isle, Ontario. The exact number of crew and passengers is unknown, but it was thought to be between 20 and 39. [2]

GEORGE SPENCER ■ Wooden bulk freight steamer of 1,361 t. and 231 ft., launched in 1884 at Cleveland
Lake Superior: Sugar Loaf Landing, near Little Marais, Minnesota, was the location of the loss of this freighter in the Big Blow of 1905. She was towing the barge AMBOY (qv) when she was struck by a terrific gale on November 28. She cut the barge loose in an effort to improve the chances of both vessels, but the wind drove the pair ashore anyway. The GEORGE SPENCER was destroyed by the pounding of waves soon after, but her crew had already made it to shore safely. [3]

SPOKANE ■ Steel bulk freight steamer of 2,357 t. and 312 ft., launched in 1886 at Cleveland
Lake Superior: The SPOKANE was the first steel freighter to operate on Lake Superior, and that lake is where she nearly ended her career as well. On September 16, 1912, the big bulk carrier was caught in a storm and driven onto Gull Rock, near Manitou Island. She broke in half and was declared a total loss by her underwriters, but was later recovered and rebuilt, lasting another 23 years. No lives were lost in the accident. [5+]

SPORT ■ Tug
Lake Huron: The tug SPORT was reported to have foundered off Lexington, Michigan, in 1920. [1]

NOAH C SPRAGUE ■ Wooden steam tug
Detroit River: All hands aboard the NOAH C SPRAGUE died when she was destroyed by an explosion at the mouth of the river. The accident occurred on November 27, 1857. [2]

J R SPRANKLE ■ Oil screw of 44 t.
Lake Erie: The exact location is not given for the loss of this vessel, which foundered in a storm on November 21, 1956. [1]

SPRAY ■ Merchant schooner
Lake Michigan: The schooner SPRAY is said to have been sunk by a white squall. [1]

ELLEN SPRY ■ Bulk freight schooner of 546 t. and 170 ft., launched in 1873 at Sturgeon Bay, WI
Lake Michigan: A reef near the Skillagallee area of Beaver Island Passage is the final resting place of this big schooner. The ELLEN SPRY was caught in a gale on November 6, 1886, struck bottom and went to pieces. She was carrying a load of coal at the time. No lives were lost. [3]

JOHN SPRY ■ Steam tug launched in 1866 at Sturgeon Bay, WI
Lake Michigan: On November 4, 1885, the tug JOHN SPRY was in port at Wrightstown, Wisconsin, when she caught fire and was destroyed, but without loss of life. [1]

GALE STAPLES ■ Wooden bulk freight steamer of 2,197 t. and 277 ft., launched in 1888 at Marine City, MI, as the steamer WILLIAM E MORELEY
Lake Superior: This large steamer was upbound with a cargo of coal when she was assaulted by a terrific gale on October 1, 1918. The northwest storm blew the freighter on Au Sable Reef, then tore her to pieces. U.S. Lifesavers took her crew off before she broke up. [5+]

M STALKER ■ Merchant schooner of 350 t. and 135 ft., launched in 1863 at Milan, OH
Lake Huron: In November of 1886, the schooner M STALKER was lost in the Straits of Mackinac following a collision with the steamer WAUBAUSHENE. She sank just off Cheboygan, Michigan. [3]

H G STAMBACK ■ Merchant brig
Lake Michigan: The brig H G STAMBACK was struck by heavy winds that capsized her and blew her to shore in 1857. Her hulk was discovered on a reef on the west side of North Manitou Island, but later slipped into deeper water. [2]

N M STANDART or **STANNARD** ■ Lumber barge or schooner-barge of 332 t.
Lake Erie: On November 18, 1880, this vessel sank five miles east of the harbor at Fairport, OH. She was carrying a load of lumber at the time of the accident. [2]

B A STANDART ■ Merchant bark
Lake Erie: The only available information on this sailing ship states that she was sunk by a white squall on the lake. [1]

R W STANDLEY ■ Propeller freighter of 350 t. and 136 ft., launched in 1872 at Chatham, Ont.
Lake Ontario: This vessel was reported to have been accidentally destroyed by fire in October of 1875. [1]

STANLEY ■ Scow
Lake Huron: Georgian Bay saw the loss of this scow in 1859, when she foundered in a storm. [1]

STAR ■ Merchant schooner, probably the 30 t. vessel of this name launched in 1841 at Oak Orchard, NY
Lake Huron: Six lives were snuffed out when the small schooner STAR foundered in a Georgian Bay storm in 1852. [1]

STAR ■ Steam tug, probably the 63 t. vessel launched in 1860 at Detroit
Lake Huron: This little steam vessel was destroyed by fire at Saginaw in 1869. [3]

STAR OF HOPE ■ 206 t. vessel of unreported type
Lake Erie: The STAR OF HOPE was reported to have stranded on Pelee Island on April 1, 1886, and probably broke up in place. [2]

STAR OF THE NORTH ■ Lumber schooner of 214 t. and 123 ft., launched in 1854 at Cleveland
Lake Michigan: A November 16, 1903 gale sent this small schooner onto a reef near the Manitou Islands and dashed her to pieces with big waves. [2]

STARLIGHT ■ Sail yacht, in use as a camp supply vessel
Lake Superior: All five persons aboard this small sail vessel were lost when she went missing somewhere off Au Train, Michigan. She sank with her cargo of lumber camp supplies on September 29, 1880. [2]

STARLIGHT ■ Merchant brig
Lake Huron: Four sailors died when this little two-master was destroyed by fire on Georgian Bay in 1883. Compare this report with the one below. [2]

STARLIGHT ■ 11 t. vessel of unreported type
Lake Huron: September, 1892, is the date given for the loss of this vessel on Georgian Bay. Four people died in the accidental fire. [1]

STARLIGHT ■ Gas screw of 26 t., launched in 1915
Lake Michigan: The M/V STARLIGHT was brand-new when she became a victim of fire on November 13, 1915. She burned on Green Bay, but with no loss of life. [1]

STARUCCA ■ Wooden passenger and package freight steamer of 1,313 t. and 218 ft., launched in 1875 at Buffalo
Lake Superior: The braced wooden steamer STARUCCA was driven on a bar near Deer Park by a frigid gale on November 15, 1887. At first she was thought to be in no danger and the crew stayed aboard, but as the storm grew in intensity, it became apparent the the vessel was not going to last. The Deer Park U.S. Lifesaving Service crew rowed their tiny surfboat though gigantic seas three times to take the frozen men off the stricken ship, and all were saved before the STARUCCA broke up and went under. [3]

GEORGE STEELE ■ Merchant schooner of 271 t. and 137 ft., launched in 1855 at Three Mile Bay, NY
Lake Huron: In October of 1898, this old schooner was stranded in a storm which put her on an inshore reef near Oscoda, Michigan. She broke up in place. [3]

H B STEELE ■ Merchant schooner of 118 t.
Lake Michigan: The schooner H B STEELE was driven ashore by a gale at Point Betsie, on the Michigan shore. She broke up during the November, 1870, storm. [1]

STEELVENDOR ■ Steel package freight motor vessel of 1,695 t. and 250 ft., launched in 1923 at Kearney, NJ
Lake Superior: Laden with a cargo of steel billets destined for the production of war materiel, the STEELVENDOR capsized and sank in heavy seas off Manitou Island, on the North Shore, on September 3, 1942. One life was lost when she went down. [3]

HENRY STEINBRENNER ■ Steel bulk freight steamer of 4,345 t. and 427 ft., launched in 1901 at Port Huron, MI
Lake Superior: Two major accidents 42 years apart marred the career of this big ore boat. She sank following a collision in the St. Marys River in 1909 and was declared a loss. But she was salvaged and returned to service. On

May 11, 1953, the now-aged steamer was laden with iron ore and battling a 75 mph gale off Isle Royale when some of her hatch covers blew off. In a big storm, green water will wash right over the decks of even the largest ships, and this is what happened to the STEINBRENNER now. Waves thundering right into her cavernous holds sent the vessel to the bottom quickly. Part of her crew had abandoned before the ship went down, but only 13 of the 30 on board lived to tell the tale. [5+]

STEINHOFF ■ Wooden propeller
Detroit River: A dock, a warehouse, and the steamer STEINHOFF were destroyed in a fire that occurred at Detroit on August 13, 1879. Two people died as a result. [1]

STELLA ■ Merchant schooner
Lake Michigan: This sail vessel was reported sunk on Lake Michigan by a white squall. [1]

WILLIAM H STEPHENS ■ Merchant schooner of 297 t. and 117 ft., launched in 1855 at Cleveland
Lake Huron: Scarecrow Island and its protecting ring of reefs lie at the southern projection of Thunder Bay, and well out of the normal shipping lane. But this schooner was scudding along the shore when she struck one of Scarecrow's outlying reefs and sank. The loss occurred on November 15, 1863. [2]

SAMUEL STEPHENSON ■ Vessel information unavailable, but may be the 175 ft. vessel of this name scrapped in 1935
Lake Huron: Some mystery surrounds this vessel which was found in the bottom of the Saginaw River when the water was exceptionally low in the 1930s. Vessels brought into shipyards for scrapping were often stripped of their valuables, then scuttled or put to the torch, and this may have been the fate of the STEPHENSON. [2]

BELLE STEVENS ■ Lumber schooner of 88 t.
Lake Michigan: Carrying a cargo of lumber and shingles, this sail vessel sank just outside the harbor of Manistee, Michigan, on November 1, 1890. [1]

FRANK B STEVENS ■ Wooden bulk freight steamer of 304 t. and 146 ft., launched in 1867 at Buffalo
Lake Erie: In May of 1919, the steamer FRANK B STEVENS sank in the harbor at Ashtabula, Ohio. She was deemed too old to attempt salvage, and was abandoned. [2]

J H STEVENS ■ Merchant schooner of 94 t. and 100 ft., launched in 1866 at Detroit
Lake Huron: The old schooner J H STEVENS caught fire and was destroyed offshore from Presque Isle, Michigan, in 1927. [2]

O STEVENS ■ Merchant bark
Lake Huron: This small sail vessel was reported wrecked in a storm on Georgian Bay in 1867. [1]

WILLIAM H STEVENS ■ Wooden package freight steamer of 1,332 t. and 212 ft., launched in 1886 at W Bay City, MI
Lake Erie: This steamboat was carrying a mixed cargo including flaxseed and copper ingots when she caught fire on September 8, 1902. The steamer burned to the waterline and sank off Clear Creek, Ont., west of Long Point. [4]

STEWART ■ Dredge barge of 293 t.
Lake Ontario: On December 23, 1931, this barge was destroyed by fire in the Welland Canal, at Welland, Ont. [1]

DAVID STEWART ■ Merchant schooner of 545 t. and 171 ft., launched in 1867 at Cleveland
Lake Erie: The schooner DAVID STEWART was lost on October 6, 1893, when she sank off Pigeon Bay, with no loss of life. She was almost destroyed by stranding near Fairport, Ohio, in 1891. [3]

ERIE STEWART ■ Bulk freight schooner of 121 ft. overall, launched in 1874 at Port Dover, Ont.
Lake Huron: Southampton, Ont., was the site of the loss of this schooner on October 7, 1907. A westerly gale struck the vessel in the harbor and drove her against a pier, where she foundered in shallow water and broke up. [1]

R G STEWART ■ Wooden passenger and package freight steamer of 197 t. and 100 ft., launched in 1878 at Buffalo
Lake Superior: The little steamer R G STEWART was transporting a small number of passengers and a cargo of cattle on June 4, 1899. She ran aground on the shore of Michigan Island, on the east side of the Apostles group, and caught fire. All but one of the 12 persons aboard survived the blaze, and some quick-thinking soul herded the cargo overboard, and most of them were saved as well. [4]

W W STEWART ■ Lighter barge of 295 t. and 160 ft., launched in 1865 at Port Huron, MI as the carferry W J SPICER
Lake Erie: This vessel had been sitting idle for seven years when she caught fire at her dock at Buffalo. She was destroyed on October 12, 1909. [2]

THOMAS D STIMSON ■ Wooden bulk freight steamer of 509 t. and 170 ft. overall, launched as the schooner-barge VIRGINIUS in 1881 at Mt. Clemens, MI
St. Clair River: On June 30, 1903, this freighter was about halfway down the St. Clair River with her load of lumber when she caught fire and was totally destroyed. [2]

H D STOCKMAN ■ Merchant schooner of 11 t. and 40 ft., launched in 1885 at Au Sable, MI
Lake Huron: The tiny schooner H D STOCKMAN was lost in a squall on Saginaw Bay in 1894. [2]

ELLA G STONE ■ Wooden tug of 42 ft. and 69 t., launched in 1881 at Algonac, MI
Lake Superior: A forest fire that swept through Duluth on October 12, 1918, destroyed this small tug at her dock. See also MENTOR. [2]

GEORGE STONE ■ Wooden bulk freight steamer of 1,841 t. and 270 ft., launched in 1893 at W Bay City, MI
Lake Erie: Five of the 18 persons aboard this vessel on October 12, 1919, lost their lives in the accident which also destroyed the ship. The steamer went hard aground on Grubb Reef, in the Pelee Passage. She caught fire after stranding, then sank near the channel. [5+]

WILLIAM STONE ■ Passenger and package freight schooner of 115 ft. overall, launched in 1896 at Vermilion, OH
Lake Michigan: Cecil Bay, in the western Straits of Mackinac, was the resting place of this little schooner, which struck bottom on the rocky shoreline and sank on October 12, 1901. [2]

STORM SPIRIT ■ Merchant schooner
Lake Huron: The schooner STORM SPIRIT was reported to have sunk following a collision which occurred in 1864. [1]

CITY OF THE STRAITS ■ Merchant schooner of 392 t. and 134 ft., launched in 1866 at Detroit
Lake Superior: Fire destroyed the schooner CITY OF THE STRAITS while she was tied to her dock at Ontonagon, Michigan, in 1896. No lives were lost, but the ship burned to the hull. [3]

STRANGER ■ Merchant schooner possibly the vessel of this name built at Bay Port, MI, in 1872
Lake Huron: In 1873, the schooner STRANGER was stranded and wrecked in Saginaw Bay, near Caseville, MI. [2]

STRANGER ■ Merchant schooner of 15 t. and 60 ft., launched in 1875
Lake Superior: This little coaster was lost in the kind of accident that all sailors feared. She was not carrying an anchor when she was dismasted in a storm on December 11, 1875, off Grand Marais, Minnesota. Those on shore tried to get a line to her, but the westerly gale just blew the schooner further and further away from shore. Her would-be rescuers could only watch in dismay as she drifted from sight. Somewhere out on the lonely lake, her crew froze to death, while the wreckage of the STRANGER was pushed to her final resting place on the Keweenaw Peninsula. [4]

STRATHMORE ■ Wooden package and bulk freight steamer of 1,101 t. and 205 ft., launched in 1871 at Detroit as the passenger and package freight steamer GORDON CAMPBELL
Lake Superior: No lives were lost, but the STRATHMORE was totally destroyed and her cargo of grain ruined when she struck the rocky bottom near Michipicoten Island. She broke up soon after, and her remains slid into deep water. Her unusual profile betrays her lineage as a mid-engined passenger ship. [4]

CHARLES A STREET ■ Wooden bulk freight steamer of 512 t. and 165 ft., launched at Grand Haven, MI, in 1888
Lake Huron: The steamer CHARLES A STREET was destroyed in an offshore fire that occurred near Richmondville, Michigan, on July 20, 1908. All of the STREET's crew were rescued from the burning ship. [3]

ELIZA H STRONG ■ Wooden bulk freight steamer of 781 t. and 205 ft., launched in 1874 at Marine City, MI, as the steamer N K FAIRBANKS (qv)
Lake Huron: On October 25, 1904, this steamer caught fire when she was abeam of Lexington, Michigan, burned to the waterline, and foundered. Her crew were able to abandon ship in time to save themselves. This ship had two other serious accidents before her final one. In 1895 she was devastated by fire near Detour, Michigan, and in 1901 she was leaking so badly in a gale on Lake Superior that she was abandoned, though she was found later, still afloat. [5+]

HELEN STRONG ■ Passenger and package freight steamer of 253 t.
Lake Erie: Two lives were lost when the steamer HELEN STRONG stranded just east of 20 Mile Creek, near Barcelona, New York. The ship had come to rest just below a 60-foot cliff and was breaking up quickly, but over 60 survivors were hauled up the cliff face to safety. The accident and magnificent rescue took place on November 2, 1846. [2]

STURGEON BAY ■ Bulk freight scow
Lake Michigan: On October 27, 1888, this scow was carrying a cargo of stone when she sank close in to shore near Manistee, Michigan. [1]

WILLIAM STURGIS ■ Merchant schooner of 263 t.
Lake Michigan: The schooner WILLIAM STURGIS stranded and was lost on September 29, 1881. She was wrecked just north of the harbor entrance at Ludington, Michigan. [1]

JOHN A STYNINGER ▪ Steamer of 117 t., launched in 1915
Lake Huron: No lives were lost when this brand-new steamer was destroyed by fire while docked at Grace Harbor, (now Grace) Michigan, 18 miles southeast of Cheboygan, Michigan. She was lost on November 12, 1915. [1]

SUCCESS ▪ Schooner of 600 t. and 135 ft., launched in 1790 at Moulmain, Burma
Lake Erie: This ship has a fascinating history and was probably the oldest operational ship afloat when she was finally lost in 1946. She was built of teak and was originally in the tea and silk trade from the Orient to Britain. In 1851, at an age when most vessels are ready for the shipbreakers, she was stationed in Australia as a waterborne prison. She was relieved of this duty in 1868, and was abandoned until scuttled in Sydney Harbor in 1885. In 1890, at age 100, she was resurrected and converted into a floating museum of the British penal system of the 18th Century. She sailed to many ports in Europe, and finally came to American shores in 1912, departing Liverpool on the same day as the ill-fated TITANIC. After many years on display along the East Coast, the ship came to the Great Lakes, where she was finally retired in 1939. On July 4, 1946, the vessel caught fire at Port Clinton, Ohio, and was destroyed, 156 years after sliding down the ways in the Far East. [4]

W J SUFFEL ▪ Package and bulk freight schooner of 126 ft. overall, launched in 1874 at Port Burwell, Ont.
Lake Erie: Another of the many victims of Long Point was the schooner W J SUFFEL. She grounded and went to pieces in a storm on November 26, 1910. [1]

JOSEPH C SUIT ▪ Wooden bulk freight steamer of 152 t. and 105 ft., launched in 1884 at Saugatuck, MI
Detroit River: In the tangle of traffic that moved up, down and across this busy waterway, the occasional collision was inevitable. The tiny JOSEPH C SUIT was tied to a wharf at Detroit on November 9, 1912, when she was rammed and sunk by the giant, brand-new sidewheeler CITY OF DETROIT III. The little steamer was a total loss. [2]

SULTAN ▪ Merchant schooner
Lake Huron: In 1873 this schooner is said to have sunk off Port Hope, on the northeast shore of Michigan's thumb. [1]

SULTANA ▪ Merchant schooner
Lake Huron: The schooner SULTANA reportedly went down somewhere on the lake in 1863. [1]

SUMATRA ▪ Schooner-barge of of 845 t., and 204 ft., launched in 1874 at Black River, OH
Lake Michigan: The schooner-barge SUMATRA was in tow of the steamer B W ARNOLD (qv) on September 30, 1896, when she was blasted by a rapidly rising westerly gale. The barge was blown down and foundered off Milwaukee with the loss of four of her crew. The rest were rescued by the ARNOLD, herself lost less than two months later. The SUMATRA had been carrying a cargo of steel railroad rails, a commodity which, at that time, was helping to end the era of wooden ships. [4]

SUMMIT ▪ Merchant schooner
Lake Huron: The SUMMIT was a small schooner that was reported stranded and lost off Tawas Point, north of Saginaw Bay, in 1872. [1]

SUN ▪ Propeller freighter of 629 t. and 192 ft.
Lake Erie: The steamer SUN was handling a three-barge tow when she was hit by a Lake Erie storm and put in distress on July 12, 1874. She cut the barges loose just before sinking abeam of Pointe Aux Pins, Ontario. All three barges reportedly made Detroit under their own sail. [2]

SUNBEAM ▪ Sidewheel passenger and package freight steamer of 400 t. and about 140 ft., launched in 1861 at Manitowoc, WI, as the steamer VICTOR
Lake Superior: A late summer gale struck this nearly new sidewheeler off the Keweenaw on August 28, 1863. According to reports, the vessel was simply torn apart by big waves and went down, taking 28 of the 29 aboard with her. When built, this vessel was equipped with the unique and highly unsuccessful Whittaker propulsion system, which was removed after her first year of use. [4]

SUNNYSIDE ▪ Merchant schooner
Lake Michigan: Carrying a cargo of ore, the schooner SUNNYSIDE stranded and broke up on the Fox Islands, in August of 1881. [1]

SUNRISE ▪ Merchant bark
Lake Huron: In 1871, the bark SUNRISE was reported to have sunk in the Straits of Mackinac, near Bois Blanc Island. [1]

SUNSHINE ▪ Schooner-barge of 516 t. and 159 ft., launched in 1854 at E Saginaw, MI, as a bark
Lake Erie: While operating as a bark, this ship capsized in a squall near Fairport, Ohio. Most of her crew died in the accident, which occurred about 1871. She was recovered and converted to a schooner-barge. [2]

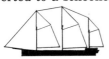

Detroit River: The end came for the old schooner-barge SUNSHINE when she caught fire on November 28, 1906, and was destroyed on the river. [3]

SUPERIOR ■ Merchant schooner or small sidewheel steamer
Lake Erie: On May 18, 1825, the SUPERIOR struck a bar off Cedar Point, near Sandusky, Ohio, and sank. Her machinery may later have been recovered. One historian suggests that she was salvaged and is the vessel below. [3]

SUPERIOR ■ Sidewheel passenger and package freight steamer of 346 t. and 126 ft., launched in 1822 at Buffalo
Lake Michigan: The small sidewheeler SUPERIOR is reported to have struck bottom and stranded offshore from New Buffalo, MI, in Oct., 1843. She broke up soon after. This is the vessel that was equipped with salvaged engines from the pioneer steamer WALK-IN-THE-WATER (qv). [4]

SUPERIOR ■ Sidewheel passenger and package freight steamer of 567 t. and 184 ft., launched in 1845 at Perrysburg, OH
Lake Superior: Pictured Rocks National Lakeshore is a beautiful slice of Lakes scenery. It is also the site of one of the most costly (in terms of life lost) shipwrecks on the big lake. On October 30, 1856, the big sidewheeler SUPERIOR was carrying a capacity load of freight and about 30 passengers when she was lost near Cascade, Michigan. She was making good weather of a storm when suddenly her rudder was ripped off and the vessel became helpless flotsam. She was literally thrown into the shallows under high cliffs, and witnesses say she fell apart within 15 minutes of striking. Sources differ on the number of lives lost, with 35 (out of 53) being the most commonly accepted. The SUPERIOR was one of the largest (and the last) ships ever to be portaged around the Sault de Ste Marie before the building of the Soo locks in 1855. [5+]

SUPERIOR ■ Schooner-barge of 306 t. and 136 ft., launched in 1861 at Detroit
Lake Huron: In 1895, this vessel, in transit without cargo, stranded and was wrecked at Oak Point, west of Pte Aux Barques, Michigan. [3]

SUPERIOR ■ Wooden propeller of 964 t. and 187 ft., launched in 1873 at Gibraltar, MI
Lake Michigan: One life was lost when this steamboat went aground in the Beaver Islands on August 28, 1898. She stranded one mile west of Gull Island lighthouse and broke up. [2]

SUPERIOR ■ Wooden steam sandsucker of 327 t. and 138 ft., launched in 1881 at Fort Howard, WI, as the sloop MENTOR
Lake Huron: Literally hundreds of strandings have occurred in the narrow Detour Channel, where the St. Marys River empties into Lake Huron. Nearly all grounded have been quickly recovered and sent on their way (a tug operator at Detour, Michigan once had a lucrative business just pulling stranded vessels off the sandbars). The sandsucker SUPERIOR was not as lucky as most. As quite often happens, the jolt of striking bottom caused her to catch fire, and the

old vessel burned to destruction on June 11, 1929. Her crewmen were able to make it to shore safely. [4]

SUPERIOR CITY ■ Steel bulk freight steamer of 4,795 t. and 429 ft., launched in 1898 at Lorain, OH
Lake Superior: As the shipping industry has grown, the need for more and more "rules of the road" have become apparent. Early ships went pretty much wherever the wanted, however they wanted. Modern skippers don't have that luxury. The tragic accident that destroyed the SUPERIOR CITY and killed 29 of her 33 crewmen is an example of the necessity of passing procedures, particularly when large vessels are involved. On August 20, 1920, the SUPERIOR CITY was downbound with iron ore and proceeding into Whitefish Bay as she had done hundreds of times. On board the 580 foot upbound freighter WILLIS L KING, things were also going routinely. The two ships signalled as they prepared to pass, but somehow signals were misunderstood and the vessels turned first one way, then the other in an effort to avoid a collision. Their efforts went for nothing. The KING plowed into the port side of the heavily-laden SUPERIOR CITY which had cut across her bow, and the latter sank very quickly. The SUPERIOR CITY was one of the first vessels designed specifically for use with the big Hewlett unloaders. The wreck was located by a diver in 1972. [5+]

CITY OF SUPERIOR ■ Wooden propeller freighter of 700 t., launched in 1857 at Cleveland
Lake Superior: On November 11, 1857, this steamer foundered at the mouth of the Eagle River, on the northwest side of the Keweenaw Peninsula. [2]

SUPPLY ■ Merchant schooner
Lake Huron: The SUPPLY was an early schooner that was reported lost on the lake in 1832. [1]

SURPRISE ■ Tug of 11 t.
Lake Huron: The tiny tug SURPRISE burned on Cask Bay, in Georgian Bay, on November 4, 1905. [2]

SURVEYOR ■ Launch
Lake Erie: This small commercial vessel was reported sunk at Ashtabula, Ohio, in 1965. [1]

SWALLOW ■ Wooden lumber hooker of 257 t. and 134 ft., launched in 1873 at Trenton, MI
Lake Erie: This small lumber steamer was lost off Lake Erie's dreaded Long Point. She sank there in a heavy storm which sent her down on October 18, 1901. [2]

SWAN ■ Wooden steam tug
Lake Huron: The tug SWAN was a victim of fire at East Saginaw, Michigan, when she burned on the Saginaw River in 1875. [1]

SWANSEA ▪ Steam passenger and freight ferry of 19 t. and 77 ft., launched in 1887 at Detroit
Lake Superior: A fire claimed this vessel in the Duluth-Superior harbor on July 28, 1926. [2]

SWEDEN ▪ Schooner-scow of 324 t.
Lake Erie: Several lives were lost when the schooner-scow SWEDEN was blown aground by a gale and broke up near Port Stanley, Ontario. She was carrying a load of lumber at the time of the October 8, 1877, accident. [3]

SWEEPSTAKES ▪ Merchant schooner of 310 t. and 141 ft., launched in 1856 at Cleveland
Lake Huron: In 1896, this schooner was reported sunk in "Big Tub," an inlet of Tobermory, Ontario, harbor. The vessel was probably recovered. One source reports the year as 1867. [3]

SWEETHEART ▪ Bulk freight schooner-barge of 538 t. and 176 ft., launched in 1867 at Detroit
Lake Huron: The schooner-barge SWEETHEART was carrying a load of lumber when she caught fire above Port Huron on July 6, 1913. The vessel burned to the hull and then sank. She had also foundered and been recovered in 1880. [3]

SWIFT ▪ Wooden bulk freight steamer of 886 t. and 192 ft., launched in 1893 at Marine City, MI, as the steamer WOTAN
Lake Michigan: On December 5, 1935, the SWIFT was just being put to bed for the winter when she caught fire at her dock and was destroyed. The accident occurred at Sturgeon Bay, Wisconsin. [2]

SYLPH ▪ Merchant schooner
Lake Erie: An early wreck at the western end of the lake was the schooner SYLPH. She was blown ashore on North Bass Island on May 12, 1824, and wrecked. Several lives were reported lost in the accident. [3]

SYRACUSE ▪ Merchant schooner
Lake Huron: In 1863, the schooner SYRACUSE sank off 40 Mile Point, at the northwest corner of the lake. [1]

SYRACUSE ▪ Steamer of 85 t. and 79 ft., launched in 1897 at Toledo
Lake Erie: On August 26, 1908, this little steamer was stranded and wrecked in Maumee Bay, off Toledo. No lives were lost, but the vessel was a total loss. [2]

HORACE TABER ▪ Lumber schooner of 269 t. and 138 ft., launched in 1867 at St. Clair, MI as the schooner AMOSKEAG
Lake Ontario: A storm that built up over the whole length of Lake Ontario caught this aged schooner on November

27, 1922. She was driven ashore on Simcoe Island, southwest of Kingston, Ontario, and pounded to pieces. The coal-laden vessel was lost with all hands. [2]

TABLE ROCK ▪ Barge
Lake Huron: In 1872, this barge foundered off Tawas Point, on the Michigan shore. [1]

TACOMA ▪ Wooden bulk freight steamer of 1,879 t. and 261 ft., launched in 1881 at Cleveland
Lake Michigan: August 23, 1914, was the last day afloat for this freighter. On that date she caught fire and was destroyed at Ludington, Michigan. [2]

TACOMA ▪ Tug of 76 t. and 73 ft.
Lake Michigan: The tug TACOMA was lost at Chicago in November of 1929 when her seams opened in a storm and she sank. [1]

TAILWINDS ▪ Trolling boat of 36 ft.
Lake Superior: The fishing craft TAILWINDS was destroyed in a boatshed fire off Port Wing, Wisconsin on July 9, 1975. [1]

TAMPA ▪ Wooden bulk freight steamer of 1,972 t. and 261 ft., launched on 1890 at W Bay City, MI
Detroit River: The exact date is not given, but the wooden steamer TAMPA was lost on the river in mid-1911. She sank as the result of a collision and lay on the river bottom until she was raised and scrapped in 1914. [2]

TARRY NOT ▪ Merchant schooner of 266 t. and 122 ft.
Lake Erie: The schooner TARRY NOT was lost on the lake in 1860, though one source says she went down on Lake Huron. [2]

TARTIN ▪ Merchant schooner of 188 t.
Lake Erie: This small schooner was bound for Toledo when she struck a reef off Point Pelee. The vessel was abandoned after she stranded on December 1, 1870. [1]

TASHMOO ▪ Steel sidewheel passenger steamer of 1,344 t. and 303 ft., launched at Detroit in 1900
Detroit River: The graceful passenger steamer TASHMOO was a famous and popular excursion vessel in the Detroit and Lake Erie area. Her career was ended by an accident that could have been one of the great shipping disasters of the Lakes, had it not been for a quick-thinking skipper. On June 18, 1936, the sidewheeler was making her usual run down the river with a full complement of passengers, when she struck a floating obstruction. A quick examination revealed that the ship had a large hole near

her bow and was taking in the Detroit River at a frightful rate. While her unwitting passengers laughed and danced, the skipper ordered down "full ahead" and steered the vessel to a dock at Amherstburg, Ontario. While her passengers were disembarking, the lovely vessel settled into the muddy bottom next to the dock. The TASHMOO was never returned to service, but was scrapped the following year. [5+]

TASMANIA ■ Bulk freight schooner-barge of 979 t. and 228 ft., launched in 1871 at Port Huron, MI, as the steamer JAMES COUCH
Lake Erie: The TASMANIA was a victim of the deadly storm that swept the Lakes on October 20, 1905. In tow of the steamer BULGARIA (qv), the big schooner-barge dropped down from the top of a big sea and hit the bottom near Southeast Shoal, in Pelee Passage. She quickly went down with all eight hands. In an unusual footnote to the accident, her anchor, which had been removed from the wreck by souvenir hunters, was returned to the wreck site in 1989. [5+]

TAWAS ■ Steam tug
Lake Huron: This towing vessel was lost off Sand Beach, Michigan, in 1874. She sank following a boiler explosion. [1]

CITY OF TAWAS ■ Merchant bark of 271 t.
Lake Michigan: The bark CITY OF TAWAS was reported to be on the beach and wrecked near St. Joseph, Michigan, in November of 1877. One source says she was lost on Lake Huron. [3]

GENERAL TAYLOR ■ Wooden propeller steamer of 462 t. and 173 ft., launched in 1848 at Buffalo, NY
Lake Michigan: The big propeller GENERAL TAYLOR was destroyed by a storm in October (3rd or 18th) of 1862. She was driven hard aground on Sleeping Bear Point, where she broke up in place. [4]

H TAYLOR ■ Merchant schooner
Lake Superior: The schooner H TAYLOR was reported as lost due to foul weather in 1876. [1]

HELEN TAYLOR ■ Bulk freight steam barge of 52 t. and 60 ft., launched in 1894 at Grand Haven, MI
Lake Michigan: This small steamer foundered off St. Helena Island, in the Straits of Mackinac, in 1923. Given up as lost by her owners, the vessel was later refloated by an amateur salvager. [4]
Lake Michigan: In January of 1930, the little HELEN TAYLOR was lost eight miles of Michigan City, Indiana. [3]

MATILDA TAYLOR ■ Package and bulk freight brig
Lake Ontario: In 1848, this little sailing vessel was driven ashore by a storm and lost two miles east of Point Breeze, New York. A barge that came to her assistance was also lost. [1]

TECUMSEH ■ Barge, possibly the 82 t. vessel built at Chatham, Ont., in 1853
Lake Huron: The barge TECUMSEH was reported as lost offshore near Port Huron, Michigan, in 1881. [1]

TECUMSEH ■ 196 t. vessel of unreported type
Lake Huron: Stranded at the eastern end of Cove Island, the TECUMSEH was lost in a storm on November 26, 1882. [1]

TECUMSEH ■ Wooden bulk freight steamer of 633 t. and 200 ft., launched in 1883 at Chatham, Ont.
Lake Huron: The steamer TECUMSEH was thought to be laid up safely at a dock at Goderich, Ontario, after the 1908 season. But on January 16, 1909, the freighter caught fire at her dock and was destroyed. [3]

TECUMSETH ■ Armed schooner of 166 t. and 76 ft., launched in 1815 at Chippewa, Ont.
Lake Huron: The TECUMSETH was a Royal Navy warship, lost in combat with the French in the harbor at Penetanguishene, Ontario, in 1817. [2]

TELEGRAM ■ Wooden passenger and package freight steamer of 134 t. and 108 ft., launched in 1885 at Waubaushene, Ont.
Lake Huron: This little vessel was destroyed in a fire which occurred at Rattlesnake Harbor, on Georgian Bay's Fitzwilliam Island, on November 1, 1908. [5]

TELEGRAPH ■ Steamer
Lake Michigan: Not much is known about this vessel which is said to have disappeared in the 1850s. She was last seen off the Beaver Islands, and legend has it that pirates from the islands waylaid the TELEGRAPH. [2]

TELEGRAPH ■ Sidewheel steamer of 107 t.
Lake Erie: Out on the lake on February 2, 1858, this small sidewheeler collided with the schooner MARQUETTE and sank, 40 miles due north of Cleveland. [1]

TEMPEST ■ Wooden bulk freight steamer of 370 t. and 138 ft., launched in 1876 at Grand Haven, MI
Lake Huron: A dockside fire destroyed this veteran steamer at a lumber wharf at Parry Sound, Ontario, on June 28, 1909. The lumber-laden ship was consumed so quickly that six of her crew died before they could escape. [5+]

TEMPEST ■ Wooden bulk freight steamer of 412 t. and 159 ft., launched in 1872 at Marine City, MI
Lake Erie: The old steamer TEMPEST was lost in heavy weather on August 27, 1918. She was 20 miles off Erie, Pennslyvania, when she began to leak faster than her pumps could handle. The vessel sank with the loss of one crewman. [4]

TEMPLETON ■ Package freight steamer or schooner
Lake Michigan: In 1893, this vessel was reported stranded and wrecked on the northwest side of Manitou Island. The TEMPLETON was reportedly carrying a cargo of 350 barrels of whiskey when she was lost. [3]

TENNIE & LAURA ■ Bulk freight schooner of 56 t. and 73 ft., launched in 1876 at Manitowoc, WI
Lake Michigan: The little schooner TENNIE & LAURA was carrying a cargo of lumber when she went down far out in Lake Michigan. She sank with the loss of one crewman, somewhere on the route between Muskegon, Michigan, and Milwaukee. [1]

S THAL ■ Merchant schooner of 55 t. and 75 ft., launched in 1881 at Oshkosh, WI
Lake Michigan: Five crew members perished when this tiny schooner foundered on the lake on November 10, 1898. [4]

THAMES ■ Wooden sidewheel steamer of 160 t. and 80 ft., launched in 1833 at Chatham, Ont.
Detroit River: The little sidewheeler THAMES was destroyed by fire at Windsor, Ontario, in December of 1838. [2]

H C THATCHER ■ Scow of 44 t.
Lake Erie: The scow H C THATCHER was sunk in the harbor at Toledo on July 25, 1884. Three lives were lost in the foundering. The vessel was light at the time of her loss. [1]

J O THAYER ■ Bulk freight schooner of 380 t. and 166 ft., launched in 1874 at Two Rivers, WI
Lake Michigan: Stranded on a sandy bar near Sheboygan, Wisconsin, on November 18, 1881, the coal-carrying schooner J O THAYER was heavily damaged and thought to be a total loss. She was, however, salvaged the following year, rebuilt and returned to service. [3]

THEANO ■ Steel package and bulk freighter of 952 t. and 255 ft., launched in 1889 at Rotterdam, Holland.
Lake Superior: This British-registered former saltie became a victim of Lake Superior's rugged coastline on November 17, 1906. Battling a tremendous gale, the steamer struck a rocky reef off Thunder Cape, at the Lakehead, and put a large hole in her bottom. The THEANO's crew was able to make it to shore safely, but the steam-

er, laden with a cargo of steel rails, slipped off the rocks and sank in deep water. [3]

THERESA ■ Steam propeller of 84 t. and 86 ft., launched in 1885 at Toronto
Lake Ontario: This little propeller was reported burned at Toronto in August of 1887. [1]

W P THEW ■ Wooden bulk freight steamer of 403 t. and 132 ft., launched in 1884 at Lorain, OH
Lake Huron: This freighter was without cargo when she was lost east of Thunder Bay Island, off Alpena, Michigan. The THEW was creeping through a fog on June 22, 1909, when she was run down and sunk by the big steel steamer WILLIAM LIVINGSTON. After the collision, the LIVINGSTON drifted away from the sinking freighter. Fortunately, another steamer which happened on the scene took the THEW's people aboard before she went down in 80 feet of water. [5+]

ALMERON THOMAS ■ Merchant schooner of 35 t. and 50 ft., launched at Bay City, MI, in 1891
Lake Huron: This tiny schooner was reported to have foundered near Point Lookout, in northwestern Saginaw Bay, in 1900. [3]

DAVID G THOMPSON ■ Propeller steamer of 182 t. and 103 ft., launched in 1883 at Kingston, Ont.
Lake Erie: Tecumseh Reef, southeast of Port Maitland, Ontario, captured this small propeller on March 26, 1927. The vessel went to pieces before she could be salvaged. [2]

EMMA E THOMPSON ■ Wooden bulk freight steamer of 276 t. and 126 ft., launched in 1875 at Saginaw, MI
Lake Huron: At Innis Island, in Georgian Bay, the bulk freighter EMMA E THOMPSON caught fire on May 28, 1914. She burned to a total loss. [3]

JACK THOMPSON ■ Lumber schooner of 210 t. and 120 ft., launched as the schooner TELEGRAPH in 1865 at Conneaut, OH
Lake Michigan: The sail vessel JACK THOMPSON was inbound with a cargo of lumber when she sank in the harbor at Chicago. The schooner went down on May 18, 1894. [3]

THOMAS THOMPSON ■ Wooden steam tug of 19 t.
Lake Erie: On November 27, 1877, this small tug sank seven miles east of Presque Isle, near Erie, PA. [1]

THORNTON ■ Merchant schooner
Lake Huron: The schooner THORNTON reportedly sank in 1870, southeast of False Detour, on the Michigan shore. [1]

THOUSAND ISLANDER ■ Steel passenger steamer of 206 t. and 166 ft., launched in 1912 at Toledo
Lake Huron: The passenger vessel THOUSAND IS-LANDER sank well offshore, abeam of Thunder Bay, Michigan, on November 21, 1928. She had encountered heavy weather while either under tow of or towing the steamer COLLINGWOOD, and went down quickly. [4]

THREE BELLS ■ Bulk freight schooner of 197 t. and 124 ft., launched in 1854 (may be the 1854 schooner-scow of this name built at Racine, WI)
Lake Michigan: In November of 1884, the schooner THREE BELLS was caught in a storm and sank in Good Harbor, on the west side of Michigan's Leelanau Penin-sula. Part of her wreckage was recovered and is now on display at a restaurant at Northport, Michigan. She was carrying a load of oak timbers when she foundered. [1]

THREE BROTHERS ■ Wooden bulk freight steamer of 583 t. and 162 ft., launched in 1888 at Milwaukee
Lake Michigan: With a load of lumber aboard, the steamer THREE BROTHERS began to sink in a storm on September 27, 1911. The only alternative to an open boat on a wind-torn lake was to run for shore. This the vessel did, striking the rocky shore of South Manitou Island. She was wrecked and abandoned, but her crew survived without casualty. [3]

THREE SISTERS ■ Merchant schooner of 47 t. and 69 ft., launched in 1901 at Fishcreek, WI
Lake Michigan: Built near the end of the schooner era, this little sailing ship was almost destroyed when she stranded in Grand Traverse Bay with heavy damage in 1905. Green Bay saw her final demise. On November 4, 1912, the THREE SISTERS was blown ashore and des-troyed by a fall gale. Four lives were lost, the approxi-mate number of crewmen for a schooner this size. [4]

THRUSH ■ Bulk freight schooner-barge of 189 ft. overall, launched in 1890 at Quebec City
Lake Ontario: The schooner-barge THRUSH was laden with coal when she filled and sank on May 16, 1916. [1]

JOHN TIBBETS ■ Merchant schooner of 250 t. and 114 ft.
Lake Erie: On July 11, 1888, the schooner JOHN TIB-BETS was wrecked at Clear Creek, seven miles west of Port Rowan, Ontario. She either foundered just offshore or was driven on the beach to break up. [2]

J H TIFFANY ■ Merchant schooner
Lake Huron: Five crewmen perished when this tall ship col-lided with the steamer MILWAUKEE (qv) and sank in the Straits of Mackinac. The schooner was lost in 1859. [2]

TIGER ■ Wooden steam tug
Lake Huron: In 1870 this tugboat was destroyed on the Saginaw River when she burned at Bay City, Michigan. [1]

TIGER ■ Dredge of 102 t. and 86 ft.
Lake Michigan: This vessel caught fire, burned and sank off the tiny village of Lakeside, Michigan, on July 26, 1929. [2]

SIR S L TILLEY ■ Wooden steamer of 769 t. and 168 ft., launched in 1884 at St. Catharine's, Ont.
Lake Erie: Carrying a cargo of general merchandise, the steamer SIR S L TILLEY caught fire and was destroyed seven miles from Fairport Ohio. The vessel burned to the hull on August 26, 1899. The shell was recovered and used as the basis for the steamer ADVANCE (qv), though much reduced in size. [4]

TIOGA ■ Steam propeller of 549 t.
Lake Erie: A fire spelled the end for this little steamer. She was carrying a load of general merchandise when she caught fire offshore and was destroyed on October 5, 1897. The burned-out hulk sank 12 miles northeast of the Point Pelee lighthouse. [1]

TIOGA ■ Iron package and bulk freight steamer of 2,230 t. and 286 ft., launched in 1875 at Buffalo
Lake Superior: Sawtooth Reef, just off Eagle River, Michi-gan, at the top of the Keweenaw Peninsula, has been one of the most deadly spots on Lake Superior. Laden with a cargo of wheat, the big, iron-hulled steamer TIOGA was making for shelter at Eagle Harbor when she struck the reef in heavy weather on November 26, 1919. The TIO-GA's crew made it to shore, but the vessel, with a gaping hole in her hull, slipped off the rocks and went down in deep water. [4]

TIP TOP ■ Scow or schooner-scow of 124 t.
Lake Ontario: July 31, 1882, was the date of the loss of this little vessel. She was carrying a cargo of stone when she reportedly foundered in the harbor at Oswego, New York. [2]

TITANIA ■ Iron steamer or yacht of 73 t. and 98 ft., launched in 1875 at Buffalo
Lake Ontario: This small iron vessel went down on Au-gust 11, 1908, near the harbor entrance at Charlotte, New York (near Rochester). [2]

N H TODMAN ■ Merchant schooner
Lake Huron: The schooner N H TODMAN foundered on the lake in 1881. [1]

TOKIO ■ Bulk freight schooner-barge of 1,385 t. and 222 ft., launched in 1889 at W Bay City, MI, as a schooner
St. Clair River: A riverine collision ended in the loss of this big schooner-barge on October 9, 1917. On that date, the TOKIO and the barge HOMER cracked heads between the Michigan towns of St. Clair and Marine City. The large sail barge sank, a total loss. [1]

TOLEDO ■ Merchant schooner
Lake Erie: An early loss along the Ontario shore was this sailing ship, reported to have broken her back in a gale and been cast ashore 1/2 mile east of the mouth of the Grand River. The accident occurred on November 20, 1838. [1]

TOLEDO ■ Steam passenger and package freight propeller of 558 t. and 200 ft.
Lake Michigan: One of the worst disasters to occur in the wreck-strewn area above Wisconsin's Door Peninsula was the sinking of the propeller TOLEDO on October 22, 1856. The vessel was reportedly raising her anchor, preparing to get underway in a storm, when the accident occurred. Perhaps the strain of the anchor's bobbing weight was too much for the ship's timbers. At any rate, she sprung some of her strakes and began to leak heavily. Before much could be done to save her or her people, the vessel went down off Port Washington. Estimates of the number lost range from 40 to a high of 55. [4]

TOLEDO ■ Steamer
Lake Huron: This steam vessel was lost at an unreported position in the Straits of Mackinac in 1869. [1]

TOLEDO ■ Merchant schooner of 136 t., and 93 ft., launched in 1843 at Oswego, NY
Lake Michigan: The little two-master TOLEDO was reported lost near Milwaukee in 1875. [2]

TOLEDO ■ Steam tug
Lake Huron: This harbor tug was destroyed by fire at Bay City, Michigan, on the Saginaw River, in 1880. [1]

TOLEDO ■ Wooden bulk freight steamer of 579 t. and 181 ft., launched in 1862 at Cleveland
Lake Superior: Downbound with a cargo of lumber, the steamer TOLEDO sank off the upper entrance to the Portage Ship Canal on September 20, 1898. Little else is reported on the accident except that the sunken wreck was later dynamited as a hazard to navigation. [3]

TOLEDO ■ Dredge barge
Lake Erie: On November 19, 1924, the dredge barge TOLEDO sank near Rattlesnake Island in a fall storm. [2]

CITY OF TOLEDO ■ Wooden package freight steamer of 413 t.
Lake Michigan: The steamer CITY OF TOLEDO was carrying a load of winter provisions when she sank in a white squall. She went down a few hundred yards offshore, seven miles north of Ludington, MI, on December 21, 1879. [3]

CITY OF TOLEDO ■ Bulk freight schooner-barge of 245 t. and 160 ft., launched in 1865 at Toledo as a steamer
Detroit River: The long career of this wooden vessel ended on July 21, 1906, when she suffered a double collision. After being rammed by an unidentified vessel, the CITY OF TOLEDO went out of control, broke her towline, and struck a bridge support. She then sank, a total loss. [2]

TOM BOY ■ Merchant schooner of 50 ft., launched in 1863
Lake Superior: On August 1, 1880, this small sailing ship went down off Presque Isle, northwest of Marquette, Michigan, on August 1, 1880. She was reportedly carrying over 2000 kegs of blasting powder when she sank. [1]

ANNIE TOMINE ■ Lumber schooner of 128 t.
Lake Michigan: On October 4, 1885, this schooner and her cargo of lumber and lath were lost when she sank five miles west of the entrance to the Grand Haven, Michigan, harbor. [1]

TONAWANDA ■ Steam freighter
Lake Michigan: One life was reportedly lost when this vessel was destroyed by an explosion while on the Chicago River. The vessel blew up on September 24, 1864. [1]

TONAWANDA ■ Wooden propeller steamer of 822 t. and 202 ft., launched in 1856 at Buffalo
Lake Erie: The propeller TONAWANDA, laden with a cargo of general merchandise, was lost on October 18, 1870. On that date she was battling a storm off Buffalo when she was disabled, then overwhelmed and destroyed. None of the crew were lost. An 1871 attempt to salvage the vessel failed. [2]

TOPEKA ■ Wooden bulk freight steamer of 1,376 t. and 228 ft., launched in 1889 at Milwaukee
Detroit River: On August 15, 1916, this self-unloading bulk freighter got the worst of a collision with the small steamer CHRISTOPHER. The TOPEKA, laden with a cargo of coal, went down off Sandwich, Ontario (now part of Windsor). She was later recovered for scrap. [2]

TOPSY ▪ Merchant schooner
Lake Michigan: The schooner TOPSY was carrying a hold and deckload of lumber when she stranded and wrecked near Waugoschance Point, in the western Straits of Mackinac. The vessel was lost on June 9, 1891. [1]

TORONTO ▪ Armed yacht, launched 1799 at Humber, Ont.
Lake Ontario: This British warship was lost in the summer of 1812 when she went aground on a rocky reef near Toronto and was destroyed. [1]

CITY OF TORONTO ▪ Sidewheel steamer of 898 t. and 207 ft., launched in 1864 at Niagara
Lake Ontario: The sidewheeler CITY OF TORONTO was lost on October 31, 1883, when she was destroyed by fire at the Muir Shipyard, at Port Dalhousie, Ontario. [2]

JOHN TORRENT ▪ Wooden steam tug of 27 t. and 50 ft., launched in 1875 at Muskegon, MI
Lake Huron: Richard's Landing, on St. Joseph Island, was the site of the loss of this small tug on May 2, 1913. She caught fire in the harbor and was destroyed. [3]

NELLIE TORRENT ▪ Wooden steam freighter of 302 t. and 140 ft., launched in 1881 at Wyandotte, MI
Lake Huron: The small steamer NELLIE TORRENT burned on the St. Marys River and was a total loss in 1899. [3]

OSCAR TOWNSEND ▪ Propeller freighter
Lake Huron: In 1891 the steamer OSCAR TOWNSEND was reported to have caught fire off Port Sanilac, Michigan, and burned to destruction. [2]

TRACY or **TRACEY** ▪ Armed snow launched in 1803 at River Rouge, MI
Lake Erie: This warship was reported wrecked at Fort Erie in 1809. She was one of the American military vessels that had been used to establish the garrison at Fort Dearborn (later Chicago) in 1803. [2]

J F TRACY ▪ Merchant schooner of 161 t. and 86 ft.
Lake Michigan: In 1886 the schooner J F TRACY went aground on the west side of Beaver Island and was wrecked just offshore. [2]

TRADE WIND ▪ Package and bulk freight schooner of 106 ft. overall, launched in 1853 at Colborne, Ont.
Lake Ontario: Another victim of fire was the schooner TRADE WIND, which was destroyed in the harbor at Kingston, Ontario, on April 15, 1909. [1]

TRADER ▪ Propeller freighter
Lake Huron: Three persons were killed when the steamer TRADER exploded and burned on the lake in 1866. [1]

TRADER ▪ Steamer
Lake Michigan: October 15, 1880, was the date of the loss of this vessel on Lake Michigan. According to reports, the vessel foundered in a storm, with ten lives lost. [2]

TRADER ▪ Scow of 291 t., launched in 1903 at Buffalo
Lake Erie: The scow TRADER went aground on Strawberry Island, in the Niagara River, and was wrecked on July 9, 1908. [2]

TRAFFIC ▪ Merchant steamer
Lake Huron: The small steamer TRAFFIC was wrecked and lost near Sebewaing, Michigan, in the southeast corner of Saginaw Bay, in 1868. [1]

TRAFFIC ▪ Steam tug
Lake Huron: The tug TRAFFIC was destroyed by fire on the Saginaw River, at Saginaw, Michigan, in 1869. [1]

TRAMP ▪ 55 t. vessel of unreported type
Lake Michigan: No date is given for the loss of this small vessel off Northport, Michigan, near Traverse City. [1]

F R TRANCHEMONTAGNE ▪ Bulk freight schooner of 133 t., launched in 1864
Lake Ontario: No lives were lost, but this small schooner was totally destroyed in an accident that occurred on October 31, 1880. The TRANCHEMONTAGNE was coming into the harbor at Oswego, New York, with her holds full of rye when she ran headlong into a breakwall, stove in her hull strakes and sank. [2]

TRANSFER ▪ Steamer
Lake Erie: In May of 1896, this steamer was reported to have foundered off Lorain, Ohio. [2]

TRANSIT ▪ Sidewheel steamer of 109 t. and 115 ft., launched in 1856 at Toronto
Lake Ontario: A fire destroyed this diminutive steamer in May of 1880. The vessel burned at Belleville, Ontario, near the eastern end of the lake. [1]

TRANSIT ▪ Wooden steam carferry of 1,057 t. and 168 ft., launched in 1872 at Walkerville, Ont.
Detroit River: On March 4, 1889, this early carferry was destroyed by fire at her moorings at Windsor, Ontario. [1]

TRANSITER ▪ Fuel tanker
Detroit River: Laden with a cargo of gasoline, this tanker exploded and burned with the loss of two lives. The accident occurred at River Rouge, Michigan, on August 9, 1941. [1]

TRANSLAKE #3 ▪ Vessel information unavailable
Lake Huron: On September 16, 1958, the TRANSLAKE #3 capsized and sank 3.5 miles from Surprise Shoal, in southwestern Georgian Bay. [2]

TRANSOIL ■ Oil tanker
Lake Erie: Two lives were lost when the tanker TRANS-OIL caught fire and was destroyed in the harbor at Toledo. The vessel was wrecked on September 26, 1942. [1]

TRANSPORT ■ Pulpwood barge of 1,595 t. and 254 ft., launched in 1880 at Wyandotte, MI, as a carferry
Lake Superior: Laden with a cargo of pulpwood, the barge TRANSPORT beached and broke up in a storm that struck her on September 22, 1942. No lives were lost in the incident, which occurred near Eagle Harbor, Michigan. [2]

TRAVELLER ■ Sidewheel steamer of 609 t. and 199 ft.
Lake Superior: This sidewheeler was at a dock at Eagle Harbor, MI, when she caught fire and was destroyed on August 17, 1865. No lives were lost in the blaze. [2]

J A TRAVIS ■ Merchant schooner of 101 t. and 106 ft., launched in 1867 at Pentwater, MI
Lake Michigan: On November 17, 1893, the schooner J A TRAVIS was laden with lumber and marble when she ran into a storm in the mouth of Green Bay. The little vessel struck bottom and sank off Cana Island. [3]

WILLIAM TREAT ■ Merchant schooner
Lake Huron: Port Albert, Ontario, north of Goderich, was the site of the foundering of this schooner in 1883. [1]

M E TREMBLE ■ Merchant schooner of of 693 t. and 198 ft., launched in 1874 at Suamico, WI
St. Clair River: A collision claimed this large schooner on September 7, 1890. The ship was in the northern part of the river when she was rammed by the steamer W L WETMORE, and quickly sank. One crewman drowned in the accident. [2]

BYRON TRERICE ■ Wooden propeller of 268 t. and 102 ft., launched in 1882 at Dresden, Ont.
Lake Erie: The small steamer BYRON TRERICE was destroyed by fire at Leamington, Ontario, in September of 1893. [1]

TRENTON ■ Wooden propeller steamer of 260 t. and 134 ft., launched in 1854 at Montreal
Lake Ontario: In March of 1858, this vessel was destroyed by fire at Picton, Ontario. [1]

TRENTON ■ 204 t. vessel of unreported type
Lake Ontario: The TRENTON was reported to have foundered off Presqu'ile Bay, Ontario, on November 22, 1879. [1]

R TRIAL ■ Merchant schooner of 36 t.
Lake Michigan: The tiny schooner R TRIAL stranded just southwest of the harbor entrance at Muskegon, Michigan, in November of 1883. She subsequently was destroyed by the action of storm waves. [2]

TRIBUNE ■ Bulk freight schooner of 276 t. and 104 ft., launched in 1847 at Chicago
Lake Michigan: Ten lives were lost when this vessel sank, a considerable number for such a small vessel. The little schooner disappeared on April 18, 1848, in upper Lake Michigan. For more than a year her fate was unknown. In November of 1849, Indian fishermen discovered her upright masts still visible below the surface off Cathead Point, at the tip of the Leelanau Peninsula. [2]

CHARLES A TRINTER ■ Gas screw of 8 t., launched in 1909
Lake Erie: No lives were lost, but the tiny TRINTER was destroyed when she caught fire and burned off Erie, Pennsylvania, on January 6, 1916. [1]

TRIUMPH ■ Vessel information unavailable, but possibly the 25 t., 60 ft. schooner launched at Sacket's Harbor, NY, in 1816
Lake Ontario: No date was given for her loss, but the TRIUMPH was described as an early merchantman. She went missing with all hands. [2]

TROY ■ Passenger and package freight steamer of 546 t. and 182 ft., launched in 1845 at Buffalo
Lake Erie: Black Rock, near the eastern end of the lake, was the site of the demise of this steamer on March 23, 1850. On that date she was carrying a cargo of general freight and a number of passengers when her boiler exploded, catching the vessel afire. Most sources say 22 persons died in the blaze. The vessel was later recovered. [4]

TROY ■ Merchant schooner of 122 t., launched in 1854
Lake Michigan: The brand spanking new schooner TROY was carrying a cargo of glass and a number of passengers when she was wrecked and sank on the east side of North Manitou Island. The accident occurred in October of 1854 and claimed 23 lives. Compare this report with the one below. [1]

TROY ■ Steam propeller
Lake Huron: The steamer TROY went down with the loss of 23 lives on October 24, 1859. She foundered in tremendous seas, 10 miles north of Pte Aux Barques. Some confusion exists between this wreck and the schooner TROY, above, and perhaps the vessel TROY, below. [1]

TROY ■ Steamer
Lake Huron: In 1860 this steamer was lost from unknown causes off Goderich, Ontario. [1]

TRUANT ■ Steam tug of 61 t.
Lake Huron: The end of this tug came on April 30, 1894, near Manitoulin Island. On that date she was at Burnt Island when she was, perhaps ironically, destroyed by fire. [2]

TUBAL CAIN ▪ Vessel information unavailable, probably a schooner
Lake Superior: A single report says this vessel sank in 1867 near Two Rivers (probably Two Harbors, Minnesota). [1]

ALVIN A or A A TURNER ▪ Wooden bulk freight steamer of 310 t. and 135 ft., launched at Trenton, MI, in 1873
Lake Huron: This vessel stranded in a big storm and was destroyed by fire off Spanish Mills (now Spanish) in the North Channel on October 18, 1905. One source says she was lost in the St. Marys River. [5]

ELIZA R TURNER ▪ Bulk freight schooner of 425 t.
Lake Erie: Two sailors died when this sailing ship went down nine miles west of Long Point. She sank on October 10, 1877. [2]

TURRET CHIEF ▪ Bulk freight turret steamer of 1,841 t. and 253 ft., launched in 1896 at Sunderland, England
Lake Superior: This steel steamer was a lesser-known victim of the Big Storm of 1913. On November 11, she was pushed ashore by huge waves and hurricane-force winds. She struck ground on the Keweenaw Peninsula, and was heavily damaged, but was later recovered and completely rebuilt, returning to service as the steamer JOLLY INEZ (qv). [5+]

TURRET CROWN ▪ Bulk freight turret steamer of 1,800 t. and 250 ft., launched in 1895 at Sunderland, England
Lake Huron: The steamer TURRET CROWN was lost on November 2, 1924. On that date she went ashore in a storm and broke up on Meldrum Point, on the north side of Manitoulin Island. Some reports say that she was driven ashore intentionally. [4]

TUSCARORA ▪ Barge of 405 t.
Lake Ontario: On October 4, 1885, the coal-carrying barge TUSCARORA sank just off the entrance to the harbor at Oswego, New York. [1]

FANNIE or FANNY TUTHILL ▪ Wooden steam tug of 27 t. and 60 ft., launched in 1873 at Saginaw, MI
Lake St. Clair: This small tug was sunk on October 1, 1905, with the loss of one of her crew of four. She was in the St. Clair Flats when she collided with the 1,000 ton steamer D C WHITNEY (qv) and quickly sank. [1]

H B TUTTLE ▪ Wooden bulk freight steamer of 845 t. and 180 ft., launched in 1871 at Cleveland

Lake Erie: The degree of damage caused to this steamer by a September 15, 1906, storm was underestimated somewhat. The coal-laden vessel had sprung a leak and sunk on the date mentioned, off Marblehead (Ohio). Salvagers succeeded in refloating the old vessel, but as she was being towed into nearby Sandusky for drydocking, she broke in two and foundered. [3]

HORACE A TUTTLE ▪ Bulk freight steamer of 1,585 t. and 250 ft., launched in 1887 at Cleveland
Lake Michigan: The TUTTLE was just leaving port at Michigan City, Indiana, with her holds full of Midwestern corn when she was overwhelmed by a fall gale. The big vessel was driven ashore and wrecked, a total loss. The accident occurred on October 26, 1898. [3]

TWILIGHT ▪ Barge or bark of 395 t.
Lake Huron: This wooden vessel was reported lost northeast of the town of Port Sanilac, Michigan, on November 18, 1877 (one source says 1887). [3]

TWILIGHT ▪ 173 t. vessel of unreported type
Lake Erie: The TWILIGHT was reportedly destroyed by fire at Tyrconnel Dock on September 5, 1891. [1]

TWIN BROTHERS ▪ Merchant schooner of 144 t., launched in 1848 at Milwaukee
Lake Michigan: A spring gale destroyed the schooner TWIN BROTHERS on March 11, 1860. The sailing ship was driven on the breakwater at Milwaukee and sank. Before her final accident, she was already known as a hard-luck ship, having been involved in at least five other serious accidents. [1]

TWO CHARLIES ▪ Merchant schooner of 87 t., launched in 1852 at Milwaukee
Lake Michigan: The port of Grand Haven, Michigan, was the site of the loss of the small schooner TWO CHARLIES on October 9, 1876. The vessel sank just south of the south pier. [1]

TWO FANNIES ▪ Merchant schooner of 563 t. and 152 ft., launched in 1872 at Peshtigo, WI
Lake Erie: The schooner TWO FANNIES was bound for Cleveland with a cargo of iron ore when she was struck by a gale and foundered off Dover, Ontario. The date of the accident is given as August 8, in either 1890 or 1896. The schooner had also been heavily damaged in a grounding in Grand Traverse Bay, Michigan, in 1879. [5]

TWO FRIENDS ▪ Merchant bark of 319 t., launched in 1873 at Port Burwell, Ont.
Lake Michigan: The small bark TWO FRIENDS was loaded with a cargo of salt when she was ripped by a sudden gale on October 16, 1880. The tall ship was thrown on a reef off the upper end of the Door Peninsula, and heavily damaged. There was no loss of life in the stranding, due to the courageous action of a local fisherman, who saved

the crew from the rigging one at a time in a tiny rowboat. According to one report, the bark was salvaged the following year. [2]

TWO WALLACES ■ Merchant schooner
Lake Superior: The schooner TWO WALLACES is said to have stranded and broken up somewhere on the big lake on November 18, 1886. [1]

TYPO ■ Merchant schooner of 335 t. and 137 ft., launched in 1873 at Manitowoc, WI
Lake Huron: The heavily trafficked offshore area between Thunder Bay and Rogers (now Rogers City), Michigan, was the location of an inordinately large number of accidents. This schooner was off Presque Isle when she collided with the propeller V H KETCHUM (qv) and sank on October 14, 1899. Reports are split as to whether four persons or nine died in the accident. [4]

U C 97 ■ World War I German mine-laying submarine, launched in 1917
Lake Michigan: The U C 97 was a war prize vessel used on the Lakes as a display ship for several years following the war. After she had served her purpose, and in line with the limitations on naval weaponry then extant, the vessel was towed out to a point offshore from Highland Park, Illinois, and sunk by gunfire from the U.S. Navy training ship WILMETTE (see EASTLAND). The sub was sunk in June of 1921, but recently there has been much interest in finding the old vessel's remains. [3]

U S 240 ■ Steel barge
Lake Erie: Bound from New York City to Cleveland with a load of sulphur, the barge U S 240 capsized and sank in a storm. The vessel went down on September 13, 1923, near Windmill Point, a few miles west of Fort Erie, Ontario. Three crewmen died when the vessel was lost. [1]

UGANDA ■ Wooden bulk freight steamer of 2,298 t. and 291 ft., launched in 1892 at W Bay City, MI
Lake Michigan: In March, April, and May of each year, the western approaches to the Straits of Mackinac are clogged with ice, as if the whole lake is attempting to shove its burden into Huron before it melts. Ships constructed of wood could not be careless when traversing these moving, grinding fields of pack ice. The wooden steamer UGANDA ran into a field near White Shoals on April 19, 1913. A cold snap froze the vessel in and she was swept along with the pack for several days, and slowly crushed as the ice-river compressed toward the Straits. When she was finally released, the vessel would no longer hold water, and she sank. [5+]

UNADILLA ■ Lumber schooner-barge of 396 t. and 153 ft., launched in 1862 at Cleveland
Lake Erie: The old schooner-barge UNADILLA was driven onto the breakwater at Cleveland by a storm which hit her on December 2, 1913. The vessel was well up on the rocks, but it was not deemed economical to salvage her, and she was abandoned. The hulk was destroyed by fire in 1915. [3]

UNCLE SAM ■ Wooden steam tug of 24 t., launched in 1874 at Saginaw, MI
Lake Huron or Michigan: The small tug UNCLE SAM was lost in the Straits of Mackinac in 1882 when she was crushed in a field of ice and sank. [2]

UNCLE SAM ■ Merchant schooner of 280 t.
Lake Erie: No date is given for the loss of this schooner when she sank near Kelley's Island, above Sandusky, Ohio. [1]

UNGANDI ■ Steam propeller
Lake Huron: Little information is available on the loss of the steamer UNGANDI in the Nipigon Strait, south of Bois Blanc Island. It is probable that this report actually refers to the wreck of the steamer UGANDA (qv). [1]

UNION ■ Wooden sidewheel steamer of 1,190 t. and 163 ft., launched in 1856 at Walkerville, Ont.
Lake Huron: In June of 1867 (one source says 1876), the steamer UNION caught fire and was destroyed at Port Huron, Michigan. [3]

UNION ■ Wooden steam tug
Lake Huron: The tug UNION was reported to have burned and sunk on Saginaw Bay in 1870. [1]

UNION ■ Wooden bulk freight propeller of 553 t., launched in 1861 at Manitowoc, WI
Lake Superior: Au Sable Point, in one of the least populated and most beautiful parts of Michigan's upper peninsula, has intercepted many ships that were moving to or from the Soo. This small steamer was downbound with a load of iron ore in her holds when she was blown up on the beach near the point by a strong westerly gale. The vessel was cast ashore on September 25, 1873, with no loss of life, and later went to pieces where she lay. [2]

UNION ■ 72 t. vessel of unreported type
Lake Erie: This little vessel was reported stranded and destroyed near Rondeau, Ontario, on September 18, 1886. [1]

UNITED KINGDOM ■ Sidewheel steamer launched in 1828 at Niagara, NY, as the steamer ALCIOPE
Lake Ontario: This early steamer was one of the first vessel wrecked near the busy port of Oswego, New York. She was reported lost in November of 1835. [2]

UNITED STATES ▪ Steel passenger and package freight steamer of 2,058 t. and 258 ft., launched in 1909 at Manitowoc, WI, as a passenger steamer, later converted to a large yacht, then to this vessel
St. Clair River: This steamer was burned to her hull at her dock at Sarnia, Ontario, on June 6, 1927. The hull and machinery were salvaged and used to construct the steamer BATISCAN, a strange-looking bulk freighter with stack forward, that served until scrapped in 1944. [4]

VALENTINE ▪ Merchant schooner
Lake Huron: In 1873 this schooner was wrecked and lost on Port Austin Reef, in northeast Saginaw Bay. [1]

FRANK L VANCE ▪ Wooden bulk freight steamer of 1,952 t. and 257 ft., launched in 1887 at Cleveland
Lake Michigan: This wooden vessel was carrying a cargo of coal when she caught fire and was destroyed off Ludington, Michigan. The ship was lost on October 4, 1910. [2]

GENERAL VANCE ▪ Wooden passenger and package freight steamer of 75 t., launched in 1838 at Perrysburg, OH (probably a sidewheeler)
Detroit River: This little steamer's short career ended at Windsor, Ontario, on June 25, 1844. One man died when the vessel exploded at her dock. [2]

VANDERBILT ▪ Steam propeller of 170 t. and 92 ft., launched in 1873 at Chatham, Ont. (one source calls her a schooner-barge)
Lake Huron: In June of 1882, this vessel was destroyed by fire near Serpent Island, in Meldrum Bay, the North Channel. Reports that claim she was lost on Sulphur Island, Thunder Bay, Michigan, are probably in error. [3]

W H or **WILLIAM H VANDERBILT** ▪ Merchant bark of 615 t., launched in 1867 at E Saginaw, MI
Lake Erie: A storm which struck this vessel on September 24, 1883, drove her ashore on the east side of Long Point. She was torn apart by the action of waves, then slipped off into deep water. [2]

SIR C T VanSTAUBENZIE ▪ Bulk freight schooner of 317 t. and 132 ft., launched in 1875 at St. Catharine's, Ont.
Lake Erie: All four of this sail vessel's crew were drowned when the schooner sank following a collision with the steamer CITY OF ERIE, on the night of September 27, 1909. The VanSTAUBENZIE, which was in ballast at the time of the wreck, went down eight miles off Long Point. [3]

LUCINDA VanVALKENBURG ▪ Merchant schooner of 301 t. and 129 ft., launched in 1862 at Tonawanda, NY
Lake Huron: A collision ended the career of the schooner LUCINDA VanVALKENBURG on June 1, 1887. She was carrying a cargo of coal when she collided in a storm with the iron propeller LEHIGH and sank near Thunder Bay light, east of Alpena, Michigan. [3]

GEORGE H VanVLECK ▪ Wooden bulk freight steamer of 1,608 t. and 238 ft., launched in 1875 at Buffalo as the steamer PORTAGE
Detroit River: Strong winds blew this steamer off her moorings and into the channel on the Detroit River on December 4, 1918. The old vessel was driven aground by the current, and was heavily damaged. She was later abandoned. [2]

VARADA ▪ Steamer
Lake Superior: The steamer VARADA was reported burned and sunk at Mineral Rock in 1915. [1]

VEGA ▪ Steel bulk freight steamer of 2,143 t. and 301 ft., launched in 1893 at Cleveland
Lake Michigan: The Big Blow of 1905 destroyed this big vessel on November 29. Laden with iron ore for Gary, Indiana, the VEGA was hurled onto the rocks of South Fox Island by tremendous seas. Her crew was able to evacuate the ship before she broke up in place. [4]

VEGA ▪ Lumber schooner of 200 t. and 118 ft., launched in 1856 at Erie, PA, as the schooner ST PAUL
Lake Michigan: The aged schooner VEGA was wrecked in the violent gale of October 20, 1905. She was docking at Ludington, Michigan, when the big seas pitched her against the pier, ripping up her sides and sinking her. [3]

VENETTA ▪ 159 t. vessel of unreported type
Lake Erie: The VENETTA was stranded and wrecked on the shore of Pelee Island on April 1, 1886. [1]

VENICE ▪ Merchant schooner of 214 t.
Lake Erie: On August 16, 1879, the schooner VENICE was driven aground on Pelee Island, near the lighthouse, and later destroyed. [1]

CITY OF VENICE ▪ Wooden bulk freight steamer of 2,107 t. and 301 ft., launched in 1892 at W Bay City, MI
Lake Erie: A collision destroyed this big ore boat on August 4, 1902. The CITY OF VENICE was downbound with a full load of iron ore when she collided with the steamer SEGUIN and sank abreast of Rondeau, Ontario. Three of the vessel's crew died in the accident. [4]

VENUS ■ Schooner-barge or schooner of 232 t. and 123 ft., launched in 1872 at New Jerusalem, OH
Lake Huron: This sail vessel was carrying a cargo of grindstones from Grindstone City, Michigan, to Milwaukee, when she was sunk on October 3, 1887. Caught in a storm, the vessel foundered near the mouth of the Black River, some miles south of the southern end of Thunder Bay, Michigan. All seven of the VENUS' crew were lost with their ship. [4]

VERANO ■ Gas screw of 102 t.
Lake Michigan: On August 28, 1946, this vessel foundered west of South Haven, Michigan. According to one report, she went down about a mile offshore. [1]

VERBENA MAY or **MAY VERBENA** ■ Steam tug
Lake Huron: The tug VERBENA MAY was reported wrecked near Stokes Bay, on the west shore of the Bruce Peninsula, in the year 1896. [1]

VERMILION or **VERMILLION** ■ Steamer (probably sidewheeler) of 385 t., launched in 1838 at Vermilion, OH
Lake Huron: Five lives were lost when the steamer VERMILION was destroyed by an offshore fire in November of 1843. The precise location of the accident is not reported. The vessel was later recovered and rebuilt. [2]

VERMONT ■ Merchant schooner, built before 1847
Lake Michigan: A single report says briefly that this vessel was lost near Grand Haven, Michigan, in 1863. [1]

VERNON ■ Wooden passenger and package freight steamer of 560 t., launched in 1886 at Chicago
Lake Michigan: This almost-new steamer suffered disaster at the hands of a Lakes gale on October 25, 1887. Bound from Glen Haven, Michigan, to Milwaukee with a cargo of general freight and a number of passengers, the little vessel was set upon by the storm and foundered near Two Rivers, Wisconsin. Estimates of the number of dead range from 36 to 41. [4]

VERNON ■ Fishing tug of 13 t.
Lake Superior: No lives were lost when this small fishing vessel went down following a collision off Grand Marais, Michigan. The VERNON was doing her usual rain-or-shine business in a dense fog when she was rammed and sunk by the big steel freighter HARVEY COLBY on August 5, 1950. The COLBY picked up the tug's crew. [2]

VIATOR ■ Steel freighter of 619 t. and 241 ft., launched in 1904 at Bodo, Norway
Lake Huron: A typically foggy condition off Thunder Bay Island resulted in the loss of this Norwegian saltie a long way from her home. The steamer was carrying a cargo of iced fish products when she collided with the steel package freighter ORMIDALE and sank. None of the crew of the VIATOR were lost in the accident. [4]

MARIE VICTOIRE ■ Merchant schooner
Lake Huron: The schooner MARIE VICTOIRE was lost in a squall on Saginaw Bay, in October of 1887. [1]

VICTOR ■ Merchant schooner of 320 t., launched in 1867 at Port Dalhousie, Ont.
Lake Huron: Upbound with a cargo of coal, the small schooner VICTOR foundered south of Sand Beach, Michigan, in a spring storm which occurred on May 30, 1888. This accident is also reported to have occurred near 40-mile Point, near Rogers City, Michigan. [3]

VICTORIA ■ Excursion steamer of 43 t. and 79 ft., launched in 1880 at London, Ont.
Thames River: The loss of this small riverine excursion boat is included here because of the large number of casualties suffered. The little steamer, just beginning her second season, was loaded (possibly overloaded) with happy passengers and was just pulling away from her dock at London, Ontario, when disaster struck. The VICTORIA capsized and sank, spilling her cargo of humanity into the river and killing about 200 of them. The May 24, 1881 accident was echoed on a similar and even more disastrous scale with the capsizing of the EASTLAND (qv) at Chicago in 1913. [2]

VICTORIA ■ Steam propeller, probably the 88 t., 76 ft. vessel built at Detroit in 1870 as the steamer SCOTIA
Lake Huron: The steamer VICTORIA was reportedly driven ashore and wrecked near Kettle Point, on the Ontario shore near the southern end of the lake. The ship was stranded by an 1884 storm. [2]

VICTORIA ■ Steam tug. possibly the 192 t., 96 ft. tug launched in 1872 at Detroit
Lake Huron: This tug was lost in 1896 when she foundered on Georgian Bay. The cause of the sinking is not reported. [2]

QUEEN VICTORIA ■ Sidewheel steamer of 652 t. and 170 ft., launched in 1861 at Hull, Quebec
Lake St. Clair: The sidewheeler QUEEN VICTORIA was destroyed near the mouth of the Thames River when she caught fire and was destroyed in September of 1883. [1]

VIENNA ■ Wooden bulk freight steamer of 1,005 t. and 191 ft., launched in 1873 at Cleveland
Lake Superior: No lives were lost, but the steamer VIENNA wound up on the bottom of Whitefish Bay in an accident which occurred on September 16, 1892. The ore boat was creeping through a thick fog when the wooden steamer NIPIGON slid out of the mist and rammed her broadside, cutting a huge hole in the VIENNA's flank and sinking her with her cargo of ore. The wreck was located in 1975. [2]

VIENNA ■ Package and bulk freight schooner of 166 t. and 102 ft., launched in 1871 at Port Burwell, Ont.
Lake Huron: The little two-master VIENNA was struck by a storm in the northwest part of the lake on October 27, 1906. The schooner was overwhelmed and foundered north by northeast of Thunder Bay Island. [3]

FRANK E VIGOR ■ Steel package and bulk freight steamer of 4,344 t. and 412 ft., launched in 1896 at Cleveland as the steamer SIR WILLIAM SIEMENS
Lake Erie: This big crane-equipped steamer was navigating the crowded Pelee Passage with a cargo of sulphur on April 27, 1944. The path of the luckless steamer crossed that of the big ore boat PHILIP MINCH, and the VIGOR was rammed near amidships. The MINCH quickly took aboard the 32-man crew of the foundering freighter, before the latter turned turtle and sank. [4]

VIKING ■ Vessel information unavailable
Lake Superior: Not much information is available on the wrecking of this vessel except that she was lost in 1912. [1]

VIOLET ■ Fishing tug of 18 t. and 48 ft., launched in 1890 at Benton Harbor, MI
Lake Michigan: On Christmas Eve, 1910, this small commercial fishing vessel was assaulted by a gale and sank off Charlevoix, Michigan. [2]

VIOLET G ■ Tug of 25 t.
Lake Superior: This tug was lost on July 21, 1927, when the big steamer AMERICA swung her against a dock and crushed her. The accident occurred at Booth Dock, Port Arthur (now Thunder Bay), Ontario. [2]

VISION ■ 59 t. vessel of unreported type
Lake Ontario: The VISION was inbound with a cargo of barley when she was destroyed by a storm and sank a mile east of the harbor entrance at Oswego, New York. She went down on November 12, 1885. [1]

VISITOR ■ Merchant schooner
Lake Erie: With her holds full of general freight, this schooner foundered off West Sister Island, on January 5, 1855. [1]

ANNIE VOIGHT or **VOUGHT** ■ Merchant schooner of 680 t. and 199 ft., launched at Fairport, OH, in 1867
Lake Michigan: This schooner, with her cargo of coal, was blown on the rocks and destroyed by a storm at South Manitou Island, Michigan, on November 21, 1892. None of her crew was lost and her cargo was partially salvaged, but the ship was a total loss. [5]

VOLUNTEER ■ Merchant schooner
Lake Huron: In 1869 it was reported that this schooner wrecked and sank in a gale, somewhere on the lake. [2]

VOLUNTEER ■ Merchant schooner of 52 t. and 50 ft., launched in 1889 at Saginaw, MI
Lake Huron: On October 14, 1893, this tiny schooner foundered on a reef located off Grindstone City, Michigan. Her crewmen were able to make it to shore safely. [3]

VOLUNTEER ■ Merchant schooner, possibly the same vessel as 1893 wreck above
Lake Huron: The small schooner VOLUNTEER was driven on a beach near Au Sable Point on the Michigan side, on July 15, 1896. She was reported broken up by waves, though none of her crew were lost. [1]

VULCAN ■ Wooden steam tug of 263 t. and 134 ft., launched in 1868 at Detroit
Lake Erie: The big tug VULCAN was towing several barges offshore from Vermilion, Ohio, when she caught fire. The vessel burned to a hulk and sank on June 8, 1893. She was the sister ship of the famous tug CHAMPION (qv). [1]

WABASH ■ Steam freighter
Lake Huron: This steamboat was lost in 1870 as a result of a collision with the vessel EMPIRE STATE. [1]

WABASH ■ Bulk freight schooner-barge
Lake Superior: The schooner-barge WABASH was upbound with a load of coal when she and her tow vessel sailed into a huge westerly gale. The thrashing vessel soon broke her towline and was cast into the rocky shallows below Pictured Rocks, east of Munising, Michigan. No lives were lost, but the vessel broke up following the November 16, 1883 accident. [2]

WABASH VALLEY ■ Wooden passenger and package freight steamer of 592 t., launched in 1856 at Buffalo
Lake Michigan: On November 22, 1860, the steamer WABASH VALLEY was caught by a following gale and thrown on a reef near Muskegon, Michigan. Her passengers and crew all made it ashore, but the vessel was dashed to pieces by the fury of the storm. [2]

T J WAFFLE ■ Wooden bulk freight steamer 149 t. and 105 ft., launched in 1914 at Westport, Ont.
Lake Ontario: On September 22, 1919, this small steamer was lost on Lake Ontario. The freighter simply went missing in heavy weather, somewhere between Oswego, New York, and the Duck Islands. The lost steamer carried a crew of eight. [3]

DAVID WAGSTAFF ■ Merchant schooner
Lake Michigan: The schooner DAVID WAGSTAFF was reported lost off Sheboygan, Wisconsin, on November 25, 1890. [1]

WAH-NE-TAH ■ Gas screw passenger and freight packet of 16 t. and 46 ft., launched in 1910 at Oshkosh, WI
Lake Michigan: None of the 22 persons aboard this vessel were injured when the little vessel caught fire and burned at Oshkosh on April 21, 1916. [2]

WAHNAPITAE ■ Lumber schooner-barge of 1,432 t. and 260 ft., launched in 1886 at W Bay City, MI
Lake Erie: The schooner-barge WAHNAPITAE was entering the harbor at Cleveland in tow of the steamer JOHN M NICOL (qv) and with a load of lumber when she was overtaken by disaster. A storm was blowing across the harbor entrance on that day, and the big barge was driven sideways into the breakwater, where she quickly filled and sank. One man died in the accident, which occurred on October 26, 1890. [2]

BELLE WALBRIDGE ■ Lumber schooner of 271 t.
Lake Michigan: On November 22, 1886, this schooner sank off the harbor entrance at Sheboygan, Wisconsin. She was carrying a cargo of telegraph poles at the time. [1]

L C WALDO ■ Steel bulk freight steamer of 4,466 t. and 480 ft., launched in 1896 at W Bay City, MI
Lake Superior: Though no lives were lost and the vessel herself survived, the story of the L C WALDO is one of the greatest in Lakes archives. On November 11, 1913, the big steamer was bound for the Soo and the Lower Lakes with her cargo of iron ore. She was battling one of the biggest, most violent storms in Lakes history, and by the time she was rounding the tip of the Keweenaw Peninsula, she was losing the fight. The ship was driven aground on desolate Gull Rock, between Passage Island and the Keweenaw, and it was immediately apparent to others in the vicinity that she was in dire trouble. The Lifesaving Service was notified and immediately set out for the wreck. While the WALDO's crew huddled together in the gale, the USLS men struggled mightily for nearly four days before finally reaching the ship and rescuing her people. The heavily damaged vessel was pulled off the rock the following year and repaired at great expense. She sailed on for 54 more years as the L C WALDO, the RIVERTON, and finally the MOHAWK DEER. Even in her old age, the vessel refused to give up to the scrapyard, just as the lifesavers had not given up in 1913. In November of 1967 the big vessel was being towed across the Atlantic to Spain for scrapping when she sprang a leak and went down for good. [5+]

WALES ■ Merchant schooner of 110 ft.
Lake Huron: The schooner WALES was abandoned near Midland, Ontario, in 1895, but it is not clear if the abandonment was due to an accident. [2]

WALK-IN-THE-WATER ■ Sidewheel passenger and package freight steamer of 358 t. and 132 ft., launched in 1818 at Black Rock (Buffalo), NY
Lake Erie: The historic steamboat WALK-IN-THE-WATER was the first steam-powered vessel on the Upper Lakes (the Canadian FRONTENAC (qv) was the first on any of the Lakes). Steamship pioneer Robert Fulton himself oversaw the installation of her engine and machinery. The vessel had a short career, however. On October 31, 1821, the little steamboat was caught by a westerly gale and driven on the rocks at Point Abino, Ontario, on the Canadian shore west of Buffalo. She went completely to pieces, but with no loss of life. Her engines were later salvaged and installed in the steamer SUPERIOR (qv). [5+]

C H WALKER ■ Merchant schooner
Lake Huron: This vessel was reported lost on the lake in 1876. The exact position of the accident is unrecorded. [1]

IDA WALKER ■ Merchant schooner
Lake Ontario: Stony Point, at the eastern end of the lake, was the final resting place of this sailing ship. Driven on a reef there on November 19, 1886, the vessel broke up soon after. The rescue of her crew was the first ever made by a Dobbins surfboat, which was later to become famous as standard equipment for American lifesaving crews. [1]

JAMES A WALKER ■ Steam propeller of 184 t. and 106 ft., launched in 1887 at Kingston, Ont.
Lake Ontario: On October 22, 1898, the small steamer JAMES A WALKER was reported to have foundered 100 yards off the beach at Nicholson Island, west of Wellington, Ontario. [1]

C B WALLACE ■ Wooden sidewheel steamer of 99 t. and 101 ft., launched in 1880 at Port Clinton, OH as the steamer J V LUTTS
Lake Erie: This little steamer was the victim of fire, which destroyed her on September 25, 1897, in the harbor at Toledo, Ohio. [2]

LOUIS WALLACE ■ Wooden steam tug of 41 t. and 54 ft., launched in 1865 at Grand Haven, MI
Lake Michigan: This wooden tug became the victim of fire on Portage Lake, near the lake entrance channel, opposite Onekama, Michigan. She was lost in 1893. [2]

ROBERT WALLACE ■ Wooden bulk freight steamer of 1,189 t. and 209 ft., launched in 1882 at Cleveland
Lake Superior: A barge laden with iron ore is a tremendous strain on the stern of a tow vessel. A towrope is said to become as hard as iron when pulling a laden barge. When both barge and tow vessel are subjected to the bucking and plunging brought on by heavy weather, some part of the system must break down. In the case of the ROBERT WALLACE, it was not the towline that parted, as was

usually the case. The WALLACE and her consort ASH-LAND were coming down the lake with loads of iron ore and fighting a storm on Nov. 17, 1902, when the unthinkable happened. The careening barge yanked against the rear of the WALLACE once too often, and the sternpost and much of the after portion of the steamer was ripped out. As the steamer quickly swamped, the ASHLAND coasted up to the scene and rescued the stricken vessel's crew. The ship went down southeast of Two Harbors, Minnesota. [4]

WALSCHIFF ■ Steel motor ship of 882 t., launched in 1952 at Lubeck, Germany
St. Clair River: One German seaman lost his life in an accident which occurred at the upper end of the river, opposite Point Edward. On Oct. 2, 1952, the WALLSCHIFF and the big ore boat PIONEER confused passing signals and collided, the laker striking the saltie amidships and sinking her. The steamer was later recovered and, since she was almost brand-new, it was considered worthwhile to tow her all the way back to Germany for repairs. [3]

WALRUS ■ Merchant schooner
Lake Michigan: In 1868, the schooner WALRUS struck Gray's Reef, east of Beaver Island, and sank. [1]

PHILIP WALTER ■ Sidewheel steamer of 102 t. and 94 ft., launched in 1872 at Sandusky, OH
Lake Erie: Eight sailors perished when this small steamer capsized and sank three miles off Lorain, OH, on June 20, 1887. She had been carrying a load of general merchandise when she was lost. Some sources say she was lost off Sandusky, OH, but a Sandusky historian places the wreck at Lorain, about 20 miles further east. The ship is sometimes listed as "P H Walters" or "Philip Walters." [4]

JOHN WALTERS ■ Merchant schooner
Lake Huron: Georgian Bay's Russel Island, near Tobermory, Ont., was the site of the loss of the schooner JOHN WALTERS in 1899. The vessel sank just offshore. [2]

GEORGE H WAND ■ Package and bulk freight schooner of 358 t. and 140 ft., launched in 1866 at Buffalo
Lake Huron: The schooner GEORGE H WAND was stranded and broken up near shore off Harbor Beach, Michigan. She was too badly damaged to be saved and was abandoned after the April 17, 1902 accident. [4]

WANDERER ■ Merchant schooner
Lake Huron: In 1883, this schooner was reported to have sunk off Kincardine, Ontario. [1]

E B WARD ■ Merchant schooner of 80 t., launched before 1847
Lake Michigan: Locational information is not given for this vessel, which was capsized by a white squall in 1870 and sank. [2]

EBER WARD ■ Wooden package freight steamer of 1,343 t. and 213 ft., launched in 1888 at W Bay City, MI
Lake Michigan: The narrowest point of the Straits of Mackinac, between Old Point Mackinac and Point La Barbe, is the spot most clogged with ice during the spring breakup. This is the area that the corn-carrying steamer EBER WARD was trying to navigate on April 9, 1909. She struck a block of floating ice and was holed, sinking into the frigid strait in less than ten minutes. Five men were lost of her crew of 16. The remains of the ship lie just west of the south pier of the Mackinac Bridge. [5+]

MARY WARD ■ Merchant steamer of 340 t. and 137 ft., launched in 1864 at Montreal as the steamer NORTH
Lake Huron: The small steamer MARY WARD was laden with a cargo of coal oil and salt when she accidentally ran aground northeast of Collingwood, Ontario, in Nottawasaga Bay. A "north'r" that followed the next day destroyed the little ship before she could be extricated. Eight crewmen as well as the MARY WARD herself were lost on November 24, 1872. The shoal area where the vessel ran aground and was subsequently demolished is still called "Mary Ward Ledges." [5+]

SUSAN WARD ■ Barge of 365 t., launched in Detroit in 1863 as a steamer
Lake Huron: An 1885 storm sank this unpowered vessel off Oscoda, Michigan. [2]

CHARLES M WARNER ■ Steam freighter of 255 ft.
Lake Huron: The wreckage of this steamer is sited off Ninemile Point, east of Cheboygan, MI. She was lost there in November of 1905 when she went aground in a storm and was reportedly broken up by wave action. The WARNER was probably ultimately recovered, as the only vessel of this name on record was still operating years later. [2]

JOHN F WARNER ■ Merchant schooner of 200 t. and 127 ft., launched in 1855 at Cleveland
Lake Huron: The small schooner JOHN F WARNER was reported lost near Alpena, Michigan, in 1890. [2]

HOMER WARREN ■ Wooden bulk freight steamer of 304 t. and 180 ft., launched in 1863 at Cleveland as the passenger steamer ATLANTIC
Lake Ontario: The steamer HOMER WARREN had her holds full of coal when she foundered from unknown causes off Pultneyville, New York. The steamer went down on October 28, 1919, with all nine of her crew (one source says 19). [5]

WARRENKO ▪ Steamer of 278 t.
Lake Ontario: On July 7, 1938, the steamer WARRENKO was lost near Kingston, Ontario, when she collided with the steamer SPRUCE BAY. [1]

WARRINGTON ▪ Wooden bulk freight steamer of 343 t. and 160 ft., launched in 1863 at Cleveland as the lighthouse tender HENRY WARRINGTON
Lake Michigan: The steamer WARRINGTON was downbound with a full load of lumber when she stranded in a summer gale near Charlevoix, Michigan. The vessel could not be freed, and was destroyed by the action of waves. The date of the accident was August 21, 1911. A vessel listed as "H Warrington" was reported wrecked on Lake Huron in 1869, and is probably the same ship. [4]

WASAGA ▪ Wooden package freight steamer of 1,619 t. and 238 ft., launched in 1876 at Buffalo as the steamer WISSAHICKON
Lake Superior: A search for shelter from a powerful gale was futile for this steamer, lost on November 7, 1910. After dropping anchor in the relative quiet of Copper Harbor, Michigan, the WASAGA caught fire, burned to the waterline, and sank. No lives were lost. [4]

GEORGE WASHINGTON ▪ Sidewheel passenger and package freight steamer of 609 t., launched in 1833 at Huron, OH
Lake Erie: The early sidewheel steamboat GEORGE WASHINGTON was a well-known carrier along the south shore of the lake until disaster ended her career on June 15, 1838. On that date she was above Silver Creek, near Dunkirk, New York, when she caught fire and was destroyed. Estimates of the number of passengers and crew who died in the catastrophe range from 30 to 50. [3]

LADY WASHINGTON ▪ Merchant sloop
Lake Ontario: A very early commercial sailing ship was this little single-mast vessel. She went missing on November 11, 1803, having last been seen off Eight Mile (or Eighteen Mile) Creek. She was carrying a cargo of chinaware when she disappeared. [2]

LADY WASHINGTON ▪ Merchant schooner of 49 t. and 60 ft., launched in 1816 at Sacket's Harbor, NY
Lake Erie: No lives were lost, but the LADY WASHINGTON was a total wreck when the schooner foundered off Sturgeon Point, New York (west of Buffalo). She went down on October 19, 1828. One source places the wreck at Sturgeon Point, Lake Huron. [3]

LADY WASHINGTON ▪ Merchant steamer of 47 t., 72 ft.
Lake Michigan: On September 14, 1890, this small steamer was carrying a cargo of general freight when she struck bottom near Seul Choix Point, east of Manistique, Michigan, and foundered. [3]

WASP ▪ Merchant schooner, may be a former warship
Lake Erie: No lives were lost when this sail vessel was driven ashore near Cunningham Creek and wrecked in 1818. [1]

WATER WITCH ▪ Steam propeller of 458 t., launched in 1863
Lake Huron: Another case of a vessel that sailed out of port and disappeared is the steamer WATER WITCH. Still in her first season of service, the steamboat went missing in a storm in November of 1863, with 28 passengers and crew on board. She is thought to have foundered northeast of Au Sable Point, off Oscoda, Michigan, and was carrying a load of copper at the time. [5]

WATERLOO ▪ Wooden steamer of 98 t., launched in 1840 at Black Rock, NY
Lake Huron: The WATERLOO was lost on the "sixth Great Lake," Georgian Bay, when she was wrecked in 1846. [2]

ALEX. WATSON ▪ Propeller steamer of 90 t. and 109 ft., launched in 1870 at Wallaceburg, Ont.
Detroit River: A single, brief report lists this steamer as wrecked on the river in June of 1871. [1]

MARY WATSON ▪ Steamer
Lake Huron: The steamer MARY WATSON was reported wrecked in a storm off Goderich, Ontario, in 1858. [1]

ANNIE WATT ▪ Steam propeller packet of 62 t. and 75 ft., launched in 1884 at Lion's Head, Ont.
Lake Huron: On August 16, 1890, the tiny steamer ANNIE WATT collided with the ship ALDERSON, off Gunn Point, Ontario, and was lost. [2]

J G WATTS ▪ Vessel information unavailable
Lake Huron: The J G WATTS was reported to have foundered on Devil's Island Bank, west of Tobermory, Ontario. She went down on November 5, 1895. [2]

WAUBIC ▪ Propeller steamer of 469 t. and 138 ft., launched in 1909 at Collingwood, Ont.
Lake Erie: The WAUBIC was the victim of a dock fire which struck her on January 18, 1938. She burned down to the hull at Kingsville, Ontario, and was thought to be a total loss. However, her hull was still serviceable and a new vessel, the ERIE ISLE, was built upon it. [3]

WAUBUNO ▪ Sidewheel passenger and package freight steamer of 146 t. and 135 ft., launched in 1865 at Port Robinson, Ont.

Lake Huron: The WAUBUNO was a popular passenger and freight boat among the coastal towns of Georgian Bay. She routinely travelled some of the most remote areas in the entire Great Lakes system. It is no wonder, then, that when the vessel failed to show up at her scheduled port of call at Parry Sound following a November 22, 1879 gale, no one was too concerned. But the WAUBUNO never showed up at all, and a search revealed precious little to indicate what had happened to the little ship. The following spring a local trapper reported having seen a "big boat" lying upside-down near Moose Point, well south of Parry Sound. Upon inspection, the derelict proved to be the WAUBUNO, without a clue visible as to what had happened, nor any trace of her 24 passengers and crew. [5+]

WAUKEGAN ■ Steel passenger and package freight steamer of 155 ft. overall, launched in 1919 at Sturgeon Bay, WI, as the tug COMMODORE
Lake Michigan: The small steamer WAUKEGAN had just been laid up for the season when disaster struck her at her winter dock at Sturgeon Bay, Wisconsin. On December 5, 1935, the vessel caught fire and was destroyed. [1]

WAUKESHA ■ Merchant schooner of 310 t. and 137 ft., launched in 1862 at Manitowoc, WI, as the NABOB
Lake Michigan: Six men died as a result of the storm that destroyed this vessel off Muskegon, Michigan, on November 7, 1896. On that date the schooner was trying to ride out the heavy weather at anchor when she became water-logged and sank. [3]

WAURECAN ■ Barge, possibly the 371 t. vessel of this name launched in 1857 at Buffalo
Lake Huron: In 1875 the barge WAURECAN foundered on the reef at Port Austin, Michigan, in northern Saginaw Bay. [1]

WAUSEDA II ■ Tug of 19 t.
Lake Huron: The tug WAUSEDA II was reportedly destroyed by fire at a dock at Fitzwilliam Island, near the mouth of Georgian Bay, on October 21, 1948. [2]

WAUWONA ■ 15 t. vessel of unreported type
Lake Huron: On June 20, 1917, the little WAUWONA was reported destroyed at Wall Island, south of Manitoulin. [1]

WAVE ■ Merchant schooner, perhaps the 44 t. schooner of this name launched in 1835 at Swan Creek, MI
Lake Huron: Two seamen died when this sailing ship was lost off Inverhuron, Ontario, in 1858. [1]

WAVE ■ Steamer
Lake Huron: The steamer WAVE was reported burned and lost at the Charity Islands, in Saginaw Bay, in 1874. [1]

WAVE CREST ■ Package and bulk freight schooner of 182 t., and 110 ft., launched in 1867 at Brockville, Ont.
Lake Ontario: The small schooner WAVE CREST was swamped and sunk off Oak Orchard Point, near Point Breeze, New York. The two-master went down on November 15, 1900. [2]

WAVERLY ■ Wooden bulk freight steamer of 1,104 t. and 191 ft., launched in 1874 at Buffalo
Lake Huron: The steamer WAVERLY was lost as the result of a collision which occurred on the night of July 22, 1903. On that date, she was struck and sunk by the steel bulk freighter TURRET CROWN (qv), off Harbor Beach, Michigan. She had also been heavily damaged in a stranding on South Manitou Island in 1887. [4]

WAVETREE ■ Merchant schooner
Lake Huron: The position of this schooner at the time of her loss is either unknown or unreported. She is said to have been lost on the Lake in 1868. [1]

WAWANOSH ■ Package and bulk freight schooner of 142 ft. overall, launched in 1873 at Sarnia, Ont.
Lake Huron: This schooner was under tow when she was struck by a gale and broke her tow cable. She went on the rocks off Oscoda, Michigan, and was pounded to pieces by storm waves. The loss occurred on December 6, 1906. [2]

WAWINET or **WAWANET** ■ Tug (possibly a yacht) of 33 t. and 87 ft.
Lake Huron: The WAWINET was lost south of Beausoliel Island off Penetang Harbor, at the south end of Georgian Bay. She sank on September 21, 1942, though one source says 1842. One report also claims that 26 people were lost in the accident. [4]

WAYNE ■ Merchant schooner
Lake Huron: In 1875 this schooner was reported stranded and wrecked at Au Sable Point, near Au Sable, Michigan. [1]

WAYNE ■ Bulk freight schooner of 322 t. launched in 1875 at Trenton, MI
Lake Ontario: No lives were lost, but this schooner and her cargo of wheat were destroyed when the WAYNE wrecked at Oswego, New York. She was entering the harbor in a storm, when she suddenly luffed to, lost steerageway, and was smashed against the breakwater. The accident occurred on December 5, 1877. [2]

ANTHONY WAYNE ■ Wooden passenger and package freight steamer of 390 t., launched at Perrysburg, OH, in 1837
Lake Erie: While carrying passengers and a cargo of liquor, this steamer suffered a boiler explosion and disastrous fire off Sandusky, Ohio. Her cargo probably fed the terrific blaze, and she was destroyed and sank very quickly. Reports of the loss of life in the April 28, 1850 tragedy vary from 38 to 69 lost. Some sources state that she had gold, specie, wines and other valuables aboard. [5+]

J L WEATHERLY ■ Steamer
Lake Erie: The steamer J L WEATHERLY was reported to have sunk in the harbor at Cleveland on May 9, 1894. [1]

NETTIE or **NETTA WEAVER** ■ Merchant schooner of 310 t.
Lake Huron: This sail vessel, the schooner NETTIE WEAVER, was destroyed in a storm on October 4, 1877. She was reported wrecked, a total loss, off Kincardine, Ontario. [2]

B L WEBB ■ Wooden propeller freighter of 843 t. and 195 ft., launched in 1856 at Detroit
Lake Superior: Waiska Bay, just west of Sault Ste. Marie, Michigan, was the site of the demise of this wooden steamer in November of 1856. One crewman lost his life when the ship stranded and burned in a gale. She was later recovered and rebuilt. [3]

H J WEBB ■ Bulk freight schooner of 432 t. and 167 ft., launched in 1869 at Vermilion, OH
Lake Huron: The exact location of the destruction of the H J WEBB on November 11, 1901, is not reported, but she is said to have gone hard aground in Georgian Bay, a total loss. [1]

CHARLES H WEEKS ■ Lumber schooner of 325 t.
Lake Huron: The WEEKS and one of her crew were lost when she foundered off Port Huron on October 6, 1889. [2]

WELCOME ■ Armed sloop of 45 t. and 60 ft., launched in 1775 at Fort Michilimackinac (Mackinaw City), MI
Lake Michigan: This small sloop warship carried troops and supplies to and from the fort that controlled the strategically-important Straits of Mackinac during the American Revolution. In 1787, she was lost with all hands in the Straits when she sank in a storm. Parts of the vessel have been recovered, and a lovely replica of her is now displayed at Michilimackinac, in the shadow of the Mackinac Bridge. [4]

WELCOME ■ Bulk freight propeller of 306 t. and 120 ft., launched as a sidewheeler at Fort Howard, WI, in 1878
Lake Michigan: The rocky approaches to Charlevoix, Michigan, with fields of boulders just below the surface, have been the death of a significant number of vessels. The small steamer WELCOME stranded off the town on September 16, 1903, and broke up from the action of waves after a salvage attempt failed. [3]

WELLAND ■ Steamer of 140 ft., launched in 1842 at Bath, Ont.
Lake Ontario: Fire destroyed this steamboat at Port Dalhousie, Ontario, in August of 1856. [2]

WILLIAM WELLHOUSE ■ Scow of 84 t.
Lake Erie: One person died when this scow, laden with a cargo of stone, collided with the schooner JANE C WOODRUFF and sank on October 15, 1880. Manhattan Mills is given as the location. [1]

WELLINGTON ■ Merchant schooner
Lake Michigan: The schooner WELLINGTON was lost on Skillagallee, east of Beaver Island in 1867. She reportedly piled ashore on the reef and was wrecked. [2]

CHANDLER J WELLS ■ Lumber schooner of 521 t.
Lake Michigan: The CHANDLER J WELLS was wrecked on November 20, 1884. While picking her way through the Beaver Islands in heavy weather, this lumber-laden ship ran aground on Whiskey Island Reef, seven miles northwest of Beaver Island Harbor Lighthouse. The ship later broke up in place. [2]

DAVID A WELLS ■ Merchant schooner of 311 t.
Lake Michigan: Eight seamen were lost when this ship sank seven miles northeast of the Chicago waterfront. The schooner and her cargo of iron ore went down on October 16, 1880. [2]

F L WELLS ■ Merchant schooner
Lake Huron: In 1868, the schooner F L WELLS was reported driven ashore and pounded to pieces near Port Bruce, Ontario. [1]

HATTIE WELLS ■ Lumber schooner of 376 t. and 164 ft., launched in 1867 at Port Huron, MI
Lake Michigan: The large schooner HATTIE WELLS was off St. Joseph, Mich., when she became caught in a heavy gale on November 6, 1912. Her crew was able to abandon ship before the schooner swamped and went down. [4]

JARVIS WELLS ■ Merchant schooner
Lake Huron: An 1879 wreck, the schooner JARVIS WELLS came ashore in a gale and was reduced to wreckage at Sand Beach, Michigan. [1]

WEND THE WAVE ■ Schooner-barge of 250 t., launched in 1867 at Ashtabula, OH, as a schooner
Lake Erie: The end came for this small schooner-barge in 1889, when she sank in Pelee Passage. [1]

WENONA ■ Merchant schooner of 496 t. and 193 ft., launched in 1857 at Cleveland
Lake Superior: On September 7, 1898, the big schooner WENONA was lost in a gale off the Keweenaw. She reportedly went down near one entrance to the Portage Ship Canal. [2]

ROBERT C WENTE ■ Wooden bulk freight steamer of 335 t. and 141 ft., launched in 1888 at Gibraltar, MI
St. Clair River: On July 1, 1927, the steamer ROBERT C WENTE was lost when she was destroyed by fire on the river. She had been a major salvage project in 1911, when she had sunk on Lake Michigan. [3]

J W WESCOTT ■ Wooden steam tug of 18 t. and 42 ft., launched in 1880 at Buffalo
Lake Superior: This small harbor tug sank with no loss of life in the harbor at Grand Marais, Michigan. She went down on October 8, 1901. [3]

WESEE ■ Wooden bulk freight steamer of 1,829 t. and 266 ft., launched in 1901 at Green Bay, WI, as the steamer ORION
Lake Erie: A blaze which occurred on November 12, 1923, destroyed this big steamer, one of the last wooden bulk freighters built. The WESEE was underway off Little Sister Island in heavy seas when she was discovered to be afire. She was beached on the island and her people were able to evacuate safely, but the vessel was destroyed. [3]

JOHN WESLEY ■ Bulk freight schooner of 302 t. and 135 ft., launched in 1872 at Toledo
Lake Erie: The WESLEY suffered a major accident on September 25, 1883, when she was blown ashore and wrecked at Windmill Point, on the Ontario Shore west of Buffalo. Thought to be a total loss, she was recovered and returned to service. [2]
Lake Huron: The WESLEY stranded near Pte Aux Barques, Michigan, in 1894. Again she was thought to be lost, but again she was recovered. [1]
Lake Huron: The now-aging JOHN WESLEY was driven hard aground by a storm which struck her on September

7, 1901. The vessel was stranded near Harbor Beach, Michigan. A survey determined that the schooner was not economically salvageable, and she was abandoned. [4]

WEST SHORE ■ Steel collier
Lake Erie: This vessel was reported to have capsized and sunk in the harbor at Buffalo in 1949. [1]

WEST SIDE ■ Lumber schooner of 334 t. and 138 ft., launched in 1870 at Oswego, NY
Lake Huron: On October 10, 1906, the schooner WEST SIDE was seeking shelter from a gale when she tried to make the difficult entry into the harbor at Parry Sound, Ontario. She was unsuccessful, being driven ashore near the harbor mouth where she was battered to pieces by storm-blown waves. [3]

B WEST ■ Steel propeller
Lake Michigan: This vessel was reported to have sunk at the mouth of Michigan's Grand Traverse Bay, near Northport. [1]

WESTERN ■ Sidewheel steamer, launched in 1833 at Chatham, Ont. as the steamer CYNTHIA McGREGOR
Detroit River: The small steamer WESTERN was lost at a wharf at Detroit on April 27, 1842. She caught fire and burned to the waterline. [2]

WESTERN METROPOLIS ■ Merchant bark
Lake Superior: In the fall of 1864, this vessel was reported stranded and broken up, but the location was not given. [1]

WESTERN RESERVE ■ Steel bulk freight steamer of 2,392 t. and 301 ft., launched in 1890 at Cleveland
Lake Superior: This vessel was the first steel freighter built for use on the Lakes. When she came out steelmen and her builders confidently predicted that her construction would put an end to disasters caused by hull failure. The vessel proved their point for only a bare two years. On August 30, 1892, the WESTERN RESERVE was in ballast and pushing her way through a summer gale when she suddenly simply broke in two and sank off Deer Park, Michigan. There was little evidence to indicate what had happened to the ship in a relatively mild gale that would explain such a complete hull failure, and there was only one eyewitness left out of the 27 aboard the steamer at the time of her foundering. The furor surrounding the tragic loss of the WESTERN RESERVE brought on a new set of rules regarding the testing of steel as to tensile strength and flexibility. [5+]

WESTERN STAR ■ Merchant schooner
Lake Huron: In 1854 this schooner was wrecked near Goderich, Ontario, and sank. [1]

WESTERN STAR ■ Steel bulk freight steamer of 4,764 t. and 416 ft., launched in 1903 at Wyandotte, MI
Lake Superior: The first of two major wrecks that this vessel suffered in her career happened in the Big Blow of November 28-29, 1905. The big steamer was off 14-mile Point, on the west side of the Keweenaw Peninsula, when a terrific windstorm and mountainous seas drove her sideways to shore. The pounding of her hull against the rocky coast led her underwriters to believe at first that the vessel was a total loss, but salvagers were later able to reclaim her. [5+]
Lake Huron: On September 24, 1915, the WESTERN STAR was blown aground and wrecked on Clapperton Island, in the North Channel. She had suffered major hull damage, but was again refloated and rebuilt. Two years later she became the Canadian steamer GLENISLA and was finally scrapped in 1963 as the PRESCOTT. [3]

WESTERN STATES ■ Steel sidewheel passenger steamer of 3,077 t. and 350 ft., launched in 1902 at Wyandotte, MI
Lake Huron: The former D & C passenger liner WESTERN STATES had been retired in 1955 and was tied to a pier at Tawas City, Michigan, for use as a floating hotel ("flotel"), when she suffered her final indignation. The once palatial steamer was an unsuccessful business venture and was being stripped when a wayward spark set her afire. The vessel was gutted by the March 21, 1959, fire and her burnt-out hull was later towed to Bay City for scrapping. The towing crew had much difficulty with the once-proud liner, which veered this way and that at the end of her tow cable. [3]

WESTFORD ■ Wooden bulk freight steamer of 140 ft. overall, launched in 1869 at Trenton, MI
Lake Huron: A victim of fire, the small steamer WESTFORD burned at Robbins' Shoal, near Georgian Bay's Johns Island, on May 27, 1904. [3]

WESTMORELAND ■ Wooden passenger and package freight steamer of 800 t. and 200 ft., launched in 1853 at Cleveland
Lake Michigan: The wooden steamer WESTMORELAND has been subject to many conflicting reports and much interest since the day she went down in the Manitou Passage, December 7, 1854. The vessel was bound for Mackinac Island with a load of winter supplies and grain for the islanders, as well as a quantity of liquor and, reputedly, over $100,000 in gold. On the date mentioned, the vessel encountered a frigid gale and began to accumulate ice on her upperworks. By the time she reached Manitou Passage the vessel was taking on water fast and was

decidedly tender from the tons of extra weight above her decks. As passengers and crew tried to abandoned ship, the vessel went down, capsizing a lifeboat and costing the lives of 17 people. Reports vary widely as to her exact position, given as Sleeping Bear Point, Platte Bay, North Manitou or South Manitou Islands, though the vessel reportedly has been located several times. [5+]

I M WESTON ■ Steam propeller of 95 t. and 96 ft., launched in 1883 at Grand Haven, MI
The only information given on the wreck of this vessel is that she was a total loss in 1902. [1]

WESTOVER ■ Steamer, possibly the 125 t., 107 ft. sidewheel tug LUTHER WESTOVER, built at W Bay City, MI, in 1877.
Lake Huron: The steamer WESTOVER was reported to have been destroyed by fire on the Au Gres River, in Saginaw Bay, in 1881. [1]

W L WETMORE ■ Wooden bulk freight steamer of 820 t. and 213 ft., launched in 1871 at Cleveland
Lake Huron: A November 29, 1901 storm drove this steamer aground on Russel Island, near Tobermory, Ontario. She had been towing two barges at the time. Though at first she was not seriously damaged, the WETMORE was later destroyed by waves. [4]

RUDOLPH WETZEL ■ Steamer or tug of 23 t.
Lake Michigan: Three lives were lost when this little steamer's boiler exploded and she sank three miles off Oak Creek, Wisconsin. The disaster occurred on October 28, 1882. [1]

WEXFORD ■ Steel bulk freight steamer of 2,800 t. and 250 ft., launched in 1883 at Sunderland, England
Lake Huron: The loss of the steel steamer WEXFORD would have been a major disaster in its own right had it not happened during the Big Storm of 1913, which sent 12 large vessels to the bottom. On November 11, the WEXFORD was off Kettle Point, Ontario, when, it is conjectured, she was simply overpowered by giant waves and terrific winds. All 17 men aboard the vessel perished when she sank. Her wreckage was located in 1975. [5+]

WHALE ■ Sandsucker-barge of 1,145 t. and 264 ft., launched in 1892 at Toledo as the carferry ANN ARBOR #2
St. Clair River: This sandsucker-barge was lost on St. Clair Flats, just outside the channel nicknamed the "snake run," in 1927. She collided with the steamer WILLIAM E COREY, sank and was abandoned. [3]

EDWARD C WHALEN ■ Steel tug of 113 t. and 76 ft., launched in 1913 at Port Arthur, Ont.
Lake Superior: This large tug was reported to have foundered off Corbiel Point on June 8, 1954. She was also reported as wrecked on Superior on October 17, 1947. [2]

FRANK W WHEELER ■ Bulk freight schooner-barge of 797 t. and 190 ft., launched in 1884 at W Bay City, MI
Lake Superior: No lives were lost when this new schooner-barge, downbound with a load of iron ore, sprang a leak and sank off Grand Marais, Michigan. The reason for her leak is somewhat of a mystery, since she was a new vessel, and the accident occurred in calm weather. The loss occurred on September 29, 1885. [2]

FRANK W or **F W WHEELER** ■ Bulk freight steamer of 1,688 t. and 266 ft., launched in 1887 at W Bay City, MI
Lake Michigan: A sandbar off Michigan City, Indiana, was the final resting place of this steamer. Laden with a cargo of coal, she hit the shallows one mile offshore and foundered on December 3, 1893. [3]

IRMA L WHEELER ■ Steam tug of 51 t. and 66 ft., launched in 1877 at Manitowoc, WI
Lake Michigan: The tug IRMA L WHEELER was lost near Charlevoix, Michigan, on Pine Lake (now Lake Charlevoix), on April 1, 1905. The WHEELER was destroyed by fire. [2]

WILLIAM WHEELER ■ Freight barge of 309 t.
Lake Ontario: On August 29, 1893, the barge WILLIAM WHEELER sank eight miles off Charlotte, New York. She was laden with a cargo of barley at the time. [1]

GEORGE J WHELAN ■ Steel steam sandsucker of 1,430 t. and 220 ft., launched in 1910 at Toledo as the bulk freighter ERWIN L FISHER
Lake Erie: The loss of this large sandsucker resulted in the deaths of 15 crewmen. The GEORGE J WHELAN was six miles off Dunkirk, New York, when her cargo of stone shifted, causing the vessel to capsize and sink. She foundered on July 29, 1930. The WHELAN had an interesting background. As a freighter she had sunk on the Lakes in 1915. After repair, she had gone to do war duty on the East Coast, where she was torpedoed in the Atlantic. After rebuilding as a sandsucker, she returned to lake service in 1919. [5+]

WHITE FOAM ■ Merchant schooner of 18 t. and 46 ft., launched in 1880 at North Island, MI
Lake Huron: The small schooner WHITE FOAM was carrying a load of lumber when she was lost in the Straits of Mackinac on September 21, 1899. On that date she sank offshore from Bois Blanc Island. [2]

WHITE OAK ■ Lumber schooner of 157 t.
Lake Michigan: Named for the material from which most Great Lakes wooden vessels were built, this small schooner was lost on October 19, 1885. She reportedly foundered five miles south of the harbor entrance at Sheboygan, Wisconsin. She was carrying a cargo of railroad ties at the time. [2]

WHITE SQUALL ■ Merchant schooner
Lake Huron: Seven crewmen died as a result of the foundering of this sail vessel in 1872. The WHITE SQUALL collided with an unnamed vessel and sank in Saginaw Bay. [1]

WHITE STAR ■ Steamer
Lake Huron: The loss of the steamer WHITE STAR occurred off Cheboygan, Michigan, in 1844. [1]

WHITE STAR ■ Merchant schooner
Lake Erie: This schooner reportedly foundered in the Pelee Passage on December 1, 1877. She went down off Point Pelee. [1]

WHITE STAR ■ Wooden bulk freight steamer of 378 t. and 136 ft., launched in 1874 at Oswego, NY, as the schooner J MARIA SCOTT
Lake Huron: The precise location for the loss of this vessel to fire is not given, but it is probable that it was at or near Port Huron, Michigan. The WHITE STAR was lost on March 9, 1901. [2]

WHITE SWAN ■ Tug
Lake Michigan: The tug WHITE SWAN was reported stranded and broken up on Skillagallee, in the Beaver Passage, in 1959. [2]

KATE WHITE ■ Steam tug of 28 t. and 62 ft., launched in 1885 at Erie, PA
Lake Erie: On August 18, 1907, the tug KATE WHITE sank near the entrance to the harbor at Fairport, Ohio. [2]

KIRK WHITE ■ Merchant schooner of 184 t., launched in 1852 at Milwaukee
Lake Huron: The schooner KIRK WHITE foundered on Saginaw Bay in 1869, perhaps in the great storm which swept the Lakes that year. [2]

D C WHITNEY ■ Wooden bulk freight steamer of 1,090 t. and 229 ft., launched at St. Clair, MI, in 1882
Lake Michigan: This steamer was one of the many victims of the reefs and shoal waters in the vicinity of Washington Island, Wisconsin, at the mouth of Green Bay. On November 25, 1905, in a tremendous storm, she was driven ashore on the island, a declared total loss. However, she was later recovered and rebuilt as the steamer GARGANTUA, and served until she was converted to a drydock in 1920. [3]

DANIEL WHITNEY ■ Merchant schooner
Lake Michigan: On August 7, 1844, the small schooner DANIEL WHITNEY was found floating six miles off the

mouth of the Kalamazoo River, on the southeast shore of the lake. All four of the vessel's crew were missing and presumed dead. [1]

GEORGE F WHITNEY ■ Merchant schooner
Lake Michigan: No good reason has ever been discovered for the disappearance of this schooner and her eight crewmen in September of 1872. She sailed away from port in fine weather and was never heard from again. Her skipper reportedly flew her ensign upside down (an international distress signal) in port the day before setting sail on her last voyage. [4]

GRACE WHITNEY ■ Bulk freight schooner-barge of 290 t. and 141 ft., launched in 1866 at Gibraltar, MI
Lake Erie: Bar Point, on the east side of the mouth of the Detroit River is near an area of convergent shipping lanes, and there have been many collisions off its shores. On July 30, 1910, the schooner-barge GRACE WHITNEY collided with the 250-foot steel freighter OGDENSBURG, and sank a few miles off the point. [2]

TRUDE R WIEHE ■ Wooden bulk freight propeller of 520 t. and 180 ft., launched in 1885 at W Bay City, MI, as the steamer ALEX FOLSOM
Lake Michigan: The freighter TRUDE R WIEHE was destroyed by fire and sunk in Portage Bay of Green Bay. She caught fire on July 21, 1910, while waiting offshore to dock. [2]

A WILCOX ■ Merchant schooner of of 130 t., built prior to 1847
Lake Michigan: Two lives were lost when this ship was wrecked in 1853. [1]

M I WILCOX ■ Package and bulk freight schooner of 377 t. and 140 ft., launched in 1868 at Toledo
Lake Erie: This sailing ship stranded and sank off the end of the pier at Ontario's southernmost town, Colchester, on May 8, 1906. None of the five men aboard her were injured. [3]

O WILCOX ■ Wooden steam tug of 159 t., launched in 1869 at Detroit
Lake Huron: The big steam tug O WILCOX was off Tawas Point, on the Michigan shore, when she foundered in a storm in 1893. The vessel reportedly went down in less than seven minutes. [2]

WILD ROVER ■ 250 t. vessel of unreported type
Lake Erie: The WILD ROVER foundered off Long Point on November 4, 1874. [1]

ALICE E WILDS ■ Bulk freight steamer of 292 t. and 136 ft.
Lake Michigan: Laden with a cargo of lumber, this propeller collided with the steamer DOUGLAS and quickly sank, 16 miles off shore, near Milwaukee. The accident took place on May 28 of 1892. [1]

W H WILLARD ■ Merchant schooner of 108 t.
Lake Michigan: The W H WILLARD was stranded and destroyed off the north pier at St. Joseph, Michigan, in a storm that struck her on November 7, 1880. [2]

WILLIAM G ■ Gas screw of 11 t., probably a fishing vessel
Lake Huron: The the small WILLIAM G was reported to have foundered six miles off Lexington, Michigan, on August 26, 1947. [1]

C P WILLIAMS ■ Merchant brig of 350 t.
Lake Huron: The brig WILLIAMS was lost near Port Austin, Michigan, at the mouth of Saginaw Bay, in 1886. She had also been seriously damaged in an 1877 accident on Lake Erie. [2]

COL. A B WILLIAMS ■ Merchant schooner of 150 ft.
Lake Huron: This sailing vessel was reported as lost in 85 feet of water, three miles below Port Sanilac, Michigan, in 1864. [2]

D G WILLIAMS ■ Merchant schooner of 118 t.
Lake Michigan: The schooner D G WILLIAMS was reported to have sunk off the south pier at Chicago, with a cargo of lumber. [1]

E C WILLIAMS ■ Merchant schooner of 175 t. and 105 ft., launched in 1849 at Charlotte, NY
Lake Erie: The E C WILLIAMS was lost in the harbor at Buffalo on September 19, 1854. On that date the little schooner collided with the steamer WESTERN WORLD and sank. [1]

WILLIS ■ Merchant schooner
Lake Ontario: The only information available on the loss of this schooner is that she just disappeared on the lake. [1]

HUNTER WILLS ■ Wooden screw tug of 84 t. and 87 ft., launched in 1878 at Sandusky, OH, as the tug LOUISE
Lake Erie: The tug HUNTER WILLS was destroyed by fire in the harbor at Erie, Pennsylvania, in 1931. [1]

ANNABELL or **ANNABELLE WILSON** ■ Bulk freight schooner-barge of 490 t. and 174 ft., launched in 1874 at Mt. Clemens, MI
Lake Erie: This purpose-built schooner-barge was carrying coal when she was lost off Dunkirk, New York, with two of her crew. She became waterlogged and sank on July 12, 1913. [4]

BELLE WILSON ■ Steamer of 186 t. and 103 ft., launched in 1881 at Picton, Ont.
Lake Huron: This little steamer went down in a late summer storm in August of 1888. She foundered on Thunder Bay, Michigan. One reports says that an 11-ton steamer of the same name was lost on Lake Ontario on August 11, 1888. [3]

D M WILSON ■ Bulk freight steam barge of 757 t. and 179 ft., launched at St. Clair, MI, in 1873
Lake Huron: One of the many ships to be lost off Thunder Bay Island, near Alpena, Michigan, the steamer D M WILSON foundered there on October 27, 1894. While entering the bay in a storm with her cargo of coal, she opened a seam, became waterlogged and sank. The crew all suvived the wreck. [3]

MABELLE or **MABLE WILSON** ■ Bulk freight schooner-barge of 1,224 t. and 242 ft., launched in 1886 at W Bay City, MI
Lake Erie: This very large schooner-barge went down on May 28, 1906. One of her eight crewmen died when the WILSON filled and sank near the west breakwater at Cleveland. The big schooner-barge was later dynamited as an obstruction to shipping. [4]

S P WILSON ■ Merchant schooner of 142 t.
Lake Michigan: The small schooner S P WILSON was lost south of Grand Haven, Michigan. She was wrecked on October 20, 1885. [1]

THOMAS WILSON ■ Whaleback bulk freight steamer of 1,712 t. and 308 ft., launched in 1892 at Superior, WI
Lake Superior: Riding with a hull full of a massive cargo like iron ore, the whaleback vessel would look almost like two separate ships. Her main deck would be nearly awash in even the calmest of water. Perhaps this low profile contributed to the accident that ended the career of the THOMAS WILSON in 1902. On June 7 the steel steamer had just left Duluth with a load of ore when she was rammed by the freighter GEORGE G HADLEY. The force of the collision cut the WILSON in two, and she sank very rapidly, with the loss of nine of the whaleback's 20 crew members. [3]

THOMAS C WILSON ■ Merchant schooner of 30 t. and 58 ft., launched in 1868 at Black River, OH
Lake Michigan: This tiny schooner had a cargo of potatoes when she stranded near Egg Harbor, in Green Bay. She went aground in the fall of 1902 and was destroyed by the action of waves and ice during the following winter. [2]

WILTRANCO ■ Barge
Lake Erie: The barge WILTRANCO was reported stranded and wrecked on October 26, 1967, with no loss of life. [1]

WIMAN ■ Steamer
Lake Huron: The WIMAN was a steam vessel that was destroyed on a reef near Pointe Aux Barques, Michigan, in 1855. [1]

CORNELIA WINDIATE ■ Merchant schooner of 322 t., launched in 1873 at Manitowoc, WI
Lake Michigan: The exact position of this wheat-laden schooner at the time of her loss can only be guessed at. She went missing with all hands in a gale on December 10, 1875, and lies somewhere in the western Straits of Mackinac. [2]

WINDSOR ■ Passenger and freight steam ferry of 250 t., launched in 1856 at Detroit
Detroit River: Probably the most destructive accident ever to hit a river ferry on the Lakes struck this little boat on April 26, 1866. The WINDSOR was preparing to depart her dock at Detroit when she was wracked by a boiler explosion and caught fire. The blaze quickly destroyed the ferry and spread to shore, destroying the dock and depot as well. At the height of the fire, courageous action by the skipper of the steamer DETROIT prevented an even greater tragedy by pushing the burning vessel out into the river to burn out and sink. After the fire had been quenched and stock taken, it was determined that 30 people had died in the blaze. The hull was recovered and converted to the vessel below. [3]
Lake Michigan: Now a schooner-barge of 238 t. and 115 ft., the WINDSOR was carrying a cargo of telegraph poles when she was caught in a storm near Cana Island, at the mouth of Green Bay, and sank, One man died in the October 1, 1893, accident. [2]

ELIJAH WINDSOR ■ Steamer of 86 t. and 85 ft., launched in 1871 at Wallaceburg, Ont.
St. Clair River: The small steamer ELIJAH WINDSOR (sometimes listed as "E Windsor") was lost on the river in November of 1901. She broke in half and sank, but the exact location is unclear, some sources saying it was at Port Huron, while others claim Wallaceburg. The year of the accident has also been reported as 1901, 1900 and 1888. [4]

WINGS OF THE WIND ■ Bulk freight schooner of 130 ft., launched in 1855 at Buffalo
Lake Michigan: This schooner was lost in May of 1866 near Chicago when she collided with the bark BALDWIN and sank. She was laden with a cargo of coal at the time. [2]

WINNANNA ■ Propeller mailboat of 199 t. and 92 ft., launched in 1907 at Midland, Ont.
Lake Huron: The mailboat WINNANNA was devastated by a fire which struck her at Tobermory, Ontario, on November 19, 1909. The vessel burned to the hull, but was rebuilt and returned to service the next year as the steamer KEENAN. [3]

CITY OF WINNIPEG ■ Package and bulk freight propeller of 889 t. and 184 ft., launched in 1870 at Gibraltar, MI, as the steamer ANNIE L CRAIG
Lake Superior: The steamer CITY OF WINNIPEG was in the harbor at Duluth with a cargo of whiskey and horses when she was struck by fire on July 19, 1881. Four lives were lost when the vessel burned to the waterline and sank. [5+]

WINONA ■ Passenger and package freight steamer of 231 t. and 110 ft., launched in 1902 at Port Stanley, Ont.
Lake Huron: A fire struck this vessel at a wharf at Spragge, Ontario in the North Channel. She was destroyed on November 13, 1931. [3]

WINSLOW ■ Wooden package freight steamer of 1,050 t. and 220 ft., launched in 1863 at Cleveland
Lake Superior: Duluth, Minnesota, was the site of the loss of this steamer on October 3, 1891. The WINSLOW caught fire at her dock and was pushed to the Flats where she was destroyed. No lives were lost, but her cargo, consisting largely of brown sugar, was completely consumed. [2]

WINSLOW ■ Bulk freight steam barge of 353 t. and 120 ft., launched in 1865 at Cleveland
Lake Huron: On August 21, 1911, the WINSLOW burned at Meldrum Bay, in the North Channel, and was a total loss. [2]

ANNIE WINSLOW ■ Merchant brig
Lake Huron: The brig ANNIE WINSLOW was reported lost on Duck Island, near the north end of Manitoulin, in 1852. [1]

KATE WINSLOW ■ Schooner-barge of 736 t. and 202 ft., launched in 1872 at W Bay City, MI
Lake Michigan: While traversing the Beaver Passage in a storm on October 14, 1897, the KATE WINSLOW was torn loose from her towing steamer. She was blown on Gray's Reef where she was dashed to pieces. [3]

R G WINSLOW ■ Merchant bark
Lake Huron or Michigan: In 1867 this square-rigger was sunk in the Straits of Mackinac. [1]

RICHARD WINSLOW ■ Merchant schooner of 885 t. and 216 ft., launched in 1871 at Detroit
Lake Michigan: The RICHARD WINSLOW is reported to have stranded on White Shoals, in the northeast quadrant of the lake, and broken up in 1898. [3]

WISCONSIN ■ Steam vessel of 700 t., launched in 1837 at Conneaut, OH (reported as a propeller, but this is probably an error, the first propeller ship on the Lakes was the VANDALIA in 1840)
Lake Erie: The steamer WISCONSIN was lost on the lake in 1853. She collided with the steamer BRUNSWICK and sank near West Sister Island. [1]

WISCONSIN ■ Steam propeller
Lake Ontario: As many as 30 lives may have been lost when this steamer met with disaster on May 21, 1867. The WISCONSIN burned to the water's edge off Cape Vincent, New York, at the head of the St. Lawrence River. [2]

WISCONSIN ■ Iron passenger and package freight steamer of 1,921 t. and 209 ft., launched in 1881 at Wyandotte, Michigan
Lake Michigan: The large package freighter WISCONSIN was carrying a cargo of machine tools when she was lost on November 29, 1929. The vessel was anchored and waiting out a storm off Kenosha, Wisconsin, when she was overpowered by weather and sank. Eighteen of the 76 passengers and crew on board were lost in the sinking. Another large vessel of this name was reported lost in 1929 on Lake Superior. [5+]

WITCH ■ Fire tug
Lake Huron: This little old tug was a popular fixture around Saginaw and Bay City, Michigan, before she was destroyed at the mouth of the Saginaw River by a fire in 1929. [2]

WITCH OF THE WEST ■ Tug of 44 t. and 60 ft., launched in 1904 at Saginaw
Lake Huron: The brand-new tug WITCH OF THE WEST was destroyed by fire in Saginaw Bay off Bay City in 1904. [2]

WOCOKEN ■ Wooden steamer of 1,400 t. and 251 ft., launched in 1870 at Cleveland
Lake Erie: Fourteen lives were lost when this steamer, laden with a cargo of coal, broke up and sank in a gale off Dunkirk, New York. The WOCOKEN was lost on October 14, 1893. [5]

LOTTIE WOLF ■ Merchant schooner of of 334 t. and 126 ft.
Lake Huron: The schooner LOTTIE WOLF was lost in Georgian Bay in October of 1879. She struck a huge submerged boulder and foundered near the north shore of Hope Island. The vessel, now covered with sand, still lies in the same spot, now dubbed "Lottie Wolf Shoal." [2]

WILLIAM H WOLF ■ Wooden bulk freight steamer of 2,265 t. and 285 ft., launched in 1887 at Milwaukee
St. Clair River: On October 20, 1921, the WILLIAM H WOLF, downbound without cargo, caught fire and was destroyed abreast of Marine City, Michigan, where she

sank after burning out. To clear the channel, the vessel was raised and resunk at another location in 1925. [5]

WOLLIN ■ Merchant schooner of 49 t. and 84 ft., launched at Milwaukee in 1855
Lake Michigan: The tiny schooner WOLLIN went aground in a spring storm on April 29, 1897, and broke up. The accident took place two miles north of the harbor entrance at Sheboygan, Wisconsin. [3]

GENERAL WOLSELEY or **WOLSEY** ■ Sidewheel steamer of 123 t. and 103 ft., launched in 1884 at Oakville, Ont.
Lake Huron: This little sidewheeler was destroyed by a blaze near Georgian Bay's Cape Croker. She caught fire in September of 1886 and was a total loss. [2]

WONDER ■ Steamer of 99 t. and 95 ft., launched in 1889 at New London, WI
Lake Erie: The small steamer WONDER sank in the harbor at Ashtabula, Ohio, after stranding on July 13, 1908. No lives were lost in the accident. [2]

WOOD DUCK ■ Bulk freight schooner of 77 t.
Lake Ontario: A November 7, 1880, gale destroyed the schooner WOOD DUCK near Oswego, New York. The vessel was carrying a cargo of barley when she was driven ashore by huge waves, where she broke up. [1]

WOOD ISLAND ■ Gas launch of 11 t. and 47 ft., launched in 1907 at Racine, WI
Lake Superior: The small motor WOOD ISLAND was lost near Five-mile Point, in the western approach to Munising, Michigan, on September 9, 1922. She was towing a broomstick raft when she suddenly exploded and burned. No lives were lost in the incident. [2]

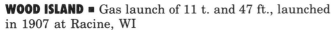

S A WOOD ■ Lumber schooner of 314 t. and 154 ft., launched in 1868 at Manitowoc, WI
Lake Michigan: The S A WOOD is one of several ships that brought her final cargo and crew home to port, despite being blasted by the worst the North Wind could throw. Partially dismasted and leaking badly from a storm that struck her on November 13, 1904, the schooner nonetheless made it to Milwaukee on short sails and willpower. One person, her skipper, had been killed by a falling spar, but the rest of the WOOD's crew lived to sail another day. The aged vessel was in too poor a condition to repair, and was abandoned. [3]

J S WOODRUFF ■ Merchant schooner
Lake Huron: The J S WOODRUFF was reported destroyed by a storm and sunk in Georgian Bay, in 1886. [2]

MARY WOOLSON ■ Bulk freight schooner-barge of 708 t. and 179 ft., launched in 1888 at W Bay City, MI
Lake Huron: One difference in the handling of sailing vessels versus powered ships is the tall ship's inability to reverse power to stop forward movement (in other words, no brakes). In several accidents this was the undoing of an otherwise sound vessel (see GUIDO PFISTER). The MARY WOOLSON was in tow of the steamer CHARLES H BRADLEY (qv) when the BRADLEY suddenly stopped, and the barge piled into her from behind. The WOOLSON sank as a result of the collision, which occurred on July 18, 1920, eight miles northeast of Sturgeon Point, near Harrisville, Michigan. The same type of accident happened to the BRADLEY again in 1931, ending her career. [4]

GEORGE WORTHINGTON ■ Merchant schooner
Lake Michigan: The schooner GEORGE WORTHINGTON was reported lost in the Straits of Mackinac, near St. Helena Island, in 1875. [1]

ALFRED P WRIGHT ■ Wooden packet of 56 t.
Lake Michigan: On November 29, 1886, this small vessel was sunk by storm waves in the harbor at Manistee, Michigan. She was later partially salvaged. [1]

ALFRED P WRIGHT ■ Wooden bulk freight steamer of 2,207 t. and 286 ft., launched in 1888 at Cleveland
Lake Superior: While sheltering from a gale in the Portage Ship Canal (Keweenaw Peninsula), the WRIGHT caught fire, burned, and sank. The accident took place on November 16, 1915, near White City, Michigan. The vessel and her cargo of wheat were a total loss, but her crew escaped the blaze. [4]

TOM WRONG ■ Merchant schooner
Lake Erie: The schooner TOM WRONG was lost near Port Burwell, Ontario. She was reportedly wrecked on a reef in 1866. [1]

WYOMING ■ Barge
Lake Huron: In 1876, this vessel was reported lost near Port Huron. [1]

WYOMING ■ Wooden bulk freight steamer of 350 t. and 154 ft., launched in 1870 at Detroit
Lake Huron: This wooden steamer ended her days off Pte Aux Barques, Michigan. While fighting heavy seas on November 12, 1904, the steamer caught fire and was destroyed. She sank just offshore from Burnt Cabin Point. [4]

YAKIMA ■ Wooden bulk freight steamer of 1,986 t. and 279 ft., launched in 1889 at Cleveland
St. Clair River: The big freighter YAKIMA strayed out of the shipping channel and went aground in the river on June 13, 1905. Before she could be pulled off her perch, the vessel caught fire and was totally destroyed. [2]

YANKEE ■ Merchant schooner, probably the 236 t., 138 ft. vessel built in 1862 at Marine City, MI, but one report says she was the 11 t., 38 ft. schooner launched at Sand Beach, MI, in 1884
Lake Huron: The YANKEE was reported lost in September of 1893 off Port Elgin, Ontario. [3]

YANTIC ■ Wooden propeller gun-bark of 836 t. and 180 ft., launched in 1864 at Philadelphia, PA
Detroit River: This vessel was an armed American sailing steamer of the type used extensively in the Civil War. The ship was permanently stationed on the Great Lakes, but by the early 20th century was considered by the U.S. Navy to be unserviceable. She remained docked at Detroit until she finally sank in 1929. [3]

YORK ■ Vessel information unavailable
Lake Superior: No date is given for the loss of this vessel, She reportedly sank off Salt Point, near the mouth of Grant's Creek, about 25 miles west of the Soo. [1]

YORK STATE ■ Merchant schooner
Lake Huron: In 1886 this vessel was lost when she foundered in Georgian Bay. [1]

YOSEMITE ■ Wooden steam freighter of 310 t. and 152 ft., launched in 1867 at Sandusky, OH
Lake Superior: On April 30, 1892, this steamer was destroyed by fire while towing two barges up Whitefish Bay. She burned to a total loss off Emerson, Michigan. [4]

YOU TELL ■ Merchant schooner
Lake Superior: The schooner YOU TELL was sailing around the southwest end of Isle Royale in a storm, when she struck a rocky shoal near Washington Island and went down. She sank on September 26, 1872. [1]

YOUNG AMERICA ■ Package freight steamer of 359 t.
Lake Ontario: A steamer with engine failure was just as helpless in a storm as a schooner with her sails blown out. Over-revving of her propeller due to the plunging of the ship could break shafts and engine parts. Storm waters could douse fires and fuel could be used up battling headwinds. Engine failure proved to be the undoing of the steamer YOUNG AMERICA. With her powerplant out, she was blown before a gale and struck ground near Oak Orchard, New York. The September 2, 1874 storm then

tore the hapless ship to pieces. She was reported carrying a "valuable" cargo. [2]

YOUNG AMERICA ■ Merchant schooner
Lake Erie: This sail vessel was reported to have foundered near Kelley's Island on August 20, 1880. She was laden with a cargo of stone at the time. [1]

YOUNG HICKORY ■ Paddle steamer of 61 t. and 82 ft., launched in 1864 at Sandusky, OH
Lake Erie: One life was lost when this little steamer sank on October 31, 1877. She went down in a storm, either off the Claybanks area near Port Burwell, Ontario, or off Bar Point. She was carrying a load of wood when she foundered. [2]

YOUNG LION ■ Wooden steam tug of 70 t., launched at Port Dalhousie, Ont., in 1862
Lake Ontario: The small steamer YOUNG LION foundered off Port Credit, Ontario, near Toronto, in November of 1874. [1]

YOUNG LYON ■ Merchant schooner
Lake Huron: The schooner YOUNG LYON foundered at an unreported position on the lake in 1874. [1]

YOUNG PHOENIX ■ Merchant schooner
Lake Erie: This early schooner sank in 1818 off Long Point. She reportedly went down quickly, but there is no report of loss of life. [1]

YOUNG ZION ■ Steamer
Lake Erie: On June 13, 1881, the steamer YOUNG ZION, loaded with a cargo of railroad iron and reportedly carrying a large amount of cash, foundered off Walnut Creek, east of Dunkirk, New York. She sank about two miles off shore. [2]

ANNIE YOUNG ■ Wooden bulk freight steamer of 1,007 t., launched in 1869 at Detroit
Lake Huron: Nine sailors died when this big (for its time) steamer caught fire and was destroyed off Lexington, Michigan. The ANNIE YOUNG was carrying a cargo of coal when she went to the bottom on October 20, 1890. [3]

WILLIAM A YOUNG ■ Bulk freight schooner-barge of 434 t. and 165 ft., launched in 1883 at Marine City, MI
Lake Huron: The area just north of Thunder Bay Island, Michigan, is dotted with the remains of more than a score of ships, including the WILLIAM A YOUNG. The barge was laden with a cargo of coal when she was swamped and sank in a storm on November 17, 1911. [5]

YUKON ■ Bulk freight schooner-barge of 1,602 t. and 270 ft., launched in 1893 at W Bay City, MI as a schooner

Lake Erie: This giant schooner-barge was a victim of the big gale of October 20, 1905. On that date the big vessel filled and sank off Ashtabula, Ohio. [5+]

ZEALAND ▪ Steam propeller freighter of 402 t. and 136 ft., launched in 1888 at Toronto as the steamer CITY OF CHATHAM
Lake Ontario: All 14 crew members died when the steamer ZEALAND foundered in a storm near Long Point, south of Prince Edward Bay, Ontario. The vessel sank on November 7, 1880. [3]

ZENITH CITY ▪ Steel bulk freight steamer of 3,850 t. and 388 ft., launched in 1895 at Chicago
Lake Huron: The well-known steamer ZENITH CITY sank in Hammond Bay, at the eastern end of the Straits of Mackinac, in 1916. She was at first thought to be a total loss, and there is no local record of her recovery, but she had a long career following the accident, not being scrapped until 1947. [4]

ZILLAH ▪ Wooden bulk freight steamer of 1,100 t. and 202 ft., launched in 1890 at W Bay City, MI, as the steamer EDWARD SMITH
Lake Superior: The old freighter ZILLAH was carrying a cargo of limestone when she encountered a particularly violent summer gale on August 29, 1926. She broke up well offshore in Whitefish Bay, but her crew were able to abandon her in time to save themselves. The wreck was located in 1975. [3]

ZIMMERMAN ▪ Sidewheel steamer of 200 ft., launched in 1854 at Niagara, Ont.
Lake Ontario: This sidewheeler was reportedly destroyed by fire at Niagara-on-the-Lake, Ontario, in August of 1863. [1]

ZOUAVE ▪ Wooden steam tug
Lake St. Clair: The ZOUAVE's entire crew of four died when the tug was destroyed by an explosion which occurred on May 25, 1862. [2]

TO THE READER

You have read information on about 3,700 Great Lakes shipwrecks. As mentioned in the introduction, this compendium does not include all the vessels ever wrecked on the Lakes, nor does it pretend to be absolutely accurate. I have used what resources were available to compile as much information as possible, and to separate the "wheat from the chaff," if possible.

If you are an avid Great Lakes shipping buff, and especially if you have intimate historical knowledge of a particular area, I fully expect that somewhere in this book you have found something that you don't agree with. If that is the case, I hope you will consider sharing this information with me for a future edition of this work. You may send this material to me, including documentation, care of the publisher: Harbor House Publishers, Inc., 221 Water Street, Boyne City, Michigan 49712.

Index of known wreck locations

HOUGHTON: E D Holton

HURON ISLS: Arctic, Pearl B Campbell, Mingoe, George Nester

HURRICANE R: Annie Coleman

ISLE ROYALE: Algoma, America, Brandon, Henry Chisholm, Comrade, Chester A Congdon, George M Cox, Cumberland, Dagmar, Emporer, Glenlyon, George R Hand, Isle Royale, Kamloops, Madeline, Monarch, Northern Belle, Henry Steinbrenner, You Tell

KALAMAZOO R: City of Allegan, Milwaukie, Daniel Whitney

KEWEENAW PENINSULA: Coralia, Samuel H Foster, Iosco, Manistee, J P Morgan Jr, G M Neelon, Olive Jeanette, Samoa, Stranger, Sunbeam, Turret Chief, L C Waldo

KEWEENAW POINT: Altadoc, City of Bangor, Bannockburn, Lac La Belle, Mesquite, Scotia

KEWEENAW WATERWAY: J Bigler, Pasadena, Charles J Sheffield

L'ANSE: Northerner

LAKE MUNUSCONG: Monteagle

LAKEPORT: C A Miesel

LAKESIDE: Lena M Nielson, Tiger

LELAND: Florida, Grand Turk, E Kanter, Ketchum, Lark, Onward, Selt, R J Skidmore

LES CHENEAUX ISLS: George E, Hattie Johnson

LEXINGTON: John Bredin, Clayton Belle, Experiment, Goliah, William Goodnow, Hydrus, Itasca, City of Port Huron, William Raynor, Kate Richmond, Sheridan, Sport, Eliza H Strong, Wabash, William G, Annie Young

LITTLE BAY DE NOC: H S Hubble

LITTLE PRESQUE ISLE: Grace Ely

LITTLE SABLE POINT: Kitty Grant

LUDINGTON: Argo, D S Austin, A T Bliss, Flint & Pere Marquette #1, Jessie Martin, Morning Light, Orphan Boy, Pere Marquette 3, J H Rutter, Charles N Ryan, Souvenir, William Sturgis, Tacoma, City of Toledo, Frank L Vance, Vega

MACKINAC ISLAND: Oliver Cromwell, Elva

MACKINAW CITY: Waldo A Avery, William H Barnum, Gertrude, Odd Fellow

MANISTEE: Abbie, Argo, Buddy, T S Christie, James Dempsey, Hattie A Estelle, Anna O Hansen, William Jones, City of Kalamazoo, Kansas, Florence Lester, Lillie E, Pere Marquette 8, Sea Lion, Belle Stevens, Sturgeon Bay, Alfred P Wright

MANITOU ISLS: Alert, Avis, Bethlehem, Alva Bradley, Lomie A Burton, Congress, Margaret Dall, Josephine Dresden, Driver, J Duvall, Ebenezer, Equator, Ray S Farr, Walter L Frost, Geneva, W H Gilcher, William T Graves, Charles H Hurd, Manitowoc, Gilbert Mollison, Montauk, H D Moore, Francisco Morazon, J B Newland, Ostrich, Queen of the Lakes, P J Ralph, J Young Scammon, Jessie Scarth, Hattie L Stamback, Star of the North, Templeton, Three Brothers, Troy, Annie Vought, Westmoreland

MANITOU PASSAGE: Free Trader, Jarvis Lord

MARINE CITY: Aztec, Badger State, William Dickenson, T S Faxton, Kalkaska, Maine, Marysville, John H Pauley, Penobscot, William H Wolf

MARQUETTE: Arizona, Alva Bradley, Florida, Charles J Kershaw, Lady of the Lake, D Leuty, Libby, Meteor, Jay C Morse, E W Oglebay, Queen of the Lakes, Siskawit, Henry B Smith

MARYSVILLE: Argonaut

MENOMINEE: Myrtle Camp, Erie L Hackley, Sidney O Neff

MIDDLE ISLAND: Major Anderson, Guillotine, Havre, Holmes, Lewis Meeker, Montana, Nonpariel, Norman, Jay Ochs, E B Palmer, Portsmouth, Lucy Raab, Annie C Raynor, Red Bottom, Kyle Spangler

MIDDLE VILLAGE: Nancy Dell

MISERY BAY: Samuel H Foster

MONROE: Fame, General Franz Sigel

MOSQUITO BEACH: Sparta

MUNISING: Manhattan, Marquette, Smith Moore, Roamer, Sparta, Wood Island, unidentified schooner

MUSKALLONGE LAKE: Pile Driver

MUSKEGON: John Bean Jr, Alvin Bronson, Henry Cort, Granada, Helen, Thomas Hume, R B King, Mackinac, Governor Mason, Muskegon, North

Shore, Nyack, L R Rockwell, Salvor, R Trial, Wabash Valley, Waukesha

NEEBISH RAPIDS: Keeweenah

NEW BUFFALO: Delaware, Superior

NINEMILE PT: F T Barney, Beaver, Harriet Ann, Maria, Charles M Warner

NORTHPORT: Badger State, Flora, Tramp, B West

OLD MISSION POINT: Alida Jane Rogers

ONTONAGON: A L Hopkins, Panama, St Clair, City of the Straits

OSCODA: Athenian, Banner, Clifton, E F Gould, J C Harrison, Jane Mason, Albert Miller, Prindiville, George Steele, Susan Ward, Water Witch, Wawanosh

OSSINEKE: William Fish

PASSAGE ISL: Ottawa, Ferdinand Schlesinger, Prindoc, L C Waldo

PENTWATER: William B Davock, Ingeborg M Forrest, George Lamont, Mercury, Anna C Minch, Novadoc, Pal, Scotia

PEQUAMING BAY: unidentified sailing vessel

PICTURED ROCKS: Elma, George, Michael Groh, Michigan, Superior, Wabash

PINE LAKE (Lake Charlevoix): Irma L Wheeler

PT BETSIE: Black Hawk, Driver, F Fitch, W C Kimball, Lawrence, C E Redfern, St Lawrence, H B Steele

PT IROQUOIS: Griffin, Samuel Mather, Monitor, Sagamore

PT ISABELLE: Sarnian

PT LOOKOUT: Thomas A Almerson, Lizzie Madden

PT MOUILLEE: Lexington

PT NIPIGON: Albemarle, Henry Clay

PT SABLE: Michigan

PTE AUX BARQUES: Albany, S P Ames, Andover, Arctic, Maggie Ashton, John J Audubon, Azov, Barbara Lynn, Berlin, A Boody, L D Cowan, Crispin, James W Curran, Dispatch, Emeu, Enterprise, A Everett, A M Foster, E M Foster, Frank H Goodyear, H Hyde, Iron Chief, Andrew Jackson, Willard Johnson, Keystone State, S H Kimball, Charles A King, Frederick A Lee, Maime, Massilon, John A McPhail, Merchant, Michigan, John Miner, Julia Minor, Mohawk, Mohegan, Mona, Montezuma, Daniel J Morrell, Naiad, H C Patter, Philadelphia, Queen City, Rocket, Charles C Ryan, St Clair, Santiago, Hunter Savidge, L Seaton, Gov. Smith, Southwestern, Superior, Troy, John Wesley, Wiman, Wyoming

PTE ISABELLE: Coralia, Sarnian

PORT AUSTIN: Austin, Jacob Betschy, S S Coe, Eugene, Howard M Hanna Jr, George W Holt, Huron, Keystone State, Matoa, Metropole, Miranda, Daniel J Morrell, Morris, Sacramento, Grace A Ruelle, Valentine, Waurecan, C P Williams

PORT CRESCENT: Monticello

PORT HOPE: Barbara Lynn, Lena Behm, E Cohen, Daisy, Racine, Sultan

PORT HURON: Amaranth, Ben Hur, Canada, Canisteo, J C Clarke, Omar D Conger, Dauntless, Cal Davis, George Dunbar, Erie, C M Farrar, Fostoria, Gladstone, Jennie Graham, B B Jones, Kewanne, Lowell, Alex Maitland, Frank Moffatt, Northerner, Ontario, John Owen, Charles S Price, Mary Pringle, William H Pringle, Reindeer, Saginaw, William Shupe, Sidney E Smith Jr, Sweetheart, Tecumseh, M E Tremble, Union, Charles H Weeks, White Star, Elijah Windsor, Wyoming

PORT SANILAC: Checotah, S C Clark, Forester, F B Gardner, City of Milwaukee, Narragansett, North Star, Rock Queen, Oscar Townsend, Twilight, Colonel A B Williams

PORT SHELDON: Dan Davis, South Haven

PORT SHERMAN: Granada

PORTAGE ENTRY: Maine, Pasadena

PORTAGE LAKE (Michigan): Music, Louis Wallace

PORTAGE LAKE (Superior): Charles H Bradley

PORTAGE SHIP CANAL: B W Arnold, Bessemer, Bon Voyage, Reed Case, Maine, Maplehurst, Nellie McGilvray, Jay C Morse, City of Montreal, Samoa, Schuykill, Toledo, Wenona

POVERTY ISL: Lake Erie

PRESQUE ISLE (Huron): Agate, Albany, American Union, Avon, Choctaw, R G Coburn, Czar, Darien,

Etruria, Fame, Harvest Queen, Ironton, Maggie, M F Merrick, Kate Moffatt, City of Naples, Nomad, Ohio, Russia, J H Stevens, Typo, William C Warren

PRESQUE ISLE (Superior): Coast Guard Launch, Favorite, Tom Boy

RABER: Rome

RICHMONDVILLE: Samuel Bolton, Charles A Street

RIVER ROUGE: Benton, Florida, Thomas Gawn, Transiter

ROCK OF AGES: Henry Chisholm, George M Cox, Cumberland

ROCKPORT: Canada, Holmes, Norman

ROGERS CITY: F T Barney, Joseph S Fay, Millard Fillmore, Messenger, Revelry

ROUND ISL: Peshtigo

SAGINAW: B C & Co, Willie Brown, Challenge, Curlew, Kate Fletcher, Little Nell, Nellie Mays, E M Miller, Kate Reid, Star, Traffic

SAGINAW BAY: Ajax, Arcturus, Bucephalus (2), Buckingham, Cygnet, George Davis, Detroit II, City of Detroit, E P Dorr, George L Dunlap, Eagle, Esperance, Eureka, Globe (2), City of Green Bay, Hector, Magic, W A Moore, Parana, Rosedale, Sacramento, Sea Gull, H D Stockman, Union, Marie Victoire, White Squall, Kirk White, Witch, Witch of the West

SAGINAW POINT: Cherokee

SAGINAW R: Antelope, Bartlett, Clay Tile, Curlew, Dormer #2, Emerald, Excelsior, Giant, Levi Johnson, Little Eastern, Charles A McDonald, Kate Reid, Relief, George E Reynolds, Marquis Roen, Salina, General Scott, H P Smith, Kittie Smoke, Star, Samuel Stephenson, Swan

SAND BEACH: (See Harbor Beach)

ST CLAIR: Gladstone, Tokio

ST CLAIR FLATS: Bothnia, Richard Burns, James Fisk Jr, Kittie M Forbes, Point Abino, Fannie Tuthill, Whale

ST CLAIR R: George T Burroughs, Fontana, Lac La Belle, Nelson Mills, Henry W Sage, Thomas D Stimson, M E Tremble, Robert C Wente, Yakima

ST HELENA ISL: California, Lawrence, J E Shaw, Helen Taylor, George Worthington

ST IGNACE: Northwest, Remora

ST JOSEPH: Nina Bailey, Champlain, Chicora, City of Duluth, Evening Star, Experiment (2), Grace Greenwood, Havana, Ithaca, Myosotis, Orion, Regulator, City of Tawas, John Torrent, Hattie Wells, W H Willard

ST MARTIN'S ISL: Emma L Coyne, Plymouth

ST MARY'S R: Agens W, Discovery, Dispatch, Frontier, General, Harriet A Hart, Keeweenah, A C Maxwell, Pontiac, Dean Richmond, Rome, Russell, Nellie Torrent

SANS SOUCI: Minnesota

SAUGATUCK: John Edward, Gotham, Kalamazoo

SAULT STE MARIE: Fur Trader, G L 37, Independence, Ontonagon, Dean Richmond, Shamrock, York

SAWTOOTH REEF: Chippewa, S R Kirby, Peninsula, James Pickands

SCAMMON COVE: Johnswood

SCARECROW ISL: Nellie Gardner, Molly T Horner, William S Stephens

SEBEWAING: Traffic

SEUL CHOIX PT: Commerce, Dreadnaught, Granger, William Home, Monitor, James D Sawyer, Lady Washington

SHOT PT: Laura Belle, Alva Bradley, George Sherman

SINGAPORE: Condor

SKILLAGALEE: Cayuga, Clarion, Condor, Julia Dean, Detroit, Joseph L Hurd, Northern Belle, Oriental, A D Patchin, Ellen Spry, Wellington, White Swan

SLEEPING BEAR BAY: J S Crouse, Rising Sun, St Nicholas

SLEEPING BEAR POINT: Atalanta, Badger State, Kate Bully, Ciscoe, Caledonia, Emily & Eliza, Gertrude, Gold Hunter, Jessie and Annie, Gilbert Knapp, James McBride, General Taylor

SOUTH HAVEN: Eagle, City of Green Bay, Hennepin, Indian, Industry, J F Johnson, Anne F Morse, Richard H, Rockaway, Florence M Smith, Verano

255

SPECTACLE REEF: Newell A Eddy, Augustus Handy, Kate Hayes, Henry J Johnson, Nightingale
SPRINGPORT: Garibaldi
STANNARD ROCK: A W Comstock, R Hallaran, Henry A Kent, Thomas W Palmer
STONY LAKE: Morning Light
STRAITS OF MACKINAC: Albany, Albemarle, Anglo-Saxon, City of Boston, Sardis Burchards, Colonel Camp, Cedarville, Henry Clay, Colonial, Colonist, Oliver Cromwell, Cygnet (2), Dauntless, Dawn, Nancy Dousman, Enterprise, Forester, E A Fulton, Granada, George H Humphrey, Jessie, Olive Lee, Little Georgy, Maid of the Mist, Maria, Marquette, Milwaukee, Minneapolis, Nightingale, Nipigon, Northwest, Perseverence, Peshtigo, Prairie State, Sandusky, J A Smith, William Stone, J H Tiffany, Toledo, Uncle Sam, Eber Ward, Welcome, Cornelia Windiate, R G Winslow
STURGEON BAY: J W Blake, Ottawa
STURGEON PT: Alvina, Tom Cochrane, Corsair, Curlew, Ida & Mary, Lodi, Neshoto, New Hampshire, Ossifrage, Oswegatchie, Commodore Perry, Ste Maries, Mary Woolson
SUGAR ISL: Seabreeze
SUMMER ISLS: C C Hand, John M Nicol, Jim Sheriffs
TAHQUAMENON BAY: Mystic
TAWAS BAY: Ferguson, Linden, Emma L Neilsen
TAWAS CITY: Griffin, Andrew A McLean, Ocean, Owen, Sea Gull (2), Western States
TAWAS PT: Goshawk, Hercules, John A McGean, Kitty Reeves, Summit, Table Rock, O Wilcox
THUNDER BAY: Adriatic, Alleghany, Baltic, Barge No 1, Bay City, Francis Berriman, B W Blanchard, Egyptian, Ellen, Elvina, Empire State, Enterprise, Oscar T Flint, Galena, Gold Hunter, Grecian, Herman Guenther, Guillotine, Gulnair, D R Hanna, Havre, Holmes, John T Johnson, Kaliyuga, Frank LaFarge, William Maxwell, Miami, Mildred, Grace Miller, Monohansett, J D Morton, New Orleans, New York, I W Nicholas, Pewabic, Roanoake, William H Stephens, Thousand Islander, Lucinda VanValkenburg, Belle Wilson
THUNDER BAY ISL: E B Allen, H P Bridge, Congress, Corsican, James Davidson, Edward U Demmer, Marion Egan, Emerald, Excelsior, Ben Franklin, W C Franz, W H Gilbert, Bela Hubbard, Julia Larsen, McDermott, Monrovia, Fred A Morse, Montana, New Orleans, Northampton, Northampton, Number 83, Ogarita, O E Parks, John Rice, Ryan, Isaac M Scott, William H Simons, W P Thew, Viator, Vienna, D M Wilson, William A Young
THUNDER BAY R: James H Hall, Shamrock
TORCH LAKE: Samoa
TRAVERSE CITY: Allegheny, Lauren Castle
TRAVERSE ISL: Lizzie A Law
TWO-HEARTED RIVER: W W Arnold, Cleveland, Annie M Peterson
VERMILION PT: Allegheny, Barge 129, W T Chappell, M M Drake, Eureka, Chauncey Hurlbut, Jupiter, Michigan, Miztec, Niagara, Joseph Paige, Frank Perew, unnamed scow
WAISKA BAY: B L Webb
WAUGOSCHANCE PT: C L Abbell, Alert, Bridgewater, Canisteo, M L Collins, Dolphin, Colonel Ellsworth, R P Flowers, Free State, Groton, Island Queen, Thomas Kingsford, W S Lyons, Maitland, Fred McBrier, Topsy
WHITE CITY: International, Alfred P Wright
WHITE LAKE: L J Conway, Day Spring, Nellie Hammond, Joseph Heald, Interlaken
WHITE R: State of Michigan
WHITE ROCK: Mary Hattie, Gibraltar
WHITE SHOALS: Circassian, W S Lyons, Uganda, Richard Winslow
WHITEFISH BAY: Coast Guard Launch, Comet, John B Cowle, William S Crosthwaite, Ora Endress, Superior City, Vienna, Yosemite, Zillah
WHITEFISH POINT: Alberta, Algosoo, Bennington, Charlie, Betha Endress, Edmund Fitzgerald, Grey Eagle, W C Griswold, Harriet A Hart, Huronton, Invincible, Major, Milan, Missoula, John Mitchell, Myron, Alex. Nimick, Nucleus, John M Osborne, Julia Palmer, Panther, Pearl, Plover, Sattelite, Saturn, William F Sauber, Servia, C J Sheffield, Adella Shores
WHITEHALL: Brightie, Contest, Anne F Morse,

Panzola II
WOOD ISLAND REEF: Chenango
WYANDOTTE: George H VanVleck

MINNESOTA

BEAVER R: Charley
BRULE PT: Mary Martini
DULUTH: Algonquin, Harry L Allen, James Bardon #7, Buffalo, E T Carrington, M D Carrington, W B Castle, F L Danforth, Josie Davidson, Cora B, Duluth, Ellwood, Erie, E P Ferry, Edward Fiske, Free Trade, J H Jeffery, Lyric, Edward J Maney, Mataafa, Mentor, M C Neff, Benjamin Noble, Onoko, Julia Palmer, Pathfinder, Quido Pfister, Record, Ella G Stone, Swansea, Thomas Wilson, City of Winnipeg, Winslow, unnamed scow
ENCAMPMENT ISL: Lotta Bernard, Lafayette
GOOSEBERRY R: Belle P Cross
GRAND MARAIS: Bob Anderson, Liberty, Siskiwit
IRON RIVER: Maple Leaf
KNIFE ISL: Niagara, Onoko
KNIFE R: Firien, Thomas Friant
LITTLE MARAIS: George Spencer
MINNESOTA PT: Sarah M Smith
PELLET ISL: Frontenac
REECE'S LANDING: Arcola
SABLE ISL: Na-Ma-Puk
SILVER BAY: Hesper
SPLIT ROCK: Algerian, William Edenborn, Criss Grover, Madiera, Maia
ST LOUIS BAY: George P Savidge
TWO HARBORS: S P Ely, Harriet B, Lewie, Rebel, Tubal Cain, Robert Wallace

NEW YORK

BARCELONA: American Sailor, American Scout, Betty Hedger, John J Boland Jr, Brandywine, Charles H Burton, Colonial, City of Detroit, Lizzie Harvey, Merida, Oneida, Helen Strong
BIG SANDY CREEK: Ariadne, Abeona
BLACK ROCK: Troy, Little Belt
BRADDOCK PT: E A Roe
BUFFALO: Abyssinia, Acme, O W Cheney, Chicago, John W Cramer, Governor Cushman, Dauntless # 12, J W Doane, Falmouth, Globe, Groton, R R Hefferd, International, Jefferson, Jordan Boys, George King, Lightship #82, Maple Leaf, B B McColl, Ada Medora, Morania #130, Myrtie, Northwest, Oakwood, William Peacock, Penobscot, Commodore Perry, Daniel D Perry, W C Richardson, Sandusky, Shawmut, South American, W W Stewart, Tonawanda, West Shore, E C Williams
CAPE ENRAGE: Frontenac
CAPE VINCENT: Ottawa, Wisconsin
CHARLOTTE: Dalhousie, Annie M Foster, Isabella, Henry Rodney, James H Shrigley, Titania, William Wheeler
DUNKIRK: Brunswick, Carlingford, Columbian, Comet, M Dousman, Robert Fulton, Golden Fleece, Good Intent, Manzanilla, Anthony McCue, Passaic, Dean Richmond, Sachem, George J Whelan, Annabell Wilson, Wocoken
EIGHT MILE CREEK: Lady Washington
FAIR HAVEN: Jeska, Thomas R Merritt, John S Parsons, Lloyd S Porter
FOUR MILE PT: Medbury
GALOO ISL: Rover
GRAND ISL: Idle Hour
GRENADIER ISL: Kingston
HARBOR CREEK: S K Martin
HORSESHOE REEF: John W Cramer, Myrtie
JEFFERSON Co: James Buckly
LEWISTON: Cibola
LITTLE SODUS BAY: Congercoal
MEXICO BAY: Hartford
MILLER'S PT: Oakwood
NIAGARA FALLS: Caroline
NIAGARA R: Detroit, Idle Hour, Jane McLeod, Daniel D Perry
NINE MILE PT: Jesse H Breck

OAK ORCHARD: Boston, Clipper, Lady of the Lake, St Lawrence, Wave Crest, Young America
OSWEGO: Albacore, David Andrews, Atlas, Baltic, Philip Becker, James G Blaine, John Burt, Calatco #2, Comet, Cormorant, Craftsman, Dauntless, William Elgin, W Y Emery, Flying Cloud, Daniel G Fort, D M Foster, B Freeman, Guide, Agnes Hope, Hattie Howard, Isabella H, William John, Hattie L Johnson, Lady of the Lake, London, Caroline Marsh, Maria Melvin, Addie Membery, David W Mills, Morey, Norwegian, Ocean Wave, Osprey, Perseverance, Eliza J Redford, Richardson, Roberval, Shannon, George B Sloan, Snowbird, Tip Top, F R Tranchemontagne, Tuscarora, United Kingdom, Vision, T J Waffle, Wayne, Wood Duck
PT AUSTIN: Abeona, George W Holt
PT BREEZE: Cuba, Matilda Taylor
PT PENINSULA: Camanche
PORTLAND: New Connecticut
PULTNEYVILLE: Dolphin, Homer Warren
RIPLEY: Mautenee, Ollie Neville, City of Rome
SACKET'S HARBOR: Annandale, J S Brooks, Oneida
SALMON R: Asp, Fair American
SILVER CREEK: Erie, H F Merry, Osceola, George Washington
SODUS: Queen of the Lakes, St Peter
STONY CREEK: Cortez
STONY ISL: North Star
STONY PT: Hinckley, Iona, Martha Ogden, Onondago, Roy, Ida Walker
STURGEON PT: Chicago, Otter, Lady Washington
THIRTY MILE PT: Nisbet Grammar, Helen Strong
TONAWANDA: Embury
VAN BUREN PT: Manzanilla, Princeton
WALNUT CREEK: Young Zion

OHIO

ASHTABULA: Ashtabula, Eli Bates, C G Breed, E S Catlin, Dixie, Dundurn, Eli, James F Joy, Keepsake, Pelican, R P Reidenbach, Genevieve Ryan, Rosa Sonsmith, Frank B Stevens, Surveyor, Wonder, Yukon
AVON LAKE: Alva B
AVON PT: Black Marlin, Hickory Stick, Fanny L Jones, Sand Merchant
BASS ISLS: M P Barkalow, Isabella J Boyce, Moses and Elias, Rainbow, May Richards, Sylph
BLACK R: Independence, Sea Bird
CEDAR POINT: Cupid, Germania, Protection, Red Cloud, Superior
CLEVELAND: Admiral, Algeria, American Eagle, Atlantic, Horace H Badger, Barge 104, Emma Blake, City of Buffalo, Caspian, Cleveco, H G Cleveland, Cossack, Charles H Davis, Donaldson, Dundee, William Grandy, John Gregory, G P Griffith, R B Hubbard, Mary, Nellie Mason, Emily B Maxwell, Lackawanna, Dan Kuntz, Junior, Kingfisher, Sophia Minch, S Neff, North Star, State of Ohio, B W Parker, James H Pellett, Pensaukee, Agnes L Potter, John Pridgeon Jr, Reindeer, Samana, Sand Merchant, Scobell, Shawnee, Silver Spray, Telegraph, Unadilla, Wahnapitae, J L Weatherly, Mabelle Wilson
CONNEAUT: Chesapeake, J C Daun, Fleetwing, Indiana, Marquette & Bessemer #2, Morning Star, John F Porter, Shenango #1
CUYAHOGA R: St Magnus, Scobell
FAIRPORT: Amelia, J J Carroll II, Augusta Ford, Franklin, Steven F Gale, John H Hill, K R Johnson, L B Johnson, Killarney, H A Lamars, L L Lamb, C B Lockwood, Merchant, New Lisbon, North Carolina, Thomas Parsons, Queen of the West, Raphael, Redbird, Sasco, Sidney E Smith, N M Standart, Sunshine, Sir S L Tilley, Kate White
GRAND R: Boxer, Ben Franklin, Olive Branch, Paulina
HURON: Alpena, Handy Boy, Leland
JOHNSON ISL: Josephine
KELLEY'S ISL: Adventure, American Eagle, William Crosthwaite, John Mark, Ohio, Margaret Olwill, C H Plummer, F H Prince, St Louis, Uncle Sam, Young America
LAKE BREEZE: Sarah E Sheldon
LAKESIDE: Alton

derbilt, Winslow
MICHIPICOTEN ISL: Bessie Barwick, Chicago, Hiram R Dixon, City of Montreal, A Seaman, J S Seaverns, Strathmore
MICHIPICOTEN R: Acadia
MIDLAND: J M Jenks, Lucknow, Luckport, Midland City, Signal, Wales
MINNECOGNASHENE ISL: Preston's Store Boat
MISSISAGI STRAIT: J S Carter, Sam Flint
MOON R: Pilot
MOOSE PT: Waubuno
MORGAN PT: Marengo
MURRAY CANAL: Major N H Ferry, Melbourne
MUSQUASH R: Chippewa
N GROS CAP: Philadelphia
NANCY ISL: Nancy
NAPANEE: Norfolk
NESTORVILLE: Harold
NIAGARA: Frontenac (2), Hamilton, Scourge, Zimmerman
NIAGARA FALLS: Caroline, Maid of the Mist, Maid of the Mist 2
NIAGARA R: Escort, Massasoit
NICHOLSON ISL: Advance, James A Walker
NIPIGON BAY: Mary E McLachlan
NIPIGON STRAIT: Neebing
NORTH CHANNEL: Abigail, Consuelo, Hiawatha, Iroquois
NOTTAWASAGA BAY: Mary Ward
OAKVILLE: P W D 114, Pinta, 4 unidentified schooners
OWEN SOUND: James Clarke, Georgian, Hibou, Silver Spray
PANCAKE ISL: Atlantic
PAPOOSE ISL: Joe Milton
PARISIENNE ISL: Aurania, V H Ketchum, Lambton
PARRY SOUND: George H Jones, Ophir, Pilot, Ella Ross, Tempest, West Side
PECHE ISL: J S Horro, Rainbow, George F Rand
PELEE ISL: Abernethy, Alameda, America, Argo, Timothy Baker, Fanny Dowell, J A Garfield, Maumee Valley, Milder, H P Murray, C K Nims, Sampson, Star of Hope, Venetta, Venice
PELEE PASSAGE: Armenia, Fayette Brown, Cardinal, Conemaugh, Jay Gould, Harsen, City of London, Orient, Charles B Packard, Specular, George Stone, Frank E Vigor, Wend the Wave
PENETANGUISHENE: Mayflower, Tecumseth
PERSEVERENCE ISL: City of Cleveland
PICKERING: A H Jennie
PICTON: Aberdeen, Burt Barnes, Robert McDonald, Trenton
PIE ISL: Barge 115
PIGEON ISL: George T Davie, Eureka
PT ABINO: Badger, Briton, Honora Carr, Manhattan, Walk-in-the-Water
PT EDWARD: Hamonic, William R Linn, Majestic, Montgomery, Orontes, Wallschiff
PT MAIMANSE: William O Brown, Charles Hebard
PT PELEE: Coaster, City of Concord, Gallatin, Grace G Gribbie, Illinois, Kelley Island, Kent, City of London, Mayflower, New Brunswick, Orient, Tartin, Tioga, White Star
PT PETRE: W J Carter, Senator Derbyshire, Charles Horn, H N Jex, Julia, Lady Moulton, Ontario
PT TRAVERSE: Condor
PTE AUX BARIL: Fred Davidson
PTE AUX PINS (Erie): O M Bond, Eau J, William M Hatch, Mountaineer, Theodore Perry, Sun
PTE AUX PINS (Superior): Avon
PORPHYRY PT: Butcher's Maid
PORT ALBERT: William Treat
PORT ALMA: Dorothy May
PORT ARTHUR: Gordon Gauthier, Kaministiquia, Thomas Maitland, H W Ritchie, St Ignace, Sarnia, Violet G
PORT BRUCE: Burlington, Constitution, Crevola, F L Wells

PORT BURWELL: George M Abell, Anzac, Bay City, E G Benedict, Robert Bruce, C O D, Dahlia, George Davis, Elliott, Everett, Forester, D Foster, Martha Freeme, Frontenac, Gibson, Globe, J A Hope, Josephine, Leviathan, Silvanus J Macy, Marjon S, Maxwell A, Missouri, Morning Star, Northern Light, Ottawa, Grace Sherman, Tom Wrong, Young Hickory
PORT COLBORNE: C B Benson, Canobie, George M Case, Emma Dietrich, Home Rule, C L Hutchinson, Joseph H, Edward Kelley, D E McFarland, F A Meyer, Osborne, Pentland, E T Peters, Raleigh
PORT CREDIT: Bismark, John By, Northman, Young Lion
PORT CREWE: D R L C #2
PORT COLLINS: Nagaho
PORT DALHOUSIE: Anna Mildred, Augusta, Belle, Delver #1, Stuart H Dunn, Northumberland, Ocean (2), Oriental, City of Toronto, Welland
PORT ELGIN: Lily Dancey, Garibaldi, Yankee
PORT GLASGOW: Mountaineer
PORT GRANBY: Bermuda
PORT HOPE: P B Locke, Monson, Nellie Theresa
PORT LAMBTON: Sachem
PORT MAITLAND: Thomas Free Battle, Commerce, George Davis, George C Finney, Florida, Guiding Star, David G Thompson
PORT MC NICOLL: John Lee Sr
PORT METCALFE: Ionia
PORT ROWAN: Mary Jane
PORT STANLEY: Baltin, H A Barr, James Buckley, Choctaw, Excelsior, Forest City, Free Trader, Herald, Lydia Mack, Marquette & Bessemer #2, Mineral State, P W D 117, City of Sandusky, Scotland, Sweden
PORT WELLER: Delaware, Muriel W, Muskallonge, Philip M
PORTSMOUTH: Simla
PRESCOTT: Southeastern
PRESQU'ILE: Emerald, John A McDonald, Pioneer, Speedy, Trenton
PRINGLE'S BAY: Anna Ruth
RONDEAU: Celtic, Colonial, Little Wissahickon, Lycoming, Theodore Perry, Picton, Racine, Lewis Ross, Union, City of Venice
RUSSEL ISL: Iron City, Neechee, Philo Scoville, John Walters, W L Wetmore
SADDLE BAG ISL: Jolly Inez
ST CATHARINE'S: Glenfinlas
ST CLAIR R: Aldrich, F A Folger, Gleniffer, Hattie, Annie Moiles, Province, Thomas D Stimson
ST IGNACE ISL: Mary Ann Hulbert
ST JOSEPH'S ISL: Hope, John Torrent
ST MICHAEL'S BAY: James Clark
SALMON PT: Hannah Butler, Henry Folger, Jessie, John R Noyes
SALMON R: Grantham
SALT PT: John A McDonald, Minnie, York
SANDWICH: (See Windsor)
SANDY ISL: William Nottingham
SARNIA: R C Brittain, Corisande, Cuyahoga, Dauntless, Essex, City of Genoa, Hamonic, Inter Ocean, Joliet, Kenosha, Simon Langell, Annie Moiles, Mollie, Ottawa, Paragon, David Scoville, Southampton, United States
SAUGEEN PENINSULA: Huron, Napoleon
SAULT STE MARIE: Independence
SCARBOROUGH BLUFFS: Alexandria, Drill Boat #3, Emerald
SCOTCH BONNET LIGHT: Manitou. Polly M Mayres
SHAWANAGA BAY: Metamora
SIMCOE ISL: Mary A Daryaw, Frontenac, Horace Taber
SISTER ISLS: Acorn, Robert Burns, Case, Cornwall, John F Eddy, Macedonian, Pearl, Visitor, Wesee, Wisconsin
SISTER ROCK: Emma
SNAKE ISL: Golden West
SOUTH BAY PT: Atlasco
SOUTH BAYMOUTH: Mary McVie, Ella Murton, San Jacinto
SOUTHAMPTON: Athens, W B Hibbard, Mazep-

pa, J H McDonald, Ontario, Saturn, Erie Stewart
SOUTHEAST SHOAL: Armenia, General Burnside, Marshall F Butters, Clarion, Commodore, Philip Minch, Walter H Oades, Charles C Packard, Smith & Post, Tasmania
SPANISH MILLS: Iroquois, Alvin A Turner
SPANISH R: Meteor
SPRAGGE: Harold, Winona
STAG ISL: Germanic, Martho, Walter R Pringle, J S Ruby
STAR SHOAL: Secret
STOKES BAY: Explorer, Verbena May
STONY PT: Onondago
STRAWBERRY ISL (Huron): Gary D
STRAWBERRY ISL (Erie): Daniel D Perry, Trader
SUPERIOR SHOALS: Arlington, Cerisoles, Inkermann
SURPRISE SHOAL: Translake #3
TALBOT: Groton
THAMES R: Ruth B
THESSALON: Oregon
THOMASVILLE: Amboy
THORNBURY: Belle McPhee
THOROLD: Geraldine Battle
THUNDER BAY: Alberta, A B Conmee, James P Donaldson, Dredge #8, Jessie Hall, Niagara, Scotiadoc
THUNDER CAPE: Maggie McRae, Monkshaven, Theano
TIMBER ISL: Kate Eccles, Florence
TOBERMORY: Alaska, Alice G, Marion L Breck, Bruce Mines, Cascaden, Forest City, City of Grand Rapids, James C King, Charles P Minch, Neechee, Newaygo, Robert K, Philo Scoville, Sweepstakes, Winnana
TORONTO: Albatros IV, Burlington, Chicoutimi, Reuben Doud, Drill Boat #3, Emerald, Erie Belle, Fearless, Finglo, Inkerman, Island Queen, Kathleen, Midland Rover, John Moore, Noronic, Olive Branch, Ontario, Picton, Queen City, Rapid City, Sligo, Theresa, Toronto
TRENTON: Alberta, Lina
TWO ISLANDS: George Herbert
VAIL'S POINT: C M Bowman, Maud L
VICTORIA ISL: Howard
WALL ISL: Wauwona
WALLACEBURG: D A Gordon, A T Kelly, Elijah Windsor
WALPOLE ISL: William Brewster
WARD ISL: Gordon Jerry
WELLAND CANAL: Geraldine Battle, Cambria, Dalhousie Rover, Europe, Idaho, Maplegrove, Robert R Rhodes, Stewart
WELLER'S BAY: Belle Sheridan
WELLER'S BEACH: Garibaldi
WELLINGTON: James A Walker
WHITE CLOUD ISL: Mystery
WIARTON: Eastnor, Okenza
WINDMILL PT: U S 240, John Wesley
WINDSOR: Barge No 7, H Dahlke, Dominion, Eighth Ohio, Huron City, Lothair, Manitoba, Pittsburg, John Plankinton, F V Specht, Thames, Topeka, Transit, General Vance
WINGFIELD BASIN: Gargantua, Shandon
WYE R: Creole
YANKEE REEF: N P Goodell
YORKSHIRE ISL: Hiawatha

PENNSYLVANIA

ERIE: Aimie, Annie Laurie, Philip D Armor, Bay City, British Lion, Chenango, Detroit, Eldorado, George M Frost, Howard S Gerken, John Grant, Isolde, McConnell, C F Michler, Nautillus, Niagara, Charles Reed, Rob Roy, Sandy Pat, Adam Shuman, Tempest, Thomas Thompson, Charles A Trinter, Hunter Wills

N GIRARD: F A Georger, John B Lyon, Rochester
PRESQUE ISLE: Charles Foster, David Foster, George M Mowbray

WISCONSIN

AJAX ISL: North West

APOSTLES ISLS: Antelope, T H Camp, Cormorant, Fred & Will, R L Ireland, Josephine, Marquette, Mayflower, Moonlight, Ontario, Ira H Owen, Pretoria, R G Stewart

ASHLAND: Tom Dowling, Keystone, Ozaukee, Pacific

BAD RIVER: Phantom

BAILEY'S HARBOR: Boaz, Capron, Challenge, Emiline, Peoria, Christine Neilson

BAYFIELD: Fedora, Ottawa, Prussia, Sevona

CANA ISL: M J Bartelme, Frank O'Connor, E P Royce, J A Travis, Windsor

CEDAR R: R J Hackett

CHAMBERS ISL: America, Jane Bell

CHEQUAMEGON PT: Lucerne

DEATH'S DOOR: Fawn, Fleetwing, Maria Hilliard, Pride, Resumption, Seaman

DOOR Co: Two Friends

DRISCO SHOAL: Ogemaw

EGG HARBOR: Thomas C Wilson

FISH ISL: L C Butts No 1

FISHERMAN SHOAL: Blazing Star, Bulgaria

GARRET BAY: Belle Laurie, Japan

GREEN BAY: Alvin Clark, Iver Lawson, Otego, Progress, Starlight, Three Sisters, Trude R Wiehe

GREEN ISL: William J Brown

HARRINGTON BEACH: John V Jones

JACKSONPORT: Australasia, Cecilia, Perry Hannah

KENOSHA: Hans Crocker, L R Doty, Hattie Earl, Lem Ellsworth, Forelle, T P Handy, Wisconsin

KEWAUNEE: Dawn, Emerald, Forward, Rouse Simmons

MADELINE ISL: Mayflower

MANITOWOC: Algoma, Walter B Allen, Ann Arbor #1, Emily Cooper, Robert C Pringle, H Rand, Silver Lake

MILWAUKEE: J M Allmendinger, Appomattox, Arrow, Barbarian, Hiran R Bond, Boston, Buckeye State, E M Carrington, Dewitt Clinton, Collingwood, Cumberland, M J Cummings, J P Decondres, Dredge #906, Ella Ellinwood, Emba, Evergreen, E M Ford, Edward E Gillen, Guiding Star, W R Hanna, Dan Hayes, Island City, Jennifer, John V Jones, Josephine, Kenosha, Laurina, A W Lawrence, Lillie E, Maine, Milwaukee, Muskegon, Nile, Norlond, North Shore, Pere Marquette 4, R G Peters, John F Porter, Prins Willem V, Reliable, Sailor Boy, St Albans, Thomas A Scott, Scow #1, Snow Drop, Sumatra, Tennie & Laura, Toledo, Twin Brothers, Alice E Wilds, S A Wood

OAK CREEK: Rudolph Wetzel

OSHKOSH: Wa-Ne-Tah

PESHTIGO: Sydney C McLouth

PILOT ISL: Berwyn, J C Gilmore, A P Nichols, Henry Norton, H M Scove

PLUM ISL: Lilly Amiot, R Kanters, O M Nelson, Pup

PORT WASHINGTON: Advance, Atlanta, Northerner, Senator, R A Seymour, Silver Cloud, Toledo

PORT WING: Roamer, Tailwinds

RACINE: Arab, Barge A, Capella, John Eggers, Evra Fuller, Laura Johnson, Elizabeth Jones, Kate Kelly, Lac LaBelle, Merchant, R G Peters, Thomas H Smith, Speed (2)

RAWLEY BAY: F J King

RED CLIFF: Ottawa

ROCK ISL: Newsboy

SAND ISL: Herring King, Kakabeka, Sevona

SHEBOYGAN: Ahanapee, Baltimore, R H Becker, Blue Belle, Challenge (2), Selah Chamberlain, Commerce, Lottie Cooper, Hannah Etty, J M Harvey, G P Heath, Hercules, May Queen, May Queen, Mediterranean, Minnehaha, Niagara, Our Son, Petrel, Phoenix, Polynesia, William A Reiss, J O Thayer, David Wagstaff, Belle Walbridge, White Oak, Wollin

SHERWOOD PT: Columbia

SISKOWIT R: John A Paige

STURGEON BAY: America, Anabel II, E G Crosby, Exile, Granite State, Robert Holland, Joseph L Hurd, LaPetite, Lakeland, Mary Mills, Ontario, Otter, S B Paige, Petoskey, Pewaukee, Jim Pullard, Sassacus, Scow #2, Sea Star, Lucia A Simpson, Swift, Waukegan

SUPERIOR: Commodore Jack Berry, Maggie Carroll, Clarence E, Courier, F L Danforth, Josie Davidson, Edward Gillen, Oden, Record

TWO RIVERS: Anna Maria, Arrow, Bessie Boalt, Oliver Culver, Dart, Francis Hinton, Lookout, Magellan, Joseph G Masten, Nevada, Planet, Racine, Scow #2, Grace Patterson, Tubal Cain, Vernon

TWO RIVERS PT: Continental, Humko, Milton

WASHBURN: City of Ashland

WASHINGTON HARBOR: Louisiana, George Presley

WASHINGTON ISL: Blazing Star, I N Foster, Halstead, Solon H Johnson, D C Whitney

WHALEBACK SHOAL: Red White & Blue

WRIGHTSTOWN: John Spry

ACKNOWLEDGEMENTS

Additional materials include U.S. and Canadian Charts of the Great Lakes; Richardson's Cruising Guides; DeLorme's Atlases of Michigan, Ohio, New York and Wisconsin; Rand McNally World Atlases (1909,1934), U.S. Weather Bureau and Weather Service Reports, and materials supplied by the Ontario Ministry of Tourism and Recreation.

I am indebted to the following institutions for the use of their collections: Mt. Pleasant Public Library; Park Library, Central Michigan University; Detroit Public Library; Great Lakes Historical Society, and especially the Clarke Historical Library, Central Michigan University.

Many individuals have also contributed information, time, and talents to this work, including: Margie Swayze, Evelyn Leasher, Dr. Patrick McMullen, Shirley Hansen, Joan Schmidt, John Fisher, Steve Adolph, Flora McMullen and dozens of others who have provided encouragement and moral support.

General Bibliography

Ackerman, Paul W., ed. *Great Lakes Dive Charts*. Chicago: Midwest Explorers League, 1985-89.

American Neptune. Various issues. Salem, MA: American Neptune.

Baker, Catherine. *Shipbuilding on the Saginaw*. Bay City, MI: Museum of the Great Lakes, 1974.

Bowen, Dana Thomas. *Lore of the Lakes*. Daytona Beach, FL: Dana T. Bowen, 1940.

_____. *Memories of the Lakes*. Cleveland: Freshwater Press, 1946.

_____. *Shipwrecks of the Lakes*. Cleveland: Freshwater Press, 1952.

Boyer, Dwight. *Ghost Ships of the Great Lakes*. New York: Dodd, Mead & Co., 1968.

_____. *Great Stories of the Great Lakes*. New York: Dodd, Mead & Co., 1966.

_____. *Ships and men of the Great Lakes*. New York: Dodd, Mead & Co. 1977.

_____. *Strange Adventures of the Great Lakes*. New York: Dodd, Mead & Co., 1974.

_____. *True Tales of the Great Lakes*. Cleveland: Freshwater Press, 1971.

Bugbee, Gordon P. *Lake Erie Sidewheel Steamers of Frank Kirby*. Belle Isle, MI: Detroit Great Lakes Model Shipbuilder's Guild, 1955.

Carter, James L. *Voyageur's Harbor*. Grand Marais, MI: Pilot Press, 1968.

Chapelle, Howard I. *The History of the American Sailing Navy*. New York: W. W. Norton/Bonanza Books, 1949.

_____. *The History of the American Sailing Ship*. New York: W. W. Norton/Bonanza Books, 1935.

Chicago Tribune. Various issues. Chicago: Tribune Publishing Co.

Detroit Free Press. Various issues. Detroit: Detroit Free Press.

Detroit News. Various issues. Detroit: Detroit News.

Doner, Mary Francis. *The Salvager*. Minneapolis: Ross and Haines, Inc. 1958.

Eliott, James L. *Red Stacks Over the Horizon*. Grand Rapids, MI: Eerdmann's, 1967.

Farmer, Silas. *History of Detroit and Michigan*. Detroit: Silas Farmer and Co., 1884.

Found, Arthur. *Lake Ontario*. American Lakes Series. New York: Bobbs-Merrill, 1944.

Great Lakes Historical Society. Museum Collections. 1990.

Greenwood, John O. *Namesakes* Series. 9 vols. Cleveland: Freshwater Press.

Harold, Steve. *Shipbuilding at Manistee*. Manistee, MI: J. B. Publications, 1979.

Harold, Steve. *Shipwrecks of the Sleeping Bear*. Traverse City, MI: Pioneer Study Center, 1984.

Hatcher, Harlan. *Lake Erie*. American Lakes Series. New York: Bobbs-Merrill, 1944.

Havighurst, Walter. *Long Ships Passing*. New York: McMillan and Co., 1942.

Heden, Karl E. *Directory of Shipwrecks of the Great Lakes*. Boston: Bruce Humphries Publications, 1966.

Hemming, Robert J. *Gales of November*. Chicago: Contemporary Books, 1981.

Hey, Chester A. *Huron County Centennial History*. Harbor Beach, MI: Harbor Beach Times, 1959.

Hilton, George W. *The Great Lakes Carferries*. Berkeley, CA: Howell-North, 1962.

History of Saginaw County, Michigan. Chicago: Chas. C. Chapman, 1881.

History of the City of Harrisville—Centennial Year. Harrisville, MI: Alcona County Review, 1953.

Inland Seas. Journal of the Great Lakes Historical Society. 45 volumes. Cleveland: Great Lakes Historical Society.

Lake Huron Observer. Port Huron, MI: Lake Huron Oberver, 1844-45.

Lane, Kit. *Shipwrecks of the Saugatuck Area*. Saugatuck Commercial Record, Saugatuck, MI, 1974.

Landon, Fred. *Lake Huron*. American Lakes Series. New York: Bobbs-Merrill, 1944.

LesStrang, Jacques. *Lake Carriers*. Seattle, WA: Salisbury Press, 1977.

Mansfield, John Brant. *History of the Great Lakes*. 2 volumes. Chicago: J H Beers, 1899.

Merchant Vessels of the United States. Various volumes 1892-1916. Washington, DC: U.S. Marine Inspection Bureau.

Michigan History. Various volumes. Lansing, MI: Michigan Historical Society.

Michigan Pioneer and Historical Collections. 37 vols. Lansing, MI: Robert Smith and Co.

Mills, John M. *Canadian Coastal and Inland Steam Vessels, 1809-1930*. Providence, RI: Steamboat Historical Society, 1979.

Musham, H. A. "Early Great Lakes Steamboats, 1816-1830", reprint from *American Neptune*. Salem, MA: American Neptune, 1946.

_____. "The Walk-In-The-Water". *American Neptune*. Salem: American Neptune, 1945.

New York Times, various issues, New York, New York.

Nute, Grace Lee. *Lake Superior*. American Lakes Series. New York: Bobbs-Merrill, 1944.

O'Brien, Michael T. *Guardians of the 8th Sea—History of the U.S. Coast Guard on the Great Lakes*. Washington: U.S. Government Printing Office, 1976.

Otis, Edna M. *Sawdust Days—When the Tawas Area was Young*. East Tawas, MI: no pub. listed, 1978.

Paasch, Capt. H. *Illustrated Marine Encyclopedia*. Reprint of 1890 work. Watford, England: Argus Books, Ltd., 1977.

Parker, Jack D. *Shipwrecks of Lake Huron*. Au Train, MI: Avery Color Studios, 1986.

Port Huron Times-Herald. Various issues. Port Huron, MI: Times-Herald.

Quaife, Milo M. *Lake Huron*. American Lakes Series. New York: Bobbs-Merrill, 1944.

Ratigan, William. *Great Lakes Shipwrecks and Survivals*. Grand Rapids, MI: Eerdmann's Publishing Co., 1960.

Saginaw News and predecessors. Various issues. Saginaw, MI: The Saginaw News.

Schultz, Gerard. *A History of Michigan's Thumb*. Self-published, 1964.

Stonehouse, Frederick. *The Great Wrecks of the Great Lakes*. Marquette, MI: Harboridge Press, 1973.

_____. *Isle Royale Shipwrecks*. Au Train, MI: Avery Color Studios, 1983.

_____. *Lake Superior's "Shipwreck Coast"*. Au Train, MI: Avery Color Studios, 1985.

_____, *Marquette Shipwrecks*. Marquette, MI: Harboridge Press, 1974.

_____. *Munising Shipwrecks*. Au Train, MI: Avery Color Studios, 1983.

_____. *A Short Guide to Shipwrecks of Thunder Bay*. Alpena, MI: B&L Watery World, 1986.

_____. *Went Missing*, 2nd edition. Au Train, MI: Avery Color Studios, 1984.

Vent, Myron H. *South Manitou Island*. Chicago: Goodway Press, 1973.

Wendt, Gordon. *In the Wake of the Walk-in-the-Water*. Sandusky, OH: G Wendt, 1984.

Wolff, Dr. Julius F., Jr. *The Shipwrecks of Lake Superior*. 2nd ed. Duluth: Lake Superior Port Cities, 1990.